The IDG Books SECRETS Advantage

The formula for a book in the *SECRETS* series is simple: Give an expert author a forum to pass on his or her expertise to readers. A *SECRETS* author, rather than the publishing company, directs the organization, pace, and treatment of the subject matter. *SECRETS* authors maintain contact with end users through feedback from articles, training sessions, e-mail exchanges, user group participation, and consulting work. Because our authors are not distanced from the reality of daily computer use, our *SECRETS* books have a strategic advantage: *SECRETS* authors are directly tied to the readers.

SECRETS authors have the experience to approach a topic in the most efficient manner, and we know that you, the reader, will benefit from a "one-on-one" relationship through the text with the author. Our research shows that readers make computer book purchases because they want an expert's take on a product. Readers want to benefit from the author's experience, and the author's voice is always present in a *SECRETS* series book. Some have compared the presentation of topic in a *SECRETS* book to sitting at a coffee break with the author and having the author's full attention.

In addition, the author is free to include or recommend useful software in a *SECRETS* book. The software that accompanies a *SECRETS* book is not intended to be casual filler but is linked to the content, theme, or procedures of the book. We know that you will benefit from the included software.

You will find what you need in this book, whether you read it from cover to cover, section by section, or simply one topic at a time. As a computer user, you deserve a comprehensive resource of answers. We at IDG Books Worldwide are proud to deliver that resource with *Word for Windows 95 SECRETS*.

Brenda McLaughlin
Senior Vice President and Group Publisher
YouTellUs@idgbooks.com

Word for Windows® 95 SECRETS™

by Doug Lowe

IDG Books Worldwide, Inc.
An International Data Group Company

Foster City, CA ♦ Chicago, IL ♦ Indianapolis, IN
Braintree, MA ♦ Dallas, TX

Word for Windows® 95 SECRETS™

Published by
IDG Books Worldwide, Inc.
An International Data Group Company
919 E. Hillsdale Blvd.
Suite 400
Foster City, CA 94404

Library of Congress Catalog Card No.: 95-81108

ISBN 1-56884-726-2

Printed in the United States of America

10 9 8 7 6 5 4 3 2 1

1B/QS/RR/ZV

Distributed in the United States by IDG Books Worldwide, Inc.

Distributed by Macmillan Canada for Canada; by Computer and Technical Books for the Caribbean Basin; by Contemporanea de Ediciones for Venezuela; by Distribuidora Cuspide for Argentina; by CITEC for Brazil; by Ediciones ZETA S.C.R. Ltda. for Peru; by Editorial Limusa SA for Mexico; by Transworld Publishers Limited in the United Kingdom and Europe; by Al-Maiman Publishers & Distributors for Saudi Arabia; by Simron Pty. Ltd. for South Africa; by IDG Communications (HK) Ltd. for Hong Kong; by Toppan Company Ltd. for Japan; by Addison Wesley Publishing Company for Korea; by Longman Singapore Publishers Ltd. for Singapore, Malaysia, Thailand, and Indonesia; by Unalis Corporation for Taiwan; by WS Computer Publishing Company, Inc. for the Philippines; by WoodsLane Pty. Ltd. for Australia; by WoodsLane Enterprises Ltd. for New Zealand.

For general information on IDG Books Worldwide's books in the U.S., please call our Consumer Customer Service department at 800-762-2974. For reseller information, including discounts and premium sales, please call our Reseller Customer Service department at 800-434-3422.

For information on where to purchase IDG Books Worldwide's books outside the U.S., contact IDG Books Worldwide at 415-655-3021 or fax 415-655-3295.

For information on translations, contact Marc Jeffrey Mikulich, Director, Foreign & Subsidiary Rights, at IDG Books Worldwide, 415-655-3018 or fax 415-655-3295.

For sales inquiries and special prices for bulk quantities, write to the address above or call IDG Books Worldwide at 415-655-3200.

For information on using IDG Books Worldwide's books in the classroom, or ordering examination copies, contact Jim Kelly at 800-434-2086.

For authorization to photocopy items for corporate, personal, or educational use, please contact Copyright Clearance Center, 222 Rosewood Drive, Danvers, MA 01923, or fax 508-750-4470.

 ™ is a trademark under exclusive license to IDG Books Worldwide, Inc., from International Data Group, Inc.

SECRETS™ is a trademark of IDG Books Worldwide, Inc.

About the Author

Doug Lowe

Doug Lowe has written more than 20 computer books, including IDG Books Worldwide's *Networking For Dummies, MORE word for Windows For Dummies*, and *The Microsoft of Network For Dummies*. He has used Word for Windows since version 1.0 and used Word for MS-DOS before that. He is a contributing editor to *DOS World* magazine and is frequent contributor to *Maximize* magazine.

ABOUT IDG BOOKS WORLDWIDE

Welcome to the world of IDG Books Worldwide.

IDG Books Worldwide, Inc., is a subsidiary of International Data Group, the world's largest publisher of computer-related information and the leading global provider of information services on information technology. IDG was founded more than 25 years ago and now employs more than 7,700 people worldwide. IDG publishes more than 250 computer publications in 67 countries (see listing below). More than 70 million people read one or more IDG publications each month.

Launched in 1990, IDG Books Worldwide is today the #1 publisher of best-selling computer books in the United States. We are proud to have received 8 awards from the Computer Press Association in recognition of editorial excellence, and three from Computer Currents' First Annual Readers' Choice Awards, and our best-selling ...For Dummies® series has more than 19 million copies in print with translations in 28 languages. IDG Books Worldwide, through a joint venture with IDG's Hi-Tech Beijing, became the first U.S. publisher to publish a computer book in the People's Republic of China. In record time, IDG Books Worldwide has become the first choice for millions of readers around the world who want to learn how to better manage their businesses.

Our mission is simple: Every one of our books is designed to bring extra value and skill-building instructions to the reader. Our books are written by experts who understand and care about our readers. The knowledge base of our editorial staff comes from years of experience in publishing, education, and journalism — experience which we use to produce books for the '90s. In short, we care about books, so we attract the best people. We devote special attention to details such as audience, interior design, use of icons, and illustrations. And because we use an efficient process of authoring, editing, and desktop publishing our books electronically, we can spend more time ensuring superior content and spend less time on the technicalities of making books.

You can count on our commitment to deliver high-quality books at competitive prices on topics you want to read about. At IDG Books Worldwide, we value quality, and we have been delivering quality for more than 25 years. You'll find no better book on a subject than one from IDG Books Worldwide.

John J. Kilcullen

John Kilcullen
President and CEO
IDG Books Worldwide, Inc.

IDG Books Worldwide, Inc., is a publication of International Data Group, the world's largest publisher of computer-related information and the leading global provider of information services on information technology. International Data Group publishes over 250 computer publications in over 67 countries. Seventy million people read one or more International Data Group publications each month. International Data Group's publications include: **ARGENTINA:** Computerworld Argentina, GamePro, Infoworld, PC World Argentina; **AUSTRALIA:** Australian Macworld, Client/Server Journal, Computer Living, Computerworld, Digital News, Network World, PC World, Publishing Essentials, Reseller; **AUSTRIA:** Computerwelt, PC TEST; **BELARUS:** PC World Belarus; **BELGIUM:** Data News; **BRAZIL:** Annuário de Informática, Computerworld Brazil, Connections, Super Game Power, Macworld, PC World Brazil, Publish Brazil, SUPERGAME; **BULGARIA:** Computerworld Bulgaria, Networkworld/Bulgaria, PC & MacWorld Bulgaria; **CANADA:** CIO Canada, ComputerWorld Canada, InfoCanada, Network World Canada, Reseller World; **CHILE:** Computerworld Chile, GamePro, PC World Chile; **COLUMBIA:** Computerworld Colombia, GamePro, PC World Colombia; **COSTA RICA:** PC World Costa Rica/Nicaragua; **THE CZECH AND SLOVAK REPUBLICS:** Computerworld Czechoslovakia, Elektronika Czechoslovakia, PC World Czechoslovakia; **DENMARK:** Communications World, Computerworld Danmark, Macworld Danmark, PC World Danmark, PC World Danmark Supplements, TECH World; **DOMINICAN REPUBLIC:** PC World Republica Dominicana; **ECUADOR:** PC World Ecuador, GamePro; **EGYPT:** Computerworld Middle East, PC World Middle East; **EL SALVADOR:** PC World Centro America; **FINLAND:** MikroPC, Tietoverkko, Tietoviikko; **FRANCE:** Distributique, Golden, Info PC, Le Guide du Monde Informatique, Le Monde Informatique, Reseaux & Telecoms; **GERMANY:** Computer Business, Computerwoche, Computerwoche Extra, Computerwoche Focus, Electronic Entertainment, GamePro, I/M Information Management, Macwelt, PC Welt; **GREECE:** GamePro, Macworld & Publish; **GUATEMALA:** PC World Centro America; **HONDURAS:** PC World Centro America; **HONG KONG:** Computerworld Hong Kong, PCWorld Hong Kong, Publish in Asia; **HUNGARY:** ABCD CD-ROM, Computerworld Szamitastechnika, PC & Mac World Hungary, PC-X Magazine; **INDIA:** Computerworld India, PC World India, Publish in Asia; **INDONESIA:** InfoKomputer PC World, Komputek Computerworld, Publish in Asia; **IRELAND':** ComputerScope, PC Live!; **ISRAEL:** PC World 32 BIT, People & Computers; **ITALY:** Computerworld Italia, Computerworld Italia Special Editions, Lotus Italia, Macworld Italia, Networking Italia, PC Shopping, PC World Italia, PC World/Walt Disney; **JAPAN:** Macworld Japan, Nikkei Personal Computing, SunWorld Japan, Windows World Japan; **KENYA:** East African Computer News; **KOREA:** Hi-Tech Information/Computerworld, Macworld Korea, PC World Korea; **MACEDONIA:** PC World Macedonia; **MALAYSIA:** Computerworld Malaysia, PC World Malaysia, Publish in Asia; **MEXICO:** Computerworld Mexico, GamePro, Macworld, PC World Mexico; **MYANMAR:** PC World Myanmar; **NETHERLANDS:** Computable, Computer! Totaal, LAN Magazine, Macworld, Net Magazine; **NEW ZEALAND:** Computer Buyer, Computerworld New Zealand, MTB, Network World, PC World New Zealand; **NICARAGUA:** PC World Costa Rica/Nicaragua; **NIGERIA:** PC World Africa; **NORWAY:** Computerworld Norge, Computerworld Privat, CW Rapport Klient/Tjener, CW Rapport Nettverk & Telecom, CW Rapport Offentlig Sektor, IDG's KURSGUIDE, Macworld Norge, Multimedia World, PC World Ekspress, PC World Nettverk, PC World Norge, PC World's Produktguide, Windows Spesial; **PAKISTAN:** Computerworld Pakistan, PC World Pakistan; **PANAMA:** GamePro, PC World Panama; **PARAGUAY:** GamePro, PC World Paraguay; **P. R. OF CHINA:** China Computerworld, China Infoworld, Computer & Communication, Electronic Product World, Electronics Today, Game Camp, PC World China, Popular Computer Week, Software World, Telecom Product World; **PERU:** Computerworld Peru, GamePro, PC World Profesional Peru, PC World Peru; **POLAND:** Computerworld Poland, Computerworld Special Report, Macworld, Networld, PC World Komputer; **PHILIPPINES:** Computerworld Philippines, PC Digest, Publish in Asia; **PORTUGAL:** Cerebro/PC World, Correio Informático/Computerworld, Mac•In/PC•In Portugal; **PUERTO RICO:** PC World Puerto Rico; **ROMANIA:** Computerworld Romania, PC World Romania, Telecom Romania; **RUSSIA:** Computerworld Rossiya, Network World Russia, PC World Russia; **SINGAPORE:** Computerworld Singapore, PC World Singapore, Publish in Asia; **SLOVENIA:** MONITOR; **SOUTH AFRICA:** Computing S.A., Network World S.A., Software World; **SPAIN:** Computerworld España, COMUNICACIONES WORLD, Dealer World, Macworld España, PC World España; **SWEDEN:** CAP&Design, Computer Sweden, Corporate Computing, MacWorld, Maxi Data, MikroDatorn, Nätverk & Kommunikation, PC/Aktiv, PC World, Windows World; **SWITZERLAND:** Computerworld Schweiz, Macworld Schweiz, PCtip; **TAIWAN:** Computerworld Taiwan, Macworld Taiwan, PC World Taiwan, Publish Taiwan, Windows World; **THAILAND:** Thai Computerworld, Publish in Asia; **TURKEY:** Computerworld Monitör, MACWORLD Turkiye, PC WORLD Turkiye; **UKRAINE:** Computerworld Kiev, Computers & Software Magazine, PC World Ukraine; **UNITED KINGDOM:** Acorn User, Amiga Action, Amiga Computing, Amiga, Appletalk, CD Powerplay, CD-ROM Now, Computing, Connexion, GamePro, Lotus Magazine, Macaction, Macworld, Open Computing, Parents and Computers, PC Home, PC Works, The WEB; **UNITED STATES:** Cable in the Classroom, CD Review, CIO Magazine, Computerworld, Computerworld Client/Server Journal, Digital Video Magazine, DOS World, Electronic, InfoWorld, I-Way, Macworld, Maximize, MULTIMEDIA WORLD, Network World, PC World, PUBLISH, SWATPro Magazine, Video Event, WebMaster; **URUGUAY:** PC World Uruguay; **VENEZUELA:** Computerworld Venezuela, GamePro, PC World Venezuela; and **VIETNAM:** PC World Vietnam   9/20/95

Dedication

This one is for Rebecca.

Credits

Publisher
Karen A.Bluestein

Acquisitions Manager
Gregory Croy

Acquisitions Editor
Ellen Camm

Brand Manager
Melisa M. Duffy

Editorial Director
Andy Cummings

Editorial Assistant
Nate Holdread

Production Director
Beth Jenkins

Supervisor of Project Coordination
Cindy L. Phipps

Supervisor of Page Layout
Kathie S. Schnorr

Project Coordinator
Sherry Gomoll

Production Systems Specialist
Steve Peake

Pre-Press Coordination
Tony Augsburger
Patricia R. Reynolds
Theresa Sánchez-Baker
Elizabeth Cárdenas-Nelson

Media/Archive Coordination
Leslie Popplewell

Graphic Coordination
Shelly Lea
Gina Scott
Carla C. Radzkinas

Project Editor
Erik Dafforn

Editors
Hugh Vandivier
Kerrie Klein

Technical Reviewer
Beth Slick

Production Staff
Shawn Aylsworth
Cameron Booker
Maridee V. Ennis
Todd Klemme
Jill Lyttle
Mark Owens
Alicia Shimer

Proofreaders
Barbara L. Potter
Gwenette Gaddis
Dwight Ramsey
Robert Springer

Indexer
Anne Leach

Cover Design
Kavish & Kavish

Acknowledgments

Let me start by thanking my family, who put up with more than the normal share of late nights and early morning absences while I finished up this book. (Someone please tell me if there really was an August this year.)

I'd also like to thank project editor Erik Dafforn for his tireless efforts throughout this project. Thanks, Erik, for not harping on me too much as deadlines came and went, then as new deadlines came and went, and, well, you know the story. As always, it's been a pleasure working with you.

Thanks also to editor Hugh Vandivier for cleaning up my sloppy language and to Beth Slick for her excellent technical review, and to Greg Croy, Melisa Duffy, and Karen Bluestein. This project has been a lot of fun; let's do it again real soon!

Thanks also to the authors of the shareware who graciously allowed me to include their software on the CD, especially to Romke Soldaat, who offered several excellent suggestions. And thanks to the beta testers of Microsoft Office 95 for sharing their insights throughout the beta test, and to the Word for Windows 95 beta support staff, especially Susan Fetter and Kevin Shaughnessey. All provided timely and accurate answers to all of my questions, even the dumb ones, and bailed me out of trouble several times.

And finally, thanks to the developers of Microsoft Word for Windows 95, for creating a program that is worth writing about. I can't wait to see what's in store for the next version of Word!

(The Publisher would like to give special thanks to Patrick J. McGovern, without whom this book would not have been possible.)

Contents at a Glance

Introduction 1

Part I: Welcome to Word for Windows 95 9
Chapter 1: What's New with Word for Windows 95 11
Chapter 2: Welcome to Windows 95 27
Chapter 3: Fundamental Word Secrets 53

Part II: Secrets of Customizing Word 67
Chapter 4: Using Templates 69
Chapter 5: Customizing Word's Startup and Appearance 121
Chapter 6: Customizing Keyboard Shortcuts, Toolbars, and Menus 139
Chapter 7: Automating Your Work with Macros 169

Part III: Secrets of Working with Word 189
Chapter 8: Managing Your Documents 191
Chapter 9: Printing Your Documents 219
Chapter 10: Working with Others 255

Part IV: Secrets of Editing 271
Chapter 11: Efficient Editing 273
Chapter 12: Using AutoCorrect, AutoText, and the Spike 293
Chapter 13: Mastering the Power Editing Tools: Spell Checker,
Thesaurus, and Grammar Checker 309

Part V: Secrets of Formatting 327
Chapter 14: Time-Honored Formatting Tips and Tricks 329
Chapter 15: All About Page Layout and Sections 359
Chapter 16: Bullets and Numbered Lists 377
Chapter 17: Tabulating Tables 389
Chapter 18: Using Styles 417

Part VI: Power Desktop Publishing Techniques 439
Chapter 19: Secrets of Typography 441
Chapter 20: Secrets of Columns, Frames,
and Desktop Publishing Effects 465
Chapter 21: Secrets of Graphics 485
Chapter 22: The Secret Applets: WordArt, Equation Editor,
and Microsoft Graph 515

Part VII: Secrets of Working with Long Documents 539

Chapter 23: Working with Outlines 541
Chapter 24: Using Master Documents 555
Chapter 25: Creating an Index, Table of Contents, or Other Table..............565
Chapter 26: Using Footnotes, Endnotes, and Cross-References 587

Part VIII: Building Word Applications 601

Chapter 27: Using OLE 603
Chapter 28: Customizing Your Documents With Fields 615
Chapter 29: Streamlining Document Creation with Forms 659
Chapter 30: Mail Merge Secrets 675

Part IX: Secrets of WordBasic Programming.................... 703

Chapter 31: WordBasic Fundamentals 705
Chapter 32: Creating Macros That Work With Documents 741
Chapter 33: Working with Dialog Boxes 771
Chapter 34: WordBasic Commands and Functions 809
Appendix A: The Word for Windows 95 SECRETS CD-ROM 849
Appendix B: The Word Document Virus Threat 853

INDEX 859

CD-License 881

Table of Contents

Introduction 1

Shhh! It's a Secret! 1
    Bug alert! 2
    The biggest Word secret of all 2
How to Use This Book 2
    Commands and such 3
    What about Word 6? 3
How This Book Is Organized 4
    Part I: Welcome to Word for Windows 95 4
    Part II: Secrets of Customizing Word 4
    Part III: Secrets of Working with Word 4
    Part IV: Secrets of Editing 5
    Part V: Secrets of Formatting 5
    Part VI: Power Desktop Publishing Techniques 5
    Part VII: Secrets of Working with Long Documents 5
    Part VIII: Building Word Applications 6
    Part IX: Secrets of WordBasic Programming 6
    Appendix A: The Word for Windows 95 SECRETS CD-ROM 6
What's Cool 6
On Your Way 7

Part I: Welcome to Word for Windows 95 9

Chapter 1: What's New with Word for Windows 95 11

New Features of Word 95 11
    Improved File⇨Open and File⇨Save As commands 12
    Improved File⇨New command 13
    The File⇨Properties command 14
    Animation 15
    The Highlighter 15
    Find and Replace All Word Forms 16
    The Tip Wizard 17
    New Help button 18
    On-the-fly spell checker 18
Compatibility with Word 6 19
New Features of Office 95 20
    Microsoft Office Shortcut Bar 20
    Binders 23
    Schedule+ 25

Chapter 2: Welcome to Windows 95 27

Learning the New Interface 27
The Desktop 28
Folders and the My Computer Icon 29

Working efficiently with folders 32
Routine file and folder operations 34
Deleting a file or a folder. 34
Renaming a file or a folder. 34
Copying a file or a folder. 34
Selecting multiple files or folders. 35
Creating a new file or folder. 35
Going up? 36
The fast track to the desktop 36
Explorer 37
Starting Explorer 38
Using Explorer 38
The Taskbar 39
Customizing the taskbar 40
Moving the taskbar 40
Using the Start button 42
Customizing the Start menu 43
Shortcuts 44
Long Filenames 46
Rules for forming long filenames 47
Short filenames 47
How Windows 95 stores long filenames 48
Whither MS-DOS? 49
MS-DOS and long filenames 50
Improved * wildcards 51
                                                                                                        52

Chapter 3: Fundamental Word Secrets **53**
Word Is Not a Typewriter 53
There Are No Codes 55
Three Document Building Blocks 56
Characters 56
Paragraphs 57
Sections 58
Styles 59
Where Formats Originate 60
Templates 62
Other Things You Should Know 62
Word commands 62
Macros 63
Fields 64
AutoText and AutoCorrect 65

Part II: Secrets of Customizing Word **67**
Chapter 4: Using Templates **69**
What Is a Template? 69
The Normal.dot template 70
Creating a New Document Based on a Template 71
Customizing the New button and Ctrl+N keyboard shortcut 72
Changing a Document's Template 73

Creating Your Own Templates 75
    Where to store your templates 75
    Converting a document to a template 77
    Creating a new template from scratch 77
    Modifying an existing template 78
Using Global Templates 78
    How Word resolves duplicate template elements 79
Using the Organizer 80
    Using Organizer to update styles in a template 81
    A macro for updating templates 82
A Gallery of Word's Templates 83
    Letters 83
    Faxes 87
    Memos 87
    Reports 87
    Press releases 103
    Resumes 103
    Business forms 103
Using Wizards 113
    Running a wizard 113
    Resetting wizard defaults 119

Chapter 5: Customizing Word's Startup and Appearance 121

The Many Ways to Start Word 121
    Using the Start button Documents menu 122
    Starting Word from My Computer or Explorer 122
    Using the Start button Programs menu 122
    Creating a shortcut on the desktop 123
    Creating a new document from the desktop, My Computer, or Explorer 124
    Using Microsoft Office Shortcut Bar 124
    Starting Word automatically 126
    Starting Word from an MS-DOS prompt 126
Word's Command-Line Switches 127
    What ever happened to the Tip of the Day? 128
Configuring the Interface 129
    Setting the View mode 130
    Working in Full Screen view 130
Customizing Pieces of the Interface 132
    Show options 133
    Window options 135
    Nonprinting Characters options 135
General Options 136

Chapter 6: Customizing Keyboard Shortcuts, Toolbars, and Menus 139

Customizing the Keyboard 139
    Creating a keyboard shortcut 141
    The point-and-click way to create a keyboard shortcut 142
    Creating a shortcut key for a style 142
    Finding out what a keyboard shortcut does 143
    Resetting keyboard shortcuts 143
    Printing your keyboard shortcuts 143
    A macro to display keyboard shortcuts 144

Customizing Word's Toolbars 147
    Word's predefined toolbars 148
    Showing and hiding toolbars 149
    A macro to toggle the Formatting toolbar 150
    Setting toolbar display options 151
    Removing toolbar buttons 152
    Adding a predefined button to a toolbar 152
    Adding a custom button to a toolbar 155
    Editing button images 156
    Stealing button images 157
    A toolbar with all of Word's built-in buttons 158
    Spacing out toolbar buttons 159
    Creating a new toolbar 160
    Deleting and renaming toolbars 160
    Resetting toolbars to their default settings 161
Customizing Word's Menus 161
    What's with the ampersand (&)? 162
    Adding a menu command 162
    Using the shortcut method to add menu commands 163
    Removing a menu command 164
    Rearranging menu commands 165
    Using separators 165
    Adding a new menu 165
    Customizing a shortcut menu 166
    Resetting menus to their default settings 167

Chapter 7: Automating Your Work with Macros 169

Macros and Templates 170
Recording a Macro 170
Macro Recording Tips 173
Running a Macro 173
More Ways to Run a Macro 174
Editing a Macro 174
    Delving into WordBasic 175
    Simple macro edits that don't require a Ph.D. in WordBasic ... 177
Using the Macros That Come with Word 177
    Macros in the Macros7.dot template 178
    Macros in the Tables.dot template 184
    Macros in the Layout.dot template 185
    Macros in the Convert.dot template 188
    Macros in the Present.dot template 188

Part III: Secrets of Working with Word 189

Chapter 8: Managing Your Documents 191

Using the File⇨Open Command 191
    Changing views 193
    Deleting and renaming documents and folders 194
    Playing favorites 195
    Setting the default document location 196
    Forcing Word to always look in Favorites 196
    Using the shortcut menu 197
    Using the Commands and Settings button 199

Opening Recently Used Documents 200
    Adding a document to a menu 201
Opening Documents Outside of Word 202
Finding Lost Files 202
    Simple searches 202
    Advanced searches 204
    Understanding And and Or 209
    Using special search characters 209
    Saving searches 211
Using the Save As Command 211
The Save All Command 214
Save Options 214
    Using AutoSave 215
    Password protecting your files 217

Chapter 9: Printing Your Documents 219

Printing Your Document 220
    Using the Print command 220
    Printing more than one copy 220
    Printing the current page 221
    Printing a range of pages 222
    Printing selected text 222
    Printing even and odd pages 223
    Printing document information 223
    Printing to a file 224
    A macro for the Print button 228
Selecting a Different Printer 229
    How to change the default printer 229
    Adding a printer 230
Setting Printer Properties 233
Setting Print Options 234
Print Preview 235
    Zooming in 237
    Shrink to fit 240
    Editing in Print Preview 242
Printing Envelopes 242
    Printing a single envelope 243
    Changing envelope options 244
    Embellishing envelopes with text and graphics 245
    Printing just the envelope 246
Printing Labels 246
    Creating custom labels 248
Sending a Fax 249
    Creating custom cover pages 252
Managing Print Jobs 253

Chapter 10: Working with Others 255

Sending a Document to Another User 255
    Using the File⇨Send command 256
    Routing a document to several users 257
    Posting a document to a shared folder 260
Using the Highlighter 260

Using the Annotation Feature 262
   Inserting annotations 262
   Creating a voice annotation 263
   Viewing annotations 263
   Removing Annotations 264
Using Revision Marks 265
   Tracking revisions as you make them 266
   Accepting or rejecting revisions 267
   Comparing document versions 268
   Merging revisions 268

Part IV: Secrets of Editing 271

Chapter 11: Efficient Editing 273

Setting the Edit Options 273
Editing Tricks 275
   Selecting text with mouse and keyboard 275
   Copy, cut, and paste 277
   Dragging and dropping 277
   Creating desktop scraps 278
   The magic of Undo and Repeat 279
Navigation Tricks 280
   Keyboard shortcuts for document navigation 280
   Going places with Edit⇨Go To 282
   A handy EditGoto macro 283
   Working with bookmarks 284
   Yes, you can go back 285
Using the Find Command 286
   Finding missing text 286
   Finding formats 289
   Finding special characters 289
Replacing Text 291

Chapter 12: Using AutoCorrect, AutoText, and the Spike 293

Using AutoCorrect 293
   What happened to SmartQuotes? 294
   COrrect TWo INitial CApitals 294
   Capitalize First Letter of Sentence 295
   Capitalize Names of Days 296
   Correct accidental usage of cAPS LOCK key 297
   Replace Text as You Type 297
   Creating AutoCorrect entries 298
   A macro to toggle AutoCorrect 299
Using AutoFormat As You Type Options 300
   Apply As You Type: Headings 301
   Borders 301
   Automatic Bulleted Lists 301
   Automatic Numbered Lists 301
   Replace Straight Quotes with 'Smart Quotes' 302
   Replace Ordinals (1st) with Superscript 302
   Replace Fractions ($^1/_2$) with fraction characters ($^1/_2$) 302
   Symbol Characters with Symbols 303

Using AutoText 303
   Creating an AutoText entry 303
   Editing an AutoText entry 305
   Assigning AutoText to a toolbar button, menu, or keyboard shortcut 305
Using the Spike 305

Chapter 13: Mastering the Power Editing Tools: Spell Checker, Thesaurus, and Grammar Checker **309**

Using the Spell Checker 309
   On-the-fly spell checking...310
   Checking a document 312
   Using the Spelling icon 313
   Spelling options 314
   Custom dictionaries 315
   Excluding text from spell checking 317
   Wild-card searches 317
   A macro for cheating at word jumbles 318
Using the Thesaurus 319
Using the Grammar Checker, or Not 320
   Checking for grammar errors 321
   Readability statistics 323
   Customizing the grammar checker 324
   A macro to insert readability statistics at the end of the document 326

Part V: Secrets of Formatting **327**

Chapter 14: Time-Honored Formatting Tips and Tricks **329**

Understanding Character and Paragraph Formats 329
A Word About Styles 330
Two Ways to Apply Character Formats 331
Using the Format⇨Font Command 332
Character Formatting Shortcuts 334
Removing Character Formatting 335
Using the Format⇨Paragraph Command 335
   Using hanging indents 337
   Setting indents with the ruler 337
 A handy pair of double indentation macros 339
Understanding Text Flow 340
Using Tabs 341
   Setting tabs with the ruler 342
   The four types of tabs 343
   Using the Format⇨Tabs command 343
   Removing all tabs 344
   Using tab leaders 344
   Running a bar tab 345
Borders and Shading 345
   Using the Format⇨Borders and Shading command 346
   Using the borders toolbar 349
   How to apply a border to a word or phrase 350
Changing Case 351

AutoFormat 354
    Using the AutoFormat command 354
    AutoFormat options 357
    AutoFormat As You Type 358
The Format Painter 358

Chapter 15: All About Page Layout and Sections 359

Understanding Sections 359
Creating Section Breaks 361
Using the File⇨Page Setup Command 362
    Margins 362
    Paper Size 363
    Paper Source 364
    Layout 365
Inserting Page Numbers 367
Headers and Footers 369
    Adding a header or footer 369
    Building a toolbar button to show headers 371
Creating Sections with Different Page Numbers 372
The Secret SectionManager Macro 373

Chapter 16: Bullets and Numbered Lists 377

Understanding Bullets and Numbered Lists 377
Using the Bullet Button 378
Creating Custom Bulleted Lists 379
Using the Numbering Button 380
Changing the Numbering Scheme 381
Creating a Multilevel List 382
Bugaboo: Problems with Bullets and Numbering 384
Using Word's Heading Numbering Feature 386

Chapter 17: Tabulating Tables 389

Understanding Tables 389
Creating Tables 391
    Creating a table using the Insert Table button 391
    Using the Table⇨Insert Table command 392
    Using the Table Wizard 393
Editing Tables 398
    Right-clicking on table cells 398
    Moving and selecting in tables 398
    Adding rows and columns 399
    Inserting cells 401
    The magic Insert Cells button 402
    Deleting cells 402
    Adjusting column width 402
Formatting Tables 404
    Using tabs in a table 404
    AutoFormatting a table 405
    Adding borders and shading to a table 406
    Merging cells to create headings 406
    Designating heading rows 407
    Splitting a Table 407

Sorting a Table 408
Using Table Formulas 409
Using a Table as a Database 411
Creating a Custom Tables Toolbar 411
Converting Text to a Table (And Vice-Versa) 414
Using the Tables7.dot Macro Template 415

Chapter 18: Using Styles 417

Understanding Styles 418
   Paragraph styles and character styles 419
   Word's built-in styles 419
Creating a Style 423
   Creating a style by example 423
   Creating a style with the Format⇨Style command 424
   Picking a name for the style 425
   Basing a style on an existing style 425
   Setting the style for the following paragraph 426
   Setting the formats for the style 426
   Adding the style to the document's template 426
Applying a Style 427
Overriding Style Formatting 427
Changing a Style 428
   Changing a style without using Format⇨Style 428
   Changing a style by using Format⇨Style 429
Deleting a Style 430
Assigning Keyboard Shortcut Keys to Styles 430
   Assigning a keyboard shortcut by using Format⇨Style 431
   Assigning a keyboard shortcut without using the Format⇨Style command 432
Viewing Style Assignments by Enabling the Style Area 432
Creating and Using Character Styles 433
Searching for and Replacing Style Formatting 434
Why Do My Styles Keep Changing Back? 435
Using the Gallery 436

Part VI: Power Desktop Publishing Techniques 439

Chapter 19: Secrets of Typography 441

Understanding Typography Terms 442
Serif Type 444
   Understanding parts of type 445
   Classifying type 445
Sans Serif Type 446
Scripts 447
Novelty Typefaces 448
Dingbats 449
Typography: More Than Just a Pretty Face 449
   Point size 449
   Line length 450
   Line spacing 451
   Alignment 452
   Kerning 453
   Character spacing 454

Avoiding Typeface Clash 455
    Picking the body text type 455
    Picking the display type 456
The Typefaces That Come with Windows 95 and Word for Windows 95 456

Chapter 20: Secrets of Columns, Frames, and Desktop Publishing Effects 465

Creating Columns 465
    Creating columns the easy way 466
    Creating columns the hard way 466
Changing the Column Width 468
Forcing a Column Break 468
Balancing Column Lengths 469
Hyphenating Your Text 469
    Automatically hyphenating a document 469
    Manually hyphenating a document 470
    Inserting an optional hyphen 471
    Inserting a non-breaking hyphen 471
Inserting a Text Frame 471
Creating an Empty Frame 473
Aligning a Frame 473
Understanding Anchors 475
Deleting a Frame 475
Desktop Publishing Effects 476
    Newsletter layouts 476
    Pull quotes 479
    Side headings 481
    Icons 482

Chapter 21: Secrets of Graphics 485

Using Clip Art and Other Pictures 485
    Using the Insert Picture command 486
    Adding a frame to a picture 488
    Adding a border to a picture 489
    Resizing and cropping a picture 489
    Editing a picture 491
    Adding a caption 491
    Using Microsoft ClipArt Gallery 493
Customizing the Picture shortcut menu 495
    Adding the Format command to the Picture shortcut menu 496
    Adding the Reset command to the Picture shortcut menu 496
    Adding the Increase Crop command to the Picture shortcut menu 497
    Adding the Decrease Crop command to the Picture shortcut menu 497
Using Word's Drawing Tools 498
    Activate the Drawing toolbar 498
    Zoom in 498
    Save frequently 500
    Don't forget Ctrl+Z 500
Drawing Simple Lines and Shapes 500
    Drawing straight and curved lines 501
    Drawing rectangles, squares, and circles 502

Drawing a polygon or freeform shape 502
Drawing a text box 504
Drawing a callout 504
Selecting Drawing Objects 506
Setting the Fill Color, Line Style, and Shadow 507
Flipping and Rotating Objects 509
Flipping an object 509
Rotating an object 90 degrees 509
Drawing a Complicated Picture 510
Changing layers 510
Aligning objects 511
Grouping objects 512
Converting Drawing Objects to a Picture Object 512

Chapter 22: The Secret Applets: WordArt, Equation Editor, and Microsoft Graph 515
WordArt 515
Creating a custom WordArt button 518
Opening the WordArt dialog box 519
Equation Editor 520
Creating an equation 521
Adding text to an equation 524
Keyboard shortcuts for Equation Editor 524
Editing an equation in a window 526
Microsoft Graph 527
Microsoft Graph terms 527
Inserting a chart 528
Finding the Insert Chart button 529
Working with the datasheet 530
Changing the chart type 530
Adding chart titles 532
Adding a label 533
Adding a legend 534
Applying an AutoFormat 534
Creating custom AutoFormats 535
Using the Chart Wizard 536

Part VII: Secrets of Working with Long Documents 539

Chapter 23: Working with Outlines 541
Understanding Outlines 541
Selecting in Outline View 543
Collapsing and Expanding the Outline 543
Collapsing and expanding body text 543
Collapsing or expanding to a specific heading level 544
Collapsing and expanding a specific heading 545
A macro to collapse body text automatically 546
Showing or Hiding Formatting 547
Promoting and Demoting Paragraphs 548
Promoting a paragraph 548
Demoting a heading paragraph 549
Dragging paragraphs to new levels 549

Editing in Outline View 550
        Deleting in Outline view 550
        Rearranging the outline 550
Printing an Outline 551
Numbering the Headings in a Document 551
Sorting a Document Alphabetically by Headings 553
Using Toolbars and Keyboard Shortcuts for Outlining 553

Chapter 24: Using Master Documents **555**

Understanding Master Documents 556
The Master Document Toolbar 557
Creating a Master Document from Scratch 557
How Word Decides Where to Break the Subdocuments 560
Inserting Existing Files into a Master Document 560
Opening a Subdocument 561
Removing a Subdocument 562
Merging and Splitting a Subdocument 562
Headers and Footers in Master Documents 562
Using Master Documents on a Network 563
Secrets of Avoiding Trouble with Master Documents 564

Chapter 25: Creating an Index, Table of Contents, or Other Table **565**

Formatting Your Document to Make a Table of Contents Easy to Create 566
Creating a Table of Contents 566
Using Other Styles to Create a TOC 568
Creating Custom TOC Styles 569
Creating a TOC by Using Field Codes 569
Creating a Table of Figures or Other Similar Tables 572
Using Styles to Create a Table of Figures 573
Tables of Authorities 574
        Marking citations in the document 574
        Creating a table of authorities 576
        Adding your own categories 577
Indexes 578
        Marking index entries manually 579
        Creating an index 580
        Marking bold and italic page numbers 581
        Marking a range of pages 581
        Marking index entries automatically from a concordance file 582
        Creating subentries 583
        Creating cross-references 584
        Formatting an index 584
Updating Tables of Contents, Tables of Figures, Tables of Authorities, or an Index 584

Chapter 26: Using Footnotes, Endnotes, and Cross-References **587**

Adding a Footnote 587
Adding an Endnote 589
Displaying and Finding Footnotes 589
Changing the Footnote Format 590
Using Different Reference Marks 590
Using a Custom Reference Mark 591

Changing the Footnote Separators 592
Converting Footnotes to Endnotes 592
Using the Secret Footnote Wizard 594
Working with Cross-References 597
Creating a Style Reference 598

Part VIII: Building Word Applications 601

Chapter 27: Using OLE 603

Understanding OLE 603
    OLE 2.0 604
    Linking vs. embedding 605
Using the Insert⇨Object Command 606
    Creating a new OLE object 606
    Inserting an existing file as an object 607
Dragging Objects into Word Documents 608
Using the Copy and Paste Special Commands 609
Editing an Object 610
Working with Links 610
Manually Updating Links 611
Converting an Object 611
Inserting and Playing Multimedia Objects 612
    Inserting a sound object 612
    Recording a sound in Word 613
Inserting a video file in a Word document 613

Chapter 28: Customizing Your Documents With Fields 615

Understanding Fields 615
Inserting a Field 617
Keyboard Shortcuts for Working with Fields 619
Another Way to Insert Fields 619
Formatting Field Results with Switches 620
    Preserving formatting when you update fields: the * mergeformat switch 620
    Capitalizing field results 620
    Setting the number format 621
    Creating custom number formats 622
    Creating custom date and time formats 623
Updating a Field 623
Preventing a Field from Being Updated 624
Field Code Reference 624
    Advance 624
    Ask 625
    Author 626
    AutoNum 626
    AutoNumLgl 626
    AutoNumOut 626
    AutoText 626
    BarCode 627
    (Bookmark) 627
    Comments 627

Compare 627
CreateDate 628
Database 628
Date 629
DDE 630
DDEAuto 630
DocProperty 631
EditTime 631
Embed 631
Eq 632
FileName 632
FileSize 633
Fillin 633
FormCheckBox 633
FormDropDown 634
FormText 634
GoToButton 634
If 635
IncludePicture 635
IncludeText 636
Index 636
Info 637
Keywords 638
LastSavedBy 638
Link 638
MacroButton 639
MergeField 639
MergeRec 640
MergeSeq 640
Next 640
NextIf 640
NoteRef 641
NumChars 641
NumPages 641
NumWords 641
Page 642
PageRef 642
Print 642
PrintDate 642
Private 643
Quote 643
RD 643
Ref 644
RevNum 644
SaveDate 644
Section 644
SectionPages 645
Seq 645
Set 648
SkipIf 648

StyleRef 649
Subject 649
Symbol 649
TA 650
TC 650
Template 651
Time 651
Title 651
TOA 652
TOC 652
UserAddress 653
UserInitials 654
UserName 654
XE 654
= (Formula) 655

Chapter 29: Streamlining Document Creation with Forms 659

Understanding Forms 659
Creating a Form Template 661
Using the Forms Toolbar 662
Creating a Text Field 663
Creating a Check Box Field 665
Creating a Drop-Down Field 666
Adding Help to a Form Field 667
Filling Out a Form 668
Using Preprinted Forms 669
Creating a Custom Form Menu 669
Using Macros in a Form 671
A Sample Form That Uses Macros 671
Exporting Form Data to a Text File 674

Chapter 30: Mail Merge Secrets 675

Understanding Mail Merge 675
Using the Mail Merge Helper 676
   Preparing the main document 676
   Preparing the data source 678
   Inserting field names in the main document 681
   Verifying your merge codes 683
Merging the documents 683
   Merging directly to the printer 684
   Merging to a new document 684
   Merging to e-mail or fax 684
   Merging a range of records 685
Using Merge Fields in the Body of a Letter 686
Using Word Fields 687
   Using a Fill-In field 688
   Using an If-Then-Else field 689
Printing Mailing Labels 690
Printing Envelopes 692
Fun Things to Do with the Data Source 694

Sorting data 695
Using a merge query 695
Understanding precedence 698
Editing the data source directly 699
Importing data from another source 701

Part IX: Secrets of WordBasic Programming 703

Chapter 31: WordBasic Fundamentals 705

The Basic Structure of WordBasic Macros 705
Rules for Writing WordBasic Instructions 707
Comments 708
Variables 709
Arrays 710
    Using the Dim instruction to define arrays 710
    Arrays with more than one dimension 711
    Sorting array values 712
Strings 712
    Concatenation 712
    String functions 713
Control Structures 715
The Goto Instruction and Labels 715
The If Statement 716
    The basic If statement 717
    Nested If statements 717
    The ElseIf structure 718
    The single-line If 719
For/Next Loops 719
    Using For/Next loops with arrays 720
    Nested For/Next loops 721
    While/Wend loops 722
    The Select Case statement 723
Error Handling 725
User Input and Output 726
    Print and Input 726
    MsgBox and MsgBox( ) 726
    InputBox$( ) 728
Getting a Word Command's Dialog Settings 730
Working with Word Commands 730
    Finding the right command 731
    Using WordBasic Help 735
    Recording the next command 736
User-Defined Subroutines and Functions 736
    Using subroutines 737
    Using functions 737
    Using shared variables 738
    Call-by-reference vs. call-by-value 739

Chapter 32: Creating Macros That Work With Documents 741

Making Sure You're In a Document Window 741
Getting the Selection 742
Using SelInfo() 743
Moving and Selecting 745
Inserting Text 748
Deleting Text 749
Formatting Text 749
Working with Bookmarks 756
Using the EditFind Command 759
Creating a Temporary Document 761
Lists of Useful Stuff 763
Using Document Variables 766
Using a Private Settings File (INI File) 767

Chapter 33: Working with Dialog Boxes 771

Using Built-in Dialog Boxes 771
Understanding Custom Dialog Boxes 773
Dialog Box Commands 775
Using the Dialog Editor 775
    Adding button controls 777
    Using the Information dialog boxes 778
    Adding option buttons and check boxes 779
    Adding text and text boxes 780
    Adding a group box 781
    Adding a picture field 781
    Deleting dialog box controls 782
    Copying the dialog box into the macro 782
    Copying a dialog box from a macro to Dialog Editor 782
    Editing the dialog box definition commands 783
Using a Custom Dialog Box in a Macro 783
    Displaying the dialog box 783
    Accessing the user's input 784
    Setting default values 785
    Putting it all together 785
Working with List Fields 788
Using Dynamic Dialog Boxes 790
    Setting up a dialog function 790
    Commands used in dialog functions 793
    A dynamic version of the CreateMsgBox macro 795
    Solving a problem with drop-down list fields 799
    A dynamic dialog box that simulates tabbed dialog boxes 801

Chapter 34: WordBasic Commands and Functions 809

WordBasic Commands and Functions
by Category 844
    String functions 844
    Numeric functions 845
    Cursor movement 845
    Scrolling 845
    Selecting 845
    Table handling 846

Paragraph formatting 846
Styles 846
View 847
Character formatting 847

Appendix A: The Word for Windows 95 SECRETS CD-ROM 849

What Is Shareware? 849
What Is Freeware? 850
The CD-ROM Itself Is Copyrighted 850
Installing the CD-ROM 850

Appendix B: The Word Document Virus Threat 853

How to Tell If You Have the
Winword.Concept Virus 855
How to Remove the Infection 855
Preventing Document Virus Infections 856
What About RTF Files? Are They Safe? 857

INDEX 859

CD-License 881

Introduction

Microsoft has done it again. On the same day that the much-anticipated new version of Windows — Windows 95 — was released, Microsoft also released a new version of its Microsoft Office suite tailored for use with Windows 95. Included in this new version of Microsoft Office is a new version of Word: Word for Windows 95, Version 7.0. Word 95 includes all of the expected upgrades required to take advantage of the new features of Windows 95: long filenames, 32-bit operation, multi-threading, and so on. But Word 95 goes further than this minimum: It also offers a host of substantial improvements to its predecessor Word 6.0, such as on-the-fly spell checking, new AutoFormat features, new Wizards, e-mail capabilities, a nifty Highlighter tool that works just like those pink and yellow highlighter pens, and much more.

The purpose of this book is to help you get the most out of Word for Windows 95. Out of the box, Word 95 is a pretty decent word processing program, about on par with the competition. With a little tweaking here and there, however, Word 95 can really sing. With this book in hand, you'll be able to produce documents that your colleagues will be certain you created with a sophisticated desktop publishing program. You'll learn shortcuts, secrets, and workarounds to common problems that you never knew existed. And, you'll be able to configure Word so that it works the way *you* want it to.

Shhh! It's a Secret!

Microsoft, in its infinite wisdom, has decided that most people don't read manuals, so why bother with them anyway. More and more, even the basic procedures required to operate a program as complex as Word are becoming "secret." But in this book, the term *secret* is reserved for those Word features that aren't documented in the manuals or the on-line help, or at least aren't documented in a way that is easy for mere mortals to discover.

Some of these secrets are powerful features that Microsoft includes with Word but decided not to tell anyone about. For example, Word comes with a Footnote Wizard that can automatically create bibliographic references that conform with MLA or Chicago Manual of Style conventions. But, you have to know where to look to find this Wizard: it isn't in any of the menus or toolbars. Similarly, Word includes a program called WordArt that lets you create fancy logos. Once again, though, you won't find this gem in any of Word's menus or toolbars.

Some of the secrets are Word features that are just downright hard to figure out how to use properly. For example, how do you set up a document that has no page numbers on the first page, then the next nine pages are numbered with Roman numerals (i, ii, iii, and so on up to ix), and the remainder of the document is numbered with Arabic numerals, starting over again at 1?

Bug alert!

Not all of the secrets are features. Some of them are outright bugs. For example sometimes Word steals portions of text when you create a numbered list by clicking the Numbering button, or it refuses to remove bold or italic formatting if the insertion point happens to be positioned just before the last character of a word.

I know it's a sobering experience to discover that Microsoft isn't flawless, but to paraphrase Forrest Gump, "Bugs Happen."

The biggest Word secret of all

The granddaddy of all Word secrets is that you do not have to be content with Word the way it works out of the box. Word is probably the most customizable piece of software ever written. You can change virtually *anything* about the way Word works. If you think Microsoft was out to lunch when its programmers populated the toolbars with buttons, scrap the standard toolbars and design your own. Do you think the menus are okay, but a few vital commands are missing? Add the commands that Microsoft forgot. Do you wish there was a keyboard shortcut to create a double underline? No problem: just create one.

This book will show you how to customize Word's menus, toolbars, and keyboard shortcuts — if you want to. Of course, you don't have to use any of this customization stuff at all; as I said, Word is an excellent word processor right out of the box. But sooner or later, you're bound to come across a feature that you'd use all the time if only it were more accessible. Such is the time when Word's capability to allow full customization comes in handy.

As if customizing the menus, toolbars, and keyboard shortcuts isn't enough, Word includes a full-fledged programming language called *WordBasic*, which you can use to create your own Word commands! These new commands — called *macros* — can range from a single line to many hundreds of lines. Fortunately, you don't need a degree in computer programming to create simple macros. Throughout this book, you'll find many examples of simple macros that plug the gaps left by Microsoft's sometimes hasty design of key features in Word. If you're interested in customizing Word to this degree, you can study these macros, type them in yourself, and even make your own modifications to the macros so that they are even more tailored to your needs. Or, you can simply copy the macros from the CD that comes with this book.

How to Use This Book

The first three chapters of this book provide some general introductory material that you should be familiar with before continuing with the rest of the book. All readers should read Chapter 1, which provides an overview of the new features of Word for Windows 95. If you are new to Windows 95, Chapter 2 will give you an overview of its most important new features. And, if you are new to Word for Windows — or if you are a Word veteran but still feel as if you haven't grasped the basics — check out Chapter 3, which gives an overview of Word fundamentals, with an emphasis on why Word works the way it does.

The rest of this book works like a reference. Start with the topic you want to learn about; look for it in the table of contents or in the index to get going. The table of contents is detailed enough that you should be able to find most of the topics you seek. If not, turn to the index, where you'll find even more detail.

Commands and such

On occasion, this book directs you to use specific keyboard shortcuts to get things done. When you see something like this:

Ctrl+Z

it means to hold down the Ctrl key while pressing the Z key and release both together. Don't type the plus sign.

Sometimes I'll tell you to use a menu command, like this:

File⇨Open

This line means to use the keyboard or mouse to open the File menu and select the Open command. (The underlined letters are the keyboard hot keys for the command. To use them, first press the Alt key. In the preceding example, you would press and release the Alt key, press and release the F key, and then press and release the O key.)

Whenever I describe a message or information you'll see on the screen, it will look like this:

Are we having fun yet?

Anything you are instructed to type appears in bold like so: Type **b:setup** in the Run dialog box. You type exactly what you see, with or without spaces.

Another little nicety about this book is that when you are directed to click one of those little buttons that litter the Word for Window's screen, a picture of the button appears in the margin. This way, you can see what the button looks like to help you find it on the screen.

What about Word 6?

While this book is written with Word for Windows 95 Version 7 in mind, it is also applicable to Word 6 users. In fact, probably 90 percent of what you read in this book applies equally to Word 6, and the 10 percent that doesn't is clearly marked. So if you haven't yet upgraded to Word for Windows 95, this book offers you a double benefit: not only does most of it apply to Word 6, but the part that applies strictly to Word 95 will help you decide whether you should upgrade.

How This Book Is Organized

The chapters in this book are organized into nine parts.

Part I: Welcome to Word for Windows 95

The chapters in this section serve as an introduction to the newest version of Word. Part I explains the new features of Word, and gives an overview of the most significant new features of Word 95 — at least those features that pertain to using Word. In addition, this section contains an important chapter — Chapter 3 — which presents an overview of why Word works the way it works — sort of a Tao of Word. This chapter is designed to trigger that lightbulb to flash on over your head by reviewing the basic assumptions that underlie the way Word operates. If you properly grasp these fundamentals, the rest of Word (well, most of it anyway) will fall right in place.

Part II: Secrets of Customizing Word

Here we go again with this stuff about "the biggest Word secret of all." This section contains chapters that explain how to use document templates, how to customize Word's appearance and change its option settings, how to customize its user interface, and how to create simple macros. I placed these chapters early in the book because they serve as foundation for the rest of the book. Throughout the rest of the book, whenever I describe a useful command that doesn't have an assigned keyboard shortcut, I'll suggest that you assign it one. I'll frequently suggest that you add new buttons to your toolbar or commands to your menus, and I'll often recommend that you create simple macros (some of them as short as a single line of text) to automate routine chores. When I do, you can refer back to these chapters for a refresher on how to complete those custom tasks.

Note

It's not necessary to read these chapters before proceeding with the rest of the book. But it will be helpful if you intend on making Word your own.

Part III: Secrets of Working with Word

The chapters in this section describe the techniques for managing your documents, which is one of the biggest changes in Word 95. Part III also explains the ins and outs of printing and sharing your work with others by using Word's groupware features.

Part IV: Secrets of Editing

The chapters in this section cover the secrets of efficiently editing your documents, from the different ways of navigating within a document, selecting text, deleting, and using Find and Replace, to the more advanced techniques of setting up and using AutoCorrect and AutoText. In addition, the spell checker, Thesaurus, and grammar checker are covered in this chapter. (By the way, I *hate* the grammar checker! Turn to Chapter 13 to see what ridiculous suggestions the grammar checker has to offer Ernest Hemingway and Abraham Lincoln.)

Part V: Secrets of Formatting

In this section, you will find details on formatting documents, including the basics of formatting characters and paragraphs. I'll unravel the mysteries of page layouts and sections, including how to get page numbers to work exactly the way you want them to. Tabs will make total sense. And, you'll learn the tricks of properly setting up bullets, numbered lists, and tables. Finally, Chapter 18 will show you how to use one of the most important of all Word features: styles.

Part VI: Power Desktop Publishing Techniques

This section extends the formatting topics that were covered in Part V into the realm of desktop publishing. You'll learn the secrets of typography, with advice on picking the right fonts to avoid the "ransom note" look. You'll also learn how to set up columns and work with frames to create some really impressive desktop publishing effects. The secrets of working with clip art and of using Word's own impressive drawing tools is covered, as are the "secret" applications that come with Word: WordArt, the Equation Editor, and Microsoft Graph.

Part VII: Secrets of Working with Long Documents

This section covers topics that don't really come into play unless your documents are relatively long. You'll learn the secrets of working with outlines and master documents, creating an index, table of contents, or other table, and creating footnotes, endnotes, and cross-references.

Part VIII: Building Word Applications

The chapters in this section show you how to use Word to solve common business problems. You'll learn how to combine objects created by different applications — such as Excel or PowerPoint — into a single document. You'll also learn how to customize documents by using Word's special field codes, how to set up fill-in-the-blank forms, and how to perform mail merges.

Part IX: Secrets of WordBasic Programming

The last section in this book is a complete tutorial in WordBasic programming. You'll learn the basics of working with the WordBasic programming language, and you'll learn how to create macros that edit your documents and that display and gather information by using custom dialog boxes.

Appendix A: The Word for *Windows 95* *SECRETS CD-ROM*

This appendix summarizes the files that you can find on the Word for Windows 95 SECRETS CD-ROM that accompanies this book, along with instructions on how to use the CD.

What's Cool

The juiciest parts of this book are the paragraphs that have an icon next to them in the margin. These icons are there to draw your attention to some cool tidbit that is worth paying attention to, even if you're just skimming through.

The following icons are used:

The Secret icon marks information that isn't readily available through normal means. You won't find this information in the manual or in the on-line help. In many cases, you won't find it anywhere else but here.

This icon marks a time-saving recommendation that can often spare you grief later.

This icon is used to mark interesting information that may shed light on why a feature works the way it does, remind you of a connection between one Word feature and another, or otherwise enlighten the subject matter.

This icon marks a feature that is new to Word for Windows 95.

Watch out. This icon is used to mark a technique or procedure that could get you into trouble if not used properly. This is not to discourage use of the feature, only to make sure that you are aware of the caveats.

This icon indicates that a macro is being presented. If you're not in the least interested in macros, this icon is your cue to skip ahead. If you are a macro junkie, this icon will quickly become your favorite. Each of these macros is included on the CD, so you don't actually have to type the macros to use them.

On Your Way

It's time to get on with it then. Roll up your sleeves and dig into Word for Windows 95. Have fun!

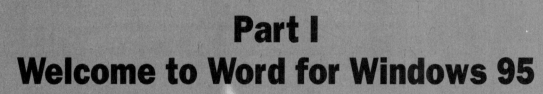

Part I
Welcome to Word for Windows 95

1   What's New with Word for Windows 95

2   Welcome to Windows 95

3   Fundamental Word Secrets

Chapter 1

What's New with Word for Windows 95

In This Chapter

▶ New features of Word 95, such as new dialog boxes to support long filenames.

▶ New features of Office 95 that affect the way you work with Word, such as Office 95's new Office Shortcut Bar and binders.

▶ New features of the other programs that come with Office 95: Excel, PowerPoint, Access, and Schedule+.

Microsoft's long-awaited replacement for its aging Windows 3.1 operating system — dubbed Windows 95 — promises many benefits for novice and advanced users alike. However, one of the most substantial features of Windows 95 — its capability to protect programs from one another — won't be realized until a new crop of Windows 95 applications takes root. Microsoft's Word for Windows 7 is the premier word processing program among this new harvest of Windows 95 programs.

Word 95 is not a thoroughly revamped version of Word. Instead, think of it more as the Windows 95 version of Word 6. There are a few minor enhancements here and there, but for the most part, the new features of Word 95 primarily support new features of Windows 95, such as long filenames. Nearly all of what you already know about Word 6 applies directly to Word 95, and most of the techniques and secrets presented in this book apply to Word 6 as well as Word 95.

New Features of Word 95

For the most part, Word 95 is simply a 32-bit, Windows 95 version of Word 6. Most of the new features described in the following sections were required simply to make Word work effectively under Windows 95.

The following sections describe the more significant new features of Word 95. You can find a list of new Word features by calling up the Help⇨Microsoft Word Help Topics command, choosing the Contents tab, and clicking on What's New.

Improved File⇨Open and File⇨Save As commands

With Windows 3.1 and Word 6, filenames were limited to eight characters plus a three-character extension. The extension indicated whether the file was a document (DOC) or a template (DOT), so users had to cram as much identifying information as possible into the eight-character filename.

Users have long grumbled about the eight-character filename limit of MS-DOS, so that was one of the first problems Microsoft addressed with Windows 95. With Windows 95, you can now use filenames as long as 255 characters. You can say good-bye to filenames like JRNL0595.DOC and LTRBOBAB.DOC and hello to filenames like "Journal for May 1995" and "Letter to Bob Abbott."

To accommodate these longer filenames, Microsoft has thoroughly revamped the standard File dialog boxes for the File⇨Open and File⇨Save As commands. Figure 1-1 shows the appearance of the new File Open dialog box.

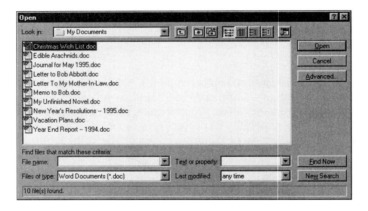

Figure 1-1: The new File Open dialog box.

Here are some of the File Open dialog box's more notable new features:

- Long filenames, which can include spaces, are supported.

- The familiar Drive and Directories controls have been replaced with a Look in control, which lets you rummage through your drives and directories (oops, I mean folders, the new Windows 95 term for directory).

- Get used to the new format for displaying files and folders. An icon is displayed next to each file to indicate the file type. Because the File Open dialog box displays only Word documents, the Word icon appears next to all of the files.

- You can use various buttons to display file details, properties, or a preview of each file's contents.

■ You can quickly search for documents that contain specific text by typing the text in the Te*xt* or property field.

The Save As dialog box is similar, as you can see in Figure 1-2. It, too, supports long filenames and lets you create a new folder. As an impressive new feature of the Save As dialog box, Word 95 will automatically suggest a filename for you, based on the contents of the first line of the document. If this first line containsa a document title, you may accept the suggested filename as is. Otherwise, you can replace it with a more pertinent filename of your own choosing.

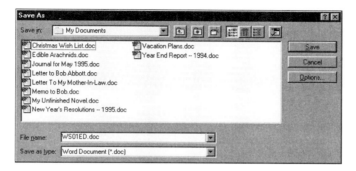

Figure 1-2: The improved Save As dialog box.

 You can create a new directory (er, folder) from the Save As dialog box by clicking the Create New Folder button. This is a welcome new feature. Before, you'd have to switch to File Manager (yuck!) just to create a new directory.

For more information about the File⇨Open and File⇨Save As commands, turn to Chapter 6.

Tip

Improved File⇨New command

The File⇨New command has been improved to provide more flexibility in the way templates are assigned to documents. In Word 6, the File⇨New command displayed a list of templates that were present in the template directory specified in the Tools⇨Options⇨File Locations dialog box (usually \WINWORD\TEMPLATE). All document templates had to be stored in this directory, and as a result, the list of templates could easily become unmanageable.

In Word 95, you can organize your templates into folders beneath the default template folder. These folders are presented in the File New dialog box as tabs, as shown in Figure 1-3. When you click a tab, Word 95 displays icons for the templates in their corresponding folder. The tab labeled General is the template folder itself, which usually contains only the NORMAL.DOT template. You can add your own templates to any of the template folders, and any folders you create under the default template folder will appear as tabs on the New dialog box if they contain at least one .DOT file.

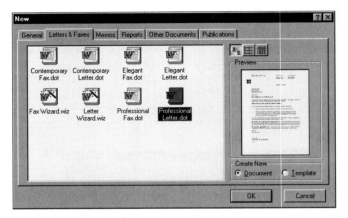

Figure 1-3: The improved File⇨New command uses tabs to organize templates.

See Chapter 6 for more information about the File⇨New command.

The File⇨Properties command

With the File/Summary info command in Word 6, you can record the following information for a document:

- Title
- Subject
- Author
- Keywords
- Comments

This useful command has been replaced by a more general File⇨Properties command, which lets you examine and set a variety of information about your document. Figure 1-4 shows the dialog box displayed when you select the File⇨Properties command.

As you can see in Figure 1-4, the information accessible via the Properties dialog box is grouped into five tabs:

- General, which displays the Windows 95 file properties for the document file (the filename, type, creation date, size in bytes, attributes, and so on).
- Summary, which includes the same summary information available in the Word 6 File⇨Summary info command.
- Statistics, which includes statistical information, including the number of characters, words, lines, and paragraphs in the document.

- Contents, which displays the contents of the document.

- Custom, which enables you to add any information to the document that you wish.

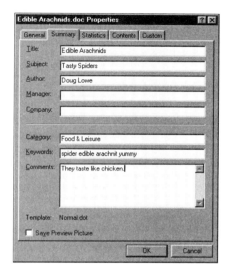

See Chapter 6 for details about using the File⟹Properties command.

Tip

Animation

Word 95 sports a flash animation feature that scrolls text up the screen in a more lively fashion than before. It's difficult to describe in a book, but you'll see what I mean the moment your typing reaches the bottom of the page and Word scrolls your text up to accommodate another line.

Unfortunately, you cannot disable this animation feature, so if your computer isn't fast enough to display the animation effect without a noticeable slowdown, you're out of luck. (Don't yell at me; I'm only the messenger.)

The Highlighter

With a new Word 95 feature called the Highlighter, you can mark portions of your document quickly, much as you would mark a printed page with a colored highlighter pen. The Highlighter tool lets you highlight text using any of four colors: blue, green, pink, and yellow.

Figure 1-5 shows the Highlighter in action. To highlight the text as shown in the figure, I clicked the Highlighter tool in the formatting toolbar and dragged over the text I wanted highlighted. You can also highlight a single word by double-clicking anywhere in the word, and you can highlight an entire paragraph by triple-clicking anywhere in the paragraph. To remove highlighting, simply drag the Highlighter tool over the text again or click to remove highlighting from individual words or paragraphs.

For details about using the Highlighter, refer to Chapter 8.

Tip

Find and Replace All Word Forms

The Find and Replace commands have a new option — Fin<u>d</u> All Word Forms — that lets you search not only for specific words but also for different forms of the same word. For example, if you search for the word *stink* and select the Fin<u>d</u> All Word Forms option, Word 95 will find not only the word *stink*, but also *stank, stunk,* and *stinking.*

If you use the Fin<u>d</u> All Word Forms option in the Replace command, Word 95 will not only find various word forms but also replace them with the correct form of the replacement word. For example, if you instruct Word to replace *stink* with *smell*, it will also replace *stank* and *stunk* with smelled, and *stinking* with *smelling.*

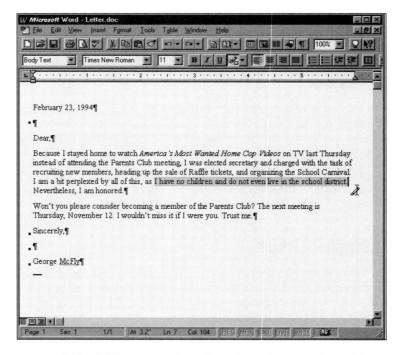

Figure 1-5: The Highlighter is an electronic version of the venerable highlighter pen.

This feature can be very useful, but it is also potentially error prone. As a result, you shouldn't use the Replace All option when replacing words using the Find All Word Forms option. Instead, you should manually confirm each replacement to ensure that Word matched up the word forms properly.

Turn to Chapter 9 for more information about the Find and Replace commands.

Tip

The Tip Wizard

The Tip Wizard lets you know when you are working inefficiently. Think of it as a quiet computer expert sitting patiently behind you, looking over your shoulder as you work. If the Tip Wizard sees you doing something in an awkward way, it jumps up and points out the error of your ways, suggesting a more efficient way to accomplish the same thing.

To activate the Tip Wizard, click the Tip Wizard button in the standard toolbar. The Tip Wizard will appear in its own toolbar, as shown in Figure 1-6.

The Tip Wizard's tips are brief and to the point. If you don't understand a tip, click the Show Me button for a more detailed explanation.

The Tip Wizard was first introduced with Excel 5.0. If you've used the Tip Wizard in Excel, you'll have no trouble using it in Word 95.

Note

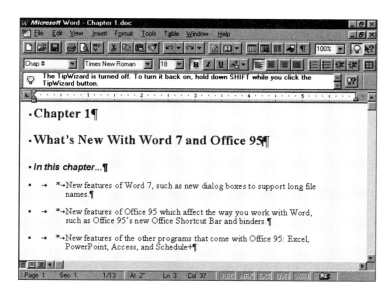

Figure 1-6: The Tip Wizard peers over your shoulder while you work, pointing out more efficient ways to use Word.

New Help button

🔃 The Help buttons in many of Word 6's dialog boxes have been replaced with a standard Help button in the title bar, next to the close button. Look back over the figures presented so far in this chapter and you'll see it, near the top right corner of each dialog box. Click this button to change the mouse pointer to a help pointer (a question mark with an arrow running through it). Then, click the help pointer on the portion of the dialog box that is causing you trouble to display help information.

On-the-fly spell checker

Word's new Automatic Spell Checking feature automatically checks your spelling as you type. You'd think this would slow Word down considerably, but the effect is barely noticeable, even on relatively slow computers. (I run a 33 MHz 486 and don't notice any delay at all.) The benefits of on-the-fly spell checking are substantial, not the least of which is that you'll quickly become both a better speller and a better typist due to the reinforcement provided by immediate detection and correction of your spelling errors.

When Automatic Spell Checking detects a misspelled word, it underlines it with a wavy red line. To correct the word, right-click it with the mouse. A list of suggested spellings will appear, as shown in Figure 1-7.

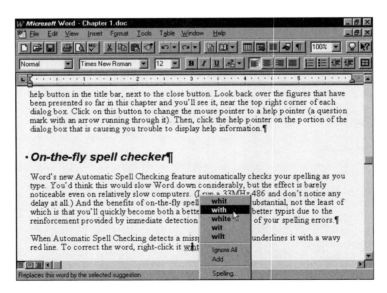

Figure 1-7: On-the-fly spell checking in action.

The 32-Bit Advantage

The biggest selling point of Word 95 is that it is a true 32-bit program, capable of taking full advantage of the new, 32-bit Windows 95 operating system. That sounds impressive, but what exactly does it mean?

From a technical standpoint, it means that Word 95 interacts with Windows 95 by using a programming interface called Win32, rather than with the older Win16 programming interface. Windows 95 can run both Win16 and Win32 applications, but it treats Win16 and Win32 applications very differently:

■ Win16 applications share a common address space, which means that an errant Win16 application can easily crash into a neighboring Win16 application, bringing both programs to a halt.

■ Win32 applications are each given a separate address space, making it difficult for a failing Win32 application to interfere with another Win32 application or with aWin16 application for that matter.

■ Win16 applications use cooperative multitasking, which means that once a program gets control of the CPU, it keeps it until the program voluntarily relinquishes control so that another program can run.

■ Win32 applications are preemptively multitasked, meaning that Windows 95 it self determines how long a program can run before it is forced to yield to another program.

The bottom-line benefits of 32-bit operation for Word 95 users include the following:

■ Improved multitasking. At least in theory, you should be able to do more things at once with the 32-bit version of Word.

■ Greater protection from errant applications. Word 95 is less likely to be trashed by a failure in another program.

■ Faster operation for certain functions. 32-bit code is not inherently faster than 16-bit code, but Win32 allows programs to spin off multiple execution threads — a feature Word 95 may exploit for operations such as background repagination.

Compatibility with Word 6

When upgrading any computer program, one of the key thoughts in the mind of any user is compatibility. Will the new software be able to access files created by the old version, and will you be able to exchange files with friends and coworkers who haven't yet upgraded to the new version?

Fortunately, Word 95 is both backward and forward compatible with Word 6. Backward compatibility means that Word 95 can open and edit documents and templates created in Word 6 without any special conversion requirements. Thus, you don't have to worry about converting your existing Word 6 documents and templates. They will work just fine in Word 95.

Forward compatibility means that you can open and edit documents and templates that you create in Word 95 in Word 6. This will be a relief to those users who need to share documents or templates with friends and coworkers who have not yet upgraded to Windows 95 and Word 95.

There are, of course, several limitations when you open a Word 95 document or template using Word 6. In particular:

■ Word 6 simply ignores any Word 95-specific features, such as the Highlighter or custom properties. If you save a document in Word 6, Word 6 removes any Word 95 highlights or custom properties.

■ Word 6 cannot deal directly with Windows 95's long filenames. Instead, Word 6 works with the 8-character filename assigned to the file by Windows 95. Thus, if you create a Word 95 document named "Letter to Bob," the filename will appear in Word 6 as "Letter~1.doc."

■ Word 6 cannot deal with Word 95's scheme for categorizing document templates by storing them in separate folders. In Word 6, any template not stored in the default template directory will not appear in the File New dialog box.

If you've created a custom spelling dictionary in Word 6, you can continue to use it in Word 95.

Word's powerful macro language, WordBasic is unchanged from Word 6 to Word 95. Prior to the release of Word 95, a rumor was floating around that Word 95 would include a version of Visual Basic for Applications (VBA), a version of Microsoft's Visual Basic that is designed for use as a universal macro language and is included with Excel. These rumors were unfounded, but Microsoft may incorporate VBA into Word in some future release. Don't hold your breath, though. Adding VBA to Word without breaking WordBasic is a monumental task.

New Features of Office 95

If you purchased Word 95 as a part of Microsoft's Office 95 suite, you have several additional new features that affect the way you work with Word 95. The following sections describe these new features.

Microsoft Office Shortcut Bar

The previous version of Microsoft Office came with a simple program called Microsoft Office Manager, or MOM for short. MOM displays a toolbar containing buttons that start the various programs included with Office. You can customize MOM so that your own programs are included in the toolbar. Other than that, however, MOM isn't very flexible.

With Office 95, Microsoft has substantially improved MOM. She is now called the Office Shortcut Bar (OSB), but is often referred to as SuperMOM. Figure 1-8 shows SuperMOM, docked to the top of the screen. (You can move SuperMOM to another edge of the screen if you wish.)

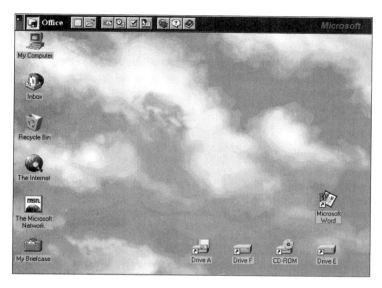

Figure 1-8: SuperMOM is a souped-up version of Microsoft Office Manager.

Unlike MOM, SuperMOM does not primarily launch programs. Instead, SuperMOM has been given a document orientation like Windows 95. From SuperMOM, you can create new documents and open existing documents, without concern for which Office application will edit the document. (That's the idea, anyway.)

For example, if you click SuperMOM's Start a Document button, it presents you with the dialog box shown in Figure 1-9. This dialog box is similar to Word 95's File New dialog box, which lets you select the template used to create a new document. However, instead of just listing Word document templates, this dialog box shows templates from all Office applications. When you select the template for the document you want to create and click OK, SuperMOM starts the correct application for the template you selected.

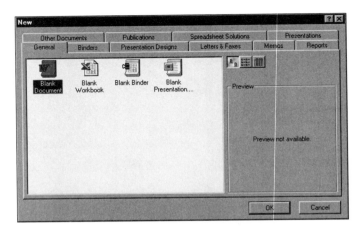

Figure 1-9: The Start a Document dialog box lets you create a new document based on a template, using any of the Office applications.

If you click the Open a Document button, SuperMOM displays an Open dialog box like the one in Figure 1-10. This dialog box is similar to Word's File Open dialog box, except that files of all types are displayed. For example, in Figure 1-10 you can see that Excel documents are intermixed with Word documents. When you select a document and click the Open button, the appropriate program will start, and the selected document will open.

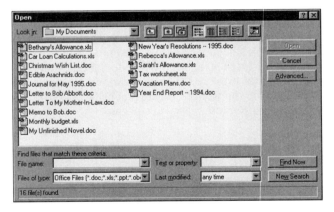

Figure 1-10: The Open a Document dialog box lets you open a document without regard to which program created the document.

Besides these document-oriented features, OSB also sports the following new features:

- You can drag the shortcut bar about and "dock" it to any of the four edges of the screen, or you can leave it floating in the middle of the screen.

- Like the Windows 95 taskbar, you can configure SuperMOM to disappear from view when not in use. It reappears when you move the mouse all the way to the edge of the screen on which it is docked.

- Like the original MOM, SuperMOM can be customized. You can add buttons to start Word or any other Office program directly, and you can add programs of your own.

- You can configure SuperMOM to display more than one toolbar.

- SuperMOM can automatically convert your Programs and Accessories folders to toolbars.

- You can configure SuperMOM with sound effects and animation.

Tip

See Chapter 4 for more information about SuperMOM.

Binders

One of the most interesting new features of Office 95 is the Microsoft Office Binder. This program lets you create binders, or special files that contain collections of document files created by other Microsoft Office applications. Each document contained in the binder is called a *section* and is analogous to a tabbed section in a real binder.

Microsoft Binder uses OLE 2 in-place editing so that you can edit the various sections that compose a binder directly from within the Binder window, regardless of which application created the document for that section. For example, when you edit a section that contains a Word document, Word's menus, toolbars, and keyboard shortcuts take over, enabling you to edit the Word document as if you were running Word. Likewise, Excel takes over when you edit a section that contains an Excel spreadsheet book.

Figure 1-11 shows Microsoft Binder in action, working with a binder that contains three sections. The column on the left side of the screen contains icons that represent the sections in the binder. As you can see, Word has taken over the rest of the Binder window so that you can edit the Chapter 1 document.

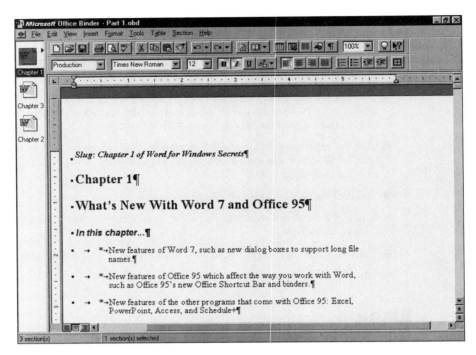

Figure 1-11: Microsoft Office Binder lets you combine documents created by any Office program into a single Binder file.

Without Binder, multifile projects are usually handled by creating a separate directory to hold the project's files. Binder has several advantages over this approach:

- You can share the entire project with a network user by mailing the binder file.

- You can print the entire project, telling Binder to number pages consecutively across all documents in the binder.

- Office ships with a set of Binder templates so that you can quickly create multidocument projects, including client billing, proposals, and more.

- The programming interface to Binder is well-documented, so you can create Binder objects using Visual Basic.

Tip

You can find detailed information about using Binder in Chapter 31.

Schedule+

Office 95 comes with an improved version of Schedule+, Microsoft's personal information manager. Figure 1-12 shows the Schedule+ windows with the contact list displayed.

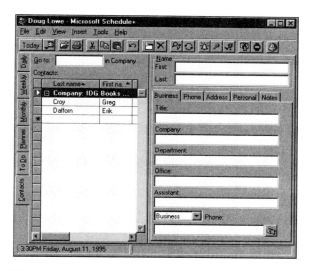

Figure 1-12: Schedule+ lets you keep a computerized address book.

Schedule+ sports the following features:

■ An appointment book that lets you schedule activities on a daily, weekly, monthly, or yearly basis. You can schedule individual activities or recurring events, such as weekly meetings, birthdays, anniversaries, and so forth.

■ Networking features that let you coordinate schedules with other network users. This feature is especially useful for scheduling meetings with other users; Schedule+ can help you determine a meeting time at which all attendees are available and can send a message to all attendees to confirm the scheduled meeting.

■ A contact list that lets you keep your address book on-line. You can integrate the contact list with Word's mail merge features.

■ A to-do list that you can tie to your appointment book and contact list.

Chapter 2

Welcome to Windows 95

In This Chapter

▶ Finding your way around the new Windows 95 user interface.

▶ Using Explorer efficiently.

▶ Discovering the secrets of long filenames.

Word 95 isn't all that much different from Word 6, but if you're switching to Word 95 and Windows 95 at the same time, prepare yourself for an uphill climb. The very fact that Word 95 runs under Windows 95 changes the way Word looks and feels. As I pointed out in the preceding chapter, most of the changes introduced with Word 95 are a direct result of the need to support Windows 95 features, such as long filenames from within Word.

This chapter describes some of the more significant improvements in Windows 95, with special emphasis on those features that affect how you work with Windows 95 application programs, including Word 95.

Learning the New Interface

To the average user, the most obvious difference between Windows 3.1 and Windows 95 is that the user interface has been thoroughly revamped. When you first begin to use Windows 95, you'll probably feel lost as you search for the familiar Program Manager groups and File Manager icons. Soon, however, you'll grow accustomed to the new look and feel of Windows 95 and begin to appreciate the subtle and not-so-subtle improvements it has to offer.

I do not intend this chapter as a tutorial on how to use the Windows 95 interface. I do, however, want to at least point out some of the more obvious differences you'll encounter right off the bat when you begin using Windows 95 and give you some hints on how you can customize the configuration of Windows 95 to suit your working style and work around its limitations.

The Desktop

In Windows 3.1, the screen background was referred to as the desktop. This rudimentary desktop served but three purposes:

- It was a place to display wallpaper, which was usually obscured by open Windows anyway and took far too large a byte out of available system resources for experienced users to take it seriously.

- It was a place where icons for minimized windows were displayed. Unfortunately, the icons were often overlaid by open windows, so you could easily lose track of which programs were running in a minimized state.

- It was a place where you could double-click to call up the Task Manager, a moderately useful program that you could also summon at any time by pressing Ctrl+Esc. The Task Manager let you switch to any running program or cancel a program that had stopped responding.

In Windows 3.1, the desktop was merely a backdrop for Program Manager, which was where most Windows users worked and, as a matter of fact, what many Windows users thought of as their "desktop." Windows 95 has eliminated Program Manager, and the desktop has been elevated as the centerpiece of the new Windows user interface. The desktop is no longer a nearly useless background, but it is the primary arena in which you will live and work in Windows 95.

Figure 2-1 shows how Windows 95 looks after startup on my system. Your system will appear different because I've customized the icons on my desktop, and you will too (if you haven't already). As you can see, no Program Manager is present, with its confusing tangle of overlapping program group windows and all-too-often obscured program icons. Instead, icons sit directly on the desktop where you can easily access them.

The icons residing on the desktop represent objects, which can be programs, folders, or data files. For example, if you're working on a Word document, you can easily drag an icon for the document onto the desktop. Then, you can start Word and edit the document simply by double-clicking on the document's icon.

When you initially set up Windows 95, your desktop is populated by several icons, depending on which options you select when you install Windows 95. The icons you are most likely to see include the following:

- **My Computer.** The My Computer icon is the principal entry point for exploring the information on your computer. I'll have more to say about My Computer in a moment.

- **Network Neighborhood.** The Network Neighborhood icon is similar to My Computer, except that it lets you access information stored on networked computers.

- **Microsoft Network.** If you installed the Microsoft Network, an icon for it will materialize on your desktop. Double-click on it to access Microsoft Network.

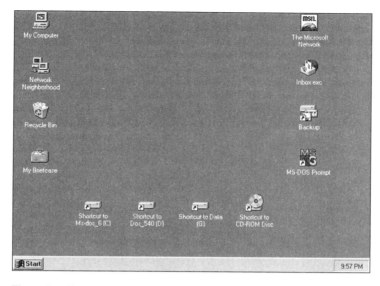

Figure 2-1: The Windows 95 desktop.

- **Inbox.** If you installed Microsoft Exchange, the Inbox icon will appear on the desktop. You can use it to read incoming electronic mail.

- **Recycle Bin.** With the Recycle Bin you can retrieve any files that you accidentally deleted, provided you haven't used the File⇨Empty Recycle Bin command to remove files permanently that have been held in limbo in the bin.

You can easily add, delete, and rearrange icons on the desktop. I'll explain how in the next sections.

Folders and the My Computer Icon

One of the most important aspects of the Windows 95 desktop is the notion of folders. Folders are nothing more than a graphical representation of disk directories. When you open a folder, Windows 95 opens a window and displays the contents of the directory in that window. Each file or subdirectory in the folder is displayed as an icon. Windows 95 determines which icon to display for each file by looking up the file's extension in the registry, the central repository for Windows configuration information. For more information about how this works, see the sidebar "How Windows 95 Keeps Track of File Types."

To access folders from the desktop, begin by clicking the My Computer icon. This opens a top-level window that represents your entire computer system. Figure 2-2 shows how the My Computer window appears on my system. Your My Computer folder will appear different, depending on how many disk drives you have.

Notice that My Computer contains an icon for both floppy disk drives (A: and B:), all hard drives, and CD-ROM drives (C: through H:), in addition to the Control Panel, Printers, and Dial-Up Networking.

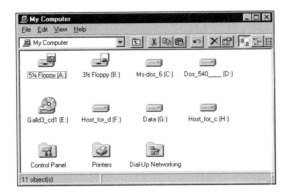

Figure 2-2: The My Computer window.

Tip

If you don't like the way individual icons appear within the folder, you can change the icon arrangement with the options available from the View menu: Large icons (the default, as shown in Figure 2-2), Small icons, List, or Details. Figure 2-3 shows how My Computer appears after the View⇨Details command is selected.

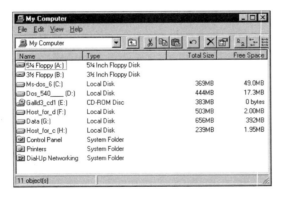

Figure 2-3: The My Computer folder with View⇨Details.

Tip

To view the contents of a drive, double-click on the icon representing the drive. Windows 95 will open a window showing the top-level folder for the drive (the drive's root directory). To view another folder, double-click on the folder's icon. You can keep double-clicking on folder icons as much as you want to navigate your way through your computer's hierarchy of folders.

Figure 2-4 shows the appearance of a typical folder containing documents of several types.

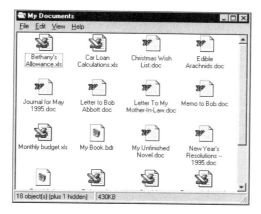

Figure 2-4: The folder containing several documents.

How Windows 95 Keeps Track of File Types

Windows 95's use of file extensions to identify the document type is a development of Associations found in previous versions of the Windows File Manager. Associations let you create a relationship between files with a given extension and a particular program. If you double-click on a file in File Manager, Windows 95 looks up the file's extension to see if an associated program exists. If so, the program executes, with the filename passed as a parameter.

Windows 95 uses a similar mechanism to keep track of file types. Windows associates the following information with each file extension:

- The file type. For Word 95, the document type is the same as for Word 6: "Microsoft Word 6.0 Document." The file type was not changed to "Microsoft Word 95.0

Document" because the actual document format has not changed from Word 6 to Word 95.

- The icon displayed when the file appears in a folder.

- Actions that you can execute from the pop-up menu that appears when you right-click the file. For a Word document, three actions are enabled: New, Open, and Print. These action sare implemented by using Dynamic Data Exchange (DDE), which lets one program send a command to another program. When you invoke one of these actions, the Windows 95 desktop starts Word and sends it a command to create a new document, open the selected document, or print the selected document.

Working efficiently with folders

Several aspects of how My Computer folders are displayed often frustrate experienced users. For example, the default behavior when you double-click on a folder icon opens up a new window to display the second folder. This seems convenient at first, but very soon you'll find your screen so cluttered with windows for open folders that you can't find your way around the desktop. Figure 2-5 shows how cluttered the desktop can appear with only six folders open.

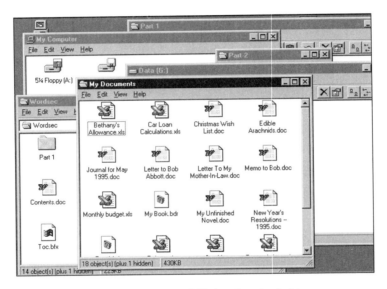

Figure 2-5: Extraneous folders can quickly inundate the desktop.

If you have this problem, open the My Computer window (double-click the My Computer icon) and then call up the View⇨Options command. The dialog box shown in Figure 2-6 will appear. Click the option button labeled "Browse folders by using a single window that changes as you open each folder." Then, click on OK. This will help prevent folder clutter.

Another folder option you might want to enable is the folder toolbar. You can activate the toolbar by selecting the View⇨Toolbar command. Table 2-1 lists the buttons that are displayed on this toolbar and describes each button's function. (If the window is too small to display the entire toolbar, you may have to enlarge the toolbar by dragging one of its sides to reveal all of the tools.)

Secret

The Cut, Copy, and Paste buttons use the same icons as the corresponding buttons on Word's toolbars. However, do not confuse the functions of these buttons. Within Word, these buttons are used to cut and paste portions of text and graphics. In a folder, these buttons cut and paste entire files and folders!

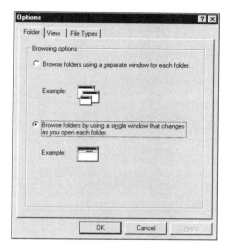

Figure 2-6: The Options dialog box for My Computer.

Table 2-1	Toolbar Buttons for Browsing Folders
Button	*What It Does*
Data (G:)	Go to a different folder. Use this drop-down list for navigating to other folders on your computer's hard or floppy drives.
	Up one level. Moves up one level in the folder hierarchy. In other words, switches to the current folder's parent folder.
	Cut. Moves the selected objects to the Clipboard.
	Copy. Places a copy of the selected objects on the Clipboard.
	Paste. Inserts the contents of the Clipboard into the current folder.
	Undo. Undoes the previous action.
	Delete. Deletes the selected objects into the Recycle Bin.
	Properties. Calls up the Properties dialog box for the selected object.

(continued)

Table 2-1 *(continued)*	
Button	*What It Does*
	Large icons. Uses large icons.
	Small icons. Uses small icons so that more objects can be displayed.
	List. Displays objects in a list with small icons.
	Details. Displays file details, including size, file type, and date modified.

Routine file and folder operations

The following sections explain how to carry out routine file and folder management operations when working with My Computer folders.

Deleting a file or a folder.

To delete a file or folder, click it to select it, press the Delete key, and click the Delete button in the toolbar, or you can use the File⇨Delete command. Windows 95 will ask whether you're sure you want to send the file to the Recycle Bin; click Yes to delete the file.

Renaming a file or a folder.

To rename a file or folder, click on it twice. Do not double-click: that will open the file or folder. Instead, click on the file or folder once, wait a moment, and click again. A rectangle will appear around the name to indicate that you can edit it. You can also rename a file or folder by selecting it and using the File⇨Rename command, or you can right-click on the file and select Rename from the context menu that appears.

Copying a file or a folder.

To copy a file or folder, drag it from one folder to another.

Note

When dragging a file, it's always a good idea to drag it by using the secondary mouse button (for right-handed users, that's the right button). When you release the mouse button after dragging the file to its destination, a pop-up menu will appear asking whether you want to move the file or folder, copy it, or create a shortcut to it (more on shortcuts later).

Selecting multiple files or folders.

To select more than one file, hold down the Ctrl key while clicking on the files you want to select. Or, click on a file, hold down the Shift key, and click another file. All files between the two files you clicked on will be selected.

Creating a new file or folder.

You can create a new file or folder by selecting the File⇨New command. A cascading menu will appear, enabling you to select the type of file that you want to create. Folder and Shortcut will always appear as options; other file types may appear as well. You can also accomplish this by right-clicking directly on the desktop to call up the shortcut menu and choosing the New command.

For Keyboard Jockeys Only

Windows 95 is designed with mouse users in mind. In keeping with Windows 3.1 tradition, however, Windows 95 provides many keyboard shortcuts for those users with rodent phobias. The following keyboard shortcuts are available when working with folders:

Keyboard Shortcut	What It Does
F2	Renames the selected file.
F3	Calls up the Find dialog box.
Alt+F4	Closes the active window.
Backspace	Opens the parent folder.
Delete	Deletes the file, placing it in the Recycle Bin.
Shift+Delete	Deletes the file without placing it in the Recycle Bin.
Enter	Opens the selected file. If the file is a program, the program is run.
Alt+Enter	Displays the selected file's property sheet.
Shift+Enter	If a folder is selected, opens Explorer.
Ctrl+A	Selects all.
Ctrl+X	Cuts the selected objects to the Clipboard.
Ctrl+C	Copies the selected objects to the Clipboard.
Ctrl+V	Pastes the objects on the Clipboard into the folder.
Ctrl+Z	Undoes the last operation.
Alt+Tab	Switches among open applications and windows.

Going up?

One frustrating limitation of working with My Computer folders is that, although you can work your way down the folder hierarchy by double-clicking on folder icons, no method seems to exist for working your way back up the hierarchy. In other words, when you open a folder, how do you return to that folder's parent folder?

Actually, you can do this in two ways. I've already mentioned both in passing, but here they are again for emphasis:

- Activate the Folder toolbar by choosing the View⇨Toolbar command. Then, click the "Up One Level" button.

- Press the Backspace key.

The fast track to the desktop

The more you use Windows 95, the more you'll come to rely on the desktop as a convenient place to drop items that you frequently access. Use the desktop for creating icons for programs so that you can quickly launch your favorite programs or create shortcuts to folders or even individual documents. You can even drag text or graphics from a program such as Word onto the desktop, drop it there, and pick it up later.

Unfortunately, even experienced Windows 3.1 users need some time to get out of the Program Manager mindset. Windows 3.1 users are used to switching directly to Program Manager from an application program by pressing Alt+Tab repeatedly until Program Manager comes to the foreground. Unfortunately, in Windows 95, the desktop is always the background. Any windows that are open will always overlay the desktop. And if you maximize a window, you won't see the desktop at all. Furthermore, the desktop never appears in the list of programs that Alt+Tab cycles through.

So how can you quickly return to the desktop so that you can access the icons you've so carefully placed there? There are three methods:

- Right-click on the taskbar to bring up its pop-up menu (you must click between the buttons on the taskbar to do this) and select the Minimize All Windows command. This instantly minimizes every open window, revealing the desktop and its icons. When you're finished working with the desktop, right-click on the taskbar again and select the Undo Minimize All command to restore the windows to their previous condition.

- Press Ctrl+Esc to call up the taskbar and press Alt+M. This also minimizes all open windows to reveal the desktop. When you're finished, right-click on the taskbar and select Undo Minimize All.

Secret

- Open a window to the hidden Desktop folder in your Windows directory. In this folder, Windows keeps track of the objects you've placed on the desktop. After you open a window for this folder, you can Alt+Tab to it to display the contents of the desktop without minimizing any other windows, as shown in Figure 2-7. As you can see, the objects in the Desktop folder aren't laid out the same as they are on the actual desktop, but they behave exactly as they do when accessed directly from the desktop. (Some desktop icons, such as My Computer and Network Neighborhood, do not appear in the Desktop folder.)

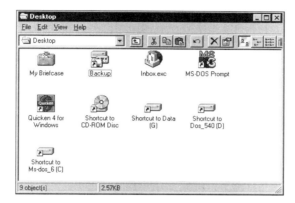

Figure 2-7: Displaying the Desktop folder.

To open the hidden desktop folder, follow these steps:

1. Double-click on My Computer to open the My Computer folder.

2. Double-click on the drive that contains your Windows folder (normally C:).

3. Double-click on the Windows folder.

4. Select the View⇨Options command.

5. Click on the View tab to display the view options.

6. Check the Show All Files option box.

7. Click on OK.

8. Double-click on the Desktop folder.

9. If you want the Desktop folder to open every time you start your computer, create a shortcut to it in the \Windows\Start Menu\Programs\ Startup folder.

Explorer

If you never used Windows 3.1 File Manager, you'll probably never use Explorer. But if you were a File Manager junkie and My Computer seems pathetically undernourished to you, you'll be relieved when you discover Explorer.

Figure 2-8 shows the Explorer window. As you can see, the Explorer window is divided into two panes, much like File Manager. On the left is a tree structure that represents your entire computer, not just the directory structure of a single drive, as in File Manager. The pane on the right shows the contents of the current folder, in this case the root folder of the C: drive.

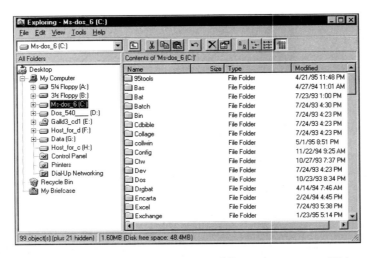

Figure 2-8: Explorer provides more advanced file management capabilities.

Starting Explorer

You can start Explorer in several ways:

■ Click on the Start button on the taskbar, select Programs, and click on Windows Explorer.

■ Click on the Start button on the taskbar, click on Run, type Explorer, and press the Enter key.

■ Right-click on My Computer or any folder icon and select Explore from the pop-up menu.

■ Select a folder in My Computer and select the File⇨Explore command, or press Shift+Enter.

■ Select the My Computer icon by clicking on it. Then, hold down the Shift key and double-click the My Computer icon, or Shift double-click on any folder icon in My Computer.

Secret

One of the most unfortunate keyboard shortcut choices Microsoft made in Windows 95 was using Shift double-click to explore a folder. The problem is that Shift single-click means to extend the selection of icons from the currently selected icon to the icon you Shift click. For example, if you select an icon at the top-right of your screen, and then Shift click an icon at the bottom-left of your screen, Windows 95 will select all of the icons in between. If you Shift double-click an icon when another icon is already selected, Windows 95 first selects all of the icons that fall between the two icons, and — believe it or not opens them all with Explorer. To explore a single icon by Shift double-clicking it, you must make sure that no other icons are already selected.

Using Explorer

All of the file operations described in the previous sections work in Explorer. Explorer's main improvement over My Computer folders is the addition of the tree pane, which allows you to navigate quickly to any drive or folder on your computer. Click on any folder in the tree to display its contents in the pane on the right side of the Explorer window.

You can expand or collapse the Explorer tree as follows:

- To expand a folder, click on the + next to the folder's icon in the tree. You can also select the folder and press the plus key on the numeric keypad or the right arrow key.

- To collapse a folder, click on the – next to the folder's icon. You can also select the folder and press the minus key on the numeric keypad or the left arrow key.

- To expand everything under a folder, select the folder and press the * key on the numeric keypad. To expand the entire Explorer tree, do this to the Desktop icon at the top of the tree.

Secret

You might notice one difference between Explorer and File Manager: File Manager is an MDI (Multiple Document Interface) application, which means that you can open more than one window within File Manager to access different drives and directories. Then, you can use File Manager's drag-and-drop feature to copy a file from one directory to another simply by dragging the file's icon from one File Manager window to another.

Explorer is not an MDI application, but you can still do this. You just have to open two separate Explorer windows. Then, you can move or copy files between folders simply by dragging the files from one Explorer window to the other.

When you drag files in Windows 95, you should do so with the right mouse button. Then, when you release the mouse button, a pop-up menu will appear asking whether you want to copy or move the file. In Windows 3.1, you had to think hard to remember whether to hold down the Shift key while dragging a file to differentiate between a move and a copy.

The Taskbar

One of the most important additions to the Windows 95 user interface is the taskbar. Initially present at the bottom of the screen, the taskbar has two basic functions:

- It provides an easy way to switch to any running program. One of the most difficult aspects of using Windows 3.1, especially for new users, was keeping track of all the windows that appear on the screen when more than one program was running. Even experienced users could lose track of programs. The taskbar displays a button for every open window. To switch to a window, simply click the window's icon in the taskbar.

- It provides an easy way to start application programs. Instead of the confusing clutter of Program Manager groups, the taskbar has a Start button that displays a simple hierarchical menu of programs. To start a program, click on the Start button to reveal the menu, move the mouse around the menu until you find the program you want to run, and click the mouse button again.

Customizing the taskbar

The default behavior for the taskbar is always to occupy the bottom of the screen, as shown in Figure 2-9. Because the taskbar is always visible, it never gets lost. This solves one of the most common problems faced by new Windows users (and experienced users, too): losing windows on the desktop. The taskbar remains visible even when you maximize a window.

Windows 95 accomplishes the always-on-top behavior of the taskbar by lying to application programs about how big the screen is. When an application is maximized, Windows reduces the reported dimensions of the screen so that the maximized window and the taskbar do not overlap. That way, the taskbar does not obscure the bottom portion of the application window. You can see this behavior in Figure 2-9: Notice that Word's status bar (which would ordinarily appear at the very bottom of the screen) appears instead just above the taskbar.

Of course, reducing the reported size of the screen results in a corresponding reduction in the amount of information an application can display. For example, keeping the taskbar visible forces Word to reduce the amount of text displayed on the screen. If you're using a 17-inch monitor with super-VGA resolution, you probably won't notice the smaller screen area. For a 13- or 14-inch monitor at standard VGA resolution (640x480), however, the reduction in screen area is noticeable.

Fortunately, Windows 95 allows you to customize the behavior of the taskbar. Right-click on a clear space in the taskbar (between buttons) to bring up the taskbar pop-up menu and select the Properties command. The taskbar properties dialog box will appear, as shown in Figure 2-10. Four options are available:

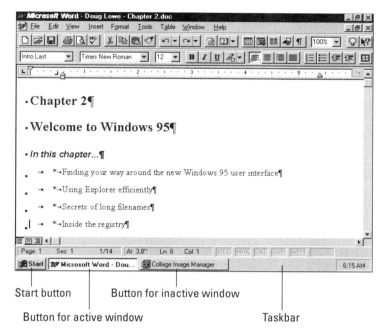

Figure 2-9: The taskbar in its default, always-visible state.

- **Always on top**. This option tells Windows 95 that whenever the taskbar is displayed, it should be visible. In other words, another window cannot overlay the taskbar.

- **Auto hide.** This option causes the taskbar to reduce itself to a line a single pixel wide at the edge of the screen when the taskbar is not being used. To call up the taskbar, simply move the mouse pointer to the thin line. The Auto hide option reduces the amount of screen real estate occupied by the taskbar when it's not in use. The screen space saved is now available to maximized applications.

- **Show small icons in Start menu.** This option reduces the size of the Start menu by using small icons.

- **Show Clock.** This option is on by default. If you disable it, the clock that appears on the right side of the taskbar will be removed.

Most experienced users should activate both Always on top and Auto hide. That way, the taskbar will always overlap any other window when it is active, but it will retreat to the very edge of the screen when not being used.

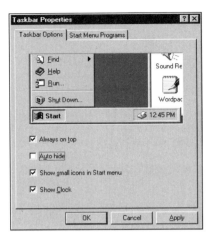

Figure 2-10: The taskbar properties dialog box.

Moving the taskbar

You can change the location of the taskbar by dragging it to any of the four edges of the screen. (The taskbar cannot float; it must be anchored to a screen edge.) To drag the taskbar, point to a clear spot on the taskbar (between buttons) and then press and hold down the left mouse button. Drag the mouse all the way to an edge of the screen. You won't see any indication that you have dragged the taskbar until the pointer reaches the edge of the screen. At that time, you'll see an outline of the taskbar. Release the mouse button to move the taskbar to the new location.

Positioning the taskbar when the Auto hide option is set can be problematic. Each of the screen's four edges potentially interferes with some aspect of using Word (and other programs as well):

■ If you move the taskbar to the right edge of the screen, it will likely interfere with application scrollbars. In other words, when you move the mouse to the right side of the screen intending to use the scrollbar, the taskbar will appear if you move the mouse too far.

■ If you place the taskbar at the top of the screen, you're liable to activate it accidentally when pointing to the window control buttons.

■ Placing the taskbar at the left edge of the screen often interferes with Word's selection bar, the left edge of the document window that allows you to select entire lines of text.

■ The least obtrusive position for the Auto hide taskbar is at the bottom of the screen. However, if Word's status bar is not visible, even the bottom placement will interfere with Word: you'll inadvertently bring up the taskbar whenever you reach for the horizontal scrollbar or the view buttons at the bottom of the Word menu.

You can also resize the taskbar to enable it to accommodate more buttons. Just position the mouse pointer over one of the edges of the taskbar long enough for the mouse pointer to change to a double-headed arrow. Then, you can drag the edge of the taskbar to increase or decrease the taskbar's size.

Using the Start button

The job of starting programs, which used to be Program Manager's purview, is now handled by the Start button, which is always available as a part of the taskbar. As Figure 2-11 shows, the Start button leads to a cascading menu structure so that you can easily start any program on your computer.

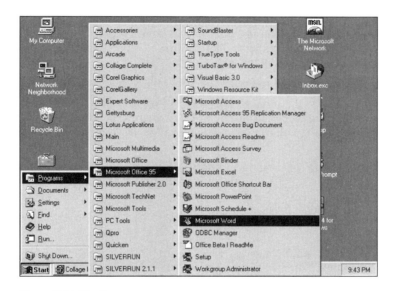

Figure 2-11: The Start menu.

Tip

You can activate the taskbar and bring up the Start menu at any time by pressing Ctrl+Esc. In Windows 3.1, Ctrl+Esc brought up the Task Manager, which let you switch between active programs. Ctrl+Esc still lets you switch between active programs because each active program appears as a button in the taskbar. By activating the Start menu, Ctrl+Esc also lets you start a new program.

The commands that initially appear on the Start menu are set by Windows and cannot be removed. They include the following:

- **Programs.** This command displays a hierarchical menu of programs. Use this command to start your application programs. Windows uses the contents of the \Windows\Start Menu\Programs folder to determine which menus and submenus to display here. When you install Windows 95 on an existing Windows 3.1 system, Windows 95 converts all of your Program Manager groups into folders subordinate to \Windows\Start Menu\Programs so that you can access your Program Manager groups through the Start button.

- **Documents.** This command displays a list of documents that you have recently opened. If you select a document from this menu, Windows 95 will automatically start the program associated with the document and open the document. Documents will automatically be collected in this menu, so you don't have to take any special action to reap the benefits of the Documents menu. If the Documents menu fills up too much, you can manually clear it via the Settings command.

- **Settings.** This is where you'll find Control Panel, Printers, and Taskbar settings.

- **Find.** This command provides access to the Windows Find facility, which lets you search for files and folders based on filename, creation date, and text contained in the file and folders.

- **Help.** This command opens the Windows 95 help facility.

- **Run.** This command lets you run any program by typing the program name or browsing for the program, just like the old File⇨Run command in Windows 3.1. You can usually get away with typing just the program name, without the complete path.

- **Shut down.** This command shuts down or restarts Windows in an orderly fashion. Also, it lets you start up your computer in MS-DOS mode so that you can run those few hyper-finicky programs that refuse to cooperate with Windows 95.

Note

Program items in the Start menu are actually shortcuts. A *shortcut* is a special type of file that contains a link to some other file — in this case, the link is to a program file. When you run a program file shortcut, Windows 95 locates the program referred to by the shortcut and runs the program. In this manner, shortcuts are analogous to Windows 3.1 PIF files. For more information about shortcuts, see the "Shortcuts" section later in this chapter.

Customizing the Start menu

Normally, any Windows program you install will automatically find its way into your Start menu. However, you can customize the Start menu by adding new programs or by removing existing programs. For example, you may want to add Word to the first-level Programs menu so that you don't have to navigate through the menu hierarchy every time you want to start Word.

To add a program to the Start menu, follow these steps:

1. Click on the Start button, move the mouse pointer to the Settings command, and click on the Taskbar command. Or, right-click the taskbar and choose the Properties command. Either way, the Taskbar properties dialog box will appear.

2. In the Taskbar properties dialog box, click on the Start Menu Programs tab to reveal the Start menu options. Then, click on the Add button. The Create Shortcut dialog box will be displayed.

3. Click the Browse button and locate the program file that you want to add to the Start menu. Double-click on the file to select it and click Next to continue.

4. Windows 95 now displays a hierarchical tree that represents the structure of the Start menu. Click on the folder in which you want the new menu item placed and click on Next.

5. Type the name as you want it to appear on the menu. Click Finish.

Normally, user programs are added to folders under \Windows\Start Menu \Programs. However, if you add a program shortcut directly to the \Windows\Start Menu folder, that program will appear directly on the Start menu, as shown in Figure 2-12.

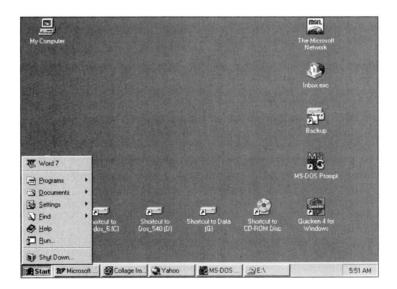

Figure 2-12: A Start menu with Word for Windows 95 added.

To remove a program from the Start menu, delete the program's shortcut from the appropriate \Windows\Start Menu folder or use the Start⇨Settings⇨Taskbar settings command to remove the program.

Shortcuts

A Windows 95 shortcut is a file that refers to another file. With shortcuts you can create references to files without having to make duplicate copies of the files themselves. For example, you can place a shortcut to your favorite application program on the desktop. Then, when you double-click on the icon for the shortcut, Windows 95 locates the program file referred to by the shortcut and runs it.

Shortcuts are one of Windows most powerful features, and they're used extensively throughout Windows 95. The following list describes just some of the uses for shortcuts:

- You can place shortcuts directly on the desktop for fast access to a program, document, or folder. I like to keep a shortcut to each of my disk drives and to a few commonly used programs on my desktop.

- Shortcuts are the basis of the Start menu. To add a program to the Start menu, just create a shortcut in the \Windows\Start Menu folder.

- You can use shortcuts to provide quick navigation of your hard disk. Just create shortcuts to the folders that you use most often in a "My Documents" folder. This is useful if you use programs that open automatically to "My Documents" and don't allow you to set the default folder (such as Microsoft's Office Shortcut Bar).

- You can place shortcuts in documents. For example, drop a shortcut to Quicken into a Word document. Then, when you double-click on the Quicken icon in the Word document, Quicken will start up.

- You can use shortcuts for objects that reside in a network. When you double-click on the shortcut, Windows 95 will attempt to access the object via the network.

- You can even place shortcuts in e-mail messages and send them to other users.

- You can use shortcuts to provide quick access to an area on the Microsoft Network on-line service (MSN). Double-click on the shortcut, and Windows 95 will automatically dial up MSN, log in, and jump to the MSN area referred to in the shortcut.

- You can quickly identify icons that represent shortcuts because the icons contain a curly arrow.

- One way to add an icon to the Start menu is simply to drag the icon from the desktop (or anywhere else) to the Start button.

You can in create shortcuts several ways. The easiest is to drag an object while holding down the right mouse button. When you release the mouse button, a pop-up menu will appear with the options Move here, Copy here, and Create shortcut here. Select Create shortcut here and type a name for the shortcut.

Shortcuts are stored on disk as files with the extension LNK. (At one time during the development of Windows 95, shortcuts were referred to as links.)

Long Filenames

One of the more ingenious new features of Windows 95 is its support for long filenames. Prior to Windows 95, filenames were limited to 11 characters: 8 characters for the name and 3 characters for the extension. Accordingly, the MS-DOS 8.3 filename convention forced users to use cryptic filenames.

With Windows 95, the 8.3 filename convention has been dropped. Filenames can now be as long as 255 characters. In addition, filenames can include embedded spaces, periods, and other punctuation. Thus, the following are all valid filenames:

```
Chapter 1
Matthews Inc. Proposal
Letter to Bob
June Sales Report
```

Of course, directories follow the same naming conventions as files so you can use long names for your directories as well.

With Windows 95, you can finally do what Macintosh users have been doing for years: create filenames that accurately describe the contents of your files. Unfortunately, you still have to follow certain rules, and it is still possible to get into trouble by misusing filenames. Also, you must contend with certain considerations when using older Windows programs that do not recognize long filenames.

Rules for forming long filenames

Just about any filename you're likely to come up with is valid under Windows 95. However, you must follow a few special rules:

■ Filenames can be as long as 255 characters.

■ Leading and trailing spaces are ignored, but spaces embedded within the filename are preserved.

■ Uppercase and lowercase letters are preserved in filenames. However, all letters are converted to uppercase when matching filenames. Thus, the following filenames are considered identical:

```
Letter to Bob
letter to bob
LETTER TO BOB
LeTtEr To BoB
```

■ Filenames may include more than one period. For example:

```
March.Sales.Report
Letter. To. Mom.
```

■ Trailing periods are ignored. Thus the following filenames refer to the same file:

```
March.Sales.Report
March.Sales.Report.
March.Sales.Report...
```

■ A complete pathname can be no longer than 260 characters.

■ Windows 95 allows you to use any character you could use to form an MS-DOS filename. In addition, the following characters are now allowed:

```
+ , ; = [ ]
```

Tip

Because a complete path is limited to 260 characters, you should be careful about using excessively long file and directory names. When you add the length of the directories together, plus the filename, plus the backslashes used to separate directories in a path, it's easier than you think to exceed the 260 character limit. Fortunately, you'll rarely have cause to use a filename longer than 30 or 40 characters.

Short filenames

Unfortunately, existing Windows 3.1 applications do not directly support long filenames. So that existing programs will be usable with Windows 95, each file is actually given two names: a long name and a short name. The short filename complies with the MS-DOS 8.3 naming convention. Thus, programs that don't know about long filenames can access the file using the short name.

For files created by programs that don't recognize long filenames, the long and short filenames are the same. For example, if you create a file named LTRBOB.DOC with Word 6, both the long and the short filenames will be LTRBOB.DOC.

For files created with long names using such Windows 95-aware applications as Word 95, Windows 95 automatically generates a short filename based on the long filename. Short filenames are generated as follows:

■ The name portion of the short filename is formed from the first six characters of the long filename, not including spaces or periods, followed by ~1.

■ The extension portion of the filename is formed from the first three characters following the last period in the long name, not including spaces.

■ If the resulting name is not unique, ~2, ~3, and so on is tried until a unique short name is found.

■ If ~9 does not yield a unique name, the name is truncated to five characters followed by ~10, ~11, and so on until a unique name is found.

Using these rules, Memo To Bob.Doc would become MEMOTO~1.DOC. If a file already exists by that name, MEMOTO~2.DOC would be used instead.

Once a file has been created, you can use either the short name or the long name to refer to the file.

When you create a long filename for a file, consider whether the file will be used by a program that doesn't yet support long filenames. If so, try to place the most meaningful information in the first six characters of the filename so that the name will be recognizable by its short filename. For example, consider this series of sales reports:

```
Sales Report for July, 1995.doc
Sales Report for August, 1995.doc
Sales Report for September, 1995.doc
```

In their long forms, these files are readily identifiable. But the short filenames will be generated as follows:

```
SALESR~1.DOC
SALESR~2.DOC
SALESR~3.DOC
```

How can you tell these files apart? On the other hand, suppose that you had given the files names such as these:

```
Jul 95 Sales Report.doc
Aug 95 Sales Report.doc
Sep 95 Sales Report.doc
```

Then, the following short names would be generated:

```
JUL95S~1.DOC
AUG95S~1.DOC
SEP95S~1.DOC
```

By placing the distinguishing information — in this case, the month and year — at the beginning of the long filename, that information is preserved in the short filename.

How Windows 95 stores long filenames

To add long filename support to Windows 95 and still remain compatible with the existing base of Windows programs, Microsoft had to figure out a way to allow long and short filenames to coexist without modifying the underlying structures used to keep track of directories and files.

Every file on an MS-DOS disk has a directory entry, a 32-byte record that includes the file's name, attributes (hidden, system, read-only, archive, or volume label), creation and modification date, starting cluster number, and file length. In Windows 95, each file's short filename is recorded with a standard directory entry. That way, existing programs can access the file without being aware of long filenames.

The long filenames are stored with additional directory entries that fit within the MS-DOS 32-byte directory entry format but utilize a special code to indicate that the directory entry is for a long filename. This code is nothing more than a clever use of the attribute bit settings found in standard directory entries. Long filename directory entries have the following four attribute bits set: hidden, system, read-only, and volume label. Setting the hidden, system, and read-only attributes is not unusual. However, setting the volume label attribute in combination with the other attributes is unorthodox. In the original design of MS-DOS, only one directory entry could have the volume label attribute, and that directory entry had to reside in the root directory. Furthermore, the volume label attribute could not be used in combination with any other attributes. By using these four attributes in combination, Microsoft essentially created a new attribute type that indicated the directory entry was for a long filename.

Each long filename directory entry can store up to 13 characters of the long filename. Thus, a long filename longer than 13 characters will require more than one directory entry to store the long filename. For example, the filename "Aug 95 Sales Report.doc" will require a total of three directory entries: one for the short filename (AUG95S~1.DOC) and two for the long filename.

Note

Long filenames are stored in Unicode, a code that uses 16 bits for each character rather than 8 bits as in standard ASCII. That's why each directory entry can hold only 13 long filename characters.

Whither MS-DOS?

Windows 95 has not abolished MS-DOS. In fact, the MS-DOS command prompt is alive and well in Windows 95. To get to it, you need only click the MS-DOS icon in the Start⇨Programs menu. An MS-DOS window will appear, in which you can run MS-DOS commands or DOS-based programs.

MS-DOS has undergone several important enhancements for Windows 95, among the more notable:

■ MS-DOS commands support long filenames. The MS-DOS implications for working with long filenames are discussed in the section, "MS-DOS and long filenames."

■ The DIR command shows long filenames, as shown in Figure 2-13.

■ You can start a Windows program directly from an MS-DOS command line simply by typing the name of the Windows program. To start Word from an MS-DOS prompt, type **WINWORD**.

■ Several familiar MS-DOS utilities such as ScanDisk and DriveSpace have been replaced with Windows counterparts.

■ Wildcards work differently. These differences are discussed in the section, "Improved * wildcards."

You can also restart your computer in a special mode called "Single MS-DOS mode." This special operating mode closely replicates the MS-DOS 6.x environment, foregoing many of the niceties of Windows 95, including multitasking and long filenames.

```
MS-DOS Prompt                                              _ □ ✕

G:\My Documents>dir *.doc

 Volume in drive G is DATA
 Volume Serial Number is 0CED-1A56
 Directory of G:\My Documents

YEAREN~1 DOC       23,040  04-28-95   9:44p Year End Report — 1994.doc
LETTER~1 DOC       23,552  04-28-95   9:45p Letter To My Mother-In-Law.doc
CHRIST~1 DOC       23,552  04-28-95   9:45p Christmas Wish List.doc
VACATI~1 DOC       23,552  04-28-95   9:45p Vacation Plans.doc
MEMOTO~1 DOC       23,552  04-28-95   9:45p Memo to Bob.doc
MYUNFI~1 DOC       23,552  04-28-95   9:46p My Unfinished Novel.doc
JOURNA~1 DOC       23,552  04-28-95   9:47p Journal for May 1995.doc
LETTER~2 DOC       23,552  04-28-95   9:47p Letter to Bob Abbott.doc
NEWYEA~1 DOC       23,552  04-28-95   9:47p New Year's Resolutions — 1995.doc
EDIBLE~1 DOC       12,800  04-29-95   6:34a Edible Arachnids.doc
        10 file(s)        224,256 bytes
         0 dir(s)     370,147,328 bytes free

G:\My Documents>_
```

Figure 2-13: The Dir command lists long filenames.

MS-DOS and long filenames

MS-DOS commands now support long filenames. However, if the filename contains embedded spaces, you must enclose the filename in quotes. For example, the following command renames "Chapter 1.doc" to Chap1.doc:

```
rename "Chapter 1.doc" Chap1.doc
```

Notice that quotes are required around the first filename because it contains an embedded space. These quotes are required whenever you work at an MS-DOS prompt or when you type a command line via the Start⇨Run command.

When typing a path, you can enclose the entire path in quotes, or just the portion of the path that includes embedded spaces. For example, both of the following commands achieve the same result:

```
cd "\wordsec\Part 1"
cd \wordsec\"Part 1"
```

When you type a filename in an MS-DOS command, you can use either the short filename or the long filename. For example, to delete a file named "Chapter 1.doc" that has a short filename of CHAPTE~1.DOC, either of these commands will do the trick:

```
del "Chapter 1.doc"
del chapte~1.doc
```

Secret

In Windows 95, the behavior of the double-dot (..) parent directory entry has been changed subtly. In previous versions of MS-DOS, you could use the double-dot in a path to back up one level in the directory hierarchy. For example, suppose the directory \Wordsec contains subdirectories Part1 and Part2. To go directly from \Wordsec\Part1 to \Wordsec\Part2, you could use this CD (change directory) command:

```
C:\Wordsec\Part1\>cd ..\Part2
```

This use of the double-dot parent entry still works. However, you can now back up two or more levels in the directory hierarchy by typing three or more periods in a row. Just type one more period than the number of directory levels you want to back up. For example, to go from \Wordsec\Part1\Pictures to \Wordsec\Part2, you can now use this CD command:

```
C:\Wordsec\Part1\Pictures>cd ...\Part2
```

Of course, you really have to be in touch with your directory structure to use this feature. But if you're a command-line jockey, you'll definitely love this feature.

Improved * wildcards

In Windows 95, the * wildcard works with a subtle difference. As you know, the * wildcard means that any combination of one or more characters can be used to match a filename. For example, the following command,

```
del abc*.doc
```

deletes any file with a name that begins with ABC and has the extension .DOC. This would include files such as ABC.DOC, ABC-1.DOC, and ABCDEFGH.DOC.

Suppose that you want to delete any file with the letters ABC anywhere in the filename. You'd be tempted to use this command,

```
del *abc*.doc
```

thinking that the asterisk before and after ABC would find files that had ABC sandwiched anywhere in the middle of the filename. In previous versions of MS-DOS, however, this won't work. The * wildcard at the beginning of the filename would cause MS-DOS to delete every file in the directory!

In Windows 95, the *abc*.doc wildcard does work as you'd expect. Rather than delete every file in the directory, it deletes only those files with the letters ABC anywhere in the filename.

Warning

Beware of the subtle difference in the way wildcards work when moving between a Windows 95 system and a system using an older version of MS-DOS. It won't take long before you get used to the new wildcard behavior and unknowingly try it on a system using an earlier MS-DOS version.

Chapter 3

Fundamental Word Secrets

In This Chapter

▶ Two common misunderstandings about Word that commonly afflict people who have used typewriters or that other word processor, WordPerfect.

▶ How Word formats characters, paragraphs, and sections.

▶ Other fundamental Word secrets, including Word commands, macros, fields, and AutoText.

You could use Word for months or even years without understanding how it works. Most Word users utilize only a small portion of Word's capabilities and settle into a routine after they learn the few procedures required to create the limited types of documents with which they work. They probably don't realize how inefficiently they've been working, all for the lack of a solid understanding of the fundamentals of how Word operates.

This chapter is an introduction to the fundamentals of Word for Windows 95 — not such fundamentals as how to type and edit text; how to open, save and print documents; or how to spell-check your work. If you've used Word for any length of time, you probably already know most of those basic procedures, and if you haven't, you'll learn soon enough. Anyway, I will cover such details in depth in later chapters. Rather, this chapter addresses the kind of fundamentals that often elude even seasoned Word veterans. If you understand the information presented in this chapter, the rest of the information in this book will make more sense.

In a way, this chapter presents the most important Word secrets of all, even though such basics wouldn't ordinarily be thought of as "secrets." If you're new to Word, pay close attention to this chapter, because it will provide you with a good foundation for what follows. If you're an experienced Word user, at least skim through this chapter, making sure you understand its salient points.

Word Is Not a Typewriter

Before I get too far into the details of how Word works, I want to clear up a common misunderstanding that often afflicts users who are new to word processing, especially users who first learned to type on a typewriter. If you learned how to type on a typewriter — as most people over 30 did — your typewriting experience may hurt you more than it will help. True, you'll be a more proficient typist if you properly position your fingers over the home row. Beware that Word's attempt to *look* like a typewriter can easily provide a false sense of security for experienced typists, for Word behaves differently than a typewriter in several subtle but important ways. For example:

- With a typewriter, every letter is the same width. If you type the letters **abcdef** on one line and then type the letters **ABCDEF** directly below on the next line, the two sets of letters will line up, like this:

  ```
  abcdef
  ```

  ```
  ABCDEF
  ```

  In Word, each letter has its own width, depending on the shape of the letter. That's what *proportional spacing* is all about. Because uppercase letters are wider than lowercase letters, the lines "abcdef" and "ABCDEF" will *not* line up on top of one another:

  abcdef

  ABCDEF

  Of course, proportional spacing is more a feature of Windows in general than of Word in particular — just about all Windows programs use proportional spacing. And Windows comes with a monospaced font called *Courier New* for those occasions when you want a printed page to look like you typed on a typewriter.

- With a typewriter, you set tab stops by maneuvering metal sliders into position. Once set, the tab stops remain set until you move them again. Not so with Word. In Word, tab stops can be different for every paragraph in a document. I've seen experienced typists on the verge of throwing solid objects at their computers in frustration over this simple fact. They toil over a paragraph, getting the tab stops and indentation settings just right; then they drop down a few paragraphs below and can't figure out why their carefully placed settings seem to have vanished.

- With a typewriter, you can use the Spacebar to indent or align text. Not with Word. The actual width of a space may vary depending on several factors, so you cannot count on spaces for indenting or aligning text.

- With a typewriter, you press the Return key at the end of every line. With Word, you press the Enter key (the computer's equivalent to the typewriter's Return key) only at the end of each paragraph. Word automatically splits each line between words. Each time you press the Enter key, Word starts a new paragraph, which can have its own indentation settings and tab stops.

These are just a few examples of how a typewriter mentality can limit the way you use Word. The thing to remember is that Word is not a typewriter. It may resemble a typewriter in superficial ways, but Word operates much differently than your typewriter.

There Are No Codes

If you cut your word-processing teeth on WordPerfect (as most of us did), you may feel that word processing with Microsoft Word is like doing a trapeze act without a net. WordPerfect relies on a convoluted set of function key commands in combination with the Ctrl, Alt, and Shift keys, which enable you to insert all sorts of codes into your document to change font, change size, adjust alignment, turn bold or italic on or off, and so on. Usually it worked, but sometimes WordPerfect documents became jumbled up for no apparent reason. When that happened, you could always rely on the safety net, otherwise known as Reveal Codes.

Reveal Codes gives you a portal into the inner workings of WordPerfect, so you can see precisely what is going on with your document. If the formatting is mixed up, Reveal Codes can help you straighten it out.

When you activate Reveal Codes, a separate window opens up, showing your document's text intermixed with special formatting codes. For example, consider the following text:

Reveal Codes gives you a *portal* into the <u>**inner workings**</u> of WordPerfect.

When viewed in Reveal Codes, this text would look something like this:

```
[Bold On]Reveal Codes [Bold Off] gives you a [Ital On]portal
[Ital Off] into the [Bold On][Und On]inner workings [Und
Off][Bold Off] of WordPerfect.
```

The formatting codes appear between brackets. For example, the [Bold On] code caused subsequent text to be formatted in boldface type, up to the next [Bold Off] code.

Word for Windows has no equivalent to WordPerfect's Reveal Codes, so when something goes awry with your formatting, you can't dissect the document as you can with WordPerfect. Word doesn't offer a Reveal Codes screen because Word does not depend on codes embedded within your document.

Remember Newton's first law of motion, which says something along the lines of, "An object in motion will continue in the same direction until some outside force acts on it"? WordPerfect works kind of that way. In WordPerfect, after text is set in motion (that is, formatted in a certain way), it continues in the same direction until some outside force — a code — acts on it. For example, once text is made bold by a [Bold On], all subsequent text is assumed to be bold until a [Bold Off] command is encountered. Pretty much all of WordPerfect's formatting is governed by similar codes.

In contrast, Word's formatting is driven not by codes, but by attributes. In Word, every character in your document has a set of attributes: font, size, style (bold, italic, underline), and so on. Likewise for paragraphs: each paragraph in your document has a set of attributes (line spacing, tab stops, indentation, justification, and so on). There are no embedded codes that turn bold on or off, set left justification, or change indentation.

Three Document Building Blocks

Word uses three types of building blocks to create documents: characters, paragraphs, and sections. These building blocks form a type of hierarchy, as follows:

- A document is made up of one or more *sections*. (Most documents have only one section.)
- A section is made up of one or more *paragraphs*.
- A paragraph is made up of one or more *characters*.

Various formatting attributes are applied to each of these building blocks. In other words, some formatting attributes are applied to characters, some are applied to paragraphs, and some are applied to entire sections. Understanding this three-layer formatting hierarchy is one of the key secrets for understanding how Word works.

Characters

The *character* is the basic unit of information in Word. Most characters are letters, numerals, or symbols. A few characters exercise special control over how text is laid out, most notably tab characters. The paragraph mark at the end of every paragraph is also a character, as are manual line breaks (Shift+Enter), manual page breaks (Ctrl+Enter), column breaks, and a handful of other esoteric characters.

Every character in a Word document carries the following formatting information along with it:

- **The font,** which indicates which typeface will be used to draw the character both on the screen and on the printed page.
- **The font size,** which determines how large the character will appear.
- **The font style:** Normal, Bold, Italic, or Bold-Italic.
- **Underline:** None, Single, Word Only, Double, or Dotted.
- **Text color.**
- **Effects:** Strikethrough, Superscript, Subscript, Hidden, Small Caps, or All Caps.
- **Spacing,** which controls the amount of space between the character and the character that follows.
- **Position,** which raises or lowers the character relative to the baseline.
- **Kerning,** which allows Word to vary the spacing between certain letter pairs for a tighter fit.

Two types of attributes that you wouldn't normally think of as *formatting* are also kept for each character:

- **Language,** which governs which language the spell checker will use when proofing the text. If the language is set to No Proofing, the text is skipped when the spell checker runs.

- **Revision marks,** which indicate whether the character has been inserted or deleted. The new Highlighter tool also uses revision marks.

Paragraphs

A *paragraph* is a group of characters terminated by a paragraph mark. The paragraph may include hundreds of characters, a single character, or, in some cases, no characters at all. Any time you press the Enter key, a paragraph mark is inserted, and a new paragraph is created.

Word treats paragraphs differently than most other word processors, and understanding how Word's paragraph formatting works is one of the keys to understanding Word. Several important formatting attributes are associated with paragraphs, not characters. Most of these formats are set via the Format⇨Paragraph command. In particular:

- **Four kinds of indentation: Left, Right, First Line, and Hanging.** Most typists and users of other word processors are used to indenting the first line of a paragraph by pressing the Tab key at the start of the paragraph. In Word, the first line indent is handled by the First Line indentation setting, and Word 95 will automatically set the First Line indentation if you press the Tab key at the start of a paragraph (unless you specifically disable this option by using the Edit tab of the Tools⇨Options command).

- **Three kinds of spacing: Before, After, and Line Spacing**. With most word processors, you add blank space between paragraphs by pressing the Enter key several times. That works in Word, but you can achieve the same effect with greater control by using the Before and After space settings. The Line Spacing setting determines how much space to leave between each line within the paragraph. If set to Single, 1.5, or Double, Word determines how much space to allow. If set to Exactly, you can specify a specific line spacing.

- **Pagination settings,** including: Widow/Orphan control, which prevents awkward page breaks that leave a single line of text stranded at the top or bottom of the page; Keep Lines Together, which guarantees that the paragraph won't be split over two pages (unless you write like Dickens); Keep With Next, which prevents Word from inserting a page break between this paragraph and the next; and Page Break Before, which directs Word to place the paragraph at the top of a new page.

- **Suppress Line Numbers,** which tells Word to skip this paragraph if automatic line numbering is used.

- **Don't Hyphenate,** which disables Word's automatic hyphenation feature for this paragraph.

Other paragraph formats are set elsewhere, so you might not think of them as paragraph formats. But they are nevertheless. These formats include the following:

- **Tabs,** which governs the location of tab stops in a paragraph. Tab stops may be set with the Format⇨Tabs command or with the ruler. Either way, the tab stops apply to *all* of the lines in the paragraph.

- **Borders and Shading,** which draws boxes around complete paragraphs or provides background shading for paragraphs.

- **Bullets and Numbering,** which adds a bullet or number character at the beginning of the paragraph.

- **Heading Numbering,** which numbers heading paragraphs.

The most important thing to remember about paragraphs is that the paragraph mark (¶) contains all of the formatting information for a paragraph. All of the format settings listed (indents, line spacing, tabs, and so on) are stored in the paragraph mark. In addition, the default character format for the paragraph is stored in the paragraph mark.

As a result, if you delete the paragraph mark, you clobber the paragraph's formatting. Exactly what happens when you delete a paragraph mark depends on how you delete the paragraph mark and whether you're using Word 6 or Word 95 and is a bit too detailed for this chapter. (See Chapter 14 for the gory details.) Still, this explains why your formatting sometimes goes haywire when you delete paragraph marks.

Tip

Paragraph marks are important enough that you always need to know where they are. If you can't see the paragraph marks in your Word documents, call up the Tools⇨Options command, click on the View tab, and click the Paragraph Marks check box. (While you're at it, click on the Tab Characters check box too because you should know where the tabs are as well.)

Sections

Sections provide the highest level of formatting available in a Word document. Sections hold formatting information culled from several sources:

- Page layout information specified on the File⇨Page Setup command, such as margins, paper size, orientation, and so on.

- Column layout specified in the Format⇨Columns command.

- Page numbers created with the Insert⇨Page Numbers command.

- Line numbers specified via the File⇨Page Setup command.

- Footnote and Endnote positioning set by the Insert⇨Footnote command.

- Headers and footers created with the View⇨Header and Footer command.

If I was giving out prizes, section formatting would win the prize for being the least coherent Word feature. Commands that control section formatting appear in four different Word menus: File, View, Insert, and Format.

Like paragraph formatting, section formatting is contained in the section mark that follows the section:

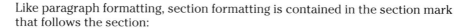

Unlike paragraphs, the first section in a document — and the only section in most documents — does not have a section mark. A section mark is assumed to be present at the end of the document, even though it does not appear on the screen. If you delete a section mark, the text in the section takes on the formatting of the following section.

Styles

A *style* is a collection of paragraph and character formats that has been given a name. After you have created a style, you can quickly apply the style to a selection of text. Then, the text takes on all of the formatting designated by the style.

Word supports two kinds of styles: paragraph styles and character styles. Paragraph styles are far and away the more popular; character styles are useful only in unusual situations and are not widely used. Paragraph styles include both paragraph and character formats. The paragraph formats in a paragraph styles such as line spacing and alignment, apply to the entire paragraph. The character format in a paragraph style is used to provide the default font, font size, and other formats for all of the characters in the paragraph.

You can always override formats obtained from a style. For example, even though a paragraph style may say that all of the characters in the paragraph are 12-point Times Roman, you can still format some of the characters in bold or italic type. This is called *direct formatting,* which always takes precedence over formatting derived from a style.

Styles are not optional in Word; *all* paragraphs in *all* Word documents have formatting applied by style, whether you realize it or not. When you create a new document, the document starts off with a single paragraph that is formatted with Word's default style, Normal. All of the paragraph and character formats associated with this default paragraph (its line spacing, alignment, font, font size, and so on) are derived from the Normal style.

Word has many built-in styles for different types of paragraphs. Normal is the default style, used for "normal" text paragraphs, such as this one. Word also has built-in styles for headings, named Heading 1, Heading 2, and so on all the way up to Heading 9. Other built-in styles are used for footnotes, endnotes, table of contents entries, index entries, and so on.

The real power of styles is that you can modify the default formats of these built-in styles, and you can create your own styles. Styles allow you to automate the process of formatting your documents. After you've set up a style for a certain type of paragraph, you never have to wade through the various Format commands to format paragraphs of that type. Just apply the style, and all of the formats associated with the style will be applied automatically to the paragraph.

And whenever you change the formatting associated with a style, all of the paragraphs to which the style has been applied will be reformated automatically.

You can apply styles to individual paragraphs in several ways. The Formatting toolbar has a Style list box that you can use to select the style for a paragraph, or you can use the Format⇨Style command. But the easiest way to assign the styles that you use most is to assign keyboard shortcuts to them. For example, I regularly use about a dozen different styles when writing a book, and each is assigned an easy-to-remember keyboard shortcut: Ctrl+Shift+B for a bulleted list, Ctrl+Shift+N for a numbered list, and so on.

Another way styles can help you automate your document formatting is by using the Style for Following Paragraph option. For example, my Heading 1 style has its Style for Following Paragraph option set to Normal. That way, whenever I create a Heading 1 paragraph, the next paragraph will be set to the Normal style without any special action on my part.

If you never work with documents longer than two pages, you may not need to use styles. Instead, just use Normal for all the paragraphs in your document and apply direct formatting as needed. If you work with longer documents, take the time to learn how to create and use styles. The time will be well spent because styles are one of the most important secrets of efficient document formatting. Styles are covered in detail in Chapter 18.

Note

Although Word has styles for paragraph and characters formats, Word does not let you create section styles. All section formatting (margins, footnote placements, and so on) must be applied by using direct formatting.

Where Formats Originate

Now that you know about character, paragraph, and section formatting and styles, let's take a closer look at the way Word determines which formats should be applied to a given character or paragraph.

To determine which character formats (font, font size, and so on) apply to a given character, Word looks at three things, in the following order:

1. Word looks at the character formats specified by the paragraph style applied to the paragraph. All of the characters in a paragraph inherit the character formatting specified by the paragraph style. For example, if the Normal style specifies 12-point Times New Roman, any characters in Normal paragraphs will be formatted in 12-point Times New Roman.

2. Word checks to see whether you have applied a character style to the character in question. If so, any character formats specified by the character style are used, overriding the formats specified by the paragraph style. Any formats that are not specified in the character style are obtained from the paragraph style. For example, if a character style named Mono specifies Courier New for the font but no font size, any characters formatted with that style will be formatted in Courier New, with whatever point size is inherited from the underlying paragraph style.

3. Word checks to see whether you have applied any direct formatting to the character. Direct formatting is applied any time you use the Format⇨Font command, one of the character formatting buttons on the Formatting toolbar, or a keyboard shortcut for character formatting. For example, if you select a character and press Ctrl+B or click the Bold button, Word displays the character in boldface. All other character formats will be drawn from the character style (if one is used) and then from the underlying paragraph style.

Paragraph formatting is a bit simpler, involving only two layers:

1. Word uses the formatting information specified by the paragraph style. Keep in mind that *all* paragraphs in a Word document are associated with a style, so all paragraphs obtain their basic format from a style.

2. Any direct formatting that you have applied to the paragraph overrides formats in the style. Direct paragraph formats are applied whenever you use the Format⇨Paragraph, Format⇨Tabs, Format⇨Borders and Shading commands, one of the paragraph formatting buttons on the Formatting toolbar, or a keyboard shortcut that applies paragraph formatting. For example, if you click on the Center button in the Formatting toolbar, the paragraph will be centered. All other paragraph formats will be taken from the paragraph style.

One of the best ways to see how this formatting works is to use the Help button in the Standard toolbar. Click on the Help button and click on any character in your document. Word will display where the formatting for the character and the paragraph that contains it is obtained, as shown in Figure 3-1.

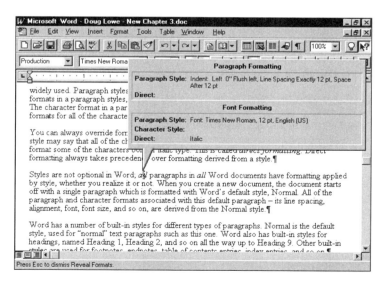

Figure 3-1: Word is happy to tell you where character and paragraph formats originate.

Templates

A *template* is a special type of Word document that is used as a model for other documents. Whenever you create a new document, the document is based on a template. The template supplies several items as a starting point for the new document, including styles, page layout information (in other words, section formatting), boilerplate text, AutoText entries, keyboard, toolbar, menu customizations made via the Tools⇨Customize command, and macros.

When you create a new document, Word copies the styles, page layout, and boilerplate text from the template into the new document. The remaining template items are kept in the template itself but remain available as if copied into the new document.

Most documents are based on the default Normal.dot template, which supplies basic margins (1" at the top and bottom, 1.25" on the sides) and built-in styles such as Normal, Heading 1, and so on. Word comes with other templates for common types of documents, such as letters, memos, and resumes. You can also create your own templates for specific document types. See Chapter 4 for a template discussion that might just make your eyes bleed.

Other Things You Should Know

The main point I wanted to relay in this chapter is how Word applies formats to characters, paragraphs, and sections via direct formatting and styles. If you understand how Word's formatting works, you'll be ready to swallow the rest of the information presented in this book.

There are a few other Word features that I want to be sure you're familiar with before I plunge into the details of putting Word to use. Although most of the following topics have entire chapters devoted to exploring their nuances in depth, these features will come up now and then throughout this book.

Word commands

Word's user interface provides three ways to invoke commands: menus, toolbars, and keyboard shortcuts. You can invoke some commands by using all three methods. For example, you can invoke the Save command from the File menu, by clicking on the Save button in the Standard toolbar, or by using the Ctrl+S keyboard shortcut. You can invoke other commands by using only one method. Examples include the Save All command, available only via the File menu; the Insert Address command, available only on the Standard toolbar; and the All Caps command, available only by using the Ctrl+Shift+A keyboard shortcut.

Word provides several hundred commands, probably more commands than any program you've ever used. Surprisingly, not even half of Word's commands are available through the menus, toolbars, and keyboard shortcuts. For example, Word has a Close command that is available on the File menu. However,

Word also has a FileCloseAll command, which closes all open files. This command is built into Word but is not available from any of Word's menus, toolbars, or keyboard shortcuts.

The first word in most Word commands indicates a command category that corresponds to one of Word's menus. For example, the FileOpen, FileSave, and FileSaveAs commands ordinarily appear on the File menu. Similarly, the EditCut, EditCopy, and EditPaste commands usually appear on the Edit menu. Other Word commands do not follow this convention, however. Examples include Bold, Italic, and Underline.

One of the best things about Word is that it lets you thoroughly customize its menus, toolbars, or keyboard shortcuts. You don't have to settle for the subset of commands that Word's developers in Redmond, Wash, think you should use. By using the Tools⇨Customize command, you can make any of the "hidden" Word commands accessible by placing it on a menu or toolbar or assigning a keyboard shortcut for it. Chapter 6 describes the secrets of customizing Word's menus, toolbars, and keyboard shortcuts.

Tip

For a quick look at the variety of commands available in Word, choose the Tools⇨Customize command. In either the Toolbars, Menus, or Keyboard tabs, select All Commands in the Categories list box. Then, you can view the entire list of Word commands in the Commands list box. See Figure 3-2.

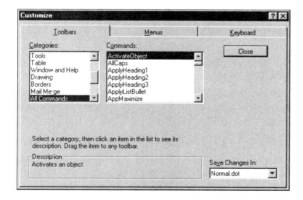

Figure 3-2: Here's how to see a list of all Word commands.

Macros

If Word's 200 or so commands aren't enough for you, you can actually create your own commands in the form of *macros*. Macros are created by using a relatively simple programming language known as *WordBasic*. If you're not into programming, you can create macros with the *Macro Recorder*, which translates your keystrokes into WordBasic commands so that you can play them back later. On the other hand, if you enjoy programming (some people actually do), you can work directly in WordBasic to create macros of considerable complexity.

Macros are a basic tool for creating custom Word applications. You'll find a general introduction to macros in Chapter 7 and several chapters devoted to the details of WordBasic programming in Part IX of this book.

Tip

One of the most interesting uses of macros is to create customized versions of Word's built-in commands. To do this, you create a macro with the same name as a built-in command by using your WordBasic skills to create an improved version of the command. Then, Word uses your macro instead of the built-in command. For example, suppose that you'd like the FileSave command to work differently: perhaps you'd like it to save *two* copies of your document, one as a backup in case the primary copy is lost. To do that, just create a macro named FileSave that saves not one but two copies of the document. Then, when you use the File⇨Save command, click on the Save button in the Standard toolbar, or press Ctrl+S, Word will invoke your FileSave macro rather than the built-in FileSave command.

Fields

Remember when I said that Word doesn't have codes? I lied, sort of. Although Word doesn't use codes for formatting purposes, it does let you insert special codes called *fields* into your document. Fields are the word processing equivalent to @functions in a spreadsheet program such as Excel. When Word comes across a field code in a document, it substitutes a calculated value for the actual field code.

For example, suppose that you want to insert today's date in your document, but you want the date to be updated whenever you edit or print the document. You could simply type the date, but when you pull up the document the next day, the date would be obsolete. You'd have to type the correct date manually each time you edit the document. That's where fields come in. Word provides a special Date field that stands for the current date. Instead of typing the date, insert a Date field. Then, Word will automatically update the date whenever you edit or print the document.

Word has 68 different field codes that you can use, ranging from simple functions, such as displaying the date, time, or page number, to more complex functions that let you create formatted equations or automate mail-merge operations. Many of these fields have one or more switches or parameters, so in a way, Word's fields compose a type of programming language that supplements the programming capabilities of WordBasic. (Of course, you don't have to be a programmer to use fields, but the proper use of some of Word's more complex field codes borders on full-bore programming.)

There are two ways to view codes when working with a document: you can view the field codes, or you can view the field results. When you view field codes, a date field would appear in your document as {DATE}. When you view field results, the date field would appear as the current date in the format 06/02/95. You can switch between viewing field codes and field results by choosing the Tools⇨Options command, clicking on the View tab, and clicking the Field Codes check box. Or, you can press Alt+F9 to alternate between viewing field codes and field results.

Many of Word's built-in features rely on codes. For example:

■ Mail merge uses such fields as {MergeField}, {MergeRec}, and {MergeSec} to control how data is inserted from the data source (that is, the list of names and addresses) into the main document (the model letter used to prepare merge letters).

■ The Table of Contents feature uses {TOC} fields to insert the table of contents and {TC} fields to mark table of contents entries.

■ The Index feature uses an {INDEX} field to create an index and {XE} fields to mark index entries.

By using fields, you can customize these features to suit your needs more closely. Chapter 28 discusses fields in detail, but descriptions of fields that are used along with specific features will pop up now and again throughout this book.

AutoText and AutoCorrect

In the old days, Word's AutoText feature was called the *Glossary*. AutoText lets you store text — anything from a single character to an entire book's worth of text — under a name. To call up the stored text, just type the AutoText name and press F3. Word automatically replaces the AutoText name with the stored text.

As an example, I'll let you in on a little secret: I hate typing Word's menu commands, such as File@->Print or Tools@->Options, over and over again. (@-> is the publisher's typesetting code for the arrow that you see between menu commands in the rest of this book.) I have problems underlining the correct letters, and the fancy arrow that appears between the menu name and the command name causes special problems. Rather than spell out these commands over and over again, I've set up AutoText entries with names that correspond to each command's shortcut keys. For example, to type File@->Print, all I do is type **fp** and press F3. Word locates the **fp** AutoText entries and substitutes it as I type.

The beauty of AutoText is that it's good for more than just text: you can store formatting information (for example, the underlines in File@->Print), field codes, special symbols, graphics, or just about anything else. Like most of Word's more useful features, AutoText entries are stored in templates. I'll have more to say about AutoText in Chapter 12.

AutoCorrect is a new feature that was introduced with Word 6. It works much like AutoText, except that you don't have to press F3 to retrieve an AutoCorrect code to expand. AutoCorrect is used mostly to correct common typographical errors, such as *adn* for *and* or *teh* for *the* (I had to disable AutoCorrect to type this sentence!). The only problem with AutoCorrect is that the AutoCorrect entry name cannot be a word you'd want to actually use because every time you type it, the word is automatically replaced with the AutoCorrect text. For example, I have an AutoText entry named *of* that expands to *Format@->Font*. This wouldn't work as an AutoCorrect entry because every time I typed the word *of*, it would automatically be expanded to *Format@->Font!*

Part II
Secrets of Customizing Word

4   Using Templates

5   Customizing Word's Startup and Appearance

6   Customizing Keyboard Shortcuts, Toolbars, and Menus

7   Automating Your Work with Macros

Chapter 4

Using Templates

In This Chapter

▶ What a template is and why templates play such an important role in using Word efficiently

▶ How the Normal.dot template supplies default settings for Word documents

▶ How to create documents that are based on a template other than the default Normal.dot template, and how to later change the template associated with a document

▶ How to create your own templates

▶ How to use global templates properly

▶ How to use the Organizer to copy styles and other template items from one template to another

▶ How to use Word's Wizards

An entire chapter on templates this early in the book may seem premature, but I want to impress upon you right from the start that templates are the key to customizing Word so that you can use it as efficiently as possible. You can use Word for years without even knowing what a template is, but if you really want to make Word your own, templates are the way. Besides, the proper use of templates will come up again and again throughout this book, so I may as well get the subject of templates out in the open.

What Is a Template?

A *template* is not a place of worship, nor is it the soft spot on the sides of your head. Instead, a template is a special type of Word document that is used as a pattern for new documents. Whenever you create a new document, that document must be based on a template. In most cases, new documents are based on the default document, named Normal.dot. Word, however, comes with a collection of alternative templates that let you quickly create documents with various formats, such as letters, memos, reports, proposals, resumes, and so forth. Using one of Word's predefined templates spares you the task of reinventing frequently used document formats.

In addition, you can create your own templates. This is the secret to customizing Word so that it works with you instead of against you. By creating a template for each type of document that you routinely create, you'll save yourself an enormous amount of time in the long run.

So what is a template?

Simply put, it is a special type of Word document file from which Word copies information whenever you create a new document. The information that is obtained from the template includes the following:

- Styles, used to apply paragraph and character formatting quickly.
- Margins and other page layout information, such as the paper size, orientation, headers, footers, and so on.
- Text, often referred to as *boilerplate text*.
- Graphics, such as a company logo.
- AutoText entries, which are sections of text you can quickly insert into your documents simply by typing a few keystrokes.
- Fields, which instruct Word to insert information, such as the time, date, document filename, page number, and so on into the document.
- Keyboard, toolbar, and menu customizations made via the Tools⇨Customize command.
- Macros, which allow you to automate routine chores.

A template is basically the same thing as a normal document, except that it is given the extension DOT rather than DOC, as normal documents are, and it contains information that isn't stored in a document, such as macros, customizations for toolbars, menus, and keyboard shortcuts, and AutoText entries. Word permits you to open and edit templates as if they were documents, and you can easily convert a document to a template by saving it as a template rather than as a document. The real difference between documents and templates lies in how you use them.

The Normal.dot template

If you do not specify a template when you create a document, Word attaches the Normal.dot template to it. Word obtains the default document format, margins, page orientation, and the standard styles such as Normal, Heading 1, Heading 2, and Heading 3 from the Normal.dot template. In other words, Normal.dot is where Word stores its default settings for any feature controlled by templates.

Normal.dot is a *global template*, which means it is always available in Word, whether the document you're working with is attached to it or not. Even if you attach a different template to a document, the settings in Normal.dot are still available because Normal.dot is a global template.

Any changes you make to Normal.dot effectively change Word's default behavior. For example, if you don't like Word's default style for Heading 1 paragraphs, you can change the Heading 1 style in Normal.dot, or you can customize the toolbars or add keyboard shortcuts to Normal.dot. By making careful changes to Normal.dot, you can change Word's behavior to suit your own working style. In effect, you can create your own individualized version of Word.

Secret

You can restore your Normal.dot template to its pristine condition by deleting it from the \Office95\Template folder. If Word discovers that Normal.dot is missing, it reverts to its original default settings and creates a new Normal.dot when you exit Word. Be aware that when you do this, you'll lose everything you've added to Normal.dot.

To create a new document based on the Normal template, call up the File⇨New command, select the Normal.dot template, and click on OK. Or, just click the New button in the Standard toolbar or press Ctrl+N. (To change the behavior of the New button or the Ctrl+N shortcut, see the section "Customizing the New button and Ctrl+N keyboard shortcut" later in this chapter.)

Creating a New Document Based on a Template

To create a document based on a template other than Normal.Dot, you must use the File⇨New command. It displays the New dialog box, as shown in Figure 4-1. From this dialog box, you pick the template on which you want to base the new document, and click on OK to create the document.

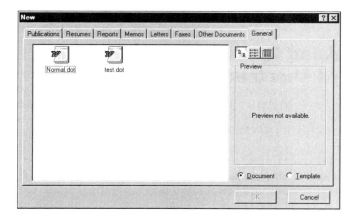

Figure 4-1: The File⇨New command lets you pick a template to base a new document on.

As you can see, the New dialog box has been thoroughly redesigned for Word for Windows 95. In Word 6, all document templates had to be stored together in a single directory, and the New dialog box presented a scrollable list of templates from which to chose. In Word for Windows 95, you can organize templates into subfolders beneath the main templates folder, and the subfolders appear as tabs in the New dialog box. You can click these tabs to see the templates in the various subfolders.

Both the Ctrl+N keyboard shortcut and the New button on the standard toolbar completely bypass the New dialog box, automatically using the Normal.Dot template for the new document. The only way to create a document based on a template other than Normal.Dot is to use the File⇨New command.

When you create a new document based on a template, any text and graphics contained in the template are automatically copied into the new document. Templates are often used for this purpose to supply text or graphics that always appears in certain types of documents. For example, a Memo template would contain a standard memo header. A Letter template would contain your letterhead. If you attach a template to an existing document, the text and graphics contained in the template are *not* copied into the document. For information about the formatting provided by each of the templates supplied with Word, see the section, "A Gallery of Word's Templates" later in this chapter.

Word also provides several Wizards, which are a specialized type of template. Wizards use WIZ as the file extension rather than DOT. If you open a wizard rather than a template, the wizard will ask you a series of questions about the content and appearance of the document you want to create. Then, it will automatically generate a document for you, complete with sample text, formatting, and styles. For more information about wizards, see the section "Using Wizards" later in this chapter.

Customizing the New button and Ctrl+N keyboard shortcut

If you prefer to use keyboard shortcuts and toolbar buttons rather than cumbersome menu commands, you may be frustrated (as I am) by the fact that both shortcuts for the File⇨New command — the Ctrl+N keyboard shortcut and the New button on the standard toolbar — create a document based on the Normal.dot template rather than displaying the New dialog box and selecting a template for the new document. Fortunately, you can change the Ctrl+N keyboard shortcut and add a toolbar button that runs the File⇨New command by displaying the New dialog box before creating a new document.

Call up the <u>T</u>ools⇨<u>C</u>ustomize command and click the Toolbars tab. Select All Commands in the <u>C</u>ategories list box and select FileNew in the Command list box, as shown in Figure 4-2.

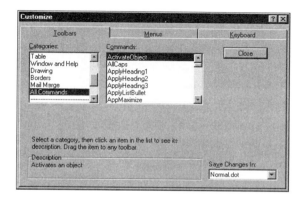

Figure 4-2: Customizing the toolbar.

Drag FileNew to the location on the toolbar where you want it to appear and release the mouse button. The custom Button dialog box will appear. Select the button image you want to use and click <u>A</u>ssign. Finally, click Close to dismiss the Customize dialog box.

Tip

For more information on creating custom toolbars, see Chapter 6. Also, if you want, you can simply replace the existing "New" button with the custom FileNew macro.

No special action is required to customize the Ctrl+N keyboard shortcut for the new FileNew macro. Because FileNew is the same name as Word's FileNew command, for which Ctrl+N is the default shortcut, pressing Ctrl+N automatically invokes the new FileNew macro and displays the New dialog box.

If you decide all of this was a mistake, call up the <u>T</u>ools⇨<u>M</u>acros command, click on the FileNew macro, and click the <u>D</u>elete button to remove the macro. No harm, no foul.

Changing a Document's Template

You can change the template attached to a document at any time. When you do, all of the macros, custom toolbars, menus, and keyboard shortcuts, as well as AutoText entries from the new template, are automatically copied into the document. Any boilerplate text or graphics in the template are *not* copied into the document. Styles from the template are copied into the document only if you select the Automatically <u>U</u>pdate Document Styles option when you attach the template.

To change the template attached to a document, use the File⇨Templates command to summon the Templates and Add-ins dialog box, illustrated in Figure 4-3. Click the Attach button to bring up an Explorer-style dialog box that takes you to your template files, select the template you want to attach to the document, and click on Open. (You may have to look in various folders to find the template you want to attach.) If you want the styles in your document to be replaced by the styles from the template you're attaching, make sure that the Automatically Update Document Styles box is checked. Then, click OK to attach the template.

If you updated styles and your document uses styles to control its formatting, the effects of the new template should be immediately visible.

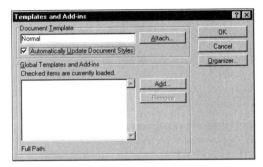

Figure 4-3: The Templates and Add-ins dialog box.

Warning

You Can't Go Back

Changing the template attached to a document is one of the few Word actions that you cannot undo with the Edit⇨Undo command. As a result, if you inadvertently attach the wrong template to a document, correcting your error can be difficult. That's because when you attach a new template, Word copies elements from the new template into the document, but does not remove elements from the document that were derived from the previous template.

To illustrate the type of problem this can cause, suppose that you're working on a document that has a handful of custom styles, and you mistakenly attach a template that has 50 custom styles. Because you used the Automatically Update Document Styles option, those 50 styles were copied into your document. The problem arises: how can you get rid of them? You can use the File⇨Templates command to attach the correct template, but the 50 styles that were copied in from the incorrect template remain in your document! There is no way to remove them easily.

To avoid this type of problem, always save your document immediately before changing templates. Then, if you're not satisfied with the results after attaching the new template, you can revert to the previously saved version of the document if necessary by closing the document without saving changes and reopening the previously saved copy of the document.

Creating Your Own Templates

Word comes with a collection of templates that let you create a wide variety of document types, but sooner or later you'll almost certainly want to create your own templates. The sections that follow explain everything you need to know about creating and using your own templates.

Where to store your templates

In Word 6, it was best to store all templates in a single directory so that you could access them from the list box displayed by the File⇨New command. With Word for Windows 95, you can organize your templates in folders within the main template folder. That way, you can keep your templates separate from the templates supplied with Word, and you can organize them according to usage.

Figure 4-4 shows an Explorer view of the folders that are created when you install Word with Office 95. Here, you can see the folders that are subordinate to the \Office95\Template folder. When you create your own templates, you should place them in one of three locations:

■ The \Office95\Template folder itself. If you place your templates here, they will appear alongside the Normal.dot template when the New dialog box is displayed. This method allows fastest access to your templates because you don't have to click any of the tabs in the New dialog box to locate your templates.

■ In one of the existing subfolders under \Office95\Template, such as Letters, Reports, or Other Documents. From here, you can click the appropriate tab in the New dialog box and see your templates alongside the templates supplied with Word. This method requires you to click the tab that corresponds to the folder your template is in but allows you to integrate your templates with the templates supplied with Word.

■ In a new folder you create under the \Office95\Template folder, such as \Office95\Template\My Templates. The new folder will appear as a separate tab in the New dialog box. This method requires an additional mouse click to access the folder that contains the templates but allows you to keep your templates segregated from the templates supplied with Word.

Note

Office 95 creates a single folder structure used to store templates for all Office 95 templates, not just Word templates. Thus, you'll find templates for Word, PowerPoint, Excel, and Access intermixed in these folders.

You can change the location of the Template directory by using the Tools⇨Options command and clicking on the File Locations tab. This brings up the dialog box shown in Figure 4-5. Here, you can set two options for template locations: User Templates and Workgroup Templates. The User Templates option normally points to \Office95\Template, and there's seldom cause to change it.

Figure 4-4: An Explorer view of the folders used to store templates.

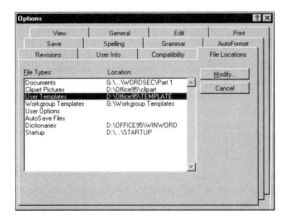

Figure 4-5: Setting the default file locations.

Use the Workgroup Templates option when you want to store templates on a network drive so that all users in a workgroup can access the same custom templates. This option is usually left blank, but if you specify a folder for it, the New dialog box lists templates from both the User Templates folder and the Workgroup Templates folder, merged into alphabetical order. In addition, subfolders of the Workgroup Templates folder will appear as tabs in the New dialog box.

Converting a document to a template

Suppose that you've been working on a document for hours, toiling with its formats until they're just the way you want them, and you realize that you might want to create other documents using the same formats. It's a simple matter to create a template from this document.

Open the document you want to use to create the template and call up the File⇨Save As command. Down at the bottom of the Save As dialog box, there's a drop-down list box labeled Save As Type, which is set to "Word Document." Change this field to "Document Template." Type a name for your template, navigate over to the folder where you want to save the template, and click OK to save the document as a template.

Now, take another look at your template. Begin by removing any unnecessary text. Remember that any text that you leave in the template will appear in any new documents you create using the template, so you want to leave only true boilerplate text that you want to appear in every document based on the template.

Tip

To delete all of the text from the document, press Ctrl+A to select the entire document and press Del.

You might also want to remove any unnecessary styles, macros, AutoText, or anything else that isn't template-worthy. When the template is just right, save it again.

Warning

You might be tempted to do a shortcut of the above procedure by opening the document, deleting text and other unnecessary elements, and choosing File⇨Save As. I caution you against this, though, because it's all too easy to delete an entire document's worth of text and accidentally use File⇨Save rather than File⇨Save As! To avert disaster, save the document as a template *before* you begin deleting massive amounts of text.

Creating a new template from scratch

To create a new template from scratch, use the File⇨New command to call up the New dialog box. First, select the existing template on which you wish to base the new template. Next, click the Template radio button (found at the bottom of the dialog box) and click OK.

Your new template will inherit whatever styles, text, and other elements were contained in the template you based it on. Now is the time to add any additional styles, macros, or other new elements to the template or to change existing template elements. In addition, you can add boilerplate text and graphics. When you're ready, use the Save command to save the template, assigning it an appropriate name and placing it in the correct folder.

Modifying an existing template

To modify an existing template, use the File⇨Open command to call up the Open dialog box. Change the Files of Type list box from "Word Documents" to "Document Templates," and locate and select the template you want to modify. Click Open to open the template, make any changes you want to make, and use File⇨Save to save the changes. That's all there is to it.

Another way to modify an existing template is to open a document based on the template and change those elements of the document that are stored in the template rather than in the document. This can be a bit confusing, however, because some elements of a document are stored only in the template. Other elements, however, are copied from the template at the time the template is attached, but subsequently stored in the document.

The following list indicates how changes to various elements of a document affect the template attached to the document:

■ **Text.** Any text you add to the document does not affect the template. The only way to change boilerplate text in a template is to edit the template directly.

■ **Direct formatting.** Any direct formatting you apply to the document affects the document only and is not copied back to the template.

■ **Styles.** Changes to a document's styles do not affect the template. Although styles are copied from the template to the document when the template is attached, subsequent changes to the styles are stored in the document and not copied back to the template. However, you can use the Organizer to copy styles back to the template. (Organizer is explained later in this chapter, in the section "Using the Organizer.")

■ **Macros.** Macros are always stored in a template, so any macros you create or modify will be stored in the template, not in the document itself. When you create a macro, you must indicate whether you want the macro stored in Normal.dot, the attached template, or another global template.

■ **Customizations.** Changes to custom keyboard shortcuts, toolbars, or menus are stored in the template. You must specify whether you want the change stored in Normal.dot, the attached template, or a global template.

■ **AutoText.** Changes to AutoText entries are stored in the template, either Normal.dot, the attached template, or a global template.

Using Global Templates

A *global template* is a template with macros, AutoText entries, and customization (keyboard, toolbar, and menu) elements that are available to all open documents regardless of which template is attached to the document. Normal.dot is a global template, which means that its elements are available even in documents that are attached to some other template. You can add your own templates to the list of global templates if you want, so that their elements will also be available globally.

Note

Only the macros, AutoText entries, and customization settings in a global template are available to other documents. Styles and boilerplate text contained in global templates are not available (unless the document happens to be attached to the template).

Tip

A global template is a great way to create a library of customized macros. You could place all your macros in the Normal.dot template, but placing them in a separate template for global macros gives you some added flexibility. For example, you can exchange your global macro template with other users without worrying about overwriting their Normal.dot templates. And you can quickly remove all of your custom macros by removing the global macro template without losing other custom items in your Normal.dot.

To add a global template, call up the File⇨Templates command. The Templates and Add-ins dialog box, which was pictured back in Figure 4-3, appears. The Global Templates and Add-ins list box contains a list of any current global templates. Click the Add button, choose the template you want to make global, and click OK. When you return to the Templates and Add-ins dialog box, the template you selected should now appear on the list. Click OK again.

When you add a global template in this manner, the template is not loaded permanently. The next time you start Word, the template will appear in the Global Templates and Add-ins list box, but it will not be checked. To activate the global template, call up the File⇨Templates command and click the global template's check box.

Tip

Fortunately, you can tell Word to automatically load *and* activate a global template by creating a copy of the template in Word's Startup directory (\Office95\WinWord\Startup). Any templates in this directory are automatically activated as global templates when Word starts.

How Word resolves duplicate template elements

When you use global templates, the possibility of duplicate template elements is very real. For example, what happens if a global template has a macro named CopyStyle and the template attached to the document has a macro also named CopyStyle? Which one takes precedence?

The following order of precedence determines which template elements to use when name conflicts occur:

1. The template attached to the document always has first priority. Any element defined in the attached template will supersede any like-named elements in Normal.dot or a global template.

2. The Normal.dot template is next. Any element that exists in Normal.dot will take precedence over a like-named element in another global template.

3. Global templates are last. Elements from global templates are used only if the attached template and Normal.dot do *not* have a like-named element.

4. If two or more global templates have identically named elements, Word uses the one that comes first in alphabetical order. For example, if "Global Template" and "My Global Macros" are both loaded as global templates and both contain a macro named CopyStyle, the one from "Global Template" will be used.

Tip

To avoid name problems like this, simply refrain from creating macros and other template elements with duplicate names. One way to do that is to ask each user to attach macro names with a unique prefix.

Using the Organizer

The Organizer is a tool designed to help you manage your templates. It lets you copy styles, AutoText, toolbars, and macros from one template to another. In addition, it lets you copy styles from a document to a template or vice versa. (Remember that AutoText, toolbars, and macros are always stored in a template, so you can't copy these elements to or from a document.)

The Organizer is especially useful when you create new styles that you want added to a template or when you modify existing styles and you want to reflect the change in the template. By default, Word stores new styles and changes to existing styles in the document itself rather than in the template where the document is attached. The Organizer allows you to copy those styles back to the template.

You cannot directly access the Organizer. Instead, you must first call up one of the following commands and click the Organizer button that appears in the command's dialog box:

- File⇨Templates
- Format⇨Style
- Tools⇨Macro

Whichever way you choose to invoke it, the Organizer displays the dialog box shown in Figure 4-6. As you can see, the Organizer dialog box includes four tabs: Styles, AutoText, Toolbars, and Macros. In each tab, the Organizer includes two lists. Initially, the list on the left shows styles in the current document or AutoText, toolbars, or macros in the current document's template. The list on the right shows styles, AutoText, toolbars, or macros from the Normal.dot template. To copy an element from the current document or template to Normal.dot, simply click the element in the left list to select it and click on the Copy button.

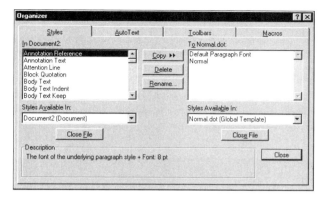

Figure 4-6: The Organizer lets you copy styles, AutoText, toolbars, and macros.

The Available In drop-down box under each list box lets you change the document or template accessed by Organizer. Initially, the Available In drop-down box under the left list includes the current document (styles only), the template attached to the current document, and Normal.dot. The Available In box under the right list includes only Normal.dot.

You can access any other document or template by clicking the left or right Close buttons. When you do, the Close button will change to an Open button. Click it, select the document or template you want to use, and click OK.

The Organizer lets you copy template elements in either direction. For example, you can click an element in the right list and click Copy to copy the element to the document or template indicated in the left list. If you select an element in the right list, Word changes several visual cues in the Organizer dialog box: the arrows on the Copy button switch sides to indicate a right-to-left copy, and the titles over the list boxes change from "In" to "To" and vice versa.

The Organizer also lets you delete or rename styles or other elements from a template or document. To delete elements, select the elements you want to delete and click the Delete button. To rename elements, select the element you want to rename (you can rename only one at a time), click the Rename button, type the new name, and click OK.

Using Organizer to update styles in a template

Suppose that you want to copy all of the styles in the current document back to the template where the document is attached. To do that, you would follow these steps:

1. Use the File⇨Templates command to call up the Templates and Add-ins dialog box and click the Organizer button.

2. When the Organizer dialog box appears, click the Styles tab if it is not already selected.

3. Click the Close File button under the list on the right side of the dialog box.

4. Click the Open File button.

5. When the Open dialog appears, change the Files of type setting to "Document templates (.dot)," select the template file you want to copy the styles to, and click the Open button.

6. Back in the Organizer dialog box, select all of the styles in the document by clicking on the first style in the left list, then scrolling to the end of the list, holding down the Shift key, and clicking on the last style in the list.

7. Click the Copy button to copy the styles from the document to the template. Word will ask for confirmation before overwriting an existing style.

8. Click Close to dismiss the Organizer.

You'd think it would be easier than that to update all of the styles in a template with styles from the document. If you find yourself doing this often, you might want to look at the macro described in the next section.

A macro for updating templates

Macro

Because Word records changes to styles and new styles in the document rather than in the template where the document is attached, you'd think there would be an easy way to transfer styles more quickly from a document to the document's templates. Unfortunately, there isn't. If you find yourself updating templates often, you might want to consider using a macro to perform this tedious task. A macro named CopyStyles is provided in the Word 95 SECRETS Sample Macros.dot template on the accompanying CD just for this purpose. Here it is:

```
Sub MAIN
Dim dlg As FileTemplates
GetCurValues dlg
template$ = dlg.Template
msg$ = "Existing styles in the template " + template$ + " will be
replaced with styles from the current document."
resp = MsgBox(msg$, "Copy Styles", 17)
If resp = 0 Then Goto UserCancel
num = CountStyles()
If num = 0 Then Goto Done
For count = 1 To num
  Organizer .Copy, .Source = FileName$(), .Destination = template$,
.Name = StyleName$(count), .Tab = 0
Next count
Done:
MsgBox Str$(num) + " styles copied."
UserCancel:
End Sub
```

This macro uses the FileTemplates WordBasic command to determine the name of the template file attached to the document. It then uses the Organizer WordBasic command to copy styles one by one from the current document to the template. Before it begins, it displays a warning dialog box that tells the user that existing styles in the template will be replaced with styles from the document. Another message indicating how many styles were copied is displayed when the macro is finished.

To use this macro, attach the WordSecrets.dot template as a global template, call up the Tools⇨Macro command, and run the CopyStyles macro. All of the styles in the currently open document will be copied to the document's template. If the CopyStyles macro does not appear in the list, change the Macros Available In field to WordSecrets.dot (global template).

A Gallery of Word's Templates

Word comes with a large collection of templates that you can use to format several common types of documents. The following sections illustrate the various templates included with Word.

Note

Many of Word's templates come in three families: Contemporary, Elegant, and Professional. You can use these template families together to create a unified design for your correspondence. You should pick one of these styles and use it whenever possible.

Letters

You'll find three templates for letters in the Letters & Faxes template folder: Contemporary Letter.dot, Elegant Letter.dot, and Professional Letter.dot. In each case, the template provides for your company name and return address, the recipient's address, the recipient's name, in addition to your name and title. The Contemporary Letter also provides a slogan that is printed at the bottom of the page. To squeeze the most from these templates, you should customize them so that your name and company information is permanently stored in the template.

Each template includes an envelope icon in the letter body that you can double-click. When you do, the template runs a macro that creates a separate document filled with tips for customizing the letter template. Before you use any of these templates, double-click the envelope and read the resulting document.

Note

Word also includes a Letter Wizard that you can use to create a letter formatted according to the Contemporary, Elegant, or Professional Letter templates. The Wizard gives you more precise control over which of the various elements common to most letters should be included, and it can supply you with several prewritten letters. The Letter Wizard is covered later in this chapter in the section "Using Wizards."

Figures 4-7, 4-8, and 4-9 illustrate the letter templates.

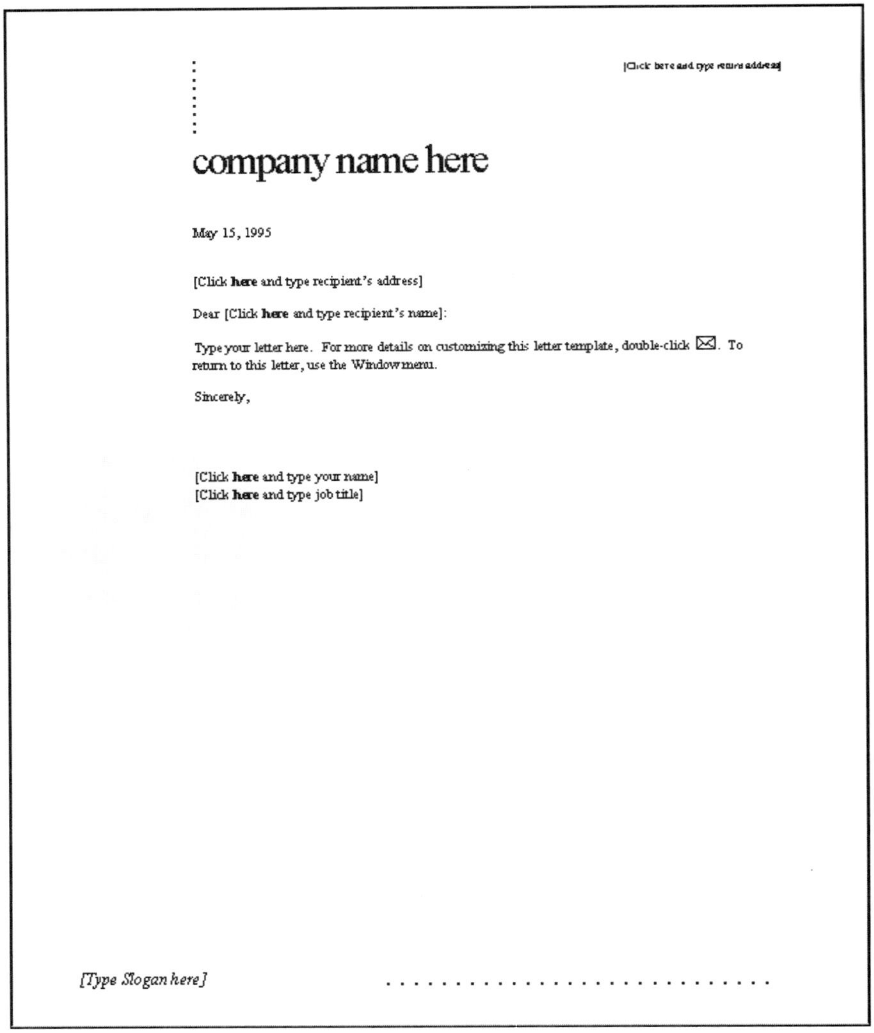

[Click here and type return address]

company name here

May 15, 1995

[Click **here** and type recipient's address]

Dear [Click **here** and type recipient's name]:

Type your letter here. For more details on customizing this letter template, double-click ✉. To return to this letter, use the Window menu.

Sincerely,

[Click **here** and type your name]
[Click **here** and type job title]

[Type Slogan here]

Figure 4-7: The Contemporary Letter.dot template.

Figure 4-8: The Elegant Letter.dot template.

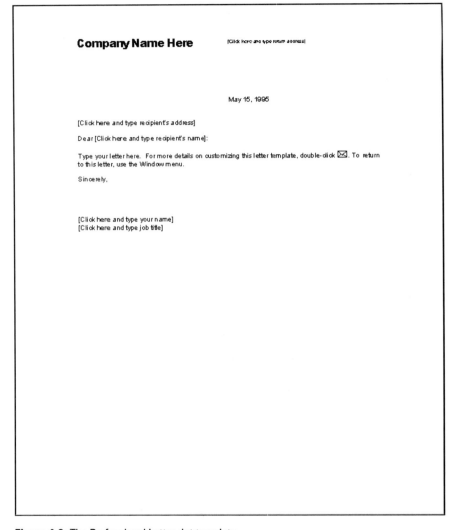

Figure 4-9: The Professional Letter.dot template.

Faxes

You'll find three fax templates in the Letters & Faxes template folder: Contemporary Fax.dot, Elegant Fax.dot, and Professional Fax.dot. These templates create a Fax Transmittal form that you can use to accompany your faxes. The form includes space for your name, the recipient's name, the fax number, the number of pages, and the priority.

Word also includes a Fax Wizard, found alongside the fax templates in the Letters & Faxes tab of the New dialog box. It constructs a fax document that includes whatever elements you want. Rather than use the Contemporary, Elegant, and Professional templates, the Fax Wizard uses its own Contemporary, Modern, and Jazzy styles. For more information about using wizards, see the section "Using Wizards" later in this chapter.

Figures 4-10, 4-11, and 4-12 illustrate the fax templates.

Memos

You'll find three templates for creating memos in the Memos template folder: Contemporary Memo.dot, Elegant Memo.dot, and Professional Memo.dot. Boilerplate text in these templates provides for standard memorandum heading information, such as From:, To:, CC:, Date:, and Re:. In addition, the body of the memo is filled with tips for using and customizing the memo templates.

A Memo Wizard is also located under the Memos tab in the New dialog box. The Memo Wizard automatically creates a memo based on the Contemporary Memo.dot, Elegant Memo.dot, or Professional Memo.dot templates and lets you select various elements of the memo. For more information about using wizards, see the section "Using Wizards" later in this chapter.

Figures 4-13, 4-14, and 4-15 illustrate the memo templates.

Reports

Reports are a bore to read, but with Word's report templates, at least they'll look good. You'll find three templates for reports in the Reports template folder: Contemporary Report.dot, Elegant Report.dot, and Professional Report.dot. These templates include a title page and two pages of text that describe how to use and customize the templates. (Unfortunately, Word does not include a wizard for automatically generating reports. However, I have made up for this deficiency by providing a Reports Wizard on the CD that comes with this book. See Appendix A for details.)

Figures 4-16, 4-17, and 4-18 illustrate the report templates.

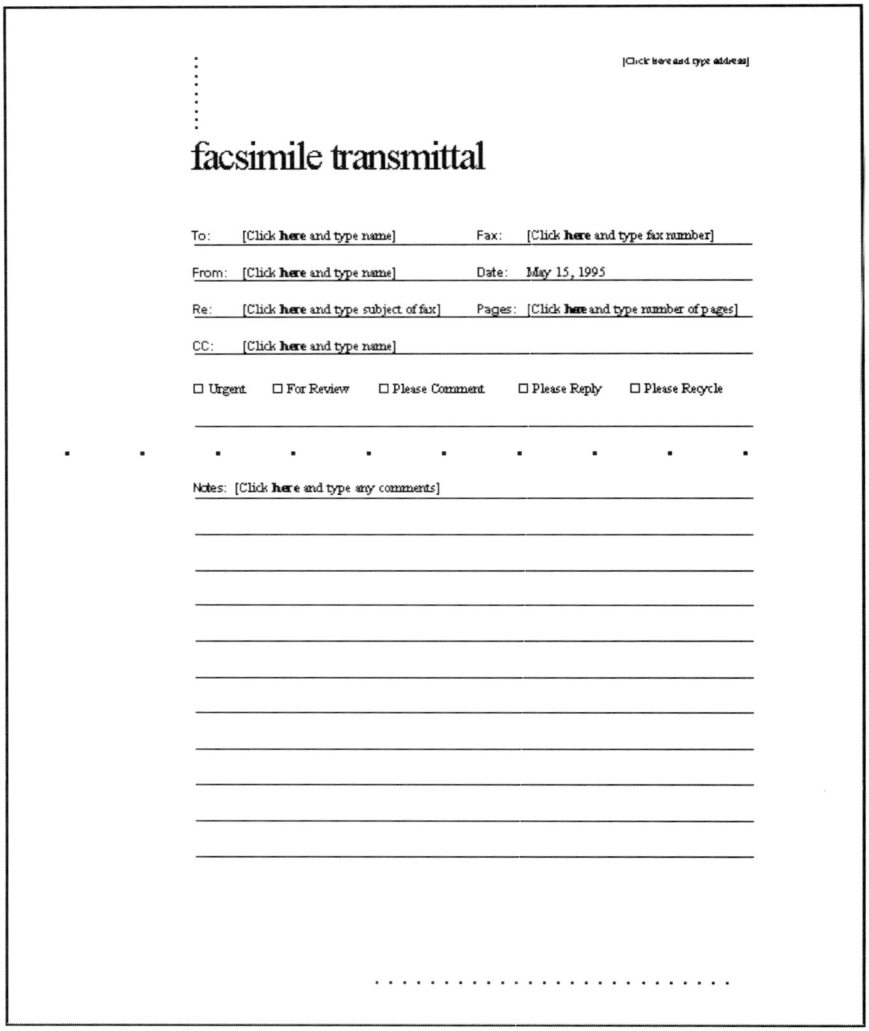

[Click here and type address]

facsimile transmittal

To:	[Click here and type name]	Fax:	[Click here and type fax number]
From:	[Click here and type name]	Date:	May 15, 1995
Re:	[Click here and type subject of fax]	Pages:	[Click here and type number of pages]
CC:	[Click here and type name]		

☐ Urgent   ☐ For Review   ☐ Please Comment   ☐ Please Reply   ☐ Please Recycle

Notes: [Click here and type any comments]

Figure 4-10: The Contemporary Fax.dot template.

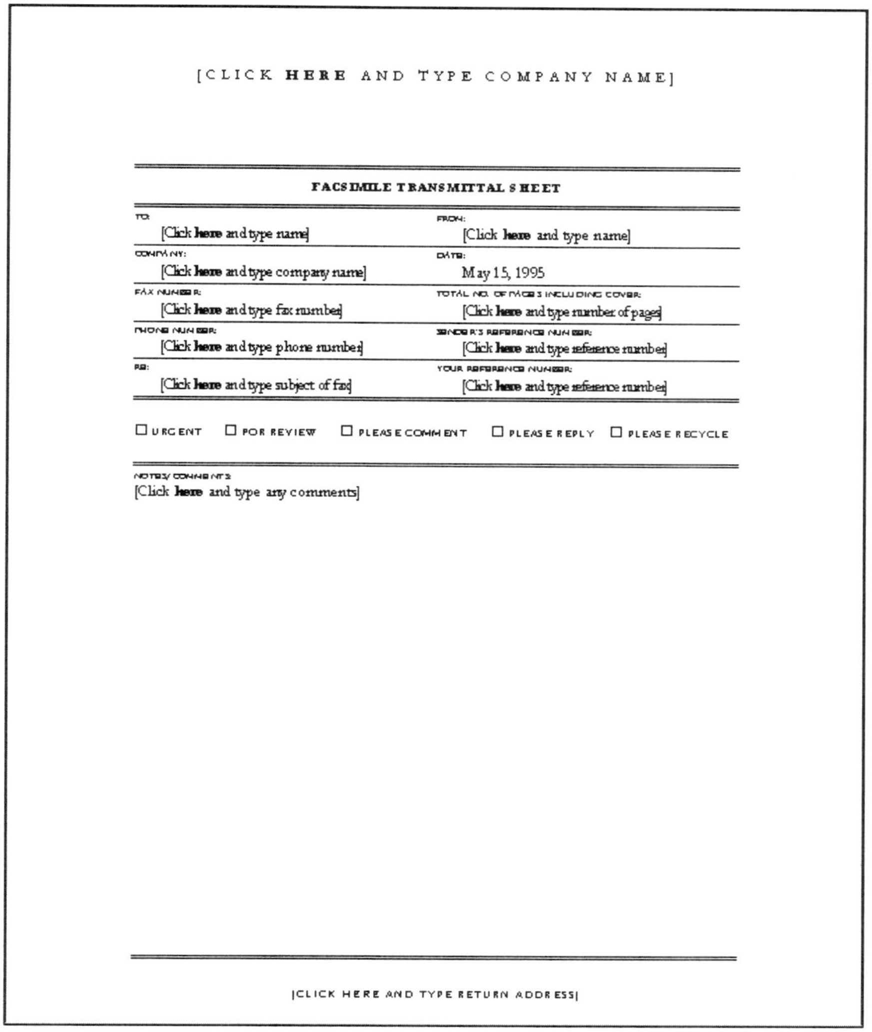

[CLICK **HERE** AND TYPE COMPANY NAME]

FACSIMILE TRANSMITTAL SHEET

TO:	FROM:
[Click **here** and type name]	[Click **here** and type name]
COMPANY:	DATE:
[Click **here** and type company name]	May 15, 1995
FAX NUMBER:	TOTAL NO. OF PAGES INCLUDING COVER:
[Click **here** and type fax number]	[Click **here** and type number of pages]
PHONE NUMBER:	SENDER'S REFERENCE NUMBER:
[Click **here** and type phone number]	[Click **here** and type reference number]
RE:	YOUR REFERENCE NUMBER:
[Click **here** and type subject of fax]	[Click **here** and type reference number]

☐ URGENT   ☐ FOR REVIEW   ☐ PLEASE COMMENT   ☐ PLEASE REPLY   ☐ PLEASE RECYCLE

NOTES/COMMENTS:
[Click **here** and type any comments]

[CLICK HERE AND TYPE RETURN ADDRESS]

Figure 4-11: The Elegant Fax.dot template

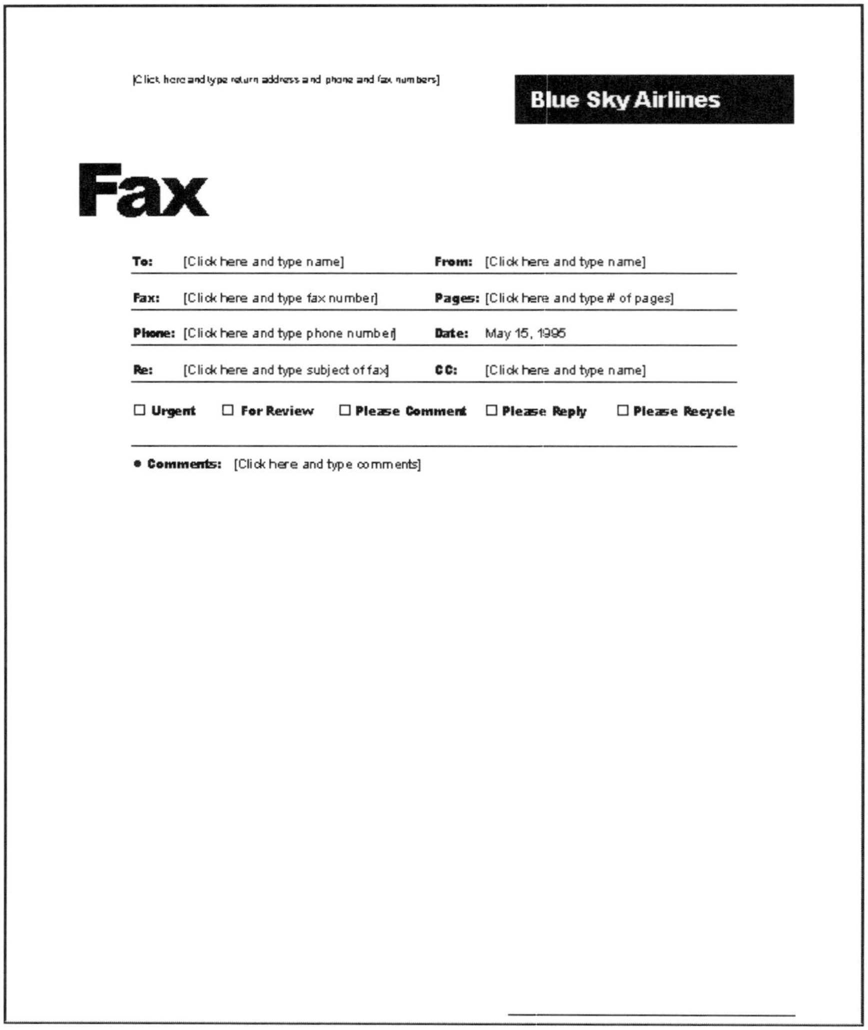

[Click here and type return address and phone and fax numbers]

Blue Sky Airlines

Fax

To: [Click here and type name]	**From:** [Click here and type name]
Fax: [Click here and type fax number]	**Pages:** [Click here and type # of pages]
Phone: [Click here and type phone number]	**Date:** May 15, 1995
Re: [Click here and type subject of fax]	**CC:** [Click here and type name]

☐ **Urgent**   ☐ **For Review**   ☐ **Please Comment**   ☐ **Please Reply**   ☐ **Please Recycle**

• **Comments:**   [Click here and type comments]

Figure 4-12: The Professional Fax.dot template.

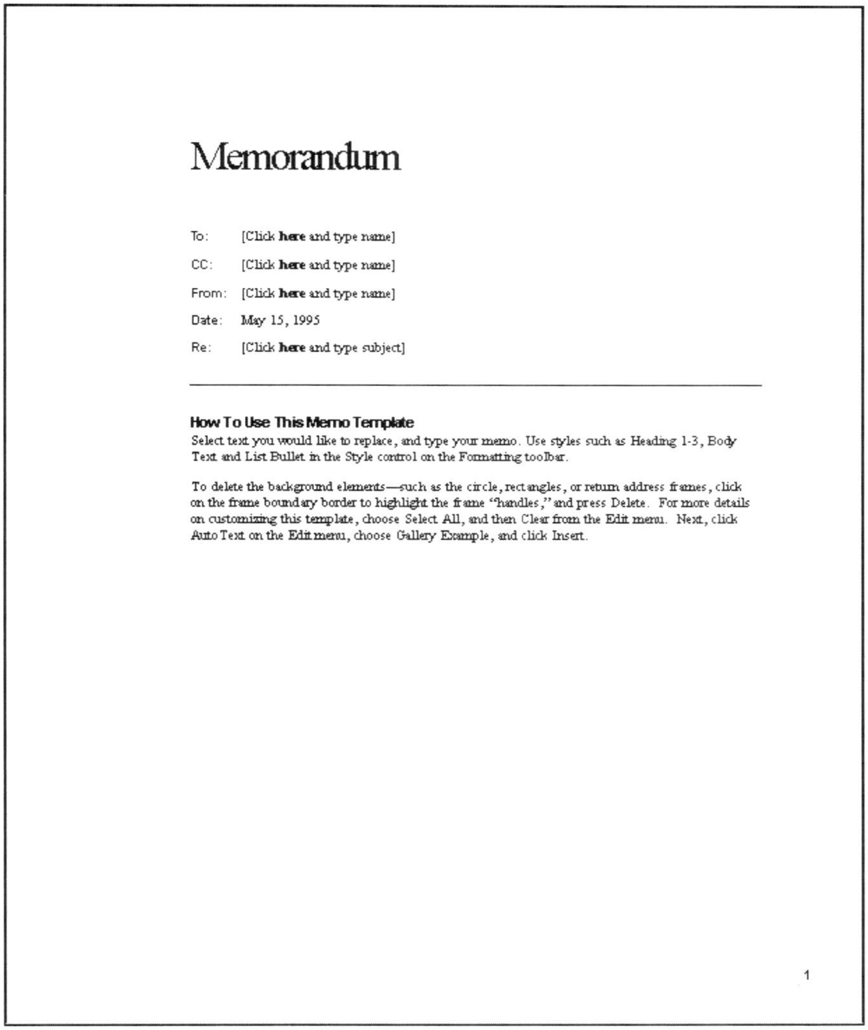

Memorandum

To: [Click **here** and type name]

CC: [Click **here** and type name]

From: [Click **here** and type name]

Date: May 15, 1995

Re: [Click **here** and type subject]

How To Use This Memo Template

Select text you would like to replace, and type your memo. Use styles such as Heading 1-3, Body Text and List Bullet in the Style control on the Formatting toolbar.

To delete the background elements—such as the circle, rectangles, or return address frames, click on the frame boundary border to highlight the frame "handles," and press Delete. For more details on customizing this template, choose Select All, and then Clear from the Edit menu. Next, click Auto Text on the Edit menu, choose Gallery Example, and click Insert.

1

Figure 4-13: The Contemporary Memo.dot template.

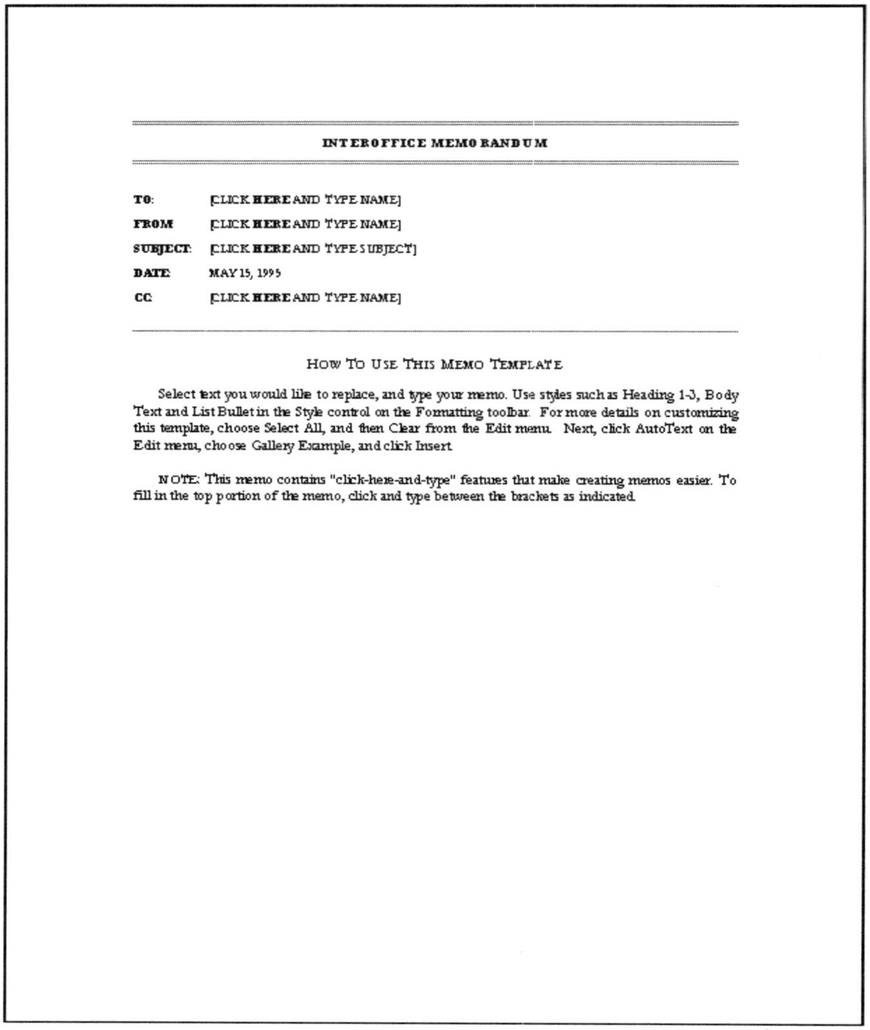

INTEROFFICE MEMORANDUM

TO:	[CLICK HERE AND TYPE NAME]
FROM:	[CLICK HERE AND TYPE NAME]
SUBJECT:	[CLICK HERE AND TYPE SUBJECT]
DATE:	MAY 15, 1995
CC:	[CLICK HERE AND TYPE NAME]

HOW TO USE THIS MEMO TEMPLATE

Select text you would like to replace, and type your memo. Use styles such as Heading 1-3, Body Text and List Bullet in the Style control on the Formatting toolbar. For more details on customizing this template, choose Select All, and then Clear from the Edit menu. Next, click AutoText on the Edit menu, choose Gallery Example, and click Insert.

NOTE: This memo contains "click-here-and-type" features that make creating memos easier. To fill in the top portion of the memo, click and type between the brackets as indicated.

Figure 4-14: The Elegant Memo.dot template.

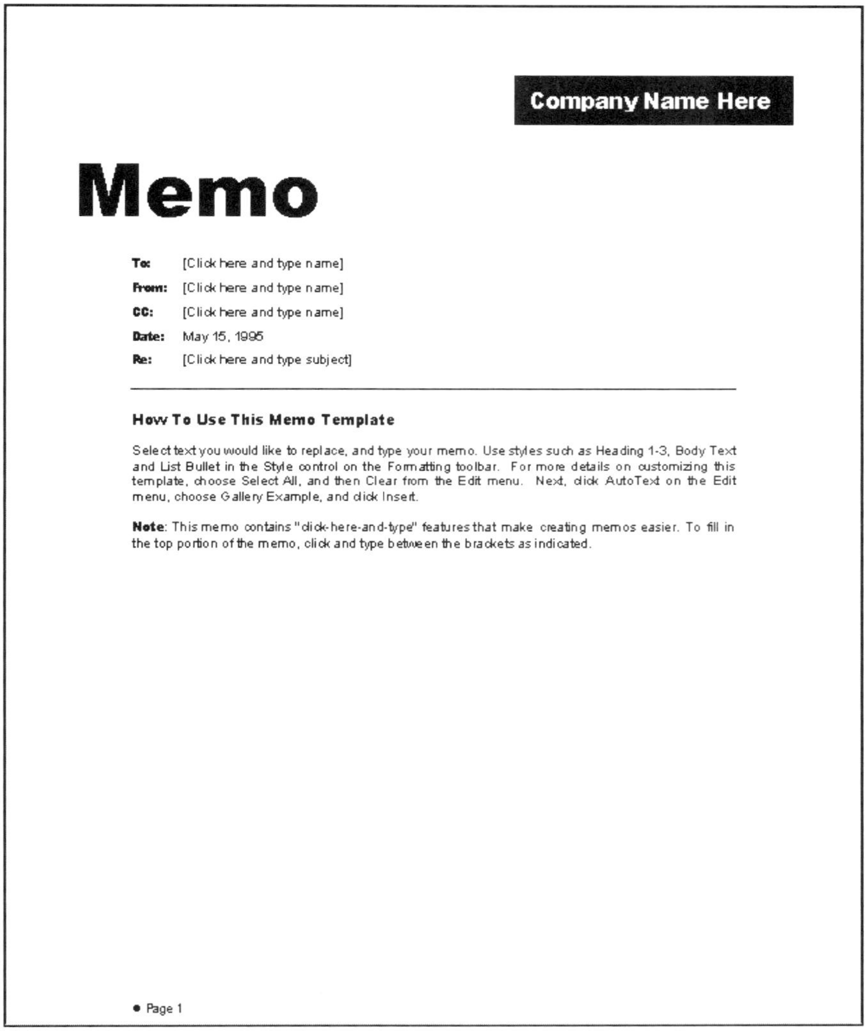

Company Name Here

Memo

To:	[Click here and type name]
From:	[Click here and type name]
CC:	[Click here and type name]
Date:	May 15, 1995
Re:	[Click here and type subject]

How To Use This Memo Template

Select text you would like to replace, and type your memo. Use styles such as Heading 1-3, Body Text and List Bullet in the Style control on the Formatting toolbar. For more details on customizing this template, choose Select All, and then Clear from the Edit menu. Next, click AutoText on the Edit menu, choose Gallery Example, and click Insert.

Note: This memo contains "click-here-and-type" features that make creating memos easier. To fill in the top portion of the memo, click and type between the brackets as indicated.

• Page 1

Figure 4-15: The Professional Memo.dot template.

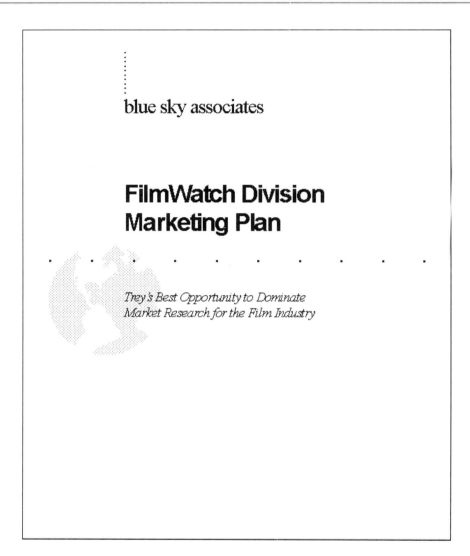

Figure 4-16a: The Contemporary Report.dot template (first page).

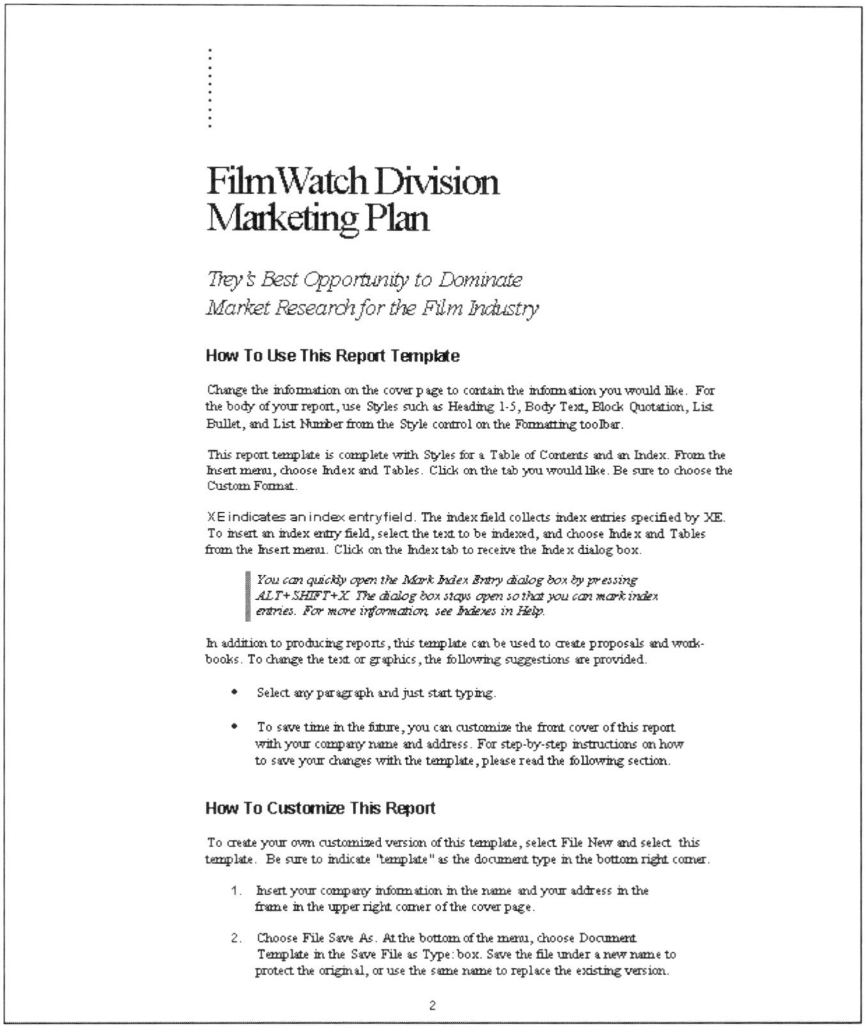

FilmWatch Division Marketing Plan

Trey's Best Opportunity to Dominate
Market Research for the Film Industry

How To Use This Report Template

Change the information on the cover page to contain the information you would like. For the body of your report, use Styles such as Heading 1-5, Body Text, Block Quotation, List Bullet, and List Number from the Style control on the Formatting toolbar.

This report template is complete with Styles for a Table of Contents and an Index. From the Insert menu, choose Index and Tables. Click on the tab you would like. Be sure to choose the Custom Format.

XE indicates an index entry field. The index field collects index entries specified by XE. To insert an index entry field, select the text to be indexed, and choose Index and Tables from the Insert menu. Click on the Index tab to receive the Index dialog box.

> *You can quickly open the Mark Index Entry dialog box by pressing*
> *ALT+SHIFT+X. The dialog box stays open so that you can mark index*
> *entries. For more information, see Indexes in Help.*

In addition to producing reports, this template can be used to create proposals and workbooks. To change the text or graphics, the following suggestions are provided.

- Select any paragraph and just start typing.

- To save time in the future, you can customize the front cover of this report with your company name and address. For step-by-step instructions on how to save your changes with the template, please read the following section.

How To Customize This Report

To create your own customized version of this template, select File New and select this template. Be sure to indicate "template" as the document type in the bottom right corner.

1. Insert your company information in the name and your address in the frame in the upper right corner of the cover page.

2. Choose File Save As. At the bottom of the menu, choose Document Template in the Save File as Type: box. Save the file under a new name to protect the original, or use the same name to replace the existing version.

2

Figure 4-16b: The Contemporary Report.dot template (second page).

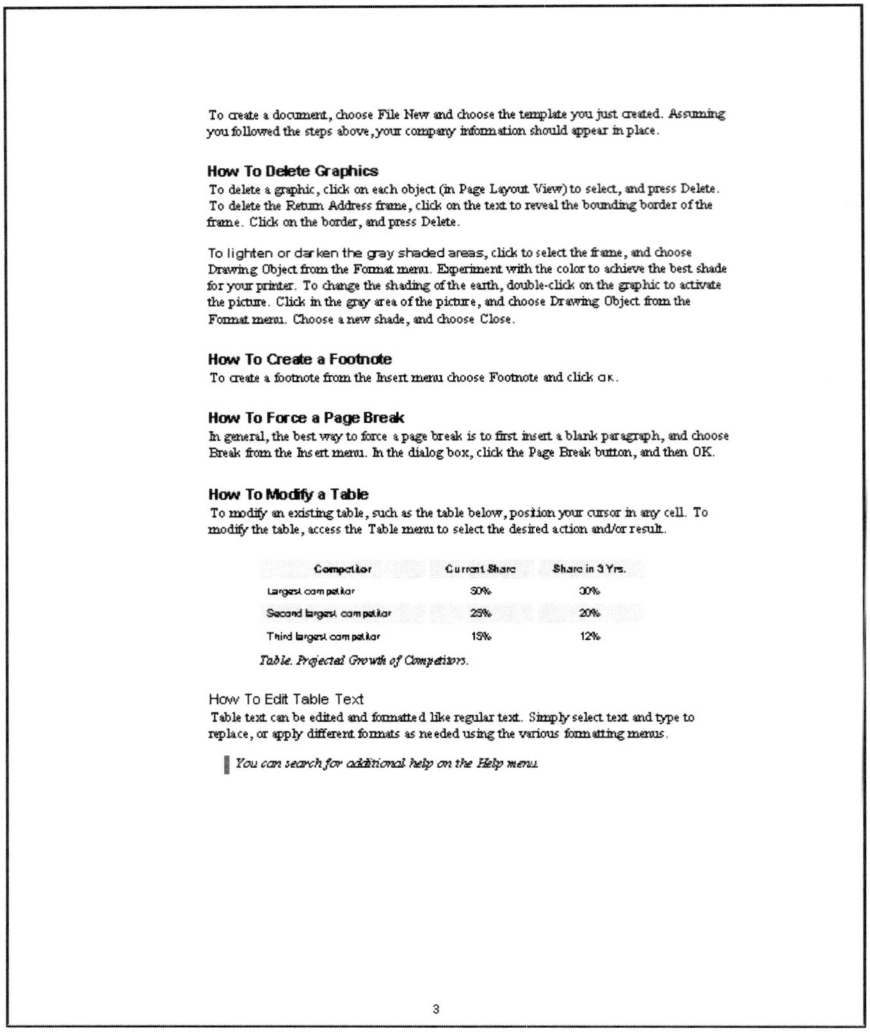

To create a document, choose File New and choose the template you just created. Assuming you followed the steps above, your company information should appear in place.

How To Delete Graphics

To delete a graphic, click on each object (in Page Layout View) to select, and press Delete. To delete the Return Address frame, click on the text to reveal the bounding border of the frame. Click on the border, and press Delete.

To lighten or darken the gray shaded areas, click to select the frame, and choose Drawing Object from the Format menu. Experiment with the color to achieve the best shade for your printer. To change the shading of the earth, double-click on the graphic to activate the picture. Click in the gray area of the picture, and choose Drawing Object from the Format menu. Choose a new shade, and choose Close.

How To Create a Footnote

To create a footnote from the Insert menu choose Footnote and click OK.

How To Force a Page Break

In general, the best way to force a page break is to first insert a blank paragraph, and choose Break from the Insert menu. In the dialog box, click the Page Break button, and then OK.

How To Modify a Table

To modify an existing table, such as the table below, position your cursor in any cell. To modify the table, access the Table menu to select the desired action and/or result.

Competitor	Current Share	Share in 3 Yrs.
Largest competitor	50%	30%
Second largest competitor	25%	20%
Third largest competitor	15%	12%

Table. Projected Growth of Competitors.

How To Edit Table Text

Table text can be edited and formatted like regular text. Simply select text and type to replace, or apply different formats as needed using the various formatting menus.

You can search for additional help on the Help menu.

3

Figure 4-16c: The Contemporary Report.dot template (third page).

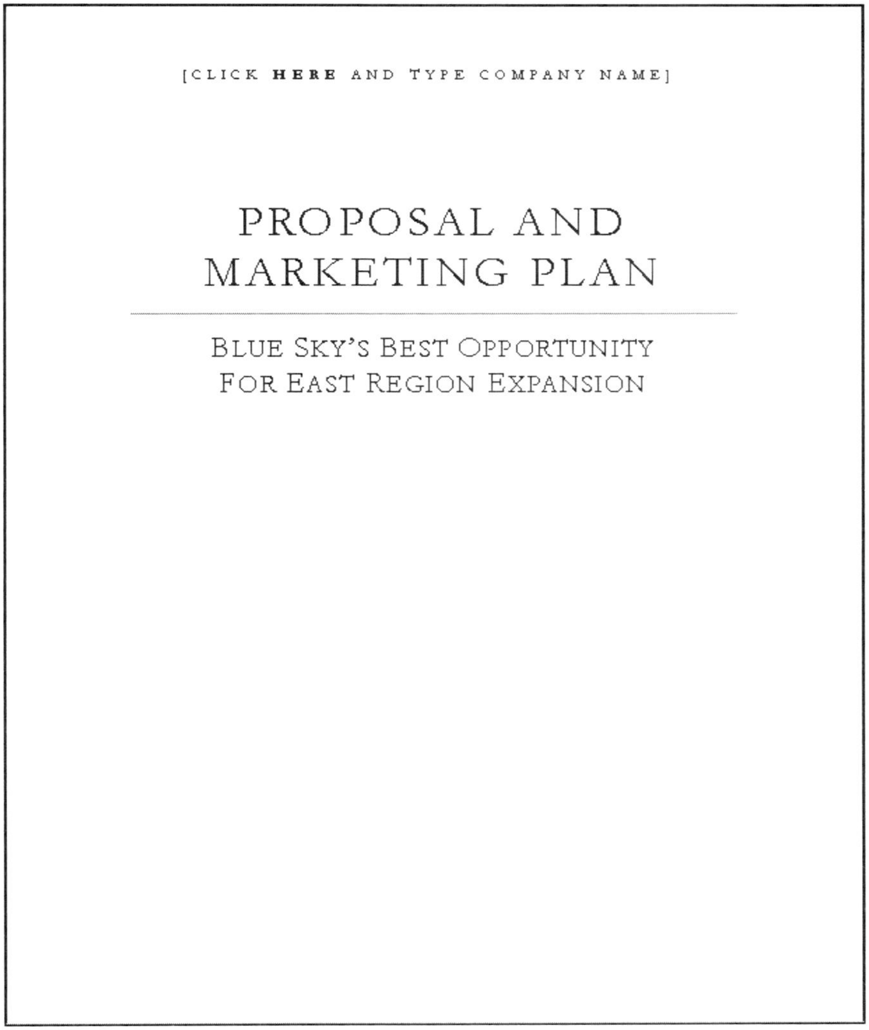

[CLICK **HERE** AND TYPE COMPANY NAME]

PROPOSAL AND MARKETING PLAN

BLUE SKY'S BEST OPPORTUNITY
FOR EAST REGION EXPANSION

Figure 4-17a: The Elegant Report.dot template (first page).

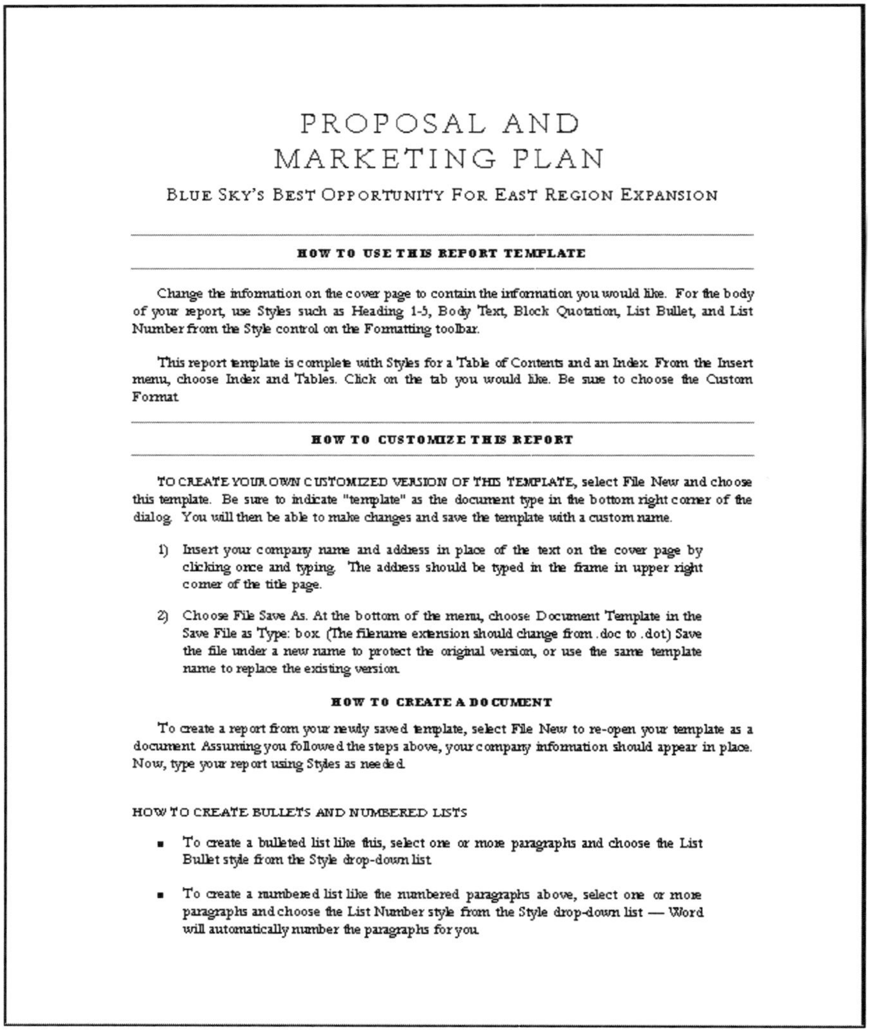

PROPOSAL AND MARKETING PLAN
BLUE SKY'S BEST OPPORTUNITY FOR EAST REGION EXPANSION

HOW TO USE THIS REPORT TEMPLATE

Change the information on the cover page to contain the information you would like. For the body of your report, use Styles such as Heading 1-5, Body Text, Block Quotation, List Bullet, and List Number from the Style control on the Formatting toolbar.

This report template is complete with Styles for a Table of Contents and an Index. From the Insert menu, choose Index and Tables. Click on the tab you would like. Be sure to choose the Custom Format.

HOW TO CUSTOMIZE THIS REPORT

TO CREATE YOUR OWN CUSTOMIZED VERSION OF THIS TEMPLATE, select File New and choose this template. Be sure to indicate "template" as the document type in the bottom right corner of the dialog. You will then be able to make changes and save the template with a custom name.

1) Insert your company name and address in place of the text on the cover page by clicking once and typing. The address should be typed in the frame in upper right corner of the title page.

2) Choose File Save As. At the bottom of the menu, choose Document Template in the Save File as Type: box. (The filename extension should change from .doc to .dot.) Save the file under a new name to protect the original version, or use the same template name to replace the existing version.

HOW TO CREATE A DOCUMENT

To create a report from your newly saved template, select File New to re-open your template as a document. Assuming you followed the steps above, your company information should appear in place. Now, type your report using Styles as needed.

HOW TO CREATE BULLETS AND NUMBERED LISTS

- To create a bulleted list like this, select one or more paragraphs and choose the List Bullet style from the Style drop-down list.

- To create a numbered list like the numbered paragraphs above, select one or more paragraphs and choose the List Number style from the Style drop-down list — Word will automatically number the paragraphs for you.

Figure 4-17b: The Elegant Report.dot template (second page).

This Style—the Block Quotation—can be used for quotes, notes or paragraphs of special interest. To use the Block Quotation Style, highlight any paragraph and choose Block Quotation from the style drop-down list on the Formatting toolbar.

MORE TEMPLATE TIPS

There are three ways to view the various style names of the template sample text

1) In Normal view, choose Tools Options. Click the View tab. In the Style Area Width box, dial up a number such as "1" and click OK. Observe the style name next to each paragraph; or

2) In Page Layout view, click on any paragraph and view the style name on the Formatting toolbar; or

3) From the Format menu choose Style Gallery. In the Preview section click on Style Samples.

HOW TO CREATE A TABLE

TO CREATE A TABLE, Choose Insert Table From the Table menu. To have it look like the below table, click Table AutoFormat on the Table menu, and then choose the Elegant format

TO MODIFY AN EXISTING TABLE, such as the table below, position your cursor in any cell. To modify the table, access the Table menu to select the desired action and/or result

COMPETITOR RANKING	CURRENT SHARE	SHARE IN 3 YRS
Largest competitor	50%	30%
Second largest competitor	25%	20%
Third largest competitor	15%	12%

■ Table: Projected growth of competitors over 3 years.

3

Figure 4-17c: The Elegant Report.dot template (third page).

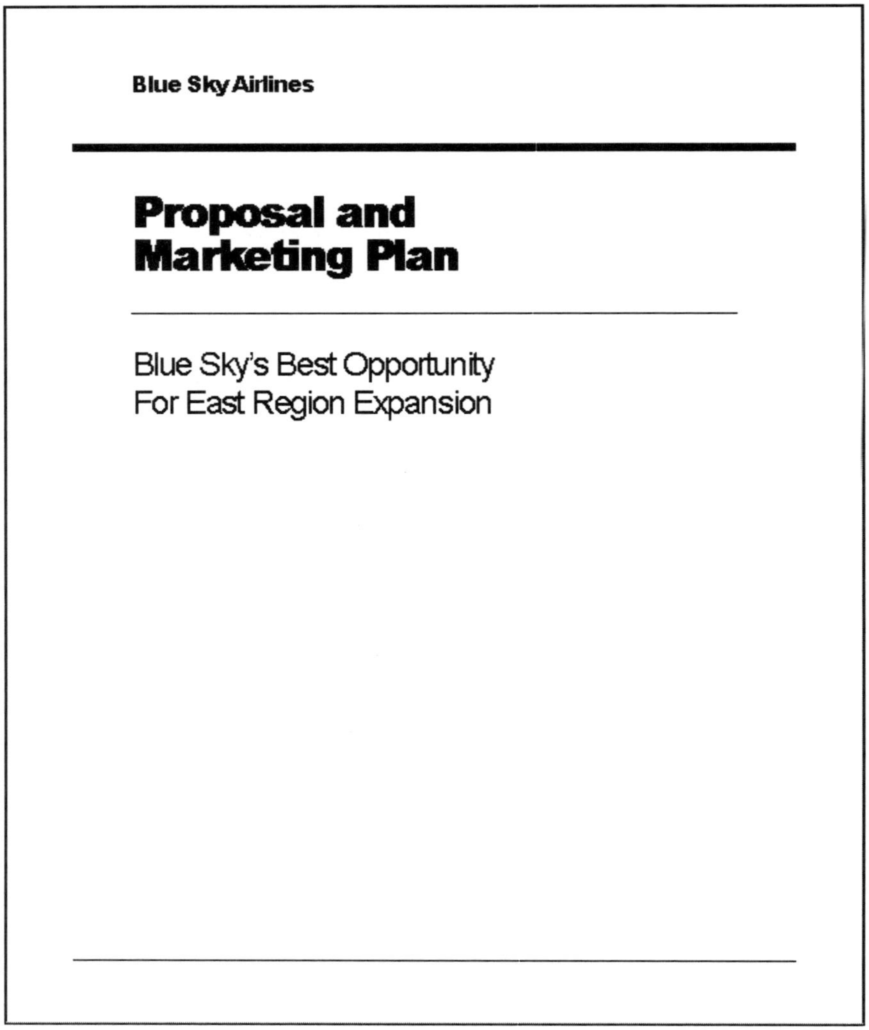

Blue Sky Airlines

Proposal and Marketing Plan

Blue Sky's Best Opportunity
For East Region Expansion

Figure 4-18a: The Professional Report.dot template (first page).

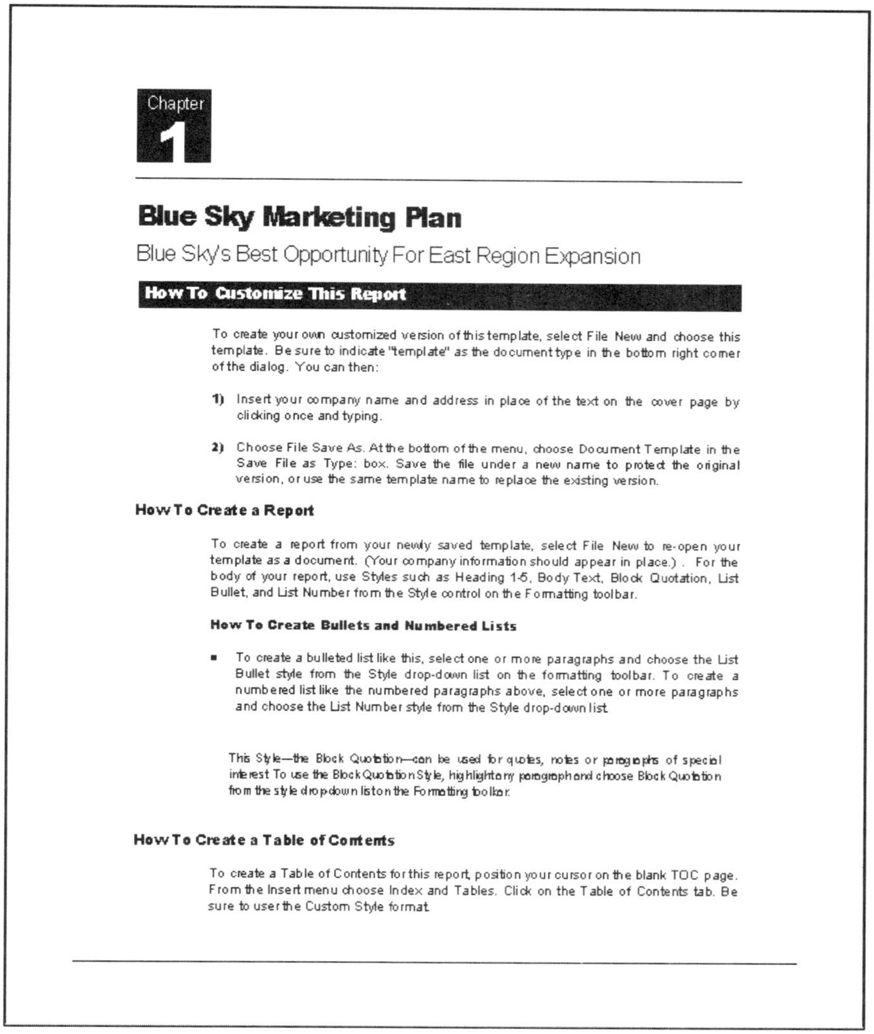

Blue Sky Marketing Plan

Blue Sky's Best Opportunity For East Region Expansion

How To Customize This Report

To create your own customized version of this template, select File New and choose this template. Be sure to indicate "template" as the document type in the bottom right corner of the dialog. You can then:

1) Insert your company name and address in place of the text on the cover page by clicking once and typing.

2) Choose File Save As. At the bottom of the menu, choose Document Template in the Save File as Type: box. Save the file under a new name to protect the original version, or use the same template name to replace the existing version.

How To Create a Report

To create a report from your newly saved template, select File New to re-open your template as a document. (Your company information should appear in place.) . For the body of your report, use Styles such as Heading 1-5, Body Text, Block Quotation, List Bullet, and List Number from the Style control on the Formatting toolbar.

How To Create Bullets and Numbered Lists

- To create a bulleted list like this, select one or more paragraphs and choose the List Bullet style from the Style drop-down list on the formatting toolbar. To create a numbered list like the numbered paragraphs above, select one or more paragraphs and choose the List Number style from the Style drop-down list.

> This Style—the Block Quotation—can be used for quotes, notes or paragraphs of special interest To use the Block Quotation Style, highlight any paragraph and choose Block Quotation from the style drop-down list on the Formatting toolbar.

How To Create a Table of Contents

To create a Table of Contents for this report, position your cursor on the blank TOC page. From the Insert menu choose Index and Tables. Click on the Table of Contents tab. Be sure to use the Custom Style format.

Figure 4-18b: The Professional Report.dot template (second page).

More Template Tips

There are three ways to view the various style names of template text

1) In Normal view, choose Tools Options. Click the View tab. In the Style Area Width box, dial up a number such as "1" and click OK. Observe the style name next to each paragraph; or

2) In Page Layout view, click on any paragraph. View the style name on the Formatting toolbar; or

3) From the Format menu choose Style Gallery. In the Preview section click on Example or Style Samples.

How To Create a Table

Choose Insert from the Table menu. Be sure to choose the Professional AutoFormat if you are using a Professional style template.

To modify an existing table, such as the table below, position your cursor in any cell. To modify the table, access the Table menu to select the desired action and/or result.

Competitor Ranking	Current Share	Share in 3 Yrs.
Largest competitor	50%	30%
Second largest competitor	25%	20%
Third largest competitor	15%	12%

• Table. Projected growth of competitors over 3 years.

How to Edit Table Text

Table text can be edited and formatted like regular text. Simply select text and type to replace, and use the Format menu to change the font and/or paragraph attributes.

How To Change a Header or Footer

In Page Layout view, choose Header or Footer from the View menu. Once activated, you can change or delete the text just like regular text. When done, click Close to exit.

To delete a ruling line in the Header or Footer, from the Format menu choose Borders and Shading. Choose None from the Preset section, and click OK.

2

Figure 4-18c: The Professional Report.dot template (third page).

Press releases

Word won't write your press releases for you, but you will find templates that will improve the odds of your press releases being read. You'll find the three templates in the Publications template folder: Contemporary Press Release.dot, Elegant Press Release.dot, and Professional Press Release.dot. Unfortunately, Word does not include a Press Release Wizard.

The press release templates include your company name, contact information, the release date, a title, and copy that you should, of course, replace with your own. Of course, you can permanently store much of this information in the template so that you don't have to change it each time.

Figures 4-19, 4-20, and 4-21 illustrate the three press release templates.

Resumes

Word won't land you a new job, but the resume templates can help you craft a resume that will outshine the competition. The three resume templates — Contemporary Resume.dot, Elegant Resume.dot, and Professional Resume.dot — are located in the Other Documents template folder. These templates contain several standard resume sections, but note that the sample text provided in the templates makes some pretty outrageous claims. You'd better tone it down a bit if you expect to be taken seriously.

The Other Documents folder also holds a Resume Wizard that helps you further customize your resume. For more information about wizards, see the section "Using Wizards" later in this chapter.

Figures 4-22, 4-23, and 4-24 illustrate the three resume templates.

Business forms

If you can't afford your own business forms, Word includes templates for three common ones: invoice, purchase orders, and weekly time sheets. You'll find the templates Invoice.dot, Purchase Order.dot, and Weekly Time Sheet.dot in the Other Documents template folder. Unlike the other templates, these do not come in Contemporary, Elegant, or Professional varieties.

As with any of the supplied templates, you can and should customize these templates. At the minimum, you'll want to store your company name and address in the template permanently. You may also want to make more drastic changes, such as adding or removing form fields. These templates use Word tables and form fields, so you should be familiar with these Word features before you start tinkering with these forms.

Figures 4-25, 4-26, and 4-27 illustrate the three business forms templates.

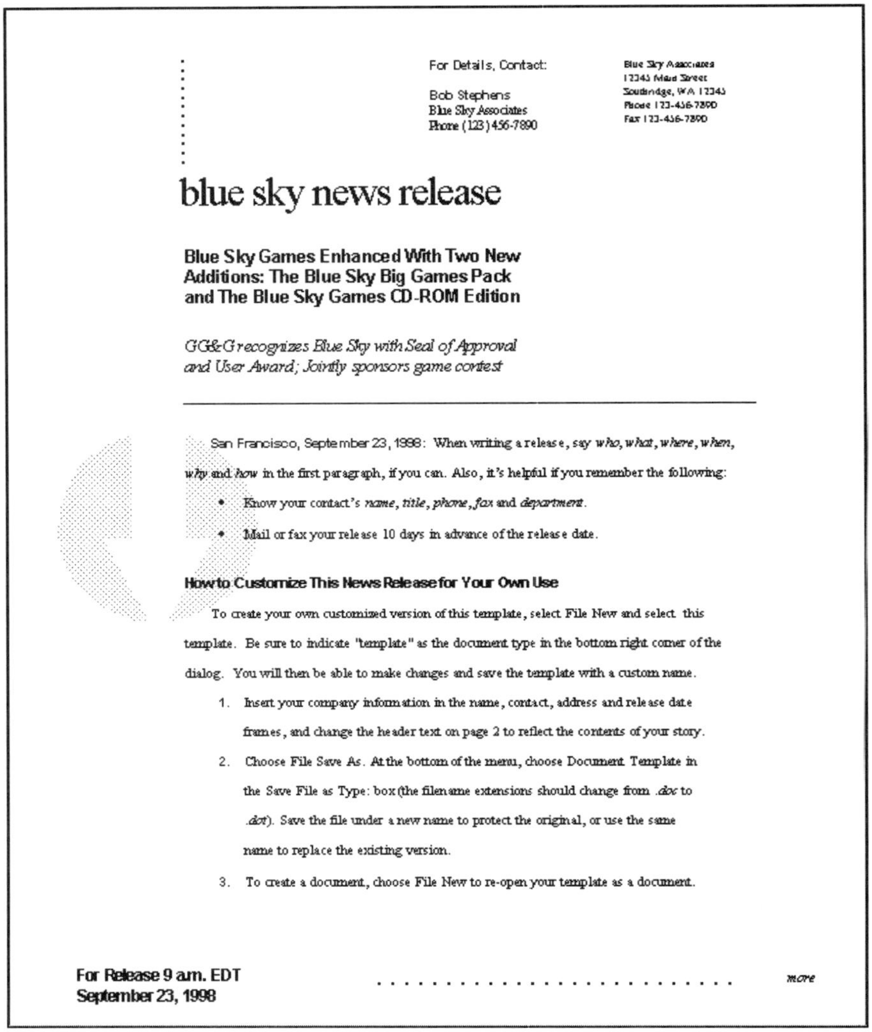

Figure 4-19: The Contemporary Press Release.dot template.

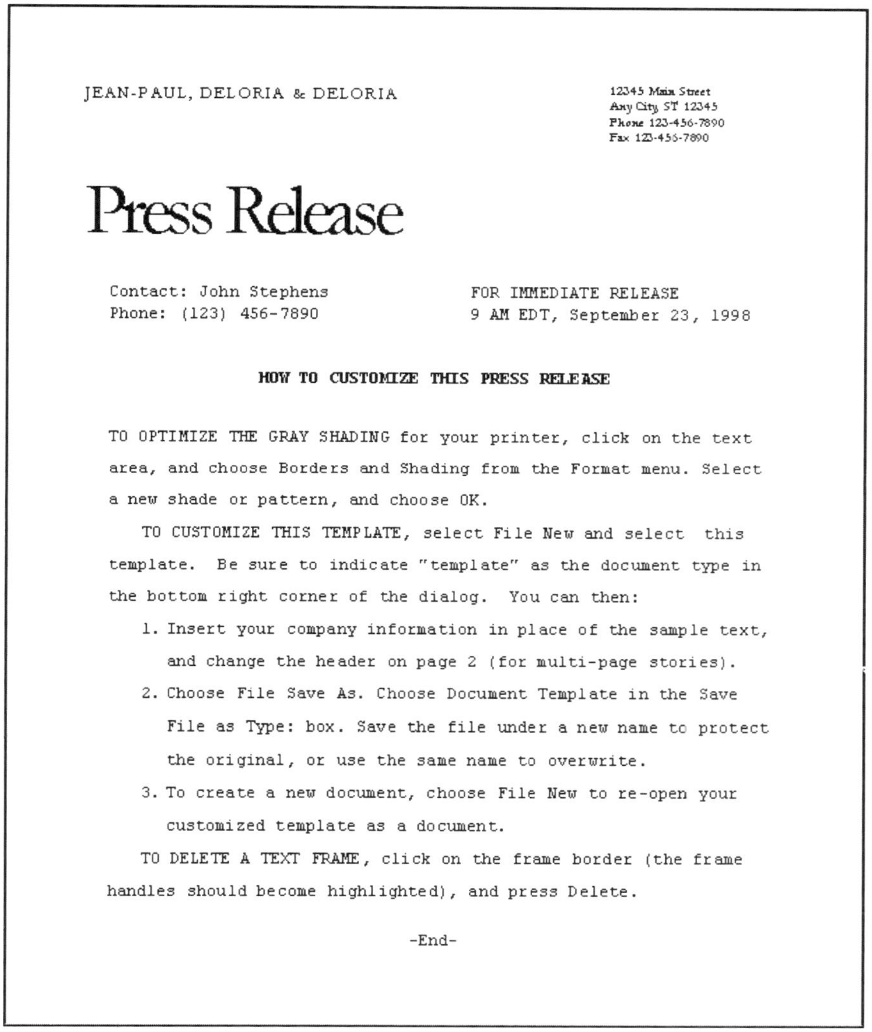

JEAN-PAUL, DELORIA & DELORIA

12345 Main Street
Any City, ST 12345
Phone 123-456-7890
Fax 123-455-7890

Press Release

Contact: John Stephens
Phone: (123) 456-7890

FOR IMMEDIATE RELEASE
9 AM EDT, September 23, 1998

HOW TO CUSTOMIZE THIS PRESS RELEASE

TO OPTIMIZE THE GRAY SHADING for your printer, click on the text area, and choose Borders and Shading from the Format menu. Select a new shade or pattern, and choose OK.

TO CUSTOMIZE THIS TEMPLATE, select File New and select this template. Be sure to indicate "template" as the document type in the bottom right corner of the dialog. You can then:

1. Insert your company information in place of the sample text, and change the header on page 2 (for multi-page stories).

2. Choose File Save As. Choose Document Template in the Save File as Type: box. Save the file under a new name to protect the original, or use the same name to overwrite.

3. To create a new document, choose File New to re-open your customized template as a document.

TO DELETE A TEXT FRAME, click on the frame border (the frame handles should become highlighted), and press Delete.

-End-

Figure 4-20: The Elegant Press Release.dot template.

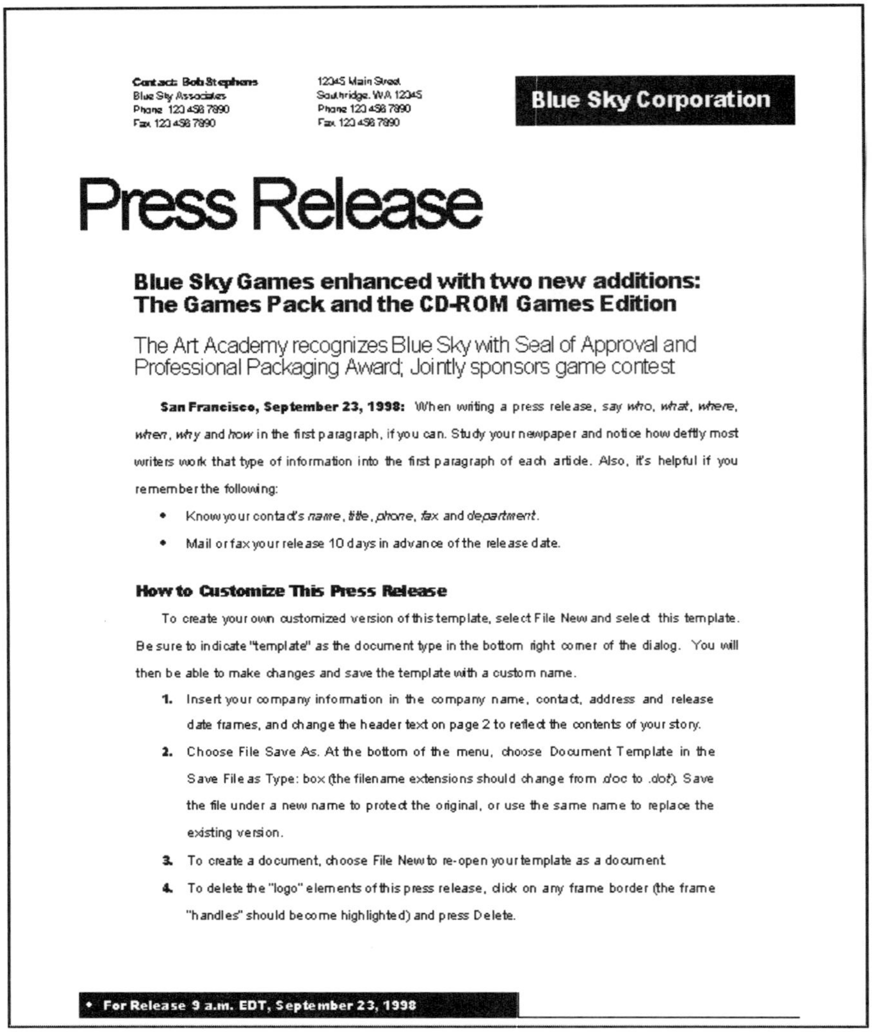

Contact: Bob Stephens
Blue Sky Associates
Phone 123 456 7890
Fax 123 456 7890

12345 Main Street
Southridge, WA 12345
Phone 123 456 7890
Fax 123 456 7890

Blue Sky Corporation

Press Release

Blue Sky Games enhanced with two new additions: The Games Pack and the CD-ROM Games Edition

The Art Academy recognizes Blue Sky with Seal of Approval and Professional Packaging Award; Jointly sponsors game contest

San Francisco, September 23, 1998: When writing a press release, say *who*, *what*, *where*, *when*, *why* and *how* in the first paragraph, if you can. Study your newspaper and notice how deftly most writers work that type of information into the first paragraph of each article. Also, it's helpful if you remember the following:

- Know your contact's *name*, *title*, *phone*, *fax* and *department*.
- Mail or fax your release 10 days in advance of the release date.

How to Customize This Press Release

To create your own customized version of this template, select File New and select this template. Be sure to indicate "template" as the document type in the bottom right corner of the dialog. You will then be able to make changes and save the template with a custom name.

1. Insert your company information in the company name, contact, address and release date frames, and change the header text on page 2 to reflect the contents of your story.
2. Choose File Save As. At the bottom of the menu, choose Document Template in the Save File as Type: box (the filename extensions should change from *.doc* to *.dot*). Save the file under a new name to protect the original, or use the same name to replace the existing version.
3. To create a document, choose File New to re-open your template as a document.
4. To delete the "logo" elements of this press release, click on any frame border (the frame "handles" should become highlighted) and press Delete.

• For Release 9 a.m. EDT, September 23, 1998

Figure 4-21: The Professional Press Release.dot template.

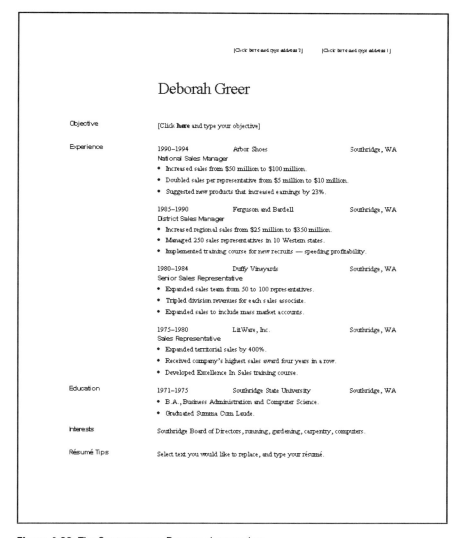

Figure 4-22: The Contemporary Resume.dot template.

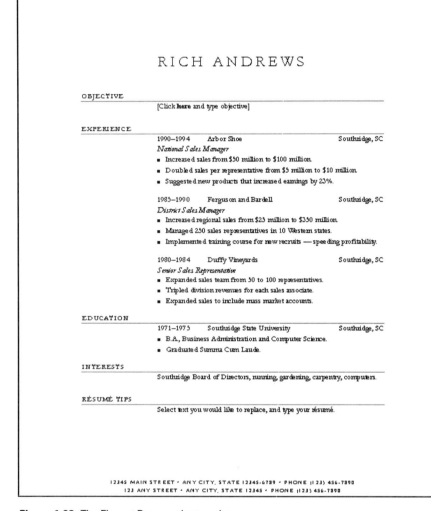

RICH ANDREWS

OBJECTIVE

[Click here and type objective]

EXPERIENCE

1990–1994   Arbor Shoe   Southridge, SC
National Sales Manager
- Increased sales from $50 million to $100 million.
- Doubled sales per representative from $5 million to $10 million.
- Suggested new products that increased earnings by 23%.

1985–1990   Ferguson and Bardell   Southridge, SC
District Sales Manager
- Increased regional sales from $25 million to $350 million.
- Managed 250 sales representatives in 10 Western states.
- Implemented training course for new recruits — speeding profitability.

1980–1984   Duffy Vineyards   Southridge, SC
Senior Sales Representative
- Expanded sales team from 50 to 100 representatives.
- Tripled division revenues for each sales associate.
- Expanded sales to include mass market accounts.

EDUCATION

1971–1975   Southridge State University   Southridge, SC
- B.A., Business Administration and Computer Science.
- Graduated Summa Cum Laude.

INTERESTS

Southridge Board of Directors, running, gardening, carpentry, computers.

RÉSUMÉ TIPS

Select text you would like to replace, and type your résumé.

12345 MAIN STREET • ANY CITY, STATE 12345-6789 • PHONE (123) 456-7890
123 ANY STREET • ANY CITY, STATE 12345 • PHONE (123) 456-7890

Figure 4-23: The Elegant Resume.dot template.

Figure 4-24: The Professional Resume.dot template.

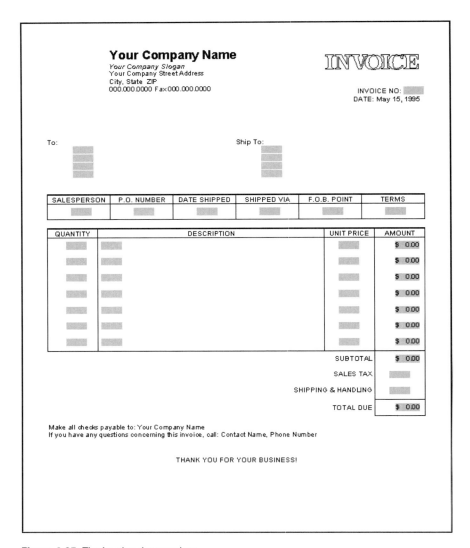

Figure 4-25: The Invoice.dot template.

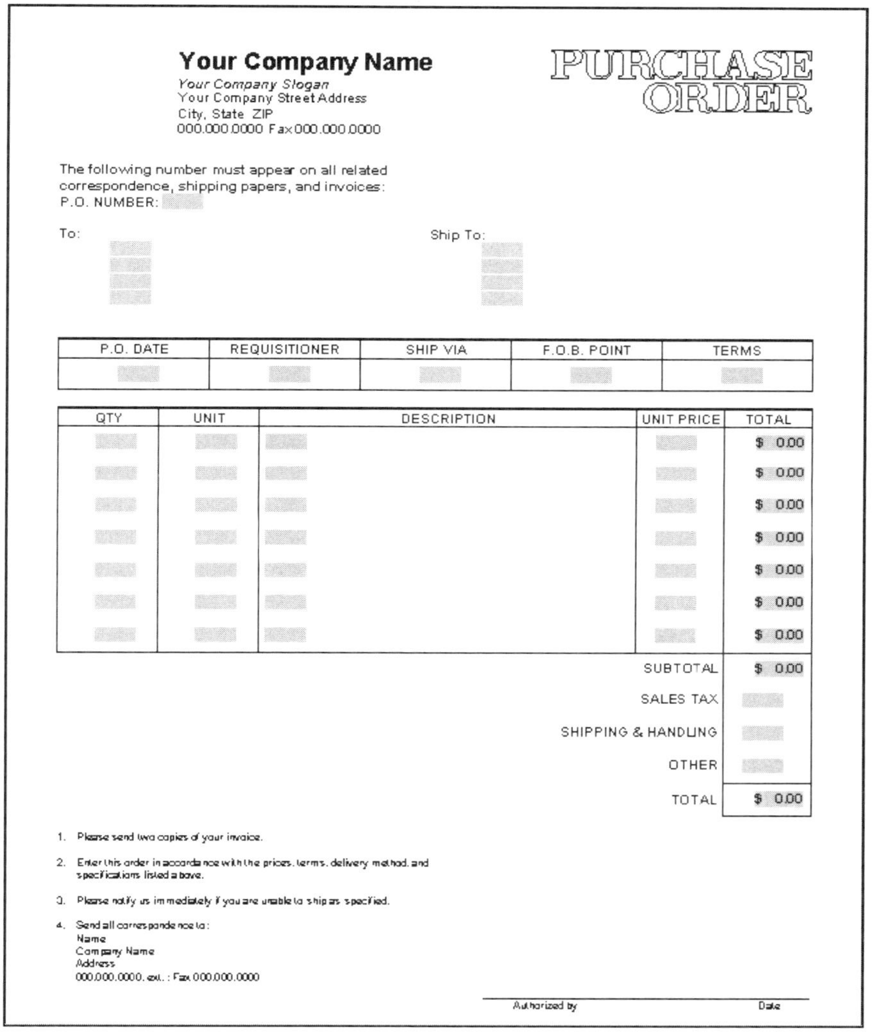

Your Company Name
Your Company Slogan
Your Company Street Address
City, State ZIP
000.000.0000 Fax 000.000.0000

PURCHASE ORDER

The following number must appear on all related
correspondence, shipping papers, and invoices:
P.O. NUMBER:

To:

Ship To:

P.O. DATE	REQUISITIONER	SHIP VIA	F.O.B. POINT	TERMS

QTY	UNIT	DESCRIPTION	UNIT PRICE	TOTAL
				$ 0.00
				$ 0.00
				$ 0.00
				$ 0.00
				$ 0.00
				$ 0.00
				$ 0.00

SUBTOTAL	$ 0.00
SALES TAX	
SHIPPING & HANDLING	
OTHER	
TOTAL	$ 0.00

1. Please send two copies of your invoice.

2. Enter this order in accordance with the prices, terms, delivery method, and
   specifications listed above.

3. Please notify us immediately if you are unable to ship as specified.

4. Send all correspondence to:
   Name
   Company Name
   Address
   000.000.0000. ext. : Fax 000.000.0000

Authorized by   Date

Figure 4-26: The Purchase Order.dot template.

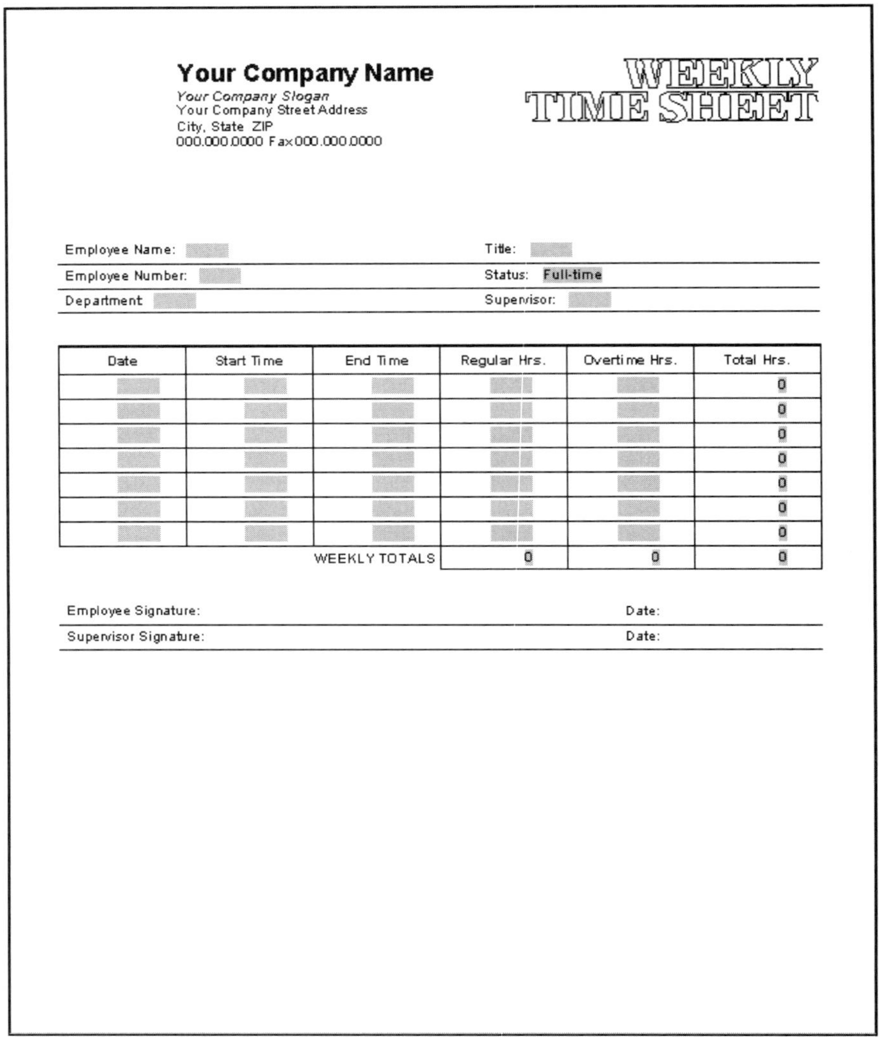

Your Company Name
Your Company Slogan
Your Company Street Address
City, State ZIP
000.000.0000 Fax 000.000.0000

WEEKLY
TIME SHEET

Employee Name: ▢   Title: ▢
Employee Number: ▢   Status: **Full-time**
Department ▢   Supervisor: ▢

Date	Start Time	End Time	Regular Hrs.	Overtime Hrs.	Total Hrs.
▢	▢	▢	▢	▢	0
▢	▢	▢	▢	▢	0
▢	▢	▢	▢	▢	0
▢	▢	▢	▢	▢	0
▢	▢	▢	▢	▢	0
▢	▢	▢	▢	▢	0
▢	▢	▢	▢	▢	0
		WEEKLY TOTALS	0	0	0

Employee Signature: Date:
Supervisor Signature: Date:

Figure 4-27: The Weekly Time Sheet.dot template.

Using Wizards

Word comes with a collection of wizards that are designed to simplify the creation of routine documents. Word's wizards include the following:

- **Agenda Wizard,** which creates meeting agendas complete with suggested topics.

- **Award Wizard,** which creates attractive certificates almost suitable for framing.

- **Calendar Wizard,** which creates monthly calendars in various formats.

- **Fax Wizard,** which creates faxes in various styles.

- **Letter Wizard,** which creates letters in various styles and includes several prewritten business letters (plus a letter to Mom for those who never write home).

- **Memo Wizard,** which creates memos with attractive headers and body text.

- **Newsletter Wizard,** which sets up a newsletter with columns and other elements.

- **Pleading Wizard,** which creates legal documents.

- **Resume Wizard,** which creates resumes with pertinent sections, such as Education, References, and so on.

- **Table Wizard,** which creates tables with various heading and border styles.

A wizard is nothing more than a special type of template that has been given the extension WIZ instead of DOC. Each wizard contains specialized macros that run automatically to prompt you for the information it needs to create the document. After you've answered the questions, the wizard creates the document for you.

Running a wizard

To run a wizard, use the File⇨New command and select a wizard instead of a template for the new document. Word loads the wizard and automatically runs it. Wizards are based on complicated WordBasic macros, which aren't particularly efficient (one of the reasons we had hoped that Word for Windows 95 would include a Visual Basic for Applications). So be patient while the wizard spends a few moments preparing its first dialog box. Once the wizard gets going, performance isn't too bad.

To illustrate how wizards work, I'll step you through one of the more popular wizards these days, the Resume Wizard. To create a resume using this wizard, start by summoning the New dialog box by using the File⇨New command. Click the Other Documents tab and double-click the Resume Wizard.wiz icon. (If the dialog box displays large icons, you may have to scroll the list to find the Resume Wizard.) Be patient while the Resume Wizard chugs and churns. Eventually, the Resume Wizard will come to life and display the dialog box shown in Figure 4-28, asking you to pick one of four basic types of resumes.

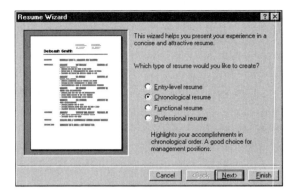

Figure 4-28: The Resume Wizard comes to life.

This dialog box shows the basic framework for all wizard dialog boxes. At the left of the dialog box is a preview of how the document you're creating will appear based on the information you've provided so far. This preview will periodically change as you work your way through the wizard.

In the right center of the dialog box are various fields and option buttons that you use to answer the wizard's questions. As you work your way through the wizard, these controls will change depending on the information the wizard is seeking.

At the bottom of the dialog box are four buttons that you use to control the wizard:

- The Cancel button bails out of the wizard without creating a document.

- The <Back button, which isn't highlighted in Figure 4-28, lets you work your way backwards through the wizard to change your answers to prior questions.

- The Next> button tells the wizard to continue with the next question.

- The Finish button tells the wizard to stop the interview and create the document now, using whatever information has been gathered so far.

In Figure 4-28, I selected a Chronological resume and clicked on Next> to move ahead. The dialog box shown in Figure 4-29 is displayed next. Here, you type your name, address, and phone number. The Resume Wizard will include this information in the resume automatically.

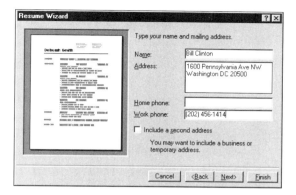

Figure 4-29: The Resume Wizard asks for your name and address.

Figure 4-30 shows the next dialog box displayed by the Resume Wizard. Here, you are asked to select which commonly used headings should be included in the resume. Initially, all of these options are checked. Note that the precise mix of sections that appear in here varies depending on which resume style you selected in the first dialog box.

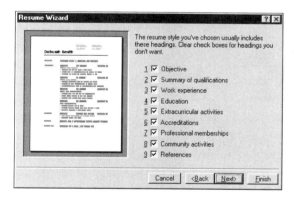

Figure 4-30: The Resume Wizard offers to include these sections in the resume.

Next, the Resume Wizard displays a list of optional sections that you can include in your resume if you wish, as shown in Figure 4-31. Again, these sections vary depending on which resume type you selected at the beginning.

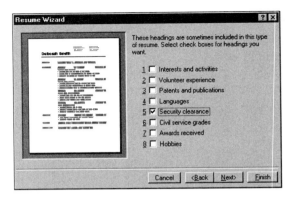

Figure 4-31: Other sections You can add to the resume.

The Resume Wizard next displays the dialog box shown in Figure 4-32, which allows you to add your own sections to the resume. To add a section, type the title as you want it to appear in the resume in the text field and click the Add button.

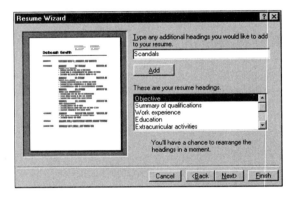

Figure 4-32: You can even add your own sections to the resume.

Next, the Resume Wizard allows you to change the order in which the sections will appear in the document by using the dialog box shown in Figure 4-33. To move a section, select it in the list box and click the Move Up or Move Down button.

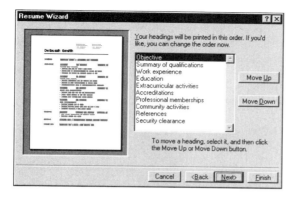

Figure 4-33: The Resume Wizard lets you juggle the order in which sections are listed in the resume.

The Resume Wizard now displays the dialog box shown in Figure 4-34, which lets you select the style to use for the resume (Professional, Contemporary, or Elegant).

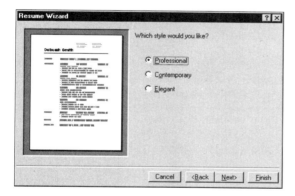

Figure 4-34: You can create a Professional, Contemporary, or Elegant style resume.

Finally, after you've answered all of the questions, you reach the checkered flag, as shown in Figure 4-35. At this point, you have three options:

- Create a cover letter to go along with the resume.

- Display help, which activates Word's on-line help to assist you as you complete the resume.

- Just display the resume, which creates the resume as a new document. This is the option you ordinarily use when a wizard is finished.

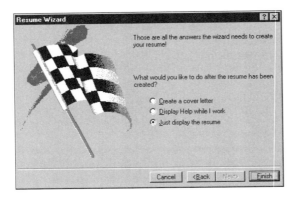

Figure 4-35: You've reached the checkered flag!

When you click the Finish button, the wizard works for a few moments and then creates the resume as a new document, as shown in Figure 4-36. You can now edit the document however you wish, filling in the blanks left by the wizard.

Note

The document is initially displayed in Page Layout view. If you prefer to work in Normal view, just click the Normal View button at the bottom of the Word window.

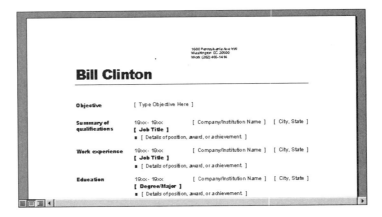

Figure 4-36: A resume created by the Resume Wizard, ready for editing.

All of the other wizards that come with Word work much the same as the Resume Wizard. Each displays a series of questions using the same dialog box format, with the same Cancel, Back, Next, and Finish controls, and each displays the checkered flag at the end with options similar to the ones shown for the Resume Wizard. Of course, the questions vary from wizard to wizard, and the document that is generated by the wizard is different. But the basic framework of all the wizards is the same.

Resetting wizard defaults

Secret

You may notice as you use Word's wizards that the answers you give persist from one use of the wizard to the next. In other words, if you select the Contemporary style for the Resume Wizard, that option will be selected by default the next time you use the Resume Wizard.

Word keeps track of the options you've chosen for each wizard in a file named Wordwiz.ini in your \Windows directory. If for some reason you want to restore all of the wizard questions to their default values, you can simply delete or rename this file. That will cause the wizards to revert to their defaults.

To restore just a single wizard to its default settings, edit the Wordwiz.ini file by using WordPad or a similar text editor. Locate the section that pertains to the wizard you want to restore to default settings and delete all of the lines pertaining to that section. For example, to restore the Resume Wizard to its defaults, you would locate the following line in Wordwiz.ini:

[Resume Wizard]

Then, delete all of this line and all of the lines that follow it, up to the beginning of the next section. (Each section consists of the name of a Wizard enclosed in brackets.)

Note

With Windows 95, Microsoft is discouraging software developers from creating their own INI files. The company is instead encouraging developers to store settings in the Windows Registry. This is just one of several examples of Microsoft not following its own advice.

Chapter 5

Customizing Word's Startup and Appearance

In This Chapter

▶ Starting Word in different ways, including a few you may not have considered

▶ Switching among Word's various views

▶ Working in full screen to display as much of your document as possible (akin to a circus high-wire act without a net)

▶ Customizing Word's View options

▶ Making Word look like WordPerfect for DOS, which is either a waste of time, an act of treason, or a cruel practical joke

The good folks at Microsoft have spent years perfecting Word's user interface. Still, they recognize that working style varies from person to person, and one person's idea of a clever shortcut might be a hindrance to another. As a result, Word lets you change almost any aspect of its "look and feel." You can add or remove elements of the user interface, such as scrollbars, the ruler, or the status bar. You can change the way Word starts. You can even change such pesky details as whether Word measures things in inches, centimeters, picas, or points.

This chapter shows you how to customize Word's startup and appearance so that it best suits your style. For more advanced customization of toolbars, keyboard shortcuts, or menus, see Chapter 6.

The Many Ways to Start Word

With Word 6 running under Windows 3.1, there were really just three ways to start Word:

1. Double-click on the Word icon in Program Manager.

2. Double-click on the Winword.exe file in File Manager.

3. Double-click on a DOC file in File Manager.

If you're lucky enough to have Microsoft Office, you can also start Word by clicking on the Word icon in the Microsoft Office Shortcut Bar (OSB).

With Word 95, there are even more ways to start Word. The following sections describe the more useful methods.

Using the Start button Programs menu

The easiest way to start Word, especially for new users, is to click on the Start button in the Windows 95 taskbar. Point to Programs and wait a moment for the Programs menu to appear; point to MS Office 95, and wait for the Office 95 submenu to appear. Then, click on Microsoft Word. (This method is analogous to double-clicking on the Word icon in Windows 3.1 Program Manager.)

Figure 5-1 shows the tangle of menus displayed when Word is finally located, at least as it appears on my system.

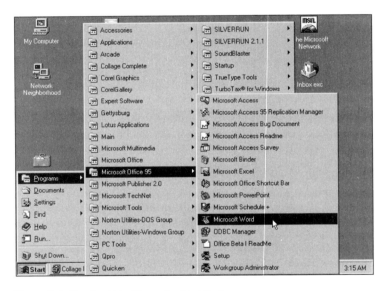

Figure 5-1: Starting Word from the Start Button.

Using the Start button Documents menu

The Start button also has a Documents menu that keeps track of documents you've recently accessed. If you call up this menu and select a Word document, Windows 95 will start Word and open the document you selected.

Starting Word from My Computer or Explorer

Another way to start Word (though not one I'd recommend) is to locate its icon in a My Computer or Explorer window and double-click on it. In a typical installation, you can find the Winword.exe for Windows program file in the C:\Office95\Winword. This is analogous to finding Winword.exe in File Manager and double-clicking it.

Figure 5-2 shows a My Computer window open to the Winword folder (on my computer, it happens to be on drive D: rather than drive C:), ready to launch Word.

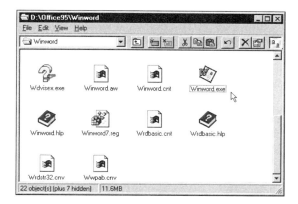

Figure 5-2: The Winword folder as displayed by My Computer.

My Computer and Explorer will also let you start Word by double-clicking on a Word document, just as in Windows 3.1 File Manager.

Creating a shortcut on the desktop

One way to start Word quickly is to create a shortcut for it on the desktop. To do this, locate the \Office95\Winword folder in My Computer or Explorer and use the right mouse button to drag the Winword.exe icon to the desktop. When you release the right mouse button, a pop-up menu will appear with several choices. Select Create Shortcut(s) Here. Windows will place an icon on the desktop with the name "Shortcut to Winword.exe." Click once on the icon's name, wait a moment, click again, and change the name to something more direct, such as "Microsoft Word." Figure 5-3 shows the resulting shortcut icon. Once this shortcut icon is in place, you can start Word by double-clicking on the icon.

Figure 5-3: A desktop icon for a shortcut to Word.

Creating a new document from the desktop, My Computer, or Explorer

You can create a new Word document in any My Computer or Explorer folder by choosing the File⇨New command and selecting Microsoft Word Document. Windows will create an empty document in the current folder. You can then double-click the icon for the new document to start Word and edit the empty document.

You can also do this at the desktop by right-clicking anywhere on the desktop and selecting New⇨Microsoft Word Document from the pop-up menu that appears. This creates an empty document on the desktop, which you can then double-click to edit.

Using Microsoft Office Shortcut Bar

If you have Microsoft Office 95, you can use the Office Shortcut Bar (OSB) to start Word. By default, OSB displays a small palette of buttons, as shown in Figure 5-4.

Figure 5-4: The Microsoft Office Shortcut Bar.

You can use two of the buttons initially displayed in the Office Shortcut Bar to start Word:

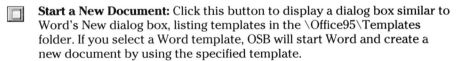 **Start a New Document:** Click this button to display a dialog box similar to Word's New dialog box, listing templates in the \Office95\Templates folder. If you select a Word template, OSB will start Word and create a new document by using the specified template.

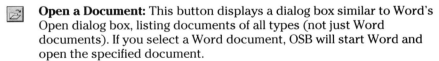 **Open a Document:** This button displays a dialog box similar to Word's Open dialog box, listing documents of all types (not just Word documents). If you select a Word document, OSB will start Word and open the specified document.

You can easily customize the OSB toolbar to include a button that starts Word directly. Right-click anywhere on OSB outside of one of its buttons and select Customize from the pop-up menu that appears. When the Customize dialog box appears, click on the Buttons tab. The dialog box shown in Figure 5-5 will appear.

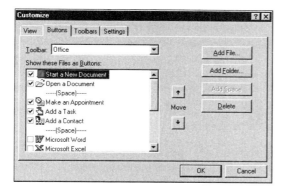

Figure 5-5: Customizing the Office Shortcut Bar.

In the Show These Files as Buttons list, find the check box for Microsoft Word and click it. Word should appear as a button on the OSB toolbar. Click OK.

If you click the Word button and Word is already running, OSB merely switches to the existing instance of Word. A new instance of Word is not started.

You can customize the OSB toolbar to include icons for any file or folder on your computer. From the Customize dialog box, click Add File to add a file — which can be a program file or a document file — or click Add Folder to add a folder.

You can also add additional toolbars to OSB. Only one of these toolbars is displayed at a time, but buttons are provided to switch from one toolbar to another. To create additional toolbars, call up the Customize dialog box by right-clicking on the OSB toolbar and choosing the Customize command; then click the Toolbars tab. OSB comes preconfigured with the following toolbars:

- **Office** (the one that is displayed by default).
- **Favorites,** which displays your Favorites folder in toolbar form.
- **Old Office,** which displays your old Microsoft Office Manager toolbar if you used Microsoft Office 4.x.
- **Desktop,** which presents the icons on your desktop as toolbar buttons.
- **MSN,** which allows you to connect to The Microsoft Network and access the Microsoft Office support forums.
- **Programs,** which presents your Start⇨Programs menu as a toolbar.
- **Accessories,** which presents you Start⇨Programs⇨Accessories menu as a toolbar.

Initially, only the Office toolbar is enabled. To enable any of the other toolbars, just click on the check box that appears next to the toolbar name. You can add additional toolbars of your own design by clicking the Add Toolbar button.

Starting Word automatically

You can set up Windows 95 so that Word launches each time you start your computer. To do so, follow these steps:

1. Click on the Start button and point to the Settings command. When the menu appears, click Taskbar.

2. When the Taskbar Properties dialog box appears, click the Start Menu Programs tab.

3. Click on Add and click Browse.

4. Locate the Winword.exe program file in the \MSOffice\Winword folder and double-click it.

5. When the Create Shortcut window reappears, click Next. Double-click the StartUp folder. (You'll probably have to scroll down the list to find it. Fortunately, the list is presented in alphabetical order.)

6. Click on Finish and then click on OK to close the Taskbar Properties window. The next time you start your computer, Word load automatically.

Starting Word from an MS-DOS prompt

In Windows 3.1, you could not start a Windows program from an MS-DOS session. If Windows 3.1 was not running, you could start Windows and load a program by listing the program name as a parameter following the `Win` command. For example, to start Windows 3.1 and Word 6, you could use a command like this:

```
win c:\winword\winword
```

However, if you started an MS-DOS command prompt from within Windows, you could not start Word from the prompt.

In Windows 95, you *can* start a Windows program from an MS-DOS prompt, whether running in a window or full screen, simply by typing the name of the program (and the path, if necessary). Because Windows keeps track of the location of the Word program file in the registry, you can start Word from an MS-DOS prompt by typing the command **winword**.

When you start Word from an MS-DOS prompt, Windows 95 starts a new instance of Word. Your MS-DOS session remains active, however, and you can switch back to it at any time by pressing Alt+Tab or by clicking on its button in the taskbar.

Note

If you "Restart your computer in MS-DOS Mode," or if you start an MS-DOS program that is set to run in MS-DOS mode, you cannot start Word. MS-DOS mode is a special mode that actually reboots your computer without running Windows. Naturally, you cannot run any Windows programs while Windows is not running.

Word's Command-Line Switches

Word 95 supports several switches that you can include on the command line. These switches are summarized in Table 5-1.

Table 5-1	Word's Command-Line Switches
Command	*What It Does*
winword *filename*	Automatically loads the specified document. You can specify more than one filename (separated by spaces) to open several documents.
winword /n	Starts Word without loading an initial empty document.
winword /a	Starts Word without loading any templates or add-ins and with default settings for options.
winword /m*macroname*	Starts Word and automatically runs the specified macro. This switch also prevents any AutoExec macro from running.
winword /m	Prevents any AutoExec macro from running.
winword /l *addin*	Starts Word and automatically loads the specified add-in (.wll) library.
winword /t *template*	Starts Word and creates a new document based on the specified template.

You can use these switches when you start Word from an MS-DOS prompt or the Start button's Run command, or you can use them when you start Word via a shortcut. To add a command-line switch to a shortcut, right-click on the shortcut to bring up the pop-up menu and select the Properties command. Click on the Shortcut tab and edit the command that appears in the Target field to include the switch you want to use. Figure 5-6 illustrates a shortcut to Word that uses a command-line switch to start Word without loading documents or templates in the StartUp folder.

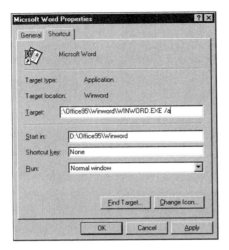

Figure 5-6: Adding a switch to a shortcut.

What ever happened to the Tip of the Day?

For some reason, Microsoft decided to drop the Tip of the Day feature from Word for Windows 95. This feature, introduced with Word 6, displayed a brief one-sentence tip each time you started Word. You could click on a button to dismiss the tip, and you could instruct Word to stop displaying the tips when you grew weary of this feature.

The good news is that Tip of the Day is still present in Word. Rather than operating as a separate feature, it's built in to the new TipWizard toolbar. When TipWizard is first activated, it displays the Tip of the Day in its toolbar. As you continue to work with Word, other tips will replace the Tip of the Day.

Tip

If you liked the Word 6 Tip of the Day feature, you can use the TipWizard to provide a similar capability. Just follow these steps:

1. Save and close any open documents.

 2. If the TipWizard toolbar is not already visible on your screen, activate it by clicking on the TipWizard button in the Standard toolbar (the TipWizard button is the lightbulb).

3. Drag the TipWizard toolbar from its default location to a position floating in the middle of the screen, as shown in Figure 5-7.

4. Exit Word.

5. Create a shortcut for Word on the desktop by right-dragging the Winword icon from the \Office95\Winword folder and selecting Create Shortcut Here when the pop-up menu appears.

6. Right-click on the shortcut icon and select the Properties command.

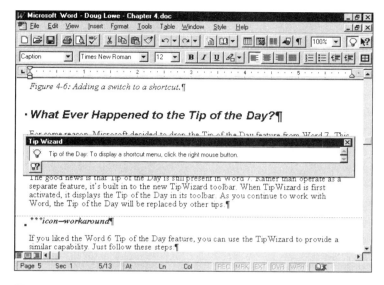

Figure 5-7: The TipWizard positioned in the middle of the screen.

7. Click on the Shortcut tab and edit the Target field so that the command line looks like this:

```
C:\Office95\WinWord\WinWord.exe /mTipWizard
```

In other words, add the /mTipWizard switch to the end of the command.

8. Close the Properties dialog box.

9. Start Word by double-clicking on the new shortcut icon you just created.

10. After reading the tip, dismiss the TipWizard toolbar by clicking on its close button (the X in the top right corner).

If you want Word to display the TipWizard when you start from the Start Programs menu, add the /mTipWizard switch to the Word shortcut located in the \Windows\Start Menu\Programs\Microsoft Office 95 folder.

If you want Word to always start this way, create a macro named AutoExec in the Normal.dot template, with the following lines:

```
Sub MAIN
TipWizard
End Sub
```

Then you can dispense with the /mTipWizard switch. For more information about creating such a macro, consult Chapter 7.

Configuring the Interface

After you customize Word's startup to your liking, you can customize its appearance by using the commands on the View menu. The following sections describe commands that let you add or remove various elements of Word's user interface.

Setting the View mode

The first four commands on the <u>V</u>iew menu let you switch among Word's various View modes:

- **<u>V</u>iew⇨<u>N</u>ormal** sets Word to Normal view, which formats text as it will appear on the printed page with a few exceptions. For example, headers and footers are not shown. This is the mode most people prefer.

- **<u>V</u>iew⇨<u>O</u>utline** activates Outline view, which lets you work with outlines established via Word's standard heading styles. For more information about using outlines, consult Chapter 23.

- **<u>V</u>iew⇨<u>P</u>age Layout** activates Page Layout view, which displays pages exactly as they will appear when printed, complete with columns, headers and footers, and all other formatting details. Word is noticeably slower in Page Layout view than in Normal view, especially when you format the document with headers and footers or use multiple columns.

- **<u>V</u>iew⇨<u>M</u>aster Document** activates Master Document view, which is really a variation of outline view that allows you to work with documents comprised of two or more subdocuments. Master documents are covered in more detail in Chapter 24.

Table 5-2 summarizes keyboard shortcuts for the first three of these commands. In addition, Table 5-2 shows the View buttons that you can use to switch to these views. The View buttons are located near the bottom of the Word window, to the left of the horizontal scrollbar. (Sorry, there is no keyboard shortcut or View button for Master Document view.)

Table 5-2	Keyboard Shortcuts and Buttons for Viewing Documents	
View Command	*Keyboard Shortcut*	*View Button*
Normal	Ctrl+Alt+N	▤
Outline	Ctrl+Alt+O	▤
Page Layout	Ctrl+Alt+P	▤

Working in Full Screen view

Some die-hard power users are proud that they've memorized all of the important keyboard shortcuts and are offended by toolbars and other controls that require the use of the mouse. To prove it, they like to work in Word's Full Screen view. In Full Screen view, the clutter of Word's title bar, menus, toolbars, rulers, status bars, and even scrollbars is eliminated. The entire screen is used to display the document, as shown in Figure 5-8. The only visible control is the floating Full Screen toolbar at the bottom right of the screen, and you can even remove it by clicking on the Close box at the top right corner of the floating toolbar. (Actually, the menu bar is also visible, as a thin row of pixels at the very top of the screen.)

Note

Switching to Full Screen view also maximizes the Word window if it is not already maximized.

·**Chapter 4**¶

·**Customizing Word's Look and Feel**¶

· *In this chapter...*¶

- → *→Adjusting Word's appearance.¶
- → *→Setting options.¶
- → *→How to create your own keyboard shortcuts so that you can quickly invoke frequently used commands.¶
- → *→How to customize Word's toolbars so that the commands you use most are available as toolbar buttons.¶
- → *→How to add new commands to Word's menus.¶

The good folks at Microsoft have spent years perfecting Word's user interface. Still, they recognize that working style varies from person to person, and one person's idea of a clever shortcut might be a hindrance to another. As a result, Word allows you to change almost any aspect of its "look and feel." You can add or remove elements of the user interface such as scroll bars, the ruler, or the status bar. If you don't like the toolbars can remove them or create your own that include just your favorite buttons. You can create your own keyboard shortcuts for the commands you use most often. You can rearrange Word's menus if you think some other arrangement would be more efficient.¶

Figure 5-8: Working in Full Screen view (with non-printing symbols visible).

In Full Screen view, you don't have toolbars to help you with routine tasks. As a result, you'll probably rely on keyboard shortcuts for the most common functions. You can also access Word's menus in Full Screen view, either by using the keyboard (for example, Alt+F to pull down the File menu) or by pointing the mouse at the almost-invisible menu bar at the top of the window. It helps to know the relative position of each menu because Word displays the menu that occupies the position to which you point.

Tip

If you intend on working in Full Screen view and using the mouse to activate menus, do not place the Windows 95 taskbar at the top of the screen with the AutoHide option enabled. If you do, the taskbar will overlay the menu bar, and the taskbar will be activated when you point to the top of the screen instead of Word's menus.

You can leave Full Screen view by clicking on the Full Screen button in the floating toolbar or by pressing the Escape key. You can also uncheck the View⇨Full Screen command.

There is no keyboard shortcut for the View⇨Full Screen command, but you can assign one by using the Tools⇨Customize command as described later in this chapter. Because the View➪Full Screen command is a toggle that alternately activates and deactivates Full Screen view, any keyboard shortcut you assign to it will work as a toggle as well. Use the keyboard shortcut once to switch to Full Screen view and use the same keyboard shortcut again to exit Full Screen view.

Customizing Pieces of the Interface

You can customize the individual components of Word's user interface by calling up the Tools➪>Options command and clicking on the View tab to reveal the Normal View Options dialog box, as shown in Figure 5-9. These options enable you to remove portions of the interface that you don't routinely use, freeing up valuable screen real estate so that you can display more or your document. These options affect Word's appearance regardless of what document is active; in other words, they are not tied to any specific document or template.

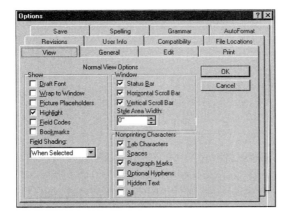

Figure 5-9: The Normal View Options dialog box.

One confusing aspect of this dialog box is that the list of options displayed varies depending on which view mode is active when you call up the Tools➪Options command. Figure 5-9 shows the options that are displayed in Normal view and Outline view. (The only difference is that in Outline view, "Normal View Options" is replaced with "Outline View Options." But the same set of options is displayed.) A slightly different set of options appears if you activate the Tools➪Options command while Page Layout view is active, as shown in Figure 5-10.

The View options are organized into three groups: Show, Window, and Nonprinting Characters. The following sections describe the options available in each of these three groups.

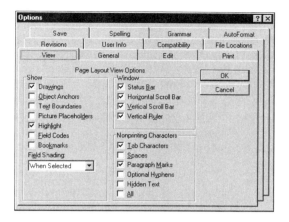

Figure 5-10: The Page Layout View Options dialog box.

Show options

The options in the Show group let you show or hide various elements displayed in the document window.

The options displayed in this group vary depending on whether you are working in Normal or Outline view or Page Layout view.

The following list summarizes the Show options that are available only in Normal or Outline view:

- **Draft Font:** This option is for users who work with computers that are too slow to keep up with Word. It instructs Word to display everything in a boring sans serif typeface and to underline any special formatting, such as italics, boldface, and so on. Frankly, I've seen few users with computers so slow that they actually benefit from using this option. Most users with computers this far out of date are still using MS-DOS 3.3 and WordPerfect 4.0. (One use for this command is to remove Word's What-You-See-Is-What-You-Get display so that users just upgrading from WordPerfect won't be frightened when italic text or bold text is actually displayed in italics or boldface on the screen.)

- **Wrap to Window:** This option tells Word to wrap text according to the width of the document window. This prevents text from being clipped on the right side of the window if the window is too narrow to display the entire text line. If you use this option, line endings may appear on the screen differently than when printed. The Wrap to Window option is usually necessary only when you are working in a small window, with unusually long lines or with an enlarged zoom setting. When Word is maximized, there is usually more than enough room to display typical line lengths at 100% zoom.

The following options are available only in Page Layout view:

- **Drawings:** If your document includes Word drawing objects, you can use this option to show each object as a simple rectangle. This is not very useful unless your document contains extremely complex drawings. (Word's drawing tools are covered in Chapter 21.)

- **Object Anchors:** If your document contains frames or drawing objects, you can use this option to show these object's anchors. The anchors normally just get in the way, so you'll probably want to activate this option only if the anchors get messed up somehow and you need to see them so that you can sort things out.

- **Text Boundaries:** This option displays lines around columns and margins so that you can see the page layout as you edit your document. If you're sensitive to the layout, this option is for you. Ami Pro, Lotus' word processor, actually displays margins in a different color so that you can discern which portion of the page is within the margins. Word has no such feature, but this option provides similar utility.

The following options are available for all views:

- **Picture Placeholders:** If you are working with a document that contains lots of embedded pictures, you might want to activate this option. It tells Word to display a simple rectangle where each picture is supposed to be displayed. This spares Word the time-consuming chore of retrieving each picture and displaying it on the screen. (Of course, you won't be able to actually see the picture unless you deactivate this option.)

- **Highlight:** If you disable this option, Word's new Highlighting feature will not be visible.

- **Field Codes:** If your document contains fields created via the Insert⇨Field command or another feature, such as a table of contents or an index , this option displays the field codes themselves rather than the formatted field. For example, if you insert a table of contents, this command will allow you to see the TOC field code rather than the table of contents itself. Use this option only when you're trying to solve a problem involving field codes or when you are impressed by some feature of a document or template, and you want to see how it works. (For example, use this option to discover how the supplied Invoice.dot template works.)

- **Bookmarks:** If you select this option, any text labeled with a bookmark will be enclosed in gray brackets. (Bookmarks, which are covered in Chapter 11, enable you to identify a location or range of text in your document by name.)

- **Field Shading:** This option lets you draw attention to fields by shading them. You can set this option to Never so that fields are never shaded, Always so that fields are always shaded, and When Selected so that fields are shaded only when they have been selected.

Window options

The options in the Window group let you activate or deactivate various elements of Word's window. The following list describes each Window option:

■ **Status Bar:** The status bar is the row of information displayed at the bottom of Word's window. It displays status information, such as the current page number, section number position on the page, whether Word is working in Overtype mode, and so on. It also displays an extended description of menu commands. If none of the information shown on the status bar tickles your fancy, uncheck this option to hide the status bar so that you can display more of your document.

■ **Horizontal Scrollbar:** If you frequently work with documents that don't fit within Word's window because they are too wide — for example, documents that include pages laid out in landscape rather than portrait orientation — the horizontal scrollbar at the bottom of the screen can come in handy. On the other hand, most users never touch the horizontal scrollbar. Unchecking this option to remove it can free up additional room for your document. But be warned: If you remove the horizontal scrollbar, you'll also lose the View buttons that appear to the left of the scrollbar. Then, you'll have to use the View menu commands or keyboard shortcuts to switch to Normal, Page Layout, or Outline view.

■ **Vertical Scrollbar:** For some users, the vertical scrollbar on the right edge of the screen is the primary method for scrolling to various portions of their documents. Others prefer to use the PageUp and PageDown keys to do their scrolling, so the vertical scrollbar just takes up space. If you don't use it, you can remove it by unchecking this option. This will increase the width of your document window slightly, allowing you to display wider lines.

■ **Style Area Width** (Normal view only): You can use this option to display the names of styles assigned to your document's paragraphs in a column called the *style area* on the left side of the screen. Normally, the style area width is set to 0", effectively hiding the style area and providing maximum room for your document's text. For users working with a smaller monitor in standard VGA mode (640x480), this is usually the best setting. If you have a larger monitor and work in a higher resolution mode, you can probably afford to give over some of your screen width to the style area. A setting of 0.6" is usually sufficient to display most style names.

■ **Vertical Ruler** (Page Layout view only): This option displays a vertical ruler on the left edge of the screen.

Nonprinting Characters options

The View options grouped under the Nonprinting Characters heading lets you control whether certain special characters should be displayed. These options are the same regardless of the View mode. The following list summarizes the options:

- **Tab Characters:** Displays tab characters as an arrow. I like to keep track of tabs, so I usually select this option.

- **Spaces:** Displays space characters as little dots. I find these dots annoying, so I usually turn this option off.

- **Paragraph Marks:** Displays paragraph symbols. I like to keep track of paragraph marks, so I usually set this option.

- **Optional Hyphens:** Displays optional hyphens (hyphens that appear only at the end of a line). Use optional hyphens only when you want to overrule Word's normal hyphenation for a specific word.

- **Hidden Text:** Displays text that has been formatted as hidden. Leave this option off if you want hidden text to be, well, *hidden*.

- **All:** This option overrides the setting for the other options and forces all special characters to be displayed.

Tip

The Show/Hide button on the Standard toolbar — the one with the paragraph mark icon — is a shortcut for the All option. When you press the button, all nonprinting characters are displayed. When you press it again, only those nonprinting characters specified in the View options are displayed. Consequently, it's best not to use the All option in the View options. Instead, select only the nonprinting characters you *always* want displayed, such as tab characters and paragraph marks. Whenever you need to see the other nonprinting characters, you can always click the Show/Hide button.

General Options

One other group of options available from the Tools⇨Options command that affects Word's user interface is the options found on the General tab, shown in Figure 5-11. The following paragraphs describe each of these options:

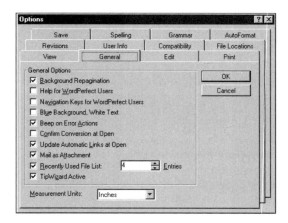

Figure 5-11: The General tab of the Options dialog box.

- **Background Repagination:** Every once in awhile, you may notice that when you stop typing for a moment, page breaks appear to dance about as if by magic. You are witnessing background repagination at work. Background repagination constantly monitors the length of your document and adjusts the positions of soft page breaks accordingly. If your computer doesn't have enough horsepower to perform background pagination without hesitation, you can disable it by unchecking this field. When background pagination is disabled, Word repaginates your document only when you print it; create a table of contents, index, or other table; or switch to Page Layout view.

  Turning off background repagination might make Word run just a bit faster, but the performance benefit usually isn't worth the price of never quite knowing on what page you're working. Therefore, I recommend you leave this option on.

- **Help for WordPerfect Users:** If you are among the myriad users just now switching from WordPerfect to Word, this option will offer some well-intentioned help whenever you try to do something the old WordPerfect way. For example, if you try to exit Word by pressing Shift+F7, you'll get a subtle reminder that Word doesn't do it that way.

- **Navigation Keys for WordPerfect Users:** This option is yet another futile attempt at making it easy for WordPerfect users to switch to Word. This one reinstates WordPerfect's insane use of the PageUp, PageDown, Home, End, and Escape keys. Word uses these keys in a much more civilized manner. You're better off learning the Word way rather than using this option so that you can pretend you're still using WordPerfect.

- **Blue Background, White Text:** This is the last straw as far as WordPerfect lookalike options are concerned. This one transforms Word's beautiful black-on-white display to white-on-blue so that Word starts to resemble DOS WordPerfect 5.1.

- **Beep on Error Actions:** This option instructs Word to let out a 10,000-decibel screech whenever you make the tiniest of mistakes.

- **Confirm Conversion at Open:** This is not some kind of option for a religious awakening, but rather instructs Word to ask for your permission before attempting to convert a non-Word document to Word.

- **Update Automatic Links at Open:** If a document contains links to other files, this option instructs Word to update those links automatically . It's usually best to leave this option on.

- **Mail as Attachment:** This option allows you to attach your documents to e-mail messages.

- **Recently Used File List:** This option allows you to specify how many files appear at the bottom of the File menu for fast opening. You can increase this setting to the default value of 4 to 9, or you can remove the recently used file list by setting it to 0. There's no reason not to set it to the maximum value of 9, although it does make the File menu a bit long.

The Great WordPerfect Look-alike Contest

If you really miss WordPerfect that much but you don't want to go back, you can use the following options in combination to make Word look and feel as much like WordPerfect for DOS as possible. I don't recommend that you use any of these options, but here they are

- **Help for WordPerfect Users.** When you're doing something the WordPerfect way, a friendly Help dialog box pops up to show you the Word way.

- **Navigation Keys for WordPerfect Users**. Restores WordPerfect's crazy use of PageUp, PageDown, Home, End, and Escape.

- **Blue Background, White Text.** Provides that nostalgic white-on-blue look.

- **View⇨Full Screen.** Eliminates all of that annoying clutter, such as menus, toolbars, scrollbars, and so on. Memorize as many commands as possible before using this one.

- **TipWizard Active:** If the TipWizard seems like a back-seat driver, you can disable it altogether by unchecking this option.

- **Measurement Units:** By default, Word uses inches as its basic unit of measure. If you prefer the metric system, you can change this option to centimeters. If you prefer to use typographical measurements, you can specify picas or points. Unfortunately, there are no options for fathoms, leagues, or cubits.

Chapter 6

Customizing Keyboard Shortcuts, Toolbars, and Menus

In This Chapter

▶ How to create your own keyboard shortcuts so that you can invoke frequently used commands quickly

▶ How to customize Word's toolbars so that the commands you use most are available as toolbar buttons

▶ How to add new commands to Word's menus

The good folks at Microsoft have spent years perfecting Word's user interface. Still, they recognize that working style varies from person to person, and one person's idea of a clever shortcut might be a hindrance to another. As a result, Word allows you to change almost any aspect of its "look and feel." You can add or remove elements of the user interface, such as scrollbars, the ruler, or the status bar. If you don't like the toolbars, you can remove them or create your own that include just your favorite buttons. You can create your own keyboard shortcuts for the commands you use most often. You can even rearrange Word's menus if you think some other arrangement would be more efficient.

There is almost no end to the amount of customization you can apply to Word's user interface, especially if you take the time to learn the WordBasic programming language to create your own macros. A certain amount of restraint is in order, because you don't want to customize Word to the point that it becomes almost unrecognizable. Still, Word's capability to adapt itself to the needs of diverse users is one reason for its success.

Customizing the Keyboard

I don't really like my mouse. Don't get me wrong: it's a good mouse, really. The mouse fits nicely in my hand, its movement is precise, and I can click and double-click with ease. But every time I reach for the mouse, I have to take one hand off the keyboard. And I can't type when my hand isn't on the keyboard. So I'm one of those keyboard junkies who loves keyboard shortcuts. I'd much rather press Ctrl+Alt+Whatever than reach for my mouse.

Word comes with plenty of built-in keyboard shortcuts, but unfortunately Word has keyboard shortcuts for commands I never use and doesn't have keyboard shortcuts for commands I use all the time. Fortunately, Word lets you completely customize its keyboard shortcuts. Customizing Word's keyboard shortcuts is one of the best ways to improve your productivity with Word, because you can assign easy-to-remember keyboard shortcuts to the commands, styles, and macros that *you* use most often.

Word lets you create keyboard shortcuts for any of the following:

- **Any Word command,** including secret commands that Word provides but are not accessible through Word's normal menus.

- **Macros.**

- **Fonts.** By creating a keyboard shortcut for your favorite fonts, you can apply character formatting without leaving the keyboard.

- **AutoText.** The normal way to invoke AutoText is to type the AutoText name and press F3. By assigning a keyboard shortcut, you can call up your favorite AutoText entries even faster.

- **Styles.** This is the most efficient way to assign the styles you use most. Several built-in styles, such as heading styles, have default keyboard shortcuts.

- **Common symbols.** Word includes keyboard shortcuts for an array of common symbols, such as ® and ©. Word lets you change the default keyboard shortcuts, although I'm not sure why you would want to do that.

A keyboard shortcut can be just about any key on the keyboard along with any combination of the Ctrl, Alt, and Shift keys. For example, Ctrl+E, Alt+Home, and Ctrl+Alt+F1 are allowable keyboard shortcuts. In addition, you can also create key-sequence shortcuts, such as Ctrl+A, X. To invoke this shortcut, press and hold the Ctrl key, press and release A, and press and release X.

Note

Keyboard shortcuts are stored in templates, so they might vary from document to document depending on which template the document is attached. Available keyboard shortcuts can also vary depending on which templates you've loaded and activated as global templates.

Some Keys Are Best Left Alone

Although you can assign almost any keyboard combination as a shortcut in Word, some keyboard combinations are best left alone. For starters, it's probably wise to avoid reassigning the most popular of Word's built-in keyboard shortcuts. For example, most users expect Ctrl+F to call up the Find command, Ctrl+W to close the current document, and Ctrl+P to invoke the Print command. You can reassign these combinations if you wish, but you do so at your peril. Imagine the mess you'd get yourself into if you created a macro named CloseAndDeleteDocFile and assigned it to Ctrl+V, the Windows-wide standard keyboard for the Paste command. 'Nuff said.

Other key combinations that are best untouched are those used to access menus via the keyboard. These include the following:

Alt+F   Alt+E   Alt+V

Alt+I   Alt+O   Alt+T

Alt+A   Alt+W   Alt+H

If you reassign any of the previous keyboard combinations, you won't be able to access the corresponding menu via the keyboard; you'll have to access the menus using the mouse.

Also there are the keyboard shortcuts used by Windows itself, such as Alt+Tab to switch tasks or Ctrl+Esc to bring up the Start menu. Fortunately, the Tools⇨Customize command simply won't let you assign these keyboard combinations. If you try to assign one of these combinations, Windows intercepts the shortcut before it ever reaches the Tools⇨Customize command.

Creating a keyboard shortcut

The most direct way to create a keyboard shortcut is to summon the Tools⇨Customize command and click on the Keyboard tab. This will bring up the dialog box featured in Figure 6-1.

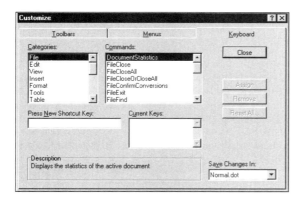

Figure 6-1: The Customize dialog box.

To create a custom keyboard shortcut, follow these steps:

1. Invoke the Tools⇨Customize command and click on the Keyboard tab.

2. To create a shortcut for a Word command, choose the command's category in the Categories list and choose the specific command in the Commands list. If you're not sure which category the command fits in, choose All Commands for the category.

   To create a shortcut for a style, macro, or other item, choose the appropriate category from the Categories list and pick the specific item. (The name of the Commands list box will change according to the category you pick.)

3. Click in the Press <u>N</u>ew Shortcut Key box and type the keyboard shortcut you want to assign. When you type the shortcut, Word will indicate whether the shortcut key you typed is already in use.

4. By default, changes are stored in Normal.dot. To save the keyboard shortcut in the template attached to the document, select the template in the Sa<u>v</u>e Changes In list box.

5. Click Assign to assign the shortcut. Then, click on Close and try out your new shortcut.

The point-and-click way to create a keyboard shortcut

You can assign a keyboard shortcut to any command that is available in Word's menus, on a visible toolbar, or to a font or style by following this procedure:

1. Press Ctrl+Alt+NumPlus (the plus sign on the numeric keypad). The mouse pointer will change to a pretzel shape.

2. Click on the command, toolbar button, font, or style that you want to assign to a keyboard shortcut. The Customize dialog box will appear, all set to assign a shortcut to the selected item.

3. Type the keyboard shortcut you want to assign in the Press <u>N</u>ew Shortcut Key field.

4. Select Normal.dot or the attached template in the Sa<u>v</u>e Changes In list box.

5. Click on Assign to assign the shortcut and click on Close.

Creating a shortcut key for a style

You can also create shortcut keys for styles from the F<u>o</u>rmat⇨<u>S</u>tyle dialog box. Just follow these steps:

1. Call up the F<u>o</u>rmat⇨<u>S</u>tyle command. The Style dialog box will appear.

2. Select the style you want to create a shortcut for and click on the <u>M</u>odify button. The Modify Style dialog box will appear.

3. Click on the Shortcut <u>K</u>ey button. This will take you to the Customize Keyboard dialog box, all set up to create a keyboard shortcut for the selected style.

4. Type the keyboard shortcut you want to assign in the Press <u>N</u>ew Shortcut Key field.

5. Select Normal.dot or the attached template in the Sa<u>v</u>e Changes In list box.

6. Click on <u>A</u>ssign to assign the shortcut and click on OK and click on Close.

Tip

To assign keyboard shortcuts to several styles, using the <u>T</u>ools⇨<u>C</u>ustomize command directly is faster than F<u>o</u>rmat⇨<u>S</u>tyle.

Finding out what a keyboard shortcut does

Secret

If you're unclear on what a particular keyboard shortcut does, call up the Tools⇨Customize command and click on the Keyboard tab. Then, click in the Press New Shortcut Key box and type the keyboard shortcut that tickles your fancy. The current assignment for that shortcut will appear if the shortcut is in use. Do *not* click the Assign button; instead, close the dialog box without assigning the shortcut.

You can use a similar technique to find out if there is a keyboard shortcut for any command, style, font, or other item. Call up the Tools⇨Customize command, click on the Keyboard tab, and find the command or other item in which you're interested. If it has a keyboard shortcut, you'll see it in the Current Keys list box.

Resetting keyboard shortcuts

You can erase all of the keyboard shortcuts stored in a template by following these steps:

1. Call up the Tools⇨Customize command and click on the Keyboard tab.

2. Select Normal.dot or the attached template in the Save Changes In list box.

3. Click on the Reset All button.

4. When the confirmation dialog box appears, click on Yes.

5. Click on the Close button.

Note

If you have keyboard shortcuts saved in both Normal.dot and the template attached to the current document, you need to use Reset All for both templates to revert completely to Word's default keyboard shortcuts. And, to make the return to default shortcuts permanent, you must save the template file as well.

Printing your keyboard shortcuts

If you've lost track of your custom keyboard shortcuts, you can print a complete list of them for the current document by following this procedure:

1. Open a document that is attached to the template with the keyboard shortcuts you want to print, or open the template itself.

2. Call up the File⇨Print command to display the Print dialog box.

3. For the Print what field, select Key Assignments.

4. Click on OK.

Keyboard assignments will be printed, starting first with the keyboard assignments derived from the template attached to the document and listing the global keyboard assignments taken from the Normal.dot template. Word's built-in keyboard shortcuts are not printed; if they were, the listing would go many pages.

A macro to display keyboard shortcuts

Another way to list the keyboard shortcuts that are available is to create a macro that retrieves the keyboard shortcuts and inserts them into a new document or displays them in a dialog box. The Wordsec.dot template included on this book's accompanying disk comes with just such a macro, named ListKeys. Listing 6-1 shows the complete listing for this macro, although you probably won't want to study it in detail unless you're a WordBasic fanatic and want to figure out how it works.

To use this macro, load the Word SECRETS Sample Macros.dot template as a global template. Open a document attached to the template you're interested in, or open the template itself. Then, call up the Tools⇨Macro command, select the ListKeys macro, and click on the Run button. The ListKeys macro will create a new document that contains a table of all the keyboard shortcuts in the template, as shown in Figure 6-2.

You might want to disable the Automatically Check Spelling option before running this macro. Otherwise, Word will likely mark most of your keyboard shortcuts as spelling errors. (This option is disabled on the Spelling tab of the Tools⇨Options command.)

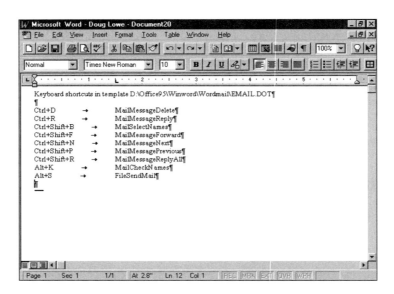

Figure 6-2: The ListKeys macro lists the keyboard shortcuts in a template.

Listing 6-1: The ListKeys Macro.

```
Sub MAIN
Count = CountKeys(1)                'Get the number of keyboard short-
cuts
If Count = 0 Then
    MsgBox "There are no custom keyboard shortcuts for this template."
    Goto Done
End If
Dim Keys(Count, 2)                  'Shortcut keys
Dim Command$(Count)                 'Commands invoked by shortcuts
Dim dlg As FileTemplates            'Get the name of the template
GetCurValues dlg
Template$ = dlg.Template
If Template$ = "" Then              'File is a template
    Template$ = FileName$(0)
End If
For i = 1 To Count
Keys(i, 1) = KeyCode(i, 1, 1)       'Get the first key of shortcut i
    Keys(i, 2) = KeyCode(i, 1, 2)   'Get the second key of shortcut
    Command$(i) = KeyMacro$(i, 1)   'Get the command for shortcut i
Next i
FileNewDefault                      'Create a new document
FormatTabs .Position = "1.5 in", .Align = 0, .Set
Insert "Keyboard shortcuts in template " + Template$ + Chr$(13) +
Chr$(13)
For i = 1 To Count
    Select Case Keys(i, 1)          'Convert the first key to a string
        Case 0 To 255
            Insert KeyText$(Keys(i, 1))
        Case 256 To 511
            Insert "Ctrl+" + KeyText$(Keys(i, 1) - 256)
        Case 512 To 767
            Insert "Shift+" + KeyText$(Keys(i, 1) - 512)
        Case 768 To 1023
            Insert "Ctrl+Shift+" + KeyText$(Keys(i, 1) - 768)
        Case 1024 To 1279
            Insert "Alt+" + KeyText$(Keys(i, 1) - 1024)
        Case 1280 To 1535
            Insert "Ctrl+Alt+" + KeyText$(Keys(i, 1) - 1280)
        Case 1536 To 1791
            Insert "Ctrl+Shift+" + KeyText$(Keys(i, 1) - 1536)
        Case 1792 To 2047
            Insert "Ctrl+Alt+Shift+" + KeyText$(Keys(i, 1) - 1792)
    End Select
If Keys(i, 2) <> 255 Then           'Convert the second key to a string
    If Keys(i, 2) < 512 Then
        Insert ", " + KeyText$(Keys(i, 2))
    Else
        Insert ", Shift+" + KeyText$(Keys(i, 2) - 512)
    End If
End If
Insert Chr$(9) + Command$(i)        'Insert a tab and the command text
```

```
InsertPara                              'Start a new line
Next i
Done:
End Sub

Function KeyText$(Key)                  'Returns text equivalent of Key
Select Case Key
    Case 8 : Keytext$ = "Backspace"
    Case 9 : Keytext$ = "Tab"
    Case 12 : Keytext$ = "Numeric 5 (Num Lock Off)"
    Case 13 : Keytext$ = "Enter"
    Case 19 : Keytext$ = "Pause"
    Case 27 : Keytext$ = "Esc"
    Case 32 : Keytext$ = "Spacebar"
    Case 33 : Keytext$ = "Pageup"
    Case 34 : Keytext$ = "Pagedown"
    Case 35 : Keytext$ = "End"
    Case 36 : Keytext$ = "Home"
    Case 37 : Keytext$ = "Down"
    Case 38 : Keytext$ = "Up"
    Case 39 : Keytext$ = "Left"
    Case 40 : Keytext$ = "Right"
    Case 45 : Keytext$ = "Insert"
    Case 46 : Keytext$ = "Delete"
    Case 48  To 90 : Keytext$ = Chr$(Key)
    Case 96  To 105 : Keytext$ = "Numeric " + Str$(Key - 96)
    Case 106 : Keytext$ = "Numeric *"
    Case 107 : Keytext$ = "Numeric +"
    Case 109 : Keytext$ = "Numeric -"
    Case 110 : Keytext$ = "Numeric ."
    Case 111 : Keytext$ = "Numeric /"
    Case 112  To 127 : Keytext$ = "F" + Str$(Key - 111)
    Case 145 : Keytext$ = "Scroll Lock"
    Case 186 : Keytext$ = ";"
    Case 187 : Keytext$ = "="
    Case 188 : Keytext$ = ","
    Case 189 : Keytext$ = "-"
    Case 190 : Keytext$ = "."
    Case 191 : Keytext$ = "/"
    Case 192 : Keytext$ = "`"
    Case 219 : Keytext$ = "["
    Case 220 : Keytext$ = "\"
    Case 221 : Keytext$ = "]"
    Case 222 : Keytext$ = "'"
    Case Else : Keytext$ = ""
End Select
End Function
```

Customizing Word's Toolbars

The good folks in Redmond, Washington, who designed Microsoft Word might be accused of indulging themselves when it comes to the toolbar feature. Not only did they equip Word with a dozen or so standard toolbars, displaying well over 100 toolbar buttons altogether, but they also threw in a bunch of additional buttons to hold in reserve, in case the original 100 aren't enough. Just for the fun of it, Figure 6-3 shows what Word's screen looks like with all ten of the predefined toolbars visible. A bit excessive, eh?

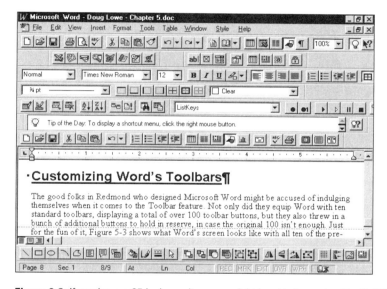

Figure 6-3: If you have a 25 inch monitor, you might be able to work with all of Word's toolbars visible.

Truthfully, though, Word's toolbars are one of best ways to customize Word to make it suit your working style. Microsoft did its best to decide which toolbar buttons would be most useful for a widest range of users, and it did a pretty good job, especially with the Standard and Formatting toolbars. Still, you're bound to find several toolbar buttons that you rarely, if ever, use. And if you think for a moment, you can probably come up with a button or two you wish you had.

For example, I almost never use right-justified paragraphs. But I frequently use hanging indents. So I've replaced the Align Right button with a custom Hanging Indent button. I even drew my own design for the button image; it took only a minute or two. Now, Word works and looks the way I want it to, not the way Microsoft thinks I should want it to work and look.

The following sections sum up the procedures for customizing Word's toolbars. Along the way, I'll pass along a few tips, secrets, and workarounds for creating custom toolbars. But, the real strength of using custom toolbars lies in the creative ways you choose to use them.

Word's predefined toolbars

Word comes with a good dozen or so toolbars. Some are fairly accessible via the View➪Toolbars command; others appear only in certain situations, such as when you switch to Outline view or display headers and footers. Table 6-1 lists all of Word's built-in toolbars and an indication of how each can be accessed.

Table 6-1	Word's Default Toolbars
Toolbar	**How to Access It**
Standard	Displayed by default. Can be controlled via the View➪Toolbars command.
Formatting	Displayed by default. Can be controlled via the View➪Toolbars command.
Borders	Can be controlled via the View➪Toolbars command or by clicking the Borders button in the Formatting toolbar.
Database	Can be controlled via the View➪Toolbars command.
Drawing	Can be controlled via the View➪Toolbars command or by clicking the Drawing button in the Standard toolbar.
Forms	Can be controlled via the View➪Toolbars command.
Macro	Automatically displayed when a macro is edited. Can be controlled via the View➪Toolbars command only when at least one macro window is opened.
Microsoft	Can be controlled via the View➪Toolbars command.
Word for Windows 2.0	Can be controlled via the View➪Toolbars command.
TipWizard	Can be controlled via the View➪Toolbars command or by clicking on the TipWizard button in the Standard toolbar.
Outlining	Automatically displayed when Outline view is activated. Can be controlled via the View➪Toolbars command only while in Outline view.

Toolbar	*How to Access It*
Master Document	Automatically displayed when Master Document view is activated. Master Document view can be activated by using the View⇨Master Document command or by clicking on the Master Document View button on the Outline toolbar. Can be controlled via the View⇨Toolbars command only while in Master Document view.
Print Preview	Automatically displayed when Print Preview is activated. Can be controlled via the View⇨Toolbars command only in Print Preview mode.
Full Screen	Automatically displayed when Full Screen mode is activated. Can be controlled via the View⇨Toolbars command only in Full Screen mode.
Macro Record	Automatically displayed when a macro is recorded. Can be controlled via the View⇨Toolbars command only while a macro is being recorded.
Mail Merge	Automatically displayed when mail merge is invoked. Can be controlled via the View⇨Toolbars command only while working in mail merge.
Header and Footer	Automatically displayed when the View⇨Header and Footer command is selected. Can be controlled via the View⇨Toolbars command only while headers and footers are visible.
Annotations	Automatically displayed when the View⇨Annotations command is selected. Cannot be controlled by the View⇨Toolbars command and cannot be customized. (In other words, this isn't really a toolbar; it just *looks* like one.)
Footnotes	Automatically displayed when the View⇨Footnotes command is selected. Cannot be controlled by the View⇨Toolbars command and cannot be customized. (Like the Annotations toolbar, this one isn't really a toolbar either.)

Showing and hiding toolbars

We'll start with the basics of making Word's toolbars appear and disappear. When you first start Word, only two of its ten toolbars are visible: the Standard toolbar and the Formatting toolbar. To display Word's other toolbars, call up the View⇨Toolbars command to display the Toolbars dialog box, shown in Figure 6-4. Click on the toolbars you want to make visible and click on OK.

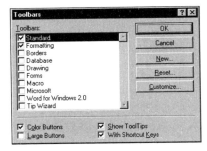

Figure 6-4: The Toolbars dialog box.

Once you have made a toolbar appear, you can change its location. Point to any part of the toolbar between buttons (in other words, the toolbars "background") and drag the toolbar to another location. You can shove the toolbar against any of the four edges of the screen (the technical term is *dock*), or you can let the toolbar float in the middle of the screen in its own window. You can also change the shape of a floating toolbar by dragging one of its edges or corners.

Tip

You can access two toolbars by clicking a button on the Standard or Formatting toolbars. To display the Drawing toolbar, click the Drawing button in the Standard toolbar. To display the Borders toolbar, click the Borders button in the Formatting toolbar.

To make a floating toolbar vanish, click the little close box in the top right corner. To make a docked toolbar vanish, call up the View⇨Toolbars command, uncheck the toolbar, and click OK. When you hide a toolbar, Word remembers the toolbar's position on the screen. Then, if you later redisplay the toolbar, Word displays it in its previous position.

Tip

A fast way to show or hide a toolbar is to right-click the background of any toolbar (click between the buttons). The pop-up menu that appears will include a list of all available toolbars, with check marks to indicate which toolbars are currently visible. Just click on the name of the toolbar you want to show or hide.

A macro to toggle the Formatting toolbar

The Formatting toolbar is one of Word's most useful, especially for new users. But after you've worked with Word long enough to master the basic formatting keyboard shortcuts (Ctrl+B for bold, Ctrl+I for italic, and so on) and you've committed to using styles for most of your formatting needs rather than directly applying font, indentation, alignment, and other attributes, the need for the Formatting toolbar is greatly reduced. Wouldn't it be great if there were a quick way to hide it to make more room for document text and quickly recall it when needed?

There is, but it involves the use of a simple macro that toggles the state of the Formatting toolbar. If the macro is run when the Formatting toolbar is visible, the macro hides it. If the Formatting toolbar is hidden when the macro runs, the toolbar is made visible.

To create the macro, call up the <u>T</u>ools⇨<u>M</u>acro command, type **ToggleFormat** in the <u>M</u>acro Name field, and click the Cr<u>e</u>ate button. Edit the macro so that it appears as follows:

```
Sub MAIN
If ToolbarState("Formatting") = 0 Then
    ViewToolbars .Toolbar = "Formatting", .Show
Else
    ViewToolbars .Toolbar = "Formatting", .Hide
End If
End Sub
```

Save your changes and use the <u>T</u>ools⇨<u>C</u>ustomize command to assign the macro to a keyboard shortcut. When the Customize dialog box appears, select the Keyboard tab, select Macros in the <u>C</u>ategories list, and then select ToggleFormat from the list of macros. Enter the keyboard shortcut you want to assign to ToggleFormat, click Assign to assign the keyboard shortcut, and click Close to close the Customize dialog box. I prefer Ctrl+Shift+F because I don't normally use this shortcut to access the Font control in the Formatting toolbar.

You'll find this macro in the Word for Windows 95 SECRETS Sample Macros.dot template on the CD-ROM.

Setting toolbar display options

At the bottom of the Toolbars dialog box (<u>V</u>iew⇨<u>T</u>oolbars) are four check boxes that control the appearance of Word's toolbars:

- **C<u>o</u>lor Buttons**: Use this option to display toolbar buttons in black and white. If you do not have a color monitor, buttons might look better if you use this option.

- **<u>L</u>arge Buttons:** If your monitor is set to a high screen resolution, such as 1,024 x 768, this option might make the toolbars more visible. Standard sized toolbar buttons look pretty tiny at high resolutions.

- **<u>S</u>how ToolTips:** If this option is selected, Word displays a brief explanation of a button's function when you hold the mouse pointer over the button for a moment.

- **With Shortcut <u>K</u>eys:** This option, new for Word 95, tells Word to include shortcut keys when it displays ToolTips. I like this option because it helps remind me of shortcut keys that I might have forgotten.

Removing toolbar buttons

If you want to remove a toolbar button, call up the Tools⇨Customize command to display the Customize dialog box and click the Toolbars tab to show the options for customizing toolbars. Or, right-click between buttons on the toolbar you want to modify and select Customize.

Now, you can drag what you want to remove from the toolbar. It doesn't matter where you drag the button, as long as you're well clear of the toolbar. When you release the mouse button, the toolbar button will be removed. Other buttons on the toolbar will adjust their position. Click Close when you're done to dismiss the Customize dialog box.

Warning

If you change your mind after removing a toolbar button, the Undo command (Ctrl+Z) will do you no good. You'll have to add the button back manually to the toolbar or use the View⇨Toolbars command's Reset option to restore the toolbar to its default configuration.

Adding a predefined button to a toolbar

Word provides quite a few buttons that aren't included in any of the predefined toolbars. For example, there are buttons for formatting text as a subscript or superscript, calling up the Find command, or inserting the current date. Although these buttons don't appear in any toolbars, they might be more useful to you than other buttons included in the predefined toolbars. If so, you can remove the buttons you rarely use and replace them with buttons you'd use more often.

To add a predefined button to a toolbar, follow these steps:

1. Call up the Tools⇨Customize command and click on the Toolbars tab, or right-click on the background of any toolbar and select the Customize command. The dialog box shown in Figure 6-5 will appear.

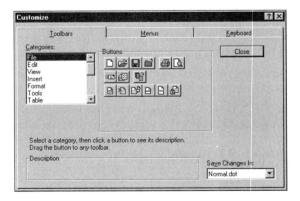

Figure 6-5: The Customize dialog box (Toolbars).

2. If necessary, make room for the new button by removing an existing button. The hard part is deciding which buttons you can part with. Because the Standard or Formatting toolbars don't have any free space, you'll have to eliminate something before you can add to those toolbars. (To remove a button, simply drag it off the toolbar.)

3. Choose the Category for the button you want to add. As you scroll through the Categories list, the predefined buttons displayed in the Buttons area change to reflect the buttons available in each category. You'll see familiar buttons, such as New, Open, and Save, plus unfamiliar ones, such as binoculars and a padlock. To determine the function of a button, click on it. A description will be displayed near the bottom of the dialog box.

4. Select the button you want to add and drag it from the Customize dialog box to the toolbar at the location where you want the button inserted. When you release the mouse button, the toolbar button you selected will be placed on the toolbar.

5. To add more buttons, repeat Steps 2-4. When you're done, click the Close button.

Table 6-2 lists some of the predefined buttons that are useful (in my humble opinion) yet don't show up on any of the more accessible toolbars. (To be sure, some of them may appear on obscure toolbars, such as Headers and Footers.)

Table 6-2	Favorite Leftover Toolbar Buttons	
Button	*Category*	*What It Does*
	File	Attempts to shrink the document so that it will fit in one page.
	File	Sends the document via electronic mail.
	File	Closes all open documents.
	Edit	Invokes the Find command.
	Edit	Repeats the last action.
	View	Shows or hides the ruler.
	View	Shows or hides field codes.
	View	Toggles Full Screen view.

(continued)

Table 6-2 (continued)

Button	Category	What it Does
	Insert	Inserts the date.
	Insert	Inserts the time.
	Insert	Inserts a WordArt object.
	Insert	Inserts an Equation Editor object.
	Insert	Inserts a footnote.
	Format	Formats the text as strikethrough.
	Format	Double-underlines the text.
	Format	Underlines the text.
	Format	Formats the text with small caps.
	Format	Formats the text with all caps.
	Format	Applies single line spacing.
	Format	Applies 1.5 line spacing.
	Format	Applies double spacing.
	Format	Creates a drop cap.
	Format	Formats the text as superscript.
	Format	Formats the text as subscript.
	Tools	Prints an envelope.

Button	Category	What it Does
🔳	Tools	Updates fields.
Σ	Table	Sums data values.
↕	Table	Sorts into ascending sequence.
↕	Table	Sorts into descending sequence.

Adding a custom button to a toolbar

If you can't find a button that meets your needs among the categories of predefined buttons, you can always create a custom button. You can create custom buttons for any of the following:

■ Any Word command

■ Macros

■ Fonts

■ Styles

■ AutoText entries

When you create a custom button, you can select one of 37 predefined custom button images, you can create your own image for the button, or you can create a text button that shows descriptive text rather than a graphical image.

To create a custom button, follow the same procedure as you would to add a predefined button to a toolbar. When you are ready to select the category, choose All Commands, Macros, Fonts, Styles, or AutoText. Then, drag the command, macro, font, style, or AutoText selection to the desired location on the toolbar of your choice. When you release the mouse button, the dialog box shown in Figure 6-6 will be displayed. Click on the button you want to use and click on Assign. To use a text button, select Text Button, type the text you want to appear on the button in the Text Button Name field, and click on Assign.

Tip

When you create a text button, Word assumes that you want to use the name of the macro, style, font, or AutoText entry as the text button name. There's usually little reason to change Word's proposed name, but if you do, try to be brief. The more text you include in the text button, the more space the button takes up on the toolbar, and toolbar space is usually at a premium.

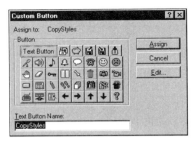

Figure 6-6: The Custom Button dialog box.

Editing button images

If you are creating a custom toolbar button image and you discover that none of the 37 supplied button images is appropriate, you can create your own button by clicking the Edit button in the Custom Button dialog box. This displays the dialog box shown in Figure 6-7, which allows you to create any button image you want. You can start with any of the 37 predefined custom buttons and work from there, or you can click the Clear button and start from scratch.

Figure 6-7: Creating your own button image.

To paint the button image, click the color you want to paint with and click in the picture area wherever you want to paint. Each square in the picture represents one pixel in the image. As you paint, you can see the effects your actions have on the full-sized version of the button image in the Preview area of the Button Editor dialog box.

The half-gray squares in the Picture area represent pixels that have no color; they allow the background color of the toolbar to show through. If you click on an empty square, it will change to the color you selected. If you click on a colored-in square, it will change to empty.

You can use the four arrow Move buttons to move the entire button image around within the square. This is helpful in case you start drawing your image and realize it isn't quite centered within the button. Just nudge it over a pixel or two by using the Move buttons. You cannot move any portion of the image off the button. If you want to clip a portion of the image, erase the portion you want clipped and use the Move buttons to move the image over.

When you're finished editing the picture, click OK.

Tip

You can edit the image on any button that's already been placed on a toolbar by calling up the Tools⇨Customize command, selecting the Toolbars tab, and right-clicking on any visible toolbar button. Select Edit Button Image from the pop-up menu to edit the button. (You can also select Choose Button Image if you'd rather start over with a new button image.)

Stealing button images

Rather than design your own buttons from scratch, it's far easier to plagiarize someone else's work. Because the Tools⇨Customize command lets you copy and paste button images, this is easier than you might at first expect. Just follow this procedure:

1. Create the button by using any of the predefined custom button design's. Select the command, macro, style, font, or AutoText entry that you want to invoke by using a custom button. It doesn't matter which button image you assign to this new button because you'll be replacing it with an image from an existing button in a moment anyway.

2. Find a button in one of Word's existing toolbars that you want to steal outright or use as the basis for the new button you created in Step 1.

3. Call up the Tools⇨Customize command and click on the Toolbars tab.

4. Right-click the button you want to copy. Then select Copy Button Image from the pop-up menu.

5. Right-click the button you created in Step 1 and select Paste Button Image from the pop-up menu. The button's image will be replaced by the image from the button you copied.

6. Right-click the button again, but this time select Edit Button Image. Edit the button however you wish. Click OK when done.

7. Click Close in the Customize dialog box when you're finished.

Secret

You can use this technique to steal button designs from other programs, provided they let you copy the button image to the Clipboard. For example, you can steal button images from Microsoft Excel by calling up Excel's Customize command, copying a button image to the Clipboard, and switching to Word and pasting the button image.

You can use a similar technique to paste *any* bitmap image onto a button. Suppose that you have a program that has a button with just the right image on it, but the program doesn't provide any direct method for copying the button image to the Clipboard. No problem. Follow these general steps:

1. Capture the button image to the Clipboard by pressing the PrintScreen key.

2. Start the Windows Paint accessory program (Start⇨Programs⇨Accessories ⇨Paint).

3. Paste the contents of the Clipboard by using the Edit⇨Paste command.

4. Zoom in on the portion of the screen that contains the button image you want to use. Select the portion of the image you want to use with the selection tool and copy it to the Clipboard.

5. Switch to Word.

6. Call up the Tools⇨Customize command.

7. Right-click the button you want to change and select Paste Button Image.

If you attempt to paste an image that is larger than the button size, Word will do its best to shrink-fit the image. This usually doesn't produce satisfactory results, however, because important details are often lost along the way. The best button pictures have strong lines and simple shapes.

A toolbar with all of Word's built-in buttons

Word comes with a total of 366 predefined button images. Some of these images are assigned to buttons on the various toolbars, while others are reserved for use by the Tools⇨Customize command. The Word for Windows 95 SECRETS Sample Macros template that's supplied on the CD-ROM contains a toolbar named Buttons Galore that lists all 366 of these buttons. (The toolbar is shown in Figure 6-8.)

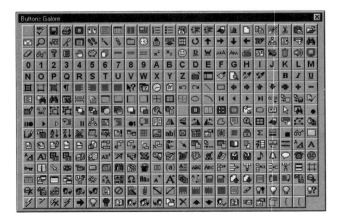

Figure 6-8: A toolbar that shows all the buttons.

You can copy images off the Buttons Galore toolbar just like you can for any other toolbar. Simply make sure the Buttons Galore toolbar is visible before you call up the Tools➪Customize command to modify a toolbar.

In case you're interested, I created the Buttons Galore toolbar by using a simple macro:

```
Sub MAIN
On Error Goto AlreadyExists
NewToolbar "Buttons Galore"
On Error Goto 0
AddButton "Buttons Galore", 1, 1, "CopyButtonImage", 0
For x = 1 To 366
    AddButton "Buttons Galore", x + 1, 1, "CopyButtonImage", x
Next x
Goto UserExit
AlreadExists:
MsgBox "The Buttons Galore toolbar already exists. Remove it and try
again!", 64
UserExit:
End Sub
```

This macro creates a toolbar that contains all of the tools arranged into a single row that extends well off the bottom of the screen. After the macro is finished, resize the toolbar by dragging its left edge to increase its width.

Spacing out toolbar buttons

In Word's default toolbars, toolbar buttons are clumped together in logical groupings, with a small amount of space left between each group of buttons. You can create or remove space between toolbar buttons by starting the Tools➪Customize command, clicking Toolbars, and dragging individual buttons left or right to add or remove space, as follows:

■ To add space between two adjacent buttons, drag one of the buttons away from the other, stopping after moving about one-fourth the width of the toolbar button. You may have to practice this a bit before you get it to work.

■ To remove space between two buttons, drag one of the buttons toward the other, stopping when the buttons are adjacent.

Take care, for as you move one button to add or remove space, other buttons on the toolbar are adjusted accordingly. You must usually fiddle with several buttons before you group the buttons just right.

You can also adjust the width of toolbar controls that use drop-down lists, such as the Formatting toolbar's Style, Font, and Font Size controls. While working in Tools➪Customize, click on the control that you want to adjust to select it and position the mouse pointer over the right edge of the control. When the mouse pointer changes to a sizing tool, you can drag the control left or right to change its width.

Creating a new toolbar

If you need to add just one or two custom toolbar buttons, you can usually find room in one of the existing toolbars by removing a button you rarely use. However, if you want to add a lot of custom buttons, you'll probably need to create your own custom toolbar. A custom toolbar can include any mixture of predefined buttons or custom buttons, so you can create a single toolbar that contains the buttons you use most from Word's various toolbars plus custom buttons of your own.

To create a custom toolbar, follow these steps:

1. Select the View⇨Toolbars command. When the Toolbars dialog box appears, click the New button. The dialog box shown in Figure 6-9 will appear.

Figure 6-9: Creating a new toolbar.

2. Type a name for your toolbar, select whether you want the toolbar stored in the global Normal.dot template or in the template attached to the document, and click on OK. Word will create an empty toolbar floating on the screen and automatically summon the Tools⇨Customize command.

3. Drag whatever tools you want onto the new toolbar. The toolbar will adjust its size to accommodate tools as you drag them on board. When you're done, click on Close to dismiss the Customize dialog box.

4. Drag the toolbar to its final resting place, floating free or docked to one edge of the screen.

Deleting and renaming toolbars

To delete a custom toolbar, call up the View⇨Toolbars command, select the toolbar you want to delete, and click the Del button. That's all there is to it.

You can rename toolbars only from the Organizer. Here is the procedure:

1. Call up the File⇨Templates command. When the Template and Add-ins dialog box appears, click Organizer.

2. In the Organizer dialog box, click the Toolbars tab. Then, select the toolbar you want to rename and click the Rename button.

3. In the Rename dialog box, type a new name for the toolbar. Click OK and click Close to dismiss the Organizer dialog box.

Resetting toolbars to their default settings

If you messed up one of the built-in toolbars beyond repair, it's time to reset it to its default configuration. To do that, call up the View⇨Toolbars command, click the toolbar you want to reset, and click Reset. A confirmation dialog box will appear to make sure that you know what you're doing; if you do, click OK.

Customizing Word's Menus

The last major item for customization is Word's menus. As with keyboard shortcuts and toolbars, Word lets you completely customize its menu structure. You can add your own commands to any of Word's default menus, you can remove commands that you seldom use or consider too dangerous for novices to use, you can rearrange menus into any configuration that you think might be more efficient than Word's default menu arrangement, and you can add your own menus. You can even tailor the pop-up menus that appear when you right-click various items within Word.

As with everything else in this chapter, custom menus are stored in document templates. To make a menu change that appears no matter what document you are editing, store the change in the Normal.dot template or a private template that is loaded as a global template. To make menu changes that appear only with specific documents, store the changes in the template attached to the document.

Customizing menus is truly one of the secrets of creating high-powered custom applications in Word. Anything you can do with a macro — which means anything that can be done at all — can be placed in a menu so that you can access it quickly. Like keyboard shortcuts and toolbars, Word lets you create menu commands for any of the following:

- **Any Word command.** You'd think that all of Word's commands would already be available as menu commands, but many are not. For example, Word's default menus do not include a Close All command to close all open documents without exiting Word, but a Word command called FileCloseAll does just that. If you think you'd use such a command, you can easily add it to the File menu.

- **Macros.** Anything you want to do that you cannot accomplish with a built-in Word command can probably be done with a macro.

- **Fonts.** You may have hundreds of fonts installed on your computer, but you routinely use only a dozen or so. If that's the case, you can add commands to apply specific fonts to an existing menu. Or, more promising still, you can create a new Font menu that lists your favorite fonts.

- **AutoText.** You can add the AutoText entries that you use most to a menu or place them on a separate menu altogether. A common use for this feature is creating a menu of boilerplate items that you can use to piece together a complete document.

■ **Styles.** Some templates have dozens of styles: too many to wade through every time you want to apply something other than Normal. If you use a relatively small collection of styles over and over again, consider creating a separate menu for them.

What's with the ampersand (&)?

Before I throw you into the depths of customizing Word's menus, I need to warn you that such work will expose you to a little whiff of programmer-speak, in the form of ampersands intermixed with menu and command names. For example, the File menu is written as &File, and the Format menu is written as F&ormat.

Did the Microsoft programmers who wrote Word suddenly develop a twitch in the index finger of their right hands when it came time to finish the Tools⇨Customize command? Not at all. Instead, they decided to use the ampersand as a symbol to indicate which character will serve as a menu or command's *hot key*: the key which the user can press in combination with the Alt key to invoke the menu or command. The hot key for the File menu is Alt+F because the ampersand precedes the F. For the Format menu, the hot key is Alt+O because the ampersand precedes the O.

Adding a menu command

When most users begin to probe the depths of Word's customization features, they discover that Word includes many commands that are not available from any of its menus: hundreds of unused commands, in fact. The fact that Microsoft left these commands off the menus should dissuade you from using them. If you find a command that you wish was available via the menus, don't gripe about it, add it to the menu! Here's the procedure:

1. Select the Tools⇨Customize command. When the Customize dialog box appears, click the Menus tab. The dialog box shown in Figure 6-10 will appear.

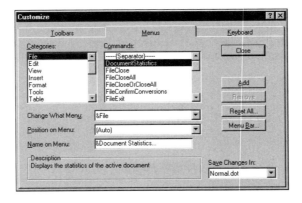

Figure 6-10: Customizing Word's menus.

2. Select the category of the command or other element you want to add to the menu from the Categories list. (Don't forget that macros, styles, fonts, and AutoText appear as categories near the bottom of the list.)

3. Select the specific command or other item from the Command list (the title of this box will change if you select the macros, styles, fonts, or AutoText categories).

4. Select the menu you want to add the command to from the Change What Menu list box. Notice that Word makes a pretty reasonable guess at which menu to use based on the command you've selected. For example, if you select the FileCloseAll command, Word presumes that you want to add it to the File menu. Pick the ApplyListBullet command, and Word will guess that you want it added to the Format menu. Change this field only if Word's assumption isn't correct.

5. Select the position where you want the command added to the selected menu. The default choice (Auto) is kind of interesting, because it tells Word to pick the location. Word makes an educated guess, placing the command near other similar commands that are already on the menu. For example, if you add the FileCloseAll command to the File menu, Word will place it right after the Close command. You can also direct Word to place the new command at the top or bottom of the menu, or you can pick a specific location for the new command.

6. In the Name on Menu field, type the command name as you'd like it to appear in the menu. Type an ampersand just before the letter that you want to serve as a hot key for the command. (Don't worry, the ampersand itself won't appear in the menu.) Word usually suggests a fairly reasonable name for the new command, complete with hot key, so you should have to change this field only if you don't like Word's suggestion.

7. Set the Save Changes In field to Normal.dot if you want your custom menu always to be available. If you want your custom menu commands to appear only in certain documents, change this field to specify the template used for those documents.

8. Click Add to add the command to the menu. You can now repeat Steps 2-7 to add other commands, or you can click Close to dismiss the Customize dialog box and check out your newly customized menus.

Using the shortcut method to add menu commands

Secret

One of Word's most obscure keyboard shortcuts is Ctrl+Alt+=, which allows you to add custom menu commands without going through the Tools⇨Customize command. To use it, follow these steps:

1. Make sure that the command you want to add to a menu is available via a keyboard shortcut or a visible toolbar button.

2. Press Ctrl+Alt+=. The mouse pointer will change to a big plus sign, but this is only to notify you that you have activated the Add Menu shortcut.

3. Press the keyboard shortcut for the command that you want added to the menus or click the appropriate toolbar button. The command will be added to the menu that Word thinks is most appropriate for the command.

You can use the shortcut method to add a style or font to the Format menu. Just press Ctrl+Alt+= and select the font or style you want to add to the menu from the drop-down lists in the Formatting toolbar.

Unfortunately, there is no way to tell Word where to insert the menu command when you use the shortcut method. If you want more precise control over the appearance of your menus, you'll have to use the Tools⇨Customize command.

Note

Is it just me, or is this shortcut not intuitive at all? Unfortunately, neither the Word manual nor the on-line help has anything to say about how to use this shortcut, so you're left to your own experimentation to figure out how it works. The first time I tried to use it, I pressed Ctrl+Alt+= and clicked on the menu at the point where I wanted to insert a new command, expecting to see the Customize dialog box suddenly appear, waiting for me to select the command to assign to the menu. That would be pretty slick, but no such luck. All of my efforts to figure out how to use this shortcut seemed to be leading nowhere, until I noticed that my Tools menu had a Customize Add Menu Shortcut command down at the bottom!

I pondered this for a moment, wondering how that command could have gotten there, when it hit me: The only way that command could have gotten there was if I pressed Ctrl+Alt+= twice in a row. The first time activated the Add Menu Shortcut feature, and the second time told Word which menu shortcut I wanted to add. I looked at my other menus and discovered that all sorts of new commands had appeared because of random keystrokes that I made while trying to figure out how to use Ctrl+Alt+=. I now had an Edit⇨Char Left command, which dutifully moved the insertion point one character to the left; it got there because I pressed the left arrow key after giving up on Ctrl+Alt+=. I also had Tools⇨Overtype command, the result of pressing the Insert key. Very strange. My only recourse was to reset my menus completely and start over. (See the section "Resetting menus to their default settings" later in this chapter for information on how to do that, in case you make the same mistake I did.)

Removing a menu command

The capability to remove commands from menus is just as important as the capability to add commands, not just because it allows you to remove custom commands you've added, but also because it lets you remove built-in commands that you never use. Such commands merely take up space on Word's already-crowded menus.

You can remove menu commands in two ways. The long way is to call up the Tools⇨Customize command, select the Menus tab, locate the menu command you want to nuke, and click the Remove button. The short way is to follow this procedure, which uses a little-known keyboard shortcut:

1. Press Ctrl+Alt+hyphen (the one next to the zero, *not* the minus key on the numeric keypad). The cursor will change to a thick horizontal bar.

2. Click the menu command that you want to remove.

Tip

The only problem with the Ctrl+Alt+hyphen trick is that it can only remove menu commands that are currently enabled. You cannot remove any commands that are grayed out. The workaround for this problem is to perform whatever action is required to enable the command you want to delete before pressing Ctrl+Alt+hyphen. For example, if you want to blow commands off the Table menu, create a table of at least one cell, select all or part of it, press Ctrl+Alt+hyphen, and click the command you want to remove.

Rearranging menu commands

Unfortunately, the Tools⇨Customize command does not provide a direct way to rearrange the items in a menu. The only way to do it is to delete the item that is out of place and recreate it at the location you prefer. This is more of a hassle than it should be: with the drag-and-drop mentality that runs throughout Windows 95 and all of Microsoft's recent application software, you'd think there would be a way to rearrange menu items by dragging them around. Maybe in Word 96…

Using separators

Word's default menus use spacers to group related commands. For example, pull down the File menu and you'll notice several groups of commands: New/Open/Close, Save/Save As/Save All, Properties/Templates, and so on. The groups are separated from one another with a horizontal line called a *separator,* and you can add or remove separators just like menu commands. To add a separator, choose Separator for the command to add. It appears at the top of the Commands list, no matter which Category is selected. To remove a separator, press Ctrl+Alt+hyphen and click on the separator you want to remove.

Adding a new menu

Besides adding commands to existing Word menus, Word lets you add completely new menus to hold custom commands. Some examples of good reasons for adding a new menu include

■ Creating a menu of commands for features you frequently use that are complicated enough to merit a separate menu. Word includes a Table menu by default because the Table feature is complicated. You can easily create a separate menu for similarly complicated features such as table of contents, indexes, and so on.

■ Creating a menu to apply the styles you use most. I do this for my own writing because it allows me to hide the Formatting toolbar. (Applying styles is the only thing I use the Formatting toolbar for anyway because I almost never change fonts or font sizes apart from styles, and I've memorized the keyboard shortcuts for its other buttons.) For those times when I do need the Formatting toolbar, I use the ToggleFormat macro, which was presented earlier in this chapter, assigned to the keyboard shortcut Ctrl+Shift+F.

■ Creating a menu to open commonly accessed documents. You can create a menu command for a specific document by opening the file you want to add to the menu and adding the FileOpenFile command to the menu.

To add your own menu, follow these steps:

1. Call up the Tools⇨Customize command and select the Menus tab.

2. Select the template that you want the custom menu added to in the Save Changes In list box (Normal.dot or another open template).

3. Click the Menu Bar button. The dialog box shown in Figure 6-11 will appear.

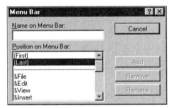

Figure 6-11: The Menu Bar dialog box, used to add or remove menus.

4. Type the name of the menu you want to add. Use an ampersand to indicate the hot key for the menu; for example, type **& Styles** to create a Styles menu.

5. Select the position in the menu bar for the new menu. The default choice is to add the menu to the end of the menu bar, but you can place it at the beginning of the menu bar or after any existing menu.

6. Click the Add button to add the menu and click Close to return to the Customize dialog box, where you can add individual commands to your new menu. When you're done, click Close. Your new menu will appear.

Customizing a shortcut menu

In addition to the menus that appear on the menu bar, Word also lets you customize the so-called *shortcut menus* that appear when you right-click on various objects within Word. In all, there are 25 different shortcut menus that you can customize:

Display Fields	Drawing Objects	Drop Caps
Endnotes	Fields	Footnotes
Form Fields	Frames	Headings
Linked Headings	Linked Text	Linked Whole Tables
Lists	Pictures	Spelling
Table Cells	Table Headings	Table Text
Table Lists	Table Pictures	Tables
Text	Toolbar Customization	Toolbars
Whole Tables		

The procedure for modifying these menus is the same for any other menu. When you call up the Tools⇨Customize Menus command, you'll find these menus listed in the Change What Menu list box after the menus that appear on the menu bar.

Just to get your creative juices flowing, here are a few ideas for commands that might be useful in individual shortcut menus:

- **Text.** This menu is displayed when normal text is right-clicked. Useful additions would include Bold, Italic, and Underline to apply character formatting; Style to change the style assigned to the paragraph; and ToolsThesaurus to look up a synonym.

- **Headings.** This menu is displayed when a paragraph formatted with one of Word's default heading styles is right-clicked. Useful additions would include ApplyHeading1, ApplyHeading2, or ApplyHeading3 to apply specific heading styles; OutlinePromote and OutlineDemote to change heading levels; and ViewOutline to switch to Outline mode.

- **Lists.** This menu is displayed when a bullet or number list is right-clicked. Useful additions would include BulletDefault and NumberDefault, which would let you quickly alternate between bullets and numbers.

Resetting menus to their default settings

If you've fouled up your menus so badly that you can't live with them anymore, you can restore them to their default configuration by calling up the Tools⇨Customize command, selecting the Menu tab, choosing which template you want to reset, and clicking on Reset All.

Chapter 7

Automating Your Work with Macros

In This Chapter

▶ Recording a simple macro.

▶ Running a macro.

▶ Editing a macro.

▶ Using the macros that come with Word.

A *macro* is a sequence of Word commands that you can play back at any time. Macros allow you to create your own customized Word commands for things you do over and over again. For example, Word comes with built-in commands to make text bold (Ctrl+B) and to make text italic (Ctrl+I), but there is no built-in command to make text bold and italic. Wouldn't it be nice if Word had a command that would apply both the bold and italic formats with a single keystroke? With macros, you can create one.

You can create macros in two ways. One is to activate the macro recorder, which records your keystrokes and commands in a macro so that you can play them back later. The other is to write macros with Word's built-in programming language, WordBasic.

This chapter shows you how to record and play back macros. It also shows you how to call up Word's macro editor so that you can view and modify a macro you've recorded or create simple macros yourself. That's enough to get you started with macros, but keep in mind that the real power of macros lies in using WordBasic. You'll find a complete course in WordBasic later in this book, in Part IX.

All macros utilize WordBasic, even macros you record by using the macro recorder. In some word processors, a macro is like a script that does little more than capture keystrokes you type and play them back later. In Word, a macro is a type of program written in the WordBasic programming language. When you record a macro with the macro recorder, Word doesn't record the actual keystrokes you type. Instead, it records the WordBasic commands which correspond to your keystrokes. For example, if you begin recording a macro and then type Alt+F to call up the File menu and O to select the Open command, Word adds a FileOpen command to your macro, not the actual keystrokes Alt+F, O.

Many of the chapters in this book present macros that you can use to automate routine chores or to take advantage of advanced Word features that are available only through macros. This chapter will give you enough information to type in those macros and run them, even though you may not understand how the macro works. I encourage you to try out as many of these macros as you can. One of the best ways to learn WordBasic is to jump right in without worrying about understanding all the details.

Macros and Templates

Macros are stored in document templates along with styles, keyboard short-cuts, custom toolbars and menus, AutoText entries, and so on. When you create a macro, Word asks whether you want to store the macro in the global Normal.dot template, the template attached to the current document, or another open template. When you run a macro, you can pick macros from Normal.dot, the current document's template, or a global template. For more information about templates, see Chapter 4.

Recording a Macro

The easiest way to create a macro, especially for users who are new to macros, is to use Word's built-in macro recorder. The macro recorder monitors your keystrokes and mouse actions and creates equivalent WordBasic commands in the macro.

Before you record a macro, take a few moments to think through what you want the macro to perform. For example, to create a macro that formats text as bold and italic, you need only press the keyboard shortcuts Ctrl+B and Ctrl+I. Clicking on the Bold and Italic buttons in the Formatting toolbar would accomplish the same thing. This is a pretty simple example, but other macros might require additional steps. Think through the steps before you begin to record your macro.

Follow this procedure to record a macro:

1. Choose the Tools⇨Macros command. This will bring up the Macro dialog box, as shown in Figure 7-1.

2. Click the Record button. The Record Macro dialog box will appear, as shown in Figure 7-2.

An alternative to choosing the Tools⇨Macro command and clicking the Record button is to double-click on the word "REC" in the status bar, at the bottom of the Word window. This calls up the Record Macro dialog box directly.

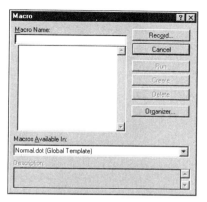

Figure 7-1: The Macro dialog box.

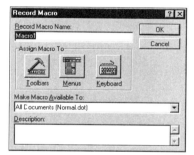

Figure 7-2: The Record Macro dialog box.

3. Type a name for the macro in the Record Macro Name field. Word will propose a name such as Macro1, but you can almost certainly come up with a better name yourself. (Unlike style names, spaces are not allowed in macro names.)

4. If you want the macro assigned to a toolbar, menu, or keyboard shortcut, click the appropriate button. The Customize dialog box will appear, ready for you to select a toolbar button, menu, or keyboard shortcut. For more information on how to use the Customize dialog box, refer to Chapter 5. If you do not assign the macro to a toolbar, menu, or keyboard shortcut, you can run the macro by using the Tools⇨Macro command.

5. Select the template where you want the macro stored by using the Make Macro Available To list box. By default, the macro will be stored in the Normal.dot template so that it will always be available.

6. Type a description for the macro in the Description field if you are so inclined.

7. Click OK to begin recording the macro. The Record Macro dialog box will disappear, the word "REC" will be highlighted in the status bar, and the Macro Record floating toolbar shown in Figure 7-3 will appear. (Also the mouse pointer will change, taking an image of a cassette tape in tow to indicate that you are in Macro Record mode.)

Figure 7-3: The Macro Record toolbar.

8. Type the keystrokes and other commands you want to record in the macro. For the BoldItalic command, press Ctrl+B, and press Ctrl+I. To record Word commands, use keyboard shortcuts, toolbars, or menu commands. Beware that anything you type, including navigation commands, such as the arrow keys, PageUp or PageDown keys, and editing keys, such as Insert and Delete will be recorded.

Tip

If you make a mistake while recording a macro, you can always use the Undo command. Each time you run the macro, the erroneous command will be executed, and then undone by the recorded Undo command. This is not very efficient, to be sure, but it works.

9. To suspend recording temporarily, click the Pause button in the Macro Record toolbar. Use this feature if you want to perform some Word action that you do not want included in the macro. For example, if you forget how to use a feature that you want to include in the macro, you can click the Pause button and call up Word's Help command. When you're ready to resume recording, click the Pause button again.

10. When you're finished, click the Stop button or double-click the word "REC" in the status bar again.

After you record a macro, you should test it by running it (see the next section) and verifying that it works the way you expect. If you made a mistake when recording, you can always record the macro again. If the macro is long and you don't want to re-record it, you can edit the macro and attempt to correct the mistake. See the section "Editing a Macro" later in this chapter.

Macro Recording Tips

Here are some tips to keep in mind as you record macros:

■ Do not make any assumptions about where the insertion point will be when you run the macro. If necessary, begin the macro with a positioning command by moving the insertion point to the beginning of the document, the beginning of the line, or the beginning of a word. (Of course, not all macros require a positioning command.)

■ Do not use the mouse to select text or navigate through the document. Word will not record these mouse actions. You can use the mouse to select menu commands or to click toolbar buttons.

■ Use Ctrl+Home or Ctrl+End to move to the beginning or end of a document. Do *not* use repeated PageUp or PageDown keys for this purpose. Three PageUps might get you to the top of your document when you record the macro, but when you run the macro, it might not. Similarly, use Home and End to move to the start or end of a line.

■ If you use the Find or Replace commands move to the beginning of the document first.

■ Avoid using dialog boxes. Word records *all* of the settings in a dialog box when you create a macro. This can result in strange side effects later. For example, you might be tempted to record the BoldItalic macro by calling up the Format⇨Font command, selecting the Bold Italic font style, and clicking OK. Unfortunately, you'll soon discover that this recorded not only the Bold Italic font style, but other character attributes as well, such as font, size, and effects. If the text to which you applied the Format⇨Font command when you recorded the macro used the Times New Roman font, any text you apply the macro to will be switched to Times New Roman.

■ Avoid any commands that depend on the contents of the document that is active when you record the macro.

Running a Macro

If you assigned a macro to a toolbar, menu, or keyboard shortcut, you can run the macro by clicking the toolbar button, choosing the menu command, or pressing the keyboard shortcut. If you did not, you can run it by following these steps:

1. Choose the Tools⇨Macro command to summon the Macro dialog box.

2. Select the macro you want to run from the list of macro names that appears in the dialog box. If the macro you want doesn't appear, try checking the Macros Available In setting. The macro might be in a different template.

3. Click Run.

More Ways to Run a Macro

The Tools⇨Macro command isn't the only way to run a macro. Here are three others:

- Use the Insert⇨Field command to insert a MACROBUTTON field in a document. Then, you can run the macro attached to the field by clicking on the macro button. See Chapter 30 for more information.

- Use the /m startup switch to start a macro automatically when you start Word. For example, to run a macro named GetReady when you start Word, use this command line:

```
winword /mGetReady
```

- Use one of the macro names listed in Table 7-1. These macros automatically run when certain events occur.

Table 7-1	Word's Auto Macros
Macro Name	*When It Runs*
AutoExec	When Word starts. This macro should be stored in Normal.dot.
AutoExit	When Word exits. This macro should be stored in Normal.dot.
AutoNew	When you create a new document based on the template that contains the AutoNew template.
AutoOpen	When an existing document is opened. This macro can reside in Normal.dot or in the template attached to the document.
AutoClose	When an open document is closed. This macro can reside in Normal.dot or in the template attached to the document.

Secret

You can prevent any of the Auto macros from running by holding down the Shift key while performing the action that would otherwise cause the macro to run. For example, to open an existing document without running its AutoOpen macro, hold down the Shift key while you use the File⇨Open command.

Editing a Macro

If you make a mistake while recording a macro, you can abandon the recording and start over. Or, you can finish the recording and edit the macro to correct the mistake. When you edit the macro, the macro's commands will appear in a separate window. You can delete or modify erroneous commands, you can insert new commands if you know how, or you can merely study the macro to try to figure out how it works.

Warning

When you edit a macro, you will be exposed to WordBasic. WordBasic is not as deadly as the Ebola virus, but it can cause severe headaches and nausea.

Here is the procedure for editing a macro:

1. Choose the Tools⇨Macro command to call up the Macro dialog box.

2. Select the macro you want to edit and click the Edit button. The macro will appear in its own document window, with a special toolbar designed for working with macros. See Figure 7-4.

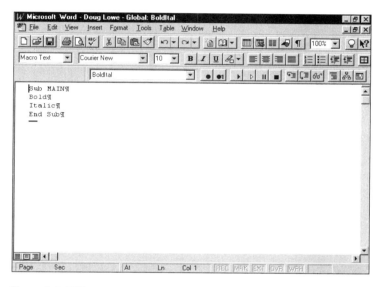

Figure 7-4: Editing a macro.

3. Make whatever changes are necessary to the macro. Correct misspelled words, delete extraneous commands, and, if you're brave, add additional commands.

4. Use the File⇨Save Template command to save your changes.

5. Use the File⇨Close command to close the macro window.

Delving into WordBasic

Later in this book, you'll find a complete tutorial on the WordBasic programming language. I don't want to begin a detailed WordBasic tutorial here, but I do want to prepare you for what to expect when you edit a Word macro.

For starters, each macro begins with the line `Sub MAIN` and ends with the line `End Sub`. These lines mark the start and finish of the macro. Other WordBasic commands can appear between these lines.

Word commands are generally written with the name of the command's menu first, followed by the name of the command, with no intervening spaces. The following table lists some common Word commands and their WordBasic command equivalents:

File⇨Open	FileOpen
File⇨Save As	FileSaveAs
Edit⇨Undo	EditUndo
View⇨Normal	ViewNormal
Format⇨Bullets and Numbering	FormatBulletsAndNumbering

WordBasic also includes a variety of other commands that are not directly accessible via the menus but invoke common Word functions. Many of these commands are assigned to keyboard shortcuts or toolbar buttons. For example:

Bold

Italic

PageDown

StartOfDocument

CenterPara

Indent

The Insert command is used to insert text into a document. For example, if you type the text **Go Figure** while recording a macro, the macro will contain an Insert command similar to this one:

```
Insert "Go Figure"
```

When you use an Insert command, any information between the quotation marks is inserted directly into the document.

WordBasic also includes an array of commands that cannot be inserted into a macro by the macro recorder, but which can be used to create sophisticated macros. These include commands for declaring local and global variables, creating your own dialog boxes, displaying messages to the user while the macro runs, controlling the execution of commands within the macro, handling errors that pop up from time to time, and so on. For more information about these statements, consult Chapter 34.

Simple macro edits that don't require a Ph.D. in WordBasic

Before you make massive changes to a macro, you need a pretty good knowledge of WordBasic. However, you can make certain types of changes without knowing much about WordBasic at all. Here is a sampling:

- **Correcting spelling errors.** If you inserted text into a document and misspelled it, don't hesitate to edit the macro to correct the misspellings. Text you insert into a document while recording a macro will be included in an Insert command in the macro. You can correct any spelling mistakes or change the inserted text altogether, provided you take care not to remove either of the quotation marks that appear before and after the text.

- **Removing extraneous commands.** If you inadvertently used a command while recording a macro and you used the Undo command to cancel the unnecessary command, you can clean up your macro by removing both the unnecessary command and the Undo command. For example, you could delete the first two lines in the following sequence:

```
Underline
EditUndo
Bold
Italic
```

- **Remove unwanted dialog box settings.** If you record a dialog box in a macro, Word will include every setting in the dialog box. You can remove those settings that you do not want to be changed by the macro. For example, if you use the Format⇨Font command to set the BoldItalic font style, the following FormatFont command will be inserted into the macro:

```
FormatFont .Points = "12", .Underline = 0, .Color = 0,
.Strikethrough = 0, .Superscript = 0, .Subscript = 0,.Hidden = 0,
.SmallCaps = 0, .AllCaps = 0, .Spacing = "0 pt", .Position = "0
pt", .Kerning = 0, .KerningMin = "", .Tab = "0", .Font = "Times
New Roman", .Bold =1, .Italic = 1, .Outline = 0, .Shadow = 0
```

This command looks complicated at first, but if you study it, you'll see that it consists of all the dialog box controls that appear on the Format⇨Font command's dialog box. The periods look strange appearing in front of each command arguments as they do, but they are required. You can safely delete the command arguments that represent dialog box controls you don't want to use so that the resulting FormatFont command looks like this:

```
FormatFont .Bold = 1, .Italic = 1
```

Using the Macros That Come with Word

When you install Word for Windows, five templates are installed in the \Winword\Macros folder (C:\MSOffice\Office95\Winword\Macros if you are using Office 95). These templates contain a collection of useful macros for various functions. To use these macros, open the template file by using the File⇨Open command or load the template as a global template. Then, run the macro via the Tools⇨Macro command. Alternatively, you can assign a keyboard shortcut, toolbar button, or menu command for the macros you use most.

The following sections describe the macros supplied with each of the templates.

Macros in the Macros7.dot template

The Macros7.dot template contains several macros you might find useful in certain circumstances. In addition to the following macros, Macros7.dot contains a Macro7 toolbar that you can use to start the macros. Once Macro7 is loaded as a global template, you can activate the Macro7 toolbar via the View⇨Toolbars command or run the macros directly from the Tools⇨Macro command.

- **DisableAutoBackup:** This macro disables the AutoBackup feature provided by the EnableAutoBackup macro and should be used only after running EnableAutoBackup. This deletes the FileSave and FileSaveAs macros that were created when you ran EnableAutoBackup and removes the Enable AutoBackup/Disable AutoBackup commands from the File menu.

- **EnableAutoBackup:** This macro provides an AutoBackup feature that makes a backup copy in a folder you specify whenever you save a file. When you run the EnableAutoBackup macro, two new macros are added to your Normal.dot template: FileSave and FileSaveAs. These two macros customize the standard FileSave and FileSaveAs commands so that a backup copy of the document is created in your backup folder. EnableAutoBackup also adds a Disable AutoBackup command to your File menu. You can use this command to disable AutoBackup temporarily. (If you do, the Disable AutoBackup command changes to Enable AutoBackup, which reinstates the AutoBackup feature.)

Note

AutoBackup is not the same thing as the Always Create Backup Copy option available in the Tools⇨Options command's Save tab. The Always Create Backup Copy stores a backup copy of the previous version of your document before saving. In contrast, the AutoBackup creates a backup copy of the file that is saved so that you have two copies of the file at all times.

- **ExitAll:** This macro is designed to provide a more efficient way to exit Word when you have several documents open. Normally, Word automatically closes every open document before exiting, prompting you one by one for whether you want to save documents that have been modified. The ExitAll macro displays a dialog box that lists all your open documents and allows you to check those documents you want saved. (Documents that have been modified because they were last saved are checked by default, but you can uncheck them if you do not want their changes saved.) Figure 7-5 shows the ExitAll dialog box. The dialog box can display only five documents at a time. If more than five files are open, you can click the More>> button to display the next group of five documents.

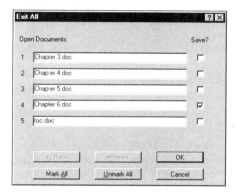

Figure 7-5: The dialog box displayed by the ExitAll macro included in the Macros7.dot template.

If you like the ExitAll macro, consider copying it to your Normal.dot template (use the Organizer to do this) and attaching it to the File⇨Exit command.

- **FindSymbol:** This macro lets you search for and replace symbols that were inserted with the Insert⇨Symbol command. It displays the dialog box shown in Figure 7-6. To specify the symbol to find, click the Find What button. This brings up Word's standard Symbol dialog box, the same dialog box that is displayed if you use the Insert⇨Symbol command. (See Figure 7-7.) To replace one symbol with another, click the Replace With button and select the replacement symbol. You can use the All, Down, and Up buttons to tell FindSymbol whether the entire document should be searched (All) or whether the search should proceed from the current location to the end of the document (Down) or to the beginning of the document (Up).

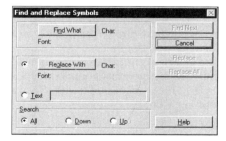

Figure 7-6: The Find and Replace Symbols dialog box.

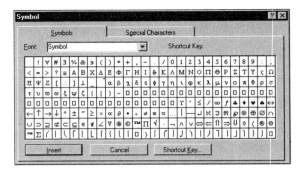

Figure 7-7: The Symbol dialog box.

- **FontSampleGenerator:** This macro creates a document that includes a table which has one row for every printable font on your computer. The table includes the name of the font and a font sample that shows a complete uppercase and lowercase alphabet, numerals, and special characters. When you run FontSampleGenerator, the dialog box shown in Figure 7-8 is displayed, informing you of how many fonts are available and asking for the point size for the font samples. Figure 7-9 shows the resulting document. Be forewarned that FontSampleGenerator can take a while to run, and the document may take a while to print, depending on your printer.

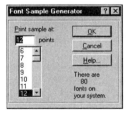

Figure 7-8: The Font Sample Generator dialog box.

- **InsertFootnote:** This macro is actually the Footnote Wizard, which automatically creates various types of footnotes formatted according to popular style manuals. The wizard asks for pertinent information and inserts a properly formatted footnote. To use this wizard, just make Macros7.dot a global template or copy the InsertFootnote macro from Macros7.dot to Normal.dot. Once in place, the InsertFootnote macro takes over for the built-in Insert⇨Footnote command, automatically invoking the Wizard whenever you insert a footnote. (This macro is new with Word for Windows 95, and is covered in more detail in Chapter 26.)

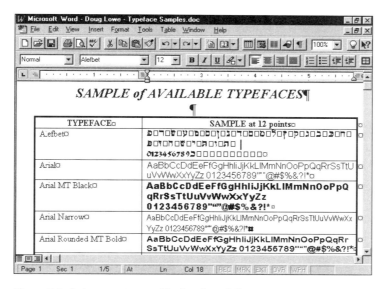

Figure 7-9: A document created by FontSampleGenerator.

■ **MindBender:** This macro plays a game that is a variation of the old Concentration card game, where you flip over pairs of cards looking for matches. When you run MindBender, you get the welcome screen shown in Figure 7-10. Click the Start Game button, and the dialog box will fill with a grid of buttons as shown in Figure 7-11. Pairs of icons stolen from Word's toolbars are scattered under these buttons. To play the game, click two of the buttons to reveal their icons. If the two icons are the same, you get credit for the match and another try. If they aren't, they are hidden again and the computer gets a turn. The game is over when the entire board has been cleared. Whoever acquires the most matches wins.

Figure 7-10: The MindBender welcome screen.

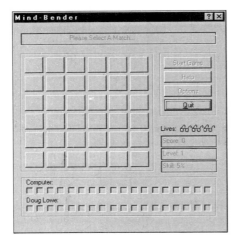

Figure 7-11: The MindBender game underway.

Secret

Game programmers can't resist the urge to throw in a secret code that gives them a way to cheat at their games. The programmer at Microsoft who wrote the MindBender macro is no exception: MindBender has a secret code that uncovers all of the hidden icons for 10 seconds so that you can see their locations and hopefully memorize a few of them. To cheat, press and hold the following keys immediately after you click the Start Game button: Ctrl, Alt, Shift, M, J, and W. (Apparently, M, J, and W are the initials of the programmer who wrote MindBender.)

■ **NormalViewHeaderFooter:** This macro lets you edit headers and footers similar to the way you could in Word 2, in a separate pane in Normal view. I don't recommend it unless you are thoroughly entrenched in the Word 2 way of dealing with headers and footers.

■ **OrganizationalChartMaker:** This macro lets you create organization charts. First, type the information for your chart as an outline by using Word's built-in heading styles to indicate the chart's hierarchy, as in Figure 7-12. Then, run the OrganizationalChartMaker macro. It will take awhile, but eventually you'll see a document that looks something like Figure 7-13.

■ **RegOptions:** This macro provides a convenient way to change the Word options stored in the Windows 95 Registry. Most of these options are better set by the Tools⇨Options command, but RegOptions is available for those who like to hack away at the Registry.

■ **SaveSelectionToTextFile:** This macro copies the selected portion of a document to a text file. You will be prompted for the name of the file.

■ **SetPrintFlags:** This macro is used when Word is having trouble printing on a specific printer. It adds entries to the Windows 95 Registry that override Word's default printing behavior for a particular printer driver. You can find more information about this macro in Chapter 9.

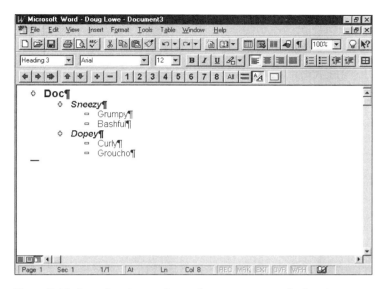

Figure 7-12: An outline that can be used to create an organization chart.

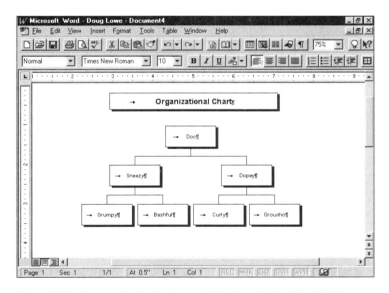

Figure 7-13: An organization chart created by OrganizationalChartMaker.

■ **SuperDocStatistics:** This macro displays just about every item of information about a document that you can imagine in a single dialog box, as shown in Figure 7-14. The row of buttons down the left side of the dialog box are equivalent to the tabs in Word's other dialog boxes. You can click on any of these buttons to display additional information about the current document. You can also create a report that lists the document information.

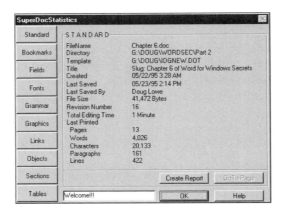

Figure 7-14: The SuperDocStatistics dialog box.

 ■ **WordPuzzler:** Remember those cheap little games your parents used to give you to keep you quiet while your family drove to the Grand Canyon? Especially the one that had a bunch of numbered squares that you were supposed to slide around until you put the numbers back into order, which you never did, and so you ended up fighting with your brother instead, and you got in trouble, and from then on you *hated* family vacations? If so, try out the WordPuzzler macro. As Figure 7-15 shows, it should bring back lots of unpleasant memories. (This macro is new with Word for Windows 95.)

Figure 7-15: The WordPuzzler macro.

Macros in the Tables.dot template

The Tables.dot template contains macros that are designed to work with tables.

■ **AccessExporter:** This macro exports a Word table to a table in a Microsoft Access database. You can create a new table, or you can append the data to an existing table. Of course, this macro won't be of much use unless you also have Microsoft Access.

■ **TableMath:** This macro makes it easier to create math formulas for Word tables. It assigns "cell names" to each table cell, much as Excel does (A1, A2, and so on), and then presents the dialog box shown in Figure 7-16 to help you prepare formulas. I discuss this macro in greater detail in Chapter 17.

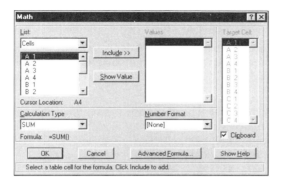

Figure 7-16: The TableMath macro.

■ **TableNumber:** This macro displays the dialog box shown in Figure 7-17, which allows you to number the rows or columns in a table. For more information, see Chapter 17.

Figure 7-17: The TableNumber macro.

 Two macros which were included in the Tables.dot template with Word 6 have been dropped from Word for Windows 95:

■ TableFillDown

■ TableFillRight

Macros in the Layout.dot template

The Layout.dot template contains macros that are designed to help you format your document and to arrange document windows.

- **ArrangeWindows:** This macro lets you quickly arrange windows into various configurations: tiled, horizontal, vertical, or cascaded. If you like it, copy it to Normal.dot or make Layout.dot a global template, and attach the ArrangeWindows macro to your <u>W</u>indow menu.

- **Cascade:** Many Windows applications have a <u>W</u>indow⇨<u>C</u>ascade command, but Word does not. This macro accomplishes the same thing and can be added to the <u>W</u>indow menu if desired.

- **DecreaseLeftAndRightIndent:** This macro decreases the left and right indents of the selected paragraphs by an equal amount, effectively widening the paragraphs. The default tab settings are used to determine how much to decrease the indent.

- **IncreaseLeftAndRightIndent:** This macro increases the left and right indents of the selected paragraphs by an equal amount, effectively making the paragraphs narrower. The default tab settings are used to determine how much to increase the indent.

- **Overscore:** This macro uses an Equation field to create *overscored* text: that is, text with a horizontal line above it.

- **PrintableCharacters:** This macro creates a new document that contains a list of all the printable characters for a given font, as shown in Figure 7-18. You can use this table to find out if a particular symbol is available and, if so, what it's ASCII code is.

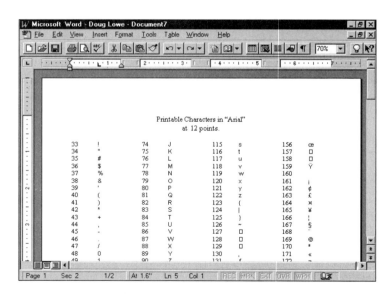

Figure 7-18: A document created by the PrintableCharacters macro.

■ **SectionManager:** This macro displays the dialog box shown in Figure 7-19, which lets you manage the format of all the sections in a document. This can be a real time-saver in documents that have many different section layouts.

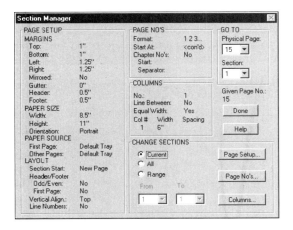

Figure 7-19: The SectionManager dialog box.

■ **TileHorizontally:** This macro arranges all of the open document windows into tiles that are stacked horizontally, one atop the other. This is useful if you have two or three open document windows, but it doesn't work well if you have more than that.

■ **TileVertically:** This macro arranges all of the open document windows into vertical tiles, placed next to each other in a left-to-right arrangement. As with TileHorizontally, this is useful when you have two or three windows open, but the more windows you have open, the less useful this macro becomes.

 Several macros that were included in the Layout.dot template with Word 6 have been dropped from Word for Windows 95. These macros include the following:

■ BaseShiftDown

■ BaseShiftUp

■ CharacterTrackIn

■ CharacterTrackOut

■ DecreaseFont

■ IncreaseFont

■ LineSpaceIn

■ LineSpaceOut

Macros in the Convert.dot template

The Convert.dot template contains two macros that are designed to convert batches of documents from one format to another. The macros are

- **BatchConversion:** This macro is a wizard that lets you convert groups of documents from one format to another by using the document converters supplied with Word. Conversion works both ways; you can convert from a foreign document format to a Word format, or you can convert Word documents to some other format.

- **EditConversionOptions:** This macro lets you set various options that Word's document converters use.

Macros in the Present.dot template

Well, actually there is only one macro in the Present.dot template:

- **PresentIt:** This macro converts a Word document to a PowerPoint presentation. To convert a document, the document must contain an outline that uses Word's standard heading styles. The PresentIt macro converts the document to an RTF file (Rich Text Format, a common format for exchanging word processing documents between different systems) and launches PowerPoint to open the RTF file.

Part III
Secrets of Working with Word

8   Managing Your Documents

9   Printing Your Documents

10   Working with Others

Chapter 8

Managing Your Documents

In This Chapter

▶ Retrieving documents with the File⇨Open command, including tricks for directing the Open dialog box to your most commonly used files

▶ Finding files that have gone astray

▶ Saving your documents, including how to set Word's file saving options

You can't get very far with Word without learning how to save and retrieve documents on disk, so you probably already know the basics of managing Word documents. Even so, Word's document management features go well beyond the basic tasks of saving and retrieving documents. This chapter covers the more advanced aspects of document management.

Using the File⇨Open Command

The most direct way to open a document is to use the File⇨Open command. There are three ways you can summon this command:

■ Choose the File⇨Open command from the menus.

■ Click on the Open button in the Standard toolbar.

■ Press Ctrl+O or Ctrl+F12. Ctrl+O is the more intuitive keyboard shortcut for the File⇨Open command ("O" is for "Open"), but Ctrl+F12 is left over from the early days of Windows, before Microsoft programmers decided that keyboard shortcuts should make sense. Rather than drop an antiquated and senseless keyboard shortcut in favor of one that makes sense and is consistent across all Windows applications (or at least is supposed to be), the Word developers at Microsoft decided to leave *both* keyboard shortcuts in place.

However you do it, the File Open dialog box as shown in Figure 8-1 will appear. If you're an experienced Word 6 user, you'll notice right away that this dialog box has been changed substantially to accommodate the Windows 95 way of accessing documents. In particular, long filenames are supported. You can run Word 6 with Windows 95, but you won't see any long filenames.

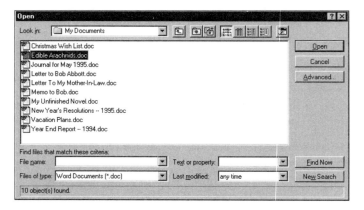

Figure 8-1: The File Open dialog box.

In Word 6, you navigated to different drives and directories by using the Drives and Directories list boxes. In Word for Windows 95, these controls have been consolidated into a single Look in control. The Look in control is a drop-down list box that includes every location where documents might be hiding: all of your disk drives, your desktop (you can store documents on the desktop by dragging them there from an Explorer window), the network, and your Briefcase (the *Briefcase* is an area where you can place files to synchronize them with files on your laptop computer). Although this list is the primary method of navigating through your drives and folders, you can still work your way down through the folder hierarchy by double-clicking on folder icons. You can move back up the folder hierarchy by clicking on the Up One Level button, which appears next to the Look in field. You can also move up one level in the hierarchy by pressing the Backspace key.

Tip

You can open more than one document at once by selecting several files and clicking the Open button. Use one of the following techniques to select several files:

- Hold down the Ctrl key while clicking on the files you want to select.

- To select a range of files, click on the first file in the range, hold down the Shift key, and click on the last file in the range.

- Click on the first file in the range you want to select and hold down the Shift key and click on the last file. Word will select the two files you clicked, plus every file in between.

- To deselect a file, hold down the Ctrl key and click the file.

Changing views

Like the Windows 95 Explorer, the File Open dialog box lets you switch among four different views of your documents. The four View buttons at the top of the File Open dialog box let you make the switch:

List: Displays a list of folders and documents with icons. This is the default view, which was shown in Figure 8-1.

Details: Displays a list of folders and documents with details, including the filename, type, size, and creation date. Figure 8-2 shows Detail view. Notice that the headers at the top of the columns are actually buttons; you can sort the list on any of the columns simply by clicking on the column's button.

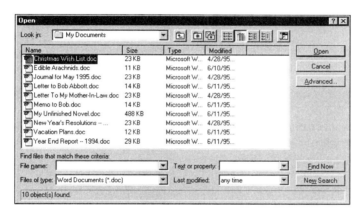

Figure 8-2: The File Open dialog box in Detail view.

Properties: Displays a panel showing various properties for the selected file, including the Title, Author, Template, Word count, and other useful information. Figure 8-3 shows Properties view.

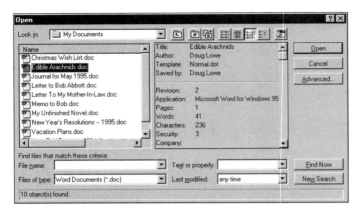

Figure 8-3: The File Open dialog box in Properties view.

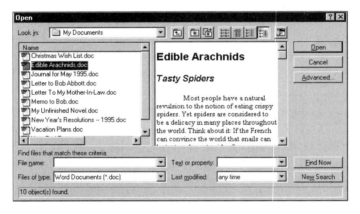

Preview: Displays a preview of the selected file, as shown in Figure 8-4.

Figure 8-4: The File Open dialog box in Preview view.

Deleting and renaming documents and folders

You can delete and rename files and folders from the File Open dialog box. Here's how:

■ To delete a file or folder, select the file or folder and press the Del key.

■ To rename a file or folder, select it by clicking on it once and then click on the filename again. A text editing box will appear around the file or folder name, allowing you to edit the name. (Don't click on it too quickly, or Word will think you double-clicked and the file or folder will open.)

Playing favorites

Some of the most useful additions to the File Open dialog box are the Favorites buttons, Look in Favorites, and Add to Favorites. These buttons, when used in conjunction with Windows 95 shortcuts, provide a convenient method of accessing commonly used documents located in various folders on your local disk drive or on network drives.

The centerpiece of the Favorites feature is a folder named Favorites, which lives in your Windows folder. You can place any documents that you frequently use in this folder, or you can create subfolders to hold your documents. Better yet, you can place *shortcuts* to your frequently used documents and folders in \Windows\Favorites. That way, you can access commonly used documents folders with just a few mouse clicks, without worrying—or even knowing—where in the disk hierarchy they reside. Unless you work with only a very small number of documents, I suggest you place only shortcuts to folders in Favorites to avoid cluttering up your Favorites folder.

Figure 8-5 shows the Favorites folder on my computer. As you can see, I've created shortcuts to various directories that correspond to projects I'm working on. (I've also created folders for each of my kids so that they don't intermingle their work with mine. If you tell enough of your friends how much you like this book, I might be able to buy my kids a computer of their own.)

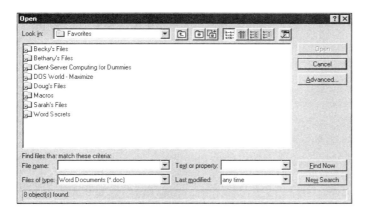

Figure 8-5: The File Open dialog box for the Favorites folder.

The File Open dialog box has two buttons that utilize the \Windows\Favorites folder:

Look in Favorites: Click on this button and you'll be instantly whisked away to the \Windows\Favorites folder.

Add to Favorites: Click on this button to create shortcuts to your commonly used documents or folders in the \Windows\Favorites folder.

When you click on the Add to Favorites button, a menu appears with two commands:

- **Add "Look In" folder to Favorites:** Creates a shortcut to the current folder in \Windows\Favorites. Use this command when you're looking at documents in a folder, you suddenly realize that you use the documents frequently, and you'd like the entire folder to be accessible from Favorites.

- **Add Selected Item to Favorites:** Creates a shortcut to the selected item — be it a document or a folder — in \Windows\Favorites. Use this command when you've clicked on a document or folder and you want to add that document or folder to Favorites.

Tip

You can also add a shortcut to Favorites outside of Word by using the right mouse button to drag a folder or document to the \Windows\Favorites folder and selecting Create Shortcut from the pop-up menu that appears when you release the mouse button.

Setting the default document location

When you call up the File Open dialog box, Word initially displays the contents of the folder indicated by the default Document File Location option setting. When you install Word for Windows 95, this option is initially set to C:\My Documents, but you can change this location by using the following procedure:

1. Call up the Tools➪Options command. The Options dialog box will appear.

2. Click on the File Locations tab.

3. Double-click on Documents. A dialog box titled Modify Location will appear.

4. In the Folder name text box, type the name of the folder you want to use for the default document location, or use the controls in the Modify Location dialog box to navigate to the folder.

5. Click on OK to return to the Options dialog box.

6. Click on Close.

Each time you use the File Open dialog command box during a Word session, Word remembers the folder that was displayed when you dismissed the dialog box and automatically redisplays the same folder the next time you use the File➪Open command. The default document location set via the Tools➪Options command is used only the first time you use the File➪Open command in a given Word session.

Forcing Word to always look in Favorites

You can set the default document location for the File➪Open command by using the Tools➪Options command and clicking on the File Locations tab. However, this sets the document location only for the first time you use the

File⇨Open command within a Word session. Thereafter, Word remembers the last location you retrieved a file from and automatically displays that folder when you use File⇨Open.

If you always want Word to display the Favorites folder when you call up the File⇨Open command, regardless of what folder you last retrieved a file from, create a macro named FileOpen in the Normal.dot template, with the following lines:

```
Sub MAIN
On Error Goto UserCancel
Dim dlg As FileOpen
GetCurValues dlg
dlg.Name = "c:\Windows\Favorites\"
Dialog dlg
FileOpen dlg
UserCancel:
End Sub
```

This macro replaces the built-in FileOpen command, always forcing the File Open dialog box to display the contents of the Favorites folder. If you use this macro, any setting you provide for the default document location via the Tools⇨Options command will be ignored.

You'll find this macro under the name FileOpenFavorites in the Secrets template on the CD-ROM that accompanies this book.

If you changed the name of the \Windows directory or installed it on a drive other than C:, you'll have to change the dlg.Name line accordingly.

Using the shortcut menu

You can right-click on a folder or document in the File Open dialog box to call up a shortcut menu, as shown in Figure 8-6.

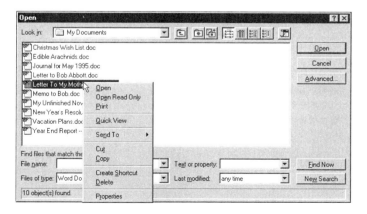

Figure 8-6: The shortcut menu for a document in the File Open dialog box.

The shortcut menu for a document contains the following commands:

- **Open:** Opens the document. This is the same as double-clicking on the document or selecting the document and clicking on the Open button.

- **Open Read Only:** Opens the document in read-only mode. This allows you to view the document, but you cannot save any changes you make.

- **Print:** Prints the document without actually opening it. The normal Print dialog box is displayed, allowing you to set the print option before printing the document.

- **Quick View:** Uses the Word quick viewer that comes with Windows 95 to view the document without actually opening it.

- **Send To:** This is one of the most useful commands to appear on the short-cut menu. It allows you to send the selected document to any of several destinations: your floppy disk drives, a fax recipient, a mail recipient, or My Briefcase. If you elect to send the document to a floppy drive, Word copies the file to the root directory of the appropriate diskette. If you send to a fax recipient, Word runs the Compose New Fax wizard to send the document via fax, provided your computer is equipped with a fax modem. If you send the document to a mail recipient, Word starts Microsoft Exchange and creates a mail message with the document embedded—you provide the address of the recipient. Finally, if you send the document to My Briefcase, the document is copied to the My Briefcase folder.

- **Cut:** Deletes the document and places it on the Clipboard. This allows you to paste it into another folder in an Explorer or My Computer window. You can also paste the file to the desktop by right-clicking anywhere in the desktop and selecting the Paste command.

- **Copy:** Copies the document to the Clipboard so that you can paste it into another folder via an Explorer or My Computer window. You can also paste the document to the desktop.

- **Create Shortcut:** Creates a shortcut to the selected document. It doesn't make much sense to have a shortcut to a document living in the same folder as the document, but once you've created the shortcut, you can drag it to another folder or to the desktop.

- **Delete:** Deletes the document or folder. You can achieve the same result by pressing the Del key.

- **Properties:** Displays the document's properties, the same as if you opened the document and chose the File⇨Properties command. File properties are covered in more detail later in this chapter.

If you right-click on a folder rather than a document, a subset of these commands appears. In addition, the shortcut menu for a document includes an Explore command, which opens a separate Explorer window for the folder.

Note

Although you can customize most of the shortcut menus that appear throughout Word via the Tools⇨Customize command, you cannot customize the shortcut menus that appear in the File Open dialog box.

Using the Commands and Settings button

The Commands and Settings button, located in the top-right corner of the File Open dialog box, displays a menu that includes commands that manipulate the selected document or that sets options that govern how the File Open dialog box works. The commands on the Commands and Settings menu include the following:

- **Open Read Only:** Opens the file for read-only access, the same as selecting the Open Read Only command from the shortcut menu when you right-click a document. This command is not available if a folder is selected.

- **Print:** Prints the document, the same as selecting the Print command from the shortcut menu when you right-click a document. This command is not available if a folder is selected.

- **Properties:** Displays the document or folder properties.

- **Sorting:** Displays the Sort By dialog box shown in Figure 8-7. This dialog box allows you to sort the document list into ascending or descending sequence according to the filename, file size, file type (based on the file extension), and last modification date. The default setting is to sort files into ascending order by filename.

Figure 8-7: The Sort By dialog box.

- **Search Subfolders:** This command tells Word to display documents in subfolders of the current folder. When you use it in Details, Properties, or Preview view, documents and folders are displayed in a tree structure, as shown in Figure 8-8. This allows you to display files in several folders at once, without using the Look in list box to change directories. The Search Subfolders command works as a toggle. In other words, it alternately sets and resets the option to search subfolders.

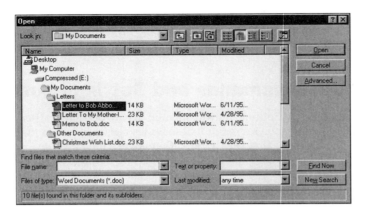

Figure 8-8: Displaying subfolders.

- **Group files by folder:** When you select the Search Subfolders option, the Group files by folder option is also automatically selected. This causes Word to sort files according to folders. If you disable this option, files from the current folder and all its subfolders are merged together and sorted into sequence according to the Sort By setting. Disabling this option also disables the folder tree displayed when you select Search Subfolders.

- **Map Network Drive:** This command allows you to assign a drive letter to a network drive, which can simplify the task of accessing files that reside on a network server.

- **Saved Searches:** This command displays a cascaded menu that lists any searches you've previously saved so that you can access them quickly. For more information about creating and using saved searches, see the section, "Saving searches" later in this chapter.

Opening Recently Used Documents

Way down at the bottom of the File menu, you'll find a list of documents that you've recently used. You can quickly reopen one of these documents by selecting it from the menu.

By default, the four most recent documents you've opened are listed on the File menu. You can change the number of files listed by following these steps:

1. Call up the Tools⇨Options command.

2. Click on the General tab.

3. Adjust the Entries spin control (located next to the Recently Used File List check box) to indicate how many documents you want listed.

4. Click on OK.

Adding a document to a menu

If you have a few specific documents that you edit all the time, you can add them to a menu. The most natural place to add a specific file is to the File menu, but you can also create a separate menu (I suggest naming it Documents) to hold your commonly used documents.

To add a command that opens a specific document to the File menu, follow these steps:

1. Open the document you want added to the File menu.

2. Call up the Tools⇨Customize command. The Customize dialog box is displayed.

3. Click on the Menus tab.

4. Select File in the Categories list.

5. Select FileOpenFile: in the Commands list.

6. When you select the FileOpenFile: command, a drop-down list box named FileOpenFile: will appear. Make sure that the document you want added to the menu is selected (if more than one document is open when you invoke the Tools⇨Customize command, one of the other documents may be selected). See Figure 8-9.

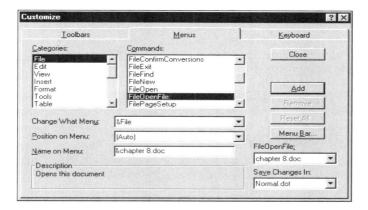

Figure 8-9: Adding a document to a menu.

7. Click the Add button and click Close to dismiss the Customize dialog box.

The document you selected should appear at the bottom of the File menu. For information about how to create a separate menu just for documents, refer back to Chapter 6.

Tip

You can also assign the FileOpenFile: command to a toolbar button or a keyboard shortcut.

Opening Documents Outside of Word

You don't have to start Word before you can open a document. In fact, you can open documents from *outside* of Word by several means. In each case, Windows 95 determines that the document you are trying to open is a Word document and automatically starts Word to edit the document. The various methods for opening a document outside of Word were covered in detail in Chapter 5, so I won't go into them again here.

Finding Lost Files

In Word 6, a separate File⇨Find File command was used to locate documents based on information in the document summary. In Word for Windows 95, the Find File command's capabilities have been enhanced and merged into the File Open dialog box, so Word for Windows 95 no longer offers a separate Find File command.

Simple searches

You can perform simple document searches by using fields that are available right on the File Open dialog box. After you have set the fields to the value you want to search for, click the Find Now button to perform the search. You can also clear the search results to prepare for a new search by clicking on the New Search button.

The following paragraphs describe the basic search fields:

- **File name:** Ordinarily, this field is left blank so that Word will display all of the files in the folder that meet the criteria specified in the File of type, Text or property, and Last modified fields. You can, however, type a wildcard filename in this field to limit the files that are displayed. For example, if you type **bob*** and press the Enter key, only those documents with filenames beginning with the letters *bob* will be displayed.

Tip

In Windows 95, the * wildcard character behaves differently than it did in Windows 3.1. Windows 95 now allows you to use the * wild-card character anywhere in a filename. For example, to display any file that begins with *a* and ends with *z*, type **a*z** in the File name field and press the Enter key. Or, to display any file that has the letters *bob* anywhere in the filename, type ***bob*** in the File name field and press Enter. (The asterisk wild card stands for "zero or more characters," so filenames that begin or end with the letters **bob** will be found.)

Secret

You can also use the File name field to navigate quickly to another location where documents are stored. Simply type an old-fashioned DOS-style path in the File name field. For example, to look in the root directory of drive D:, type **d:** in the File name field and press the Enter key. To display the contents of the Projects folder on drive C:, type **c:\projects** and press Enter.

■ **Files of type:** This field lets you select the type of files to be listed in the File Open dialog box. It contains the following options:

    * All Files (*.*)

    * Word Documents (*.doc)

    * Document Templates (*.dot)

    * Rich Text Format (*.rtf)

    * Text Files (*.txt)

    * Word (Asian Versions) 6.0 - 7.0 (*.doc)

    * Lotus 1-2-3 (*.wk1, *.wk3, *.wk4)

    * Schedule+ Contact List (*.scd)

    * Personal Address Book (*.pab)

    * MS-DOS Text with Layout (*.ans)

    * Text with Layout (*.asc)

    * Windows Write (*.wri)

    * WordPerfect 5.x (*.doc)

    * WordPerfect 6.x (*.doc, *.wpd)

    * Microsoft Excel Worksheet (*.xls, *.xlw)

    * Word 3.x - 5.x for MS-DOS (*.doc)

    * Word 6.0 for MS-DOS (*.doc)

    * RFT-DCA (*.rft)

    * Works 3.0 for Windows (*.wps)

    * Works for MS-DOS 3.0 (*.wps)

    * Works 4.0 for Windows (*.wps)

    * WordStar for Windows 1.0 - 2.0 (*.wsd)

    * WordStar 3.3 - 7.0 (*.ws*)

The Files of type setting is nothing more than a filename filter that shows only files with particular extensions. For example, if you select Word Documents (the default setting), any file with a DOC extension is displayed, whether the file is actually a Word document or not. Several of the file types share a common file extension. For example, Word Documents, Word for MS-DOS, and WordPerfect all use *.doc. Using any of these File type settings will result in the same set of files being displayed.

Furthermore, Word automatically detects the document type if you open a non-Word document and invoke the appropriate conversion routine. So setting the File type field to WordPerfect 5.x doesn't mean that you can open only WordPerfect documents. All it does is limit the files displayed in the File Open document to files with the DOC extension.

- **Te_x_t or property:** This field allows you to display only those documents
  that contain a certain word or phrase. For example, to show only those
  documents that contain *Bud Abbot,* type **Bud Abbot** in the Te_x_t or property
  field. Word searches not only the document text, but the document properties as well. So any documents that were authored by Bud Abbot will be
  displayed as well, even if the name *Bud Abbot* does not appear in the body
  of the document.

- **Last _m_odified:** This drop-down list lets you display only those files that
  have been modified today, yesterday, this week, last week, this month, last
  month, or anytime. The last modified date is updated each time you save a
  document.

Advanced searches

The File Open fields described in the previous sections are usually enough to
locate your documents. For more advanced searches, you can click on the
Advanced button in the File Open dialog box to call up the Advanced Find
dialog box, shown in Figure 8-10.

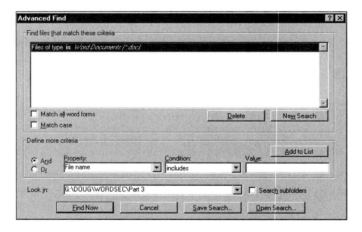

Figure 8-10: The Advanced Find dialog box.

If you're familiar with the Word 6 Find File command, you'll notice right away
that this dialog box represents a radical departure from the way Word 6
handled advanced searches. In Word 6, the Advanced Search dialog box
consisted of three separate tabbed sections that let you fill in search values for
the file location, summary information, and timestamp.

Word for Windows 95 takes a different approach to advanced search criteria. Instead of a series of fill-in-the-blank fields, Word for Windows 95 asks you to build a list of search criteria one line at a time. When you initially call up the Advanced Find dialog box, the first search criteria line is already provided, based on the location information specified in the File Open dialog box. For example, the first search criteria in Figure 8-10 is

`Files of Type is Word Documents (*.doc)`

Most search criteria lines include three items: a property, a condition, and a value. In the previous example, the property is `Files of Type`, the condition is `is`, and the value is `Word Documents (*.doc)`.

You can add additional lines to the search criteria. For example, to search for files that were created on or after April 1, 1995, you would add this line:

`Creation Date on or after Saturday, April 1, 1995`

You can add additional lines to the search criteria by following this procedure:

1. If the criteria list contains more than one line, click on the line after which you want to add the new line.

2. Select the property you want to match from the Property drop-down list box. Table 8-1 lists the properties you can search for. To search for a property that isn't in the list (such as a custom property), just type the property name.

3. Select the condition from the Condition drop-down list box. The conditions available in this list box vary depending on which property is selected. Table 8-2 lists the condition settings available for various Property types.

4. Type a value in the Value field, if appropriate. Some property/condition combinations do not require values. See the section "Using special search characters" later in this chapter for details about typing values into this field.

5. Select the And or Or radio button. If you select And, both the criteria you are adding and the previous criteria must be met for the file to be selected. If you select Or, either the criteria you are adding or the previous criteria must be met. For a complete explanation of how these options work, see the section "Understanding And and Or."

6. Click on Add to List. The criteria will be added to the list.

Table 8-1	Properties for Advanced Searches	
Property	*Type*	*Source*
Application name	Text	The name of the application that created the file
Author	Text	File⇨Properties Summary tab
Category	Text	File⇨Properties Summary tab
Comments	Text	File⇨Properties Summary tab
Company	Text	File⇨Properties Summary tab
Contents	Text	File⇨Properties Contents tab
Creation date	Date	File⇨Properties Statistics tab
Filename	Text	File⇨Properties General tab
Files of type	Text	File⇨Properties General tab
Format	Text	???
Hidden slides	Number	PowerPoint documents
Keywords	Text	File⇨Properties Summary tab
Last author	Text	???
Last modified	Date	File⇨Properties Statistics tab
Last printed	Date	File⇨Properties Statistics tab
Last saved by	Text	The name of the user who last saved the file
Lines	Number	File⇨Properties Statistics tab
Manager	Text	File⇨Properties Summary tab
Multimedia Clips	Number	PowerPoint documents
Notes	Number	PowerPoint documents
Number of characters	Number	File⇨Properties Statistics tab
Number of pages	Number	File⇨Properties Statistics tab
Number of words	Number	File⇨Properties Statistics tab
Paragraphs	Number	File⇨Properties Statistics tab
Revision	Text	File⇨Properties Statistics tab
Security	Text	???
Size	Number	File⇨Properties General tab
Slides	Number	PowerPoint documents
Subject	Text	File⇨Properties Summary tab
Template	Text	File⇨Properties Summary tab
Text or property	\Text	Document text
Title	Text	File⇨Properties Summary tab
Total edit time	Number	File⇨Properties Statistics tab

Table 8-2	Conditions for Advanced Searches
Condition	*Explanation*
Text fields	
Includes	The field must contain the text specified in the Value field. This is equivalent to placing an asterisk (*) wildcard before and after the value.
Begins with	The field must begin with the text specified in the Value field. This is equivalent to placing an asterisk (*) wildcard after the value.
Ends with	The field must end with the text. This is equivalent to placing an asterisk (*) wild card before the value.
Numeric fields	
Equals	The field must match the value exactly.
Does not equal	Any value other than the specified value is accepted.
Any number between	Lets you specify a range of values. In the Value field, you should specify the low and high values separated by the word *and*. For example, *10 and 100*.
At most	The same as the familiar Less Than Or Equal To (< =) operator.
At least	The same as the familiar Greater Than Or Equal To (> =) operator.
More than	The same as the familiar Greater Than (>) operator.
Less than	The same as the familiar Less Than (<) operator.
Date fields	
Yesterday	The date matches yesterday's date.
Today	The date matches today's date.
Last Week	The date is from the previous week.
This Week	The date is from the current week.
Last Month	The date is from the previous month.
This Month	The date is from the current month.
Any time	The date doesn't matter.
Anytime between	The date falls within a range of dates. The Value field should specify two dates separated by *and*. For example, *01/01/95 and 12/31/95*.
On	The date matches a specific date value.
On or after	The date matches or follows a specific date value.
On or before	The date matches or precedes a specific date value.
In the last	Lets you specify a date or time range, such as *30 days* or *2 hours*.

To remove a line from the search criteria, click on the line to select it and click the Del button. Notice that the settings for the line you deleted are placed in the Property, Condition, and Value fields so that you can use them as the starting point for a new line. Although there is no way to edit a criteria line directly, you can edit a line by deleting it, making whatever changes need to be made, and clicking the Add to List button to add the line back.

After you have set up the search, you must click Find Now to perform the search.

The following paragraphs describe four other Advanced Find controls:

- **Match all word forms:** If you check this check box, Word uses the same word-form matching routine that is available in the Edit⇨Find command. Thus, if you select Match all word forms and search for documents containing the word *run*, documents containing *ran, runs,* and *running* will be located as well.

- **Match case:** Normally, Word disregards case when searching files. For example, if you search for files containing the word *Bozo,* files containing *Bozo, BOZO, bozo,* or even *bOzO* would be found. If you check the Match case check box, the case must match exactly as you typed it. Thus, Word would find files that contain only the word *Bozo,* with only the *B* capitalized.

- **Look in:** This list box works the same as the Look in control in the File Open dialog box.

- **Search subfolders:** If you check this check box, Word searches not only in the folder specified in the Look in field, but in any of that folder's subfolders as well.

Note

Although the Advanced Find dialog box does not include the File name, Files of type, Text or property, or Last modified fields found in the File Open dialog box, these options are available as items in the Property drop-down list box. When you call up the Advanced Find dialog box, any entries you've made for those fields are translated into search criteria lines. For example, if you specified **bob** for the File name field, *Word Documents (*.doc)* for the Files of type field, *delinquent* for the Text or property field, and *Yesterday* for the Last modified field, and you clicked on Advanced, Word would preset the following criteria lines:

```
File Name includes bob
Files of Type is Word Documents (*.doc)
Text or Property includes delinquent
Last Modified yesterday
```

Understanding And and Or

Advanced Find has provisions that search for files that meet two or more conditions, such as files created on or before 12/31/94 and containing the word *Johnson*. You can also search for files that meet either of two conditions. For example, you might want to list files that were created on or before 12/31/94 or that have *John Smith* listed as the author.

As you add lines to the search criteria, Word assumes that you want to search for files that match all of the criteria you specify. For example, suppose that I wanted to search for any document that contains a chapter I've written about Microsoft Word. I could set up the following search criteria:

```
Files of Type is Word Documents (*.doc)
Author includes Doug Lowe
Keywords includes Word
```

In this example, Word will search for files that meet all three of the criteria listed. In other words, the file must be a Word document, the author must be *Doug Lowe,* and the Keywords property must include *Word*. If even one of these criteria is not met, the file will not be included in the search results. (Of course, for this search to be effective, I would have to be diligent about setting the Keywords property whenever I create new documents.

On the other hand, suppose that I want to search for documents I've written about Word or PowerPoint. In that case, I could set up the following search criteria:

```
Files of Type is Word Documents (*.doc)
Author includes Doug Lowe
Keywords includes Word
 OR: Keywords includes PowerPoint
```

In this search, Word would find Word documents with *Doug Lowe* listed as the author and *Word* or *PowerPoint* listed as a keyword.

To switch from And to Or when adding search criteria, click on the Or button in the Define More Criteria group. To revert to And, click on the And button.

Using special search characters

You can use special characters in the Value field when you set up search criteria. Table 8-3 lists the various characters you can use. The first two (* and ?) are wildcard characters that work just like they do in filenames. The other special characters let you create more advanced searches.

Table 8-3	Special Search Characters
Character	**What It Does**
*	A multiple-character wildcard. Any combination of characters, including no characters at all, will match the wildcard. For example, *b*b* will match *bob*, *bard*, *board*, and so on.
?	A single-character wildcard. Any single character matches the wild card. For example, *b?b* matches *bib, bob, bab,* and so on.
& or space	Tells Word to look for files that contain both the word listed before the ampersand or space and the word listed after the ampersand or space. For example, if you search for *billy bob* or *billy & bob*, the document must contain both *billy* and *bob* to be matched.
,	Tells Word to look for files that contain either the word listed before the comma or the word listed after the comma. For example, if you search for *billy, bob*, Word finds all documents that contain the word *billy* or the word *bob*.
~	Tells Word to look for files that do *not* have the word that follows the tilde. For example, *~Clinton* means to look for files that do not include the word *Clinton*.
" "	Tells Word to treat the characters that fall within the quotes as a single word. This is the proper way to search for a phrase rather than a single word. For example, to search for documents that contain the phrase "Who laid the rails," enclose the phrase in quotes. Otherwise, Word will interpret the spaces between the words as And operators, causing it to find any document that contains the words *Who, laid, the,* and *rails*.

Tip

Using the search characters listed in Table 8-3 can eliminate the need to create multiple search criteria lines. For example, I previously showed a search criteria that used two lines to search for files with *Word* or *PowerPoint* listed as keywords. You could perform same search as follows:

```
Files of Type is Word Documents (*.doc)
Author includes Doug Lowe
Keywords includes Word, PowerPoint
```

Warning

Be careful when using special characters in complex search criteria that includes OR conditions. You can easily yourself twist into knots and wind up creating a search that makes no sense. For example, see if you can guess what the following criteria does:

```
Files of Type is Word Documents (*.doc)
Author includes Tommy Smith
OR: Author includes ~Mary Jones
```

This search will find any document that was written by Tommy Smith, plus any document that was *not* written by Mary Jones. Because any document that was written by Tommy Smith was obviously *not* written by Mary Jones, the first Author criteria is redundant. The following search would achieve identical results:

```
Files of Type is Word Documents (*.doc)
Author includes ~Mary Jones
```

If you're not careful, you can create searches that can't possibly find any documents. Here is a simple example:

```
Files of Type is Word Documents (*.doc)
Keywords includes Bogota ~Bogota
```

Obviously, a file cannot both contain and not contain the word *Bogota*.

Saving searches

If you find yourself repeating the same searches, you can save the search so that you don't have set it up again each time you need to use it. After you have saved a search, you can rerun it at any time by calling up the File⇨Open command, clicking the Commands and Settings button, selecting the Saved Searches command, and choosing the saved search you want to run.

To save a search, follow these steps:

1. Call up the File⇨Open command and click the Advanced button.

2. Set up the search criteria exactly the way you want it saved.

3. Click the Save Search button. The dialog box shown in Figure 8-11 will appear.

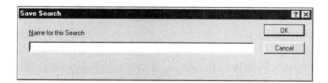

Figure 8-11: The Save Search dialog box.

4. Type the name you want the search saved under. Use a name that describes the documents found by the search, such as "Letters to Wilson."

5. Click on OK.

Using the Save As Command

The Save As command saves a new file or an existing file under a different name. There are two ways you can summon this command:

■ Choose the File⇨Save As command from the menus.

■ Press F12.

You can also invoke the Save As command by using the Save command for any document that has not yet been saved to disk:

- Choose the File⇨Save command from the menus for a document that has not yet been saved to disk.

- Click on the Save button in the Standard toolbar for a document that has not yet been saved to disk.

- Press Ctrl+S or Shift+F12 for a file that has not yet been saved to disk. Ctrl+S is easy to remember because "S" stands for Save.

Figure 8-12 shows the Save As dialog box, displayed when you invoke the Save As command. As you can see, this dialog box shares many features and controls with the File Open dialog box.

Figure 8-12: The Save As dialog box.

To save a document, call up the Save As command, navigate to the folder where you want to save the document, type a new name for the document, and click on the Save button.

If you want to replace an existing document with the current document, double-click on the document you want replaced. Word will display a dialog box asking whether you really want to replace the document. If you click on Yes, the existing document will be overwritten by the document you are editing.

Tip

When you first call up the Save As dialog box, Word takes a wild guess that the text in the first paragraph of the document should be used as the filename. This makes sense if the first paragraph is the title of the document, but, more often than not, you'll want to type a more sensible document name.

Like the File Open dialog box, the Save As dialog box contains several buttons. The following paragraphs describe the function of each of these buttons:

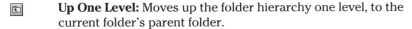 **Up One Level:** Moves up the folder hierarchy one level, to the current folder's parent folder.

Look in Favorites: Calls up the \Windows\Favorites folder. For a more complete discussion of the Favorites folder, refer back to the section titled "Playing favorites" earlier in this chapter.

Create New Folder: Creates a new folder as a subfolder of the current folder. You will be prompted to type a name for the new folder.

List: Displays a list of folders and documents with icons. This is the default view, which was shown back in Figure 8-12.

Detail: Displays a list of folders and documents with details, including the filename, type, size, and creation date.

Properties: Displays a panel showing various properties for the selected file, including Title, Author, Template, Word count, and other useful information.

Commands and Settings: Displays a menu listing several commands that can be applied to the selected folder or document.

Notice that the Save As dialog box also includes a Save as type list box. Normally, this field is set to Word Document (*.doc) so that documents are stored in Word format. You can change this setting to save a document in another format.

Warning

Not all file types support all of Word's formatting features. Any special formatting that isn't supported by the file type will be lost when you save the file. So if you're going to save your masterpiece in one of these formats, you may want to keep a version in Word format, too.

Why Doesn't My Save As Command Work?

If you are having trouble saving documents, you may have contracted a unique virus that has surfaced recently. Unlike other viruses, which infect program files, this virus attacks Word documents. It takes advantage of the fact that Word allows you to use an AutoOpen macro that is automatically executed whenever a document is opened. The Word virus hides itself in an AutoOpen macro. Then, when you open an infected document, the virus transfers itself into your Normal.dot template, where it infects new documents you create.

One of the symptoms of this virus is that the Save As command begins to misbehave: It won't allow you to change the document format. That's because the virus actually changes your documents to templates. Once a document has been converted to a template, you cannot use the Save As command to change it to another document format.

For more information about this virus, consult Appendix B. There, you will find instructions about how to tell if you have been infected and how to purge your Word files of the virus.

The Save All Command

The File➪Save All command saves all open documents. If you are working on several files at once, this command saves you the hassle of switching to each document window and saving the document. (Save All will also save any open templates.)

Save Options

If you click on the Options button on the Save As dialog box or if you use the Tools➪Options command and click on the Save tab, you'll see the dialog box shown in Figure 8-13. This dialog box controls the settings for several options that affect how documents are saved.

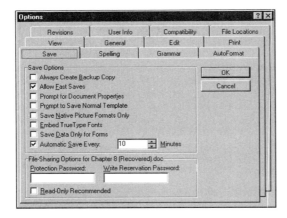

Figure 8-13: The Save Options dialog box.

The following paragraphs describe the effect each of these options has:

■ **Always Create Backup Copy:** If this option is selected, Word always saves the previous version of the document as a backup copy each time it saves the document. The backup copy uses the extension BAK.

Warning

Do not rely on the Always Create Backup Copy option as your only backup of important documents. The backup copy created by this option resides on the same drive and in the same folder as the document itself. As a result, if a disk failure or other problem renders the drive or folder inaccessible, the backup copy will be inaccessible as well. Always back up important documents to a separate disk drive or to tape.

■ **Allow Fast Saves:** If you work with large documents that take a long time to save, you can select the Allow Fast Saves option to speed things up. This option tells Word to save only those parts of the document that have changed since the last time the document was saved. The changes are written to the end of the document file.

The disadvantages of Fast Saves are twofold. First, although the Fast Saves feature makes it faster to save files, it becomes correspondingly slower to open files. Second, the size of the document increases each time you save it with Fast Saves enabled because changes to the document are written to the end of the file.

■ **Prompt for Document Properties:** If you want to use document properties, such as summary and keyword information, you should enable this option. Then whenever you save a file for the first time, Word will prompt you for the summary information.

■ **Prompt to Save Normal Template:** This option forces Word to ask for your permission before saving changes to the Normal.dot template. If you're concerned about proliferating changes to this template, enable this option.

■ **Save Native Picture Formats Only:** Saves only the Windows version of imported graphics.

■ **Embed TrueType Fonts:** Saves TrueType fonts in the document file. This increases the size of the document file but enables you to copy the file to another system without worrying about whether the other system has the fonts that are used in the document. If your document uses only the basic Times New Roman and Arial fonts, if you don't plan on using the document on another system, or if you're sure the other system has all the fonts used by the document, don't bother with this option.

■ **Save Data Only for Forms:** Saves just the data for a form. This is useful if you create a new document based on a template that includes a form, and then you want to save just the data, not the form itself. For more information about forms, see Chapter 29.

■ **Automatic Save Every *n* Minutes:** This option automatically saves your document at regular intervals. The default setting is to save the document every 10 minutes, but you can change the time interval if you wish. For more information, see the following section, "Using AutoSave."

Using AutoSave

The AutoSave function is enabled by the Automatic Save Every *n* Minutes check box in the Tools⇨Options Save command. This option works differently than you might expect. Rather than automatically issue the equivalent of a File⇨Save command each time the AutoSave interval elapses, the AutoSave option saves a special recovery version of the document in a separate folder.

The AutoSave file is normally stored in the folder indicated by the system TEMP variable (usually, C:\TEMP) and uses the file extension ASD (for AutoSave Document). The filename itself is generated automatically and is usually something meaningless, such as ~WRAD418.

The ASD file is used whenever Word restarts itself after a failure, such as a power loss or if Windows crashes. You can tell that Word has used the ASD file by looking at the title bar: The word *(Recovered)* will appear after the document name.

Tip

The use of AutoSave does not preclude the need to save your work frequently. Keep in mind that AutoSave does *not* save changes to your document file. It is designed only to facilitate recovery should your computer crash. You should still be in the habit of pressing Ctrl+S every few minutes as you work so that your latest changes are permanently committed to disk.

Secret

AutoSave and Word's attempts at document recovery are not always perfect. In fact, I usually find that after a system failure, the original copy of my documents are more current that the AutoSave versions that Word tries to use for recovery. Unfortunately, determining whether the AutoSave document is more current than the original document is not as easy as it should be because Word won't let you open the original document without first saving the restored AutoSave file. Here's how I resolve this dilemma:

1. Save the recovered AutoSave file by using the Save As command. For the new filename, I use the word *Recovered* followed by the original filename. Thus, the recovered version of Chapter 8.doc would be Recovered Chapter 8.doc.

2. Open the original saved document (for example, Chapter 8.doc).

3. Compare the original saved document (Chapter 8.doc) with the recovered AutoSave file (Recovered Chapter 8.doc) to see which one is more current. If the AutoSave file is more current, close the original document and use the Save As command to save the recovered AutoSave file by using the original document name, replacing the outdated original document.

Using the AutoBackup Macros

Word comes with two macros that extend the backup capabilities of the Save and Save As commands by always storing *two* copies of each document, one to serve as a backup copy. This is not the same thing as the Always Create Backup Copy option, which saves the *previous* version of the document using BAK as the file extension. The AutoBackup macros save a second copy of the document in a folder you specify. The backup folder can be on the same drive, or it can be on a different drive, including a disk drive or a network drive.

To use the AutoBackup macros, you must first load the Macro70.dot template as a global template with the File⇨Template command. Then you can run the EnableAutoBackup macro by using the Tools⇨Macro command. When you do, you'll be prompted to enter the location for your backup files. Type the drive and path where you want the backup files stored and press Enter.

The EnableAutoBackup macro creates two macros, named FileSave and FileSaveAs. These macros effectively replace the built-in FileSave and FileSaveAs commands. Here is what the FileSave macro looks like:

```
Sub MAIN

On Error Goto CANCELLED

FileSave

Backdir$

=GetPrivateProfileString$
("HKEY_CURRENT_USER\Software
\Microsoft\Word\7.0\Options",
"BAK-PATH", "")

If
UCase$(FileNameInfo$(FileName$(),
5)) = UCase$(backdir$)
```

```
Then

MsgBox "You have AutoBackup en-
abled and are attempting to save a
file into your backup directory.
A copy will not be created.", 64

Goto CANCELLED :

EndIf

CopyFile
FileNameInfo$(FileName$(),1),
Backdir$

CANCELLED:

End Sub
```

This macro starts by saving the file by using the built-in FileSave command. Then, it retrieves the backup folder location from the registry (it was put there by the EnableAutoBackup macro) and runs a CopyFile command to copy the document to the backup location. The FileSaveAs macro is similar.

The EnableAutoBackup macro also adds a new command to the File menu: Disable Auto Backup. When you run this command, the Disable AutoBackup macro runs. This macro, in turn, deletes the FileSave and FileSaveAs macros. As an added bonus, it replaces the Disable Auto Backup command with an Enable Auto Backup command, so you can reinstate AutoBackup without going through the Tools⇨Macro command again.

Password protecting your files

Word allows you to protect your sensitive files from snooping eyes by using passwords. You can apply two types of passwords to your documents:

■ A Protection Password prevents users who do not know the password from opening the file. Use this password for files that you don't want unauthorized users to examine.

■ A Write Reservation Password prevents users who do not know the password from saving the file. Use this password for files that you don't want unauthorized users to modify.

To password protect a document, follow these steps:

1. Open the document.

2. Call up the Tools⇨Options command and click the Save tab.

3. Type the password in the Protection Password or Write Reservation Password field (or both, if you want to provide a different password for each type of access). Word displays asterisks as you type the password. This prevents Looky-Lous from seeing your password as you type it.

4. When Word prompts you to reenter the password, type it again, exactly as you did the first time.

5. Click OK.

6. Save the file.

After the file is password protected, Word will prompt you (or anyone else) to enter the password before allowing you to open the document with the dialog box shown in Figure 8-14.

Figure 8-14: The Password dialog box.

Here are some tips for working with passwords:

- Do not forget your password! If you forget, there is no way to access your data.

- Don't use different passwords for every document. You'll never remember them all. Instead, use the same password for all your documents.

- Do not write your password down on a Post-It note and stick it on your computer monitor.

- Use a password you already know, such as your network login password. That way, you don't have to remember an extra password.

- Don't use obvious passwords, such as your kids' names, your spouse's name, your dog's name, or the name of your boat.

To remove password protection from a file, open the file (you'll have to supply the password to do it), call up the Tools⇨Options command, click Save, highlight, and delete the password. Click OK and save the file.

Chapter 9

Printing Your Documents

In This Chapter

▶ Printing documents using the Print button

▶ Printing documents using the Print command, which allows you to control settings, such as the number of copies to be printed, which pages should be printed, and so on

▶ Setting up a convenient macro that adds extra functions to the Print button

▶ Telling Word what printer you want to use when you have more than one printer available

▶ Adding a new printer to your computer

▶ Setting printer properties and print options

▶ Using the Print Preview feature to check your document's formatting before committing it to paper

▶ Printing envelopes and labels

▶ Faxing a document

▶ Managing print jobs once you've sent them to the printer

Printing is one of the main reasons most of us even bother to use our computers. After all, what would be the point in carefully crafting a Word document, spreadsheet, or database report if we couldn't create a printed copy of our work to show off to our friends and colleagues?

Unfortunately, printing is also one of the most frustrating aspects of using a computer. Even seemingly simple documents, such as one-page memos, can look great on the screen but come out of the printer looking terrible.

The good news is that printing is dramatically improved in Word for Windows 95. Windows 95 itself has improved printing features. Microsoft completely rewrote most of the printing subsystem for Windows 95 (well, okay, it borrowed some from Windows NT). The dreaded Print Manager is long gone, replaced by a sophisticated 32-bit print spooler that you can control simply by clicking on desktop printer icons. And, many of the hassles of installing and configuring printers under Windows 3.1 are eliminated by the new Plug and Play feature, which can often automatically recognize and configure a printer immediately after you plug it in to the computer.

The printing features of Word itself have been improved, too. Background printing is now handled as a separate thread — a technique that improves performance and stability and simply wasn't possible under Windows 3.1. In addition, Microsoft has worked to correct many of the irritating little bugs that plagued printing in Word 6.

Printing can still be an iffy proposition in Word for Windows 95, however, especially if you do anything unusual, such as try to print a page loaded with graphics on a printer that doesn't have much memory. And, you'd better make sure your hair is firmly attached before trying to print envelopes.

Printing Your Document

 The easiest way to print a document is to click the Print button that appears in the Standard toolbar. Clicking this button prints a single copy of your entire document. This simple little button handles probably 90 percent of most people's printing needs (including my own). The rest of this chapter is devoted to that other troublesome 10 percent.

Tip

Actually, saying the Print button prints a single copy of an entire document isn't quite accurate. The Print button invokes the Print command using the current settings in the Print dialog box. Thus, if you use the File⇨Print command to print 10 copies of a document, the next time you use the Print button, 10 copies of the document will be printed. Anytime you use the File⇨Print command to change the print settings, be sure to change them back to their default values before using the Print button during the same Word session. (After you exit Word, the Print dialog box settings are restored to their defaults the next time you start Word.)

Using the Print command

If you need to print anything other than a single copy of an entire document, you'll need to bring up the Print dialog box. You can do that in one of two ways:

- Use the File⇨Print command.
- Press Ctrl+P.

This brings up the Print dialog box, as shown in Figure 9-1.

Printing more than one copy

You can print more than one copy of a document by setting the Number of copies field to the number of copies you want printed.

Tip

If you are printing more than one copy of a document that contains complex graphics, you might want to uncheck the Collate option. When unchecked, the Collate option prints multiple copies of each page. For example, if you print three copies uncollated, you'll get three copies of page 1, followed by three copies of page 2, and so on.

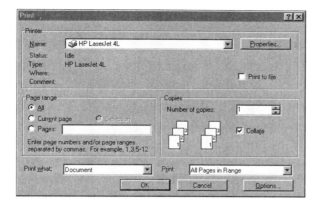

Figure 9-1: The Print dialog box.

When the print job is done, you'll have to sort out the pages manually, but the improvement in printing time might make up for the extra time spent sorting pages. Why? Because most printers can print multiple copies of a single page at the printer's maximum rated speed, no matter how long it took to print the first copy of the page. For example, the printer may spend 15 minutes figuring out how to print the first copy of a complex page, but the second and third copies will print almost immediately. When checked, the Collate option prints each copy of the document separately. If one of the pages has a particularly complicated graphic that takes 15 minutes to print, you'll spend a total of 45 minutes waiting for the printer to print that page for each copy of the document.

Printing the current page

Word's default printing behavior prints all of the pages in the current document, but you can change this default to print a single page or a range of pages.

To print a single page, follow these steps:

1. Place the insertion point anywhere in the page you want to print.
2. Press Ctrl+P or use the File⇨Print command to call up the Print dialog box.
3. Click on the Current page option button.
4. Click on OK.

Printing a range of pages

To print a range of pages

1. Press Ctrl+P or use the File⇨Print command to call up the Print dialog box.

2. Type the page range in the Pages text box. For example, to print the first four pages of the document, enter **1-4** in the Pages field. To print a single page, just type the page number. There is no need to concoct a one-page range (**3-3**, for example) to print a single page.

3. Click OK.

Note

You can print more than one range of pages by separating the page ranges with commas. For example, if you enter **1-3,11-15,19,22-25**, you'll print pages 1, 2, 3, 11, 12, 13, 14, 15, 19, 22, 23, 24, and 25. The only rule is that the numbers have to be in order. For example, you could not specify 1-3, 19, 11-15, 22-25.

Secret

If your document contains sections that have their own page numbering, you can refer to these sections by typing the letter **s** followed by the section number immediately following a page number. Although it is not required, you can also use the letter **p** to differentiate page number from section numbers. For example, both **1s2** and **p1s2** means page 1 of section 2.

To print a range of pages in a section, specify the section on both the first and last page in the range. For example, to print pages 1-5 of section 2, type **p1s2-p5s2** in the Page field.

To print an entire section, type the letter **s** followed by the section number. For example, **s3** prints all of the third section.

Printing selected text

You can also print a specific selection of text. Follow these steps:

1. Highlight the text you want to print. The text can be less than one page, or it can span multiple pages. It does not have to begin at the top of a page or end at the bottom of a page.

2. Press Ctrl+P or choose the File⇨Print command to bring up the Print dialog box.

3. Click the Selection option button. (This button is available only if a range of text is selected when you call up the Print command.)

4. Click OK.

Note

Word does not maintain the text's positioning on the page when printing a selection of text. In other words, even though the selected text might fall in the middle of the page, Word prints the selection starting at the top of the page.

Printing even and odd pages

If you want to print, say, all the odd-numbered pages of a document, use the Print list box to choose Odd Pages. Do the same for even-numbered pages.

Printing document information

The Print what list box lets you print information about your document rather than the document itself. The Print what list box includes the following options:

- **Document:** Prints the contents of the document. This is the default choice.

- **Summary Info:** Prints the summary information displayed by the File⇨Properties command, such as the author's name, document title, and so on. You can also include summary information with every printout by choosing the Tools⇨Options command, clicking on the Print tab, and selecting the Summary Info option as shown in Figure 9-2.

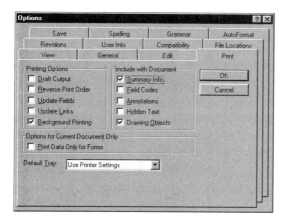

Figure 9-2: The Print Options dialog box.

- **Annotations:** Prints annotations separately from the document. To print annotations together with the document, choose the Tools⇨Options command, click on the Print tab, and select the Annotations option.

- **Styles:** Prints a description of the styles stored in the document.

- **AutoText Entries:** Prints the AutoText entries for the document.

- **Key Assignments:** Prints the custom keyboard assignments that are available for the document.

Printing to a file

In some instances, you might want to save printed output in a file rather than send it directly to a printer. The most common reason for doing this is if you want to use a printer that is attached to another computer, and the other computer does not have a copy of Word for Windows 95. The print to file feature allows you to create a special *print file,* transfer the file to the other printer (usually via diskette), and send the print file to the other computer's printer.

To print to a file, follow these steps:

1. Choose the File⊏⊅Print command or press Ctrl+P to bring up the Print dialog box.

2. Select the printer where you ultimately will print the file.

Note

It is very important that you select the correct printer driver for the printer that will eventually print the file. Otherwise, the printer will probably not be able to print the file properly.

3. Click the Print to file check box.

4. Click OK. The Print to File dialog box will appear, as shown in Figure 9-3.

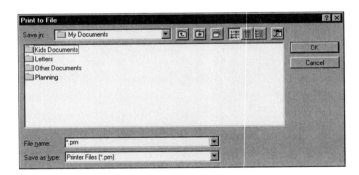

Figure 9-3: The Print to File dialog box.

5. Type the name of the file you want to create. The default extension for the file is PRN.

6. Click on OK.

You can print the created file to any printer that matches the printer selected when you created the print file. You can even print it on a computer that does not have Windows 95 installed.

To print the file on a computer running Windows 3.1

1. Start File Manager, or switch to File Manager if it is already running.

2. Choose the File⊏⊅Copy command, or press F8.

3. In the From field, type the complete filename and path for the print file.

4. In the To field, type **LPT1** if the printer is attached to the first printer port (most are). If the printer is attached to the second or third printer port, type **LPT2** or **LPT3**.

5. Click OK.

To print the file from an MS-DOS prompt, type **copy *filename* LPT1:**

Unfortunately, you cannot directly print a print file by using Windows 95. This is a feature that the designers of Word for Windows 95 allowed for, but the Windows 95 developers didn't. However, there is a workaround you can use that will allow you to print print files in Windows 95:

1. Create an MS-DOS batch file named PRINTER.BAT that contains the following line:

   ```
   copy %1 lpt1:
   ```

   To create this batch file, start Notepad (located in the Start⇨Programs⇨Accessories menu) and type the preceding Copy command. Then, use the File⇨Save command to save the file in the \Windows\Command folder and use the File⇨Exit command to close Notepad.

2. Open a My Computer or Explorer window and navigate to the \Windows\Command folder, right-click the Printer.bat file, and choose the Properties command. When the Properties dialog box appears, click the Program tab.

3. Change the Run list box to Minimized and click the Close on exit check box. See Figure 9-4.

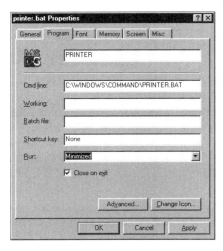

Figure 9-4: Properties for the PRINTER.BAT batch file.

4. Click OK.

5. Back in the Explorer or My Computer window, choose the View⇨Options command, and click on the File Types tab. The dialog box shown in Figure 9-5 will appear.

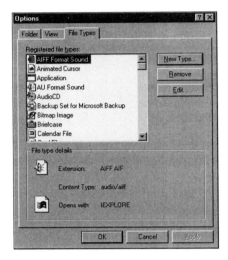

Figure 9-5: The File Types tab of the Options dialog box.

6. Click the New Type button. The Add New File Type dialog box will appear, as shown in Figure 9-6.

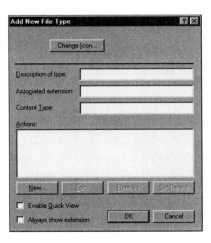

Figure 9-6: The Add New File Type dialog box.

7. Type **Print File** in the Description of type field.

8. Type **PRN** in the Associated extension field.

9. Click on the New button. The New Action dialog box will appear as shown in Figure 9-7.

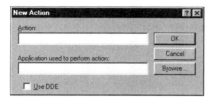

Figure 9-7: The New Action dialog box.

10. Type **print** in the Action field.

11. In the Application used to perform action field, type **c:\windows\command\printer.bat**.

12. Click on OK to return to the New Action dialog box.

13. Click on the Change Icon button. A list of icons will appear; select one you think is fitting for print files. Figure 9-8 shows the one I prefer.

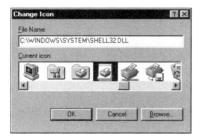

Figure 9-8: Selecting an icon for print files.

14. Click on OK and then click on Close twice.

This workaround lets you send print files to the printer much as you would print any other type of document. You can right-click on the print file's icon and select Print from the quick menu, or you can drag the print file's icon to a printer icon. (It's not a perfect solution, however. For example, if you drag the print file to a printer icon, Windows 95 will change the default printer to the one where you drag the file.)

A macro for the Print button

If you like the Print button but wish it had a bit more functionality, the following macro, named ShiftPrint, may be just what you need. If you replace the standard Print button with a button assigned to this macro, you'll have the following options:

■ Click the ShiftPrint button to print a single copy of the entire document, the same as when you click the standard Print button.

■ Hold down the Shift key and click the ShiftPrint button to call up the Print dialog box.

■ Hold down the Ctrl key and click the ShiftPrint button to print the current page.

Macro

The macro itself is fairly simple:

```
Declare Function GetAsyncKeyState Lib "user32"(nVirtKey As Long) As
Integer
Sub MAIN
On Error Goto UserCancel
If GetAsyncKeyState(16) < 0 Then
    Dim dlg As FilePrint
    GetCurValues dlg
    Dialog dlg
    FilePrint dlg
Else
    If GetAsyncKeyState(17) < 0 Then
        Dim dlg As FilePrint
        GetCurValues dlg
        dlg.Range = 2
        FilePrint dlg
    Else
        FilePrintDefault
    End If
End If
UserCancel:
End Sub
```

The Declare Function statement at the beginning of the macro must come *before* the Sub MAIN statement.

If you don't want to bother typing this macro in, you'll find it in the Word for Windows 95 SECRETS Sample Macros.dot template that is on the CD-ROM that accompanies this book.

Secret

This macro illustrates the technique for determining whether a key such as Shift or Ctrl is pressed by using the Windows API GetAsyncKeyState function. This, of course, has nothing to do with printing, but if you're into WordBasic coding, you might find this technique useful.

Selecting a Different Printer

Windows 95 designates one of your printers as your default printer, the one to which documents are printed unless you specify otherwise. Many users have more than one printer available to them (for example, a local printer and one or more network printers). If you have more than one printer available, you need to know how to print to a printer other than the default printer. Here's the procedure:

1. Call up the File⇨Print command.

2. Select the printer you want to use in the Name list.

3. Set any other print options you need.

4. Click OK.

 This procedure is a substantial improvement over Word 6, where you couldn't change the printer name from the File⇨Print command. Instead, you had to call up the File⇨Print command and click the Printer button to call up a separate dialog box that allowed you to change the printer. Now, you can change the printer directly from the Print dialog box.

How to change the default printer

If you find yourself selecting a different printer more often than not, you may want to change your default printer. Here is the procedure:

1. In the Windows 95 Start menu, select the Settings command and choose Printers. The Printers folder will appear, as shown in Figure 9-9.

Figure 9-9: The Printers folder.

2. Double-click on the printer you want to make the default printer. A Printer window such as the one shown in Figure 9-10 will appear.

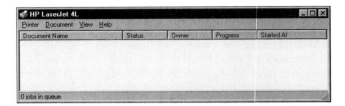

Figure 9-10: A printer window for a Hewlett-Packard HP LaserJet 4L printer.

3. Choose the Printer⇨Set as default command.

4. Close the printer window and the Printers folder by clicking on the close box (the X in the top-right corner of the window).

Adding a printer

If you install a new printer on your computer, you must setup the printer in Windows 95 before you can print to it. You do that from Start\Settings\Printers. Get your Windows 95 CD or diskettes ready and then follow this procedure:

1. In the Start menu, select the Settings command and select Printers. The Printers folder will appear. (It was illustrated in Figure 9-9.)

2. Double-click on the Add Printer icon. This starts a Wizard that leads you step by step through the process of adding a printer. Figure 9-11 shows the first screen displayed by the Add Printer Wizard.

Figure 9-11: The Add Printer Wizard welcome screen.

3. Click Next>. The Add Printer Wizard asks for the make and model of the printer you want to add, as shown in Figure 9-12.

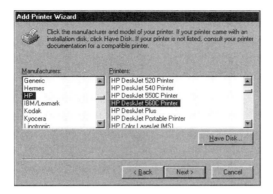

Figure 9-12: The Add Printer Wizard asks what kind of printer you want to add.

4. Select the manufacturer of your printer from the Manufacturers list and then select the printer model from the Printers list. In Figure 9-12, I selected HP (Hewlett-Packard) as the Manufacturer and HP DeskJet 560C Printer as the Printer. (You can quickly move your way through the list of printer manufacturers by typing the first letter of the manufacturer you want to see.)

Note

If the printer you want to add does not appear in the list, you'll have to add the printer by using the installation disk that came with the printer. Insert the disk in the floppy disk drive and click Have Disk.

5. When you've selected the proper printer, click Next>, to proceed. The Add Printer Wizard next asks which port the printer is attached to, as shown in Figure 9-13. Most printers will be attached to the LPT1: port. If your computer is equipped with two printer ports, you'll have to choose between LPT1: and LPT2:.

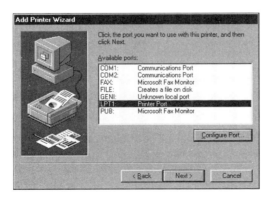

Figure 9-13: The Add Printer Wizard asks to which port the printer is attached.

Note

If you are installing a printer driver for a printer you don't actually have, you can select FILE: as the printer port. This is similar to selecting Print to File in Word's Print dialog box, except that when you select FILE: as the printer port, Windows 95 *always* prints to a file when you print to this printer.

6. Click Next> to proceed. The Add Printer Wizard next asks for a name for the printer, as shown in Figure 9-14.

Figure 9-14: The Add Printer Wizard asks for a name.

7. If you don't like the name suggested by Windows 95, change it. You can also elect to have the new printer set as the default printer by clicking the Yes option button.

8. When you're ready, click Next>. The Add Printer Wizard offers to print a test page, as shown in Figure 9-15.

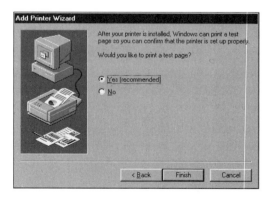

Figure 9-15: The Add Printer Wizard offers to print a test page.

9. If you want to print the test page, select <u>Y</u>es. If you don't (for example, if the printer isn't yet physically installed), click <u>N</u>o.

10. Click Finish to complete the installation of the printer. The Add Printer Wizard may ask you to insert your Windows 95 CD or one of the floppy disks so that it can retrieve the appropriate driver files.

Tip

It's a good idea to always install the Generic/Text Only driver. Configure the Generic/Text Only printer to print to FILE. This provides an easy way to create a standard text file from virtually any Windows application.

I also recommend that you add a PostScript printer, even if you don't actually have one. This will enable you to create PostScript file output that you can take to a print shop or a typesetting shop for high-resolution output. It also allows you to create Encapsulated PostScript Files (EPS), which you can insert as pictures in Word documents. When adding the PostScript printer, select the HP Laserjet 4/4M PostScript driver and configure it also to print to FILE (unless you actually have such a printer, of course).

Setting Printer Properties

The Print dialog box's <u>P</u>roperties button lets you change various settings that are specific to the type of printer you are using. For example, Figure 9-16 shows the Properties dialog box for a Hewlett-Packard HP LaserJet 4L printer. Most printer drivers have Paper settings similar to the ones shown in this figure. The other options available from this dialog box vary from one printer to the next. You'll have to check the documentation that came with your printer for the details on how each option works.

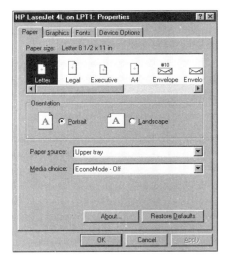

Figure 9-16: Printer properties for an HP LaserJet 4L laser printer.

Fortunately, the default settings for these printer properties are usually appropriate for most users, so you probably won't need to change printer properties.

Setting Print Options

The Tools⇨Options command has a Print tab that lets you set several important printing options, as shown in Figure 9-17. You can also access these options from the Print dialog box by clicking the Options button.

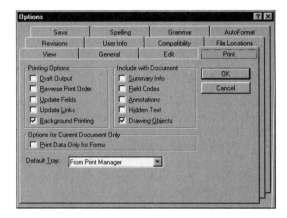

Figure 9-17: Print options.

The first group of Printing Options controls printing behavior:

- **Draft Output:** Directs Word to leave out complicated formatting to speed up printing. Which type of formatting gets axed depends on the printer type.

- **Reverse Print Order:** Tells Word to print pages backward, starting with the last page of the document and working back toward the first page. (I hope you don't read this book like that.)

- **Update Fields:** Updates the contents of fields before printing.

- **Update Links:** Updates information linked into Word from other files before printing. This option is necessary only if you have files on a network and you want to be sure that the most current versions are included in your printout.

- **Background Printing:** Enables you to continue working while Word prints your document. If Word slows down dramatically with background printing enabled, you may as well disable this feature.

The Include with Document group of options lets you tell Word what document information you want included in the printout:

- **Summary Info:** All of the information that appears on the Summary tab in the document's Property dialog box will be included along with the document. This is not the same as selecting Summary Info in the Print dialog box's Print what field. That prints just the summary information, not the document itself. Setting the Summary Info option here in the Print options tab prints the summary information *and* the document.

- **Field Codes:** Check this option if you want to print field codes (such as { SEQ Tables * MERGEFORMAT }) rather than the calculated value of each field. Ordinarily, you should leave this option unchecked. If you are having trouble with the document, selecting this option and printing it can sometimes help you isolate problems with field codes.

- **Annotations:** If annotations have been added to the document, check this option to print them on a separate page.

- **Hidden Text:** If the document has any hidden text that you want printed, check this option. The whole idea behind hidden text is to let you include text in the document that doesn't appear when the document is printed, so this option is ordinarily left off.

- **Drawing Objects:** This is the option to check if you want to include drawing objects — shapes, text boxes, and callouts created by using Word's drawing tools — in your printout. Disable this option if your document contains complicated drawing objects that take a long time to print and you want to print out a quick draft copy of the document without the drawings.

The Print options tab has two other options:

- **Print Data Only for Forms**: Use this option if you use Word's form fields to fill in forms, but you are printing the document on preprinted forms. It tells Word to print the data in the form fields, but not to print the form itself.

- **Default Tray:** This option tells Word from which paper tray the printer should draw paper. This option changes the paper source that Word uses by default. You can also change the paper source on a per-document basis by using the File⇨Page setup command and clicking on the Paper Source tab.

Print Preview

Print Preview is Al Gore's favorite Word command: It saved more trees last year than the spotted owl by letting you examine how your document will appear when printed without actually committing it to paper. By previewing the document on-screen, you can correct formatting problems before sending the document to the printer.

To preview a document, click on the Print Preview button in the Standard toolbar or choose the File⇨Print Preview menu command. Figure 9-18 shows a document displayed in Print Preview.

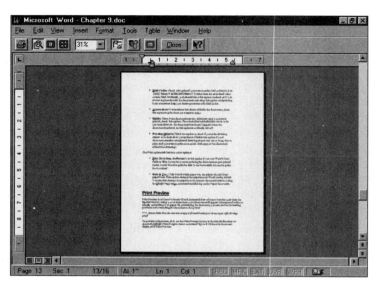

Figure 9-18: Print Preview.

As you can see in Figure 9-18, Print Preview displays its own toolbar with buttons for various functions that are often used when previewing documents. The Print Preview toolbar includes buttons shown in Table 9-1.

Table 9-1	Print Preview Toolbar Buttons	
Button	*Name*	*What It Does*
	Print	Prints the document.
	Magnifier	Lets you zoom in to a specific portion of the document. For more information about using this tool, see the section "Zooming in."
	One Page	Displays one complete page, as shown in Figure 9-18.
	Multiple Pages	Displays more than one page on the screen.
28%	Zoom Control	Lets you manually set the zoom factor.
	Rulers	Shows or hides the horizontal and vertical rulers so you can adjust margins.

Button	Name	What it does
	Shrink to Fit	Shrinks the document to make it fit on one fewer page. See the section "Shrink to fit" for more information.
	Whole Screen	Removes the title bar, menus, status bar, and toolbars so that the maximum amount of information is displayed on the screen.
Close	Close	Leaves Print Preview.
	Help	Displays help on any area you click.

Zooming in

Print Preview normally displays a full document page so that you can quickly spot formatting problems, such as misplaced headers or footers, inappropriately placed page breaks, and so on. On most monitors, you can't actually read any text when a whole page is shown. So, to scrutinize your document's formatting more closely, you need to zoom in.

The easiest way to zoom in for a close look at your document is to click on the Magnifier button in the Print Preview toolbar. The mouse pointer will change to a magnifying glass. Click on the area of the document you want to look at more closely, and Word will zoom in on that area, as shown in Figure 9-19.

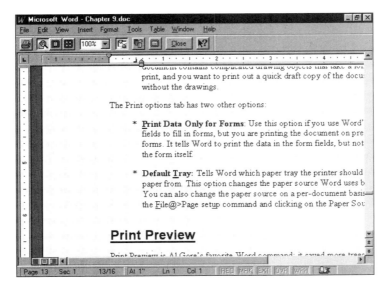

Figure 9-19: Zooming in on a document.

Once you've zoomed in, you can zoom back out by clicking the mouse button again. (It doesn't matter where you click to zoom out.)

Another way to zoom in is to change the zoom factor manually in the Zoom Control. You can type any zoom percentage you want, or you can select from one of the preset zoom factors available in the Zoom Control's list. You can zoom out to see more of your document, or you can zoom in to larger than full size, such as 150% or 200%.

In addition to percentages such as 50%, 75%, and 100%, the Zoom Control offers the following choices:

■ **Page width:** Zooms in as close as possible so that the entire width of the page is still visible.

■ **Whole page:** Zooms out to the default whole-page setting, in which one entire page is visible.

■ **Two pages:** Zooms way out so that two complete pages are visible, as shown in Figure 9-20.

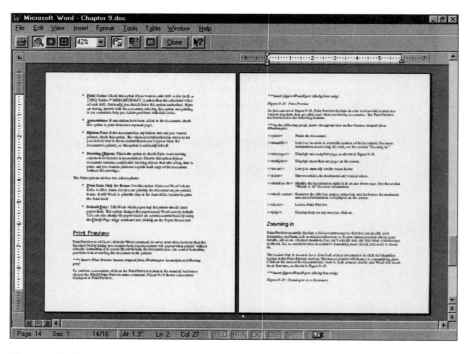

Figure 9-20: Zooming out to show two pages.

You can use the Multiple Pages button to zoom out even farther so that more than two pages is visible. When you click on the Multiple Pages button, a menu drops down as shown in Figure 9-21. Click on it and drag to indicate the number of pages you want displayed.

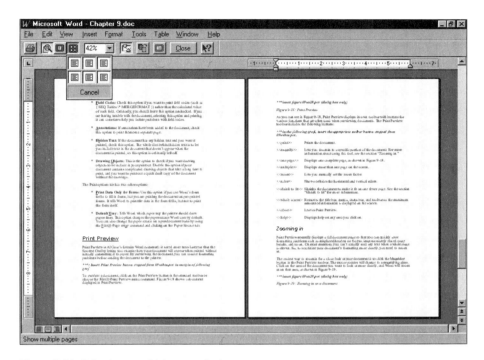

Figure 9-21: Selecting a multiple-page display.

When using the Multiple Pages tool, you can drag the mouse pointer past the end of the control to display more than the six pages that initially appear. The maximum number of pages you can display depends on the page size and your video resolution. For 8.5 x 11 pages, the maximums are

640 x 480	12 pages (2 x 6)
800 x 600	18 pages (3 x 6)
1,024 x 768	50 pages (5 x 10)

Figure 9-22 shows a display of 50 pages (5 x 10) at 1,024 x 760.

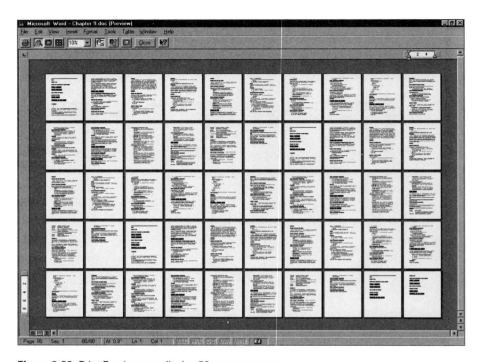

Figure 9-22: Print Preview can display 50 pages at once.

Shrink to fit

If you've ever been frustrated by a document with a last page that contains only a line or two of text, you'll love the *Shrink to Fit* feature. It nips and tucks your document in a bold effort to eliminate that last short page. Sometimes it works, and sometimes it doesn't, but it's always worth the effort to eliminate that embarrassing one-line last page.

To try to make a document fit into one fewer page, follow these steps:

1. Switch to Print Preview by clicking on the Preview button or by using the File⇨Print Preview command. Shrink to Fit is available only in Print Preview mode.

2. Click on the Shrink to Fit button in the Print Preview toolbar.

Word tries everything in its power to make the document fit into one less page. If the document is only a line or two long, Word can often make the adjustment by reducing the point size slightly and adjusting the line spacing. If the last page is much longer than a line or two, the odds of successfully shrinking it are substantially reduced.

Note

Word may decide to do something ridiculous like shrink your text to 6-point type. If that happens, just press Ctrl+Z to undo the whole mess.

If Word doesn't succeed at shortening your document, here are a few tricks you can try:

■ Play with the margins. A slight adjustment to the top and bottom margins may get a line or two more on each page. A change to the left and right margins may get more text on each line, thus reducing the total number of lines in the document.

■ Try a different font. Some fonts, such as Century Schoolbook, take much more space than, say, Times New Roman. If you don't believe me, take a look at Figure 9-23, which shows this paragraph formatting in several different fonts. See the difference? For more information about fonts, check out Chapter 19.

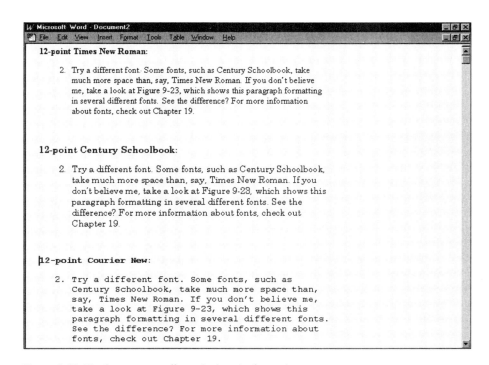

Figure 9-23: The font you use affects the length of your document.

■ If all else fails, you can always rewrite a portion of your document to make it shorter. Your readers will probably appreciate it.

Secret

By placing the Shrink to Fit button on the Print Preview toolbar and not making it available through the menus or a keyboard shortcut, Microsoft gives the impression that you can only use Shrink to Fit while in Print Preview. Not so. You can use the Shrink to Fit command from Normal or Page Layout view as well. Just use the Tools⇨Customize command to add the ToolsShrinkToFit command to a menu, toolbar, or keyboard shortcut. You'll find ToolsShrinkToFit listed under the All Commands category.

Editing in Print Preview

You can even edit your document while in Print Preview. Just zoom in to the portion of the document you want to edit. If the mouse pointer is a magnifying glass, click the Magnifier button to restore the mouse pointer to an I-beam. Then, click in the text where you want to edit and begin typing.

Note

You can do more than simple edits while working in Print Preview. In fact, nearly all of Word's editing and formatting features are available to you while working in Print Preview. You can access Word commands by using the menus, which remain visible, or by using keyboard shortcuts, which remain active. All toolbars except for the Print Preview toolbar are hidden when you switch to Print Preview, but you can even call them back by using the View⇨Toolbars command.

Printing Envelopes

Note

This section describes how to print envelopes one at a time. For information about mass printing envelopes as part of a mail merge, refer to Chapter 30.

Word's Tools⇨Envelopes and Labels command is specially designed for printing single envelopes or sheets of labels. See the section "Printing Labels" for information about labels; this section describes how to print envelopes.

There are two ways to print an envelope with the Tools⇨Envelopes and Labels command: You can print the envelope immediately, or you can insert the envelope in the document as a separate section and print it later. By inserting the envelope into the document, you can save it and not have to go through the Tools⇨Envelopes and Labels command the next time you send a letter to the same individual.

Secret

You can create a toolbar button to call up the Envelopes and Labels dialog box quickly. Choose the Tools⇨Customize command, click on the Toolbars tab, select the Tools category, and drag the Envelope icon to the toolbar of your choice.

Printing a single envelope

To print a single envelope, follow these steps:

1. Open or create a document – such as a letter — that contains the address you want to appear on the envelope.

2. Highlight the address you want to appear on the envelope. If you skip this step, Word will attempt to find the address in the document automatically. This will work in many cases, but to be sure, highlight the address first.

Tip

Another way to mark the address in the document is to assign it the bookmark name EnvelopeAddress. Then, you do not have to highlight the address or worry about Word trying to find the address automatically. See Chapter 11 for information about creating bookmarks.

3. Choose the Tools⇨Envelopes and Labels command. The Envelopes and Labels dialog box will appear, as shown in Figure 9-24.

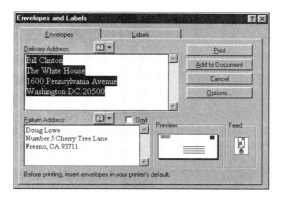

Figure 9-24: The Envelopes and Labels dialog box.

4. Check the delivery address and the return address to make sure that they are correct. Make any necessary changes. If you are using envelopes that already have your return address printed on them, click the Omit check box.

5. Ensure that the printer is ready to print an envelope. If necessary, manually feed an envelope into the printer. Double-check the Feed indicator at the bottom-right corner of the Envelopes and Labels dialog box to confirm that you and Word agree on how the envelope will be fed into the printer.

6. Click the Print button to print the envelope.

Changing envelope options

If your envelopes are not printing correctly, you may need to fiddle with the envelope options. From the Envelopes and Labels dialog box, click the Options button to bring up the Envelope Options dialog box, shown in Figure 9-25.

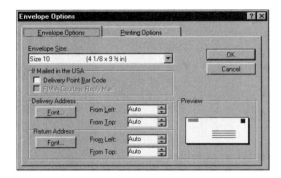

Figure 9-25: The Envelope Options dialog box (Envelope Options tab).

The following options are available in the Envelope Options tab:

- **Envelope Size:** Lets you select from a list of predefined standard envelope sizes. You can also select Custom Size, which brings up the dialog box shown in Figure 9-26, allowing you to specify any size envelope you want.

Figure 9-26: The Envelope Size dialog box.

- **Delivery Point Bar Code:** Adds a special bar code immediately above the address line, which the post office can use to speed delivery.

- **FIM-A Courtesy Reply Mail:** Adds a FIM-A mark that helps the post office identify your mail as business reply mail. If your envelopes have a FIM-A mark preprinted on them, do not select this option.

- **Delivery Address:** The controls in this group let you change the font and positioning for the delivery address.

- **Return Address:** The controls in this group let you change the font and positioning for the return address.

If you click the Printing Options tab, another set of options is displayed, as shown in Figure 9-27.

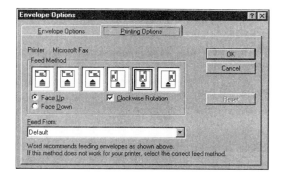

Figure 9-27: The Envelope Options dialog box (Printing Options tab).

The Feed Method group of controls lets you inform Word of how you will feed envelopes into your printer. You can select the path the paper takes through the printer, the paper's orientation, and whether the paper is inserted face up or face down. It is crucial that you set these options so that they match the orientation of the envelopes as you feed them into your printer. If you do not, Word will print the address upside down, in the wrong location, or not at all. Word is preprogrammed to know how envelopes are fed into the most popular types of printers, so you should have to mess with these controls only if Word doesn't recognize your printer.

Embellishing envelopes with text and graphics

You can embellish your envelopes with graphic logos or text messages by clicking the Add to Document button rather than the Print button in the Envelopes and Labels dialog box. This inserts the envelope as a separate section at the start of the document. After the envelope has been inserted into your document, you can add text or graphics to it. For example, you can add your company logo by importing it from a picture file or by drawing it using Word's drawing tools. Or, you can add a greeting or a marketing message ("You May Have Already Won Ten Billion Dollars!") to the envelope.

Switch to Page Layout view when you do this so that you can place text and graphics accurately on the screen. Then, you can place the text or graphics in a frame and drag the frame to the desired position on the envelope. Here are some possible methods for creating graphic images for placement on envelopes:

- Use Word's built-in drawing tools.

- Use WordArt, an applet that comes with Word and is adept at creating logos.

- Draw a bitmap image using Paint, one of the accessories that comes with Windows 95.

- Use the Insert⇨Symbol command to insert a symbol using the Wingdings font.

If you routinely want to add text or graphics to your envelopes, follow this procedure:

1. Choose the Tools⇨Envelopes and Labels command, adjust the envelope options, and click Add to Document.

2. Add a graphic or text to the envelope.

3. Highlight the text or graphic. If it is in a frame, be sure to select the frame itself, too.

4. Choose the Edit⇨AutoText command.

5. Type **EnvelopeExtra1** in the Name field.

6. Click Add.

If you have a second graphic or textual element on your envelopes, you can create a second AutoText entry named EnvelopeExtra2. When Word prints envelopes, it looks for these two special AutoText entries and automatically places them on the envelope if they exist. Therefore, you have created the EnvelopeExtra1 and EnvelopeExtra2 entries, you can print envelopes with custom graphics or text simply by calling up the Tools⇨Envelopes and Labels command, setting the envelope options, and clicking Print.

Printing just the envelope

If you have added an envelope to your document via the Tools⇨Envelopes and Labels command, the envelope is inserted into the document as page 0. As a result, you can print just the envelope by calling up the Print dialog box and typing **0** in the Pages field.

Printing Labels

You can also use the Envelopes and Labels command to print labels. As with Envelopes, Word can automatically extract the address to print on the labels. You can instruct Word to print a single label or an entire sheet of identical labels. You can also create a new document formatted for labels and edit the individual labels any way you see fit. I frequently use this option to print labels for file folders.

Here is the procedure for printing labels, either a single label or an entire sheet of identical labels:

1. Find out what kind of labels you have. Word works best with Avery labels, but you can customize the labels for any size.

2. Choose the Tools⇨Envelopes and Labels command and click on the Labels tab. Figure 9-28 shows the resulting dialog box.

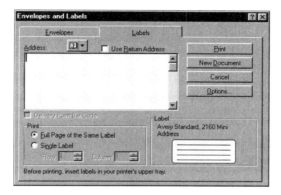

Figure 9-28: The Labels tab of the Envelopes and Labels dialog box.

3. If Word finds an address in the document or if you highlighted the address before calling up the Tools⇨Envelopes and Labels command, the address will appear in the Address field. If it is incorrect or if no address appears, type one now.

Note

Naturally, if you are printing labels for something other than addresses (for example, name tags or file folders), you won't actually want an address to appear in the Address field. Instead, the Address field should contain whatever you want to appear on the labels.

4. Click Options to call up the Label Options dialog box, shown in Figure 9-29.

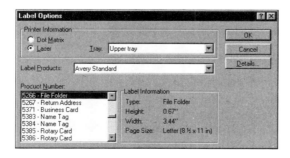

Figure 9-29: Setting label options.

5. Select the type of labels you are using by choosing the Avery Standard, Avery Pan European, or Other in the Label Products drop-down list box and selecting the correct label type in the Product Number list box. If your label type isn't on the list, see "Creating custom labels."

6. Click OK to return to the Envelopes and Labels dialog box.

7. To print an entire page of identical labels, click Full Page of the Same Label. To print a single label, click Single Label and adjust the Row and Column settings to indicate which label you want to print.

8. Insert a sheet of labels in the printer and click Print. Alternatively, you can click the New Document button to create a document formatted for the labels. You can then save the document and print it later. You can also edit the individual labels.

Tip   If you're not sure which direction to insert the labels into your printer, consult the documentation that came with the printer. Or, draw an arrow on a plain sheet of paper indicating the direction in which you feed the paper and test print the labels on the paper. This will help you judge whether you should insert the labels face up or face down. (It's always a good idea to print a test page on plain paper before using a sheet of labels anyway.)

Creating custom labels

If your labels don't appear in the list of predefined labels, you'll have to create a custom label format. To do so, select the Custom label type and click the Details button. This will bring up either the Custom Laser Information dialog box illustrated in Figure 9-30 or the Custom Dot Matrix Information dialog box, depending on which type of printer is selected. The two are identical except for the title.

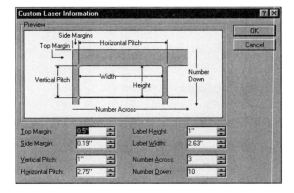

Figure 9-30: The Custom Laser Information dialog box.

To set up your custom label, enter appropriate values for each of the eight fields in this dialog box:

- **Top Margin:** The distance between the top of the sheet and the top of the first label.

- **Side Margin:** The distance between the left edge of the sheet and the left edge of the first margin.

- **Vertical Pitch:** The distance between the top of one label and the top of the label beneath it.

- **Horizontal Pitch:** The distance between the left edge of one label and the left edge of the label to its right.

- **Label Height:** The height of each label.

- **Label Width:** The width of each label.

- **Number Across:** The number of labels in each row.

- **Number Down:** The number of labels in each column.

Notice that as you change these values, the diagram in the Preview window changes to reflect the settings you've entered. When you're satisfied with the layout, click OK. Word will ask whether you're sure that you want to change the label format; click Yes to proceed.

Sending a Fax

With Windows 95 and Office 95, sending a fax is easier than ever before. Windows 95 comes with Microsoft Fax, a serviceable fax utility that can be used on its own to send and receive fax documents or in combination with Word to fax Word documents.

Note

To use Microsoft Fax, your computer must be equipped with a fax modem, the modem must be connected to a phone line, and Windows 95 must be properly configured to recognize the modem. If Windows 95 does not recognize your modem, choose the Settings⇨Control Panel command from the Start menu and double-click the Modems icon to configure the modem.

Here is the procedure for sending a document via fax:

1. Create a new document or open an existing document that you want to send.

2. Call up the File⇨Print command.

3. Select Microsoft Fax as the Printer.

4. Click OK. The Compose New Fax dialog box will appear, as shown in Figure 9-31.

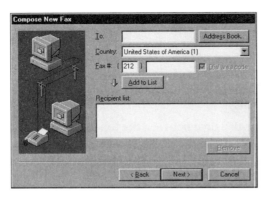

Figure 9-31: Entering the recipient's name and fax number.

5. Type the name of the person you want to send the fax to in the To field, and the fax number in the Fax # field. Then, click on the Add to List button so that the name appears in the Recipient list.

6. Click on Next> to proceed. The Compose New Fax dialog box will ask whether you want to send a cover page, as shown in Figure 9-32.

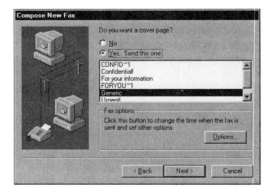

Figure 9-32: Microsoft Fax asks whether you want to include a cover page.

7. Select the cover page you want to send, or choose No if you do not want to send a cover page. For information about creating a custom cover page, see the section, "Creating custom cover pages" later in this chapter.

8. If you want to send the fax at a later time or change other faxing options, click the Options button, set the options however you want, and click OK to return to the Compose New Fax dialog box.

9. Click Next> to proceed. Microsoft Fax will ask you for information to include on the cover page as shown in Figure 9-33.

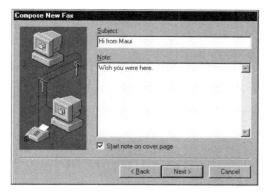

Figure 9-33: Microsoft Fax asks for information to include on the cover page.

10. Type the cover page information and click Next to proceed. Microsoft Fax asks for one final confirmation before proceeding, as shown in Figure 9-34.

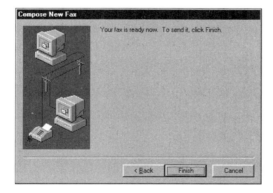

Figure 9-34: Do you really want to send this fax?

11. Click Finish to send the fax. Microsoft Fax will schedule the fax to be sent. Eventually, the fax modem will dial the number, send the fax, and hang up. During the entire process, the Microsoft Fax Status dialog box will keep you informed of its progress. See Figure 9-35.

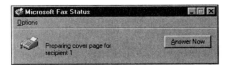

Figure 9-35: The Microsoft Fax Status dialog box.

 If you don't want the Microsoft Fax dialog box to remain on your screen, just click its close button. This does not stop your fax from being sent; it just dismisses the Status dialog box. A small fax icon appears in the corner of the Windows 95 task bar next to the clock. You can click this icon at any time to recall the Status dialog box.

Creating custom cover pages

Microsoft Fax comes with several built-in cover pages: Generic, For Your Information, Confidential, and Urgent. You can use one of these cover pages, or you can create your own cover page by using the Microsoft Fax Cover Page Editor. You'll find it hidden in the Start menu under Programs⇨Accessories⇨Fax.

Figure 9-36 shows the Cover Page Editor at work. It is a specialized word processor that lets you set up a single page of text and graphics and insert fields that are drawn from the Sender's and Recipient's addressing information. The easiest way to create a custom cover page is to open one of the supplied cover pages, edit it, and save it under a new name. Cover pages have filenames with CPE as their extension, and the standard cover pages are stored in the \Windows folder.

To insert a field, use the Insert menu, which offers several dozen specific fields, arranged as follows:

- **Recipient:** Name, Fax Number, Company, Street Address, City, State, Zip Code, Country, Title, Department, Office Location, Home Telephone Number, Office Telephone Number, To: List, and CC: List.

- **Sender:** Name, Fax Number, Company, Address, Title, Department, Office Location, Home Telephone Number, and Office Telephone Number.

- **Message:** Note, Subject, Time Sent, Number of Pages, and Number of Attachments.

You can find complete information about using the Cover Page Editor in the Cover Page Editor's Help command.

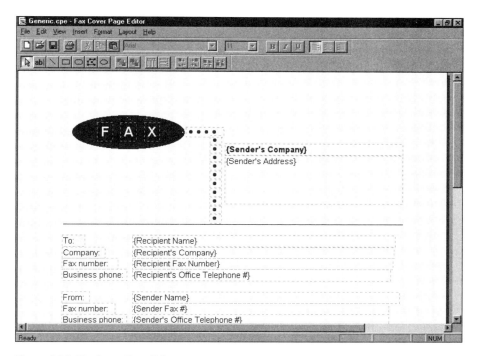

Figure 9-36: The Cover Page Editor.

Managing Print Jobs

Like Windows 3.1, Windows 95 uses a print spooler to handle the actual printing of your documents. When Word for Windows 95 sends data to the printer, the print spooler intercepts the data and writes it temporarily to a disk file. This enables the print spooler to handle more than one print job at a time.

Unlike Windows 3.1, Windows 95 does not have a Print Manager program that manages the jobs that have been sent to the printer. Instead, the print spooler is an integral component of Windows 95.

To manage the jobs that have been sent to a printer, you just double-click on the printer's icon in the Printers folder, accessible from My Computer or the Start menu's Settings⇨Printers command. Or, double-click on the printer icon that appears in the corner of the task bar (next to the clock) when a document is printing. Either way, the print queue window will appear, as shown in Figure 9-37.

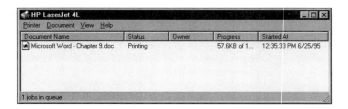

Figure 9-37: The print queue window lets you manage documents that have been sent to the printer.

The following commands are available for managing documents as they print:

- **Printer⇨Pause Printing:** This command temporarily suspends printing. Use this command if you need to stop the printer for a moment while you change paper, clear a paper jam, or delay printing until a more convenient time. (You can often achieve the same result by pressing your printer's On-Line or Ready button, but many newer printers — including mine — don't have such a button.) To resume printing, select the command again.

- **Printer⇨Purge Print Jobs:** Deletes the print job currently printing and all print jobs waiting to be printed.

- **Printer⇨Set as Default:** Makes the printer the default printer.

- **Printer⇨Properties:** Calls up the Properties dialog box for the printer so that you can adjust the printer settings.

- **Printer⇨Close:** Closes the print queue window. This does *not* suspend printing or delete print jobs that haven't been printed yet.

- **Document⇨Pause Printing:** Pauses the selected print job. Select the job you want to pause before choosing this command.

- **Document⇨Cancel Printing:** Deletes the selected print job. Select the job you want to pause before choosing this command.

- **View⇨Status Bar:** Shows or hides the status bar at the bottom of the window.

- **Help:** Displays help information about managing print jobs.

Chapter 10

Working with Others

In This Chapter

▶ Sending documents to other users, including routing a document to a list of users for review and comment

▶ Using the Highlighter, a new Word for Windows 95 feature designed to draw attention to portions of a document

▶ Using the Annotation feature to add your comments to a document or to review another user's comments

▶ Using the Revision Marking feature to see document changes made by other users

The first computer networks were created so that users could share expensive I/O devices, such as printers and disk drives, and send electronic mail messages to one another. Modern networks still provide these basic features, but until recently, most computer application programs were not "network aware." They could access data on network disk drives and print documents on network printers, but they treated such network resources as printers and disk drives as nothing more than extensions of local resources.

The combination of Word for Windows 95 and Windows 95 puts the network to better use than simple file and printer sharing and e-mail. Word for Windows 95 makes it easy for a group of users to work collaboratively on a document. These users can send the document back and forth across the network from user to user, each adding comments by using the Annotation feature and scrutinizing each other's changes with the Revision Marking feature. The underlying networking capabilities of Windows 95 handle most of the details of using the network automatically, so Word users are free to focus on their work rather than on the network.

Sending a Document to Another User

Word for Windows 95 provides a File⇨Send command, which allows you to send a copy of the current document to one or more network users. Word 6 provided this command as well, but with Word for Windows 95, the File⇨Send command is integrated with Microsoft Exchange, the universal e-mail client that comes with Windows 95. With Exchange in place, you can use the File⇨Send command to send the current document to a user on your local network or to a user with whom you communicate via an information service, such as the Microsoft Network, CompuServe, or the Internet.

Using the File⇨Send command

To send a document as an e-mail message to another user, follow these steps:

1. Create or open the document that you want to send.

2. Choose the File⇨Send command. Your disk will churn for a moment and then Microsoft Exchange will display the New Message dialog box as shown in Figure 10-1. Notice that the document itself has been inserted into the message as an attachment.

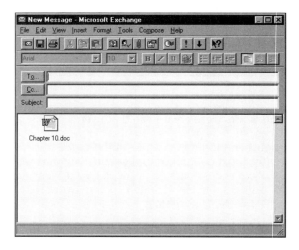

Figure 10-1: Sending a document as an e-mail message.

Note

Depending on how Microsoft Exchange is configured on your system, you may first be asked to select a *profile*, which controls settings such as where incoming mail is stored and which information services are used to deliver outgoing mail. Usually, you will have only one profile, named MS Exchange Settings, in which case you can simply click OK. If several profiles are available, choose the one you want to use and click OK.

To have Microsoft Exchange automatically use a specified profile each time it starts, double-click on the Inbox icon on your desktop, choose the Tools⇨Options command, and set the "Always use this profile" setting.

3. Type the recipient's e-mail address in the To field. If you don't know the e-mail address, click the T_o... button to bring up your address book. Search the address book for the recipient's name. When you find the name, double-click it, and click OK to return to the New Message dialog box.

Note

You can type more than one name in the To field to send the message to several users. Just separate the names with semicolons.

4. If you want copies of the message sent to other users, type those users' names into the Cc field. You can search the address book for names for the Cc field by clicking the _Cc... button.

5. Type a subject for your message in the Subject field.

 6. Click the Send button.

Of course, setting up a working e-mail system is a bit of a challenge, certainly more detailed that I can go into in a book on Word. You'll have to check with your network administrator for details on how to send e-mail messages over your network.

Routing a document to several users

If you want to send a document to more than one user, you don't have to use the File⇨Send command repeated for each user. Instead, use the File⇨Add Routing Slip command. It lets you set up a list of e-mail recipients and send the document to each one. The File⇨Add Routing Slip command lets you choose between one of two methods for sending the document to multiple users:

■ You can send the document to the users on the list one at a time. When the first user receives the document, that person can review it, modify it, and add annotations. Then, the first user forwards the document to the next user in the list with the File⇨Send command. When the last user in the list receives the document, that person uses the File⇨Send command, which automatically returns the document to you with all of the users' revisions and annotations in place, awaiting your review.

■ You can send a separate copy of the document to all of the users on the list at once. Then, each user reviews, revises, and annotates the document and uses the File⇨Send command to return the document to you. You wind up with multiple versions of the document, which you can review independently or combine by using the Merge Revisions feature, described later in this chapter.

Here is the procedure for routing a document to several users:

1. Create or open the document you want to route.

2. Choose the File⇨Add Routing Slip command. The Routing Slip dialog box will appear, as shown in Figure 10-2.

Figure 10-2: The Routing Slip dialog box.

3. Click the A<u>d</u>dress button to bring up the Address Book dialog box, shown in Figure 10-3.

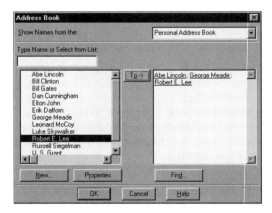

Figure 10-3: The Address Book dialog box.

4. For each person you want to route the document to, click on the person's name in the list and click the T<u>o</u>-> button to add that user's name to the list. Keep adding names until the list is complete.

Note

If a name doesn't appear in the list, it may be in a different address book. Select the correct address book from the <u>S</u>how Names from the: list box. If the name isn't in an address book, you can add it by clicking the <u>N</u>ew button.

5. When the routing list is complete, click the OK button to return to the Routing List dialog box. The names you selected will appear in the routing list, as shown in Figure 10-4.

Figure 10-4: The Routing List dialog box with names.

6. If you don't like the Subject proposed by Word, change it to something more appropriate.

7. Type a message in the Message Text field, for example, to provide instructions to the users receiving the routed document or to set a deadline.

Word automatically adds instructions that tell users how to return the document to you, so you don't have to include similar instructions in the Message Text field.

8. Select One After Another or All at Once as the routing method.

9. Check the Return When Done check box so that users can return the document to you automatically by using their File⇨Send command.

10. If you want to track the status of your document, check the Track Status check box. You will receive mail when each user forwards the document to the next user in line. That way, you'll be able to tell who is sitting on the document.

11. Set the Protect For setting as follows:

- **Revisions:** Users can modify the document, but revisions are tracked. That way, you can see what changes have been made to the document.

- **Annotations:** Users cannot modify the document, but they can add annotations.

- **Forms:** If the document contains form fields, the user can make changes only to the fields. Use this option when you want users to fill out a form, but you don't want them to change the layout of the form itself. For more information about forms, see Chapter 29.

- **None:** Users can freely modify the document. Revisions are not automatically tracked.

12. When you're ready to send the document along its way, click Route.

Note

If you go to all the trouble to set up the routing list but then realize you want to work on the document a bit more, click Add Slip instead of Route. This sets up the routing slip but doesn't actually send the document. You can then use the File➪Send command to send the document to the recipients listed on the routing slip.

Posting a document to a shared folder

Microsoft's Exchange Server product provides a feature called *shared folders,* which allow network users to access documents stored in a common folder without the hassles of setting up shared network drives. If Exchange Server was available on your network when Word was installed, you can use the File➪Post to Exchange Folder command to copy the document to the shared folder.

Using the Highlighter

The Highlighter is a tool that allows you to draw attention to a portion of a document by shading it with a background color similar to a highlighter pen. It is intended to be used in workgroup settings. For example, you might use it to highlight a portion of a colleague's document that you think needs to be reworked. When you send the document back to your colleague, that person will be able to find the highlighted section of text easily.

 To highlight text, click the Highlighter button in the Formatting toolbar and paint the text you want highlighted by dragging the special highlighter pointer over the text. Alternatively, you can double-click a word to highlight the entire word, or you can triple-click a paragraph to highlight the entire paragraph. When you're finished highlighting, click the Highlighter button again.

Another way to use the Highlighter tool is to select the text you want to highlight first and then click the Highlighter button. The selected text is immediately highlighted, and the mouse pointer does not change to the Highlighter tool.

Secret

There is no keyboard shortcut for the Highlighter tool, but you can assign one by using the Tools➪Customize command. Look for the Highlight command under the Tools category.

The default color for the Highlighter is yellow, but you can change colors by clicking on the arrow next to the Highlighter button. This reveals a menu that offers the four most common color choices for highlighting: Yellow, Green, Blue, and Pink and also None, which you can think of as a fifth highlight color.

Secret

If you hold down the mouse button and drag down past the bottom of the Highlight color menu, you can reveal three more colors below the four that initially appear. You can also drag to the right to reveal eight more colors, for a total of 16. See Figure 10-5. Frankly, the four colors that initially appear in the Highlight color menu are the most useful. It won't do you much good to highlight text with Black or Dark Blue because the background color is so dark that it renders the text unreadable.

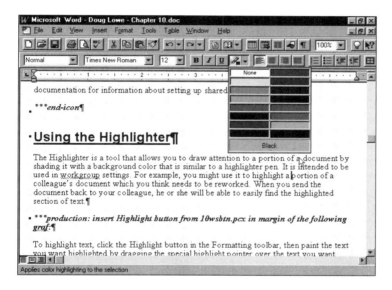

Figure 10-5: The secret Highlight colors.

You can set the default Highlight via the Revisions tab of the Tools⇨Options command. You can also access these options by calling up the Tools⇨Revisions command and clicking the Options button.

To remove highlighting, repaint the area where you want to remove highlighting. Or, select None as the highlight color and highlight away. Highlighting will be removed from everything you paint, and you won't have to worry about accidentally highlighting areas that weren't already highlighted.

Tip

Another surefire way to remove highlighting is to open the document by using Word 6 and save the file. Word 6 doesn't recognize Word for Windows 95's Highlight feature, so any highlighting you've applied to the document will be removed when you save the file in Word 6.

Using the Annotation Feature

The Annotation feature lets other people add commentary to your document, which you can later say that you reviewed and carefully considered before rejecting their suggestions as ludicrous. It's a great feature to use if you want people to think that you're a team player or if you want to foster the appearance of cooperative work. Heck, it's also a good feature to use if you really do want to be a team player or if you want to work cooperatively with your cohorts.

Inserting annotations

An *annotation* is a way of commenting on a part of a document without modifying the document. When you insert an annotation, Word adds a hidden annotation mark to the text at the location of the annotation and then adds your comments to a separate *annotation pane,* which is keyed to the annotation marks. You can then return later and view each of the comments.

To insert an annotation, follow these steps:

1. Select the text where you want to add commentary. If the text is really long, just move the cursor to the end of the text. If you select the text before creating the annotation, Word highlights the text later when you display the annotation.

2. Use the Insert⇨Annotation command, or just press Ctrl+Alt+A. Either way, an annotation mark is inserted as hidden text following the text you selected. Then, the screen is split in two, revealing the annotations in the bottom portion of the screen. Word refers to this as the annotation pane, and it's right. Figure 10-6 shows a Word screen with the annotation pane visible.

3. Type your comments. They are added to the annotation pane at the correct position.

4. Click the Close button to dismiss the annotation pane and return to the document.

Notice how the annotation marks in the document are keyed to annotations in the annotation pane. Word uses your initials (it gets them from the User Info options), followed by a sequence number. For example, the first annotation I created in Figure 10-6 is identified as DL1, the second is DL2, and so on. Under this scheme, several people can add annotations to a document, and you can easily determine which comment came from each person.

If you're going to insert a bunch of annotations, you can leave the annotation pane open. After typing an annotation, just click the mouse anywhere in the document. Both the document pane and the annotation pane remain visible. Find the next bit of text you want to comment on, select it, and press Ctrl+Alt+A to insert another annotation.

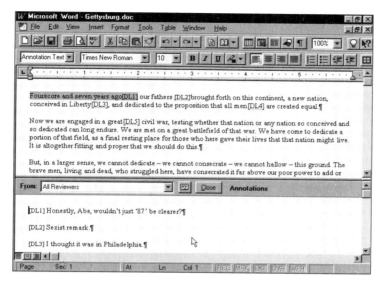

Figure 10-6: The annotation pane.

Creating a voice annotation

If you have a sound card, a microphone, and more disk space than you know what to do with, you can add a voice annotation by clicking the cassette-tape button in the Annotation Pane. This starts the Windows sound recorder, which you can use to insert a sound object in the annotation. Click the red Record button, record your message, click the Stop button, and close the Sound Recorder dialog box. A sound icon will appear in the annotation.

To play the voice annotation, open the annotation pane and double-click on the sound icon.

Note

I'm not kidding when I say that sounds take a lot of disk space. When I added the three annotations visible in Figure 10-6 as voice annotations, the Gettysburg.doc file grew from 13K to 253K. Each second of voice annotation requires about 22K of disk space.

Viewing annotations

To view annotations that people have added to a document, open the annotation pane by using the View⇨Annotations command. You can then scroll through the document pane or the annotation pane to look at annotations along with the corresponding document text. Notice that as you scroll through either pane, the other pane scrolls in sync. When you select an annotation by clicking it in the annotation pane, the document pane is scrolled to the text to which the annotation refers, and the referenced text is highlighted.

If the document contains annotations created by more than one user, you can restrict the annotation pane so that it shows just one user's comments by choosing that user from the F<u>r</u>om drop-down list. To display all annotations regardless of who inserted them, select All Reviewers.

Tip

If you want to copy an annotation directly into the document, select the annotation text you want to copy. Press Ctrl+C, click in the document at the location where you want the text inserted, and press Ctrl+I.

If the annotation pane is too big or too small, you can change its size. Hold the mouse steady over the top edge of the annotation pane for a moment, and the mouse cursor changes to a double arrow. You can hold down the left mouse button and drag the annotation pane up or down to increase or decrease its size.

Tip

Word does not have a keyboard shortcut to go to the next annotation. Word does have a GoToNextAnnotation command, however, which you can assign to a keyboard shortcut with the <u>T</u>ools⇨<u>C</u>ustomize command. Word also has a GoToPreviousAnnotation command.

You can print annotations by calling up the <u>T</u>ools⇨<u>O</u>ptions command, clicking the Print tab, and checking the <u>A</u>nnotations check box. Then, when you print the document, the hidden text that marks the annotation locations is printed along with the document, and the annotations are printed on a separate page after the document has been printed. In addition, the annotations page includes the page number to which each annotation refers. (If you want to print just the annotations page without printing the document, call up the <u>F</u>ile⇨<u>P</u>rint command and select Annotations for the <u>P</u>rint What field.)

Removing Annotations

To remove an annotation, highlight the hidden annotation mark in the document text and press the Delete key. If the annotation marks aren't displayed, click the Show/Hide Paragraph button on the Standard toolbar. Believe it or not, Word doesn't provide a quick way to wipe out all annotations in a document. To delete all annotations, you have to delete each one individually.

Macro

You can, however, create a macro that will delete all annotations for you:

```
Sub MAIN
On Error Goto UserExit
If MsgBox("Remove annotations?", "Annotations", 52) = - 1 Then
    Dim dlg as ToolsOptionsView
    GetCurValues dlg
    HiddenOption = dlg.Hidden
    ToolsOptionsView .Hidden = 1
    ViewAnnotations 0
    EditReplace .Find = "^a", .Wrap = 1, .ReplaceAll
    ToolsOptionsView .Hidden = HiddenOption
End If
UserExit:
End Sub
```

This macro first displays a dialog box asking whether you want to delete annotations. If you do, it closes the annotation pane and uses a Replace command to remove all annotation marks. Because the Replace command will not be able to find the annotation marks unless hidden text is visible, the ToolsOptionsView command is first used to reveal hidden text. After the annotations are removed, the hidden text view option is restored to its prior setting. (You'll find this macro named RemoveAnnotations in the Word for Windows 95 SECRETS Sample Macros.dot template on the CD.)

Using Revision Marks

Wouldn't you like to see what changes have been made to a document? This would be a great help to anyone in charge of maintaining corporate bylaws, legal documents, records about investments in failed savings and loans, congressional testimony, and so on. It would also be a great feature for anyone who distributes a document to coworkers for revision, allowing you to see what changes your friends have tried to sneak past you.

With Word's revision marks, you can. Revision marks let you indicate what changes have been made to a document. Any text that is deleted is shown with a line running through it (*strikethrough*). Text that has been inserted is underlined. And any line that contains a change is marked with a vertical line in the margin, so you can quickly scan through a document to find changes. Figure 10-7 shows an example of a document with revision marks. This section shows you how to create revision marks like these.

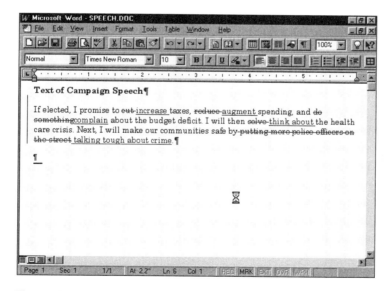

Figure 10-7: A document with revision marks.

Tracking revisions as you make them

The easiest way to create revision marks is to turn on the revision marking feature before you begin editing your document. Word then keeps track of revisions as you make them. You can print the document with or without the revision marks, and you can later accept or reject the revisions.

Follow these steps to begin marking revisions:

1. Call up the Tools⇨Revisions command. The Revisions dialog box appears, as shown in Figure 10-8.

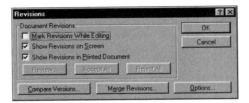

Figure 10-8: The Revisions dialog box.

2. Check the Mark Revisions While Editing check box. This step causes Word to keep track of the revisions you make while editing the document.

3. If you do not want the revisions to appear on-screen while you edit the document, uncheck the Show Revisions on Screen check box. The revision marks normally appear on-screen as you type. This can be annoying, so you may want to uncheck this box. As long as the Mark Revisions While Editing check box is checked, Word tracks revisions whether the revision marks are shown on-screen or not.

4. If you do not want to print the revision marks, uncheck the Show Revisions in Printed Document check box. Revision marks are usually printed when you print the document. Uncheck this box to omit the revision marks when the document is printed. You can always check this box later to print the document with revision marks.

5. Click OK. The Revisions dialog box is whisked away. The letters *MRK* are highlighted in the status bar at the bottom of the screen to remind you that revisions are being tracked.

To disable revision marking, call up the Tools⇨Revisions command again, uncheck the Mark Revisions While Editing check box, and click OK. I sometimes do this to correct a simple and obvious typographical error that doesn't need to be highlighted by a revision mark. Then, I turn revision marking back on.

Tip

You can quickly call up the Revisions dialog box by double-clicking on the letters *MRK* in the status bar.

Note

The three check boxes in the Revisions dialog box work independently of one another. Mark Revisions While Editing tells Word whether to keep track of revisions while you edit your document. The other two control whether revisions marks are displayed or printed.

If you click the Options button in the Revisions dialog box, Word lets you customize the highlighting and colors used to mark inserted text, deleted text, and changed lines, plus the positioning of the vertical line.

Accepting or rejecting revisions

When you have accumulated a bunch of revision marks, sooner or later you will want to accept or reject the revisions. If you accept the revisions, the changes are permanently incorporated into the document, and the revision marks are removed. If you reject the changes, the document reverts to its previous state and the revisions are deleted along with the revision marks.

To accept or reject revisions, follow these steps:

1. Call up the Tools⇨Revisions command, or double-click MRK on the status bar. Either way, the Revisions dialog box appears.

2. Click Accept All to accept all revisions, or Reject All to reject all revisions. Either way, Word asks you a confirming question, such as "Are you nuts?" Click Yes to continue.

3. Click the Close button, which returns you to your document.

Tip

Skim through your document to confirm that revisions have indeed been accepted or rejected as you intended. It should be obvious.

If you have second thoughts, press Ctrl+Z. The revision marks are restored.

Revision marks accumulate in a document until you either accept or reject them. You can therefore collect a set of revision marks over a period of days or weeks and then deal with them all by accepting or rejecting them.

If you would rather accept or reject revision marks one by one, click the Review button. This action calls up the Review Revisions dialog box, shown in Figure 10-9. From this dialog box, you can click one of the Find buttons to find the next or previous revision mark and then click Accept or Reject to dispense with the revision. To streamline the search even more, check the Find Next After Accept/Reject check box. Then, Word automatically moves to the next revision mark after you click Accept or Reject.

Figure 10-9: The Review Revisions dialog box.

Comparing document versions

Word tracks revisions only when you activate revision marks with the
Tools⇨Revisions command. If you forget to activate revision marking, you can
still re-create revision marks by comparing a document with an earlier version
of the same document. Word does its best to mark text that has been inserted
or deleted from the older version of the document.

Tip

Follow these steps to compare documents:

1. Open the newer version of the two documents that you want to compare.

2. Call up the Tools⇨Revisions command. The Revisions dialog box appears.

3. Click the Compare Versions button. The Compare Versions dialog box
   appears, which looks almost like the File Open dialog box.

4. Choose the file to which you want to compare the current file. In other
   words, choose the older version of the file you opened in Step 1.

5. Click OK. Word compares the files and automatically inserts revision marks
   in the newer document.

Don't expect Word to insert revision marks perfectly when it compares documents. Word is good at marking minor revisions, but some revisions may
confuse Word and cause it to insert wacky revision marks. It's better to mark
revisions as you make them, if possible.

Tip

You can call up the Tools⇨Revisions command and click the Review button to
accept or reject revisions selectively after comparing the documents.

Merging revisions

If a document has been given to several users who have each made revisions,
you can merge the various revisions together, provided that each user edited
the document with revision marking active. Just follow these steps:

1. Open the document edited by the first user whose revisions you want to
   incorporate into the final document.

2. Choose the Tools⇨Revisions command.

3. Click the Merge Revisions button. This brings up the Merge Revisions dialog box, shown in Figure 10-10. (This dialog box is identical to the Open dialog box except for the title.)

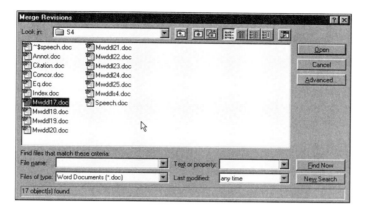

Figure 10-10: The Merge Revisions dialog box

4. Select the original version of the document and click Open. The revisions and annotations in the first document are merged into the second document.

5. Inspect the revisions and accept or reject them as appropriate.

6. Save the file.

7. Repeat steps 1-6 for each version of the document.

Note

Word offers a more streamlined method for merging revisions of documents that have been sent to multiple users via the File➪Add Routing Slip command with the All At Once option. When you receive the returned mail message, double-click on the document icon. Word will open the document and ask whether you want to merge revisions.

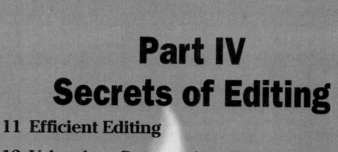

Part IV
Secrets of Editing

11 Efficient Editing

12 Using AutoCorrect, AutoText, and the Spike

13 Mastering the Power Editing Tools: Spell Checker, Thesaurus, and Grammar Checker

Chapter 11

Efficient Editing

In This Chapter

▶ Configuring Word's editing options for efficient operation

▶ Efficient methods of editing your documents

▶ Getting from one place to another fast

▶ Using the Go To command and bookmarks, plus a simple macro that cures a serious defect in the Go To command

▶ Using the Find and Replace commands

This chapter focuses on the most fundamental aspect of using Word: editing text. I presume that you already know the basics of editing text, or you wouldn't have made it this far. So, the emphasis here is on learning those extra tricks that can help make you more productive, but that might not be immediately apparent to a novice user. I'll start by describing Word's Edit options.

Setting the Edit Options

The first step in improving the *efficiency* of your editing skills is to set Word's editing options correctly. As each user's editing needs vary, there are no right and wrong option settings, so you need to evaluate each option according to your needs.

Figure 11-1 illustrates the Edit tab of the Tools⮂Options command, and the following list describes each of the edit options:

■ **Typing Replaces Selection:** If you highlight text by dragging the mouse over it or by holding down the Shift key while moving the cursor and then typing something, the whatever-it-was-you-typed obliterates the whatever-it-was-you-highlighted. This behavior can really drive you bonkers, especially if you're in the habit of highlighting text to apply formatting, such as boldface or italic. Fortunately, you can turn this feature off by unchecking the Typing Replaces Selection box. Many Word users prefer this option turned off.

■ **Drag-and-Drop Text Editing:** More commonly known as "dragon dropping," this feature lets you move text by selecting it and dragging it with the mouse. If it annoys you, turn it off by unchecking this field.

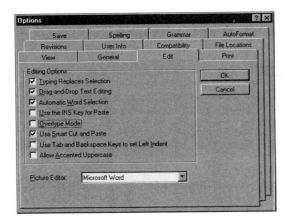

Figure 11-1: Word's editing options, available via the Tools⟳Options command.

- **Automatic Word Selection:** When this option is on, dragging the mouse selects whole words: The highlighted portion of text skips ahead of the mouse pointer a word at a time and skips back to the beginning of the word if you start dragging in the middle a word. This option drives some people crazy, but I find it kind of convenient. Word doesn't begin the word-at-a-time behavior until you've highlighted more than one word. Thus, you can highlight individual characters within a single word, but after you drag the mouse past the end of a word, Word switches to word-at-a-time highlighting.

- **Use the INS Key for Paste:** Makes the Insert key double as a shortcut for the Edit⟳Paste command. This is for people who can't remember that Ctrl+V is already the keyboard shortcut for Edit⟳Paste (which you might think is pretty convenient until you reach the part later in this chapter where I tell you that Ctrl+V is one of the three most important keyboard shortcuts — not just in Word for Windows 95 — but in all of Windows, and that you should commit those keyboard shortcuts to memory before you go to bed tonight). Using the Insert key as a shortcut for Edit⟳Paste is a crutch I don't recommend because the default Ctrl+V is the standard Paste key for all Windows programs.

- **Overtype Mode:** Puts Word into Overtype mode, in which any text you type obliterates text on-screen. I have no idea why you would want to do this. As far as I can tell, there is no logical reason for Overtype Mode to even exist, except perhaps as a cruel joke. Whether you check this option or not, you can press the Insert key to switch between Insert and Overtype modes unless you checked the Use the INS Key for Paste option. (As luck would have it, the Insert key is adjacent to the Del and Home keys, which are both useful keys in their own respect.) If you have the unfortunate habit of hitting the Insert key when you mean to hit the Home or Del keys, use the Tools⟳Customize command to remove the Insert key as a shortcut for toggling Overtype mode. You'll still be able to toggle Overtype mode by double-clicking on the letters OVR in the status bar.

- **Use Smart Cut and Paste:** Adjusts spaces before and after text you cut and paste so that you don't end up with two spaces between some words and no spaces between others. Leave this option checked; it's too good to turn off.

- **Use Tab and Backspace Keys to set Left Indent:** This option drives me crazy: If you press the Tab key at the start of a paragraph, it increases the paragraph's first line indent by .5" and deletes the tab character. Likewise, the Backspace key "lets out" the first line indent. I prefer to set these settings myself, thank you.

- **Allow Accented Uppercase:** Lets you put accents on capital letters when text is formatted as French. I don't know a lick of French, so I can't tell you if this is a good idea or not.

- **Picture Editor:** Lets you use a graphics program other than Word to edit imported graphics.

Editing Tricks

This book is a bit too advanced to present a primer on editing. I presume that you know how to move the cursor around, how to type, how to use the Backspace and Del keys, and so on. The following sections are devoted to a few less obvious editing tricks that you may not know.

Selecting text with mouse and keyboard

The easiest way to select text is by dragging the mouse over the text you want to select. As I've already mentioned, this dragging behavior is influenced by the setting of the Automatic Word Selection option. If this option is selected, Word constrains the selection to whole words once you drag the mouse past a single word. This can be convenient but can also interfere with precise text selection.

You can also use the following mouse actions to select text:

- Another way to select a block of text with the mouse is to click at the start of the block, hold down Shift, and click at the end of the block. Everything in between will be selected.

- To select a single word, double-click on the mouse anywhere on the word.

- To select an entire paragraph, triple-click on the mouse anywhere on the paragraph.

- To select an entire sentence, hold down Ctrl and click on the mouse anywhere in the sentence.

- To select a column of text, hold down Alt, press and hold the left mouse button, and drag. Drag the mouse left or right to increase or decrease the width of the column selected, and drag the mouse up or down to extend the column up or down. (This technique is most useful after you've arranged text into columns by using tabs, and you want to rearrange the columns.)

Some of the mouse selection techniques require you to click on the *selection bar,* that invisible but ever-present narrow band to the left of the text:

- Click on the selection bar once to select an entire line of text.
- Double-click on the selection bar to select an entire paragraph.
- Triple-click on the selection bar to select the entire document.
- To select several paragraphs, double-click on the selection bar to select the first paragraph, hold down the mouse button after the second click, and drag the mouse up or down the selection bar to select additional paragraphs.

In a table, you can select individual cells, columns, or rows:

- To select a cell, click the mouse on the cell. To select several cells, hold down the left mouse button and drag the mouse across the cells you want to select.
- To select an entire column, click on the top gridline of the column. The mouse pointer changes to a down arrow when it's in the right position to select the column. You can select several columns by dragging the mouse in this position.
- To select an entire row, click on the selection bar to the left of the row. To select several rows, drag the mouse in the selection bar.

Table 11-1 summarizes the keyboard shortcuts that are available for selecting text.

Table 11-1	Keyboard Shortcuts for Selecting Text
Keyboard Shortcut	**What It Does**
Ctrl+A	Selects entire document.
Ctrl+NumPad5	Selects entire document.
Alt+NumPad5	Selects entire table.
F8	Extends the selection, similar to holding down the Shift key or dragging the mouse. After pressing F8, the selection will be extended as you move the insertion pointer.
Ctrl+Shift+F8	Extends a column selection.

Copy, cut, and paste

Table 11-2 summarizes the three most important keyboard shortcuts in all of Windows.

Table 11-2	The Three Most Important Word Keyboard Shortcuts
Keyboard Shortcut	*What It Does*
Ctrl+C	Copies the selected text to the Clipboard.
Ctrl+X	Cuts the selected text to the Clipboard. The original text is removed from the document.
Ctrl+V	Pastes the contents of the Clipboard at the insertion point.

Word's Standard toolbar has buttons for these functions, and you can access them via the Edit menu, but memorizing and using the keyboard shortcuts is far more convenient. As a plus, you'll discover that just about all Windows programs — including Windows itself — honor these keyboard shortcuts.

If you have trouble remembering these shortcuts, consider first that they are positioned adjacent to one another on the bottom row of the keyboard. Then consider the following memory aids:

- **Ctrl+X:** The *X* is reminiscent of the X drawn to cross out something you want removed.

- **Ctrl+C:** The *C* is short for Copy.

- **Ctrl+V:** The *V* is reminiscent of a proofreading mark (a caret) that indicates where something should be inserted.

Dragging and dropping

Drag-and-drop editing was first introduced with Word for Windows 2.0, refined in Word 6 to allow you to drag and drop text between two open documents, and refined even further in Word for Windows 95 to allow you to drag and drop text between Word and other application programs that support drag-and-drop editing, including the Windows desktop.

In its simplest form, drag-and-drop editing allows you to move text from one location in a document to another by using the mouse only, without using the Clipboard. You simply highlight the text you want to move and use the mouse to drag the text to a new location. When you release the mouse button, the text is cut from its original location and pasted to the new location.

Tip

If you hold down the Ctrl key while dragging text, the text is copied rather than moved to the new location.

You can drag and drop text between two open documents, but both documents must be visible on the screen. It would be nice if Word let you press Ctrl+F6 to switch between open documents while dragging the text, but no dice. Instead, you must ensure that both documents are visible (a quick way to accomplish this is to use the Window⇨Arrange All command) and drag the text from one document window to another.

Note

According to Windows 95 convention, you should be able to drag text with the right mouse button, and Word should display a pop-up menu when you release the right button, with such options as Copy Text Here or Move Text Here. This would be a convenient way not to have to remember to hold down the Ctrl key to copy rather than move text, but apparently the Word for Windows 95 developers decided to ignore this Windows 95 convention. You can, however, right-drag text *outside* of Word to the desktop, where a pop-up menu appears as expected.

Creating desktop scraps

New in 95

Word for Windows 95 now allows you to drag text completely away from Word into another application. The target application for this type of drag-and-drop edit is usually Windows 95 itself or, more precisely, the Windows 95 desktop. When you drag text out of Word for Windows 95 onto the Windows 95 desktop, the text is placed in a *document scrap* and given its own icon, as shown in Figure 11-2. You can then drag the text back into a Word for Windows 95 document at a later time: a few minutes later or a few days later. The scrap can sit on the desktop indefinitely. You can also double-click on the scrap icon to open the scrap as a document.

Document scraps are a great way to move bits and pieces out of one or several documents for use later in another document. In essence, they allow your desktop to double as a super-Clipboard, capable of holding not just one but many text snippets that can be pasted together later. (Just be careful that your Windows 95 desktop doesn't become cluttered with scraps just like your real desk!)

Tip

If you find yourself needing to create more than a few scraps and you don't want your desktop to become cluttered, create a folder called "Scrapbook" (or whatever name that suits your fancy) and drag the scraps into it instead of to the desktop. Then, you can close or minimize the Scrapbook folder to hide the scraps.

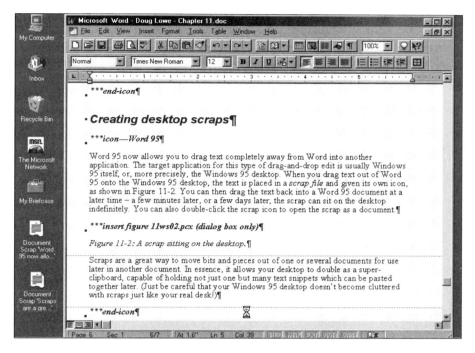

Figure 11-2: Two document scraps sitting on the desktop.

The magic of Undo and Repeat

The Undo command is one of those commands that most Word users far too often neglect. I use it all the time, not because I'm always making mistakes (although I make my share of them), but because it encourages me to try new things. For example, I might want to see how a line of text looks in boldface. If I don't like it, I undo it. Or, I might want to try moving a paragraph to another location. Don't like it? Undo it.

You can access the Undo command from the Edit menu, but Undo is used frequently enough that you should simply memorize its keyboard shortcut: Ctrl+Z. While you're at it, go ahead and memorize the keyboard shortcut for an almost equally useful command: Repeat, Ctrl+Y. The Repeat command, as its name implies, repeats the last action. If you just used the Format⇨Font command to make a bevy of formatting changes all at once, click on some more text that you want similarly formatted and press Ctrl+Y. Those same formats will be applied to the text.

Repeat repeats just about any action you can do in Word, including Undo. When the most recent command is Undo, the Repeat command becomes the Redo command: It redoes the action undone by the Undo command. Undo and Redo are a perfect combination for people who can't decide whether they like something or not.

Unlike most word processors, Word keeps track of more than one recent action. In fact, you can undo up to 100 recent actions. To undo more than one action at a time, click on the down arrow in the Standard toolbar's Undo button to reveal a list of the 100 recent undoable actions. Drag the mouse to select the actions you want to undo, and release the mouse to undo them all in one fell swoop. See Figure 11-3.

Figure 11-3: Undoing more than one command.

The Redo button in the Standard toolbar has a similar capability to redo up to 100 recently undone actions.

Navigation Tricks

Most Word users know that they can navigate through their documents by using the cursor arrow keys, the PageUp and PageDown keys, and the scrollbars. The sections that follow describe some more advanced methods of navigating through your document.

Keyboard shortcuts for document navigation

Quite a few keyboard shortcuts are designed to transport you to just about any part of your document you might want. Table 11-3 summarizes them.

Table 11-3 Keyboard Shortcuts for Navigating Through Documents	
Keyboard Shortcut	*What It Does*
Up/Down Arrows	
Up	Previous line
Down	Next line
Ctrl+Up	Previous paragraph
Ctrl+Down	Next paragraph
Alt+Up	Previous object
Alt+Down	Next object

Keyboard Shortcut	*What It Does*
Left/Right Arrows	
Left arrow	Left one character
Right arrow	Right one character
Ctrl+Left arrow	Left one word
Ctrl+Right arrow	Right one word
Alt+Left arrow	Left one word (same as Ctrl+Left arrow)
Alt+Right arrow	Right one word (same as Ctrl+Right arrow)
Page Up/Page Down	
PageUp	Previous screen
PageDown	Next screen
Ctrl+PageUp	Top of window
Ctrl+PageDown	Bottom of window
Ctrl+Alt+PageUp	Previous page
Ctrl+Alt+PageDown	Next page
Alt+PageUp	Top of column
Alt+PageDown	Bottom of column
Home/End	
Home	Beginning of line
End	End of line
Ctrl+Home	Beginning of document
Ctrl+End	End of document
Other	
Alt+F1	Next field
Shift+F1	Previous field
F11	Next field (Same as Alt+F1)
Shift+F11	Previous field (Same as Shift+F1)
Ctrl+F6	Next document window
Shift+Ctrl+F6	Previous document window
F5	Go to; calls up the Go To dialog box
Shift+F5	Go back to the previous insertion point

Going places with Edit⇨Go To

The Go To command allows you to jet over to any of several specific locations in your document. You can call up the Go To command from the Edit menu (Edit⇨Go To), by pressing F5, or by double-clicking on the page number portion of the status bar at the bottom of the Word window. Whichever way you choose, the Go To dialog box appears, as shown in Figure 11-4.

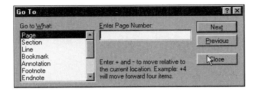

Figure 11-4: The Go To dialog box.

The Go To dialog box is used most often to go to a specific page number. To do that, simply type the page number into the Enter Page Number field, click on Go To (the Next button changes to a Go To button the moment you type a page number), and click on Close or press the Escape key to dismiss the Go To dialog box.

Besides going to a specific page, you can also go to a *relative page:* that is, a page number relative to the current page number. To move forward *n* pages, type +*n* (for example +1 or +7). To move back *n* pages, type -*n* (for example -3 or -50).

Pages aren't the only places where you can use the Go To command. The Go To What field can also be set to

- A section
- A line
- A bookmark
- An annotation
- A footnote
- An endnote
- A field
- A table
- A graphic
- An equation
- An object

The Go To dialog box features one of the most irritating buglets in all of Word (one that I had hoped they would fix in Word for Windows 95). The problem is that the Go To dialog box stays on the screen after Word has found the page and has taken you to it. If you Go To Page 11, you have to press the Escape key to dismiss the Go To dialog box before you can begin working on Page 11. Microsoft would probably tell you that it designed the feature that way; that most users, after going to page 11, don't want to do anything to page 11 but want instead to go to page 23; and that making them press F5 again would be a nuisance. Poppycock! The Go To dialog box should disappear after taking you to wherever it is you want to go. It shouldn't stick around like an unwanted houseguest. Get used to hitting the Escape key whenever you use Go To.

A handy EditGoto macro

If the Go To command irritates you as much as it does me, try replacing it with the following EditGoto macro. This macro pops up the dialog box shown in Figure 11-5, asking for a page number. If you type a page number and press Enter, Word goes to that page number and dismisses the dialog box. You can also type a relative page number (that is, +3 or -7, for example). The A̲dvanced button calls up the built-in Go To command, which you can then use as usual.

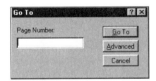

Figure 11-5: The EditGoto macro's dialog box.

To create the macro, call up the T̲ools⇨M̲acro command, type **EditGoto** as the macro name, and click on Cr̲eate. Type in the macro exactly as follows:

```
Sub MAIN
Begin Dialog UserDialog 320, 100, "Go To "
    Text 10, 15, 113, 13, "Page Number: ", .Text1
    TextBox 10, 33, 160, 18, .PageNo$
    PushButton 213, 13, 88, 21, "&Go To", .Goto
    PushButton 213, 37, 88, 21, "&Advanced", .Advanced
    CancelButton 213, 61, 88, 21
End Dialog
Dim dlg As UserDialog
buttonchoice = Dialog(dlg, 1)
Select Case buttonchoice
    Case 1
        Dest$ = dlg.PageNo$
        EditGoTo .Destination = Dest$
    Case 2
```

(continued)

```
            Dim GoTodlg As EditGoTo
            GetCurValues GoTodlg
            Dialog GoTodlg
        Case Else
    End Select
    End Sub
```

Click on the Save button to save your work, return to a document window, and test the macro by pressing F5. (This macro is found in the Word for Windows 95 SECRETS Sample Macros.dot template on the CD-ROM.)

Working with bookmarks

A *bookmark* is a name you assign to a location in a document or a selection of text. For example, I assigned a bookmark name every time I introduced a figure when I wrote this chapter. This way, I can quickly find the first reference to every figure in this chapter.

To create a bookmark, position the insertion point where you want to place the bookmark and press Ctrl+Shift+F5. This brings up the Bookmark dialog box, shown in Figure 11-6. Type the name of the bookmark and click Add.

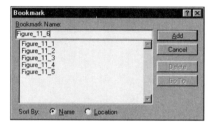

Figure 11-6: Adding a bookmark.

The bookmark name can be a maximum of 20 characters in length and can include letters and numbers, but no spaces, punctuation, or special symbols except the underscore character (_). The name must begin with a letter. Notice that the Add button doesn't become active until you type a valid bookmark name, and if you type an incorrect bookmark name (for example, if you include a space or any special character except the underscore), the Add button is deactivated.

You can create a bookmark for a selection of text rather than for a specific insertion point location, but there's usually little reason to bother selecting the text. If the only reason you are creating the bookmark is to go to it later, don't bother selecting a range of text; just place the insertion point at the location you want to return to and create a bookmark.

After you've created a bookmark, you can go to it at any time by pressing Ctrl+Shift+F5 to call up the Bookmark dialog box, clicking on the bookmark you want to go to, and clicking on the Go To button.

You can also go to a bookmark by calling up the Edit⇨Go To command, selecting Bookmark in the Go To What list, selecting the bookmark in the Enter Bookmark Name drop-down list, and clicking Go To. Going to the bookmark by using Ctrl+Shift+F5 is a lot easier, though.

Secret

Actually, you don't have to select Bookmark in the Go To What list if you remember the bookmark name. Simply type the bookmark name in the Enter Page Number field and press the Enter key. Word is smart enough to figure out that what you entered was a bookmark, not a page number.

To delete a bookmark, press Ctrl+Shift+F5 to call up the Bookmark dialog box, select the bookmark you want to delete, and click Del.

Although the most obvious reason for using bookmarks is to help you quickly locate a particular portion of a document, bookmarks serve many other workhorse functions within Word. Several important Word features use bookmarks to perform their magic:

- Form fields
- Index entries that involve page ranges
- Cross references
- Envelope text, such as delivery address and return address
- GOTOBUTTON fields that allow you to create a rudimentary hypertext document
- Tables of contents and tables of authorities

In addition, bookmarks often play a crucial role in macros that manipulate specific portions of text. In particular, macros often use several predefined bookmarks that allow the macro to access the current character, paragraph, or text selection. For more information about these predefined bookmarks, see Chapter 32.

Yes, you can go back

Secret

Most Word users don't know about the Go Back command because it doesn't appear on any menus or toolbars. The only way to access it is via its keyboard shortcut, Shift+F5, and if you didn't read the manual, you'd probably never stumble across it on your own. Yet, the Go Back command can be very useful. Word remembers the last five locations at which you've edited your document, and each press of Shift+F5 returns you to one of those previous editing locations.

The only limitation of the Go Back command is that it always returns to the point of the most recent editing. Sometimes you need to quickly mark a location in your document to which you can return later. Two macros, when assigned to custom toolbar buttons, can really help out in such situations. The first, called WhereWasI, creates a bookmark named "WhereWasI" at the current location. The second, called GoToWhereWasI, goes to the "WhereWasI" bookmark.

The WhereWasI macro consists of just one line:

```
Sub MAIN
    EditBookmark .Name = "WhereWasI", .Add
End Sub
```

The GoToWhereWasI macro is equally simple:

```
Sub MAIN
    EditBookmark .Name = "WhereWasI", .Goto
End Sub
```

To make these macros easily accessible, create toolbar buttons for them or assign keyboard shortcuts.

Using the Find Command

The Edit➪Find command lets you search for text anywhere in your document. It also lets you search for specific formats, such as a particular font or style, and special symbols, such as paragraph marks or annotations.

You summon the Find command by choosing Edit➪Find from the menu or by pressing Ctrl+F. Unfortunately, there is no toolbar button for the Find command, but you can add one if you're willing to customize your toolbars. Word even supplies a predefined toolbar button image that looks like a set of binoculars.

However you invoke it, the Find command displays the Find dialog box, as shown in Figure 11-7. The following sections explain how to use this dialog box for various searches.

Figure 11-7: The Find dialog box.

Finding missing text

You can use the Edit➪Find command to find text anywhere in a document. Just follow these steps:

1. Choose Edit➪Find or press Ctrl+F to summon the Find dialog box.

2. Type the text you want to find in the Find What field.

3. Click on the Find Next button.

4. Wait a second while Word searches your document. When it finds the text, it highlights it on-screen. The Find dialog box remains on-screen so that you can click on Find Next to find yet another occurrence of the text.

5. When it can find no more occurrences of the text, Word displays an appropriate message.

You can bail out of the Find dialog box at any time by clicking on Cancel or pressing the Escape key.

You can change the direction of Word's search by changing the setting in the Search drop-down list box. Three choices are available:

■ **Down:** Starts the search at the position of the insertion point and searches forward toward the end of the document.

■ **Up:** Searches backward from the insertion point, toward the beginning of the document.

Note

Both the Down and Up options search until they reach the bottom or top of the document and then ask whether you want to continue searching the rest of the document.

■ **All:** Searches the entire document without regard to the position of the insertion point.

Check the Match Case option before beginning the search if it matters whether the text appears in uppercase or lowercase letters. This option is handy when you have, for example, a document about Mr. Smith the blacksmith.

Speaking of Mr. Smith the blacksmith, use the Match Whole Word Only option to find your text only when it appears as a whole word. If you want to find the text where you talk about Mr. Smith the blacksmith's mit, for example, type **mit** in the Find What text box and check the Match Whole Word Only option. That way, the Find command looks for *mit* as a separate word. It doesn't show you all the *mit*s in Smith and Blacksmith.

Check the Use Pattern Matching option if you want to include wildcard characters or other search operators in the Find What field. Table 11-4 summarizes the search operators you can use if you select this option.

Table 11-4   Advanced Search Operators for the Find Command

Operator	*What It Does*
?	Finds a single occurrence of any character. For example, **f?t** finds *fat* or *fit*.
*	Finds any combination of characters. For example, **b*t** finds any combination of characters that begins with *b* and ends with *t*, such as *bat*, *bait*, *ballast*, or *bacteriologist*.

(continued)

Table 11-4 *(continued)*

Operator	*What It Does*
#	Any numerical digit.
[*abc*]	Finds any one of the characters enclosed in the brackets. For example, **b[ai]t** finds *bat* or *bit* but not *bet* or *but*.
[*a-c*]	Finds any character in the range of characters enclosed in the brackets. For example, **b[a-e]t** finds *bat* or *bet* but not *bit* or *but*.
[!*abc*]	Finds any character except the ones enclosed in the brackets. For example, **b[!ai]t** finds *bet* or *but* but not *bat* or *bit*.
@	Finds one or more occurrences of the previous character. For example, **10@** finds *10, 100,* or *1000*.
{*n*}	Specifies that the preceding character must be repeated exactly *n* times. For example, **10{2}** finds *100* but not *10* or *1000*.
{*n,*}	Specifies that the preceding character must be repeated at least *n* times. For example, **10{2,}** finds *100* or *1000* but not *10*.
{*n,m*}	Specifies that the preceding character must be repeated from *n* to *m* times. For example, **10{2,3}** finds *100* or *1000* but not *10* or *10000*.
<	Finds the following text only if it appears at the beginning of a word. For example, **<pre** finds *predestined* and *prefabricated* but not *appreciate* or *apprehend*.
>	Finds the preceding text only if it appears at the end of a word. For example, **ing>** finds *interesting* and *domineering* but not *ingenious* or *ingest*.

Check the Sounds Like option if you're not sure exactly how to spell the text for which you're searching. Word will use a phonetic algorithm to search for words that are pronounced the same as the word you seek. For example, if you search for **your** with the Sounds Like option on, Word will stop when it finds *you're*. Don't expect too much from this option, however. For example, if you typed **low** in the Find What field, you'd expect it to find *Lowe*, but it doesn't.

With Word for Windows 95, a new option, Find All Word Forms, has been added to the Find command. If this option is selected, Word looks for alternative forms of most verbs. For example, if you search for **run**, Word will find *runs, running,* and *ran.* It's smart enough to know about certain oddball words, such as *go:* If you search for **go**, Word will find not only *goes, going,* and *gone,* but also *went.* Searching for **be** finds *is, was, am, are, were, being,* and *been.*

Don't expect miracles, however. Find All Word Forms doesn't pick up every imaginable word form, especially where nouns are concerned. For example, a search for **introduction** doesn't pick up *introductory,* and **religion** doesn't catch *religious.* Find All Word Forms is more adept at finding alternative word forms for verbs than for nouns.

Finding formats

To find specific types of formatting, choose the Edit⇨Find command. The keyboard shortcut is Ctrl+F. Either way, the Find dialog box appears. Click on the Format button and choose the type of format you want to search for from the pop-up menu. The following options are available:

- **Font**: Allows you to search for specific font formatting. You can search for specific fonts or for such font formatting as bold, italics, font size, and so on.

- **Paragraph**: Allows you to search for specific paragraph formatting, such as indentation and alignment.

- **Tabs**: Allows you to search for paragraphs with specific tab settings.

- **Language:** Allows you to search for paragraphs formatted for a particular language.

- **Frame**: Allows you to search for specific frame formatting.

- **Style**: Allows you to search for paragraphs formatted with a particular style.

- **Highlight**: Allows you to search for highlighted text.

Make sure that the Find What field itself is blank; otherwise, the Find command searches for specific text that's formatted with the style you specify.

Finding special characters

You can also use the Find command to search for special characters, such as em dashes or annotation marks. Call up the Find command and click on the Special button to reveal a list of special characters that you can search for, shown in Figure 11-8. Select the character you want to search for and click on Find Next to begin the search.

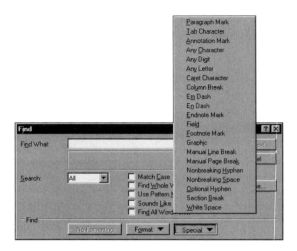

Figure 11-8: Searching for special characters.

When you select a special character, Word inserts a code into the Find What field. If you know the code, you can bypass the Special button and its huge menu by typing the code directly into the Find What field. You can also use these codes when invoking the EditFind command from a macro. Table 11-5 summarizes the codes.

Table 11-5	Search Codes for Special Characters
Character	*Code*
Paragraph mark	^ p
Tab character	^ t
Annotation mark	^ a
Any character	^ ?
Any digit	^ #
Any letter	^ $
Caret character	^ ^
Column break	^ n
Em dash	^ +
En dash	^ =
Endnote mark	^ e
Field	^ d
Footnote mark	^ f
Graphic	^ g

Character	Code
Manual line break	^ l
Manual page break	^ m
Nonbreaking hyphen	^ ~
Nonbreaking space	^ s
Optional hyphen	^ -
Section break	^ b
White space	^ w

Replacing Text

You can use the Edit⇨Replace command to replace all occurrences of one bit of text with other text. Here is the procedure:

1. Choose Edit⇨Replace or press Ctrl+H to summon the Replace dialog box, as shown in Figure 11-9.

Figure 11-9: The Replace dialog box.

2. Type the text you want to find in the Find What field and type the text you want to substitute for the Find What text in the Replace With field.

3. Click on the Find Next button. When Word finds the text, it highlights it on-screen.

4. Click on the Replace button to replace the text.

5. Repeat the Find Next and Replace sequence until you're finished.

As for the Find command, you can use the Match Case, Find Whole Word Only, Use Pattern Matching, Sounds Like, and Find All Word Forms options. The latter is even smart enough to properly replace alternative word forms with the correct version of the replacement text. For example, if you replace **run** with **walk**, Word will replace *running* with *walking* and *ran* with *walked*.

If you're absolutely positive that you want to replace all occurrences of your Find What text with the Replace With text, click on the Replace All button. This step automatically replaces all remaining occurrences of the text. The only problem is that you're bound to encounter at least one spot where you didn't want the replacement to occur. Replacing the word **mitt** with **glove**, for example, changes *Smith* to *Sgloveh* (and no, *Sgloveh* is not the Czechoslovakian form of the name *Smith*).

Because Word is not 100 percent confident in its capability to properly replace all alternative word forms, you'll receive a warning message if you select the Find All Word Forms option and click on Replace All. Find All Word forms is tricky enough that you should verify each replacement.

Chapter 12

Using AutoCorrect, AutoText, and the Spike

In This Chapter

▶ How to use AutoCorrect, a feature that "automagically" corrects common typing errors *as you make them* and has a few other tricks up its sleeve as well

▶ How to use Word's AutoFormat As You Type options, which are really AutoCorrect options in disguise

▶ How to use AutoText, a feature that lets you store short words or phrases, larger sections of text, such as paragraphs or whole pages, or even complicated graphics for easy recall

▶ Using the Spike, a nifty feature that works like a cumulative Clipboard that gathers text from various locations in your document and pastes it into a single location

This chapter covers three advanced editing features of Word: AutoCorrect, AutoText, and the Spike. You can get along without these features (although the AutoCorrect feature is activated by default when you install Word), but knowing what they are and how they work is very worthwhile. Depending on the type of documents you create, these features may or may not prove invaluable.

Using AutoCorrect

AutoCorrect — originally introduced with Word 6 and enhanced a bit for Word for Windows 95 — monitors your typing, carefully watching for common typing mistakes and fixing them quicker than you can say "Bob's Your Uncle." For example, type **adn** and AutoCorrect changes it to *and*. Typing **teh** becomes *the;* **recieve** becomes *receive*. You get the idea. AutoCorrect has other features as well: It corrects capitalization, including accidental use of the Caps Lock key, and it lets you insert special symbols.

AutoCorrect is controlled from the Tools⇨AutoCorrect command, which brings up the dialog box shown in Figure 12-1. This dialog box lets you activate specific AutoCorrect features. In the figure, all AutoCorrect features are enabled, but you might find that one feature or another doesn't suit your fancy. If that's the case, use the Tools⇨AutoCorrect command to disable the feature you don't like.

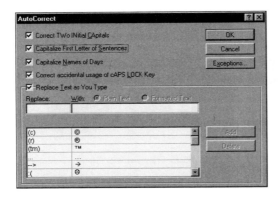

Figure 12-1: The AutoCorrect dialog box.

Note

I'm not sure why the AutoCorrect dialog box wasn't incorporated into the Tools⇨Options command because these options seem to belong with the options on the Tools⇨Options dialog box's Edit tab. In fact, one of those options (Use the Tab and Backspace Keys to Set Left Indent) almost seems like an AutoCorrect feature to me. The only thing I can figure is that the Tools⇨Options dialog box already has 12 tabs, and there just wasn't room to squeeze in the AutoCorrect options.

Note

AutoCorrect settings, including specific AutoCorrect entries used to replace typing, are treated as a Word option rather than as a template or document option. Thus, any changes you make to the AutoCorrect settings will be available no matter what document or template you use.

The following sections describe each of the AutoCorrect options in detail.

What happened to SmartQuotes?

If you're an experienced Word 6 user, the first thing you may notice about the AutoCorrect dialog box is that the SmartQuotes option has disappeared. Not to worry; Word still handles SmartQuotes. The option has simply been moved to the AutoFormat tab of the Tools⇨Options command. It is covered in more detail later in this chapter.

COrrect TWo INitial CApitals

If you're an average typist, you probably have the bad habit of occasionally leaving the Shift key down a bit too long when typing the initial capital letter of a sentence or a proper noun. The result is that two letters of the word wind up being capitalized rather than just one. If this option is enabled, AutoCorrect watches for this mistake and changes the second capital letter to lowercase.

This is a very useful feature, unless of course you *want* to type the first two letters of a word in capitals. As an example, I had a devil of a time typing the heading for this section. AutoCorrect kept correcting my capitalization. When I typed *COrrect*, Word changed it to *Correct*. One way around this is to type *COrrect*, let Word change it to *Correct*, then go back and change the lowercase *o* to capital. But guess what? The next time you accidentally type *COrrect*, Word doesn't correct your mistake. Why? Because AutoCorrect's default behavior is to watch for any capitalization it corrects that you immediately change back. It remembers those words and doesn't correct them in the future.

You can click the Exceptions button to call up the AutoCorrect Exceptions dialog box, as shown in Figure 12-2. This dialog box contains two *exception lists* (that is, specific words that should not be corrected): one for INitial Caps and the other for First Letter. Figure 12-2 shows the list for INitial CAps. As you can see, the exception list includes the four words in the heading for this section. Word automatically added these words because the Automatically Add Words to List check box is checked. To disable Word's capability of remembering which words you do not want it to correct, uncheck this box. (I have it un-checked on my system because I've found that Word is all too likely to add words that don't belong in the exception list.)

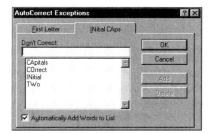

Figure 12-2: The INitial CAps exception list.

You can remove a word from the exception list by clicking the word to select it and clicking the Del button. To add a word of your own, type the word with the first two letters capitalized in the Don't Correct field and click Add.

Capitalize First Letter of Sentence

If you choose the Capitalize First Letter of Sentence option, Word will automati-cally ensure that the first letter of each sentence is capitalized. The poet e. e. cummings should have used this feature.

The Capitalize First Letter of Sentence option works by looking for periods or other sentence-ending punctuation. This presents a problem when you want to use an abbreviation that ends with a period: Word is liable to capitalize the word following the abbreviation, thinking that the previous sentence has come to an end. Fortunately, Word provides an extensive exception list that includes many common abbreviations. To access it, click the Exceptions button and click the First Letter tab. See Figure 12-3.

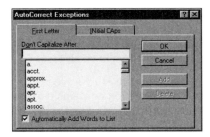

Figure 12-3: The First Letter exception list.

If the Automatically Add Words to List option is on, Word will watch for any words it automatically capitalizes that you then immediately uncapitalize. Word assumes that the preceding word is an abbreviation and should be added to the list. Because Word is likely to add a word that doesn't belong on the exception list, I've disabled this option on my system.

To remove a word from the exception list, select the word and click Del. To add a word, type the word in the Don't Capitalize After field and click Add.

Capitalize Names of Days

If this option is enabled, Word always capitalizes the first letter of the names of days: Monday, Tuesday, Wednesday, and the like. Thus, if you type **thursday**, Word automatically changes it to *Thursday*.

Tip

Unfortunately, Word doesn't have an option that also capitalizes the names of months (January, February, and so on). However, you can easily add AutoCorrect entries to capitalize month names. Just set up the following AutoCorrect entries:

Replace	*With*
january	January
february	February
march	March

…and so on, through December. For instructions on setting up your own AutoCorrect entries, see the section "Replace Text as You Type."

Correct accidental usage of cAPS LOCK key

This AutoCorrect feature is new for Word for Windows 95, and I love it. I frequently press the Caps Lock key by mistake when reaching for the Shift key. With this option enabled, Word watches for the tell-tale pattern of inverted capitalization: a word that begins with a lowercase letter and then continues with uppercase letters. When it detects the pattern, it corrects the incorrectly capitalized letter and disables the Caps Lock key.

Replace Text as You Type

This option is the heart of AutoCorrect; the other options are merely gravy. At its core, AutoCorrect is a list of replacements that should be made whenever certain words are typed. For example, whenever you type **adn**, Word should automatically substitute *and*. Word will make these substitutions only if the Replace Text as You Type check box is selected.

Word comes with an extensive list of built-in AutoCorrect entries. Some of these entries correct commonly misspelled words, such as *adn* for *and* and *teh* for *the*. Others provide a convenient way to insert special symbols quickly. Table 12-1 summarizes these AutoCorrect entries.

Table 12-1	Built-In AutoCorrect Entries for Creating Symbols
Replace	*With*
(c)	Copyright symbol: ©
(r)	Registered symbol: ®
(tm)	Trademark symbol: ™
...	Elipses: ...
—>	Small right arrow: ⇨
<—	Small left arrow: ⇦
==>	Big right arrow: →
<==	Big left arrow: ←
<=>	Double arrow: ⇔
:)	Happy face: ☺
:(	Sad face: ☹
:|	Neutral face: ☺

Secret

You can use the Undo command to undo a change made by AutoCorrect. For example, if you type —> and do *not* want it converted to an arrow, press Ctrl+Z immediately after Word changes it to the arrow. The text will be restored to —>.

Creating AutoCorrect entries

To add your own AutoCorrect entries, type the text you want to be replaced in the Replace field, followed by the text you want to replace it with in the With field. For example, if you want to set up an AutoCorrect entry so that every time you type **february**, Word replaces it with *February,* type **february** in the Replace field, type **February** in the With field, and click Add.

If you want Word to preserve the formatting for an AutoCorrect entry, first type the replacement text in your document and format it however you want. Then select the text and call up the Tools⇨AutoCorrect command. The replacement text will be placed in the With field. All you have to do is type the Replace field and click Add.

That is how you can add additional symbols to the AutoCorrect list. For example, suppose that you routinely use the open book symbol in the Wingdings font. Follow these steps to add it as an AutoCorrect entry so that whenever you type **<b>**, the open book symbol is inserted:

1. Choose the Insert⇨Symbol command. The Symbol dialog box will appear. Select the Wingdings font and click on the open book symbol, as shown in Figure 12-4.

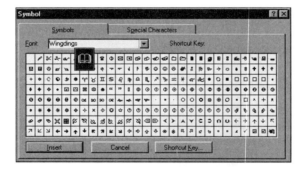

Figure 12-4: Inserting the open book symbol into a document.

2. Click the Insert button to insert the symbol into the document and click Close to close the Symbol dialog box.

3. Use the mouse to highlight the symbol you just inserted.

4. Call up the Tools⇨AutoCorrect command. The AutoCorrect dialog box will appear with the book symbol already placed in the With field, as shown in Figure 12-5.

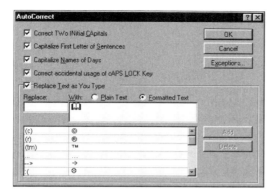

Figure 12-5: Creating an AutoCorrect entry for the open book symbol.

5. Type **<b>** in the Replace field.

6. Click Add and click Cancel to dismiss the AutoCorrect dialog box.

Now, whenever you type **<b>**, Word will automatically substitute the open book symbol formatted in the Wingdings font.

A macro to toggle AutoCorrect

Because the type of writing I do frequently requires me to type words with weird spelling or goofy capitalization, I often need to toggle AutoCorrect features on and off. Toward that end, I use a macro named ToggleAutoCorrect, which I've assigned the keyboard shortcut Ctrl+period. Whenever I want to turn off AutoCorrect, I press Ctrl+period. To turn it back on, I press Ctrl+period again.

You can find the ToggleAutoCorrect macro in the Word SECRETS.Dot template that comes with this book, or you can create it yourself. Call up the Tools⇨Macro command, type **ToggleAutoCorrect** for the macro name, and click on Create. Then, type in the following macro:

```
Sub MAIN
Dim dlg As ToolsAutoCorrect
GetCurValues dlg
If dlg.ReplaceText = 1 Then
    dlg.ReplaceText = 0
    dlg.SmartQuotes = 0
    dlg.InitialCaps = 0
    dlg.SentenceCaps = 0
    dlg.CapsLock = 0
    dlg.Days = 0
Else
    dlg.ReplaceText = 1
    dlg.SmartQuotes = 1
    dlg.InitialCaps = 1
```

```
        dlg.SentenceCaps = 1
        dlg.CapsLock = 1
        dlg.Days = 1
End If
ToolsAutoCorrect dlg
End Sub
```

Finally, assign the macro to the Ctrl+period keyboard shortcut, or whatever other shortcut you'd rather use.

This macro alternately sets and resets all of the AutoCorrect options as a set. If you wish, you can tailor the macro by omitting lines for AutoCorrect options you don't want toggled.

Using AutoFormat As You Type Options

Word has another feature called AutoFormat, which automatically improves the formatting of documents that were written with little concern for appearance. However, Microsoft tacked on a variety of AutoCorrect-like features to AutoFormat. These features apply document formatting as you type. If you call up the Format⇨AutoFormat command and click the Options button, or if you call up the Tools⇨Options command, click the AutoFormat tab and select the AutoFormat As You Type option button. You'll see the dialog box shown in Figure 12-6.

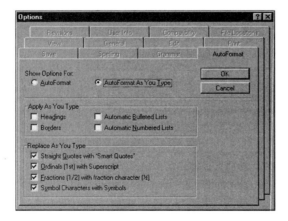

Figure 12-6: The AutoFormat As You Type options.

Personally, I fail to see the logic in creating a separate category of options for what are really AutoCorrect options. One could argue that the first group of AutoFormat options automatically applies paragraph formatting, which is out of the realm of AutoCorrect. But, the remaining options, such as converting ordinals like 1st to 1st, are AutoCorrect pure and simple. Go figure.

Apply As You Type: Headings

Whenever you type a line that starts with a capital letter, has no ending punctuation, and is at least 20 percent shorter than the maximum line length, Word makes the paragraph a heading if this option is selected. Frankly, the rules for AutoFormatting headings as you type are too restrictive. What if the heading needs to be more than one line long? (Some do.) What if the heading ends with a question mark? What if you need to use two or more levels of headings? It's much easier to memorize the keyboard shortcuts for applying Word's built-in heading styles: Ctrl+Alt+1 for a Heading 1, Ctrl+Alt+2 for a Heading 2, and so on. Verdict: ☞ Thumbs down.

Borders

If you type three or more hyphens, underscores, or equal signs in a row and this option is selected, Word deletes the characters and instead applies a border to the top of the paragraph. You get a thin line for dashes, a thick line for underscores, or a double line for equal signs. This is a pretty neat feature. Verdict: ☝ Thumbs up.

Automatic Bulleted Lists

If you start a paragraph with a bullet character (an asterisk, hyphen, "o," or >) followed by a space or tab, Word removes the bullet character and the space or tab and instead formats the paragraph as a bulleted list. This is pretty convenient for users who haven't yet learned how to use the Bullets button in the Formatting toolbar, but I don't particularly care for it. Verdict: ☞ Thumbs down.

Tip

For more information about bullets, see Chapter 16.

Automatic Numbered Lists

If you start a paragraph with a number followed by a period, space, or tab; Word removes the number and instead formats the paragraph as a numbered list. This is OK for users who haven't yet learned how to use the Numbering button in the Formatting toolbar, but it drives me batty. Usually, if I start a paragraph with a number followed by a tab, it's because I'm creating a numbered list in a format that is too complicated for the Numbering button to handle, and I don't want to take the time to mess with Word's multilevel numbered list feature. For simple numbered lists, I always just click the Numbering button anyway. Verdict: ☞ Thumbs down.

Tip

For more information about numbered lists, see Chapter 16.

Replace Straight Quotes with 'Smart Quotes'

This option tells Word to replace ordinary apostrophes and quotation marks automatically with curly quotes and apostrophes. The trick of it is figuring out whether to use the left or right variety of curly quote or apostrophe. The left variety should appear to the left of quoted material; the right quote or apostrophe should appear to the right. Word does its best to figure it out, and usually gets it right. If there is a character immediately following the apostrophe or quote, Word replaces it with a left quote or apostrophe. If there is a nonblank character immediately before the quote or apostrophe, Word replaces it with a right quote or apostrophe. Verdict: 👍 Thumbs up, with the following caveat:

The Smart Quotes feature works most of the time, but it bombs when you want to use a simple curly apostrophe. For example, try typing **Stop 'n Go**. You can't do it: Word insists on turning the apostrophe the other way 'round. (See, I did it again: bet you can't!)

Tip

You might be able to concoct some type of macro that will let you directly insert a left curly apostrophe, but there's a simpler way. Simply type *two* apostrophes in a row. Word will curl them both: the first one left, the second one right: ' '. Now go back and delete the first one.

Secret

SmartQuotes is such a useful feature that you have little reason to turn it off. If you need to type an ordinary, noncurled apostrophe or quote once in awhile, try this trick: type the apostrophe or quote and press Ctrl+Z (Undo). I was surprised when I first tried this to discover that the Undo command treats typing the apostrophe or quote and converting it to a curly form as two separate actions. When you press Ctrl+Z, Undo undoes the SmartQuote action, leaving you with a plain apostrophe or quote.

Replace Ordinals (1st) with Superscript

This option replaces ordinal numbers, such as 1st, 2nd, 3rd with properly formatted superscripts: 1st, 2nd, and 3rd. This is really nothing that AutoCorrect can't accomplish, but it is convenient. For most people, ordinals are one of the main reasons to use superscripts (the other being footnotes), so automatically converting them in this way is a real convenience. Verdict: 👍 Thumbs up.

Replace Fractions (1/2) with fraction characters ($^1/_2$)

The standard Windows character set, which most fonts adhere to, includes three fraction characters: $^1/_2$, $^1/_4$, and $^3/_4$. Prior to Word for Windows 95, the most convenient way to access these characters was via the Insert⇨Symbol command. With this option enabled, however, Word for Windows 95 automatically converts 1/2, 1/4, and 3/4 to their fraction equivalents. Verdict: 👍 Thumbs up.

Too bad the Windows character set doesn't include a few other fractions, at least 1/3 and 2/3. Sigh.

Symbol Characters with Symbols

This option does two things:

■ It replaces two hyphens with a typographical dash called an em dash, so called because it is about as wide as a capital letter *M*. For example — this is an em dash.

■ It replaces two hyphens preceded and followed by a space with an en dash, so called because it is about the width of a capital letter *N*. For example, June – July, Aug – Sep, and so on.

Secret

With only these two characters under its control, the Symbol Characters with Symbols feature could just have easily been implemented by using AutoCorrect. But apparently Microsoft has more substantial plans in store for this feature. We'll have to wait for the next release of Word to find out.

Using AutoText

Word's AutoText feature lets you store words, phrases, or longer portions of text and graphics under a user-defined name. To recall the stored text, you simply type the AutoText name and press F3, the AutoText key. For example, you might store your address in an AutoText entry named *addr*. Then to include your address in a document, you just type **addr** and press F3.

An AutoText entry can contain more than text; it can also contain complete formatting information as well as graphics. In essence, an AutoText entry can contain any part of a Word document that you can select.

Judicious use of AutoText can often help speed up your typing. I generally use AutoText on a project-by-project basis. For example, while writing this book, I found that I frequently need to refer to specific Word commands: for example, Tools⇨Options or File⇨Print. Rather than retype these commands over and over again, I've created AutoText entries for most of them. The AutoText name for each is the two-letter hot-key sequence for the command. For example, Tools⇨Options is *to* and File⇨Print is *fp*. It's a lot easier to type **fp** and press F3 than to type **File⇨Print**, underlines and all.

Creating an AutoText entry

To create an AutoText entry, type and format the text exactly as you want it to be stored. Then, select the text and call up the Edit⇨AutoText command. The AutoText dialog box will appear, as shown in Figure 12-7. Word suggests the text itself as the AutoText Name, but you'll want to change it to something more succinct. For example, I would type **ex** for the Name in Figure 12-7 and click Add to create the AutoText entry.

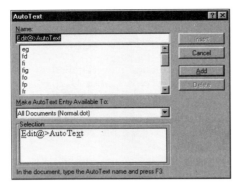

Figure 12-7: Creating an AutoText entry.

AutoCorrect and AutoText Compared

Word's AutoCorrect and AutoText features are similar enough that you can easily become confused about which is which, and which feature you should use in a given situation. The following table should help clarify the difference between AutoCorrect and AutoText.

AutoCorrect	AutoText
Associates a name with stored text, formatting, and graphics.	Associates a name with stored text, formatting, and graphics.
Entries are automatically recalled when you type the entry name followed by a space or punctuation.	Entries are manually recalled when you type the entry name and press the AutoText key (F3).
AutoCorrect is intended for correcting simple spelling errors or typing special symbols.	AutoText is intended for storing commonly used text for quick recall.
AutoCorrect entries are stored with Word options and are always available.	AutoText entries are stored in templates and are available only when the template is open.
AutoCorrect entries cannot be recalled from a macro.	AutoText entries can be recalled from a macro.
AutoCorrect provides other typing-related features, such as SmartQuotes, capitalization correction, and so on.	AutoText is just AutoText.

Secret

Do you remember what I said way back in Chapter 3 about the importance of paragraph marks: that all paragraph formatting is stored in the paragraph mark? This key Word concept comes into play when you create AutoText entries. If you want the AutoText entry to retain its paragraph formatting, you must select the paragraph mark along with the rest of the text before you create the AutoText entry. If the paragraph mark is not included in the AutoText entry, the text will pick up its paragraph formats from the paragraph where the AutoText entry is inserted.

Editing an AutoText entry

Tip

You cannot directly edit an AutoText entry. You have to follow a roundabout procedure such as the following:

1. Switch to a new document.

2. Insert the AutoText entry by typing its name and pressing F3.

3. Edit the entry however you want.

4. Select the entire entry.

5. Call up the Edit⇨AutoText command and save the entry by using the same name it was previously saved under.

Assigning AutoText to a toolbar button, menu, or keyboard shortcut

You can access AutoText entries from the Tools⇨Customize command, which means that you can assign them to toolbars, menus, and keyboard shortcuts. Then, you can recall the AutoText entry by clicking on its button, choosing its menu command, or using the assigned keyboard shortcut without worrying about or even knowing the AutoText entry's name.

For example, Figure 12-8 shows a customized toolbar that contains buttons that insert boilerplate clauses into a church's order of worship. When the church secretary prepares the order of worship each week, he or she simply clicks on the appropriate buttons to include the various components that will be used in that week's worship service. Creating a toolbar of this sort is useful for any type of document that must be regularly assembled from a collection of recurring paragraphs.

Using the Spike

In the last chapter, I said that the most important keyboard shortcuts in Word for Windows 95 are the basic cut-and-paste keys: Ctrl+X to cut text to the Clipboard, Ctrl+C to copy text to the Clipboard, and Ctrl+V to paste text into your document from the Clipboard. These keys are great as far as they go, but at times you really need a more powerful cut-and-paste feature.

Figure 12-8: A toolbar that features AutoText entries.

Suppose, for example, that you want to create a new document by moving information from a half-dozen existing documents. Using regular cut-and-paste, you would employ a procedure something like the following:

1. Create a new document.

2. Open a document containing something you need to move.

3. Cut the text you need to the Clipboard.

4. Switch back to the new document.

5. Paste the text from the Clipboard into the new document.

6. Repeat Steps 2 through 5 until the new document is assembled.

This procedure works, but it involves a great deal of unnecessary switching back and forth between documents. What if you could just cut text to the Clipboard without obliterating the Clipboard's existing contents? Then, you could simply cut the text you need from one document, open another document and cut some more text, and so on until you've cut all the text you need. Next, you switch to the new document and paste in all that text with one swift keystroke.

Word enables you to do precisely that by using an obscure little feature known as the *Spike*. The Spike has nothing to do with volleyball, punk rock hairstyles, or Snoopy's little brother. Rather, the Spike is a kind of super-Clipboard that accumulates bits and pieces of text, graphics, or whatever else you place on it. Then with a single keystroke, it inserts its entire contents into a document. Follow this procedure to use the Spike:

1. Select the text, graphics, or whatever else you want to move from the initial document and place on the Spike.

2. Press Ctrl+F3. Ctrl+F3 is the magic "Cut-to-Spike" key. The selected text or graphics is deleted from the document and added to the Spike.

3. Perform Steps 1 and 2 again for other bits of text and graphics that you want accumulated on the Spike. You can open other files to collect information from several documents to put on the Spike.

4. After you've gathered up all the text and graphics you need, position the cursor at the point in the target document where you want everything inserted.

5. Press Ctrl+Shift+F3. Ctrl+Shift+F3 is the magic "Put-the-Spike-Here" key. All the text and graphics on the Spike are inserted into the target document.

The Spike is kind of a peculiar gadget. One of its most annoying oddities is that you cannot place anything on the Spike without simultaneously deleting it from the document's text. Too bad. Word really should have a "Copy-to-Spike" key to complement its "Cut-to-Spike" key, but it doesn't.

Tip

One way around the problem of not being able to copy text to the Spike is to use the following sequence of keys: Ctrl+C, Ctrl+F3, Ctrl+V. This procedure copies the selection to the Clipboard, cuts the selection to the Spike, and then inserts the copy of the selection from the Clipboard back into the document at its original location. This leaves a copy of the text in the Spike that you can later paste into a document by pressing Ctrl+Shift+F3. (If you're really adventurous, record this key sequence as a macro and assign it to the keyboard combination Ctrl+Alt+F3 — your very own "Copy-to-Spike" command.)

Note

The Spike is actually a special AutoText entry. If you call up the Edit⇨AutoText command, you'll find an AutoText entry named Spike that contains the text you've collected.

Chapter 13

Mastering the Power Editing Tools: Spell Checker, Thesaurus, and Grammar Checker

In This Chapter

▶ Using Word's spell checker to avoid embarasing speling erors

▶ Using the thesaurus to help avoid repetition, reiteration, and redundancy

▶ Using the grammar checker if you want, but I don't really think it does much good, so why bother

This chapter shows you how to tap into three Word tools designed to help you improve your writing: the spell checker, the thesaurus, and the grammar checker. These three tools are sometimes collectively referred to as Word's *proofing tools,* because they assist in the task of proofreading your document.

Using the Spell Checker

I was voted Worst Speller in the Sixth Grade. Not that this qualifies me to run for vice president or anything, but it shows how much I appreciate computer spell checkers. Spelling makes no sense to me. I felt a little better after watching *The Story of English* on Public Television. Now at least I know who to blame for all the peculiarities of English spelling: the Angles, the Saxophones, and the Norms (especially the guy from "Cheers").

Thank goodness for Word's spell checker. It works its way through your document, looking up every word in its massive list of correctly spelled words and bringing any misspelled words to your attention. It performs this task without giggling or snickering. It gives you the opportunity, in fact, to tell it that *you* are right and *it* is wrong, and that it should learn how to spell words the way you do.

You can use Word's spell checker in one of two fundamentally different ways. You can have it watch over your shoulder as you type and gasp in horror every time you commit a spelling error, or you can wait until the document is finished and then have it check the spelling for the entire document. Either way, the spell checker is pretty thorough. Hope you have thick skin.

Secret

Although Word's spelling dictionary is fairly thorough, it does have some rather embarrassing omissions. Try creating a new document by using Word's Resume Wizard. The Wizard will insert a paragraph listing your accreditations. Unfortunately, even though Microsoft's own wizard inserts the word *accreditations* into the document, someone forgot to add *accreditations* to Word's spelling dictionary. The dictionary contains *accreditation* and *accreditation's*, but not *accreditations*. As a result, the word will be flagged as a misspelling.

On-the-fly spell checking

The easiest way to check your document's spelling is to enable Word's new on-the-fly spell checking option. If Word doesn't already check your spelling as you type, call up the Tools⇨Options command, click the Spelling tab, and check the Automatic Spell Checking check box.

When the Automatic Spell Checking option is enabled, Word underlines any misspelled words with a wavy red line as shown in Figure 13-1. (I tried to convince IDG Books Worldwide to pop for an expensive four-color printing process so that you could actually see the red lines in Figure 13-1. The folks at IDG informed me that they would be glad to oblige, but the cost would be deducted from my next royalty check. I then realized that you could probably figure out that the wavy line under the misspelled words in Figure 13-1 is supposed to be red.)

Note

Word doesn't beep, chime, or yell at you when you misspell a word. As a result, unless you watch the screen as you type, you may not immediately notice a spelling error. So it's a good idea to check the screen periodically, even if you are a 90-word-per-minute touch typist who never looks up.

If you make a spelling mistake, you can go back and correct the word. After you've done that, Word will remove the wavy red underline. Alternatively, you can right-click the word to bring up a quick menu of suggested spellings, as shown in Figure 13-2. Click the correct spelling for the word to replace the misspelled word with the correct spelling automatically.

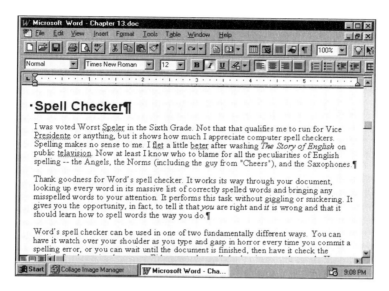

Figure 13-1: Automatic Spell Checking in action.

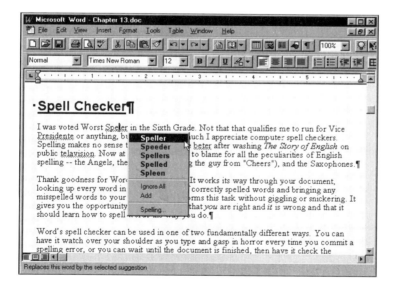

Figure 13-2: Correcting a spelling mistake.

The quick menu that appears when you right-click a misspelled word also shows the following commands:

- **Ignore all:** This command tells Word to ignore this misspelling, not only here but throughout the document. When you ignore the misspelling, Word removes the wavy red underlines.

Note

If you've told Word to ignore a few too many misspelled words, you can call up the Tools⇨Options command, click the Spelling tab, and click the Reset Ignore All. Word will immediately restore the wavy red underlines for any words that you previously told Word to ignore.

- **Add:** This command tells Word to add the misspelled Word to a custom dictionary so that Word will not flag it as a misspelling in the future. Use this command for those rare occasions when you come across a word that is spelled correctly, but which Word doesn't recognize. (This occurs frequently with proper names or in technical writing.) See the section "Custom dictionaries" later in this chapter for more information about custom dictionaries.

- **Spelling...:** This command brings up the Spelling dialog box for a full-fledged spell check.

Checking a document

If you don't use the Automatic Spell Checking feature, you can still check the spelling for a document after the fact. There are three ways to begin a spell check:

- Call up the Tools⇨Spelling command.

- Press F7.

 - Click the Spelling button in the Standard toolbar.

Whichever you choose, Word begins checking your spelling. When Word finds a misspelled word, it displays the Spelling dialog box, as shown in Figure 13-3.

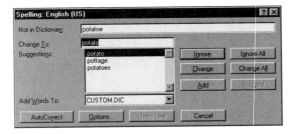

Figure 13-3: The Spelling dialog box.

You then have the following options:

- **Ignore:** If the word is correctly spelled as it is or if you want to spell it incorrectly on purpose (for example, if you're creating a menu for a restaurant called *The Koffee Kup*), click the Ignore button.

- **Ignore All:** Click this button to tell Word to ignore not only this occurrence of the word, but subsequent occurrences of the same word, too.

- **Change:** If the word really is misspelled, choose the correct spelling from the list of suggested spellings that appears in the dialog box and click the Change button. If the correct spelling doesn't appear among the suggestions, type the correct spelling in the Change To field and click the Change button.

- **Change All:** If you think the spelling error will crop up again, click Change All. This tells Word to correct any subsequent occurrences of the same error automatically.

- **Add:** If the word is correctly spelled and you want to add it to a custom dictionary, click Add. Word will add it to the current custom dictionary, as indicated in the Add Words To list box. (Custom dictionaries are explained later in this chapter.)

- **Suggest:** If you have disabled the Always Suggest option (see the section, "Spelling options" later in this chapter for more information), you can click the Suggest button so that Word will look up possible correct spellings in its dictionary.

- **AutoCorrect:** If you realize that you make this same spelling mistake over and over again, click AutoCorrect. Word will add the misspelled word and its correct spelling as an AutoCorrect entry. That way, Word will automatically correct the spelling error without even bothering to ask.

- **Options:** Brings up the Spelling Options dialog box, the same as if you had chosen the Tools⇨Options and clicked the Spelling tab.

- **Undo Last:** Reverses the action you took for the last misspelled word displayed by the Spelling dialog box.

If Word detects a repeated word (that is, the same word occurring twice in a row), it displays a variation of the Spelling dialog box that gives you two choices: Ignore or Delete. If you want the word to be repeated, click Ignore. To delete the second occurrence of the repeated word, click Delete.

Using the Spelling icon

 When Automatic Spell Checking is enabled, you'll find a Spelling icon in the form of an open book at the bottom of the Word window, near the right edge of the status bar. This icon indicates the status of your document's spelling:

Word is spell checking the document. The pencil is animated to give the feeling of motion. When you have enabled the Automatic Spell Check option, the pencil moves whenever you are typing.

    The document contains one or more spelling errors. You can go directly to the next spelling error by double-clicking on the Spelling icon.

    The document does not contain any spelling errors.

Note

You can double-click on the Spelling icon to go to the next misspelled word.

Spelling options

You can set options for Word's spell checker by choosing the Tools⇨Options and clicking the Spelling tab, or by clicking the Options button from the Spelling dialog box. Either way, the spelling options are displayed in the Options dialog box as shown in Figure 13-4.

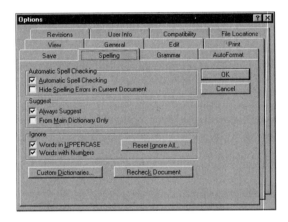

Figure 13-4: Spelling options.

The following paragraphs describe the proper use of each of the spelling options:

- **Automatic Spell Checking:** Use this option if you want Word to check your spelling automatically as you type.

- **Hide Spelling Errors in Current Document:** Hides the red wavy underline that marks misspelled words.

- **Always Suggest:** If your computer is fast enough that searching the dictionary for correct spellings doesn't slow down your spell check too much, leave this option selected. However, if you find that Word spends an inordinate amount of time each time you advance to the next misspelling, turn this option off.

- **From Main Dictionary Only:** Select this option if you do not want Word to consult your custom dictionaries when suggesting words.

- **Ignore Words in UPPERCASE:** Tells Word not to look up words that are in all uppercase. Many common acronyms and business names, including FEMA (Federal Emergency Management Agency) and IBM are not in the dictionary. With this option selected, Word won't even bother to spell check them if you type them in all uppercase.

- **Ignore Words with Numbers:** Technical documents are often filled with words that intermix text and numbers and shouldn't be spell checked. Win95 is one example. Other examples include product part numbers or government form numbers, such as BX-104 and 1040-A. With this option enabled, Word doesn't bother to look up any word that contains a mixture of letters and numbers.

- **Reset Ignore All:** This is the button you click to tell Word to forget about all those times you have chosen the Ignore All button while spell checking your document.

- **Custom Dictionaries:** This button brings up a separate dialog box for managing custom dictionaries and is described in the next section.

- **Recheck Document:** Use this button to force Word to recheck the spelling of a document after you've changed spelling options.

Custom dictionaries

Word comes with a large dictionary of spellings, called the *main dictionary*. As exhaustive as the main dictionary is, it isn't comprehensive. Many technical fields have their own specialized jargon, and new words are being invented every day (especially in Washington).

That's where custom dictionaries come in. A *custom dictionary* is a list of words (spelled correctly, of course) that supplements the main dictionary. Words are added to a custom dictionary when you click the Add button or when you select the Add command from the pop-up menu that appears when you right-click a misspelled word.

By default, Word sets up and maintains a single custom dictionary, named Custom.dic. This dictionary hides out in the \Windows\MSApps\Proof folder, although you can change this location by using the File Locations tab of the Tools⇨Options command.

If all of your writing needs are similar, a single custom dictionary is adequate. However, some people need more than one custom dictionary. For example, if you're an attorney by day and a Chaucer scholar by night, you probably don't want to store all of Chaucer's weird spellings in your default Custom.dic dictionary. After all, a contract or a will with spellings such as *commissioun* (*commission*), *symple* (*simple*), or *statut* (*statute*) probably wouldn't hold up in court.

For this purpose, Word lets you set up and maintain more than one custom dictionary, and you can have more than one dictionary active at once. Alternative custom dictionaries are created in the same folder as the default Custom.dic (\Program files\Common files\Proof), and must use the extension .DIC.

To manage custom dictionaries, Call up the Tools⇨Options command and click on the Spelling tab. The Spelling options will appear. (Refer back to Figure 13-4 if you're not sure what this dialog box looks like.) Click the Custom Dictionaries button to summon the Custom Dictionaries dialog box, as shown in Figure 13-5.

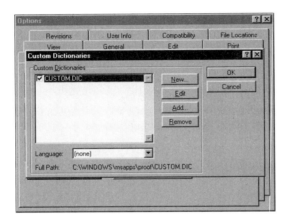

Figure 13-5: The Custom Dictionaries dialog box.

All of the available custom dictionaries will appear in the Custom Dictionaries list. To enable a custom dictionary, click on it to check its check box. To disable a custom dictionary temporarily, uncheck its check box.

Four buttons are provided for managing custom dictionaries:

■ **New:** Click this button to create a new custom dictionary. Word will prompt you for a name for the new dictionary.

■ **Edit:** Opens the selected dictionary so that you can edit its word list. A custom dictionary is nothing more than a simple ASCII text file, with one word per line. This simple structure allows you to edit the dictionary by using any text editor. Word simply opens the dictionary by as a text file.

■ **Add:** Displays an Add Custom Dictionary dialog box that is similar to the File Open dialog box. It allows you to browse your hard disk for dictionary files to be added to the Custom Dictionary list.

■ **Remove:** Removes a custom dictionary from the Custom Dictionary list. This does not actually delete the file; it merely deletes Word's knowledge of the file.

Excluding text from spell checking

Sometimes, you want to prevent Word from spell checking a range of text, either a text selection or an entire paragraph. For example, you might quote a passage from Chaucer or Shakespeare, and you do not want Word to flag its misspelled words every time you spell check the document.

To prevent Word from spell-checking text, select the text in question and call up the Tools⇨Language command. Select (no proofing) as the language for the text and then click OK. Word will skip over the text formatted with (no proofing) whenever it does a spell check.

Wild-card searches

Secret

A little-known feature of Word's spell checker is that you can perform wildcard searches against the main dictionary. This can be useful for solving crossword puzzles or looking for words that rhyme. Here is the procedure:

1. Call up the Tools⇨Spelling command and click the Spelling button, or press F7. Either way, the Spelling dialog box will appear.

2. Disregard the first misspelling identified by Word. Instead, type the wild-card search pattern you want to use in the Change To field. You can use a question mark for one character or an asterisk to search for more than one character. For example, to search for words that end in -ution, type *ution.

3. Click the Suggest button. Word will display the first 20 words that match your wildcard search, as shown in Figure 13-6. (Unfortunately, there's no way to get past the 20-word limit.)

Figure 13-6: Using the spell checker with wild-cards.

Here are some other examples of wild-card searches:

- *Under* finds words of any length that begin with *under-*. More than 20 words match this wild-card, so Word doesn't display them all. You will see *under-achiever*, *underbelly*, and some other interesting ones.

- *Def* ment* finds words of any length that start with *def-* and end with *-ment*. Three words will be found: *defacement, deferment,* and *defilement.*

- *f??nt* finds five letter words that begin with *f-* and end with *-nt*. The following five words will be found: *faint, feint, flint, fount,* and *front.*

A macro for cheating at word jumbles

Macro

Word's built-in spell checker has the little-known capability to take a jumbled-up collection of letters and put back in the right order. For example, give it the letters *rmtoucpe,* and it spews forth *computer.* Give it *dnre,* and it emits *nerd* and *rend.*

Unfortunately, the Microsoft people decided that the company that syndicates those "Jumble" puzzles in newspapers might sue them if they made this feature available to just anybody, so they hid it deep within the bowels of Word, where only those who have the courage to tackle WordBasic may find it. To use the "Jumble" feature, you have to write a macro:

```
Sub MAIN
Dim Matches$(20)
Begin Dialog UserDialog 396, 200, "The UnJumbler", .UnJumbler
    Text 9, 12, 145, 13, "Word to UnJumble:", .Text1
    Text 9, 31, 71, 13, "Matches:", .Text2
    TextBox 166, 10, 213, 18, .Word
    ListBox 11, 54, 192, 120, Matches$(), .Matches
    PushButton 245, 49, 134, 21, "UnJumble", .UnJumble
    PushButton 291, 81, 88, 21, "Done", .Done
End Dialog
Dim dlg As UserDialog
Dialog dlg
End Sub


Function UnJumbler(id$, action, suppval)
Dim Matches$(20)
If action = 2 Then
    If id$ = "UnJumble" Then
        On Error Resume Next
        Word$ = DlgText$("Word")
        ToolsGetSpelling Matches$(), Word$, "", "", 2
        DlgListBoxArray "Matches", Matches$()
        UnJumbler = - 1
        DlgFocus "Word"
    End If
End If
End Function
```

When you run the UnJumbler macro, the dialog box shown in Figure 13-7 appears. Type the scrambled word in the Word to UnJumble field and then click the UnJumble button. The macro unscrambles the word and displays the results in the Matches list. You can unscramble as many words as you want before clicking the Done button to end the macro.

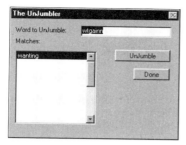

Figure 13-7: The UnJumbler macro. Cheaters never prosper.

Unfortunately, the UnJumbler can't deal with multiple words. If you type two or more words in the Word to UnJumble field, the UnJumbler ignores them. And you're on your own if the letters represent two or more scrambled-up words.

Tip

Try the UnJumbler on Scrabble puzzles, too. It works only when there is a solution that uses all seven letters, which occurs quite frequently. I tried it on a recent puzzle, with the following results:

l-e-t-a-y-h-h (second letter double)	healthy (17 points)
b-d-r-e-m-a-l (triple word score)	marbled (36 points)
g-v-s-n-i-k-i	Vikings (15 points)
e-a-n-r-d-t-g	granted (9 points)

With a 50-point bonus for each seven-letter word, that's a score of 277. Not bad for someone whose editor says he doesn't know how to spel.

You can use the UnJumbler to find six-letter words from a seven-letter Scrabble rack with a little work. Type in just six of the seven letters and click the UnJumble button. Try it seven times, leaving out a different letter each time, to find the best word.

Using the Thesaurus

The thesaurus allows you to look up words with similar meanings. I use it all the time to try to add some variety to my writing. For example, rather than say that Word has a *bunch* of proofing features, I might use the thesaurus to remind me that I could also say that Word has *a lot* of proofing features, or perhaps a *bevy* of proofing features.

To call up the thesaurus, place the insertion point in the word you want to look up and press Shift+F7. The Thesaurus dialog box will appear, as shown in Figure 13-8.

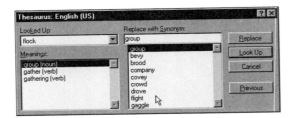

Figure 13-8: The Thesaurus.

If a suitable alternative appears in the Thesaurus dialog box, select it and click the Replace button. The original word in your text will be replaced by the selected alternative.

If a suitable alternative doesn't appear, do not be discouraged, depressed, broken-hearted, or shattered. Perhaps one of the suggested alternatives is close, but not quite right. If so, double-click on it to see a list of its synonyms. Or, if several words appear in the Meanings list, double-click on one of them to see a different list of synonyms. You can continue in this fashion as much as you want.

Using the Grammar Checker, or Not

I think Word's much-touted grammar checker is a letdown. This is not because there's anything wrong with it. Actually, as grammar checkers go, it's pretty good. In my opinion, though, grammar checkers are a waste of time. They aren't really intelligent enough to distinguish between genuine grammatical errors and stylistic license, so the majority of the messages generated by the grammar checker will most likely be incorrect.

Consider Figure 13-9, in which the grammar checker has flagged the first sentence of Ernest Hemingway's masterpiece, *The Old Man and the Sea*, as sexist. The checker wasn't smart enough to realize that this is fictional narrative and the word *man* is entirely appropriate. It suggests replacing *man* with *person*, *human being*, or *individual*. Somehow I doubt that *The Old Human Being and the Sea* would have been as compelling a title.

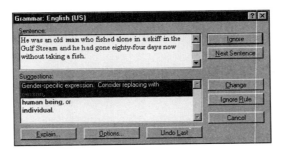

Figure 13-9: The grammar checker doesn't like Hemingway's writing much.

I thought that maybe Hemingway was an isolated example, so I pulled another book off my shelf: *A Brief History of Time* by Steven Hawking. Instead of fiction, this one is a technical book, albeit intended for a mass audience. *A Brief History of Time* spent more than 100 weeks on *The New York Times* bestseller list and sold millions of copies. It is perhaps the best written technical book I've ever read. For some reason, Hawking's prose, which is crystal clear to any human reader, seems to stump Word's grammar checker. When it comes to the sentence:

> Most people would find the picture of our universe as an infinite tower of tortoises rather ridiculous, but why do we think we know better?

The grammar checker suggests replacing the underlined *do* with *does*. Go figure. The grammar checker went on to suggest that Hawking had used incomplete sentences, left his prepositions hanging in the wrong places, and was prone to use run-on sentences, as if the book would have spent even more time on the bestseller list if Hawking had used shorter sentences.

I've run the grammar checker on many other specimens of outstanding writing, with similar results. The "Gettysburg Address" is guilty of passive voice and run-on sentences; Winston Churchill mixes up his prepositions; Thomas Jefferson should have used more periods; and so on.

One line of reasoning in favor of using the grammar checker is that it can help a poor writer become more proficient. This would be possible, were it not for the fact that the grammar checker is just as apt to offer bad advice as good. How is a poor writer supposed to know the former from the latter?

If you must use the grammar checker, feel free to ignore its advice. And, by all means call up the Tools⇨Options command, click the Grammar tab, and click Customize Settings and review the rules used by the grammar checker. Disable any rules you don't agree with or find the grammar checker cannot reliably detect. The section "Customizing the grammar checker" explains how.

Checking for grammar errors

The basic procedure for running the grammar checker is simple. To start the ball rolling, open the document you want to check and invoke the Tools⇨Grammar command. If you want to check only part of the document, select the portion you want checked first. Either way, the grammar checker jumps right into checking the document. When it finds what it believes to be an error, it displays a dialog box similar to the one that was shown back in Figure 13-9.

You can respond to the grammar checker's messages by clicking any of the buttons that appear on the grammar checker dialog box:

- **Ignore:** Tells the grammar checker to ignore the alleged error. This is the button you will click nine times out of ten (with the possible exception of Cancel).

- **Next Sentence:** Many times, the grammar checker will report multiple errors for a single sentence. You can often tell when the grammar checker isn't going to be able to make heads or tails out of a sentence. For example, the grammar checker usually has trouble with headings, captions, and other bits of text that aren't complete sentences. Rather than wade through message after message for these non sentences, you can click <u>N</u>ext Sentence to direct the grammar checker to skip ahead to the next sentence.

- **<u>C</u>hange:** This button allows you to edit the sentence directly in the Grammar dialog box and then record your change in the document.

- **Ignore <u>R</u>ule:** When you get tired of the grammar checker constantly misdiagnosing writing flaws, you can click Ignore <u>R</u>ule. This tells the grammar checker to cease from warning you about violations of the rule that triggered this message.

- **<u>E</u>xplain:** Displays a description of the rule that caused the sentence to be flagged as a possible error. Some of the explanations are brief; others are elaborate grammar lessons. For example, Figure 13-10 shows an explanation that was triggered by Abraham Lincoln's use of the word *which* in the following sentence from the Gettysburg Address:

  > It is for us the living, rather, to be dedicated here to the unfinished work <u>which</u> they who fought here have thus far so nobly advanced.

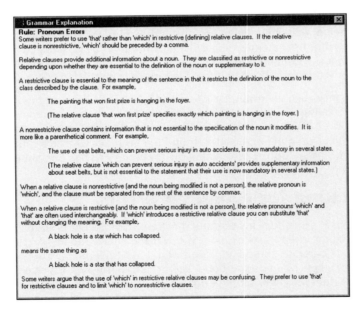

Figure 13-10: The grammar checker's explanation of why Lincoln should have considered *that* instead of *which*.

- **<u>O</u>ptions:** Calls up the Options dialog box so that you can change the behavior of the grammar checker. These options are described in the section "Customizing the grammar checker" later in this chapter.

- **Undo <u>L</u>ast:** Undoes the last grammar checker action.

■ **Cancel:** My favorite button on the Grammar dialog box.

Readability statistics

After the grammar checker finishes its futile effort at tearing apart your prose, it does an often useful analysis of your document's readibility by using several well-known methods for determining the "grade level" of your document. Figure 13-11 shows these readability statistics, in this case, calculated for the very chapter you are reading now.

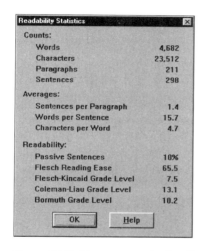

Figure 13-11: The grammar checker displays readability statistics.

The first two sections of the Readability Statistics dialog box show various counts and averages compiled from your document. Then, the following readability statistics are shown:

■ **Flesch Reading Ease:** Computes document readability based on the average number of syllables per word and the average number of words per sentence. Scores range from 0 (zero) to 100. Most good writing falls in the range of 60 to 70. The higher the number, the more readable the text.

■ **Flesch-Kincaid Grade Level:** Computes document readability based on the average number of syllables per word and the average number of words per sentence, similar to the Flesch Reading Ease measurement. However, the resulting score is stated as a grade-school level. For example, a score of 8.0 means that an eighth-grader should be able to read and understand the document. Most writers shoot for seventh- to eighth-grade level on this scale.

■ **Coleman-Liau Grade Level:** Another grade-school level measurement, based on characters per word and words per sentence.

■ **Bormuth Grade Level:** Yet another grade-level measurement, also based on characters per word and words per sentence.

Notice that the different grade-level measurements give wildly different results. A small variation would be understandable, but in Figure 13-11, the Flesch-Kincaid measurement says a seventh-grader should be able to read and understand this chapter; the Bormuth measure says it is fit for high school sophomores, and the Coleman-Liau measurement says that only high-school graduates should attempt to read it.

The moral of the story is: Don't put too much stock in these statistics. They are helpful as a general guide, but don't take them too seriously.

Customizing the grammar checker

You can use the Tools⇨Options command to customize the grammar checker so that it checks only for specific types of grammatical errors. Call up the Tools⇨Options command and click on the Grammar tab to see the options shown in Figure 13-12.

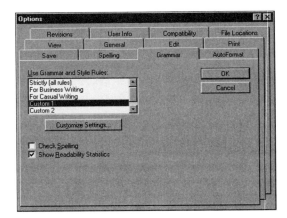

Figure 13-12: Setting the grammar checker's options.

These options allow you to select one of three preconfigured grammar checking styles: Strictly (all rules), For Business Writing, and For Casual Writing. In addition, you can choose one of three custom styles: Custom 1, Custom 2, and Custom 3.

Each of these grammar checking style options represents a different combination of the grammar checker's 50 or so rules. For example, Business Writing checks for questionable prepositions, contractions, and archaic expressions; Casual Writing does not.

You can change the specific rules that are checked by any of these options by selecting the option in the Use Grammar and Style Rules list box and clicking the Customize Settings button. This brings up the dialog box shown in Figure 13-13.

Figure 13-13: The Customize Grammar Settings dialog box.

Here, you can choose which specific rules to check for. Notice that the list box at the center of the dialog box actually displays two distinct lists of rules depending on the setting of the <u>G</u>rammar and <u>S</u>tyle option buttons. In addition, you can tell the grammar checker how sensitive it should be to split infinitives, consecutive nouns or prepositional phrases, and long sentences.

Secret

Surprisingly, Word does not provide any way directly to summon the Readability Statistics dialog box that was presented in the previous section without first running the grammar checker. However, you can use the Customize Grammar Settings dialog box to set up the Custom 1 setting so that it ignores all of the built-in grammar rules. That way, when you run the grammar checker, it will display the Readability Statistics dialog box without any intervening Grammar warnings.

To set up the grammar checker to work this way, follow these steps:

1. Choose the <u>T</u>ools⇨<u>O</u>ptions command and click the Grammar tab.

2. Select "Custom 1" in the <u>U</u>se Grammar and Style Rules list box.

3. Click the Cus<u>t</u>omize Settings button.

4. In the Customize Grammar Settings dialog box, uncheck all of the <u>G</u>rammar rules that appear in the list box.

5. Click the <u>S</u>tyle option button and uncheck all of the rules that appear.

6. Change the Split <u>I</u>nfinitives, Consecutive <u>N</u>ouns, and Prespositional <u>P</u>hrases options to "Never."

7. Change the Sentences Containing More <u>W</u>ords Than field to 999.

8. Click OK to return to the Options dialog box and click OK again.

A macro to insert readability statistics at the end of the document

The following macro is on the Word for Windows 95 SECRETS Sample Macros.dot template under the name InsertStats. It inserts a table at the end of the current document that shows readability statistics for the document, as shown in Figure 13-14.

```
Sub MAIN
numstats = CountToolsGrammarStatistics()
Dim GrammarArray$(numstats - 1, 1)
ToolsGrammarStatisticsArray GrammarArray$()
EndOfDocument()
InsertPageBreak
TableInsertTable .NumColumns = 2
Style "Normal"
Bold 1
Insert "Readability Statistics"
NextCell
Bold 1
InsertDateTime
For i = 0 To numstats - 1
    NextCell
    Insert GrammarArray$(i, 0)
    NextCell
    Insert GrammarArray$(i, 1)
Next i
TableSelectTable
TableColumnWidth .AutoFit
BorderLineStyle 1
BorderInside
BorderLineStyle 2
BorderOutside
CharRight
End Sub
```

Readability Statistics	09/12/95
Words	271
Characters	1,180
Paragraphs	3
Sentences	10
Sentences per Paragraph	3.3
Words per Sentence	27.1
Characters per Word	4.2
Passive Sentences	40%
Flesch Reading Ease	68.2
Flesch Kincaid Grade Level	9.1
Coleman-Liau Grade Level	14.2
Bormuth Grade Level	10.9

Figure 13-14: The Readability Statistics table inserted by the InsertStats macro.

To create this macro, choose the Tools⇨Macros command, type **InsertStats** in the Macro Name field and then click Create. Type the macro in exactly as shown above. If you find this macro useful, you may want to use the Tools⇨Customize command to attach it to a menu or toolbar button.

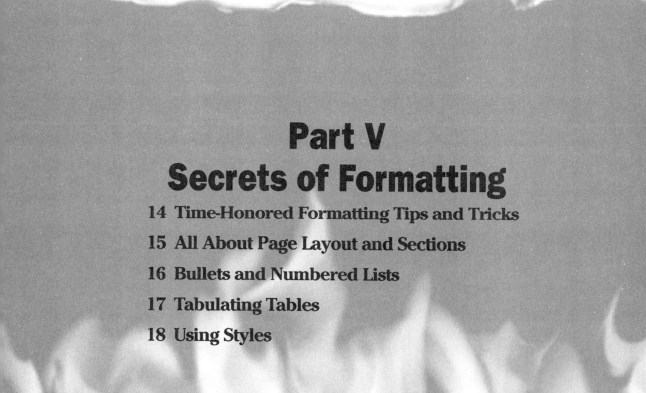

Part V
Secrets of Formatting

14 Time-Honored Formatting Tips and Tricks

15 All About Page Layout and Sections

16 Bullets and Numbered Lists

17 Tabulating Tables

18 Using Styles

Chapter 14

Time-Honored Formatting Tips and Tricks

In This Chapter

▶ The basics of applying character and paragraph formats, including the most useful keyboard shortcuts and toolbar buttons

▶ The ins and outs of using tabs, including the proper way to set up tab leaders to create a row of dots across the line or a fill-in-the-blanks form

▶ The proper way to apply borders and shading

▶ All about the AutoFormat command, even though I don't think it's particularly useful

▶ Several handy macros, including one that increases and decreases indentation from both sides of the line, and an improved version of the Change Case command

If you've been using Word for any length of time, you already know how to apply basic formatting to characters and paragraphs. This chapter describes all of the formatting options that are available for characters and paragraphs from the Format menu, along with the keyboard and button bar shortcuts you can use to apply them quickly. Much of this material may seem like review, but I urge you to read the entire chapter. Sometimes even veteran Word users come across a so-called "basic" feature that they never knew existed.

Understanding Character and Paragraph Formats

Before I dive into the details of using the specific formats for characters and paragraphs, I want to review the basics of how character and paragraph formatting works. I presented this information back in Chapter 3, but it's important enough that I'll reiterate it here.

Characters are the basic unit of information in a Word document. A character can be a letter, number, or any other symbol you can type (or insert by using the Insert⇨Symbol command). Characters can carry basic formatting information, such as font, size, attribute (bold, italic, underline, and so on), color, and so forth. However, most characters carry none of these formats. Instead, they inherit their formatting from the paragraph that contains them.

A *paragraph* is a stream of characters that ends with a paragraph mark. The paragraph mark is created when you press the Enter key. Paragraphs carry the basic character formatting information that applies to all of the characters in the paragraph, and they carry paragraph formatting, such as indentation, spacing, tab settings, borders and shading, and so on.

Perhaps the most important concept to understand in all of Word is that paragraph formats are stored inside the paragraph mark. For example, if you place the insertion point somewhere in the middle of a paragraph and use the Format⇨Paragraph command to change the indentation, the indentation setting will be stored in the paragraph mark at the end of the paragraph, and the new setting will apply *to the entire paragraph.*

This is one of the key differences between Word and most other word processors — most notably WordPerfect. In WordPerfect, any change to indentation applies at the beginning of the line where you insert the indentation code. As a result, it is possible for the indentation of a paragraph to change in the middle of the paragraph. Not so with Word. Because the indentation format is kept in the paragraph mark at the *end* of the paragraph, the entire paragraph can have but one indentation setting.

Tip

Because the paragraph marks play such a vital role in formatting, I recommend that you always make them visible. If you cannot see the paragraph marks in your Word documents, call up the Tools⇨Options command, click on the View tab, and select the Paragraph Marks option.

A third level of formatting that applies in Word is *section formatting*, which controls page layout formats such as margins, columns, headers and footers, page numbers, and so on. I'll defer discussion of section formats until the next chapter.

A Word About Styles

No discussion of formatting would be complete without mention of *styles,* which are nothing more than named collections of formats. Word for Windows 95 lets you use two types of styles: paragraph styles and character styles. When you apply a paragraph style, Word obtains the formatting information for the paragraph from the style. The paragraph style governs not only the paragraph formatting, such as indentation and spacing, but also the default character style for the paragraph. Although less popular, character styles let you apply formats to characters within a paragraph.

A complete discussion of styles is beyond the scope of this chapter, but you'll find everything you could possibly want to know about styles (and probably more) in Chapter 18. For now, two key points about styles are worth remembering:

- Paragraphs and characters draw their basic formatting information from styles. Any formats applied directly to paragraphs or characters by using the techniques described in this chapter serve to override the formatting information obtained from the styles.

- *All* paragraphs in a Word document are formatted by styles. In other words, styles are not optional. By default, new paragraphs are formatted with the Normal paragraph style. The Normal style is set up for 10-point Times New Roman, with no indentation or added line spacing.

Two Ways to Apply Character Formats

You can apply character formats before you type or after you type.

To apply formatting before you type, follow these steps:

1. Type up to the point at which you want your new formatting to apply.

2. Choose the format you want to use by using the Format⇨Font command, a keyboard shortcut, or a toolbar button.

3. Type away. The format you chose will be applied to the text as you type.

4. When you're done, use the Format⇨Font command, keyboard shortcut, or toolbar button again to turn off the special character formatting.

To apply character formats to text you've already typed, follow these steps:

1. Highlight the text where you want to apply the format.

Note

   To apply a special format to a single word, just click on the mouse any-where in the word. You don't have to actually highlight the word.

2. Choose the format you want to use by using the Format⇨Font command, a keyboard shortcut, or a toolbar button. The highlighted text will receive the new format.

You can remove formatting in the same way that you apply it. For example, if a word is italicized, you can remove the italics by clicking anywhere in the word and pressing Ctrl+I, or by selecting the entire word and pressing Ctrl+I.

Secret

The good programmers at Microsoft left a rather embarrassing bug in Word for Windows 95: The trick of removing formatting by clicking anywhere in the word and using a keyboard shortcut or toolbar button will not work if you happen to click between the last letter in the word and the next to the last letter. For example, type the word ***bug*** and then move the insertion point between the *u* and the *g* and press Ctrl+I. The word will become italic. Now press Ctrl+I again. The word should return to normal type, but it doesn't. Press the left arrow to move the insertion point between the *b* and the *u* and then press Ctrl+I: The text reverts to normal. But, any time the insertion point is positioned between the next to last and last letters of a word, you cannot remove formatting by using the formatting shortcuts or toolbar buttons.

Using the Format⇨Font Command

You can apply all of Word's basic character formats with the Format⇨Font command, which summons the dialog box shown in Figure 14-1. For the most popular formatting options, keyboard shortcuts and toolbar buttons are provided so that you don't have to trudge through this tedious dialog box. But for those formats with keyboard shortcuts that you can't remember and for those that have no shortcuts, the Format⇨Font command is the only option.

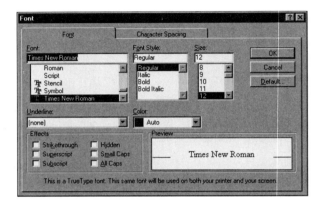

Figure 14-1: The Font dialog box (Font tab).

The Format⇨Font command is the only way to apply the following formats to characters:

■ Dashed underline

■ Color

■ Strikethrough

■ Character spacing

These formats have no keyboard assignments or toolbar buttons. If you use them frequently, refer back to Chapter 6 for instructions on how to create keyboard shortcuts or toolbar buttons for them.

The following formatting options are available under the Font tab of the Format⇨Font command:

■ **Font:** Selects the font to use for the selected text. (Strictly speaking, Microsoft should have used the term *typeface* rather than font because Times New Roman Bold is a different font than Times New Roman Italic, but both are members of the Times New Roman typeface. Sigh.)

■ **Font Style:** Allows you to select Regular, Italic, Bold, or Bold Italic text.

- **Size:** Specifies the size of the type in points (a point is 1/72 of an inch). You can type any point size into the Size field (including fractions, such as 12.5), or you can select from the commonly used sizes in the list box.

- **Underline:** Allows you to select from one of several underlining styles: (none), Single, Words Only, Double, or Dotted.

Note

The wavy red underlines you see from time to time are displayed on the screen by the spell checker whenever you misspell a word. You cannot manually apply that type of underline with the Format⇨Font command.

- **Color:** Select a color for the text from the drop-down list.

- **Effects:** You can select from among the following special effects: Strikethrough, Superscript, Subscript, Hidden, SMALL CAPS, and ALL CAPS.

Note

When you use Small Caps or All Caps, Word remembers which letters are typed in uppercase and which are lowercase. Thus, you can revert to normal mixed-case type by removing the Small Caps or All Caps option.

Notice that two pairs of the Effects check boxes are one-or-the-other options: Superscript/Subscript and Small Caps/All Caps. You can select only one of each pair. That makes complete sense, of course: Text cannot be both a superscript and a subscript, nor can you format text as both small caps and all caps.

If you click on the Character Spacing tab, the Character Spacing options will appear, as shown in Figure 14-2.

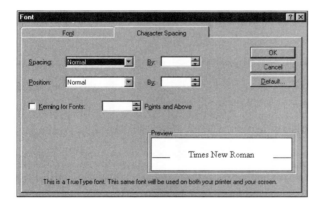

Figure 14-2: Character Spacing options.

The following formatting options are available from the Character Spacing tab of the Font dialog box:

- **Spacing:** Normal, Expanded, or Condensed. If you select Expanded or Condensed, you must then set the By field to indicate how many points the space between individual characters will be increased or decreased. You can experiment with different settings for these fields to create letters that appear scrunched together or spaced out. (This option is not where you set the spacing between lines. That's done via the Format⇨Paragraph command, which is described later in this chapter.)

- **Position:** Normal, Raised, or Lowered. If you select Raised or Lowered, you then indicate how many points above or below the baseline you want the text moved in the By field.

- **Kerning for Fonts:** Kerning means to adjust the amount of space between certain combinations of letters that would otherwise appear to have too much space between them. If you check this field, you can also set the minimum character size for which kerning should be used. This is handy because kerning problems are more noticeable at larger type sizes.

Tip

Chapter 19 explains the character spacing options described previously in greater detail.

When you have finished setting these options, click on OK. The formats you selected will be applied to the selected text. If no text was selected, the new formats will be used for text you subsequently type.

Character Formatting Shortcuts

Word comes preconfigured with keyboard shortcuts and toolbar buttons that allow you to apply the most commonly used character formats quickly. Table 14-1 lists these shortcuts.

Table 14-1	Character Formatting the Easy Way	
Toolbar Button	*Keyboard Shortcut*	*What It Does*
B	Ctrl+B	**Bold**
I	Ctrl+I	*Italic*
U	Ctrl+U	Underline (Continuous)
	Ctrl+Shift+W	Word Underline
	Ctrl+Shift+D	Double Underline

Toolbar Button	*Keyboard Shortcut*	*What It Does*
	Ctrl+Shift+A	ALL CAPS
	Ctrl+Shift+K	SMALL CAPS
	Shift+F3	Changes Case
	Ctrl+=	Subscript
	Ctrl+Shift+=	Superscript
[Times New Roman ▼]	Ctrl+Shift+F	Changes font
[12 ▼]	Ctrl+Shift+P	Changes point size
	Ctrl+]	Increases size one point
	Ctrl+[	Decreases size one point
	Ctrl+Shift+>	Increases size to next available size
	Ctrl+Shift+<	Decreases size to previous available size
	Ctrl+Shift+Q	Switches to Symbol font (Greek Tragedy)
	Ctrl+Shift+S	Changes style
	Ctrl+Shift+Z	Removes character formatting
	Ctrl+Spacebar	Removes character formatting

Removing Character Formatting

To remove any character formats you've applied, highlight the text and press Ctrl+Spacebar. The text will revert back to the character format specified for the Normal style.

Using the Format⇨Paragraph Command

The Format⇨Paragraph command is the gathering place for all of Word's paragraph formats. Figure 14-3 shows the dialog box that appears when you summon this command.

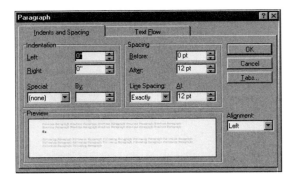

Figure 14-3: The Paragraph dialog box.

You can apply the following formats from the Paragraph dialog box:

■ **Indentation:** Sets the left and right indentation for the paragraph. The Left and Right fields normally show the indentation in inches, but you can change the unit of measure to any of the options listed in Table 14-2.

■ **Special:** Sets special indentation types. The most common is First Line, which sets the indentation for the first line of the paragraph. Hanging can be used to create hanging indents, in which every line but the first line of the paragraph is indented. (A separate section is devoted to hanging indents later in this chapter.)

■ **Spacing:** Sets the amount of space to leave before and after each paragraph. See Table 14-2 for the valid units of measure for these fields.

■ **Line Spacing**: Sets the amount of space to provide between each line. Specify Single, 1.5 Lines, or Double to let Word decide on the exact line spacing based on the font size. Or, you can specify an exact line spacing by selecting Exactly and setting the At field to the line spacing you want to use.

Warning

You can create problems for yourself if you use the Exactly option for Line Spacing and later change the font size. That's because Word doesn't adjust the line spacing to reflect the new font size. For example, if you set Line Spacing to Exactly 14 pt and change the font size to 24 pts, the line spacing won't be tall enough to accommodate the large font size, and you'll end up with chopped-off characters.

■ **Alignment:** Sets the alignment for the paragraph to Left, Centered, Right, or Justified.

Table 14-2	Units of Measure for Indentation and Spacing
Example	*Unit of Measure*
0.5 in	Inches
0.5"	Inches
1.5 cm	Centimeters (There are 2.54 centimeters in an inch.)
36 pt	Points (There are 72 points in an inch.)
3 pi	Picas (There are 6 picas in an inch.)
2 li	Two lines

Using hanging indents

A *hanging indent* is a paragraph in which every line except the first is indented. Hanging indents are commonly used along with bullets or numbers to create lists. Figure 14-4 shows several examples of hanging indents.

Creating a hanging indent in Word is one of the things that annoys experienced WordPerfect users more than anything else. In WordPerfect, you just press F4 (the Indent key), and the rest of the paragraph is indented at the nearest tab stop. For example, to create the hanging indent shown in the last example in Figure 14-4, you would type **_Hanging Indent_** in bold italic, press F4, and type the rest of the paragraph.

Creating a hanging indent is a little more complicated in Word. In Word, you create a hanging indent by calling up the Format⇨Paragraph command that sets the Special indentation field to Hanging and typing the amount of indentation in the By field. Word automatically places a tab stop at this location. Then, you would type **_Hanging Indent_** in bold italic, press the Tab key, and type the rest of the paragraph. (You can also create the hanging indent by dragging the hanging indent tool on the ruler, as described in the next section.)

Tip

The bullets and numbering feature automatically sets hanging indents for you. Chapter 16 covers this feature.

Setting indents with the ruler

You can also set paragraph indents by using the indentation controls on the ruler. There are four controls for adjusting indentation by using the ruler, as shown in Figure 14-5.

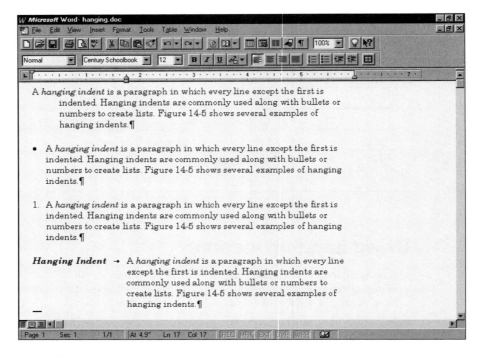

Figure 14-4: Examples of hanging indents.

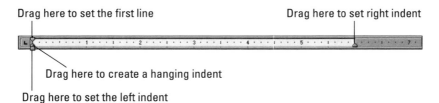

Figure 14-5: Ruler controls for setting paragraph indentation.

You can drag any of these tools to adjust the paragraph indentation. To set a hanging indent, drag the hanging indent tool to the right. The first line indent tool will remain in place, and a tab stop will automatically be created so that you can tab the first line to the indentation point.

Creating Custom Toolbar Buttons for Hanging Indents

If you use hanging indents frequently, you may want to create custom toolbar buttons to increase and decrease the hanging indent. To do so, follow these steps:

1. Call up the Tools⇨Customize command and click on the Toolbars tab. Note that throughout the following steps, the Customize dialog box will remain on-screen.

2. Choose All Commands in the Categories field and drag the HangingIndent and Unhang commands to any available location in the Formatting toolbar. Don't worry which button image you select for the new buttons because you will change it in the remaining steps.

3. Right-click on the Increase Indent button in the Formatting toolbar and choose the Copy Button Image command.

4. Right-click on the new Increase Hanging Indent button and choose the Paste Button Image command.

5. Right-click on the new Increase Hanging Indent button again and choose the Edit button image command.

6. Edit the button image so that it looks like this:

7. Repeat Steps 3-6, copying and pasting the image from the Decrease Indent button onto the new Unhang button and editing the image so that it looks like this:

A handy pair of double indentation macros

One type of indentation I frequently require is a double-indent, where both the left and right margins are indented, but Word has no automatic way to create this feature. Because I use this often when I include quotations in my writing, I've devised a pair of macros, one to increase both indents and the other to decrease both indents, and I've assigned them to toolbar buttons with custom images.

Both of these macros take into account that some users do not work with inches as their default unit of measure. As a result, the macros first change the unit of measure to picas and add or subtract 3 from the current left and right indents to increase or decrease the indentation by .5 inch (six picas are in an inch). After setting the left or right indentations, the macros then reset the unit of measure to the previous unit.

To create the first macro, call up the Tools⇨Macro command, type **IncreaseBothIndents** as the macro name, and click on Create. Then, type in the macro exactly as follows:

```
Sub MAIN
Dim tog As ToolsOptionsGeneral
GetCurValues tog
OldUnits = tog.Units
ToolsOptionsGeneral .Units = 3
On Error Goto UserError
Dim fp As FormatParagraph
GetCurValues fp
RightIndent$ = fp.RightIndent
LeftIndent$ = fp.LeftIndent
FormatParagraph .RightIndent = Str$(Val(RightIndent$) + 3),
.LeftIndent = Str$(Val(LeftIndent$) + 3)
UserError:
ToolsOptionsGeneral .Units = OldUnits
End Sub
```

Click on the Save button to save your work and return to a document window. Now, call up the Tools⇨Customize command and click on the Toolbars tab. Select Macros for the Categories list and drag the IncreaseBothIndents macro to any available space on the Formatting toolbar (or any other toolbar, if you prefer). Pick a button image (it doesn't matter which one). Next, right-click on the Increase Indent button, choose the Copy Button Image command, right-click on the new Increase Both Indents button, and choose the Paste Button Image command. Right-click on the Increase Both Indents button again, choose the Edit Button Image command, and edit the button so that it looks like this:

Follow the same procedure to create the second macro, but replace the FormatParagraph command near the end of the macro with this command:

```
FormatParagraph .RightIndent = Str$(Val(RightIndent$) - 3),
.LeftIndent = Str$(Val(LeftIndent$) - 3)
```

Name the second macro DecreaseBothIndents, and edit its button image to look like this:

You'll find both of these macros in the Word for Windows 95 SECRETS Sample Macros.dot template on the CD-ROM.

Understanding Text Flow

If you call up the Format⇨Paragraph command and click on the Text Flow tab, you'll see the dialog box shown in Figure 14-6.

The following paragraphs describe the function of each of the text flow settings:

- **Widow/Orphan Control:** This setting prevents Word from splitting a paragraph across pages if a single line would be left stranded at the bottom of one page or at the top of the next page. Widow/Orphan Control is on by default and should be left on for most documents.

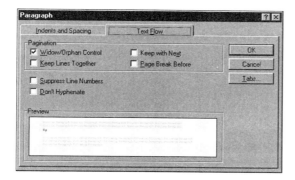

Figure 14-6: The Text Flow tab of the Paragraph dialog box.

- **Keep Lines Together:** If you have a paragraph that should not be split across pages, use the Keep Lines Together option. Then, Word will bump the paragraph over to the next page if the paragraph won't fit. Do not use this option on long paragraphs unless you want to leave large amounts of empty space at the bottom of your pages.

- **Keep with Next:** This option forces Word to place the paragraph on the same page as the following paragraph. It is used most often with heading paragraphs to prevent the heading from being stranded at the bottom of a page.

- **Page Break Before:** This option forces Word to insert a page break before the paragraph so that the paragraph always begins at the top of a page. Use it for chapter or section headings when you want each chapter or section to start on a new page.

- **Suppress Line Numbers:** If you are using Word's line numbering feature, this option tells Word to skip the numbers for this paragraph. Chapter 16 covers line numbering.

- **Don't Hyphenate:** If you use Word's hyphenation feature, this option instructs Word to skip hyphenation for the paragraph in question. Hyphenation isn't too important for single-column documents, but it does become a factor when you create documents with two or more columns. Chapter 20 covers hyphenation.

Using Tabs

Tabs are a part of paragraph formats, just like indentation, alignment, and line spacing. As a result, when you set tabs, the new tabs apply only to the paragraph the insertion point is in, or, if a range of text is selected, to the selected paragraphs. In addition, whenever you press the Enter key, the new paragraph inherits the tab stops of the previous paragraph.

The following sections describe the ins and outs of using tabs.

Setting tabs with the ruler

The easiest way to set tabs is with the ruler. Here is the procedure:

1. If the ruler isn't visible, use the <u>V</u>iew⇨<u>R</u>uler command to make it visible.

2. Type the text that you want lined up with tabs. If you want, type several paragraphs. Press the Tab key once and only once between each column of information that you want lined up, even if the information doesn't line up just yet.

3. Select the paragraph or paragraphs where you want to set tabs. If you're setting tabs for just one paragraph, click the mouse anywhere in the paragraph. If you're setting tabs for more than one paragraph, drag the mouse to select at least some text in each paragraph.

4. Click the mouse on the ruler at each spot where you want a new tab stop. The text you typed in Step 2 will automatically snap to under the tabs you create, as shown in Figure 14-7.

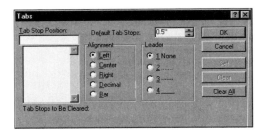

Figure 14-7: The Tabs dialog box.

5. Make any last-minute adjustments that are required to line up the text just the way you want. You can move a tab you've already created by clicking on and dragging the tab marker with the mouse and sliding it to the new location. When you release the mouse button, text in the currently selected paragraphs is adjusted in the new tab position.

Default tab stops are placed every .5 inches. However, each time you create a new tab stop, any default tab stops to the left of the new tab stops are deleted. In other words, default tab stops exist only to the right of tab stops you create.

You can remove a tab stop from the ruler by clicking on the tab stop you want to remove and dragging it straight down off the ruler. When you release the mouse, the tab stop is deleted.

The four types of tabs

Word lets you create four types of tab alignments: left, center, right, and decimal. To change the type of tab that's created when you click on the ruler, click on the Tab Alignment button at the far left edge of the ruler. Each time you click on the button, the picture on the button changes to indicate the alignment type, as shown in Table 14-3.

Table 14-3	Tab Types	
Tab Symbol	**Tab Type**	**Explanation**
⌊	Left tab	Text is left aligned at the tab stop.
⌊	Center tab	Text is centered over the tab stop.
⌋	Right tab	Text is right aligned at the tab stop.
⌊	Decimal tab	Numbers are aligned at the decimal point over the tab stop. For numbers that do not include a decimal point, the decimal tab works the same as a right tab, so the numbers are still lined up properly. Thus, decimal tabs are the best way to line up a column of numbers whether or not the numbers include a decimal point.

Note

In spite of the recent political shifts in Washington, *left* tabs are still the most popular type of tab.

You can call up the Tabs dialog box by double-clicking on the lower-half of the ruler. Watch where you double-click, though, because the first click adds a tab stop. As a result, you'll have to click on Clear to remove the tab stop that was inadvertently created.

Using the Format⇨Tabs command

If you have an unexplainable aversion to the ruler, you can set tab stops by using the Format⇨Tabs command instead. Just follow these steps:

1. Call up the Format⇨Tabs command. The Tabs dialog box will appear, as shown back in Figure 14-7.

2. Type the position where you want the new tab stop to appear in the Tab Stop Position field.

3. Select the Alignment option you want for the new tab stop (Left, Center, Right, Decimal, or Bar). (Bar will explained later, in the section "Running a bar tab.")

4. Select the tab leader type for the tab stop. If you don't want leaders, choose 1. None. (Leaders will be explained later, in the section "Using tab leaders.")

5. Click on Set.

6. Repeat Steps 2–5 for any other tab stops you want to create.

7. Click on OK to dismiss the Tabs dialog box.

Removing all tabs

To remove all tab stops, highlight the paragraphs where you want to remove the tab stops. Then, choose the Format⇨Tabs command or double-click in the bottom half of the ruler to summon the Tabs dialog box. Click on the Clear All button to remove the tabs and click on OK to return to the document.

Using tab leaders

Tab leaders are commonly used in price lists, tables of contents, or other lists to help draw the eye from one item to its counterpart across the page. You can also use tab leaders to create fill-in-the-blanks forms. Just look at the table of contents of this book for an excellent example of tab leaders.

Word lets you create three types of leaders: dots, dashes, and solid lines. Dots and dashes are the leader type you'll use for lists; solid lines are what you'll use for forms.

If you want the tab leader to end at a certain location, create a left-aligned tab at that location and use the leader type of your choice. This technique is commonly used to create fill-in-the-blank forms. For example, the following line uses two left-aligned tab stops with solid-line leaders, one at 2.5", the other at 5":

Name: _____Rank: _____

Notice that there is no space whatsoever between the end of the first solid-line leader and the word *Rank*. To insert a small amount of space, you could type a few spaces, or you could create another tab, say at 2.625":

Name: _____ Rank: _____

If you are going to use dot or dash leaders to connect items in a list, you usually use right- or decimal-aligned tabs. For example, the following list is formatted with a single right-aligned dot-leader tab stop at 4.5":

5.25" Double Density... *360KB*

5.25" High Density *1.2MB*

3.5" Double Density... *720KB*

3.5" High Density *1.44MB*

Running a bar tab

You must be 21 to use this feature in most states.

One of the more unusual things you can do with tabs is create vertical bars between columns of information, like this:

Hawkeye	James T. Kirk	Gilligan
B.J.	Mr. Spock	The Skipper
Charles	Dr. McCoy	The Professor
Hot Lips	Mr. Chekov	Mary Ann
Radar	Mr. Sulu	Ginger
Col. Potter	Lt. Uhura	Mr. Howell
Father Mulcahy	Nurse Chapel	Mrs. Howell

Here, the vertical bars between the columns are actually special deviant versions of tab stops. To create them, follow these steps:

1. Create some tab stops on the ruler. You'll have to create *two* tab stops for each column of information you need, about 1/8 inches apart.

2. Choose the Format⇨Tabs command to summon the Tabs dialog box.

3. Change every other tab stop to a bar tab by clicking the tab stop, selecting Bar as the alignment type, and clicking the Set button.

4. Click OK.

5. Adjust the positioning of the tabs if you want.

Bar tabs aren't like regular tab stops in that the Tab key doesn't stop at them. As a result, you use only one tab character between each column.

If the bar tab extends above or below the line, it's because the paragraph format calls for extra space above or below the paragraph. Use the Format⇨Paragraph command to remove the Above or Below space. (If you need the extra space, add it to the adjoining paragraphs instead.)

Tip

Bar tabs are a crude way of making tables. A far better way to create tables with ruled lines is to use Word's Table feature, which is covered in Chapter 17.

Borders and Shading

You can apply a border and background color to a paragraph by calling up the Format⇨Borders and Shading command or by using the Borders toolbar. As with most Word features, the toolbar is convenient, but the Format⇨Borders and Shading command gives you more control.

Tip

This section describes how to apply borders and shading to paragraphs. You can also use borders and shading with frames and tables. See Chapters 17 and 20 for more information.

Using the Format⇨Borders and Shading command

To apply a border by using the Format⇨Borders and Shading command, follow these steps:

1. Select the paragraph or paragraphs where you want to apply the border and background shading.

2. Choose the Format⇨Borders and Shading command. The Paragraph Borders and Shading dialog box will appear, as shown in Figure 14-8.

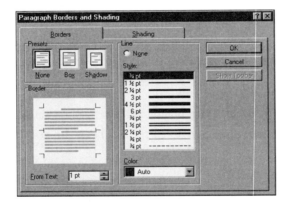

Figure 14-8: The Paragraph Borders and Shading dialog box (Borders tab).

3. Select the border type you want. To draw a simple box around the paragraph or paragraphs, click on Box. For a shadow effect, click on Shadow. Otherwise, click on the various edges of the paragraphs represented in the Border area to indicate which edges you want a border to appear.

   The line in the middle of the Border area allows you to create borders between successive paragraphs that have the same border formatting. The line at the bottom of the Border area applies a border only to the last of a series of bordered paragraphs.

4. Select the line style you want to use from the Style list. Various line widths and styles such as double lines and dashed lines are available.

   You can change line styles as you apply individual borders so that a paragraph can have a thin border at the top and a thick border at the bottom.

5. Click on the Shading tab to display the Paragraph Borders and Shading options, as shown in Figure 14-9.

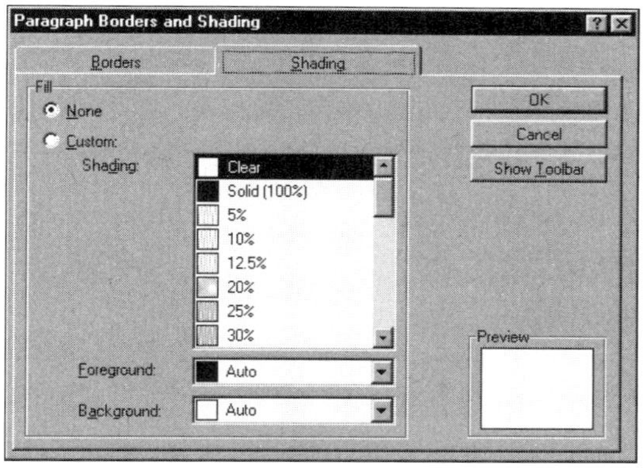

Figure 14-9: The Paragraph Borders and Shading dialog box (Shading tab).

6. Select the shading option you want to use.

7. Click on OK.

By default, the borders are placed one point from the text they surround. If that placement is too tight for you, you can increase the spacing by adjusting the From Text value in the Paragraph Borders and Shading dialog box (Borders tab).

Tip If you choose the Box or Shadow border style, any adjacent paragraphs that are also formatted with Box or Shadow borders will be included in the same box, as shown in Figure 14-10.

If you would rather box each paragraph separately, you must place an unboxed paragraph mark between each boxed paragraph, as shown in Figure 14-11. These "spacer" paragraphs need not contain any text, and you might want to vary their before or after spacing so that the boxed paragraphs are spaced the way you want.

Secret To create white-on-black characters, format the characters as white (use the Format⇔Font command) and apply solid black shading to the paragraph.

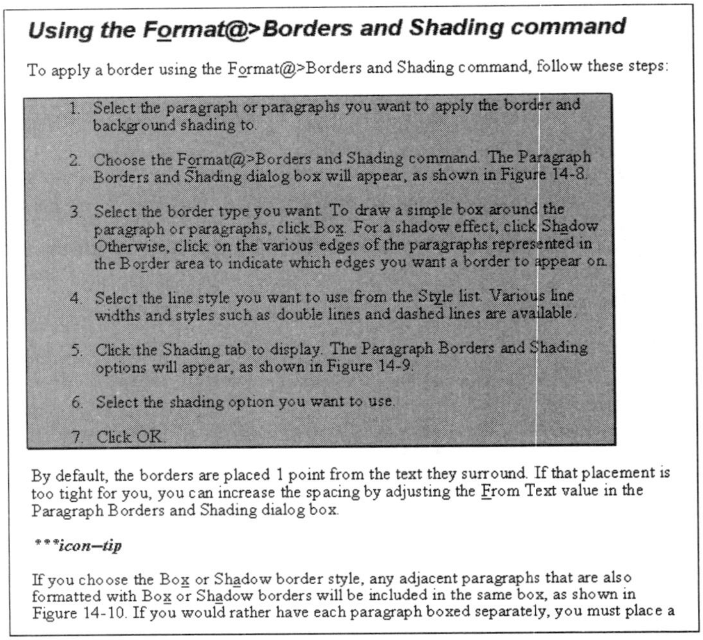

Using the Format@>Borders and Shading command

To apply a border using the Format@>Borders and Shading command, follow these steps:

1. Select the paragraph or paragraphs you want to apply the border and background shading to.
2. Choose the Format@>Borders and Shading command. The Paragraph Borders and Shading dialog box will appear, as shown in Figure 14-8.
3. Select the border type you want. To draw a simple box around the paragraph or paragraphs, click Box. For a shadow effect, click Shadow. Otherwise, click on the various edges of the paragraphs represented in the Border area to indicate which edges you want a border to appear on.
4. Select the line style you want to use from the Style list. Various line widths and styles such as double lines and dashed lines are available.
5. Click the Shading tab to display. The Paragraph Borders and Shading options will appear, as shown in Figure 14-9.
6. Select the shading option you want to use.
7. Click OK.

By default, the borders are placed 1 point from the text they surround. If that placement is too tight for you, you can increase the spacing by adjusting the From Text value in the Paragraph Borders and Shading dialog box.

***icon–tip

If you choose the Box or Shadow border style, any adjacent paragraphs that are also formatted with Box or Shadow borders will be included in the same box, as shown in Figure 14-10. If you would rather have each paragraph boxed separately, you must place a

Figure 14-10: Adjacent paragraphs are contained in the same box or shadow border.

Using the Format@>Borders and Shading command

To apply a border using the Format@>Borders and Shading command, follow these steps:

1. Select the paragraph or paragraphs you want to apply the border and background shading to.

2. Choose the Format@>Borders and Shading command. The Paragraph Borders and Shading dialog box will appear, as shown in Figure 14-8.

3. Select the border type you want. To draw a simple box around the paragraph or paragraphs, click Box. For a shadow effect, click Shadow. Otherwise, click on the various edges of the paragraphs represented in the Border area to indicate which edges you want a border to appear on.

4. Select the line style you want to use from the Style list. Various line widths and styles such as double lines and dashed lines are available.

5. Click the Shading tab to display. The Paragraph Borders and Shading options will appear, as shown in Figure 14-9.

6. Select the shading option you want to use.

7. Click OK.

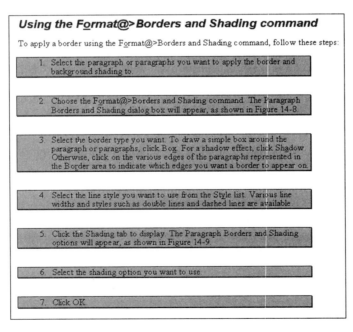

Figure 14-11: To create separate adjacent box or shadow paragraphs, use nonbordered "spacer" paragraphs.

Using the borders toolbar

Another way to apply borders and shading quickly is to call up the Borders toolbar, shown in Figure 14-12. The formatting toolbar includes a Borders button. Click it once to summon the Borders toolbar; click it again to hide the Borders toolbar.

Figure 14-12: The Borders toolbar.

Table 14-4 summarizes the function of the controls on the Borders toolbar.

Table 14-4	**The Borders Toolbar**
Tool	*What It Does*
[¾ pt ——— ▼]	Selects the line style for the border
▣	Adds a border on the top of the paragraph
▣	Adds a border on the bottom of the paragraph
▣	Adds a border on the left of the paragraph
	Adds a border on the right of the paragraph
⊞	Adds a border between adjacent paragraphs
▣	Adds a box-style border
▦	Removes borders.
[☐ Clear ▼]	Sets the shading style

Note You can mix and match border styles. For example, try formatting a paragraph with a 6-point top border and 1-point bottom, left, and right borders, as shown in Figure 14-13. Experiment with different combinations until you find one that creates the effect you want.

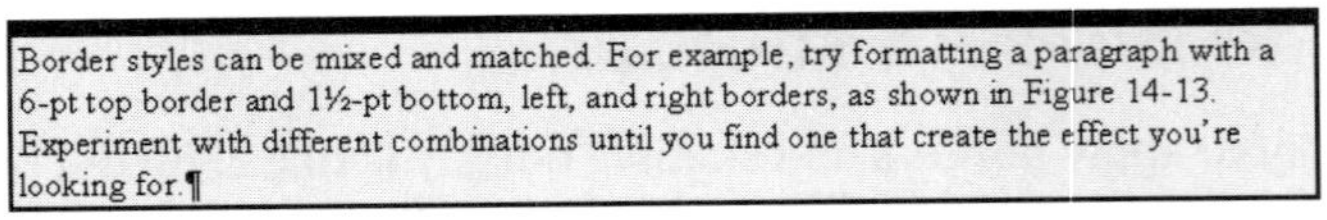

Border styles can be mixed and matched. For example, try formatting a paragraph with a 6-pt top border and 1½-pt bottom, left, and right borders, as shown in Figure 14-13. Experiment with different combinations until you find one that create the effect you're looking for.¶

Figure 14-13: You can combine borders to achieve interesting effects.

How to apply a border to a word or phrase

Secret

The Borders and Shading command applies borders to entire paragraphs. There is a way to apply a border to an individual word or phrase within a paragraph, however. For example, you can create an effect similar to this:

Sometimes it is nice to place a border around a single word.

You can achieve this effect through the use of an EQ field code. Field codes are covered in detail in Chapter 28, so I won't go into the details of how to use the EQ field code here. However, you can use the following macro, named WordBorder, to place a border around any selected text automatically:

Macro

```
Sub MAIN
    If SelType() = 2 Then
        InsertField .Field = "EQ \x(" + CleanString$(Selection$()) +
")"
    End If
End Sub
```

To create this macro, call up the Tools⇨Macro command, type **WordBorder**, and click on Create. Type the macro as shown above and press Ctrl+S to save the macro in your Normal.dot template. Alternatively, you can retrieve the macro from the Word for Windows 95 SECRETS Sample Macros.dot template on the CD-ROM.

To make the macro convenient to use, use the Tools⇨Customize command to assign the macro to a keyboard shortcut, toolbar button, or menu. The Word for Windows 95 SECRETS Sample Macros.dot template includes a toolbar that provides a button for this and many other macros included in this book.

To use the macro, you must first select the text you want to place a border around. If you do not select any text, the macro exits without doing anything.

Note

If you select more text than will fit on a single line, the field code will display !Error. This is because the EQ field result cannot span more than one line. If you receive the !Error result, press Ctrl+Z to undo the macro and try again with less text selected.

Changing Case

The Format➪Change Case command is useful when you want to change the case of a sentence, paragraph, or other arbitrary selection of text. For example, you can use it to capitalize an entire selection, just the first letter of the selection, or the first letter of each word.

To use the Format➪Change Case command, follow these steps:

1. Select the text whose case you want to change.

2. Call up the Format➪Change Case command. The Change Case dialog box, shown in Figure 14-14, will appear.

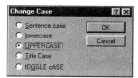

Figure 14-14: The Change Case dialog box.

3. Pick the capitalization option you want to apply to the selection.

4. Click on OK.

An easier way to change case is to use the keyboard shortcut Shift+F3. Each time you press Shift+F3, Word "cycles" through a different case option. As a result, you can just keep pressing Shift+F3 until the text is capitalized the way you want.

Unfortunately, the programmers at Microsoft decided that they could try to anticipate the type of case change you want to make based on how much text you select. If you select one sentence or more, the Shift+F3 shortcut alternates among the following options:

- all lowercase

- ALL UPPERCASE

- Initial Capital Letters (Title Case)

If you select more than one full sentence, Shift+F3 alternates among a *different* set of options:

- all lowercase

- ALL UPPERCASE

- First capital letter (Sentence case.)

This might seem to make sense at first, but unfortunately it doesn't deal well with headings, which are typically one sentence or less. For headings, Shift+F3 would be better if it alternated among the following options:

■ all uppercase

■ First capital letter (Sentence case.)

■ Initial Capital Letters (Title Case)

Unfortunately, Word insists on throwing headings into the one-sentence-or-less category because headings do not include a period and therefore are never longer than one sentence. As a result, you cannot quickly convert a heading from Sentence Case to Title Case and vice versa. Frankly, Shift+F3 would be much more useful if Microsoft had tried not to anticipate what type of case you wanted and simply allowed Shift+F3 to always cycle through all five case options without regard to how much text is selected.

Here is a macro that does precisely what I just described, cycling through all five Change Case possibilities without regard to how much or how little text is selected:

```
Sub MAIN
Sel$ = LCase$(Selection$())
If Len(Sel$) = 1 Then
    ChangeCase
    Goto Bail
End If
PrevSel$ = GetDocumentVar$("WordSecChangeCaseSelection")
If PrevSel$ = Sel$ Then
    Counter$ = GetDocumentVar$("WordSecChangeCaseCounter")
Else
    Counter$ = "-1"
    SetDocumentVar "WordSecChangeCaseSelection", Sel$
End If
Ctr = Val(Counter$) + 1
If Ctr > 5 Then Ctr = 0
If Ctr = 3 Then Ctr = 4
ChangeCase(Ctr)
SetDocumentVar "WordSecChangeCaseCounter", Str$(Ctr)
Bail:
End Sub
```

To create this macro, call up the Tools⇨Macro command and type **ChangeCase** in the Macro Name field. Then, click on Create and type the macro in exactly as shown. If you'd rather not bother with typing the macro in yourself, you'll find it in the Word for Windows 95 SECRETS Sample Macros.dot template on the CD-ROM supplied with this book.

Because the ChangeCase macro is given the same name as the built-in Word command that is assigned to Shift+F3, the ChangeCase macro will automatically be invoked when you press Shift+F3.

The ChangeCase macro is an excellent example of how a seemingly simple task can become difficult to implement. The built-in ChangeCase command accepts a number from 0–5 indicating which type of case conversion to perform, as follows:

0	Sets the text to all lowercase
1	Sets the text to all uppercase
2	Capitalizes the first letter of each selected word
3	Capitalizes the first letter of the selection
4	Capitalizes the first letter of each selected sentence
5	Toggles the case of each selected letter

The macro works by first calling ChangeCase with 0, and then with 1, then 2, and so on. After it gets to 5, it resets itself to 0, so the cycle continues endlessly as long as you keep pressing Shift+F3.

To accomplish this seemingly simple task, the macro must know what value it called ChangeCase with the last time it was executed. The easiest way to do that is to create a *document variable* (a macro variable that is actually stored with the document) that can be checked each time.

To complicate matters, the macro should know when it is being run the first time for a given text selection. To do that, the macro stores a second document variable that contains the contents of the previous selection. Then, the current selection is compared with the previous selection to see whether it is the same.

The one drawback to this approach is that the value of the two document variables is stored on disk with the document when you use the File⇨Save command. Fortunately, only a small amount of disk space is required to store these variables, unless of course you select an unusually large portion of text before invoking the ChangeCase macro. (If you want to eliminate this problem, you could create a custom FileSave macro that would delete the two document variables before saving the document to disk.)

One final complication is that the ChangeCase macro command includes an additional type of case conversion: 3, which arbitrarily capitalizes the first letter of the selection without changing any other characters in the selection. This case conversion option isn't particularly useful when cycling through the various case conversion options because the conversion to title case has already capitalized the first letter of the selection and the first letter of every other word in the selection. Thus, the ChangeCase macro simply skips over this case conversion option.

AutoFormat

Word's AutoFormat feature attempts to format an otherwise unformatted document automatically. Microsoft apparently had pretty lofty ambitions for the AutoFormat feature. Here is how the feature is described in the *User's Guide* for Word 6.0:

> *"After you've typed a document, you can have Word format the text by choosing AutoFormat from the Format menu.*
>
> *"Word analyzes each paragraph and determines how the paragraph is used in the document (for example, as a heading or an item in a bulleted list). Word then applies a* style, *a preset group of formats, appropriate for that item."*

I'll be honest with you: I'm not a big fan of Word's AutoFormat command. It is a well-intentioned feature, but it doesn't work well in actual practice. The basic problem is that in order to use it, you have to know how to work with styles. After you learn how to use styles, you'll see that it takes only a single mouse click or a swift keyboard shortcut to apply the correct style for each paragraph as you type. And for many paragraphs, you can set up the style so that the *next* paragraph is automatically formatted with the correct style.

After you learn these few simple mouse clicks and keyboard shortcuts, you'll realize that it's far more efficient to format the document correctly in the first place. Otherwise, you type away without regard to formatting and hope that Word can properly figure out which paragraphs are headings and which are merely one-line paragraphs or where a numbered list begins and ends. Don't set your hopes too high. Word can only partially figure these things out, and you're going to have to spend more time reviewing and correcting Word's formatting errors than you would have spent formatting the document correctly in the first place.

The one occasion on which I do sometimes use AutoFormat is when I'm looking at a document that I obtained somewhere else, such as from CompuServe or The Microsoft Network, which was created as a straight text file with no formatting whatsoever. In that case, I will often run the file through AutoFormat just to make it a little more readable. But for routine use, I do not recommend that you rely on AutoFormat to do your work for you. It isn't that sophisticated, and it's not that difficult to learn how to apply the proper formatting yourself.

Using the AutoFormat command

All that being said, here's how to use the AutoFormat command:

1. Open a document that has not been formatted. For example, Figure 14-15 shows a text document containing instructions about Internet mail that I recently downloaded from CompuServe. Because it is a text-only document, it contains no formatting whatsoever.

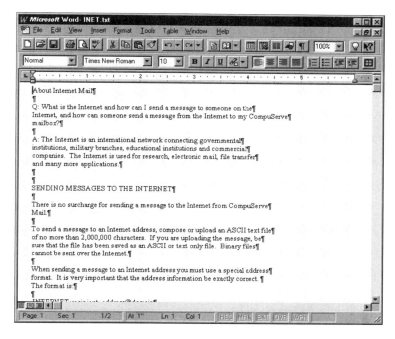

Figure 14-15: A document sorely in need of formatting.

2. Call up the Format⇨AutoFormat command. The AutoFormat dialog box will appear, as shown in Figure 14-16.

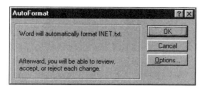

Figure 14-16: The AutoFormat dialog box.

3. Click on OK. Word will grind and whir as it formats your document. When it is finished, the dialog box shown in Figure 14-17 will appear.

Figure 14-17: The AutoFormat command is finished.

4. Click on <u>A</u>ccept. The dialog box will vanish, and you can inspect the results. Figure 14-18 shows how the unformatted document shown in Figure 14-15 was handled.

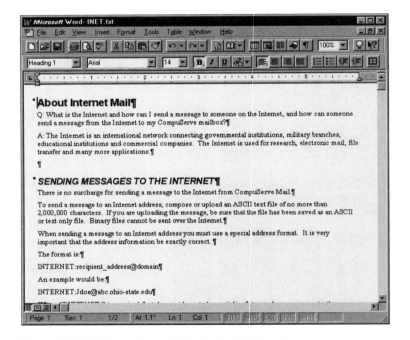

Figure 14-18: A document gussied up by the AutoFormat command.

As you can see, AutoFormat managed to format headings and body text in this document properly. However, you should still review the document for any glaring errors.

If you click on the Review Changes button, Word will take you on a guided tour of the formatting changes it made, allowing you to accept or reject each change individually. I don't usually bother with this step, primarily because I don't trust AutoFormat to anything with formatting matters anyway. For the occasional text-only file that I just want to be a bit more readable, I just click on Accept so that all changes will be automatically accepted, and I review the document and make any adjustments necessary to correct obvious formatting mistakes.

If you suddenly realize that using AutoFormat was a huge mistake, just click on the Reject All button. All of AutoFormat's changes will be nullified.

AutoFormat options

You can customize the behavior of the AutoFormat command by clicking on the Options button when the AutoFormat dialog box appears, or by choosing the Tools⊃Options command and clicking on the AutoFormat tab. Either way, the AutoFormat Options dialog box will appear, as shown in Figure 14-19.

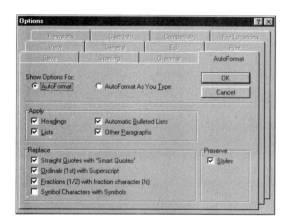

Figure 14-19: The AutoFormat Options dialog box.

These options let you tell Word which types of automatic formatting it should attempt. Specifically:

- **Headings:** Tells Word to look for paragraphs that look like headings and apply appropriate heading styles.

- **Lists:** Looks for numbered lists and replaces manually typed numbers with numbered list styles.

- **Automatic Bulleted Lists:** Looks for paragraphs that look like bulleted lists and replaces them with bullet paragraph styles. Among other things, Word looks for asterisks and hyphens as tell-tale signs of intended bulleted lists.

■ **Other Paragraphs:** Formats other paragraphs, including body text, inside address lines, and salutations.

■ **Straight Quotes with 'Smart Quotes':** Replaces boring apostrophes and straight quote marks with their curly equivalents.

■ **Ordinals (1st) with Superscript:** Automatically formats so-called "ordinal" numbers typed out as 1st, 2nd, or 3rd with superscripts, as in 1st, 2nd, and 3rd.

■ **Fractions (1/2) with fraction characters ($^{1}/_{2}$):** Works for 1/2, 1/4, and 3/4.

■ **Symbol Characters with Symbols:** Replaces (c), (r), and (tm) with the symbols ©, ®, and ™.

■ **Preserve Styles:** Tells Word not to change any paragraphs you have already formatted with styles.

AutoFormat As You Type

Microsoft insists that the AutoFormat As You Type features belong with the AutoFormat command, but I can't agree. To me, they belong with the AutoCorrect feature. As a result, I presented AutoFormat As You Type back in Chapter 12, along with the AutoCorrect and AutoText features.

The Format Painter

The Format Painter allows you to copy the character formatting from one selection of text and apply it to other text in the document. For example, suppose that you have formatted some text in 14-point Century Gothic bold, with character spacing expanded by one point. The Format Painter allows you to instantly format more text with those same attributes. Here's how:

1. Highlight the text whose format you want to copy.

2. Click on the Format Painter button (the one with the paintbrush on it). The mouse pointer will change shapes, to an insertion bar with a paintbrush in tow. The formatting of the selected text will be "sucked up" by the Format Painter.

3. Drag the mouse over the text you want to reformat. The format previously "sucked up" by the Format Painter will be applied to whatever text you drag the mouse over. You can also click on the mouse in the midst of a word to apply the format to the entire word.

Personally, I'm not a big fan of the Format Painter because it defeats the purpose of using styles. All of the formatting applied by the Format Painter is applied as direct formatting. If you really want all of your headings to be 14-point Century Gothic bold with one point expanded character spacing, you're better off applying this formatting via one of the standard heading styles. That way, you can be sure that *all* your headings will be formatted properly.

Chapter 15

All about Page Layout and Sections

In this chapter

▶ Understanding the relationship between sections and page layout

▶ Creating section breaks

▶ Setting margins, page size, orientation, and other basic page formats

▶ Adding page numbers to the bottom or top of your document pages

▶ Creating headers and footers

Sections are the third piece of the Word formatting puzzle after character and paragraph formats. In this chapter, you'll learn all about setting up basic page formats by using sections. Many of the features presented in this chapter are best used when combined with other Word features to solve specific page layout problems. For examples, turn to Chapter 20.

Understanding Sections

Sections are the basis of Word's page layout formatting. Most documents consist of only a single section, so all of the pages in the document receive the same formatting. If some of the pages require different formatting, you can break up the document into two or more sections, each with its own page format.

Sections control the following formatting information:

■ The size of the paper

■ The left, right, top, and bottom margins

■ The orientation of the paper: whether the document is printed "portrait," where the height is bigger than the width, or "landscape," where the width is the larger measurement

- The number and spacing of columns

- Header and footer information, including the positioning of the header or footer as well as its appearance

- Footnotes and endnotes, again including the positioning and appearance of the footnotes and endnotes

- Page numbering

- Line numbering

One of the most confusing aspects of working with sections is that a single page can contain more than one section. For example, a page might start off with a single-column layout, then switch to two columns, and then switch back to a single column. Such a page would comprise of three sections.

Unfortunately, Word does not include one convenient "Format⇨Section" command that allows you to set all of these formats from one convenient location. In fact, most of the section formats are not even set from the Format menu at all. Instead, section formatting is scattered about the Word menus:

- **File⇨Page Setup:** This command lets you set basic page formatting information, such as margins, the position of headers and footers, and paper size and orientation.

- **View⇨Header and Footer:** This command displays the header and footer area so that you can customize the headers and footers.

- **Insert⇨Break:** This command lets you create a new section that has the same format as the previous section.

- **Insert⇨Page Numbers:** This command adds a page number to the header or footer, lets you vary the page numbering style, and allows you to set the starting page number for the section.

- **Insert⇨Footnote:** This command lets you create footnotes or endnotes and control their appearance and position.

- **Format⇨Columns:** This command lets you set the number of columns and the size and spacing for each column.

All documents contain at least one section. In documents with only one section, the section formatting information is stored in the last paragraph mark of the document, along with the last paragraph's paragraph formats. If a document contains two or more sections, the end of each section except the last is indicated by a section break, which looks like this:

━━━━━━━━━━━━━━━━━━━━━━━━━━━━End of Section━━━━━━━━━━━━━━━━━━━━━━━━━━━━━

The section break contains the section formatting information just as a paragraph mark contains paragraph formatting. As a result, if you delete a section break, the sections before and after the break will be combined and the formatting information from the section that followed the break will be used.

Creating Section Breaks

You can create a new section in several ways. One is to use the Insert⇨Break command. This method allows you to create a new section that will inherit the formatting of the previous section. You can then make whatever formatting changes you want to the new section. To create a new section in this manner, follow these steps:

1. Position the insertion point at the spot where you want the new section to begin.

2. Choose the Insert⇨Break command. The Break dialog box will appear, as shown in Figure 15-1.

Figure 15-1: The Break dialog box, used to create a section break.

3. Choose one of the four section break types:

   - **Next Page**: Creates a new section that will begin at the top of the following page.

   - **Continuous:** Creates a new section that will begin on the next line of the same page. This type of section break is commonly used when changing the number of columns on a page.

   - **Even Page:** Creates a new section that begins on the next even numbered page.

   - **Odd Page:** Creates a new section that begins on the next odd numbered page.

4. Click OK.

Note

You can also use the Insert⇨Break command to create a page break or a column break. A page break simply skips the text to the top of the next page without starting a new section. A column break skips to the top of the next column. For more information about column breaks, see Chapter 20.

Several of the commands that apply formatting to sections also let you create new sections. These commands include an Apply To field that lets you choose from among these options:

- **This Point Forward:** This is the option to select if you want to create a new section. Word will insert a section break and apply whatever formatting you select to the following section.

- **Whole Document:** Select this option to apply a layout format to all of the sections in the document.

- **This Section:** Use this option to apply formatting just to the current section. This option does not appear in the Apply To drop-down list box if the document consists of only one section.

Using the File⇨Page Setup Command

The File⇨Page Setup command controls many page layout formats. When you call up this command, it will display the Page Setup dialog box, which sports four separate tabbed sections. The following sections describe each of the four tabs.

Margins

Figure 15-2 shows the Margins tab of the Page Setup dialog box.

Figure 15-2: The Page Setup dialog box (Margins tab).

Normally, this dialog box contains the following options:

- **Top**: Sets the distance from the top of the page to the first line of text. The default is 1".

- **Bottom:** Sets the distance from the bottom of the page to the last line of text. The default is 1".

- **Left:** Sets the distance from the left edge of the page to the start of the text. The default is 1.25".

- **Right:** Sets the distance from the right edge of the page to the end of the text. The default is 1.25".

- **Gutter:** Sets the an additional amount of margin space for pages that are to be bound. The space is added to the left margin unless the Mirror Margins box is checked, in which case the space is added to the inside margin.

- **Header:** Sets the distance from the top of the page to the header area. The default is 0.5".

- **Footer:** Sets the distance from the bottom of the page to the footer area. The default is 0.5".

- **Apply To:** Determines whether the settings will apply to the Whole Document, This Section, or This Point Forward.

If you select the Mirror Margins check box, the Margins tab changes, as shown in Figure 15-3.

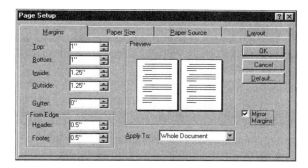

Figure 15-3: Mirrored margins.

As you can see, the Left and Right options change to Inside and Outside. This allows the margins for each page to alternate: On odd numbered pages, the inside margin is on the left; on even-numbered pages, the inside margin is on the right. Any additional space provided for by the Gutter field is added to the inside margin.

Paper Size

The Paper Size tab of the Page Setup dialog box is shown in Figure 15-4.

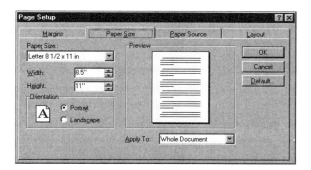

Figure 15-4: Setting the paper size and orientation.

The Paper Size tab includes the following options:

- **Paper Size:** Sets the paper size. The drop-down list allows you to pick from a variety of paper sizes, including Letter, Legal, and various other envelope sizes.

- **Width:** Sets the width of the paper. This field is automatically set when you choose a Paper Size. If you change the value of this field, the Paper Size field will change to "Custom Size."

- **Height:** Sets the height of the paper. This field is also set automatically according to the Paper Size you select, and changing the height will automatically change Paper Size to "Custom Size."

- **Portrait:** Orients the paper in an upright position, where the height is greater than the width.

- **Landscape:** Orients the paper sideways so that the width is greater than the height. When you switch from Portrait to Landscape (and vice versa), the Height and Width values are automatically swapped.

- **Apply To:** Determines whether the settings will apply to the Whole Document, This Section, or This Point Forward.

Paper Source

The Paper Source tab, shown in Figure 15-5, provides options that enable you to specify that the first page of the document will be printed on paper drawn from a different source than the paper used for the rest of the document. For example, you may specify that the first page be printed on paper manually fed in to the printer, and the rest of the document printed on paper drawn from the paper tray. This is used mostly for two-page letters, where the first page is printed on manually fed letterhead, and subsequent pages are printed on plain paper in the printer's paper tray. (The options that appear on this tab may vary a bit depending on the type of printer you have installed.)

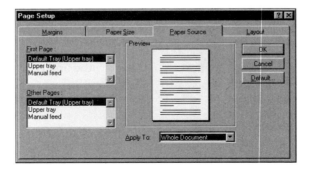

Figure 15-5: Setting the paper source.

Layout

The Layout tab, shown in Figure 15-6, sounds more exciting than it really is. "Layout" conjures up hopes of an all-encompassing dialog box wherein you can control at least the major aspects of your document's layout. Alas, the lowly Layout tab should have been named "Leftovers" because it contains nothing but a few obscure layout options that apparently didn't seem to fit anywhere else.

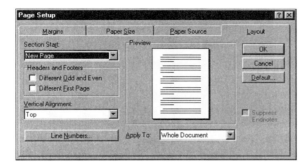

Figure 15-6: The Layout Options That Didn't Fit Anywhere Else But We Couldn't Bring Ourselves To Leave Them Out dialog box.

Here's the lowdown on the Layout options:

- **Section Start:** This drop-down list box offers essentially the same options that are available on the Insert⇨Break command. It lets you change the section break type for the current section. For example, if you created the section originally specifying "Odd Page" and you want to change it to "New Page," this is where you make the change. (This is a pretty lame place to put this option, if you ask me. You initially set this option in the Insert⇨Break command; why should you have to come to the File⇨Page Setup command's Layout tab to change it? What Word desperately needs is a Format⇨Section command.)

- **Different Odd and Even** and **Different First Page**: These two options let you set up different header and footers for even and odd pages or for the first page in a section. This is useful if you are printing on both sides of the page or if you don't want the header to appear on the first page.

- **Vertical Alignment:** Top, Center, or Justified. Top is the norm. Use Center if you want to center a title in the middle of the page and don't want to press the enter key 10 or 12 times to center it. (I've never found a use for Justified. If you do, write a letter to Bill Gates thanking him for this very useful feature.)

■ **Line Numbers:** Calls up the dialog box shown in Figure 15-7, which lets you print line numbers. You can select any starting line number, the increment to count lines by (5 or 10 is usually specified here), and whether line numbering is to restart for each page or section or should be continuous for the entire document.

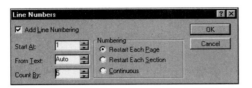

Figure 15-7: Setting up line numbers.

This feature is loved by lawyers and Shakespeare scholars alike. Figure 15-8 shows an example of a document formatted with line numbers. Notice that the title line at the top of the page is not figured into the line numbers. There are two ways to achieve this. First, you can call up the Format⇨Paragraph command, click the Text Flow tab, and select the Suppress Line Numbers option for the heading paragraph. Alternatively, you can create a continuous section break immediately after the title and turn off line numbering for the section that contains the title.

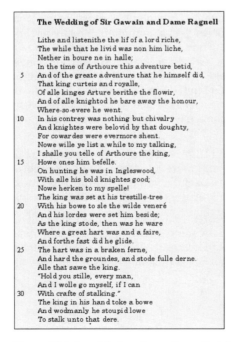

Figure 15-8: I can't believe I actually studied this stuff in college.

Inserting Page Numbers

Headers and footers, which I'll describe in detail later in this chapter, are for putting information at the top or bottom of each page. The most common type of information to be put in a header or footer is the page number. If all you want to appear in your header or footer is a page number, you don't have to mess with headers and footers at all. Instead, just use the Insert⇨Page Numbers command and follow these steps:

1. Choose the Insert⇨Page Numbers command. This will summon the Page Numbers dialog box, shown in Figure 15-9.

Figure 15-9: The Page Numbers dialog box.

2. Choose the position of the page numbers by using the Position drop-down list box. The choices are Bottom of Page or Top of Page.

3. Choose the alignment of the page numbers by using the Alignment drop-down list box. The choices are Left, Center, Right, Inside, and Outside. (Inside and Outside apply only if you are using mirrored margins for two-sided printing.)

   As you set the page number position and alignment, the Preview box is updated so that you can see the positioning of the number.

4. If you want the page number to be printed on the first page, check the Show Number on First Page option.

5. Click OK.

If you are not content with the page numbers Word shows when you use the Insert⇨Page Numbers command, click the Format button when the Page Numbers dialog box appears. The Page Number Format dialog box will appear, as shown in Figure 15-10.

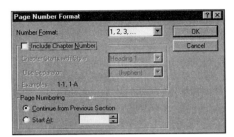

Figure 15-10: The Page Number Format dialog box.

This dialog box lets you control several aspects of page numbering. For starters, you can change the page number format by selecting an option from the Number Format drop-down list box. You can choose normal Arabic numbering (1, 2, 3...), uppercase or lowercase letters (A, B, C... or a, b, c...), or uppercase or lowercase Roman numbering (I, II, III... or i, ii, iii...).

You can select the Include Chapter Number option to create compound page numbers that include a number drawn from a heading paragraph, such as 1-1, 1-2, and so on. Follow these steps:

1. Format the chapter headings by using one of Word's built-in heading styles (most likely, Heading 1).

2. Use the Format⇨Heading Numbering command to number the headings automatically. Specify the numbering type and click OK.

3. Choose the Insert⇨Page Numbers command and click the Format button to summon the Page Number Format dialog box.

4. Check the Include Chapter Number check box and indicate which style is used for the chapter titles and which character you want to use as a separator between the chapter number and the page number (a hyphen, period, colon, or a dash).

5. Click OK to return to the Page Numbers dialog box and click OK to insert the page numbers into the document.

The Page Number Format command also lets you set a starting page number for the document or section. Usually, you'll use Continue from Previous Section so that page numbers will be continuous throughout the document. However, if you created a separate section for front matter — such as a title page, table of contents, and so on — it is customary to restart the page numbers for the first chapter of the document at page 1.

Secret

When you insert a page number by using the Insert⇨Page Numbers command, the page numbers are inserted in the header or footer area as a framed paragraph formatted with the built-in Page Number style. The easiest way to change the font for the page numbers is to use the Format⇨Style command to modify the Page Number style.

Headers and Footers

The Insert⇨Page Numbers command is great if all you want to appear at the top or bottom of a page is a plain, unadorned page number. Fortunately, Word provides the View⇨Headers and Footers command so that you can create fancier headers and footers.

Adding a header or footer

To add a header or footer, use the View⇨Header and Footer command. This switches you into Page Layout view and activates the header and footer area so that you can edit the header and footer. The body of your document remains visible, but it is dimmed to indicate that you cannot edit it. See Figure 15-11.

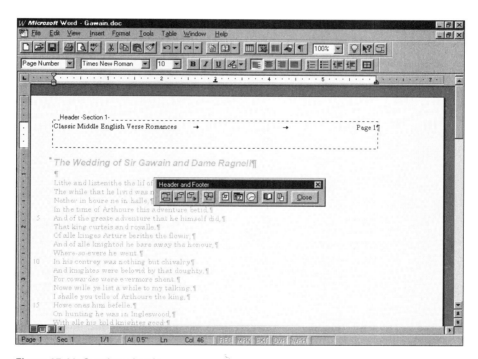

Figure 15-11: Creating a header.

After you have activated the View⇨Header and Footer command, you can use the Header and Footer toolbar to work with headers and footers. Table 15-1 describes the function of each button on this toolbar.

Table 15-1	The Buttons on the Header and Footer Toolbar
Button	**What It Does**
🔲	Switches from the header to the footer area. To switch back to the header, click the button again.
🔲	Inserts the page number. Unlike the Insert⇨Page Number command, this does not insert the page number in a frame. Instead, the page number is placed at the insertion point.
🔲	Inserts the Date.
🔲	Inserts the Time.
🔲	If the document has more than one section, moves to the header for the previous section.
🔲	If the document has more than one section, moves to the header for the next section.
🔲	If the document has more than one section, links the current header to the header for the previous section so that both sections will use the same header.
🔲	Calls up the File⇨Page Setup command so that you can change the placement of the header or footer.
🔲	Hides the document text altogether. Click it again to restore the hidden text.
Close	Returns to Normal view.

You can type anything you want in the header or footer areas, and you can apply any type of formatting you want. By default, Word creates a center-aligned tab stop dead set in the middle of the page and a right-aligned tab stop at the right margin. As a result, you can use the tab key to create a header that has some text flush against the left margin, some more text centered on the page, and still more text flush against the right margin.

Tip

You can often spruce up the appearance of the page by adding a border line beneath the header or above the footer. Just use the Format⇨Borders and Shading command, or call up the Borders toolbar and click away.

You can also use the Insert⇨Field command to insert interesting information in the header. Table 15-2 lists some of the fields that you might find useful in headers and footers. For information about using fields, see Chapter 31. You'll also find descriptions of these fields in Chapter 28.

Table 15-2	Fields That Are Useful In Headers and Footers
Field	*What It Does*
Date	Displays the date (same as clicking the Date button, except that you can change the format).
Time	Displays the time (same as clicking the Time button, except that you can change the format).
Author	Displays the author's name recorded in the document properties.
FileName	Displays the filename.
NumPages	Displays the number of pages. Useful for creating page numbers, such as *1 of 14*.
Title	Displays the document Title taken from the document properties.
Ref	Inserts the text indicated by a bookmark.
StyleRef	Inserts the text for the first or last paragraph on the page formatted with a given style. Useful for creating dictionary-type headings, such as *infamy - inflection*.
RevNum	Inserts the revision number of the document. (This isn't as useful as it sounds, because the revision number is incremented every time you save the document. If you take my advice and save your work every five minutes or so, your revision numbers won't be very meaningful.)

Note

It may seem weird that to "create" a header or footer, you use a command that's placed on the View menu. It makes sense, though, when you realize that *all* Word documents have headers and footers. As a result, you don't use the command to "create" a header or footer. All the View⇨Headers and Footers command does is allow you to view the header and footer area so that you can edit headers and footers, adding your own text and formatting.

Building a toolbar button to show headers

If you create a lot of documents that have headers and footers, you may want a more convenient way to access them than working your way through the View menu. Unfortunately, Word's standard toolbars do not have a Header button, but you can create one yourself if you want. Here's how:

1. Choose the View⇨Headers and Footers command so that the Headers and Footers toolbar is visible.

2. Call up the Tools⇨Customize command and click the Toolbars tab.

3. Change the Categories list to All Commands and scroll the Commands list until you find the ViewHeaders command.

4. Drag the ViewHeaders command off the Customize dialog box and onto the Standard or Formatting toolbars (or whatever other toolbar where you want to add it). When Word offers to let you choose a button image for the ViewHeaders button, click Cancel. This will create a blank button.

5. Right-click the Switch Between Header and Footer button and choose the Copy Button Image command. (You'll probably have to move the Customize dialog box out of the way so you can reach the Headers and Footers toolbar.)

6. Right- click the blank Headers button and choose the Paste Button Image command.

7. The button image for the new Headers button is pretty close to what we want, but it accentuates the footer rather than the header. Right- click it again and choose the Edit Button Image command and edit the button as shown in Figure 15-12. Click OK to accept the edited button image and click Close to dismiss the Customize dialog box.

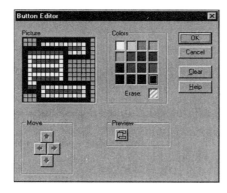

Figure 15-12: The edited button image for the custom Header button.

Creating Sections with Different Page Numbers

Many documents require sections that have different page number formats. For example, many documents require that the first page or two — a cover page and perhaps an inside title page — have no page numbers at all. Then, a section of "front matter" begins, including a table of contents, an acknowledgments page, and perhaps a preface, forward, or introduction, which should be numbered with Roman numerals (i, ii, and so on.). Then, the body of the document begins, which should be numbered with with Arabic numerals starting with 1.

To create a document of this sort, you must use sections to format groups of pages with different numbering schemes. No special action is required for the first group of pages: the ones with no page numbers.

To create the proper page numbering for the front matter, follow these steps in Normal or Page Layout view:

1. Place the insertion point at the beginning of the front matter. (If you have already inserted a page break so that the first page of the front matter will begin at the top of a new page, delete the page break. In the next step, you will insert a section break that will cause the front matter to start atop a new page.)

2. Choose the Insert⇨Break command.

3. Choose Next Page.

4. Click OK to insert the break.

5. Choose the View⇨Header and Footer command.

6. Click the Switch Between Header and Footer button to switch to the footer (unless you positioned the page numbers at the top of the page).

7. Click the Same as Previous button to detach the footer from the previous section's footer.

8. Click the Close button to return to Normal or Layout view.

9. Choose the Insert⇨Page Numbers command.

10. Set the Position and Alignment options however you want.

11. Click the Format button.

12. For the font matter, choose the Roman numeral number format (i, ii, iii...) in the Number Format list box.

13. Select Start At 1.

14. Click OK to return to the Page Numbers dialog box and click OK to insert the page numbers.

You can follow a similar procedure to begin a new section of page numbering for the body of the document by using Arabic numerals rather than Roman numerals.

The Secret SectionManager Macro

Secret

Earlier in this chapter, I said that what Word desperately needs is a Format⇨Section command. Word does come with a little-known macro that comes pretty close. It's called SectionManager, and it resides in the Layout7.dot template in the \MSOffice\Winword\Macros folder. It provides a single point of control for the various Word feature related to sections.

To make this macro available, you must load the Layout7.dot template as a global template by following these steps:

1. Choose the File⇨Templates command.

2. Click the Add button.

3. Locate the Layout7.dot template in the C:\MSOffice\Winword\Macros folder and then click OK.

4. Back in the Templates dialog box, click OK to return to the document.

To use the SectionManager macro, choose the Tools⇨Macro command, select the SectionManager macro, and click Run. The SectionManager macro will display the dialog box shown in Figure 15-13. (If you cannot find the SectionManager macro, make sure that the Macros Available In list box indicates "All Active Templates.")

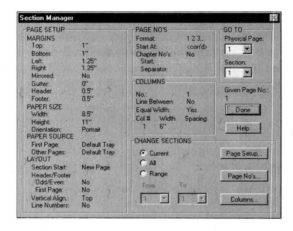

Figure 15-13: The Section Manager dialog box.

The Section Manager dialog box displays all of the information about the current section:

- **PAGE SETUP:** This information is culled from the File⇨Page Setup command and includes margins, paper size, paper source, and Layout information.

- **PAGE NO'S:** This information comes from the Insert⇨Page Numbers command.

- **COLUMNS:** This information is taken from the Format⇨Columns command.

The Section Manager offers the following groups of controls:

- **GO TO:** These controls allow you to go to a specific page or section. The Section Manager dialog box will be updated to reflect information for the section you go to. If you go to a page number, the information for the first section on that page will be shown.

- **CHANGE SECTIONS:** These controls allow you to change the section formatting for the current section, all sections, or a range of sections. You can click Page Setup, Page No's, or Columns to change the page setup, page numbers, or column formatting for the section or sections you choose.

- **Done:** Click Done when you want to quit the Section Manager.

- **Help:** Click Help to call up a brief help screen.

About the only section formatting option that isn't covered by Section Manager — and unfortunately it is an important one — is the Same As Previous header and footer option, which links headers and footers across sections.

Secret

Unfortunately, not even Microsoft's programmers are perfect when it comes to developing bulletproof macros. The SectionManager macro would be a great tool for inspecting the section formatting of complicated documents, but sometimes it doesn't work. In particular, it won't work reliably for any document in which the first paragraph of any section is framed. The problem is that whenever you tell SectionManager to go to a specific section, it moves the insertion point to the beginning of the section and issues a FilePageSetup command to obtain the page setup information. Unfortunately, the FilePageSetup command is unavailable when the insertion point is within a frame, so the SectionManager macro ends abruptly with an error message.

It turns out that Microsoft's own Newsletter Wizard creates newsletter documents in which the first paragraph of the first section is housed in a frame. As a result, you can't use SectionManager to inspect the sections in documents created by the Newsletter Wizard.

Chapter 16

Bullets and Numbered Lists

In This Chapter

▶ Understanding how bullets and numbers are tied to Word's paragraph formatting

▶ Creating bulleted lists using the Bullets button or the Format⇨Bullets and Numbering command

▶ Creating numbered lists using the Numbering button or the Format⇨Bullets and Numbering command

▶ Creating fancy multilevel lists

▶ Breaking the bad news: sometimes Word becomes confused and gobbles up portions of the text you're trying to format as a bulleted or numbered list

▶ Using a related numbering feature that adds numbers to your heading paragraphs

Glance through this book and you'll see many examples of bulleted and numbered lists. Both are excellent ways to add emphasis to a series of important points or to add a sense of order to items that fall into a natural sequence. This chapter shows you how to use Word's built-in bulleting and numbering features to create such lists quickly.

Understanding Bullets and Numbered Lists

You can create bulleted and numbered lists the hard way, by inserting bullet symbols or by typing numbers yourself and using a hanging indent to format the list properly. There's a better way through. Word allows you to add a bullet or a number to each paragraph. The bullet or number is a part of the paragraph format and adds the bullet character or the number so that you don't have to do so. Word also automatically sets the tabs and indents so that the bullets and numbers line up properly, and Word even takes on the job of keeping the numbers in a numbered list in sequence. As a result, if you add or delete a paragraph or rearrange paragraphs in the list, the numbers reorder themselves automatically.

The trick to using bullets and numbers is realizing that Word considers them a part of the paragraph format, just like other paragraph formats, such as indentation, spacing, and alignment. As a result, you do not have to type the bullet character or the number manually. Word supplies them automatically because of the paragraph formats.

Because bullets and numbers are paragraph formats, you can easily apply them to paragraph styles. While this may not be worth the effort to do so for simple bulleted and numbered lists, it is certainly worthwhile if you want to set up a complicated multilevel list.

Using the Bullet Button

The easiest way to create a bulleted list is by using the Format toolbar's Bullet button. Here's the procedure:

1. Type one or more paragraphs where you want to add bullets.

2. Select the paragraphs you want to add bullets to by clicking and dragging the mouse over them.

3. Click the Bullet button on the Formatting toolbar.

When you create a bulleted list this way, Word uses a default bullet character (normally a small dot) and creates a .25" hanging indent. (If the paragraphs already have hanging indents, the original indentation settings are preserved.) If you want to change the default bullet character, see the next section "Creating Custom Bulleted Lists."

To create a bulleted list as you type, format the first paragraph with a bullet. When you're finished typing the first paragraph, press the Enter key. The bullet format will carry over to the next paragraph. You can continue in this fashion, propagating the bullet to subsequent paragraphs as you type them. When you're done, press the Enter key and click the Bullet button again to deactivate bullets for the selected paragraphs.

You can add paragraphs to a bulleted list by positioning the insertion point at the end of one of the bulleted paragraphs and by pressing Enter. Because the bullet is part of the paragraph format, it carries over to the new paragraph.

What if you want to have several paragraphs associated with a single bullet? You could apply the bullet to the first paragraph in the group and manually create a .25" hanging indent for the subsequent paragraphs. An easier way is to press Shift+Enter instead of Enter at the end of all but the last of the paragraphs in the group. Shift+Enter forces the text to a new line, which gives the appearance of starting a new paragraph. As far as Word is concerned, however, the entire group is a single paragraph, so only one bullet is applied.

To remove bullets, just click the Bullet button again. It works like a toggle, so pressing it once adds bullets and pressing it again removes them. To remove bullets from an entire list, select all the paragraphs in the list and click the Bullet button.

Think of the old six- shooter whenever you create bulleted lists. More than six bullets in a row is pushing the limits of most reader's patience. Also, don't leave one bullet standing by itself. Bullets are used to mark items in a list, and it takes more than one item to make a list.

Tip

Without a doubt, the best way to work with bullets is to create a bullet style. That way, you can customize the bullet style all you want. With a bit of work, you can even mimic a check mark or create your own custom bullet design. Assign a keyboard shortcut, such as Ctrl+Shift+B, to your custom bullet style, and you're on your way.

Creating Custom Bulleted Lists

You don't have to remain content with the boring black-dot bullet character that Word uses by default. Here's how you can create a bulleted list with bullets of your own choosing:

1. Highlight the paragraphs you want to convert to a bulleted list.

2. Choose the Format⇨Bullets and Numbering command. The Bullets and Numbering dialog box will appear, as shown in Figure 16-1. Because this dialog box has three tabs, you may have to click the Bulleted tab to show the bullet possibilities.

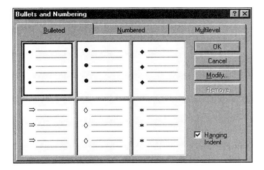

Figure 16-1: Bulleted options in the Bullets and Numbering dialog box.

3. If you like one of the six bullet formats shown in the dialog box, click it and click OK. You're done.

4. Otherwise, choose one of the six bullet formats you would like replaced with a custom format and click the Modify button to bring up the Modify Bulleted List dialog box, as shown in Figure 16-2.

5. Modify the bullet format any way you want. You can adjust the bullet character, point size, color, and indentation. The Preview box shows you how the bulleted list will appear.

6. You can use any character you want for the bullet character by clicking the Bullet button. This brings up the Symbol dialog box, shown in Figure 16-3.

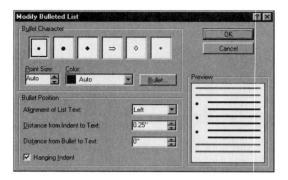

Figure 16-2: The Modify Bulleted List dialog box.

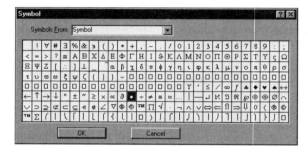

Figure 16-3: The Symbol dialog box.

7. Pick the bullet character you want to use. The Symbol font, which is initially shown when the Symbol dialog box is displayed, has only a few interesting bullet characters. For a better selection of bullet characters, switch to the Wingdings font. Wingdings has a great selection of bullet characters, including pointing fingers, smiley faces, grumpy faces, Siskel-and-Ebert style thumbs up and thumbs down, peace signs, time bombs, and a skull and crossbones. (If all you want is a simple check mark, look at the bottom row, fourth from the right.)

8. Click OK to return to the document and to see the results of your custom bullet format.

Using the Numbering Button

The easiest way to create a numbered list is to use the Numbering button. Here are the steps:

1. Type one or more paragraphs that you want number.

2. Select them all by dragging the mouse over them.

3. Click the Numbering button on the Formatting toolbar.

When you use the Numbering button to create a numbered list, Word uses a default numbering format and establishes a .25" hanging indent for each paragraph. (If the paragraphs are already formatted with hanging indents, the original indentation settings are kept.) You can change the numbering scheme if you want. To find out how, see the next section "Changing the Numbering Scheme."

Word does its level best to keep the list in order. If you add or delete a paragraph in the middle of the list, Word renumbers the paragraphs to preserve the order. If you add a paragraph to the end of the list, Word assigns the next number in sequence to the new paragraph.

Note

To remove numbering from a numbered paragraph, select the paragraph and click the Numbering button. To remove numbering from an entire list, select all of the paragraphs in the list and click the Numbering button.

Tip

If you insert a non-numbered paragraph in the middle of a numbered list, Word breaks the list in two and begins numbering from 1 again for the second list. However, if you simply turn off numbering for one of the paragraphs in a list, Word suspends the numbering for that paragraph and picks up where it left off with the next numbered paragraph.

Changing the Numbering Scheme

1, 2, 3 is not the only way to count. Word is tolerant of alternative counting preferences, such as A, B, C, or even Romanesque I, II, and III. If you want to use one of these alternative counting schemes, just follow these steps:

1. Highlight the paragraphs you want to format with fancy numbers.

2. Choose the Format⇨Bullets and Numbering command to bring up the Bullets and Numbering dialog box. You may have to click the Numbered tab to display the numbering options, as shown in Figure 16-4.

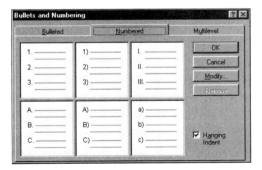

Figure 16-4: Numbering options.

3. If you like one of the six numbering formats shown in the dialog box, click it. Then, click OK and go home.

4. Otherwise, click the Modify button to bring up the Modify Numbered List dialog box, as shown in Figure 16-5.

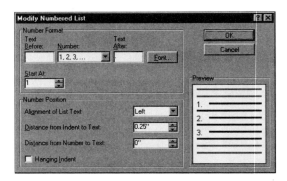

Figure 16-5: The Modify Numbered List dialog box.

5. Adjust the numbering scheme any way you want. You can type text to be included before and after the number (for example, you can surround the number with parentheses or brackets), change the number format, and play with the indentation. For example, you might add the word *Chapter* before the numbers and change the numbering format to One, Two, and so on.

6. Click OK.

In addition to normal number formats like 1, 2, 3...; A, B, C...; or I, II, III..., you can specify One, Two, Three...; 1st, 2nd, 3rd...; or First, Second, Third.... You can also specify a different font for the numbers by clicking the Font button when the Modify Numbered List dialog box appears. The font is applied not only to the number but also to the Text Before and Text After.

Note

Word's oddball numbering formats work even with unreasonably long lists. Try it and see for yourself: Word knows how to spell "one-thousand one-hundred and eighty-seventh." It also knows that the Roman numeral equivalent is MCLXXXVII.

Creating a Multilevel List

Single-level lists are interesting enough, but Word's numbering feature becomes even more interesting when you use it to create multilevel lists. If creating lists of this sort is your cup of tea, you'll love this feature.

To create a multilevel list, just follow these steps:

1. Type the text you want to make into a multilevel list. Don't worry about the numbers yet. Adjust the indentation of each paragraph as you go to reflect the numbering levels by using the Increase Indent and Decrease Indent buttons.

2. Choose the Format⇨Bullets and Numbering command. The Bullets and Numbering dialog box will appear. Select the Multilevel tab to see the multilevel numbering options, as shown in Figure 16-6.

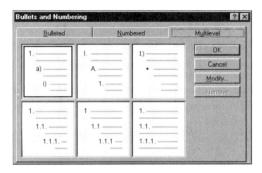

Figure 16-6: Creating a multilevel list.

3. Click the multilevel numbering format you like and click OK.

4. To create a custom multilevel numbering scheme, click the Modify button. The Modify Multilevel List dialog box will appear, as shown in Figure 16-7.

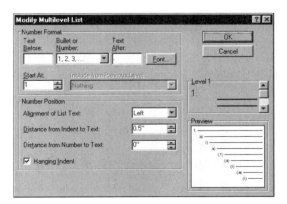

Figure 16-7: Customizing a multilevel list.

5. The Modify Multilevel List dialog box is where you customize each level of a multilevel list. Only one level of the list is shown at a time, as indicated by the Level box. Move the scrollbar to change levels. Then, format each level however you want. You can format each level as a bullet or a number by choosing the bullet or number format from the Bullet or Number drop-down list box.

6. Click OK when you are finished.

Tip

The multilevel list feature is useful for small lists with two or three levels. But if you really just want to create an outline, use the Outline feature instead. You'll find details on creating outlines in Chapter 23.

Bugaboo: Problems with Bullets and Numbering

I hate to be the bearer of bad news, but Word's bulleting and numbering feature has a few insidious bugs lurking just beneath the glossy veneer. None of these bugs are insurmountable, but they're significant enough to sometimes drive you crazy. I had hoped that these bugs would be corrected with Word 95, but noooo.

For starters, Word will screw up any bullet or numbered paragraph that actually does begin with a number. For example, let's make a list of favorite classic Disney movies:

Snow White

Sleeping Beauty

101 Dalmatians

Cinderella

Select all four paragraphs, click the Numbering button, and the list will end up looking like this:

1. Snow White

2. Sleeping Beauty

3. Dalmatians

4. Cinderella

Word decided that the *101* in *101 Dalmatians* was extraneous, so it unceremoniously dropped it. You have to go back and retype **101**.

If you had clicked the Bullets button instead of the Numbering button, Word would have displayed a dialog box asking "Do you want to replace the existing numbers with bullets?" Of course, you wouldn't suspect that it means the *101* in *101 Dalmatians*, so you click Yes. Your bulleted list then becomes:

- Snow White

- Sleeping Beauty

- Dalmatians

- Cinderella

Same nonsense. Go back and retype **101**, or say "No" when Word asks whether you want to replace the numbers.

It gets worse. Word thinks that any word three characters or fewer that ends with a period is a number that you manually typed and decided to replace with a bullet or automatic numbering. Let's make a list of our favorite magazines:

Time

Newsweek

U.S. News and World Report

Mad

Now, highlight it and click Numbering. Surprise:

1. Time

2. Newsweek

3. News and World Report

4. Mad

Word apparently thinks *U.S.* is a number to be discarded, no questions asked. Once again, the Bullets button asks the question, "Do you want to replace the existing numbers with bullets?" If you click Yes, *U.S.* will be wiped out.

Now for the pièce de résistance. Let's make a list of 800 numbers you can call for customer service:

1-800-555-1234

1-800-555-5678

1-800-555-9012

Now, select all three paragraphs and click the Numbering tool. Poof! The phone numbers disappear altogether, leaving you with only a blank numbered list:

1.

2.

3.

Sometimes Word will decide to handle the phone numbers with letters instead:

a)

b)

c)

It just depends on how cranky Word is. The problem is that Word thinks it is dealing with a multilevel list, and sometimes it has trouble deciding where to come in on which level. You can further confuse Word by starting each paragraph with a tab or by indenting the paragraphs.

Warning

If one of these bugs reaches out and bites you, press the Undo key (Ctrl+Z) right away. You can click the Bullets or Numbering buttons again to remove the bullets or numbers, but that won't restore your text: You'll wind up with blank paragraphs where your text once stood.

Using Word's Heading Numbering Feature

If you just want to add numbers to a document's headings, you can do so with Word's heading numbering feature. To use heading numbering, you must apply the appropriate heading styles—Heading 1, Heading 2, Heading 3, and so on—to your heading paragraphs. Then, when you apply heading numbering, all of the heading paragraphs in the document are automatically numbered according to the numbering scheme you pick.

Note

Because heading styles are inherently multilevel, the heading numbering feature is similar to the multilevel numbering feature. Don't mix up these two features, however. Heading numbering applies numbers to all of the headings in your document, whereas a multilevel list applies numbers only to the paragraphs that you indicate.

Here is the procedure for adding heading numbers to your document:

1. Format your document's headings by using Word's standard heading styles (Heading 1, Heading 2, and so on).

2. Choose the Format⇨Heading Numbering command. The Heading Numbering dialog box appears, as shown in Figure 16-8.

3. Pick the heading style you want and click OK.

4. If none of the predefined numbering styles tickles your fancy, click Modify to summon the Modify Heading Numbering dialog box, as shown in Figure 16-9. As you can see, this dialog box bears a remarkable resemblance to the Modify Multilevel List dialog box. To set the number format for a particular heading level, move the scrollbar in the Level box. When you're done, click OK.

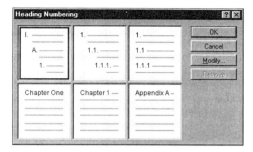

Figure 16-8: The Heading Numbering dialog box.

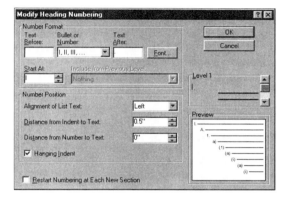

Figure 16-9: The Modify Heading Numbering dialog box.

If you plan on using heading numbering, add the numbering to your heading styles so you don't have to add it manually later. Choose the Format⇨Style command and select any of the heading styles. Then, click Modify, click Format, choose the Numbering command, and pick the number format you want.

To remove heading numbers, call up the Format⇨Heading Numbering command and click the Remove button in the dialog box.

Heading numbering always applies to all of the paragraphs in a document formatted with a given style. As a result, you cannot selectively apply it to some heading paragraphs but not to others. You can, however, set it up so that heading numbers are omitted for certain heading levels. Choose the Format⇨Heading Numbering command, click Modify, slide the Level scrollbar to the heading level for which you want numbers omitted, and pick None for the Bullet or Number field.

Chapter 17

Tabulating Tables

In This Chapter

▶ Setting up and using Word tables

▶ Letting Word handle the dirty work of formatting table cells using the Table AutoFormat command

▶ Editing a table by inserting and deleting cells, columns, and rows

▶ Formatting table cells yourself

▶ Using advanced table features, such as merging and splitting cells, splitting a table, and creating functions to perform calculations on table cells

▶ Creating your own customized toolbar with buttons for commonly-used table functions

This chapter describes the ins and outs of formatting text and graphics into tables. Word's table feature is remarkably versatile, so it pays to learn how it works.

Understanding Tables

You can think of a *table* as a mini-spreadsheet within your Word document. It consists of *rows* and *columns,* with *cells* at the intersections of each row and column. Each cell can contain text or graphics, and you can format it in any way you wish. Figure 17-1 shows a simple Word table.

Survey Results¶				
Word Feature¤	Like it¤	Hate it¤	**What is it?**¤	¤
Mail Merge¤	20%¤	70%¤	10%¤	¤
Table of Contents¤	10%¤	40%¤	50%¤	¤
Styles¤	25%¤	60%¤	15%¤	¤
Macros¤	5%¤	80%¤	15%¤	¤

Figure 17-1: A simple table.

Each cell can contain one or more paragraphs of text, and text automatically wraps within its cell. Whenever text wraps to a new line, Word automatically increases the height of the row if necessary to accommodate the new line of text. This is where the versatility of tables becomes apparent. The table in Figure 17-1 could be created using tabs rather than the Table feature; in fact, it would probably be easier to create the table using tabs. Consider the table in Figure 17-2, however. To create a table such as this using tabs, you'd have to break the lines for each column manually, using the Tab key to separate columns from one another.

	Advantages	Disadvantages
Tabs	Easy to set up for simple tables.	Difficult to use if text must span several lines within a column.
Table	Can apply any type of formatting within each cell. Text automatically wraps within cells.	More difficult to set up than tabs.

Figure 17-2: A more complex table.

Figure 17-3 shows how this table appears in Word when it is being edited. Notice in the ruler how each table column has its own margins and indentation settings. (The ruler's indentation doohickeys are only visible for the column the insertion point is in; in this example, the first column is active.) Notice also that dotted gridlines appear around the table cells. These gridlines help you see the layout of the table as you are editing the table. They do not appear when the table is printed.

Note

If you do not see gridlines when you work with tables, choose the Table⇨Gridlines command.

Notice also that each cell has a little box in it, called the *end-of-cell marker*. You can think of these markers as the paragraph marks for cells. In fact, end-of-cell markers are not displayed unless paragraph marks are also displayed. If you don't see paragraph marks or end-of-cell markers in your documents, choose the Tools⇨Options command, click the View tab, and select the Paragraph Marks check box. Or, click the Show/Hide ¶ button in the standard toolbar.

A Word table can contain as many as 31 columns. The number of rows is unlimited. When you create a table, Word adjusts the size of each column so that the table fits between the left and right margins. Each column is initially set to the same size, but you can adjust the size of individual columns later, and you can adjust the width of the entire table.

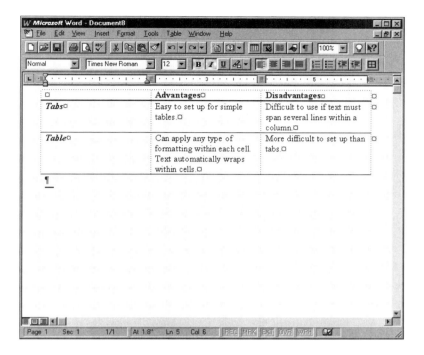

Figure 17-3: How the table appears in Word.

Creating Tables

The following sections describe several methods for creating tables.

Creating a table using the Insert Table button

The Insert Table button, which resides on the Standard toolbar, is the fastest way to create a simple table. When you click on this button, a drop-down grid appears, as shown in Figure 17-4. Drag the mouse down and across the grid until the correct number of columns and rows is selected and release the button to create the table at the insertion point. (Naturally, you should place your insertion point where you want the table inserted first.)

Figure 17-4: Using the Insert Table button.

The number of rows and columns that the Insert Table button can create depends on the resolution of your computer monitor:

Screen Resolution	Table Size
640x480	15x9
800x600	20x20
1,024x768	27x25

Secret

The Insert Table button is limited not only by the screen resolution, but also by the button's placement toward the right side of the Standard toolbar. As you drag the table grid to the right, you hit the right margin at only 9 columns when working in 640x480 mode. However, if you use the Tools⇨Customize command to relocate the Insert Table button farther to the left in the Standard toolbar, you can increase the number of columns to as many as 31, which is the maximum number of columns any table can contain.

Using the Table⇨Insert Table command

If you prefer the dialog-box approach to creating a table, use the Table⇨Insert Table command. The advantages of using this command over the Insert Table button are that you can pick an arbitrary number of rows and columns, and you can access the Table Wizard and Table AutoFormat features. (Beware that as you work with tables, the contents of the Table menu is liable to change depending on what is selected when you call it up.)

Follow these steps to create a formatted table using the Table⇨Insert Table command (the Table Wizard will be covered in a later section):

1. Position the insertion point where you want to insert the new table.

2. Choose the Table⇨Insert Table command. The Insert Table dialog box will appear, as shown in Figure 17-5.

3. Use the spin controls to set the number of rows and columns you want to create in the Number of Columns and Number of Rows fields.

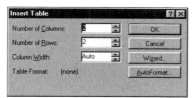

Figure 17-5: The Insert Table dialog box.

4. If you want to apply an AutoFormat to the table, click on the AutoFormat button. This will bring up the Table AutoFormat dialog box, which lets you choose from more than a few predefined table formats. Pick the format you want to apply and click OK to return to the Insert Table dialog box. (For a more complete description of the Table AutoFormat dialog box, see the section "AutoFormating a table" later in this chapter.)

5. Click OK to insert the table.

Using the Table Wizard

Word's Table Wizard can do much of the dirty work involved with setting up and formatting a table. To use it, follow these steps:

Note

The exact sequence of steps involved in creating a table may vary somewhat from the following, based on the instructions you provide for the Table Wizard.

1. Position the insertion point where you want to insert the table.

2. Choose the Table⇨Insert Table command. The Insert Table dialog box will appear. (If you forgot what it looks like, refer back to Figure 17-5.)

3. Click on the Wizard button. The Table Wizard dialog box will appear, as shown in Figure 17-6.

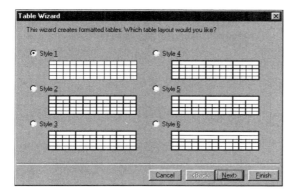

Figure 17-6: The Table Wizard rears its ugly head.

4. Select the table style you want.

5. Click on Next>. The Table Wizard continues, as shown in Figure 17-7.

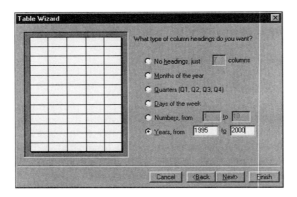

Figure 17-7: The Table Wizard asks for column headings.

6. Select the type of table column headings you want to use. In Figure 17-7, I selected the years from 1995 to 2000. Other choices include months, quarters, days of the week, and simple numbers. The selection you make here also determines how many columns will appear in the table.

7. Click on Next>. The Table Wizard continues, as shown in Figure 17-8.

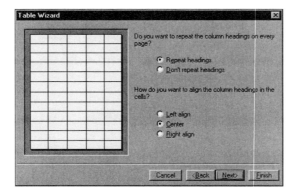

Figure 17-8: The Table Wizard asks how column headings should be aligned.

8. Answer the questions about whether you want the headings repeated on each page (only important for long tables) and whether you want the column headings left-aligned, centered, or right-aligned.

9. Click on Next>. The Table Wizard continues, as shown in Figure 17-9.

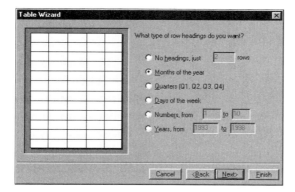

Figure 17-9: Now it wants to know about row headings.

10. Select the type of table row headings you want to use. In Figure 17-9, , I selected the <u>M</u>onths of the year to use for row headings. Note that the selection you make here also determines how many rows will appear in the table.

11. Click on <u>N</u>ext>. The Table Wizard continues, as shown in Figure 17-10.

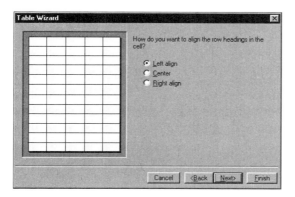

Figure 17-10: The Table Wizard asks how you want to align the row headings.

12. Select the alignment for the row headings: left, centered, or right.

13. Click on <u>N</u>ext>. The Table Wizard continues, as shown in Figure 17-11.

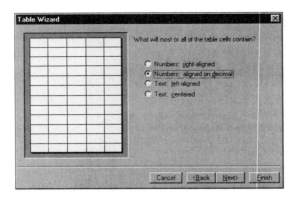

Figure 17-11: Now, it wants to know how to align the data.

14. Select the alignment for the data that will appear in the table cells. You can select from two numeric formats (right-aligned or decimal-aligned) or two text formats (left-aligned or centered).

15. Click on Next>. The Table Wizard continues, as shown in Figure 17-12.

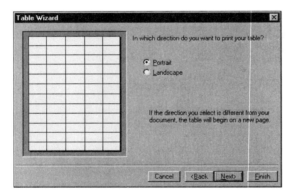

Figure 17-12: The Table Wizard wants to know which way to print your table. Will it ever end?

16. Select whether you want the table to use Portrait or Landscape orientation.

17. Click on Next>. The Table Wizard continues, as shown in Figure 17-13.

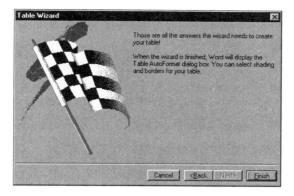

Figure 17-13: The checkered flag is out. It's almost finished now.

18. Finally! Tell the Table Wizard whether you need help after the table is created and click on Finish.

19. Stretch your muscles for a moment, but don't get up. In just a moment, the Table AutoFormat dialog box will appear, as shown in Figure 17-14.

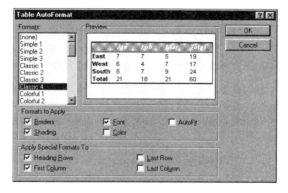

Figure 17-14: Pick an AutoFormat for the table.

20. Select the formatting you want applied to the table and click OK.

21. Figure 17-15 shows what the finished product should look like.

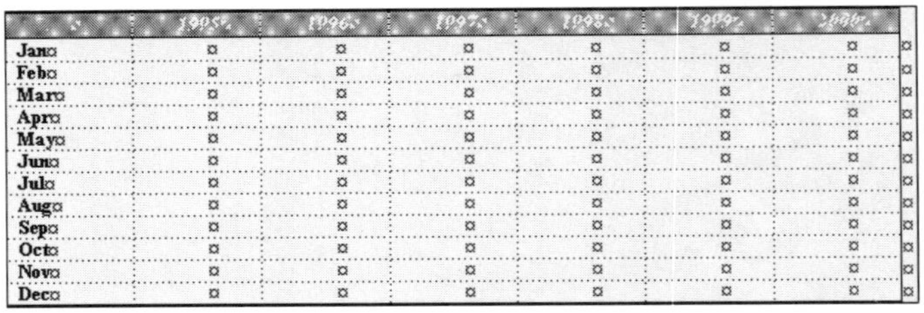

Figure 17-15: A finished table.

Editing Tables

The following sections describe the procedures for basic table-editing tasks: selecting cells, adding and deleting rows and columns, and changing column widths.

Right-clicking on table cells

Just about everything you would want to do to a table cell is accessible on the shortcut menu that appears when you right-click on the cell. Different combinations of commands will appear depending on whether you select a single cell, a range of cells including an entire column or row, or an entire table.

Moving and selecting in tables

You can move from cell to cell in a table using any of the keyboard shortcuts listed in Table 17-1.

Table 17-1 Keyboard Shortcuts for Moving Around in a Table	
To Move to This Cell	*Use This Keyboard Shortcut*
Next cell in a row	Tab
Previous cell in a row	Shift+Tab
First cell in a row	Alt+Home
First cell in a column	Alt+Page Up
Last cell in a row	Alt+End
Last cell in a column	Alt+Page Down
Previous row	Up Arrow
Next row	Down Arrow

You can combine the keyboard shortcuts listed in Table 17-1 with the Shift key to extend the selection over a range of cells. In addition, you can select the entire table by placing the insertion point anywhere in the table and pressing Alt+Numeric 5 (the 5 on the numeric keypad).

You can also select various portions of a table using the mouse actions listed in Table 17-2.

Table 17-2	Mouse Actions for Selecting Cells In A Table
To Select This	*Use This Mouse Action*
A single cell	Move the mouse over the left edge of the cell until the mouse pointer becomes a right-pointing arrow and click.
An entire row	Move the mouse just past the left edge of the leftmost cell in the row until the mouse pointer changes to a right-pointing arrow and click.
An entire column	Move the mouse just above the topmost cell in the row until the mouse pointer changes to a down-pointing arrow and click.
A range of cells	Drag the mouse across the rectangular area of cells you want to select.

Adding rows and columns

To add a new row or column to a table, use the Table⇔Insert command. Depending on whether you have selected an individual cell or a range of cells, one or more complete rows, or one or more complete columns, this command will appear in the Table menu as Table⇔Insert Cells, Table⇔Insert Rows, or Table⇔Insert Columns.

To add new rows to a table, follow one of these procedures:

- To insert a new row within the body of a table, select the row where you want to insert the new row and choose the Table⇔Insert Row command. The new row will be inserted above the selected row.

- To insert several rows, select the number of rows you want to insert and choose the Table⇔Insert Row command. The new rows will be inserted above the selected rows. For example, Figure 17-16 shows two rows about to be inserted into a table.

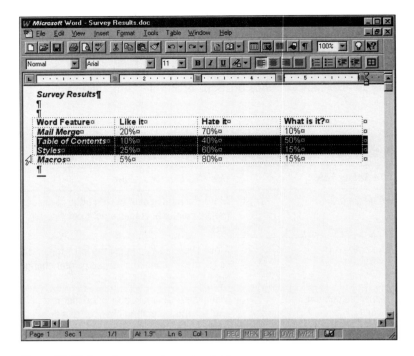

Figure 17-16: Inserting several rows in a table.

■ To insert a new row at the bottom of the table, move the insertion point to the last cell in the last row of the table and press the Tab key.

To add new columns to a table, follow one of these procedures:

■ To insert a new column within the body of the table, select the column where you want to insert the new column and choose the Table⇨Insert Column command. The new column will be inserted to the left of the selected column.

■ To insert several columns, select the number of columns you want to insert and choose the Table⇨Insert Column command. The new columns will be inserted to the left of the selected columns.

■ To insert a new column at the right of the table, move the mouse pointer immediately above the end-of-row markers to the right of the table until the pointer changes to a solid black down-pointing arrow and click to select the markers, as shown in Figure 17-17. Then, choose the Table⇨Insert Column command. A new column will be inserted to the right of the table. (The new column may extend past the right margin. You may need to adjust the widths of one or more columns so the table will fit within the margins.)

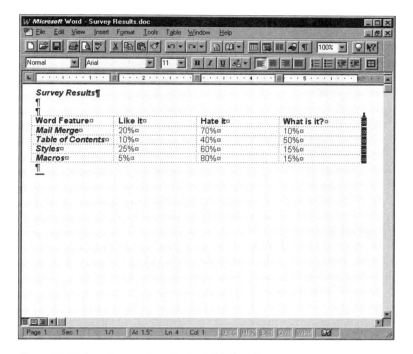

Figure 17-17: Inserting a column to the right of a table.

Inserting cells

Word will also allow you to insert individual cells within a table. Start by highlighting the cell or cells where you want to insert the new cells. Then, choose the Table⇨Insert Cells command. The Insert Cells dialog box will appear, as shown in Figure 17-18.

Figure 17-18: The Insert Cells dialog box.

If you want to add new cells above the selected cells and shift the unselected cells in the same rows down, choose the Shift Cells Down option. If you want to insert the new cells to the left of the selected cells, with extra cells being added to the affected rows, choose the Shift Cells Right option. Then, click OK.

The magic Insert Cells button

Secret

The Insert Table button has a peculiar feature: it changes to an Insert Cell button when the selection pointer is placed inside a table. You can use this button to insert cells into the table quickly. How it works depends on what cells are selected when you use it:

■ If an entire row of cells is selected or if no cells are selected, the Insert Cell button inserts a new row.

■ If an entire column is selected, the Insert Cell button inserts a new column.

■ If a range of cells is selected, the Insert Cell button calls up the Insert Cells dialog box.

Deleting cells

If you want to delete the contents of one or more cells, select the cells and press the Del key. The contents of the cells will be deleted, but the cells them-selves will remain in place.

To remove one or more rows or columns from the table completely, select the rows or columns you want to delete and choose the Table⇨Delete command. (It will appear in the Table menu as either Table⇨Delete Rows or Table⇨Delete Columns.)

To remove a range of cells in the table completely, select the cells you want to remove and choose the Table⇨Delete Cells command. The Delete Cells dialog box will appear, as shown in Figure 17-19.

Figure 17-19: The Delete Cells dialog box.

Select whether you want to shift the surrounding cells up or left to fill the void left by the deleted cells or to just delete entire rows or columns and click OK.

Adjusting column width

When Word creates a table, it initially makes each column the same width. This isn't appropriate for many tables, however, because the data in each column is rarely uniform in size. For example, the first column of a table may contain the names of famous composers, and the second column may list their birth dates. Obviously, the first column should be wider than the second.

Fortunately, Word doesn't impose uniform column widths. You can manually adjust the width of each column individually, or you can let Word automatically adjust the width of each column based on the contents of the column.

To adjust the width of an individual column manually, drag the gridline to the right of the column to increase or decrease the column width. Alternatively, you can drag the column marker that appears in the ruler, as shown in Figure 17-20. Either way, the width of the columns to the right of the one you adjust is automatically adjusted so that the width of the entire table remains the same.

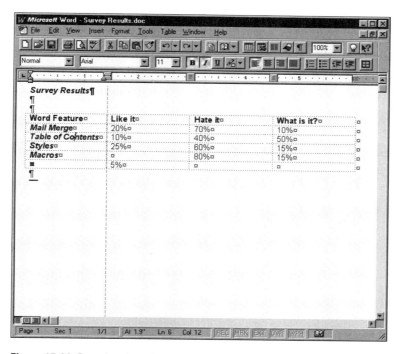

Figure 17-20: Dragging the column marker.

Tip

If you hold down the Alt key while adjusting column width, the width of each column will be displayed in the ruler.

Another way to change column width is to choose the Table⇨Cell Height and Width command and click on the Column tab. The dialog box shown in Figure 17-21 is then displayed.

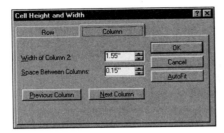

Figure 17-21: Manually setting column widths.

From this dialog box, you can set the width of each column to a precise measurement, and you can change the spacing between columns. The Cell Height and Width dialog box shows the column width and spacing for one column at a time. Use the Previous Column and Next Column buttons to move from column to column.

If you click the AutoFit button, Word will automatically adjust the width of each column to accommodate the widest text in each column. Usually, the best way to adjust the column widths for a table is to first use AutoFit and then make any additional adjustments that are necessary.

Formatting Tables

You can format the contents of table cells just as you format any other document text in Word. You can change the font, font size, add bold, italics, and underlines. You can even add borders and shading to individual cells. Most of this formatting is pretty straightforward. The following sections describe the trickier aspects of formatting tables.

Using tabs in a table

You can set tab stops for individual cells or a range of table cells. Tabs in tables work pretty much the way they do outside of tables, with two important exceptions:

- To insert a tab character into a cell, you must press Ctrl+Tab. Simply pressing the Tab key moves you to the next cell without inserting the tab character.

- If you add a decimal tab to a table cell, the text in the cell is automatically aligned over the decimal tab. You do not have to press Ctrl+Tab to move the data to the tab stop.

AutoFormatting a table

The Table⇨Table AutoFormat command is designed to spare you the hassle of formatting your tables cell-by-cell. Although it can't always give you the exact look for your table, it can often bring you close. You can then go back and tweak individual cell formats until your table is perfectly formatted.

To AutoFormat a table, follow these steps:

1. Create a table using the Insert Table button in the Standard toolbar or the Table⇨Insert Table command. Create the correct number of rows and columns and type in your data. If appropriate, use the first row and column as headings.

2. Click the mouse anywhere in the table.

3. Choose the Table⇨Table AutoFormat command. The Table AutoFormat dialog box will appear, as shown in Figure 17-22.

4. Select the table format you like from the Formats list. As you scroll through the list of available formats, the Preview box shows how a sample table would appear with the format applied.

5. Select which formatting elements you want applied to the table by checking or unchecking the appropriate boxes. For example, if you don't have headings in the first row (or if you don't want the headings formatted in a special way), uncheck the Heading Rows box.

6. Click OK.

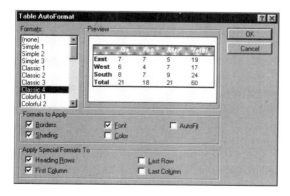

Figure 17-22: The Table AutoFormat dialog box.

Tip

You can change the AutoFormat applied to a table at any time. Just click anywhere in the table and summon the Table⇨Table AutoFormat command again, or, right-click in the table and choose the Table AutoFormat command.

Adding borders and shading to a table

Borders and shading can make a ho-hum table come alive. You can create a complete grid for your table, or you can use borders more judiciously, adding rules between rows or perhaps just at the top and bottom of the table. With the Borders toolbar, you can experiment with different combinations of borders until you find one that looks just right.

You can apply borders and shading to individual cells or ranges of cells by following these steps:

1. Click on the Border tool in the Formatting toolbar to summon the Border toolbar.

2. Select the cell or cells where you wish to add a border or shading.

3. Click on the appropriate border button to add a border above or below, on the left or right, around an entire range of cells, or on the interior borders of a range of cells. To remove a border, click the button again.

4. To shade a cell or cells, pull down the shading list box and select the shading you want.

Note

For more information about using borders and shading, including how to use the Format⇨Borders and Shading command, see Chapter 14.

Merging cells to create headings

If your table requires a heading that spans more than one column, you can use the Table⇨Merge Cells command. For example, Figure 17-23 shows a table in which the cell that contains the heading "Survey Results" has been merged so that it spans three columns.

	Survey Results		
	Like it	Hate it	What is it?
Mail Merge	20%	70%	10%
Table of Contents	10%	40%	50%
Styles	25%	60%	15%
Macros	5%	80%	15%

Figure 17-23: A table with a multicolumn heading.

To create a multicolumn heading such as the one shown in Figure 17-23, follow these steps:

1. Create the table as usual. For the heading that will span several columns, type the text into the cell over the first column you want the heading to span.

2. Highlight the cells in the row where you want to create a multicolumn heading in.

3. Choose the Table⇨Merge Cells command. The cells will merge into one gigantic cell that spans several columns.

4. If you want the heading centered over the cells, click on the Center button in the Formatting toolbar or press Ctrl+E.

If you want to separate cells that you merged, select the merged cell and choose the Table⇨Split Cells command. When Word asks you how many columns to split the cell into, specify the number of columns the merged cell spans.

The Table⇨Table AutoFormat command does not deal very well with merged cells. If you must use both features in the same table, format the table with Table⇨Table AutoFormat first and then merge the cells to create a multicolumn heading.

Note

Designating heading rows

If you have an unusually long table that spans more than one page, you can designate the top row or rows of the table to serve as heading rows, which are automatically duplicated at the top of each page. Select the row or rows you want to use for headings (the top row of the table should be included in the selection) and choose the Table⇨Headings command. Then, Word will duplicate the selected rows at the top of each page where the table appears.

To stop using heading rows, choose the Table⇨Headings command again.

Splitting a Table

Suppose you've created a large table and decide that you'd like to drop a paragraph of normal text right in the middle of the table, between two of its rows. In other words, you want to divide the table into two smaller tables. To do that, just select the row where you want the table divided and choose the Table⇨Split Table command. Word divides the table into two and inserts a blank paragraph between the two tables.

What about splitting a table vertically, creating two side-by-side tables? Unfortunately, there is no way to do this in Word. However, you can simulate two side-by-side tables by using an empty table column to create an empty space between two separately bordered areas of the table, as shown in Figure 17-24. Here, what appears to be two tables is actually a single table: the space between them is an unused column.

Secret

Red Team	
Higgens	23
Crouter	21
Newman	21
Henman	17
Ray	15

Blue Team	
Owens	25
Marshall	22
Wilson	19
Smith	19
Olsen	14

Figure 17-24: Creating the appearance of two side-by-side tables.

Sorting a Table

You can sort the rows of a table using the Table⇨Sort command. Here is the procedure:

1. Select the rows you want to sort. For the best results, select entire rows, and leave out any heading rows you don't want sorted. Usually, you'll want to sort the entire table, except for headings.

2. Choose the Table⇨Sort command to display the Sort dialog box, shown in Figure 17-25.

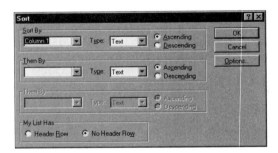

Figure 17-25: The Sort dialog box.

3. Set the column you want to sort the table by and the type of sort you want. By default, the Sort dialog box sorts data into ascending sequence based on the first selected column. But, you can pick a different column to sort by, or you can choose to sort in descending sequence, and you can tell Word whether the column contains text, numbers, or dates. You can also sort up to three columns. (This setting tells Word which columns to use to determine the sorted order. Keep in mind that Word keeps rows together when it sorts them.)

4. If your selection includes a heading row that you do not want sorted, check the Header Row option.

5. Click OK.

Using Table Formulas

If you can't afford a real spreadsheet program, you can use Word tables as sort of a poor man's spreadsheet. Like a spreadsheet, Word tables let you enter data into rows, columns, and cells. The tables even let you perform simple calculations on cells using formulas similar to spreadsheet formulas.

The most common use of formulas in a Word table is to add a row or column of cells. Here is the procedure:

1. Select the cell where you want the total to appear.

2. Choose the Table⇨Formula command to display the Formula dialog box, shown in Figure 17-26.

Figure 17-26: The Formula dialog box.

3. Double-check the formula proposed by Word. Word takes its best guess for the cells you want to add. If you insert a formula to the right of a row of numbers, Word assumes you want to add the numbers to the left. If you place it beneath a column of numbers, Word assumes you want to add the cells above.

4. Click OK.

5. Double- check the results to make sure the numbers are added up correctly. Yes, your computer does know how to add and subtract (unless it's a Pentium), but the formula might be set up to calculate the total differently than you expect.

Besides adding a range of numbers, Word can perform a whole list of other functions. Table 17-3 summarizes the most common of these functions. For information about additional functions you can use, see Chapter 28. The most useful are Average, Product, Count, Max, and Min. In the Formula dialog box, you can use the Paste Function list box to select functions other than Sum.

Table 17-3	Formulas Most Commonly Used In Tables
Formula	**Explanation**
AVERAGE( )	The average of a list of cells.
COUNT( )	The number of items in a list of cells.
MAX( )	The largest value in a list of cells.
MIN( )	The smallest value in a list of cells.
PRODUCT( )	The product of a list of cells (that is, all of the cell values multiplied together).
SUM( )	The sum of a list of cells.

Note

Word formulas use a reference system to refer to individual table cells just like a spreadsheet program. Each column is identified by a letter, starting with A for the first column, B for the second column, and so on. After the letter comes the row number. Thus, the first cell in the first row is A1, the third cell in the fourth row is C4, and so on. You can construct cell references in formulas as follows:

- A single cell reference, such as *B3* or *F7*.

- A range of cells, such as *A2:A7* or *B3:B13*.

- A series of individual cells, such as *A3,B4,C5*

- *ABOVE* or *BELOW*, referring to all the cells in the column above <u>or below</u> the current cell.

- *LEFT* or *RIGHT*, referring to all the cells in the row to the left <u>or to the right</u> of the current cell.

You can also construct simple math expressions such as *C3+C5*100*. You can use any of the standard mathematical operators:

+	Addition
-	Subtraction
*	Multiplication
/	Division
%	Percent

You can also control the format of numbers that appears in formulas by editing the <u>N</u>umber Format field in the Formulas dialog box. The <u>N</u>umber Format drop-down list includes several predefined formats. If you wish, you can create your own number formats using the characters listed in Table 17-4.

Table 17-4 **Characters Used To Build Your Own Number Formats**

Character	Explanation
0 (zero)	Displays a single digit of the result. If the result digit is zero, "0" is displayed. Use this to insure that a minimum number of digits is displayed. For example, 00.00 will display the value 1.01 as 01.01.
#	Displays a single significant digit of the result, but does not display leading zeros .
x	Used as the right most digit on the right of the decimal point to round the result value at this digit. Use this in the right most decimal position to display a rounded result.
. (decimal point)	The decimal point.
, (digit grouping symbol)	Separates series of three digits. For example, ##,##0.00.
- (minus sign)	Adds a minus sign to a negative result or adds a space if the result is positive or 0 (zero).
+ (plus sign)	Adds a plus sign to a positive result a minus sign to a negative result, or a space if the result is 0 (zero).
%, $, *, and so on	Displays the specified character.
'text'	Adds text to the result. Encloses text in single quotation marks.

Note

You can provide separate number formats for positive, negative, and zero values by separating the number formats with semicolons. For example, ##,##0.00;(##,##0.00) provides for negative numbers to be enclosed in parentheses, whereas ##,##0.00;(##,##0.00);n/a displays negative numbers in parentheses and zero values as "n/a."

Using a Table as a Database

Word tables are the basis for the database used when using the Mail Merge feature. As a result, I won't discuss the database uses of tables here. Instead, I refer you to Chapter 30, where you'll learn the ins and outs of using tables as a mail merge data source.

Creating a Custom Tables Toolbar

Considering the number of commands available on the Table menu, it's surprising that Word doesn't include a Tables toolbar button. What makes this even more surprising is that although no built-in toolbar is available, Word does supply a number of toolbar buttons for table functions. You can add these buttons to an existing toolbar, or you can create your own custom Tables toolbar.

Figure 17-27 shows the Toolbars tab of the Customize dialog box with Tables selected in the Categories list. As you can see, there are several table-related buttons from which to choose. Table 17-5 lists the function of each of these buttons.

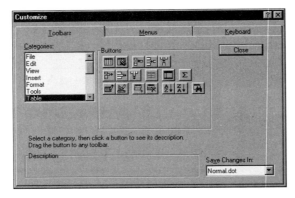

Figure 17-27: The Tools Customize command leads you to a collection of Table buttons.

Table 17-5	Buttons for Table functions
Button	*What It Does*
▦	Inserts a table, or, if the insertion pointer is in a table, inserts a row or column.
▦	Inserts an Excel worksheet.
▦	Inserts one or more cells.
▦	Inserts one or more rows.
▦	Inserts one or more columns.
▦	Deletes one or more cells.
▦	Deletes one or more rows.
▦	Deletes one or more columns.

Table 17-5 *(continued)*

Button	What It Does
	Alternately shows and hides gridlines.
	Calls up the AutoFormat dialog box.
	Inserts an =SUM formula
	Displays a form for entering data one row at a time.
	Adds or deletes a field to the form.
	Adds a row to the table.
	Deletes a row.
	Sorts the table into ascending sequence.
	Sorts the table into descending sequence.
	Searches for information in a table.

Figure 17-28 shows the toolbar I use when working with tables. You can build this toolbar yourself, but you'll find a copy of it in the Word Secrets.dot template that comes with this book.

Figure 17-28: The custom Tables toolbar.

If one of the buttons in the Tables toolbar doesn't look familiar, it's because it is a custom button I created myself to AutoFit a column's width. Unfortunately, there is no TableAutoFit command that you can easily assign a button to, so you have to create a simple macro for it and design your own button. To create the macro, call up the Tools⇨Macro command, type **TableAutoFit** in the Macro Name field, and click on Create. Then type the macro exactly as follows:

```
Sub MAIN
TableColumnWidth .AutoFit
End Sub
```

Close the macro, save it, and call up the Tools⇨Customize command, click on the Toolbars tab, select Macros in the Categories list, and drag the TableAutoFit macro to a toolbar. When Word offers to assign a button image, click on the Edit button, and edit the button image as shown in Figure 17-29.

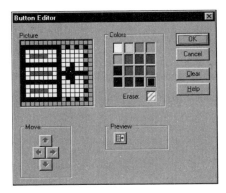

Figure 17-29: Creating the AutoFit button image.

Converting Text to a Table (And Vice Versa)

If you have tabular information that you did not originally enter as a table, you can use the Table⇨Convert Text to Table command to convert the text to a table. Word will automatically create a table for you, making its best guess at how many rows and columns the table should contain based on the format of the data you highlighted. This is especially useful if the information was originally created outside of Word, for example, as a simple text file that used tabs to align information into columns.

To convert text to a table, first highlight the text you want to convert and then choose the Table⇨Convert Text to Table. The dialog box shown in Figure 17-30 will be displayed.

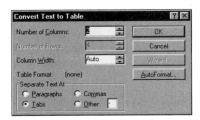

Figure 17-30: Converting text to a table.

The main thing to pay attention to here is the character Word will use to determine what text goes into each cell: tabs, paragraph marks, commas, or any arbitrary character you'd like to use. Word will usually deduce the proper character based on the text you highlight, but it's worth double-checking.

You can also convert an existing table to text. Select the table you want to convert and choose the Table⇨Convert Table to Text command to summon the dialog box shown in Figure 17-31.

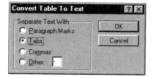

Figure 17-31: Converting a table to text.

Choose whether you want to use paragraph marks, tabs, commas, or some other character to separate the text for each table cell, then click OK to convert the table to text.

Using the Tables7.dot Macro Template

One final thing you should know about tables before we move on is that Word for Windows 95 comes with a template with several macros designed for use with tables. The macro is named Tables7.dot and lives in the \Winword\Macros folder (\Msoffice\Winword\Macros if you have installed Microsoft Office).

To activate the Tables7.dot template, follow these steps:

1. Choose the File⇨Templates command. The Templates and Add-ins dialog box will appear.

2. Click on the Add button.

3. Browse until you find the Tables7.dot template.

4. Click it, and click OK.

5. Click OK again to dismiss the Templates and Add-ins dialog box.

Once you have loaded this template, you have access to three macros:

■ **AccessExporter:** Converts a Word table to a database table that Microsoft Access can process. This macro comes in handy if you have a large mail merge data source you'd like to convert to Microsoft Access.

■ **TableMath:** This macro ostensibly simplifies the task of creating table formulas, but in actual practice it has just the opposite effect. I'd avoid it if I were you.

■ **TableNum:** This macro inserts a column that numbers the rows in the table, or inserts a row that numbers the columns.

To use these macros, choose the Tools⇨Macro command, select Tables7.dot in the Macros Available In field, and double-click on the macro you want to run.

Chapter 18

Using Styles

In This Chapter

▶ Understanding how styles work, including the difference between character and paragraph styles

▶ A list of the built-in styles that come with Word

▶ How to create your own styles, using one of two techniques: the easy way and the hard way

▶ Applying styles to the paragraphs in your document, including how to assign keyboard shortcuts to styles

▶ Viewing the style area and searching for and replacing styles with the Find and Replace commands

Styles are one of the best Word features that most people don't use. I can understand the reluctance to go to all the bother of setting up and using styles for simple documents such as letters and short, one- or two-page memos, but for serious word processing, styles are a must.

Styles are the secret to freeing yourself from the tyranny of Word's Format menu. They enable you to apply a bevy of formatting commands with a single keystroke or mouse click. Plus, they allow you to change the formatting of common document elements, such as headings or bulleted lists, with a sweep of your hand.

Styles are a great formatting tool precisely because they enable you to forget about formatting altogether and focus on the structure of your writing. Once you set up styles, you won't have to think in terms of fonts, sizes, indents, and tabs. Instead, you can think in terms of headings, body text, lists, and other structural elements of your document.

Another benefit of styles — especially in an office setting — is that they allow everyone to benefit from the experience of whoever sets up the style. Only one user in the office needs to master all of the formatting features of Word. The other users need to learn only how to apply styles to create great-looking documents.

Understanding Styles

Styles are integral to the way Word works. Even if you've never heard of styles, you are already using them. All Word documents start off with several pre-defined styles, including that ubiquitous Normal style, which governs the default appearance of paragraphs in your document. You cannot create a Word document without using at least the Normal style.

Styles consolidate the formatting information provided by a host of Word commands, as summarized in Table 18-1.

Table 18-1	Formatting Commands Included in Styles
Command	**Formats Included**
Format⇨Font	Font name, style (regular, bold, italic, or bold italic), and special character attributes, such as small caps or superscripts, as well as character spacing and kerning.
Format⇨Paragraph	Left and right indentation, first line indentation and hanging indents, line spacing, before and after spacing, and text flow (widow/orphan control, keep with next, and so on).
Format⇨Tabs	Tab stop positions, tab types, leader tabs, and bar tabs.
Format⇨Borders and Shading	Borders and line styles as well as fill shades.
Tools⇨Language	Alternative dictionaries for spelling and hyphenation.
Format⇨Frame	Frame containing text and graphics.
Format⇨Bullets and Numbering	Numbered or bulleted lists.

With all of these formats stored together under one name, you can imagine how much time styles can save you. For example, suppose that you want to format headings with 16-point Arial Bold, 18 points of space above the heading and 6 points below, and with a line drawn beneath the paragraph. You'd have to bounce the mouse all over the place to format a heading like this manually. Or, you can create a style and apply it with a single click of the mouse or a keyboard shortcut.

Styles enable you to apply Word formats you don't know how to use or can't remember. For example, you may not know how to set up a customized bullet that uses a skull and crossbones instead of a boring dot. But, if you can talk your friendly local Word guru into setting up a style formatted with that kind of bullet, you can effortlessly apply the fancy bullet style, without even knowing how to create the evil-looking bullets manually.

Suppose that you decide that the skull and crossbones might not appeal to your new clientele. No problem. Just change the style to use a different bullet character, and — *voilà!* — all the paragraphs formatted with the style will instantly be changed. No need to search the document manually and make the changes individually.

Styles are stored along with your text in the document file. Thus, each document can have its own collection of styles, and styles with the same name can have different formatting characteristics in different documents. For example, a style named *Bullet List* may have ordinary round bullets in one document but check marks or skull and crossbones in another.

You can store styles in templates, which means that new documents start off life with a fresh store of styles inherited from the template on which they are based. Templates were described in detail in Chapter 4; if necessary, refer back to that chapter for a refresher course on how templates work.

One final benefit of using styles is that some Word features — Table of Contents and Outline view in particular — work best when you use styles for your headings and body text. In fact, I wouldn't even bother using these features without also using styles. You *can* mark table of contents entries and outline levels by using field codes, but styles are much easier.

Paragraph styles and character styles

Word lets you create and use two types of styles: paragraph styles and character styles. Paragraph styles apply to entire paragraphs, whereas character styles apply only to selected characters within a paragraph. In most situations, paragraph styles are far more useful than character styles. So much more useful, in fact, that most people (myself included) never bother with character styles. Throughout the rest of this chapter, the term *style* refers to paragraph styles unless I specifically mention character styles.

Word's built-in styles

The Normal.dot template (which all new documents are based on unless you specifically choose a different template) contains 69 built-in paragraph styles and 6 built-in character styles. Tables 18-2 and 18-3 list these styles, along with an indication of the formatting that is applied for each of the styles.

Note

You won't see all of these styles in the Formatting toolbar's Styledrop-down list unless you hold down the Shift key when activating the drop-down.

Table 18-2	Word's Built-In Paragraph Styles
Style	*Formatting*
Annotation Text	Normal
Body Text	Normal + Space After 6 pt.
Body Text Indent	Normal + Indent: Left 0.25", Space After 6 pt.
Caption	Normal + Bold, Space Before 6 pt., Space After 6 pt.
Closing	Normal + Indent: Left 3"
Endnote Text	Normal
Envelope Address	Normal + Font: 12 pt., Indent: Left 2", Position: Center Horiz. Relative To Page, 0.13" From Text Horiz., Bottom Vert. Relative To Margin, Width: Exactly 5.5", Height: Exactly 1.38"
Envelope Return	Normal
Footer	Normal + Tab stops: 3" Centered, 6" Right Flush
Footnote Text	Normal
Header	Normal + Tab stops: 3" Centered, 6" Right Flush
Heading 1	Normal + Font: Arial, 14 pt., Bold, Kern at 14 pt., Space Before 12 pt. After 3 pt., Keep With Next
Heading 2	Normal + Font: Arial, 12 pt., Bold, Italic, Space Before 12 pt. After 3 pt., Keep With Next
Heading 3	Normal + Font: Arial, 12 pt., Space Before 12 pt. After 3 pt., Keep With Next
Heading 4	Normal + Font: Arial, 12 pt., Bold, Space Before 12 pt. After 3 pt., Keep With Next
Heading 5	Normal + Font: Arial, 11 pt., Space Before 12 pt. After 3 pt.
Heading 6	Normal + Font: 11 pt., Italic, Space Before 12 pt. After 3 pt.
Heading 7	Normal + Font: Arial, Space Before 12 pt. After 3 pt.
Heading 8	Normal + Font: Arial, Italic, Space Before 12 pt. After 3 pt.
Heading 9	Normal + Font: Arial, 9 pt., Bold, Italic, Space Before 12 pt. After 3 pt.
Index 1	Normal + Indent: Hanging 0.14", Tab stops: 6" Right Flush…
Index 2	Normal + Indent: Left 0.14" Hanging 0.14", Tab stops: 6" Right Flush…

Style	*Formatting*
Index 3	Normal + Indent: Left 0.28" Hanging 0.14", Tab stops: 6" Right Flush…
Index 4	Normal + Indent: Left 0.42" Hanging 0.14", Tab stops: 6" Right Flush…
Index 5	Normal + Indent: Left 0.56" Hanging 0.14", Tab stops: 6" Right Flush…
Index 6	Normal + Indent: Left 0.69" Hanging 0.14", Tab stops: 6" Right Flush…
Index 7	Normal + Indent: Left 0.83" Hanging 0.14", Tab stops: 6" Right Flush…
Index 8	Normal + Indent: Left 0.97" Hanging 0.14", Tab stops: 6" Right Flush…
Index 9	Normal + Indent: Left 1.11" Hanging 0.14", Tab stops: 6" Right Flush…
Index Heading	Normal + Font: Arial, Bold
List	Normal + Indent: Hanging 0.25"
List 2	Normal + Indent: Left 0.25" Hanging 0.25"
List 3	Normal + Indent: Left 0.5" Hanging 0.25"
List 4	Normal + Indent: Left 0.75" Hanging 0.25"
List 5	Normal + Indent: Left 1" Hanging 0.25"
List Bullet	Normal + Indent: Hanging 0.25", Bullet
List Bullet 2	Normal + Indent: Left 0.25" Hanging 0.25", Bullet
List Bullet 3	Normal + Indent: Left 0.5" Hanging 0.25", Bullet
List Bullet 4	Normal + Indent: Left 0.75" Hanging 0.25", Bullet
List Bullet 5	Normal + Indent: Left 1" Hanging 0.25", Bullet
List Continue	Normal + Indent: Left 0.25", Space After 6 pt.
List Continue 2	Normal + Indent: Left 0.5", Space After 6 pt.
List Continue 3	Normal + Indent: Left 0.75", Space After 6 pt.
List Continue 4	Normal + Indent: Left 1", Space After 6 pt.
List Continue 5	Normal + Indent: Left 1.25", Space After 6 pt.
List Number	Normal + Indent: Hanging 0.25", Auto Numbering
List Number 2	Normal + Indent: Left 0.25" Hanging 0.25", Auto Numbering

continued

Table 18-2 *(continued)*

Style	Formatting
List Number 3	Normal + Indent: Left 0.5" Hanging 0.25", Auto Numbering
List Number 4	Normal + Indent: Left 0.75" Hanging 0.25", Auto Numbering
List Number 5	Normal + Indent: Left 1" Hanging 0.25", Auto Numbering
Macro Text	Font: Courier New, 10 pt., English (US), Flush left, Line Spacing Single, Widow/Orphan Control, Tab stops: 0.33", 0.67", 1", 1.33", 1.67", 2", 2.33", 2.67", 3"
Message Header	Normal + Font: Arial, 12 pt., Indent: Hanging 0.75", Border: Box (Single), Border Spacing: 1 pt., Pattern: 20%
Normal	Font: Times New Roman, 10 pt., English (US), Flush left, Line Spacing Single, Widow/Orphan Control
Normal Indent	Normal + Indent: Left 0.5"
Signature	Normal + Indent: Left 3"
Subtitle	Normal + Font: Arial, 12 pt., Centered, Space After 3 pt.
Table of Authorities	Normal + Indent: Hanging 0.14", Tab stops: 6" Right Flush...
Table of Figures	Normal + Indent: Hanging 0.28", Tab stops: 6" Right Flush...
Title	Normal + Font: Arial, 16 pt., Bold, Kern at 14 pt., Centered, Space Before 12 pt. After 3 pt.
TOA Heading	Normal + Font: Arial, 12 pt., Bold, Space Before 6 pt.
TOC 1	Normal + Tab stops: 6" Right Flush...
TOC 2	Normal + Indent: Left 0.14", Tab stops: 6" Right Flush...
TOC 3	Normal + Indent: Left 0.28", Tab stops: 6" Right Flush...
TOC 4	Normal + Indent: Left 0.42", Tab stops: 6" Right Flush...
TOC 5	Normal + Indent: Left 0.56", Tab stops: 6" Right Flush...
TOC 6	Normal + Indent: Left 0.69", Tab stops: 6" Right Flush...
TOC 7	Normal + Indent: Left 0.83", Tab stops: 6" Right Flush...
TOC 8	Normal + Indent: Left 0.97", Tab stops: 6" Right Flush...
TOC 9	Normal + Indent: Left 1.11", Tab stops: 6" Right Flush...

Table 18-3	Word's Built-In Character Styles
Style	**Formatting**
Annotation Reference	Default Paragraph Font + Font: 8 pt.
Default Paragraph Font	The font of the underlying paragraph style
Endnote Reference	Default Paragraph Font + Superscript
Footnote Reference	Default Paragraph Font + Superscript
Line Number	Default Paragraph Font
Page Number	Default Paragraph Font

Creating a Style

If none of the predefined styles that comes with Word meets your needs, you can create your own style. The following sections describe two approaches to making your own styles.

Creating a style by example

Usually, the easiest way to create a new style is to format a paragraph with all of the formats you want the style to use, and to create a new style by using the paragraph as an example. Here is the procedure:

1. Pick a paragraph that you think is a likely candidate for creating a style.

2. Format the paragraph with the style that you would like to serve as the base style for the new style you are about to create. Usually, this will be the Normal style.

3. Adjust the paragraph's formatting until you format the paragraph just right.

4. With the insertion point in the paragraph, press Ctrl+Shift+S or click the Style list box on the Formatting toolbar. (The Style list box is the left-most box on the Formatting toolbar.)

5. Type a descriptive name for the style. Spaces are acceptable, so the style name can consist of more than one word. For practical purposes, however, you should avoid typing a name so long that it doesn't fit in the style list box.

6. Press Enter to add the style to the document.

Creating a style with the Format⇨Style command

The other way to create a style is with the Format⇨Style command. This method is not as easy as the style-by-example method, but it does provide greater flexibility. Start by choosing the Format⇨Style command. The Style dialog box will appear, as shown in Figure 18-1.

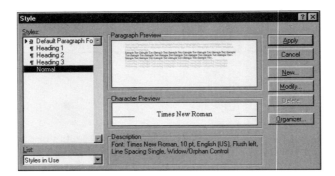

Figure 18-1: The Style dialog box.

To create a new style, click the New button. The New Style dialog box will appear, as shown in Figure 18-2.

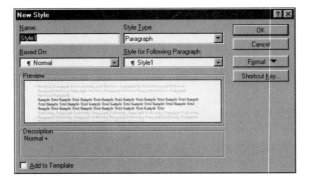

Figure 18-2: The New Style dialog box.

Picking a name for the style

Type the name for your new style in the <u>N</u>ame field. You can type any name you want, but try to be as descriptive as possible. I usually prefer to use names that describe the function of the paragraph rather than the details of its formatting. For example, I prefer *Salutation* or *Poetry Quotation* to *Indented Paragraph* or *Double-Spaced*.

Secret

Word actually lets you assign *two* names to each style: a main style name and an alias. The *alias* is usually a short, two- or three-character code that you can type quicker than the full style name. To assign an alias, type the full style name, a comma, and the alias. For example:

```
Poetry Quotation,pq
```

In this example, *pq* will serve as an alias for *Poetry Quotation*.

Basing a style on an existing style

You should also realize that you can *base* one style on another style. When a style is based on another style, all of the formats of the base style are inherited. The new style then specifies only those formats which differ from the base style.

As an example, suppose that you want to create a style for a poetry quotation. You want your quotations to be set in the same typeface as the rest of the document, except in italic, and you want it indented .5" from the left and right. When you create the Poetry Quotation style, you would base it on Normal so that it would inherit all of the basic formats: font, font size, line spacing, and so on. Then, you would provide additional formats for the Poetry Quotation style: italic, left indent .5", and right indent .5".

When Word describes the formatting for a style, it indicates the base style and the additional formatting unique to the style in this manner:

```
Normal + Italic, Indent: Left 0.5", Right 0.5"
```

In other words, the Poetry Quotation style is the Normal style plus italics and 0.5" left and right indentation.

Basing styles on one another in this fashion is a very valuable tool. Suppose that the Normal style is formatted to use Times New Roman, but you later decide you'd rather set the entire document in Century Schoolbook. If you set up your styles properly, you need to change only the Normal style. Then, all paragraphs formatted with the Normal style or with any style based on Normal will reflect the font change.

Setting the style for the following paragraph

Normally, when you press the Enter key to create a new paragraph, the new paragraph assumes the same style as the previous paragraph. In some cases, that's exactly what you want it to do. However, for some styles, the style of the following paragraph is almost always a different style. For example, a paragraph formatted with the Heading 1 style is rarely followed by another Heading 1 paragraph. Instead, a Heading 1 paragraph is usually followed by a Normal paragraph.

Instead of always changing the style assigned to a new paragraph in situations like this, you can specify the style for the next paragraph with the Format⇨Style command. Then, when you press the Enter key, the new paragraph is assigned the style you specified. This little trick can almost completely automate the chore of formatting your documents.

Setting the formats for the style

To set the formats for the style, click the Format button to reveal a drop-down menu that contains the following commands:

- Font
- Paragraph
- Tabs
- Border
- Language
- Frame
- Numbering

Use these commands to bring up the standard Word formatting dialog boxes to apply whatever formats you want associated with the style. For example, if you want the style to use italic characters, select the Font command and pick Italic as the font style.

Adding the style to the document's template

If you want the style to be available for other documents that use the same template, click the Add to Template check box. If you leave this option unchecked, the new style will be available only in the current document. (If you need a quick refresher on templates, refer back to Chapter 4.)

Applying a Style

To apply a style to a paragraph or to change the style applied to a paragraph, place the insertion point anywhere in the paragraph where you want to apply the style. Then, pick the style you want to apply from the style drop-down list box in the Formatting toolbar.

For a keyboard-only method, press Ctrl+Shift+S and type the name of the style and press Enter. Be aware that this is a little error-prone, however. If you type a style name that doesn't exist, Word simply creates a new style that uses the name you type. So, for example, if you intend on applying the Heading 1 style, but you type **Headign 1** instead, Word will create a new style called Headign 1. That's probably not what you had in mind.

Secret

This is where that Alias style name comes in handy. For example, if you created a style named Figure Caption, you wouldn't want to have to type in Figure Caption every time you apply the style. However, if you gave the Figure Caption an alias of Fig, you could apply the Figure Caption by typing Ctrl+Shift+S, Fig, and pressing Enter.

Tip

If you have pulled down the drop-down style list by clicking on its down-arrow button with the mouse, you can quickly move to a style in the list by typing the first letter of the style's name. Also, if the style that you are looking for doesn't appear in the style list, hold down the Shift key and click the down arrow next to the style list box. Sometimes Word doesn't list all of the available styles unless you do this.

You can apply a style to two or more adjacent paragraphs by selecting a range of text that includes all of the paragraphs you want formatted and applying the style.

Tip

If you want to find out which style is applied to a paragraph, click anywhere in the paragraph and look at the style field in the Formatting toolbar. Alternatively, you can use the Tools⇨Options, View command to reveal the style area. Then, the name of each paragraph's style is displayed next to the paragraph. (More on the style area in a moment.)

Overriding Style Formatting

All of the formatting a paragraph needs is usually provided by the paragraph style. However, in some cases, additional formatting is required. For example, several words in the paragraph may need the emphasis of bold or italic type. You can override any of the formats provided by the paragraph style by applying formats directly to the paragraph or to selected characters within the paragraph. These overriding formats are called *direct formats*.

In the case of direct paragraph formats, such as indentation or alignment, such formatting is lost if you later decide to apply a different style to the paragraph. For example, if you apply the Normal style to a paragraph and then add 12 points of space above the paragraph, the extra space is lost if you apply a different style to the paragraph.

But direct character formats are a different story. Word holds on to direct character formats that you've applied when you change the paragraph's style. For example, if you create a paragraph formatted with the Normal style, make a few words italic and a few others bold, and apply another style to the paragraph, the italics stay italics and the bold stays bold.

Well, most of the time, anyway. Sometimes, Word *does* override direct character formats when you change paragraph styles. This happens when you select a block of text in the paragraph and change the paragraph style. If more than half of the selected text has had direct formatting applied, all of the direct formatting in the paragraph is removed — not just the direct formatting in the part of the paragraph that was selected, but in the entire paragraph. (I'm still trying to figure out the logic behind this rule. If it makes sense to you, I envy your keen powers of intuition.)

Changing a Style

You can change the formatting of an existing style in two ways: with or without the Format⇨Style command. Because the Format⇨Style command is a cumbersome beast, I recommend the second procedure.

Changing a style without using Format⇨Style

To change a style without using the Format⇨Style command, first find a paragraph that is formatted with the style you want to change and then change the paragraph's formatting by applying direct formats. For example, you can change the paragraph's font by selecting the entire paragraph and choosing a new font in the Font drop-down list box found in the Formatting toolbar.

Once you have reformatted the paragraph to your liking, reapply the style to the paragraph by selecting the same style from the Style list in the Formatting toolbar. When you do this, the Reapply Style dialog box will appear, as shown in Figure 18-3.

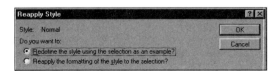

Figure 18-3: The Reapply Style dialog box.

As you can see, the Reapply Style dialog box presents you with two options: you can either update the style with the changes you've made to the paragraph or you can discard the changes and reapply the style as it was. Assuming you want to update the style to reflect the changes you've made (that's the default choice), just click OK or press Enter.

Note

If your attempts at reformatting the paragraph prove utterly unsatisfactory and you decide that you liked it better the way it was, reapply the style and pick the second choice in the Reapply Style dialog box ("Reapply the formatting of the style to the selection").

Tip

When you redefine a paragraph style by using the selection as an example, Word uses the formatting of the first character in the selection to set the character formatting for the paragraph style. Usually, this detail poses no unusual problems, but it can help explain some seemingly funny behavior that occurs now and then when redefining styles. For example, if an entire paragraph is set in Times New Roman, but the first word is italic, the entire paragraph will be changed to italic if you select the whole paragraph and redefine the style. To avoid this, don't select the entire paragraph but begin the selection *after* the italicized text.

Changing a style by using Format⇨Style

Modifying a style by example is the easiest way to make a few minor stylistic adjustments. However, you can only make certain style changes, such as the Based On style or the Style for Following Paragraph, from the Format⇨Style command.

To modify a style by using the Format⇨Style command, follow these steps:

1. Choose the Format⇨Style command. The Style dialog box will appear. (Refer back to Figure 18-1 if you don't remember what it looks like.)

2. Select the style you want to modify in the Styles list.

3. Click Modify to summon the Modify Style dialog box, as shown in Figure 18-4.

4. To change the format of the style, click the Format button to reveal the mini-Format menu and choose any of the menu commands to summon an appropriate formatting dialog box.

5. Click OK to return to the Style dialog box and click Close to return to the document.

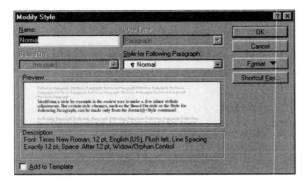

Figure 18-4: The Modify Style dialog box.

Deleting a Style

If you no longer need a style, you can delete it by choosing the Format⇨Style command, selecting the style you want to delete, and clicking the Delete button.

Any paragraphs that were formatted with the style will revert to Normal. In my opinion, that's not how Word should handle paragraphs formatted with deleted styles: better they should be formatted with the style on which the deleted style was based. For example, if you have a style named Quotation, which is based on another style named Body Text, any paragraphs formatted with the Quotation style should revert to Body Text when you delete the Quotation style. Instead, they revert to Normal. Oh well.

Assigning Keyboard Shortcut Keys to Styles

To make styles easier to use, you can assign keyboard shortcuts to the styles you use most often. Then, you can apply those styles simply by pressing the keyboard shortcut. Not surprisingly, you can assign keyboard shortcuts in two ways: with and without the Format⇨Style command.

Four of Word's predefined paragraph styles already have keyboard shortcuts associated with them:

Ctrl+N	Normal
Ctrl+Alt+1	Heading 1
Ctrl+Alt+2	Heading 2
Ctrl+Alt+3	Heading 3

You can assign more than one keyboard shortcut to a style if you want. You can also create keyboard shortcuts with virtually any combination of keyboard keys by using the Shift, Ctrl, and Alt keys alone or in combination. For example, you could assign Ctrl+K, Alt+K, Ctrl+Shift+K, or even Ctrl+Alt+Shift+K.

For more information about working with keyboard shortcuts, refer back to Chapter 6.

Tip

Assigning a keyboard shortcut by using Format⇨Style

To create a keyboard shortcut by using the Format⇨Style command, choose the Format⇨Style command. Next, select the style you want to assign a shortcut to and click the Modify button. When the Modify Style dialog box appears, click the Shortcut Key button. The Customize dialog box will appear, as shown in Figure 18-5.

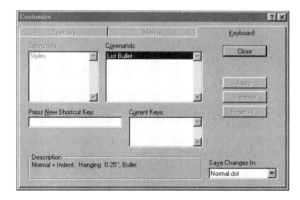

Figure 18-5: Assigning a keyboard shortcut to a style.

Type the keyboard shortcut you want to assign to the style and click Assign to assign the keyboard shortcut and return to the Modify Style dialog box. Click OK to return to the Style dialog box and click Close to return to your document. You can now assign the style quickly by placing the insertion point anywhere in the paragraph where you want to assign the style and pressing the assigned keyboard shortcut.

Assigning a keyboard shortcut without using the Format➪Style command

The following procedure describes how you can assign a keyboard shortcut without venturing into the Format➪Style command. This is one of those procedures that I think is really cool, except that I never seem to remember the weird keyboard shortcut you have to use to start the procedure, so I always wind up using the Format➪Style command anyway.

1. Press Ctrl+Alt+Gray plus. That's the gray plus sign key on the numeric keypad, way over at the far right side of the keyboard. (See what I mean? Do you really think you'll remember that?)

⌘ 2. Notice how the mouse cursor changes to a pretzel.

3. Choose the style from the Style list box on the Formatting toolbar by clicking the down arrow next to the Style list box and clicking the style where you want to assign a shortcut. I know that pointing and clicking while the mouse pointer looks like a pretzel is weird, but it works. When you successfully click on the style, Word displays the Customize dialog box, ready for you to type a shortcut.

4. Type the keyboard shortcut that you want to use.

5. Click Assign to assign the shortcut to the style. Then click OK and Close.

Viewing Style Assignments by Enabling the Style Area

The style area, a narrow band on the left-hand edge of the document window, displays the name of the style assigned to each paragraph in your document. Figure 18-6 shows what Word looks like with the style area activated.

To activate the style area, call up the Tools➪Options command and click the View tab. Then, set the Style Area Width field to 0.6 or 0.7. A narrower setting won't be able to display the complete style name. Much larger, however, is just a waste of screen real estate.

The only problem with the style area is that it restricts the width of the document window. If you can't see the entire width of your text with the style area enabled, you'll probably want to leave it off. If you are working on a small monitor in 640x480 mode, you probably don't have enough screen real estate to spare for the style area. In 800x600 or larger, there's plenty of room for the style area.

After you have enabled the style area, you can adjust its width by dragging the line that separates it from the rest of the document window. To remove the style area altogether, drag the line all the way to the left of the window or call up the Tools➪Options command and set the Style Area Width text box to 0.

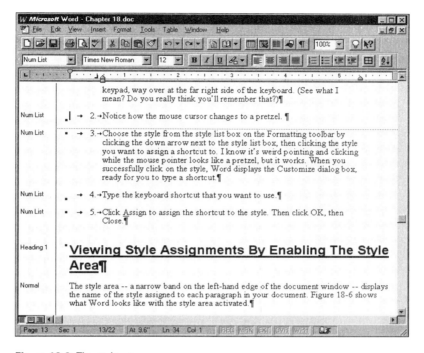

Figure 18-6: The style area.

Tip

You can select an entire paragraph by clicking on the paragraph's style name in the style area.

Note

The style area is visible only in Normal and Outline views. The Style Area Width field won't appear at all if you call up the Tools⇨Options command while Word is in Page Layout view.

Creating and Using Character Styles

Word has a little-known and seldom-used feature called *character style,* which enables you to create styles applied to specified characters rather than entire paragraphs. Creating a character style is just like creating a paragraph style, except that when the New Style dialog box appears, you set the Style Type field to Character. Then, your formatting options are limited to Font and Language settings.

To apply a character style, select the range of characters you want to apply the style to and apply the style by using the Style list box on the Formatting toolbar or by typing the style's keyboard shortcut.

You can distinguish character styles from paragraph styles in style lists because paragraph styles have a paragraph mark next to them. Character styles have an underlined a next to them.

Like paragraph styles, character styles can be based on other styles. To make the character style inherit the font formats of the underlying paragraph style, base the character style on the special style name *(underlying properties)*.

Secret

Referencing Text in a Header or Footer

Frankly, I don't use character styles much. It's just as easy to apply direct formatting over the default paragraph character format for simple formats such as bold and italic. However, here's an obscure use for character styles that can come in handy from time to time: when used in conjunction with the Insert⇨Field command, a character style can be used to place any selected text from the document in your page headers. For example, you could highlight a key phrase on each page of your document and apply the character style to it. Then, Word will automatically place that text at the top of the page. Here is how to set it up:

1. Create a character style that you will use to mark text you want placed in the header. Give it a name such as "Header Text" and base it on *(underlying properties)*.

2. Use the View⇨Header and Footer command to edit the header. Then, use the Insert⇨Field command to call up the Insert Field dialog box.

3. In the Insert Field dialog box, select "Links and References" in the Categories list and select StyleRef in the Field Names list. Then, type **Header Text** (or whatever name you used in Step 1) following the word STYLEREF in the Field Codes text box and click OK.

4. Close the Header by clicking the Close button on the Headers and Footers toolbar.

5. In the document, select the text you want to appear in the header and apply the Header Text style to the selection. The text will instantly appear in the header.

6. Go to another page and apply the Header Text style to text on that page. The header for that page will show the text you just selected.

On each page, the header will show the first text formatted with the Header Text style. If there is no text on the page formatted with Header Text, the text from the previous page will be used.

Searching for and Replacing Style Formatting

The Edit⇨Find command allows you to locate every paragraph that is formatted with a given style. Just call up the Edit⇨Find command (the keyboard shortcut is Ctrl+F), click the Format button, and choose Style from the pop-up menu. The Find Style dialog box will appear, as shown in Figure 18-7.

Figure 18-7: The Find Style dialog box.

Select the style that you want to find and click OK to return to the Find dialog box. The style name will be shown in the Format text box, just below the Find What text box. Make sure that the Find What text box is blank; otherwise, the Find command searches for specific text that's formatted with the style you specify. To begin the search, click the Find Next button.

To replace paragraph styles, follow a similar procedure with the Edit⇨Replace command. When the Replace dialog box appears, click in the Find What text box and use the Format button to choose the style you want to find. Next, click in the Replace With text box and use the Format button again, this time to choose the style that you want to replace for the Find What style. Next, use the Find Next and Replace buttons to find and replace style formatting. Or, if you're feeling brave, throw caution to the wind and just click Replace All.

Why Do My Styles Keep Changing Back?

One of the most common problems encountered when using styles is that changes you make to your styles don't seem to last. You toil over a style until the document looks just right, print it, and then save the file. But, the next time you open the document, it looks just the way it did before you changed the style. It's as if you forgot to save your changes.

If this is happening to you, call up the File⇨Templates command and uncheck the Automatically Update Document Styles. The Automatically Update option tells Word that whenever you open the document, the styles in the document's template should be copied into the document. This causes any changes you made to the document's styles to vanish; without warning, Word replaces the styles you so carefully crafted with the styles in the template.

The Automatically Update Document Style option is useful when you make changes to a template's styles, and you want documents based on the template to be updated automatically to reflect the look of the new styles. But, be warned that any changes made to the styles in individual documents will be lost.

Using the Gallery

The Style Gallery (Format⇨Style Gallery) is designed to let you quickly change the look of a document by copying the styles in from any template. It displays a list of all the templates that are available on your computer, along with a preview window that shows how your document would appear if formatted with the styles in that template, as shown in Figure 18-8.

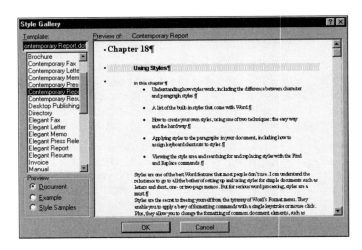

Figure 18-8: The Style Gallery.

You can click on different templates to get a thumbnail view of how each template will affect the document's formatting. Then, when you have decided on a template to use, click OK to copy the styles from the selected template into the document. If you want to leave the document as is, click Cancel instead.

Secret

The Style Gallery preview is sensitive to the view mode that is active when you call up the Format⇨Style Gallery command. If you are in Normal view or Outline view, Style Gallery will display the document preview in Normal view. If you are in Page Layout view, you'll see the preview in Page Layout view. If you really want to see what your document will look like when formatted with a different template's styles, switch to Page Layout view before calling up the Style Gallery.

The Style Gallery actually provides three ways you can preview the formatting supplied by a template. The default option is to show how the current document would appear when formatted by the template. This is useful for seeing what impact a template's styles will have on your document, but it doesn't give you an idea of the range of styles that are included in the template. That's because if a particular style isn't used in the current document, it won't appear in the Style Gallery preview area.

Style Gallery's other two views are designed to counter this deficiency. If you click <u>E</u>xample, you will see an example of text formatted with the template's styles drawn from the template itself. Each template can provide its own example, so the designer of the template can be sure to highlight those styles that show off the template's capabilities. Figure 18-9 shows an example of Style Gallery with a template example visible.

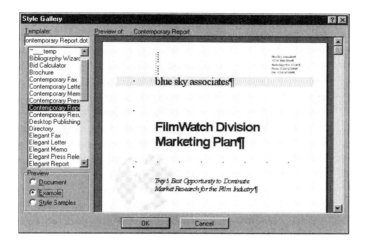

Figure 18-9: Style Gallery can preview a template by using an example stored in the template.

Secret

The example that is displayed when you select a template in Style Gallery and when <u>E</u>xample is selected is simply an AutoText entry stored in the document under the name Gallery Example. If you want Style Gallery to be able to preview your own templates, just create an example formatted the way you want it displayed, select the example text, and use the <u>E</u>dit⇨AutoTe<u>x</u>t command to create a Gallery Example AutoText entry.

If you select <u>S</u>tyle Samples, Style Gallery displays the name of each style in the template, with each style name formatted with its style, as shown in Figure 18-10.

Secret

Actually, <u>S</u>tyle Samples works much like <u>E</u>xample: All it does is display the contents of an AutoText entry named Gallery Style Samples. To display a style sample for one of your own templates, just add a Gallery Style Samples AutoText entry to the template. You can put anything you want in this AutoText entry, but if you want your template to behave like Word's supplied templates, Gallery Style Samples should contain one line for each style, containing the style name and formatted with the style.

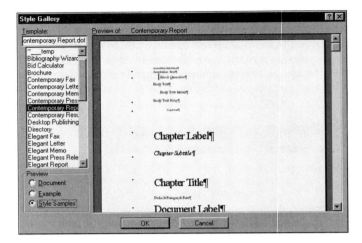

Figure 18-10: Style Gallery can also display samples of the styles contained in a template.

Part VI
Power Desktop Publishing Techniques

19 Secrets of Typography

20 Secrets of Columns, Frames, and Desktop
    Publishing Effects

21 Secrets of Graphics

22 The Secret Applets: WordArt, Equation Editor,
    and Microsoft Graph

Chapter 19

Secrets of Typography

In This Chapter

▶ Understanding the intricacies of typography, including the basic types of type

▶ Why there's more to typography than choosing a typeface

▶ The typefaces that are supplied with Windows 95 and Word for Windows 95/Office 95

Back where I come from, there are people who do nothing all day but study type. They are called *typographers*. They work in musty type foundries that smell of molten lead and spend most of their free time cleaning their hands and coming up with cute names for new type designs like *Pandemonium* or *Bologna Book* or *Vogon Old Style*.

Now, through the magic of Windows, you too can be a typographer. Why print all of your documents using Arial and Times New Roman like everybody else when typefaces that are more attractive and more useful are readily available. A surprising number of Windows application programs come with extra typefaces, including Word for Windows 95 and Office 95. The CD at the back of this book has a collection of free fonts, and a few hundred shareware fonts that you can use if you pay a small registration fee to the copyright owner. If that's not enough, some programs, such as CorelDraw!, come with *hundreds* of typefaces. You can purchase CD-ROMs packed with hundreds of typefaces for as little as $29.95. You can even find typefaces for free on on-line services such as The Microsoft Network or CompuServe.

Of course, the dark side of this story is that After you have all those typefaces, you don't know what to do with them. The proper use of typefaces can make your documents look like a professional with impeccable taste did them. Improper use can have the same effect as hanging a yellow diamond sign on your computer that reads "Amateur Desktop Publisher On Board."

Typography (the study of type) can be a fascinating subject. Entire books have been written about it, books that are worthy of a quiet evening read while resting in a lush leather recliner with a glass of sherry and a pipe nearby. If you don't have a leather recliner and you're fresh out of sherry and quiet evenings, this chapter will have to suffice. It gives you a few quick pointers that won't make you an expert in typography but that will help you avoid the most obvious typographical blunders.

Note

Desktop publishing uses two basic kinds of type fonts: *PostScript* and *TrueType*. PostScript is the more popular among desktop publishing gurus, but TrueType is far and away the more popular among normal people because support for TrueType is built into Windows 95. Using PostScript requires not only a more expensive PostScript printer but also a special software program called *Adobe Type Manager*, or *ATM*. Fortunately, if your Windows 95 configuration is configured with Adobe Type Manager and PostScript fonts are installed on your computer, Word for Windows 95 can work equally well with TrueType or PostScript fonts.

Understanding Typography Terms

Typography is kind of like wine tasting: it has its own fancy terminology. Typographers say things like "*Vogon Old Style* has a delicately balanced variation in stroke weight, with just a hint of angularity in the serifs to drive the message forward without being precocious. This, combined with its full but gentle bouquet and a tangy but fruity finish, make it the ideal choice for your yard sale sign."

Then, they'll look at you, expecting you to nod your head knowingly and say, "But, of course."

You certainly don't need to have such refined taste when it comes to picking type, but you should at least understand some basic terms:

- **Typeface:** A typeface is a design for a set of letters, along with numerals and punctuation marks to go along with it. The typeface includes both upper-case and lowercase letters. For example, Times Roman is the name of one of the most popular typefaces.

- **Typeface family:** A group of closely related typefaces. For example, Times Roman, Times Bold, Times Italic, and Times Bold Italic. The bold, italic, and bold italic forms of a family are considered separate typefaces, but members of the same family.

- **Font:** A complete set of type for a particular typeface and size. For example, 10-point Avant Garde and 12-point Avant Garde are two distinct fonts.

In the days of lead type, the distinction between font and face was important because a typesetter had only certain fonts representing a particular family. For example, the typesetter had only 9-, 10-, and 12-, and 14-point Times fonts for each face in the Times family. If you wanted 13-point Times Roman, you were out of luck.

The distinction between font and face is not so important anymore because Windows can create fonts of any point size you want. Thus, if you have the Times Roman typeface, you can display it in any size you want. If 11 is too small but 12 is too big, you can even print it in 11.5 point!

Windows actually muddles the terminology by using the term *font* to mean *typeface family*. When you format characters in Word for Windows, you specify the font (such as Times New Roman), the size (such as 11 point), and the style (bold, italic, or bold italic). Actually, all three of these combined is what a typographer calls a *font*.

Here are several other terms you need to be aware of before we go any further:

- **Proportional spacing:** In the days of typewriters and daisy-wheel printers, every letter occupied the same width on the line. In proportionally-spaced fonts, each character has its own width, according to the design of the letter. For example, the letter *M* is wider than the letter *i*. Proportional spacing was once a novelty reserved for high-powered desktop publishing, but it is taken for granted nowadays.

- **Monospacing:** Monospace type is type where each letter is the same width. It is still commonly used in certain situations. Windows comes with one monospaced typeface, Courier New, which is designed to look like it was printed on a typewriter.

- **Body text:** Body text is the main text of your document. The most important criteria for selecting a typeface for body text is legibility. In most documents, body text consists of paragraph upon paragraph of rather ordinary-looking words. You should choose a body text that doesn't distract the readers as they read.

- **Display type:** Display type is used for headings, captions, titles, and anything else that isn't body text. Text set in display type is usually brief — often just a few words — so legibility isn't the only factor to consider. The display type usually contrasts in some way with the body text type, adding variety to a page that would otherwise be filled with boring and lifeless body text.

When selecting type for body and display text, keep in mind that the typefaces you use for body text and display type need to be carefully coordinated. One of the easiest ways to mess up an otherwise good-looking page is *typeface clash* (and the Typeface Clash Police are everywhere, you know). See the section "Avoiding Typeface Clash" later in this chapter for advice on picking typefaces for body text and display type that work well together.

Some documents have more than one kind of display type. For example, a newsletter has display type in the nameplate, masthead, headings, pull quotes, jumplines, and so on. Try to limit the number of different typefaces you use for these elements. If you don't, your document ends up looking like a ransom note, and it will take forever to print.

Serif Type

Serif type is type that has little feet at the bottom of the letters. These little feet enable the type to walk smoothly across the page in Michael Jackson moonwalking style. Figure 19-1 shows the difference between a serif and sans serif *h* up close so that you can see what I am talking about.

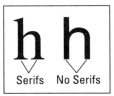

Figure 19-1: What a serif really is.

Figure 19-2 shows some examples of seriffed typefaces.

Times New Roman comes with Windows.

Book Antiqua is not antiquated.

Then There's Bookman Old Style.

Century Schoolbook is an excellent study.

Garamond MT is a good choice for tight fits.

Figure 19-2: Some seriffed typefaces.

In each of the typefaces in Figure 19-2, the serifs at the bottoms of the letters create the faint illusion of a baseline that aids the eye as it moves across the page.

Tip

Serif type is usually the best kind of type to use in paragraphs of text. The serifs make it easier for the eye to follow a line of text across the page and then jump down to the next line.

Serifs also occur at the tops of some letters, like at the top of a capital *T* or *F* and a lowercase *p* or *y*. Serifs at the tops of letters are called *head serifs*. That means they can boss the lowly *foot serifs* around.

The most commonly used serif typeface is Times Roman. Windows 95 comes with a TrueType typeface called *Times New Roman*, which is equivalent to Times Roman.

Understanding parts of type

Ever wonder what all the doohickeys and deelybobs found in a typical type design are called? Probably not. But, just in case, Figure 19-3 and the following definitions give you the lowdown.

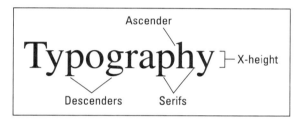

Figure 19-3: Type parts.

- **Serifs:** The little feet at the tops and bottoms of letters.

- **Descender:** The part of the letter that hangs down below the line (such as the lines in *j*, *p*, and *y*).

- **Ascender:** The part of the letter that rises above the body of the letter (such as the lines in *b*, *d*, and *h*).

- **X-height:** The height of a lowercase letter *x*, which usually governs the height of other lowercase letters and the appearance of the ascenders.

Classifying type

Serif typefaces used to look alike to me, until I became interested in them and started looking at them more closely. Actually, there's a world of difference between various serif typefaces. The shapes of the serifs vary from face to face, as does the x-height, the design of ascenders and descenders, the thickness of the strokes, the contrast between thick and thin portions of the stroke, the shape of the enclosed spaces in letters like *a* and *e*, and other subtle details of the design.

Collectors love to classify things, and type collectors are no different. Here are a few of the categories commonly used to group related typefaces:

- **Old Style:** Old Style typefaces are influenced by the very first typefaces, originating in the late 15th century. One of the great type designers of this era was Aldus Manutius, after whom the software company Aldus is named. (And you always thought Aldus' last name was PageMaker.)

  Many typefaces identify themselves as Old Style faces; for example, Bookman Old Style, Century Old Style, and Goudy Old Style. Others, such as Garamond and Times New Roman, do not.

  Some of these typefaces were developed in the 20th century. The designation *Old Style* doesn't mean that the typeface is old; it just means that it uses design elements common to other Old Style typefaces.

- **Transitional:** This style was originated in the mid-18th century by John Baskerville. Baskerville pioneered improved printing techniques that enabled typefaces to use finer strokes safely. Examples of Transitional typefaces are Americana, Baskerville, and Caledonia.

- **Modern:** The Modern style isn't really modern, but dates to the 18th century and the type designer Giambattista Bodoni. Modern typefaces have a strong vertical orientation that some say gives the entire category a picket-fence look. It includes serifs that are very thin and nearly flat. The most commonly used modern typeface today is Bodoni.

- **Clarendon:** Clarendon typefaces were first used in the mid-19th century. Like Modern typefaces, they have a strong vertical orientation. However, they also have generous serifs, usually cut square off the edge and are not so flat. This makes them exceptionally readable, and among the most widely used typefaces categories. Examples include Bookman, Century Schoolbook, and Cheltenham.

Sans Serif Type

Sans serif typefaces don't have serifs. Figure 19-4 shows some examples.

Without serifs to scoot the eye across the line, sans serif types are difficult to read in large stretches. Sans serif types are best used for headlines, captions, notes, and other short bursts of text. Use them in full paragraphs only if you want to appear trendy.

Probably the most widely used sans serif typeface is Helvetica. Windows doesn't come with Helvetica, but it does come with Arial, an equivalent TrueType typeface. Because Arial is supplied with Windows, it is a bit overused. If you have an alternative sans serif typeface, consider using it instead.

Notice in Figure 19-4 how the Century Gothic typeface has a very geometrical look to it. It's almost as if the whole typeface is constructed of perfect circles and straight lines. Appearances can be deceiving, though. Study this typeface carefully and you'll notice subtle variations in the seemingly perfect circles and

Arial comes with Windows

Arial narrow gives a tighter fit

Century Gothic goes around in circles

Impact is a bold effort

Figure 19-4: Sans serif typefaces.

lines. (Try turning the book around and looking at the type upside-down to make the differences more apparent.)

Scripts

Scripts are typefaces that are designed to mimic handwriting. Some scripts look like ornate, hand-drawn calligraphy and are usually used in formal invitations. Other scripts look like they were spontaneously drawn. Figure 19-5 shows examples of both types.

Brush Script MT

Matura MT Script Capitals

Vivaldi

Monotype Corsiva

Figure 19-5: Various script typefaces.

Keep in mind that scripts are usually difficult to read, especially in smaller sizes. Don't use them for large expanses of text.

Tip

Don't use script types to imitate a hand-written signature. It's too much of a desktop cliché. If you want to add a computer printed signature to your documents, use a scanner to scan your signature and then include it as a graphic. If you don't have a scanner, take your signature to a copy center that has computers. They'll scan it for you, probably for about $10.

Novelty Typefaces

Novelty typefaces are typefaces so weird that they defy categorization. Figure 19-6 shows some examples.

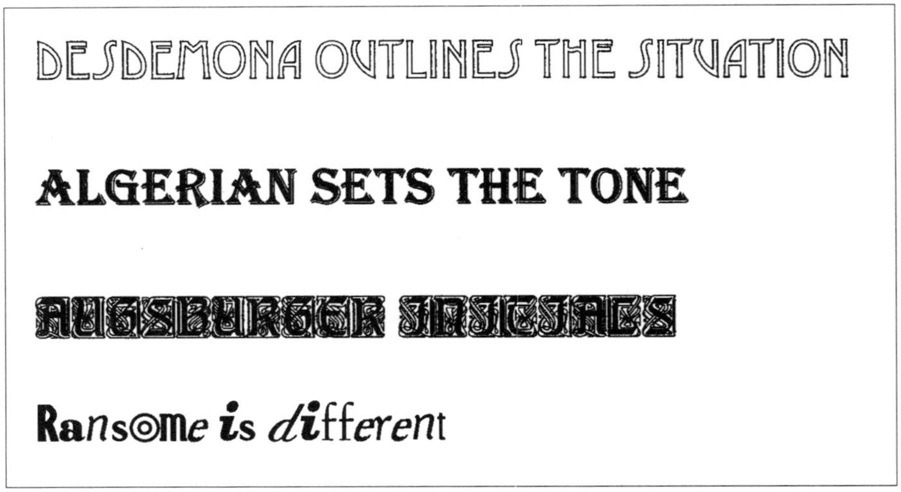

DESDEMONA OUTLINES THE SITUATION

ALGERIAN SETS THE TONE

AUGSBURGER INITIALS

Ransome *is different*

Figure 19-6: Novelty typefaces.

See? You can chose from hundreds of typefaces like this.

Note

Be careful about how you use these typefaces. Most of them are intended only for decorative use. Some of them can evoke a certain atmosphere, such as the Gold Rush days. Others just look goofy.

You can often find typefaces that represent your favorite TV show: *Star Trek*, *The Brady Bunch*, *The Flintstones*, *The Jetsons*, and so on. These are fun for a comical effect.

My favorite novelty typeface is Klingonese (Star Trek fans will know what I'm talking about). I haven't found any use for it because none of the characters are recognizable to humans and I don't know any Klingons, but I think it's cool that someone actually took the time to create this typeface.

Dingbats

One final font category you need to know about is *dingbats*. These are typefaces that don't contain letters of the alphabet. Instead, they contain symbols, such as bullet characters, ballot boxes, check marks, and other embellishments.

Windows 95 comes with a dingbats font called Wingdings. Word for Windows 95 and Office 95 provide an additional dingbat font called Monotype Sorts. To access the symbols contained in these fonts, use the Insert⇨Symbol command and select Wingdings or Monotype Sorts as the font.

Typography: More Than Just a Pretty Face

Picking a typeface is only the first step in creating type that looks good. Other aspects to consider are the point size, line length, line spacing, and alignment.

Point size

When you create a new document by clicking the New button, Word bases the new document on the Normal template (Normal.dot). The default text format for documents based on the Normal.dot is 10-point Times New Roman. Considering that the left and right margins in the Normal template are 1.25, creating text lines a full 6-inches long, either this font is way too small or the line is way too long. Type a few paragraphs of text in 10-point Times New Roman on a 6-inch line, and you'll see what I mean.

One obvious way to improve the legibility of documents based on Normal.dot is to increase the point size to 11- or 12-point type. As you increase the point size, the amount of text that fits on each line naturally goes down and the text becomes more readable. This increase eases the burden on the eye, probably saving you money in the long run by reducing your need for eyeglasses. If you make this change to the Normal style in your Normal.dot, all of your document will be more legible.

Not all typefaces, however, appear to be the same size at a given point size. For example, consider the following examples from A.A. Milne's *Winnie the Pooh*, both set in 12-point type:

- **Times New Roman (12 point)**

  The Old Grey Donkey, Eeyore, stood by himself in a thistly corner of the forest, his front feet well apart, his head on one side, and thought about things. Sometimes he thought sadly to himself, "Why?" and sometimes he thought, "Wherefore?" and sometimes he thought, "Inasmuch as which?"

- **Century Schoolbook (also 12 point)**

  The Old Grey Donkey, Eeyore, stood by himself in a thistly corner of the forest, his front feet well apart, his head on one side, and thought about things. Sometimes he thought sadly to himself, "Why?" and sometimes he thought, "Wherefore?" and sometimes he thought, "Inasmuch as which?"

Notice how much larger the second example looks, even though both samples are the same point size? This is partly because the design of Century Schoolbook has a slightly larger x-height than Times New Roman, but also because Century Schoolbook has longer serifs than Times New Roman, which leaves more space between the letters.

There is no magic point size to use in all circumstances. Some typefaces are very readable in 9-point type, and others are not. Most of the time, your body text should be set in 10-, 11-, or 12-point type.

Tip

Increasing the point size isn't the only way to make Normal.dot more legible. Another alternative is to shorten the line length by increasing the margins. See the next section, "Line length," for more about the relationship between point size and line length.

Line length

The Normal.dot template sets the left and right margins to 1.25" each, which results in a 6-inch line length on standard 8.5" x 11" paper. That's almost always too wide, especially if you stick with the Normal.dot default 10-point Times New Roman font. You need to reel 'er in a bit.

Unfortunately, there is no hard and fast rule for setting the proper line length. It varies depending on the typeface, point size, and the spacing between lines. All these factors work together. In other words, if you use a larger typeface and a larger point size and increase the amount of space between the lines, you can use a longer line length.

For example, here are two samples of text set in 9-point Times New Roman, with different line lengths:

The Old Grey Donkey, Eeyore, stood by himself in a thistly corner of the forest, his front feet well apart, his head on one side, and thought about things. Sometimes he thought sadly to himself, "Why?" and sometimes he thought, "Wherefore?" and sometimes he thought, "Inasmuch as which?"

The Old Grey Donkey, Eeyore, stood by himself in a thistly corner of the forest, his front feet well apart, his head on one side, and thought about things. Sometimes he thought sadly to himself, "Why?" and sometimes he thought, "Wherefore?" and sometimes he thought, "Inasmuch as which?"

The only real test for getting the line length right is to print some samples and read them. However, there are a few rules of thumb that graphics designers follow when setting the line length. One is that the length of the line should average about 50-60 characters; another is that each line should hold about eight to 10 words. Yet another rule of thumb is the one-and-a-half-alphabets rule: Type the lowercase alphabet one and a half times, like this:

abcdefghijklmnopqrstuvwxyzabcdefghijklm

That should be about the length of one line. These rules of thumb however, are meant to be applied to two- or three-column layouts. For single-column layouts, these rules usually result in lines that are too short.

Tip

To adjust the line length, set the page layout margins by using the File⇨Page Setup command rather than grabbing the margin controls on the Ruler and sliding them. Dragging the ruler's margin controls sets the left and right indents on a paragraph-by-paragraph basis instead of adjusting the margins for the entire page. If you want to adjust only one paragraph, using the ruler is the way to go.

Line spacing

Line spacing refers to the amount of space added between lines of text. Consider these samples, each set in 10-point Times New Roman but with varying amounts of line spacing:

- **Line spacing: exactly 10 points**

  The Old Grey Donkey, Eeyore, stood by himself in a thistly corner of the forest with his front feet well apart and his head on one side, and thought about things. Sometimes he thought sadly to himself, "Why?" and sometimes he thought, "Wherefore?" and sometimes he thought, "Inasmuch as which?"

- **Line spacing: exactly 12 points**

  The Old Grey Donkey, Eeyore, stood by himself in a thistly corner of the forest with his front feet well apart and his head on one side, and thought about things. Sometimes he thought sadly to himself, "Why?" and sometimes he thought, "Wherefore?" and sometimes he thought, "Inasmuch as which?"

- **Line spacing: exactly 14 points**

  The Old Grey Donkey, Eeyore, stood by himself in a thistly corner of the forest with his front feet well apart and his head on one side, and thought about things. Sometimes he thought sadly to himself, "Why?" and sometimes he thought, "Wherefore?" and sometimes he thought, "Inasmuch as which?"

Increasing the line spacing enables you to run the line longer and use a smaller point size or use a larger point size on a smaller line. In both cases, the extra line spacing adds definition to each line. To change the line spacing in Word for Windows, use the Format⇨Paragraph command and adjust the Line Spacing and At settings.

Extra line spacing beyond the type size is called *leading* because back in the old days of lead type, the extra space was added by inserting thin strips of lead between the lines of type. If you set the line spacing to Single, Word adds a bit of extra leading. How much depends on the size of the type and the typeface you've selected. It usually works out pretty well, but if you want precise control, set the line spacing to Exactly instead. (You then also have to set the number of points for the line spacing.)

Alignment

The type of paragraph alignment you use affects the legibility of type, too. Word enables you to use four types of alignment: Left, Centered, Right, and Justified. Body text is either left-aligned or justified. Headings are usually either left-aligned or centered. You can set the text alignment by clicking one of the alignment buttons in the Formatting toolbar or by calling up the Format⇨Paragraph command and adjusting the Alignment setting.

Justified text gives your document a more formal appearance, but it has another important benefit as well: justified text usually crams more text onto each line, resulting in fewer lines of text. That's why almost all newspapers set text in justified columns. If you're tight on space, consider using justified text.

Be careful about justified text in narrow columns, though. Word sometimes throws in an excessive amount of space between words to get the line to justify, as shown here:

> Sometimes he thought
> sadly to himself, "Why?"
> and sometimes he thought,
> "Wherefore?"   and
> sometimes he thought,
> "Inasmuch as which?"

Notice the enormous gap in the fourth line. You could throw a Linotype machine through it.

You can fix problems like this usually by throwing in an optional hyphen. To do that, press Ctrl+- where you want the word to be hyphenated. If the word is anywhere near the end of the line, Word hyphenates it. For example:

> Sometimes he thought
> sadly to himself, "Why?"
> and sometimes he thought,
> "Wherefore?" and some-
> times he thought,
> "Inasmuch as which?"

In this example, I hyphenated the word *something*. That solved the problem in the fourth line, but introduced a new problem in the fifth line. To correct the new problem, hyphenate again:

> Sometimes he thought
> sadly to himself, "Why?"
> and sometimes he thought,
> "Wherefore?" and some-
> times he thought, "Inas-
> much as which?"

This is a lot of work, isn't it? That's why I avoid justified type whenever possible.

Note

You can set up Word to hyphenate your documents automatically. Skip ahead to the next chapter to find out how.

Kerning

Kerning refers to making minor adjustments to the space between specific pairs of characters. Kerning is required because certain letter combinations tend to look as if they are spaced too far apart, especially at larger type sizes. For example, Figure 19-7 shows two samples of type. The first line is not kerned. As you can see, the amount of white space in the letter combinations *Yo*, *Ve*, and *Wo* appears excessive. The second line shows the same text set in the same typeface but with Word's kerning feature activated. You can see that Word closed up the space for these letter combinations, giving the entire line a more balanced appearance.

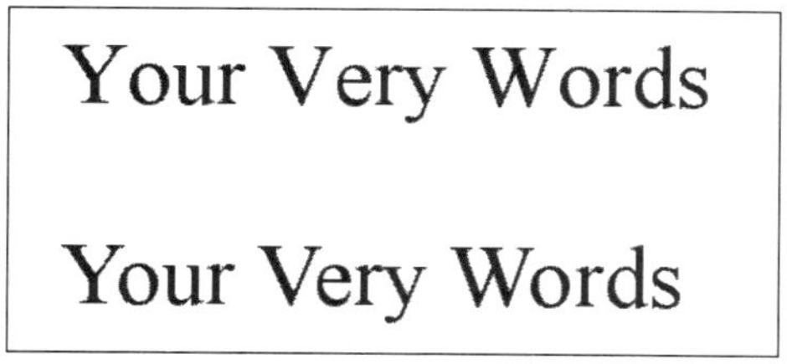

Your Very Words

Your Very Words

Figure 19-7: How kerning can improve the appearance of text.

To activate Word's kerning feature, follow these steps:

1. Select the text you want kerned.

2. Call up the Format⇨Font command and click the Character Spacing tab. The dialog box shown in Figure 19-8 will appear.

3. Click the Kerning for Fonts option button.

4. Type the minimum size you want Word to begin kerning. In the example, Word will apply kerning to fonts 18 points and larger.

5. Click OK.

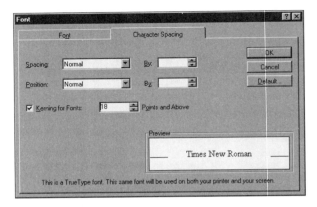

Figure 19-8: The Character Spacing tab of the Font dialog box.

Character spacing

Word also lets you adjust the spacing between characters (often called *tracking*), which gives your fonts a tighter or looser feel, depending on whether you decrease or increase the space. For example, the following example shows text set in 12-point Times New Roman with normal character spacing:

> The Old Grey Donkey, Eeyore, stood by himself in a thistly corner of the forest, his front feet well apart, his head on one side, and thought about things. Sometimes he thought sadly to himself, "Why?" and sometimes he thought, "Wherefore?" and sometimes he thought, "Inasmuch as which?"

The following example shows the same text set with an additional one-half point character spacing:

> The Old Grey Donkey, Eeyore, stood by himself in a thistly corner of the forest, his front feet well apart, his head on one side, and thought about things. Sometimes he thought sadly to himself, "Why?" and sometimes he thought, "Wherefore?" and sometimes he thought, "Inasmuch as which?"

And in this example, the letter spacing is reduced by one-half point:

> The Old Grey Donkey, Eeyore, stood by himself in a thistly corner of the forest, his front feet well apart, his head on one side, and thought about things. Sometimes he thought sadly to himself, "Why?" and sometimes he thought, "Wherefore?" and sometimes he thought, "Inasmuch as which?"

As you can see, minor adjustments to the character spacing can have a dramatic impact on the appearance of the text. To change the letter spacing, follow this procedure:

1. Select the text whose letter spacing you want to adjust.

2. Call up the Format⇨Font command and click the Character Spacing tab.

3. Use the spin control for the Spacing field to increase or decrease the amount of character spacing.

4. Click OK.

Avoiding Typeface Clash

Faced with a bewildering array of typographical choices, what's a poor Word user to do? Here is some well-intentioned advice on picking fonts to use for body text and display type.

Picking the body text type

The main criterion for selecting a body type is legibility. Unfortunately, legibility is not an either/or proposition. Some typefaces are easy to read in some circumstances and hard to read in others. Several factors work together to make text easy or hard to read. The typeface, point size, the length of the line, and the amount of space between the lines all work together to create or destroy legibility.

That being said, here are a few rules of thumb for picking a good, legible typeface for body text:

■ **Use a serif typeface for body text.** The point of serifs is to make text more legible. You can use sans serif typefaces for body text if you know what you're doing, but the safest way to create legible body text is to stick to a serif typeface.

■ **Whatever typeface you use, adjust the point size, line length, and line spacing to improve legibility.** No type looks good when set in 9 point on a 6-inch line with no additional line spacing.

■ **Don't bother with Times New Roman.** Times was originally designed for newspapers (the *London Times*, actually). The design goals were something like this: "Design a typeface that enables us to cram as much text as possible onto one line and print the newspaper on overworked presses and cheap paper. Make sure that the text is still readable even if the press doesn't pick up and deposit quite enough ink on the page, or if the paper has been sitting in the rain for two hours." Unless you're trying to save paper or you want a newspaper look, you can almost certainly find a better typeface. As an added bonus, you'll stand out from the crowd. *Everybody* has Times New Roman, but not everybody has Vogon Old Style.

Picking the display type

Display type is usually used in short bursts: short headings, captions, titles, and so on. So legibility isn't necessarily the most important consideration when choosing a display type. Other factors, such as how much it contrasts with the body text and what kind of atmosphere is created, are important as well.

The safest way to pick a display type is to opt for a sans serif typeface. That's why Windows 95 includes Arial, a Helvetica look-alike. Arial works with Times New Roman and just about any other serif typeface. Like Times New Roman, though, it's a bit overused. If you have another sans serif typeface at your disposal, consider using it instead.

If you want, you can also safely use a variation of the body text typeface for display type. For example, if the body text is 11-point Century Schoolbook, you may set headings as 14-point Century Schoolbook Bold and captions as 10-point Century Schoolbook Italic.

Warning

Don't mix different serif typefaces unless you know what you're doing. Some serif typefaces work well together, but others do not, and the subtleties are beyond the reach of most of us. Some designers marvel at your ingenuity in combining Goudy Old Style with Cheltenham, while others turn pale and begin to feel nauseous just thinking about it. Don't risk it.

The Typefaces That Come with Windows 95 and Word for Windows 95

The following sections show samples of the typefaces that are available to all Word for Windows 95 users. Times New Roman and Arial are supplied with Windows 95; the others are supplied with Word for Windows 95 or Office 95.

ALGERIAN

ALGERIAN
ALGERIAN ITALIC

ABCDEFGHIJKLMNOPQRSTUVWXYZ
1234567890

ABCDEFGHIJKLMNOPQRSTUVWXYZ
1234567890

THE OLD GREY DONKEY, EEYORE, STOOD BY HIMSELF IN A THISTLY CORNER OF THE FOREST, HIS FRONT FEET WELL APART, HIS HEAD ON ONE SIDE, AND THOUGHT ABOUT THINGS. SOMETIMES HE THOUGHT SADLY TO HIMSELF, "WHY?" AND SOMETIMES HE THOUGHT, "WHEREFORE?" AND SOMETIMES HE THOUGHT, "INASMUCH AS WHICH?"

Arial

Arial
Arial Bold
Arial Italic
Arial Bold Italic

ABCDEFGHIJKLMNOPQRSTUVWXYZ
abcdefghijklmnopqrstuvwxyz
1234567890

ABCDEFGHIJKLMNOPQRSTUVWXYZ
abcdefghijklmnopqrstuvwxyz
1234567890

The Old Grey Donkey, Eeyore, stood by himself in a thistly corner of the forest, his front feet well apart, his head on one side, and thought about things. Sometimes he thought sadly to himself, "Why?" and sometimes he thought, "Wherefore?" and sometimes he thought, "Inasmuch as which?"

Arial Narrow

Arial Narrow
Arial Narrow Bold
Arial Narrow Italic
Arial Narrow Bold Italic

ABCDEFGHIJKLMNOPQRSTUVWXYZ
abcdefghijklmnopqrstuvwxyz
1234567890

ABCDEFGHIJKLMNOPQRSTUVWXYZ
abcdefghijklmnopqrstuvwxyz
1234567890

The Old Grey Donkey, Eeyore, stood by himself in a thistly corner of the forest, his front feet well apart, his head on one side, and thought about things. Sometimes he thought sadly to himself, "Why?" and sometimes he thought, "Wherefore?" and sometimes he thought, "Inasmuch as which?"

Arial Rounded MT Bold

Arial Rounded MT Bold
Arial Rounded MT Bold Bold
Arial Rounded MT Bold Italic
Arial Rounded MT Bold Bold Italic

ABCDEFGHIJKLMNOPQRSTUVWXYZ
abcdefghijklmnopqrstuvwxyz
1234567890

ABCDEFGHIJKLMNOPQRSTUVWXYZ
abcdefghijklmnopqrstuvwxyz
1234567890

The Old Grey Donkey, Eeyore, stood by himself in a thistly corner of the forest, his front feet well apart, his head on one side, and thought about things. Sometimes he thought sadly to himself, "Why?" and sometimes he thought, "Wherefore?" and sometimes he thought, "Inasmuch as which?"

Book Antiqua

Book Antiqua
Book Antiqua Bold
Book Antiqua Italic
Book Antiqua Bold Italic

ABCDEFGHIJKLMNOPQRSTUVWXYZ
abcdefghijklmnopqrstuvwxyz
1234567890

ABCDEFGHIJKLMNOPQRSTUVWXYZ
abcdefghijklmnopqrstuvwxyz
1234567890

The Old Grey Donkey, Eeyore, stood by himself in a thistly corner of the forest, his front feet well apart, his head on one side, and thought about things. Sometimes he thought sadly to himself, "Why?" and sometimes he thought, "Wherefore?" and sometimes he thought, "Inasmuch as which?"

Bookman Old Style

Bookman Old Style
Bookman Old Style Bold
Bookman Old Style Italic
Bookman Old Style Bold Italic

ABCDEFGHIJKLMNOPQRSTUVWXYZ
abcdefghijklmnopqrstuvwxyz
1234567890

ABCDEFGHIJKLMNOPQRSTUVWXYZ
abcdefghijklmnopqrstuvwxyz
1234567890

The Old Grey Donkey, Eeyore, stood by himself in a thistly corner of the forest, his front feet well apart, his head on one side, and thought about things. Sometimes he thought sadly to himself, "Why?" and sometimes he thought, "Wherefore?" and sometimes he thought, "Inasmuch as which?"

Braggadacio

Braggadacio
Braggadacio Italic

ABCDEFGHIJKLMNOPQRSTUVWXYZ
abcdefghijklmnopqrstuvwxyz
1234567890

ABCDEFGHIJKLMNOPQRSTUVWXYZ
abcdefghijklmnopqrstuvwxyz
1234567890

The Old Grey Donkey, Eeyore, stood by himself in a thistly corner of the forest, his front feet well apart, his head on one side, and thought about things. Sometimes he thought sadly to himself, "Why?" and sometimes he thought, "Wherefore?" and sometimes he thought, "Inasmuch as which?"

Britanic Bold

Britanic Bold
Britanic Bold Bold
Britanic Bold Italic
Britanic Bold Bold Italic

ABCDEFGHIJKLMNOPQRSTUVWXYZ
abcdefghijklmnopqrstuvwxyz
1234567890

ABCDEFGHIJKLMNOPQRSTUVWXYZ
abcdefghijklmnopqrstuvwxyz
1234567890

The Old Grey Donkey, Eeyore, stood by himself in a thistly corner of the forest, his front feet well apart, his head on one side, and thought about things. Sometimes he thought sadly to himself, "Why?" and sometimes he thought, "Wherefore?" and sometimes he thought, "Inasmuch as which?"

Brush Script MT

Brush Script MT
Brush Script MT Bold

ABCDEFGHIJKLMNOPQRSTUVWXYZ
abcdefghijklmnopqrstuvwxyz
1234567890

The Old Grey Donkey, Eeyore, stood by himself in a thistly corner of the forest, his front feet well apart, his head on one side, and thought about things. Sometimes he thought sadly to himself, "Why?" and sometimes he thought, "Wherefore?" and sometimes he thought, "Inasmuch as which?"

Century Gothic

Century Gothic
Century Gothic Bold
Century Gothic Italic
Century Gothic Bold Italic

ABCDEFGHIJKLMNOPQRSTUVWXYZ
abcdefghijklmnopqrstuvwxyz
1234567890

ABCDEFGHIJKLMNOPQRSTUVWXYZ
abcdefghijklmnopqrstuvwxyz
1234567890

The Old Grey Donkey, Eeyore, stood by himself in a thistly corner of the forest, his front feet well apart, his head on one side, and thought about things. Sometimes he thought sadly to himself, "Why?" and sometimes he thought, "Wherefore?" and sometimes he thought, "Inasmuch as which?"

Century Schoolbook

Century Schoolbook
Century Schoolbook Bold
Century Schoolbook Italic
Century Schoolbook Bold Italic

ABCDEFGHIJKLMNOPQRSTUVWXYZ
abcdefghijklmnopqrstuvwxyz
1234567890

ABCDEFGHIJKLMNOPQRSTUVWXYZ
abcdefghijklmnopqrstuvwxyz
1234567890

The Old Grey Donkey, Eeyore, stood by himself in a thistly corner of the
forest, his front feet well apart, his head on one side, and thought about
things. Sometimes he thought sadly to himself, "Why?" and sometimes he
thought, "Wherefore?" and sometimes he thought, "Inasmuch as which?"

Colona MT

Colona MT
Colona MT Bold
Colona MT Italic
Colona MT Bold Italic

ABCDEFGHIJKLMNOPQRSTUVWXYZ
abcdefghijklmnopqrstuvwxyz
1234567890

ABCDEFGHIJKLMNOPQRSTUVWXYZ
abcdefghijklmnopqrstuvwxyz
1234567890

The Old Grey Donkey, Eeyore, stood by himself in a thistly corner of the forest, his
front feet well apart, his head on one side, and thought about things. Sometimes he
thought sadly to himself, "Why?" and sometimes he thought, "Wherefore?" and
sometimes he thought, "Inasmuch as which?"

DESDEMONA

DESDEMONA
DESDEMONA BOLD
DESDEMONA ITALIC
DESDEMONA BOLD ITALIC

ABCDEFGHIJKLMNOPQRSTUVWXYZ
ABCDEFGHIJKLMNOPQRSTUVWXYZ
1234567890

ABCDEFGHIJKLMNOPQRSTUVWXYZ
ABCDEFGHIJKLMNOPQRSTUVWXYZ
1234567890

THE OLD GREY DONKEY, EEYORE, STOOD BY HIMSELF IN A THISTLY CORNER OF THE FOREST,
HIS FRONT FEET WELL APART, HIS HEAD ON ONE SIDE, AND THOUGHT ABOUT THINGS.
SOMETIMES HE THOUGHT SADLY TO HIMSELF, "WHY?" AND SOMETIMES HE THOUGHT,
"WHEREFORE?" AND SOMETIMES HE THOUGHT, "INASMUCH AS WHICH?"

Footlight MT Light

Footlight MT Light
Footlight MT Light Bold
Footlight MT Light Italic
Footlight MT Light Bold Italic

ABCDEFGHIJKLMNOPQRSTUVWXYZ
abcdefghijklmnopqrstuvwxyz
1234567890

ABCDEFGHIJKLMNOPQRSTUVWXYZ
abcdefghijklmnopqrstuvwxyz
1234567890

The Old Grey Donkey, Eeyore, stood by himself in a thistly corner of the forest, his front feet well apart, his head on one side, and thought about things. Sometimes he thought sadly to himself, "Why?" and sometimes he thought, "Wherefore?" and sometimes he thought, "Inasmuch as which?"

Garamond MT

Garamond MT
Garamond MT Bold
Garamond MT Italic
Garamond MT Bold Italic

ABCDEFGHIJKLMNOPQRSTUVWXYZ
abcdefghijklmnopqrstuvwxyz
1234567890

ABCDEFGHIJKLMNOPQRSTUVWXYZ
abcdefghijklmnopqrstuvwxyz
1234567890

The Old Grey Donkey, Eeyore, stood by himself in a thistly corner of the forest, his front feet well apart, his head on one side, and thought about things. Sometimes he thought sadly to himself, "Why?" and sometimes he thought, "Wherefore?" and sometimes he thought, "Inasmuch as which?"

Haettenschweiler

Haettenschweiler
Haettenschweiler Italic

ABCDEFGHIJKLMNOPQRSTUVWXYZ
abcdefghijklmnopqrstuvwxyz
1234567890

ABCDEFGHIJKLMNOPQRSTUVWXYZ
abcdefghijklmnopqrstuvwxyz
1234567890

The Old Grey Donkey, Eeyore, stood by himself in a thistly corner of the forest, his front feet well apart, his head on one side, and thought about things. Sometimes he thought sadly to himself, "Why?" and sometimes he thought, "Wherefore?" and sometimes he thought, "Inasmuch as which?"

Impact

Impact
Impact Italic

ABCDEFGHIJKLMNOPQRSTUVWXYZ
abcdefghijklmnopqrstuvwxyz
1234567890

ABCDEFGHIJKLMNOPQRSTUVWXYZ
abcdefghijklmnopqrstuvwxyz
1234567890

The Old Grey Donkey, Eeyore, stood by himself in a thistly corner of the forest, his front feet well apart, his head on one side, and thought about things. Sometimes he thought sadly to himself, "Why?" and sometimes he thought, "Wherefore?" and sometimes he thought, "Inasmuch as which?"

Kino MT

Kino MT
Kino MT Bold
Kino MT *Italic*
Kino MT Bold Italic

ABCDEFGHIJKLMNOPQRSTUVWXYZ
abcdefghijklmnopqrstuvwxyz
1234567890

ABCDEFGHIJKLMNOPQRSTUVWXYZ
abcdefghijklmnopqrstuvwxyz
1234567890

The Old Grey Donkey, Eeyore, stood by himself in a thistly corner of the forest, his front feet well apart, his head on one side, and thought about things. Sometimes he thought sadly to himself, "Why?" and sometimes he thought, "Wherefore?" and sometimes he thought, "Inasmuch as which?"

MS Linedraw

MS Linedraw
MS Linedraw Bold
MS Linedraw Italic
MS Linedraw Bold Italic

ABCDEFGHIJKLMNOPQRSTUVWXYZ
abcdefghijklmnopqrstuvwxyz
1234567890

ABCDEFGHIJKLMNOPQRSTUVWXYZ
abcdefghijklmnopqrstuvwxyz
1234567890

The Old Grey Donkey, Eeyore, stood by himself in a thistly corner of the forest, his front feet well apart, his head on one side, and thought about things. Sometimes he thought sadly to himself, "Why?" and sometimes he thought, "Wherefore?" and sometimes he thought, "Inasmuch as which?"

Matura MT Script Capitals

Matura MT Script Capitals
Matura MT Script Capitals Bold
Matura MT Script Capitals Italic
Matura MT Script Capitals Bold Italic

ABCDEFGHIJKLMNOPQRSTUVWXYZ
abcdefghijklmnopqrstuvwxyz
1234567890

ABCDEFGHIJKLMNOPQRSTUVWXYZ
abcdefghijklmnopqrstuvwxyz
1234567890

The Old Grey Donkey, Eeyore, stood by himself in a thistly corner of the forest, his front feet well apart, his head on one side, and thought about things. Sometimes he thought sadly to himself, "Why?" and sometimes he thought, "Wherefore?" and sometimes he thought, "Inasmuch as which?"

Playbill

Playbill
Playbill Bold
Playbill Italic
Playbill Bold Italic

ABCDEFGHIJKLMNOPQRSTUVWXYZ
abcdefghijklmnopqrstuvwxyz
1234567890

ABCDEFGHIJKLMNOPQRSTUVWXYZ
abcdefghijklmnopqrstuvwxyz
1234567890

The Old Grey Donkey, Eeyore, stood by himself in a thistly corner of the forest, his front feet well apart, his head on one side, and thought about things. Sometimes he thought sadly to himself, "Why?" and sometimes he thought, "Wherefore?" and sometimes he thought, "Inasmuch as which?"

Times New Roman

Times New Roman
Times New Roman Bold
Times New Roman Italic
Times New Roman Bold Italic

ABCDEFGHIJKLMNOPQRSTUVWXYZ
abcdefghijklmnopqrstuvwxyz
1234567890

ABCDEFGHIJKLMNOPQRSTUVWXYZ
abcdefghijklmnopqrstuvwxyz
1234567890

The Old Grey Donkey, Eeyore, stood by himself in a thistly corner of the forest, his front feet well apart, his head on one side, and thought about things. Sometimes he thought sadly to himself, "Why?" and sometimes he thought, "Wherefore?" and sometimes he thought, "Inasmuch as which?"

Wide Latin

Wide Latin
Wide Latin Bold
Wide Latin Italic
Wide Latin Bold Italic

ABCDEFGHIJKLMNOPQRSTUVWXYZ
abcdefghijklmnopqrstuvwxyz
1234567890

ABCDEFGHIJKLMNOPQRSTUVWXYZ
abcdefghijklmnopqrstuvwxyz
1234567890

The Old Grey Donkey, Eeyore, stood by himself in a thistly corner of the forest, his front feet well apart, his head on one side, and thought about things. Sometimes he thought sadly to himself, "Why?" and sometimes he thought, "Wherefore?" and sometimes he thought, "Inasmuch as which?"

Chapter 20

Secrets of Columns, Frames, and Desktop Publishing Effects

In This Chapter

▶ Creating columns

▶ Adjusting column width

▶ Forcing a column break

▶ Hyphenating your text

▶ Putting your text in frames

▶ Using columns and frames for various desktop publishing effects

If you use Word to create newsletters, brochures, and other stuff that you really should be doing on a desktop publishing program such as Adobe PageMaker, Corel Ventura, or even Microsoft Publisher, you'll be happy to know that Word enables you to create beautiful two- or three-column layouts. (Actually, you can create as many as 11 columns on an 8.5" x 11" page, but unless you use really small type and supply your readers with a magnifying glass, that's not such a good idea.)

This chapter jumps head-first into setting up newspaper-style columns in Word and tackles a related feature: hyphenation. Hyphenation isn't such a big deal in single-column layouts, but after you add two or three columns to a page, hyphenation can be the key to making the columns look good. After dealing with columns and hyphenation, this chapter turns to frames, which allow you to place text and graphics in arbitrary locations on the page.

Creating Columns

Columns are a sectional thing: when you create multiple columns, the column layout is applied to the entire section. If the entire document consists of but one section, the column layout applies to the entire document. If you want part of the document to have one column and another part to have two or three columns, you have to create two or more sections to accommodate the different column layouts.

Creating columns the easy way

Here is the easiest way to create multiple columns in your document:

 1. Click the Columns button on the Standard toolbar. The drop-down menu shown in Figure 20-1 will appear.

Figure 20-1: The Columns button.

2. Click and drag the mouse to pick the number of columns you want. When you let go, the document will be formatted with the number of columns that you chose.

If you want only a part of your document to be formatted in columns, select the part you want to columnize (*columnate? encolumn?*), click the Columns button, and choose the number of columns you want. This creates a separate section for the text formatted in columns, with section breaks before and after the text you selected.

When you create a two-column layout, you probably expect to see both columns side by side on-screen. That happens only if you switch to Page Layout view by using the View⇨Page Layout command. In Normal view (View⇨Normal), the text is formatted according to the width of the column, but the columns are not displayed side by side on-screen.

For a quick glimpse of how the columns appear when printed, use the File⇨Print Preview command. When you've seen enough, click the Close button to return to your document.

Don't forget that the magic Undo command (Ctrl+Z) can instantly restore your document to a single column if you decide that changing to two or three columns was a mistake.

The Columns button enables you to set the number of columns, but it doesn't enable you to control the size of each column or the amount of space between columns. To do these latter actions, you need to use the Format⇨Columns command, described next.

Creating columns the hard way

The Columns button enables you to set the number of columns, but it doesn't enable you to control the size of each column or the amount of space between columns. To do these latter actions, you need to use the Format⇨Columns command. Here is the procedure:

1. Move the cursor to the point in the document where you want the columns to begin. If you want to apply columns to the entire document, it doesn't matter where you put the cursor.

2. Choose the Format➪Columns command. The Columns dialog box will appear, as shown in Figure 20-2.

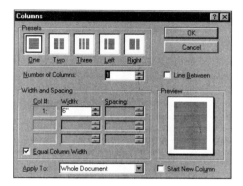

Figure 20-2: The Columns dialog box.

3. Click one of the five preset column layouts. If you want more than three columns, use the Number of Columns control to set the number of columns you want. Notice that the Left and Right preset layouts provide for a narrow column and a wide column side by side.

4. If you want to change the width of the columns, change the Width field. To change the amount of space between columns, change the Spacing field.

5. If you want a vertical line to appear centered in the space between columns, click the Line Between check box.

6. If you want the new column layout to begin at the cursor position, choose This Point Forward from the Apply To list box. Word adds a section break at the cursor position and applies the column layout to the new section. Thus, text that follows the cursor is formatted in columns, but text that comes before it is not.

7. Click OK.

If you check the Equal Column Width check box, Word balances the columns evenly. If you uncheck this check box, you can create columns of uneven width.

Tip

Using the Apply To: This Point Forward option is the way to create a headline or title that spans the width of two or three columns. Start by creating the headline, using a large font and centering it. Then, use the Format➪Columns command to create a two- or three-column layout. Set the Select Apply To field to This Point Forward to throw the columns into a new section so that the headline remains in a single column.

Changing the Column Width

 If you don't like the width of columns that you've created, you can change them at any time. One way to change column width is to call up the Format⇨Columns command and play with the Width and Spacing fields. An easier way is to click and drag the *column marker*, the box-like separator between columns in the ruler (shown in the margin).

If you check the Equal Column Width check box in the Columns dialog box, all of the column markers move in concert so that equal column widths are preserved. Otherwise, you can adjust the column markers individually.

You can drag the column marker by its center, which adjusts the width of the columns to the left and right of the marker, preserving the width of the marker that represents the amount of space between columns. Or, you can drag the marker by its left or right edge, which adjusts only the left or right column, with a corresponding change to the amount of space between columns.

As a general rule, however, you should try to keep the gap between the columns the same width even if you are working with columns of unequal width. Otherwise, you create an unbalanced look.

Tip

When adjusting column width by dragging the column marker, hold down the Alt key before clicking the mouse. Doing so causes Word to display measurements that show the width of each column and the size of the space between columns.

Don't forget that any formatting applied to paragraphs in columns is still in effect. If you gave a paragraph a left indent of .5", the paragraph is indented a half inch from the left column margin. This effectively reduces the column width.

Forcing a Column Break

Left to its own devices, Word will automatically decide when the time has come to jump text from the bottom of one column up to the top of the next column. There are times, however, when you want to intervene and insert a column break of your own.

Follow these steps to force a column break:

1. Place the cursor where you want the new column to begin.

2. Press Ctrl+Shift+Enter or use the Insert⇨Break command, check the Column Break option, and click OK.

In Normal view, a column break is indicated in the text by a solid line running all the way across the screen. In Page Layout view, the column break is obvious when you see the text jump to the next column.

Tip

Don't try to create two or three columns of equal length by inserting column breaks where you think the bottom of each column should fall. Instead, see the next section "Balancing Column Lengths."

Balancing Column Lengths

Most of the time, the last column of text will not line up evenly with the bottom of the page. Instead, the text will end midway down the page, creating columns that are not the same length. In many cases, this is acceptable. But, if you want to force Word to adjust the length of each column automatically so that all the columns are the same length, follow these steps:

1. Position the insertion point at the end of the last column.

2. Choose the Insert⇨Break command.

3. Choose Continuous.

4. Click OK.

This continuous section break will balance all of the columns in the section so that they are of equal length and will start a new section without forcing a page break.

Hyphenating Your Text

Word has the capability of automatically hyphenating words. You can set it up so that words are hyphenated as your type them, or you can wait until after you've typed your text and then automatically hyphenate the document. Hyphenating as you type can slow down Word, especially if you don't have a blazingly fast computer. Thus, I suggest that you type your document first and then hyphenate it.

Automatically hyphenating a document

Here is the procedure for hyphenating a document automatically:

1. Type your text without worrying about hyphenation at all.

2. Choose the Tools⇨Hyphenation command. The Hyphenation dialog box will appear, as shown in Figure 20-3.

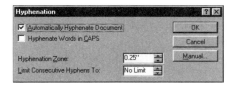

Figure 20-3: The Hyphenation dialog box.

3. Check the Automatically Hyphenate Document check box.

4. Check the Hyphenate words in CAPS check box if you want words made up of all capital letters to be hyphenated. Leave this unchecked if your writing includes specialized jargon that appears in all capitals and should not be hyphenated.

5. Adjust the Hyphenation Zone if you're picky. This zone is the area within which Word tries to end each line. If necessary, Word hyphenates words that cross into this zone.

6. Set the Limit Consecutive Hyphens To list box to 3 or 4. Two or three hyphens in a row are OK, but Word's default setting for this field places no limit to the number of consecutive lines that Word can hyphenate. You don't want to see a column with 10 hyphenated lines in a row.

7. Click OK and watch as Word hyphenates the document.

8. Check the results. You may not be happy with Word's hyphenations, so you should always check the results and make any necessary corrections.

Manually hyphenating a document

If you'd rather confirm each hyphenation Word makes, you can manually hyphenate your document. Here is the procedure:

1. Choose the Tools⇨Hyphenation command.

2. Click the Manual button. Word will begin looking for words that need to be hyphenated. When it finds one, it will display the dialog box shown in Figure 20-4.

Figure 20-4: The Manual Hyphenation dialog box.

3. If you agree with the proposed hyphenation, click Yes. Word will hyphenate the word and continue its search.

4. If you want to hyphenate the word at a different location, click the location where you want the hyphenation and click Yes.

5. If you do not want the word hyphenated, click No.

Inserting an optional hyphen

If you want to cause Word to hyphenate a word at a particular spot, place the cursor where you want the work hyphenated and press Ctrl+– (that's the hyphen next to the zero on the main part of the keyboard). Pressing this creates an *optional hyphen*, which is displayed only when the word falls at the end of a line.

Warning

Do *not* hyphenate words simply by typing a hyphen. It may work for the time being, but if you later edit the text so that the hyphenated word no longer falls at the end of a line, the hyphen still appears, now in the middle of the line where it does not belong. Use Ctrl+– instead.

Inserting a non-breaking hyphen

There are cases where you want to use a hyphen in a compound word, but you don't want the word to be split up at the end of the line because it might look funny. For example, *G-Men*. In that case, you should use Ctrl+Shift+– rather than the hyphen key alone to create the hyphen. Word displays the hyphen, but does not break the word at the hyphen. This is called a *non-breaking hyphen*.

Inserting a Text Frame

Suppose that you're writing along, minding your own business, when you realize that you might just like to put some special highlighting on that sentence you just typed: **Getting Congress to do the will of the people is like teaching tricks to Africanized Killer Bees.** Rather than just making it bold, you think it would be great to put it in a box alongside the main text and make the main text flow around it, just like in Figure 20-5.

The following steps provide the framework for inserting text into a frame:

1. Type the text you want to frame as a separate paragraph at a point that's near where you want the final framed text to appear. The positioning doesn't have to be exact, though, because you can move it after you've placed it in a frame. In Figure 20-5, I typed the quote I want to frame as a separate paragraph just before the heading "Inserting a Text Frame."

2. Select the paragraph (by triple-clicking it) and call up the Insert⇨Frame command. A frame can contain more than one paragraph of text. If you try to create a frame from *less* than a paragraph of text, Word inserts a paragraph mark at the end of the text you framed.

3. If Word asks whether you want to switch to Page Layout view, respond Yes. You can work with framed text in Normal view, but you can't adjust its positioning on the page. Because moving the text around on the page is the main reason for framing it, it only makes sense to switch to Page Layout view now. After you've finished playing with the frame, you can switch back to Normal view if you want.

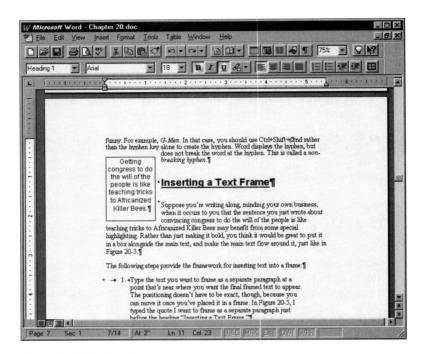

Figure 20-5: Wrapping a frame around text.

4. Word inserts a frame and places the text in it. Initially, it will look something like the frame shown in Figure 20-6.

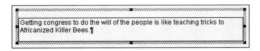

Getting congress to do the will of the people is like teaching tricks to Africanized Killer Bees.¶

Figure 20-6: How text appears when first framed.

5. Drag the frame to its new size and location. To change the size of the frame, drag it by one of the handles at the corners or on the sides of the gray frame box. To move the frame, drag the frame from any point on the gray frame box between the handles.

You can tell when the mouse pointer is in position to move or resize a frame by watching for the pointer to change shapes. When the pointer changes to a two-headed arrow, you can drag the frame edge or corner to resize the frame. When the pointer changes to a regular arrow that has a four-cornered arrow attached to its tail, you can drag the frame to move it to a new location.

6. Reformat the text within the frame. For example, you may want to change the font, font size, alignment, shading, and so on. Word will automatically add a border when you created the frame, so you don't have to take extra steps to draw a box around the frame. (However, you can later use the Format⇨Borders and Shading command to remove the border or apply shading.)

When you switch back to Normal view, the framed paragraph will appear with proper formatting, but it will not be displayed in its final location on the page. Instead, it will be displayed in the location at which you originally typed the text in Step 1. You can see the frame's position on the page only when you switch to Page Layout view.

Note

You can also create frames with the Insert⇨Picture command. I'll have more to say about this in Chapter 21.

Creating an Empty Frame

If you want to create an empty frame that you can later fill with text, a picture, drawing, or graph, follow these steps:

1. Use the View⇨Page Layout command to switch to Page Layout view. You must be in Page Layout view to insert a frame.

2. Don't select anything. If you select any text or graphics, Word will try to put the selection into the frame when you perform the next step. To create an empty frame, make sure that no text or graphics are selected.

3. Choose the Insert⇨Frame command. The mouse pointer will change to a cross-hair cursor.

4. Drag the cross-hair cursor to create your frame. Start by placing the cross-hair cursor where you want the top-left corner of the frame to be placed. Then, click and drag the mouse to create a frame of the correct size.

5. Move the frame if you didn't place it right by dragging it by the edges.

6. Select the frame and start typing text or use the Insert⇨Picture command to put a picture in the frame.

Keep in mind that frames don't do much good unless you put something in them. You can create the frame and then insert text or a picture (or both) into it, or you can type the text or insert the picture and then create the frame — it doesn't matter much which way you do it.

Aligning a Frame

You can use your mouse to drag a frame to any location on-screen, but if you want to ensure that the frame is placed at a specific location, use the Format⇨Frame command instead. This command brings up the Frame dialog box, pictured in Figure 20-7. Its controls enable you to control the position of a frame on the page.

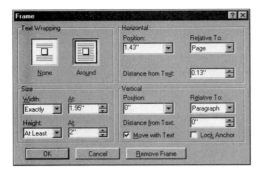

Figure 20-7: The Format Frame dialog box.

Here's the lowdown on the various Frame dialog box controls:

- **Text Wrapping:** To wrap your text around a frame, click Around. To interrupt your text when the frame appears and resume it after the frame, click None.

- **Size:** Controls the Width and Height of the frame. You can leave both fields set to Auto to make Word figure out how big the frame should be. Or, you can change either field to Exactly and then type a number in the corresponding At field to set the width or height precisely.

- **Horizontal:** Controls the horizontal left-to-right position of the frame. In the Position field, you can type a measurement or you can choose Left, Right, Center, Inside, or Outside and allow Word do the measuring for you. (Inside and Outside are used when even- and odd-numbered pages have different margins. Inside means left on a right-hand page and right on a left-hand page; outside means left on a left-hand page and right on a right-hand page.)

   In the Relative To field, you can choose Page, Margin, or Column. This option tells Word where to measure from when applying the Position setting. For example, to place the frame flush left against the margin, set the Position field to Left and the Relative To field to Margin. To line it up against the right edge of the column, set Position to Right and Relative To to Column.

   Distance from Text is where you tell Word how much empty space to leave between the right and left edge of the frame and any text that wraps around the frame. Increase this option if the text seems too crowded.

- **Vertical:** Sets the vertical, up-and-down position of the frame. You can type a number in the Position field or set it to Top, Bottom, or Center and let Word figure it out.

   Set the Relative To field to Page, Margin, or Paragraph to control placement of the frame. For example, to sit the frame down on the bottom margin, set Position to Bottom and Relative To to Margin. To place a frame one inch below a particular paragraph, set Position to 1" and Relative To to Paragraph.

Check the <u>M</u>ove With Text check box if you want the frame to travel along with the paragraph where it's anchored. If extensive editing causes the anchor paragraph to move to the next page, the frame moves to the next page, too. If you want to force the frame to stay on the same page even if the anchor paragraph jumps pages, uncheck the <u>M</u>ove With Text check box. See the following section, "Understanding Anchors," for an explanation of what I mean by the *anchor paragraph*.

Understanding Anchors

Every frame is *anchored* to a particular paragraph. When you move a frame around on the page, Word automatically picks up the frame's anchor and drops it on the nearest paragraph. This is the paragraph that is referred to when you set the Frame dialog box's Vertical R<u>e</u>lative To field to Paragraph. When you switch to Normal view, the frame is displayed immediately before the paragraph where it is anchored.

If you don't want Word to change the paragraph where a frame is anchored when you move the frame, check the Loc<u>k</u> Anchor field in the Frame dialog box. Then, the frame anchor remains in the same paragraph even if you move the frame about the page.

You can actually see the anchors in Page Layout view if you click the Show/Hide Paragraph Marks button on the Standard toolbar. When you select a frame, the paragraph where it is anchored has a little anchor next to it. You can change the anchor paragraph by dragging the anchor from paragraph to paragraph, and you can pop up the frame dialog box by double-clicking the anchor. Shiver me timbers!

Deleting a Frame

The easiest way to rid yourself of a frame is to select it and press the Del key. However, this deletes not only the frame but its contents as well. Word enables you to delete the frame without deleting the text or pictures contained in the frame. The contents of the frame are returned to their proper position on the page, and all is well.

To remove a frame without destroying its contents, follow this procedure:

1. Select the frame.

2. Conjure up the F<u>o</u>rmat⇨Fra<u>m</u>e command. The Frame dialog box will appear.

3. Click the <u>R</u>emove Frame button.

Keep in mind that the whole point of a frame is to relocate some text or graphics on the page. If you remove the frame, the text or graphics it contains is zapped back to its original location within the text.

Tip

To delete a frame along with its contents, select the frame and press the Del or Backspace keys.

You can use the Format⇨Borders and Shading command to hide the border in a frame, but that's not the same as removing the frame itself. To remove the frame itself, you must use the Format⇨Frame command and click the Remove Frame button.

Desktop Publishing Effects

The following sections describe just a few of the practical applications for columns and frames, occasionally combined with other formatting features that were covered in previous chapters.

Newsletter layouts

Creating an attractive newsletter can really tax your ability to work with columns and frames. Even so, the basic section layout of a newsletter is generally pretty straightforward. Most newsletter designs call for just two sections. The first, formatted for a single column, contains the nameplate and related materials: the name of the newsletter, a slogan or subtitle, date and volume information, and publisher information. The second section begins with a continuous section break so that it doesn't jump to a new page and splits the page into two or more columns. It is within this section that the newsletter's articles are placed.

Within these sections, frames are used to create elements that contrast the rigid structure of the newsletter columns. For example, a table of contents might be framed in a box that spans the width of two columns, and a pull quote might be framed so that it straddles several columns.

For an example of how sections, columns, and frames can be used to create a complicated newsletter layout, run the Newsletter Wizard that comes with Word for Windows 95. Start by choosing the File⇨New command. Then, when Word asks for the template to base the new document on, click on the Publications tab and double-click on the Newsletter Wizard.wiz icon. Answer the Newsletter Wizard's questions however you want, click Finish, and watch as the Wizard builds a skeleton newsletter for you. Figure 20-8 shows a sample of the type of newsletter layout the Newsletter Wizard can produce.

The Newsletter Wizard uses a two-section approach to formatting its newsletters. The nameplate, consisting of the newsletter title, volume, and date, is in the first section. The second section begins with a continuous section break and is formatted into three columns.

You can't always tell how a document as complex as the newsletter in Figure 20-8 is put together by looking at it in Page Layout view. Figure 20-9 shows this same document in Normal view, at a reduced zoom setting so that all of the first section and most of the second section fits on the screen.

Figure 20-8: A newsletter layout generated by the Newsletter Wizard.

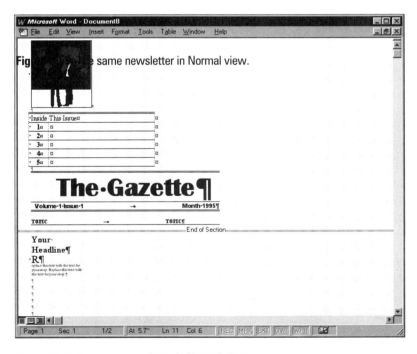

Figure 20-9: The same newsletter in Normal view.

Switching to Normal view reveals some surprising things about the way this document is formatted. Notice that the very first item in the document is not the newsletter title as you would expect, but the graphic that appears in the middle of the page in Figure 20-8. This graphic has been framed and then moved with the mouse to its final resting position, which actually falls within the next section.

Similarly, the next item after the graphic is the table of contents. This is constructed by using the Word's Table feature, placed in a frame, and relocated to the bottom of the page.

Finally, the newsletter title appears, followed by the publication information. The last line in the first section is the topic heading line, which spans the entire width of the layout.

An alternative to using a two-section approach to create the nameplate portion of the newsletter page is to use a single section with multiple columns. Then, the nameplate itself is placed in a frame and the frame's width is dragged over some or all of the newsletter columns. Figure 20-10 shows an example of a newsletter that I formatted in this way. It is formatted entirely in a single section.

Figure 20-10: A newsletter formatted with just one section.

This newsletter is formatted on a three-column layout, with the first column narrower than the rest. The measurements for this page layout are as follows:

Top & Bottom Margin:	0.5"
Left & Right Margin:	1.0"
Column 1 Width:	1.5"
Columns 2 and 3 Width:	2.5"
Space Between Columns:	0.25"

To create the shaded first column, I simply applied 50 percent shading to a paragraph and pressed the Enter key to create as many paragraphs as were necessary to fill the column to the bottom of the page. This isn't elegant, but it works. Then, I typed the nameplate information, framed it by using the Insert⇨Frame command, and dragged the frame to increase its width to span the second and third columns. I then went back and filled in the information in the first column, deleting paragraph marks as necessary so that the shaded paragraphs wouldn't extend into the second column.

Finally, I typed the articles and the article headings. I inserted the clip art graphic in-line by using the Insert⇨Picture command; no frame is needed to place this clip art in the desired location.

As you can see, there are many approaches to setting up multicolumn newsletter layouts. All of the approaches have one thing in common: they all involve a lot of fiddling around to balance columns, line up the illustrations in the proper location, and so on.

Pull quotes

A *pull quote* is a short quotation pulled out of an article, either verbatim or in paraphrased form, and given special treatment. Its purpose is to pique the reader's interest so that he or she will be drawn to read the article.

You can often create pull quotes simply by typing them in place and formatting them in an alternate typeface, a larger point size, and perhaps with a border above and below. To create fancier pull quotes, especially those that straddle column boundaries as shown in Figure 20-11, you must create the pull quote in its own frame.

Follow these steps to create a pull quote like the one in Figure 20-11:

1. Type the text that you want to appear in the pull quote. Place the text near the point where you want it to appear, but don't worry about the exact positioning. Once you put the quote in a frame, you can easily move it about the page.

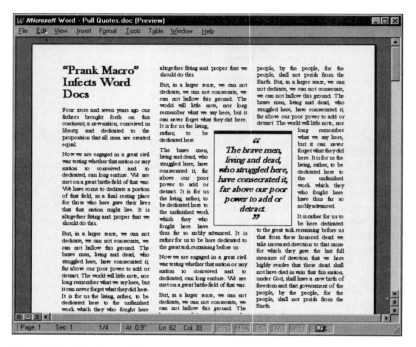

Figure 20-11: A pull quote draws the reader in to an article.

2. Format the pull quote however you want. In Figure 20-11, I used a larger italic version of the body text typeface, centered the paragraph, and placed the quotation marks on separate lines. Then, I increased the size of the quotation marks. When I increased their size, the quotation marks disappeared behind the text above them, so I had to use the Format⇨Font command to lower them a bit.

3. Double-click in the pull-quote paragraph to select it.

4. Use the Insert⇨ Frame command to place the pull quote paragraph in a frame.

5. Adjust the frame's size and position however you want. Place the pull quote frame in a location that is not too close to the spot where the quote appears in the article, and make sure that you place it in the middle of paragraphs, not between them. If you place the pull quote between paragraphs, the reader might think the pull quote is a heading.

6. Use the Format⇨ Borders and Shading command to add a border to the pull quote. In Figure 20-11, I used a thin border for the left, right, and bottom edge of the frame and provided a thicker border at the top. Other border designs can be just as effective.

Side headings

A *side heading* is a heading that appears in a separate column next to the text it relates to, as in Figure 20-12. Intuition would suggest that side headings should be easy to create by giving body text paragraphs a generous left indent and formatting the heading paragraph with a hanging indent. But, this works only when the heading consists of only one line. To create multiline side headings, such as the ones in Figure 20-12, you have to use frames.

Although side headings can be difficult to set up, you can easily create a style for side headings. Then, creating a side heading is as easy as applying a style.

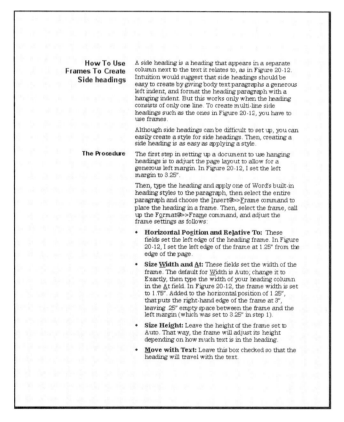

Figure 20-12: Side headings.

The first step in setting up a document to use side headings is to adjust the page layout to allow for a generous left margin. In Figure 20-12, I set the left margin to 3.25".

Then, type the heading and apply one of Word's built-in heading styles to the paragraph, select the entire paragraph, and choose the Insert⇨Frame command to place the heading in a frame. Then, select the frame, call up the Format⇨Frame command, and adjust the frame settings as follows:

- **Horizontal Position and Relative To:** These fields set the left edge of the heading frame. In Figure 20-12, I set the left edge of the frame at 1.25" from the edge of the page.

- **Size Width and At:** These fields set the width of the frame. The default for Width is Auto; change it to Exactly and type the width of your heading column in the At field. In Figure 20-12, the frame width is set to 1.75". Added to the horizontal position of 1.25", that puts the right-hand edge of the frame at 3", leaving .25" empty space between the frame and the left margin (which was set to 3.25" previously).

- **Size Height:** Leave the height of the frame set to Auto. That way, the frame will adjust its height depending on how much text is in the heading.

- **Move with Text:** Leave this box checked so that the heading will travel with the text.

When you use the Insert⇨Frame command, a border will automatically be placed around your text. Use the Format⇨ Borders and Shading command to remove the border.

After you have the heading set up just right, reapply the appropriate heading style so that the frame format is stored as a part of the style. Then, you can create additional hanging heads just by applying the style.

Icons

If you've ever wondered how to create margin icons such as those found in this book, wonder no more. Margin icons are easy to create by using frames. In fact, a margin icon is essentially the same as a side heading, except that instead of text, the icon shows a picture. Figure 20-13 shows an example.

You can use any clip art image that is appropriate as a margin icon. Place the insertion point at the point where you want the icon to appear, choose the Insert⇨Picture command, and insert the picture. Next, use the Insert⇨Frame command to wrap a frame around the picture and drag the frame to the margin where you want it to appear.

Note

You can also use any of the special characters available in the Wingdings or Monotype Sorts fonts as an icon character, too. Just increase the point size to make the character large enough and format it as you would a side heading.

Tip

After you get a margin icon formatted properly, create an AutoText entry for it. Then you won't have to go through the steps of manually applying the frame and moving it each time you need to use the icon.

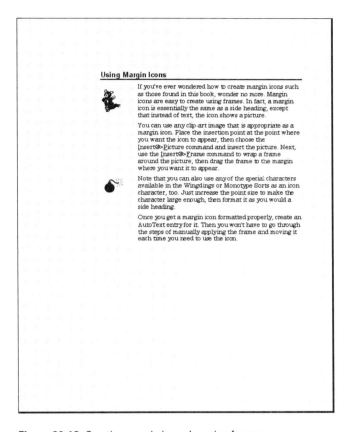

Figure 20-13: Creating margin icons by using frames.

Chapter 21

Secrets of Graphics

In This Chapter

▶ Inserting pictures into your document

▶ Sizing and cropping clip art pictures

▶ Creating your own pictures by using Word's drawing tools

This chapter covers Word's graphics features. For starters, we'll take a look at adding predrawn pictures — that is, clip art — to your Word documents. Then, we'll examine Word's built-in drawing tools, which aren't as advanced as you'll find in a full-featured drawing program like CorelDraw! but will let you spice up your documents with a little something here and a little something there.

Using Clip Art and Other Pictures

Word comes with 104 clip art images that you can incorporate into your documents to add pizzazz. In addition to these images, you can also insert picture files in any of the following formats:

■ Windows bitmap (BMP)

■ Windows metafile (WMF)

■ Tagged Image Format (TIF)

■ Encapsulated Postscript (EPS)

■ Targa (TGA)

■ AutoCAD 2-D (DXF)

■ Computer Graphics Metafile (CGM)

■ PC Paintbrush (PCX)

■ CorelDraw (CDR)

■ Word Perfect Graphics (WPG)

■ HP Graphics (HGL, PLT)

■ Macintosh PICT (PCT)

- Micrographx Designer/Draw (DRW)
- Compuserve GIF (GIF)
- KODAK Photo CD (PCD)
- JPEG (JPG)

It's important to realize that Word lets you work with two very different types of clip art pictures: *bitmap images* and *vector images*. A bitmap is an image file that stores each dot — called a *pixel* — that makes up the image. The standard Windows format for bitmaps is BMP, but Word supports other popular bitmap formats such as PCX, GIF, and JPG.

Bitmap images can vary tremendously in quality, depending primarily on the resolution used to create the image. The higher the resolution, the larger the file: quality bitmap clip art images are often 100K apiece or more. As a rule of thumb, the smaller the bitmap file, the poorer it will look when displayed in larger sizes. Bitmap files that are very small (say, 10K or less) are best displayed in small, postage-stamp sized frames.

Vector images do not comprise a bunch of individual dots; instead, a vector image file stores information about the actual shapes that make up the picture. A vector image file must be redrawn by the computer every time it is viewed. This slows down the display, but allows for more precision, especially as the picture is scaled. The standard Windows format for vector images is WMF (which stands for Windows MetaFile), but Word also supports several other popular formats, including CorelDraw! (CDR) and AutoCad (DXF).

Using the Insert Picture command

The easiest way to insert a picture into a document is to use the Insert⇨Picture command. Start by positioning the insertion point right where you want to insert the picture and call up the Insert⇨Picture command. The Insert Picture dialog box will appear, as shown in Figure 21-1.

Tip

If you don't see the picture preview when you call up the Insert⇨Picture command, click the Preview button located near the top-right corner of the dialog box. Keep in mind that Word must retrieve the picture from disk to display its preview, so activating the picture preview slows down the Insert Picture dialog box a bit.

When you find the picture you want to add, click it to select it and click OK. To search for files of a specific type, select the file type you want to look for in the Files of type field. You can also enter a complete or partial filename in the File name field, and the other controls work just as they do for the Open dialog box.

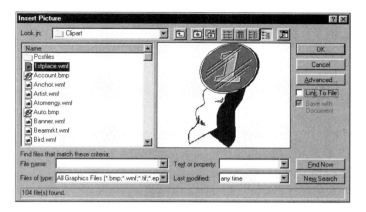

Figure 21-1: The Insert Picture dialog box.

Tip

All too often, a picture inserted into a document looks like it has been cut off at the knees. For example, look at Figure 21-2. Here, I've tried to add a lovely picture of a Heffalump to some otherwise dry prose, just to cheer things up a bit, but the Heffalump picture seems to be cut off.

> All to often, a picture inserted into a document looks like it's been cut off at the knees. For example, look at Figure 21-2. Here, I've tried to add a lovely picture of a Heffalump to some otherwise dry prose, just to cheer things up a bit, but the Heffalump picture seems to be cut off.

Figure 21-2: Alas, the Heffalump is cut off.

The problem is a common but simple one: the paragraph has been formatted with Exact line spacing. Because the paragraph format says that the lines should be a certain point size, Word lops the top off the picture. Call up the Format⊃Paragraph command and change the line spacing to Single, and the full picture will appear, as shown in Figure 21-3. (Alternatively, you can place the picture in a frame, as described later in this chapter.)

If you choose Link To File, the picture will be linked to the original file. Then, you can double-click the picture to edit it. When you do, the program that originally created the file will be activated so that you can edit the picture.

Tip

When you choose the Link To File option, the Save with Document also becomes available. This option, which is normally set, instructs Word to create a link to the original file but also to store a copy of the file in the Word document. If you disable this option, a copy of the file is not stored in the Word document. This reduces the size of the Word document. If you transfer the document to another computer, make sure that you transfer any linked but not saved pictures, too.

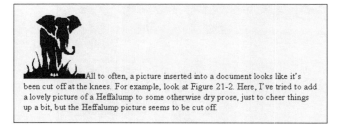

All to often, a picture inserted into a document looks like it's been cut off at the knees. For example, look at Figure 21-2. Here, I've tried to add a lovely picture of a Heffalump to some otherwise dry prose, just to cheer things up a bit, but the Heffalump picture seems to be cut off.

Figure 21-3: Changing the paragraph line spacing to Single solves the problem.

Adding a frame to a picture

Suppose that you're rambling along, typing some boring prose about a dull subject such as using clip art when it occurs to you that a picture of a Heffalump would be appropriate right about now. You conjure up the Insert⇨Picture command and discover that Word does indeed come with a clip art picture of a Heffalump. But, when you insert it, the Heffalump stands there all by itself, on its own line as shown in Figure 21-4. It's as if all of the text in the document is stuffed with fluff, afraid to meet the Heffalump face to face, probably aware that wherever you find a Heffalump, a Woosle is probably not far off.

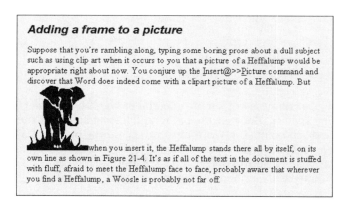

Adding a frame to a picture

Suppose that you're rambling along, typing some boring prose about a dull subject such as using clip art when it occurs to you that a picture of a Heffalump would be appropriate right about now. You conjure up the Insert@>>Picture command and discover that Word does indeed come with a clipart picture of a Heffalump. But

when you insert it, the Heffalump stands there all by itself, on its own line as shown in Figure 21-4. It's as if all of the text in the document is stuffed with fluff, afraid to meet the Heffalump face to face, probably aware that wherever you find a Heffalump, a Woosle is probably not far off.

Figure 21-4: The Heffalump scares the rest of the text away.

Well, just slap a frame on that picture and the text cuddles up right next to it as if Heffalumps are what text likes best of all. Look at Figure 21-5 and you see what I mean.

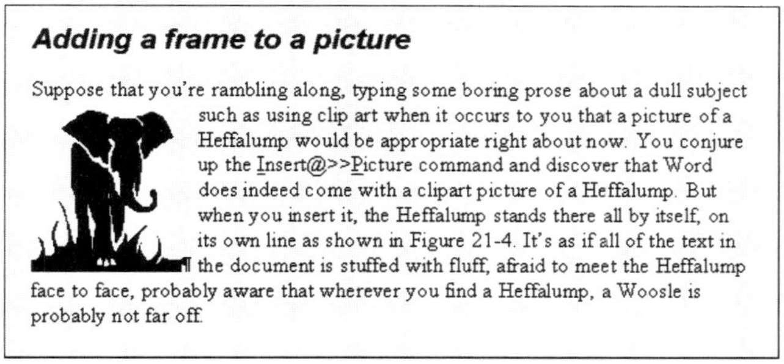

Adding a frame to a picture

Suppose that you're rambling along, typing some boring prose about a dull subject such as using clip art when it occurs to you that a picture of a Heffalump would be appropriate right about now. You conjure up the Insert@>>Picture command and discover that Word does indeed come with a clipart picture of a Heffalump. But when you insert it, the Heffalump stands there all by itself, on its own line as shown in Figure 21-4. It's as if all of the text in the document is stuffed with fluff, afraid to meet the Heffalump face to face, probably aware that wherever you find a Heffalump, a Woosle is probably not far off.

Figure 21-5: Putting the Heffalump in a frame gives the text enough courage to come back.

To frame a picture, follow these steps:

1. Use the Insert⇨Picture command to insert a picture. If the top of the picture looks like it has been cut off, use the Format⇨Paragraph command to set the Line Spacing to anything other than Exactly.

2. Click the picture to select it.

3. Use the Insert⇨Frame command to slap a frame on the picture. Or, right-click the picture and choose the Frame Picture command.

4. Drag the frame by the handles to resize it or drag it by the frame box to move it. The text will flow right around the frame. Experiment with different locations and sizes until you see just the effect you want.

If the text insists on leaving an excessive amount of space above or below the picture, click the picture and call up the Format⇨Paragraph command. Check the Before and After spacing; if it is anything but zero, set it to zero and click OK. That should remove the excess space.

To delete a framed picture, just click the frame and press the Del key.

Adding a border to a picture

Unlike text frames, Word does not automatically wrap a border around picture frames. If you want the frame to have a border, select the frame, and use the Format⇨Borders and Shading command to apply the border. Or, you can right-click the picture and select Borders and Shading from the shortcut menu that appears.

Resizing and cropping a picture

You can change the size of a picture by clicking on the picture to select it and dragging any of the handles on the corners or edges of the picture. If you drag by one of the edge handles, the picture will be distorted in the direction you drag. For example, the three bears shown in Figure 21-6 are all derived from the same clip art. The first one is too tall, the second one is too short, but the third one is just right.

Figure 21-6: The three bears: how a single clip art image can be manipulated to create different effects.

If you want to change the size of a picture without distorting it, drag it by one of the corner handles.

Word also lets you *crop* pictures, which means that a portion of the picture is cut off. To crop a picture, hold down the Shift key while dragging one of the corner or edge handles. The mouse pointer will change to a cropping tool. If you drag one of the handles *away* from the picture, you create a negative crop. In other words, the cropping area becomes larger than the picture itself. In this case, Word fills the empty space with white.

For more precise control over sizing and cropping, you can select the picture and call up the Format⇨Picture command. This brings up the dialog box shown in Figure 21-7. Here, you can manually adjust the size of the picture, either by providing an actual measurement or a percentage scaling factor. You can also provide a cropping measurement for each edge of the picture: Left, Right, Top, and Bottom.

Tip

If you have resized or cropped a picture beyond all hope of recognition, you can restore it to its original form by calling up the Format⇨Picture command and clicking the Reset button.

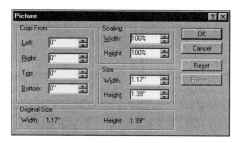

Figure 21-7: The Format Picture dialog box.

If you have placed a border around a picture, you may find that the border is a bit too close for comfort. Fortunately, you can use cropping to add some space between the border and the picture. You could do this by holding down the Shift key and dragging the edges away from the picture, but you'll have trouble making sure that the extra space is evenly distributed around the picture. Instead, click the picture and choose the Format⇨Picture command. Then, set the Left, Right, Top, and Bottom cropping measurements to a negative amount, such as –0.2.

Editing a picture

If you select a picture and choose the Edit⇨Picture command (or right-click the picture and choose Edit Picture from the shortcut menu), Word takes you to a separate window that allows you to edit the picture by using Word's drawing tools. If the picture is a bitmap image (for example, BMP, PCX, or GIF), you won't be able to do anything meaningful to it with Word's drawing tools, except perhaps add a border or embellish the picture with captions.

However, if the picture is a vector image, Word allows you to edit it by using Word's built-in drawing tools. These tools are covered later in this chapter, so I won't go into them in detail here. The main thing to remember is that when you edit a picture from within Word, you are actually editing only the copy of the picture that has been inserted into your document. You are *not* editing the actual picture file that was retrieved from disk when you use the Insert⇨Picture command.

Secret

Apparently, Microsoft at one time thought other software companies would like to let their drawing programs — rather than Word's drawing tools — be used to edit images within Word. As a result, if you pull up the Tools⇨Options command and click the Edit tab, you'll see a drop-down list box titled Picture Editor. Unfortunately, there is only one option in this list: Microsoft Word.

Adding a caption

Word lets you automatically add captions to pictures. For example, Figure 21-8 shows a caption added to a picture. This caption was created by the Insert⇨Caption command. The figure number was supplied automatically and is updated automatically as pictures are added and removed from the document. In addition, Word provides a mechanism that allows you to refer to the figure number in the text, automatically keeping such figure references in sync with the figures to which they refer.

Secret

You can add captions anywhere in your document, not just attached to a picture. Captions work best if they are attached to pictures, charts, tables, or framed text.

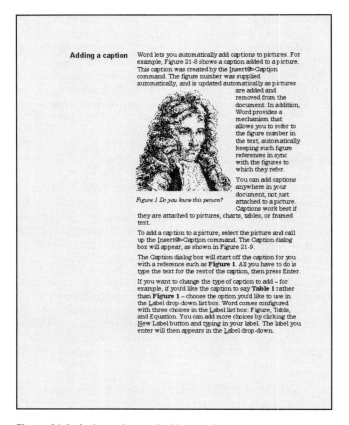

Figure 21-8: A picture inserted with a caption.

To add a caption to a picture, select the picture and call up the Insert⇨Caption command. The Caption dialog box will appear, as shown in Figure 21-9.

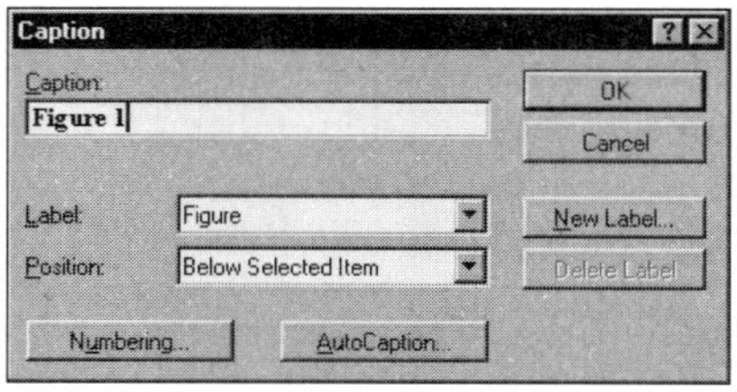

Figure 21-9: The Caption dialog box.

The Caption dialog box will start off the caption for you with a reference such as *Figure 1*. All you have to do is type the text for the rest of the caption and press Enter.

If you want to change the type of caption — for example, if you'd like the caption to say *Table 1* rather than *Figure 1* — choose the option you'd like to use in the Label drop-down list box. Word comes configured with three choices in the Label list box: Figure, Table, and Equation. You can add more choices by clicking the New Label button and typing in your label. The label you enter will then appear in the Label drop-down.

You can also change the position of the caption by altering the selection in the Position drop-down list box, and you can change the numbering scheme to Roman numerals or letters by clicking the Numbering button.

The AutoCaption button leads to the AutoCaption dialog box, shown in Figure 21-10. This dialog box lets you instruct Word to insert captions automatically whenever certain types of objects are inserted into your document. Click the object types you'd like to have automatically captioned (you can select more than one), pick a label, and click OK. In Figure 21-10, I set up AutoCaptions for Microsoft Word Tables, using Table as the label.

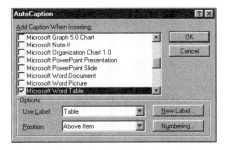

Figure 21-10: Using the AutoCaption dialog box to tell Word to add captions automatically whenever certain types of objects are added to your document.

Using Microsoft ClipArt Gallery

Secret

If you purchased Word as a part of Microsoft Office 95, or if you have installed a version of Microsoft's PowerPoint Microsoft Publisher, you have access to a little gem called Microsoft ClipArt Gallery. This program makes it easier to find clip art because it arranges your clip art files into categories, and it presents thumbnail views that show 12 images at a time.

ClipArt will automatically configure itself to include clip art supplied with various Microsoft programs, including Word, PowerPoint, and Publisher. In addition, you can add your own graphics to ClipArt Gallery. Thus, ClipArt Gallery can provide one-stop shopping for all of the clip art files on your computer.

ClipArt Gallery is designed for use with PowerPoint or Publisher, so Word doesn't provide any direct way to access it. However, you will find it listed in the Insert⇨Object command. To use the ClipArt Gallery from Word, follow these steps:

1. Position the insertion point where you want the clip art inserted.

2. Choose the Insert⇨Object command.

3. Select "Microsoft ClipArt Gallery" from the list of Object types.

4. Click OK. The ClipArt Gallery will appear, as shown in Figure 21-11.

5. Select the clip art image you want to insert. You can select a category from the Categories list to help narrow your search.

6. When you have found the clip art you want to insert, click Insert.

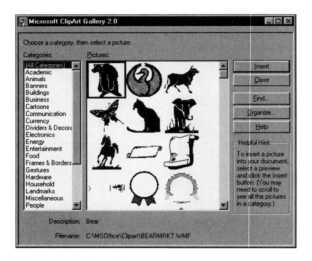

Figure 21-11: ClipArt Gallery helps you quickly locate clip art.

To add your own clip art to ClipArt Gallery, click the Organize button. This displays the dialog box shown in Figure 22-12.

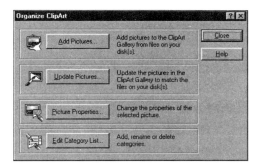

Figure 21-12: The Organize ClipArt dialog box.

The Organize ClipArt dialog box offers the following choices:

- **Add Pictures:** Adds clip art files from your disk to the ClipArt Gallery.

- **Update Pictures:** Refreshes ClipArt Gallery's thumbnail images of your clip art files. Use this if you have replaced existing clip art files on your disk with newer versions, and you want the Gallery's thumbnails to match.

- **Picture Properties:** Allows you to set the category and type a description for the selected picture.

- **Edit Category List:** Allows you to create new categories or rename or delete existing categories.

To add a collection of clip art from a folder on your disk, first use Edit Category List to create a new category for the clip art. Then, use Add Pictures to add the pictures.

Customizing the Picture shortcut menu

When you right-click a picture, a shortcut menu appears containing several useful commands. By default, the Picture shortcut menu contains the following commands:

- Cut
- Copy
- Paste
- Edit Picture
- Borders and Shading
- Caption
- Frame Picture

The following sections describe four commands and macros that can be added to this menu to make it more useful: Format, Reset, Increase Crop, and Decrease Crop.

Adding the Format command to the Picture shortcut menu

First, you can add the Format⇨Picture command to the shortcut menu. To do that, follow these steps:

1. Choose the Tools⇨Customize command.

2. Click the Menus tab.

3. In the Change What Menu field, select Pictures (Shortcut).

4. In the Categories field, select Format.

5. In the Command field, select FormatPicture.

6. Change the Name on Menu field to "&Format...".

7. Click Add.

8. Click Close.

Now, insert a picture and right-click the picture to verify that the Format command has been added.

Adding the Reset command to the Picture shortcut menu

The next command to add to the Pictures shortcut menu is a macro that automatically resets the picture to its original size. This is equivalent to choosing the Format⇨Paragraph command and clicking the Reset button.

To create the macro and assign it to the Picture shortcut menu, follow these steps:

1. Choose the Tools⇨Macro command.

2. Type **ResetPicture** in the Macro Name field.

3. Click the Create button.

4. Type the macro in exactly as shown below:

```
Sub MAIN
FormatPicture .CropTop = 0, .CropBottom = 0, .CropLeft = 0,
.CropRight = 0, .ScaleX = "100%", .ScaleY = "100%"
End Sub
```

5. Click the Save button and click Yes when Word asks whether you are sure you want to save changes.

6. Follow Steps 1 through 3 from the procedure described previously under "Adding the Format command to the Picture shortcut menu," except choose Macros for the Categories, select the ResetPicture macro, type **&Reset** in the Name on Menu field, and click Add. Then click Close.

Adding the Increase Crop command to the Picture shortcut menu

An IncreaseCrop command would come in handy from time to time, allowing you to increase the cropping factor evenly in all directions. To add the Increase Crop command to the shortcut menu, create a macro named IncreaseCrop and type the macro instructions exactly as follows:

```
Sub Main
Dim fp As FormatPicture
GetCurValues fp
NewCropTop$ = Str$(Val(fp.CropTop) + 0.05) + Chr$(34)
NewCropBottom$ = Str$(Val(fp.CropBottom) + 0.05) + Chr$(34)
NewCropLeft$ = Str$(Val(fp.CropLeft) + 0.05) + Chr$(34)
NewCropRight$ = Str$(Val(fp.CropRight) + 0.05) + Chr$(34)
FormatPicture .CropTop = NewCropTop$, .CropBottom = NewCropBottom$,
.CropLeft = NewCropLeft$, .CropRight = NewCropRight$
End Sub
```

Then, use the Tools⇨Customize command to add the IncreaseCrop command to the Picture shortcut menu. Set Name on Menu to "Increase Crop."

Adding the Decrease Crop command to the Picture shortcut menu

To add the Decrease Crop command to the shortcut menu, create a macro named DecreaseCrop. The macro should appear exactly as follows:

```
Sub Main
Dim fp As FormatPicture
GetCurValues fp
NewCropTop$ = Str$(Val(fp.CropTop) - 0.05) + Chr$(34)
NewCropBottom$ = Str$(Val(fp.CropBottom) - 0.05) + Chr$(34)
NewCropLeft$ = Str$(Val(fp.CropLeft) - 0.05) + Chr$(34)
NewCropRight$ = Str$(Val(fp.CropRight) - 0.05) + Chr$(34)
FormatPicture .CropTop = NewCropTop$, .CropBottom = NewCropBottom$,
.CropLeft = NewCropLeft$, .CropRight = NewCropRight$
End Sub
```

The only difference between this macro and the IncreaseCrop macro is that the plus signs are replaced with minus signs in the third through sixth lines.

Once again, use the Tools⇨Customize command to add the Decrease macro to the Picture shortcut menu. Set the Name on Menu field to "Decrease Crop."

Using Word's Drawing Tools

If you don't have a clip art picture that meets your needs, you can always use Word's drawing tools to create your own picture. Word's drawing tools aren't as powerful as the tools provided with a full-featured drawing program such as CorelDraw! or Adobe Illustrator, but they are powerful enough to create some fancy pictures. Before I delve into the specifics of how to use each tool, this section describes a handful of general tips for drawing pictures.

Activate the Drawing toolbar

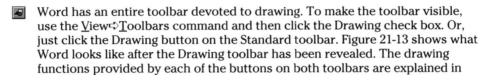 Word has an entire toolbar devoted to drawing. To make the toolbar visible, use the View➪Toolbars command and then click the Drawing check box. Or, just click the Drawing button on the Standard toolbar. Figure 21-13 shows what Word looks like after the Drawing toolbar has been revealed. The drawing functions provided by each of the buttons on both toolbars are explained in this chapter.

Notice that Figure 21-13 shows a new document created by using one of the templates provided with Word 95. Many of these templates use drawing objects to create interesting graphic effects.

Note

Word's drawing tools work only in Page Layout view. Word automatically switches to Page Layout view when you activate the Drawing toolbar.

Tip

After you have drawn something on your document, you should probably stick to Page Layout view for the duration. When you switch back to Normal view, drawing objects are disconcertingly hidden from view. You can easily forget about the drawing objects when you switch back to Normal view.

Zoom in

When you work with Word's drawing tools, increase the zoom factor so that you can draw more accurately. I usually work at 200 percent when I'm drawing. To change the zoom factor, click the down arrow next to the Zoom Control tool (near the right side of the Standard toolbar), choose a zoom factor from the list or click the zoom factor, type a new zoom percentage, and press Enter.

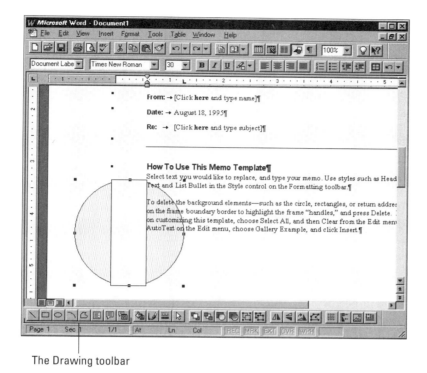

The Drawing toolbar

Figure 21-13: Word with the Drawing toolbar enabled.

Before you change the zoom factor to edit an object, select the object you want to edit. That way, Word zooms in on that area of the page. If you don't select an object before you zoom in, you probably will have to scroll around to find the right location.

Tip

If you are drawing a particularly complicated drawing, you can also draw the object much larger than you intend its final form to be. This enables you to work on the finer points of the object's detail. When the drawing is finished, you can group the individual objects that make up the drawing and resize the drawing to its final size.

Tip

Save frequently

Drawing is tedious work. You don't want to spend two hours working on a particularly important drawing, only to lose it all just because some joker on the other side of the world drops a bomb on your backyard. There are two ways to prevent catastrophic loss from incidents such as these: by pressing Ctrl+S frequently as you work and by working in a hardened bunker located a minimum of 60 feet underground. For most people, pressing Ctrl+S frequently is the more practical alternative.

Don't forget Ctrl+Z

Don't forget that you're never more than one keystroke from erasing a mistake. If you do something that leaves your picture worse off than it was when you started, you can always press Ctrl+Z to undo your last action. Ctrl+Z is my favorite and most frequently used Word key.

Drawing Simple Lines and Shapes

Word provides an entire row of drawing tools, located on the Drawing toolbar. Table 21-1 shows you what each of these drawing tools does.

To draw an object, just click the button that represents the object you want to draw and then use the left mouse button to draw the object. It's not always as simple as that. You can find in the following sections detailed instructions for drawing with the more important tools.

Table 21-1	Word's Basic Drawing Tools
Drawing Tool	*What It Does*
�	Draws a straight line. You can later change the attributes of the line to create thick lines, dashed lines, or lines with arrowheads.
◻	Draws rectangles. To make a perfect square, hold down the Shift key while you draw.
○	Draws circles and ovals. To create a perfect circle, hold down the Shift key while you draw.
◱	Draws an arc (not the kind Noah used, but a curved line). To create a perfect quarter-circle arc, hold down the Shift key while you draw.
⌂	Draws freeform shapes.
▣	Draws a text box.
▤	Draws a callout, which resembles a text box but has a line sticking out from it.

Tip

If the Drawing toolbar has disappeared, you can make it appear again by using the <u>V</u>iew⇨<u>T</u>oolbars command and checking the Drawing box or by clicking the Drawing button on the Standard toolbar.

Tip

If you make a mistake, you can delete the object you just drew by pressing the Del key and trying again. Or, you can change its size or stretch it by clicking it and dragging its handles.

Table 21-2 summarizes some handy shortcuts you can use while you're drawing.

Table 21-2	Drawing Shortcuts
Shortcut	*What It Does*
Shift	Hold down the Shift key to force lines to be horizontal or vertical, to force arcs and ellipses to be true circles, or to force rectangles to be squares.
Ctrl	Hold down the Ctrl key to draw objects from the center rather than from end to end.
Ctrl+Shift	Draws from the center and enforces squareness.
Double-click	Double-click one of the buttons on the toolbar to draw several objects of the same type.

Drawing straight and curved lines

To draw a straight line, follow these steps:

1. Click the Line tool.

2. Point to where you want the line to begin.

3. Press the left mouse button and drag to where you want the line to end.

4. Release the mouse button.

The procedure for drawing an arc is the same as drawing a line except that you click the Arc button rather than the Line tool.

You can use the F<u>o</u>rmat⇨Drawing <u>O</u>bject command to change the line color, thickness, dashes, and arrowheads for a line or arc. Or, you can use buttons on the Drawing toolbar to change these attributes. Last but not least, you can right-click the picture and choose Format Drawing Object from the shortcut menu. See the section "Setting the Fill Color, Line Style, and Shadow," later in this chapter.

Tip

You can force a line to be perfectly horizontal or vertical by holding down the Shift key while you draw.

The ends of an arc are always 90 degrees apart. In other words, an arc is always one-quarter of a circle or ellipse.

Drawing rectangles, squares, and circles

To draw a rectangle, follow these steps:

1. Click the Rectangle tool.

2. Point to where you want one corner of the rectangle to be.

3. Press the mouse button and drag to where you want the opposite corner of the rectangle to be.

4. Release the mouse button.

The procedure for drawing a circle or ellipse is the same as drawing a rectangle except that you click the Ellipse button rather than the Rectangle tool.

You can use the Format⇨Drawing Object command to change the fill color or the line style for a rectangle or circle. You can also use the buttons on the Drawing toolbar to change the color and line style. See the section "Setting the Fill Color, Line Style, and Shadow," later in this chapter.

Tip

To create an even square or a perfectly round circle, hold down the Shift key while you draw.

Drawing a polygon or freeform shape

A *polygon* is a shape that has many sides and has nothing to do with having more than one spouse (one is certainly enough for most of us). Triangles, squares, and rectangles are polygons, but so are hexagons and pentagons, as is any unusual shape with sides that all consist of straight lines.

Word's Freeform button is designed to create polygons, with a twist: not all the sides have to be straight lines. The Freeform button lets you build a shape with sides that are a mixture of straight lines and freeform curves. Figure 21-14 shows three examples of shapes I created with the Freeform tool.

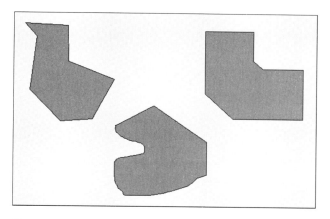

Figure 21-14: Three freeform shapes courtesy of the Freeform button.

Follow these steps to create a polygon or freeform shape:

 1. Click the Freeform tool.

2. Click where you want the first corner of the object to be.

3. Click where you want the second corner of the object to be.

4. Keep clicking wherever you want a corner to be.

5. To finish the shape, click near the first corner, the one you created in Step 2. You don't have to be exact; if you click anywhere near the first corner you put down, Word assumes that the shape is finished.

To draw a freeform side on the shape, keep holding down the mouse button when you click at a corner and then draw the freeform shape with the mouse. When you reach the end of the freeform side, release the mouse button. Then, you can click again to add more corners. The second shape in Figure 21-9 includes one freeform side.

 You can reshape a polygon or freeform shape by selecting it and clicking the Reshape button on the Drawing toolbar and then dragging any of the handles that appear on the corners.

Tip

If you hold down the Shift key while you draw a polygon, the sides are constrained to 30- and 45-degree angles. The third shape in Figure 21-9 was drawn in this way.

You can also use the Freeform button to draw a multisegmented line, called an *open shape*. In an open shape, the beginning point does not connect to the ending point. To draw an open shape, follow the procedure just described, but skip Step 5. Instead, double-click or press the Esc key when the line is finished.

Drawing a text box

A *text box* is similar to a frame in that it contains text and you can move it around the page to place the text precisely where you want it. The primary differences between a text box and a frame are that text boxes don't adjust their size automatically based on how much text you type in them and you can't add a text box by using a style. Text boxes don't usually stand by themselves, but you typically use them in combination with shapes drawn with the other drawing tools.

Drawing a text box is pretty much the same as drawing a rectangle. Follow these steps:

1. Click the Text button.

2. Point to where you want one corner of the text box to be.

3. Press the left mouse button and drag to where you want the opposite corner of the text box to be.

4. Release the mouse button.

5. Type some text.

Drawing a callout

A *callout* is a special kind of text box that has a line attached to some other object, as shown in Figure 21-15. In the figure, I used callouts to label the various parts of a clip art picture.

Figure 21-15: Callouts.

Follow this procedure to create callouts while maintaining your sanity:

1. Click the Callout tool.

2. Click where you want to attach the callout line.

3. Drag the mouse to where you want the callout text to appear. When you release the mouse, a big 1-inch-square callout box appears.

4. Type some callout text. The text is inserted in the callout box.

5. The callout box will probably be too big, so you'll have to adjust it by dragging it by the handles.

As you drag a callout box around the screen, the callout line automatically adjusts itself so that it always points at the object to which you attached it. You can use the Line Style button to add an arrowhead to the callout line. See the section, "Setting the Fill Color, Line Style, and Shadow" later in this chapter.

You can change the callout format by clicking the Format Callout button. This step pops up the dialog box shown in Figure 21-16, where you can choose from four different callout styles and customize the size and shape of the callout line. If you select a callout before you click the Format Callout button, the format applies to the callout you selected. If you do not select a callout before you click the button, the format becomes the default for all callouts you subsequently create.

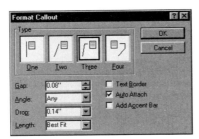

Figure 21-16: The Format Callout dialog box.

The Format Callout dialog box also offers the following three options:

■ **Text Border:** Places a box around the callout text.

■ **Auto Attach:** Causes Word to move the callout line automatically to the right or left of the callout text as the you move the position of the text or the end point of the callout line.

■ **Add Accent Bar:** Adds a vertical line to the end of the callout line.

Figure 21-17 shows callouts with various combinations of text borders and accent bars.

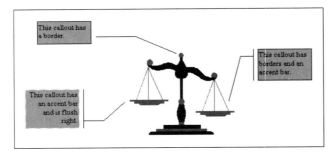

Figure 21-17: Formatted callouts.

Selecting Drawing Objects

After you've added drawing objects to a document, you need to know how to select those objects so that you can move them, resize them, fill them with color, or delete them without remorse. Here are the tricks for successfully selecting drawing objects:

■ You can usually select an object by moving the mouse pointer over the object and clicking it. As a visual clue, the mouse pointer changes from the normal I-beam pointer to an arrow when it is in position to select a drawing object.

■ If an object is hiding stubbornly behind text and the mouse pointer won't change to the arrow, click the Select Drawing Objects button on the Drawing toolbar to change the mouse pointer to an arrow that can select *only* drawing objects. Click the Select Drawing Objects button again to return the mouse pointer to normal. If you still can't get at the object, look ahead to the section "Changing layers."

■ To select more than one object at a time, hold down the Shift key while clicking on the objects.

■ If you've selected several objects and you want to deselect one of them, click on the unwanted object again while holding down the Shift key.

Setting the Fill Color, Line Style, and Shadow

Word drawing objects have various attributes you can change:

■ **Fill color:** The interior color of an object.

■ **Line color:** The color of the lines that outline the object (or in the case of a line or arc, the color of the line or arc itself). If the object has no line color, the lines are not visible.

■ **Line style:** The thickness and style of the lines that outline the object, including dashed lines and arrowheads.

To change any of these object attributes, follow these steps:

1. Select the object or objects you want to change.

2. Use the appropriate button to change the color or style, as summarized in Table 21-3.

Table 21-3	Tools for Setting Colors and Line Styles
Drawing Tool	**What It Does**
	Sets the fill color.
	Sets the line color.
	Sets the line width and style.

When you use these buttons to change the color or style, the selected object changes. In addition, any new objects you create assume the new color or style.

Alternatively, you can use the Format⇨Drawing Object command to change colors and line styles, or right-click the object and select the Format Drawing Object command. This command pops up a dialog box that has three tabs. The first, Fill, is shown in Figure 21-18. It lets you control the color and pattern used to fill the interior of the object.

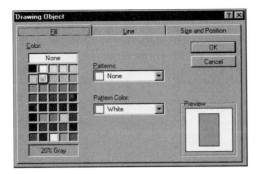

Figure 21-18: The Drawing Object dialog box (Fill tab).

The second tab of the Drawing Object dialog box is Line. Shown in Figure 21-19, it lets you control the color, style, and thickness of the border drawn around the object. For certain types of objects, you can also add arrowheads to the line ends.

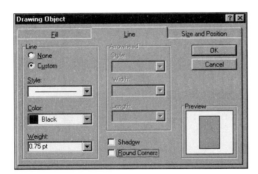

Figure 21-19: The Drawing Object dialog box (Line tab).

The third tab, Size and Position, is shown in Figure 21-20 and lets you execute precise control over the positioning of the object. Of the options on this tab, the one you're most likely to use is Lock Anchor: it ensures that the graphic object will always appear on the same pages as the text paragraph where the object is anchored.

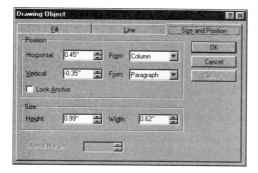

Figure 21-20: The Drawing Object dialog box (Size and Position tab).

Flipping and Rotating Objects

To *flip* an object means to create a mirror image of it. To *rotate* an object means to turn it about its center. Word lets you flip objects horizontally or vertically and rotate objects in 90-degree increments.

Flipping an object

Word lets you flip an object vertically or horizontally to create a mirror image of the object. To flip an object, follow these steps:

1. Select the object you want to flip.

 2. Click the Flip Horizontal or Flip Vertical button on the Drawing toolbar.

Rotating an object 90 degrees

You can rotate an object in 90-degree increments by following these steps:

1. Select the object you want to rotate.

 2. Click the Rotate Right button on the Drawing toolbar.

3. To rotate the object 180 degrees, click the Rotate button again.

4. To rotate the object 270 degrees (the same as rotating it 90 degrees to the *left*), click the Rotate button again.

Drawing a Complicated Picture

After you add more than one object to a page, several problems often arise: what happens when the objects overlap? how do you line up objects so that they don't look like they were thrown at the page from a moving car? and how do you keep together objects that belong together? The following sections show how to use Word features to handle overlapped objects, align objects, and group objects.

Changing layers

Whenever you have more than one object on a page, the potential exists for objects to overlap one another. Like most drawing programs, Word handles this problem by layering objects like a stack of plates. The first object you draw is at the bottom of the stack, the second object is on top of the first, the third is atop the second, and so on. If two objects overlap, the one that's at the highest layer is the one that wins; objects below it are partially covered.

So far, so good. But, what if you don't remember to draw the objects in the correct order? what if you draw a shape you want to tuck behind a shape you've already drawn? or what if you want to bring an existing shape to the top of the pecking order? No problem. Word lets you change the stack order, moving objects to the front or back so that they overlap just the way you want.

To complicate matters even more, Word has two distinct layers in which objects can be drawn: one in front of the text, the other behind the text. Objects in front of the text obscure any text that happens to fall behind it. Objects behind the text are obscured by text that happens to overlap it.

Word provides four toolbar buttons for changing the stacking order. These buttons are summarized in Table 21-4.

Table 21-4	Toolbar Buttons for Layering Objects
Drawing Tool	*What It Does*
	Brings an object to the front of other objects at the same layer.
	Sends an object behind other objects at the same layer.
	Brings an object to the layer in front of the text.
	Sends an object to the layer behind the text.

Layering problems are most obvious when objects have a fill color. If an object has no fill color, any objects behind it are allowed to show through. In this case, the layering doesn't matter much.

Aligning objects

Nothing looks more amateurish than objects dropped randomly on the page with no apparent concern for how the objects line up with one another. Word provides several features that let you line up objects as you draw them:

■ **Snap to Grid:** When this mode is on, the entire page is overlaid by an invisible grid to which objects are aligned. Whenever you create a new object or move an existing object, it automatically sticks to the nearest gridline. To turn Snap to Grid mode on or off, click the Snap to Grid button on the Drawing toolbar. The dialog box shown in Figure 21-21 will appear. The Snap To Grid option controls whether the grid is active: if this option is checked, drawing objects will align to the grid; otherwise, they won't. Check or uncheck the Snap To Grid option and click OK.

If you want to change the grid spacing, adjust the Horizontal or Vertical spacing fields. For more precise alignment, you can also change the Horizontal Origin and Vertical Origin fields: they control the position relative to the top-left corner of the page at which the grid begins.

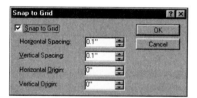

Figure 21-21: The Snap To Grid dialog box.

■ **Align Drawing Objects button:** Lets you select several objects and then line them up. You can align the objects horizontally to the top, bottom, or center of the objects, or vertically to the left edges, right edges, or centers.

To align objects, simply select all the objects you want to align (hold down the Shift key while clicking each object) and click the Align Drawing Objects button. The Align dialog box appears, as shown in Figure 21-22. Click the type of alignment you want and click OK. You can center objects to each other or to the page. When you align objects to each other, the last object you select serves as the anchor point: it remains stationary, while the other objects are moved to align with it.

Tip

Be ready at the Ctrl+Z key when you use the Align command. Aligning often doesn't work the way you want, but pressing Ctrl+Z lets you quickly reverse a boo-boo before anyone notices.

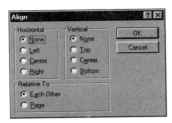

Figure 21-22: The Align dialog box.

Grouping objects

A *group* is a collection of objects that Word treats as though it were one object. Using groups properly is one of the keys for putting simple shapes together to make complex pictures because groups allow you to move or copy more than one object at a time.

To create a group, follow these steps:

1. Select all the objects that you want included in the group.

2. Click the Group button on the Drawing toolbar.

To take a group apart so that Word treats the objects as individuals again, follow this procedure:

1. Select all the grouped objects that you want to separate.

2. Click the Ungroup button on the Drawing toolbar.

Tip

Word lets you create groups of groups. This capability is useful for complex pictures because it lets you work on one part of the picture, group it, and then work on the next part of the picture without worrying about accidentally disturbing the part you have already grouped. After you have several such groups, select them and group them.

Converting Drawing Objects to a Picture Object

The Create Picture lets you create a new picture object, which is then inserted into your document as if it had been placed there by the Insert⇨Picture command. You can convert existing drawing objects to a picture, or you can start from scratch by clicking the Create Picture button with nothing selected.

To create a picture from existing drawing objects, use Word's drawing tools to draw directly on the document. Then, select the objects you want to be a part of the picture — grouping them if you wish — and click the Create Picture button. The drawing objects will be converted to a picture.

To create a picture from scratch, click the Create Picture button with nothing selected. Word will open a picture editing window, as shown in Figure 21-23. You can then draw your picture by using Word's drawing tools. Click Close Picture to return to the document.

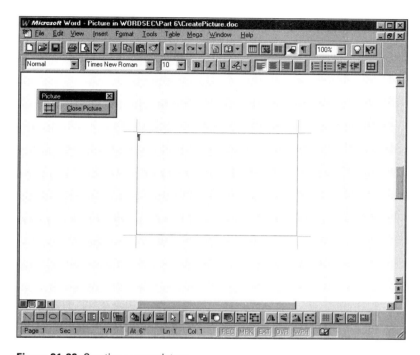

Figure 21-23: Creating a new picture.

Secret

The opposite of creating a picture from Word drawing objects would be to separate out a picture object into its component Word drawing objects. Although no menu command or toolbar button appears to provide this function, Word does have a built-in DrawDisassemblePicture command that does the trick. To use it, follow these steps:

1. Select the picture object you would like to convert to Word drawing objects.

2. Choose the Tools⇨Macro command.

3. Select "Word Commands" for the Macros Available In field.

4. Select DrawDissamblePicture for the Macro Name field.

5. Click Run.

The picture object will be converted to individual Word drawing objects.

Chapter 22

The Secret Applets: WordArt, Equation Editor, and Microsoft Graph

---

In This Chapter

▶ WordArt

▶ Equation Editor

▶ Microsoft Graph 5

Microsoft Word comes with a collection of OLE-enabled applications that are designed not to be used by themselves, but from within Word via the Insert⇨Object command. This chapter describes these applications. (For more information about OLE in general, see Chapter 27.)

Note

If you cannot find one of these applications when you call up the Insert⇨Object command, you probably did not install the application when you installed Word 95 or Office 95. Just rerun the Word 95 or Office 95 setup program and install the missing component.

WordArt

WordArt is a program that allows you to create fancy logos which consist of text that has been folded, spindled, and mutilated to create interesting designs. Figure 22-1 shows several examples of the types of logos you can create with WordArt.

To create a logo with WordArt, follow this procedure:

1. Choose the Insert⇨Object command. The Insert Object dialog box will appear, as shown in Figure 22-2.

2. Select Microsoft WordArt 2.0 from the Object Type list and click OK. There will probably be many other object types that have infiltrated the list; if so, just scroll until you find WordArt 2.0. Also, you may find an entry for WordArt 1.0. If so, skip it. When you finally find Microsoft WordArt 2.0, click

Figure 22-1: WordArt at work.

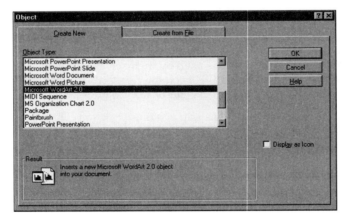

Figure 22-2: The Object dialog box.

OK to conjure up WordArt. Like the other OLE 2.0 add-ons, WordArt and Word will take a few moments to discuss how the Seahawks should fare next season. Then, WordArt takes over Word's menus and toolbars as any good OLE 2.0 application should, replacing Word's menus and toolbars with its own, as shown in Figure 22-3.

3. Type some clever text in the Enter Your Text Here dialog box. Click the Update Display button to transfer your text from the dialog box into the WordArt object.

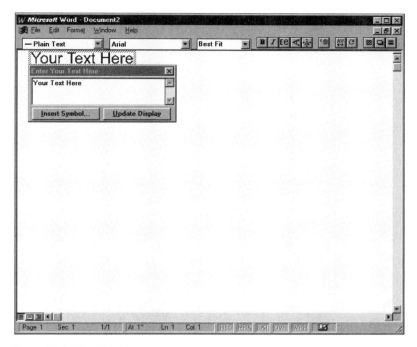

Figure 22-3: WordArt takes over.

Note

If you make subsequent text changes, remember to click Update Display again so that the changes are reflected in the WordArt object.

4. Pick a shape from the shape list at the left side of the toolbar. The text will be skewed to conform to the shape you pick.

5. Fool around with other WordArt controls. The various controls available on the WordArt toolbar are summarized in Table 22-1. Experiment as much as you want until you get the text looking just right. Figure 22-4 shows an example of how WordArt appears after the text has been manipulated.

6. Click anywhere outside the WordArt frame to restore Word to its normal state so that you can continue working on the document.

Tip

Don't forget that in Word's eyes, a WordArt object is not text; it is a graphic created as an OLE object. You can't edit it just by clicking on it and typing. Instead, you have to double-click on it to conjure up WordArt and edit the text from within WordArt.

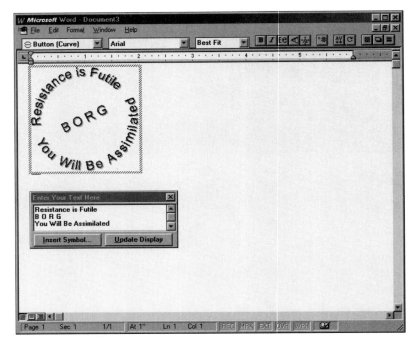

Figure 22-4: WordArt after text has been entered and manipulated.

Creating a custom WordArt button

I think it's kind of crazy that Microsoft plants a button right on the Standard toolbar for inserting an Excel worksheet (which is something most of us rarely do) but leaves off the button for WordArt. Fortunately, Word does come with a built-in WordArt button; it's just not assigned to the standard toolbars. The WordArt button is illustrated in the margin next to this paragraph. To add it to a toolbar, follow these steps:

1. Choose the Tools⇨Customize command and click the Toolbars tab.

2. Pick Insert in the Categories list box.

3. Drag the WordArt button from the Customize dialog box onto the toolbar where you want it located.

4. Click Close.

Table 22-1		WordArt Tools
Tool	**Name**	**What It Does**
`⊖ Button (Curve) ▼`	Shape	Selects the shape for the WordArt.
`Arial ▼`	Font	Selects the font used to display the text.
`Best Fit ▼`	Size	Selects the font size.
`B`	Bold	Makes the text bold.
`I`	Italic	Makes the text italic.
`EE`	Even Height	Makes all characters the same height, whether they are uppercase or lowercase.
`◁`	Flip	Flips letters on their sides.
`↔`	Stretch	Stretches the text to fill the selected shape.
`▤`	Align	Displays a menu of alignment choices (Center, Left, Right, plus three types of justification).
`AV`	Spacing Between Characters	Displays a dialog box that lets you adjust character spacing.
`C`	Rotate	Displays a dialog box that lets you rotate the text.
`▨`	Shading	Selects a pattern or color for the text.
`▢`	Shadow	Selects one of several shadow types for the text.
`▣`	Border	Adjusts the thickness of the text outline.

Opening the WordArt dialog box

Secret

If you don't like the way WordArt takes over Word's menus and button bars, you can work with WordArt in a single dialog box that contains all of its controls. This dialog box is shown in Figure 22-5.

To summon this dialog box, first create a normal WordArt object by using the technique previously described. Then, click outside of the WordArt object to return to the document. Finally, right-click the object and choose the Open WordArt 2.0 command.

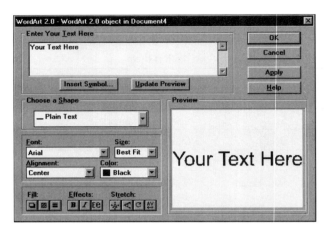

Figure 22-5: WordArt in a dialog box.

Equation Editor

Steven Hawking wrote in the preface to his book, *A Brief History of Time,* that his editor warned him that every mathematical equation he included in the book would cut the book's sales in half. So he included just one: the classic $e=mc^2$. See how easy that equation was to type? The only trick was remembering how to format the little *2* as a superscript.

I think the truth is that Hawking's editor didn't want to mess with more complicated equations. He probably didn't know about Word's Equation Editor program. With Equation Editor, you can create all sorts of complicated equations with relative ease. Figure 22-6 shows a whole covey of equations. I don't have a clue what any of them mean, but they sure were easy to create.

Equation Editor is a special version of a gee-whiz math program called MathType, from Design Science. Equation Editor is included with Word 95, PowerPoint 95, and Office 95. If you have PowerPoint and already know how to use its Equation Editor, you're in luck — they're identical.

Equation Editor has its own complete help system. After you're in Equation Editor, press F1 or use the Help command to call up complete information about using it.

$$\mu_{r,x} = Y_x \pm t_\alpha S_{y,x} \sqrt{\frac{1}{n} + \frac{(X - \overline{X})^2}{\sum X^2 - n\overline{X}^2}} \qquad \sigma_p = \sqrt{\frac{\pi(1-n)}{n}} \sqrt{\frac{N-n}{N-1}}$$

$$t = \frac{\overline{X}_A - \overline{X}_B}{\sqrt{\frac{(n_A - 1)s_A^2 + ((n_B - 1)s_B^2}{n_A + n_B - 2}} \sqrt{\frac{1}{n_A} + \frac{1}{n_B}}} \qquad f(x) = y = \sqrt[3]{\frac{x-1}{x^2 + 1}}$$

$$\sqrt{(x - h - c)^2 + (y - k)^2} = \left| h + \frac{c}{e^2} - x \right| e \qquad I = \frac{\sum \left(\frac{p_n}{p_0} \times 100 \right) v}{\sum v}$$

$$t = \frac{b}{\frac{s_{Y,X}}{\sqrt{\sum X^2 - n\overline{X}^2}}} \qquad d_1^* = -z_{\alpha/2} \sqrt{P_c(1 - P_c)\left(\frac{1}{n_A} + \frac{1}{n_B} \right)}$$

Figure 22-6: Equations run amok.

Creating an equation

To add an equation to a document, follow these steps:

1. Use the Insert⇨Object command. The Object dialog box will appear.

2. Choose Microsoft Equation 2.0 from the Object Type list and click OK. This step summons Equation Editor, which argues with Word for a few moments about who's really in charge. Then, it replaces Word's menus with its own and pops up a floating toolbar that's chock full of buttons for inserting mathematical symbols, as shown in Figure 22-7.

3. Start typing your equation. The variables and basic operators, such as plus and minus signs, are easy enough: just type them on the keyboard. But how do you get those fancy symbols, like square root and summation? The answer lies in the floating Equation toolbar.

4. To add a symbol that's not on the keyboard, use one of the buttons in the top row of the Equation toolbar. Each button yields a menu of symbols, most of which only Robert Oppenheimer could understand. There's nothing special about the tools in the top row of the Equation toolbar: they simply insert special characters into your equation. These symbol buttons are summarized in Table 22-2. The magic of Equation Editor lies in the template buttons found in the bottom row on the toolbar, summarized in Table 22-3. These template buttons let you build the parts of the equation that have elements stacked on top of one another, such as fractions, superscripts, and roots.

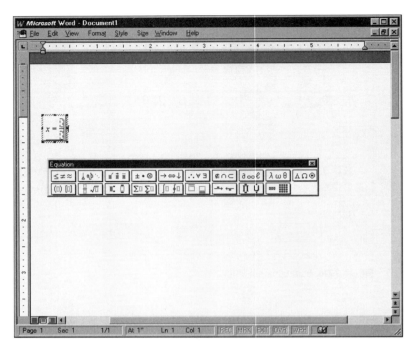

Figure 22-7: Creating an equation with the Equation Editor.

5. To add a stacked symbol, use one of the buttons in the bottom row of the Equation toolbar. Each button in the bottom row of the toolbar is attached to a menu of *templates,* which you use to create stacked symbols (not to be confused with document templates, which are altogether different). Most templates include a symbol and one or more *slots,* in which you type text or insert other symbols. Back in Figure 22-7, for example, I used a template to create a fraction. You can see that the fraction template consists of a horizontal stroke with a slot for the numerator above and the denominator below.

To complete this fraction, I can type a number in each slot. Or, I can add another symbol or template to make the equation more interesting. Most equations consist of templates nestled within the slots of other templates. The beauty of it is that Equation Editor adjusts the equation on-the-fly as you add text or other templates to fill a slot. If you type something like **ax**^{2} **+bx+c** in the top slot, for example, Equation Editor stretches the fraction bar accordingly.

To move from one template slot to the next, press the Tab key.

6. When you're finished, click anywhere outside the equation. Equation Editor bows out, enabling Word to restore its menus and toolbars. You can now drag the equation object to change its size or location.

Tip

Sometimes Equation Editor leaves droppings behind and obscures the clean appearance of the equation. When that happens, use the View➪Redraw command to clean up the equation.

Table 22-2: Equation Editor's Symbol Buttons

Button	*Symbols It Accesses*
≤ ≠ ≈	Greater-than-or-equal-to, less-than-or-equal-to, not-equal-to, equivalent signs, and other similar symbols.
∔ ab ⋱	Spacing symbols and various types of elipses.
▯′ ▯̂ ▯̈	Character embellishments, such as primes, hats, bars, and dots. (These items are often called diacriticals or accents.)
± • ⊗	A collection of standard math operators that aren't found on the keyboard.
→ ⇔ ↓	Various and sundry arrows.
∴ ∀ ∃	Logical operators.
∉ ∩ ⊂	Set theory symbols.
∂ ∞ ℓ	Miscellaneous symbols.
λ ω θ	Greek letters.
Λ Ω ⊛	More Greek letters.

Table 22-3: Equation Editor's Template Buttons

Button	*Templates It Accesses*
(▯) [▯]	Big parentheses, brackets, braces, and their ilk.
▯/▯ √▯	Templates for creating fractions and roots.
▯ ▯	Templates with little boxes above or below for superscripts and subscripts.
Σ▯ Σ▯	Summation templates for using that big Greek Fraternity Sigma thing.
∫▯ ∮▯	Integral templates. (I knew I should have paid more attention in Calculus class!)
▯ ▯	Templates with bars above or below.
→ ←	Arrows with templates above or below for text.
∏ ∐	Templates for working with sets.
▫▫▫ ▦	Matrices of templates.

Adding text to an equation

Equation Editor watches any text you type in an equation and does its best to figure out how the text should be formatted. If you type the letter **x**, for example, Equation Editor assumes that you intend for the x to be a variable, so the x is displayed in italics. If you type **cos**, Equation Editor assumes that you mean the cosine function, so the text is not italicized.

You can assign several different text styles to text in an equation:

- **Math:** The normal equation style. When you use the Math style, Equation Editor examines text as you type it and formats it accordingly by using the remaining style types.

- **Text:** Text that is not a mathematical symbol, function, variable, or number.

- **Function:** A mathematical function, such as sin, cos, or log.

- **Variable:** A letter that represents an equation variable, such as a, b, or x. Normally formatted as italic.

- **Greek:** Letters from the Greek alphabet that use the Symbol font.

- **Symbol:** Mathematical symbols, such as +, =, summation, integral, and so on. Based on the Symbol font.

- **Matrix-Vector:** Characters used in matrices or vectors.

You can change the text style by using the Style commands, but you should normally leave it set to Math. That way, Equation Editor can decide how each element of your equation should be formatted.

Tip

On occasion, Equation Editor's automatic formatting doesn't work. Type the word **cosmic**, for example, and Equation Editor assumes that you want to calculate the cosine of the product of the variables m, i, and c. When that happens, highlight the text that was incorrectly formatted and use the Style⇨Text command.

Note

Don't use the Spacebar to separate elements in an equation: let Equation Editor worry about how much space to leave between the variables and the plus signs. The only time you should use the Spacebar is when you're typing two or more words of text formatted with the Text style.

The Enter key has an interesting behavior in Equation Editor: It adds a new equation slot, immediately beneath the current slot. This key is sometimes a good way to create stacked items, but it's best to use an appropriate template instead.

Keyboard shortcuts for Equation Editor

Unlike most of the other OLE applications described in this chapter, Equation Editor is loaded with helpful keyboard shortcuts. You have my deepest sympathies if you are forced to use Equation Editor often enough to commit these keyboard shortcuts to memory, but just in case, they are listed in Table 22-4.

Table 22-4	Keyboard Shortcuts for Equation Editor
Keyboard Shortcut	*What It Does*
Navigating and editing keys	
Tab	Moves to the end of the current slot; if the insertion point is already at the end of the slot, moves to the beginning of the next slot.
Shift+Tab	Moves to the end of the preceding slot.
Ctrl+Tab	Inserts a tab character.
Ctrl+D	Redraws the equation.
Ctrl+Y	Selects all.
Ctrl+Shift+L	Left-align.
Ctrl+Shift+C	Center.
Ctrl+Shift+R	Right-align.
Applying styles	
Ctrl+Shift+=	Applies Math style.
Ctrl+Shift+E	Applies Text style.
Ctrl+Shift+F	Applies Function style.
Ctrl+Shift+I	Applies Variable style.
Ctrl+Shift+G	Applies Greek style.
Ctrl+Shift+B	Applies Matrix-Vector style.
Inserting symbols	
Ctrl+K, I	Infinity (∞).
Ctrl+K, A	Arrow ($\rightarrow$).
Ctrl+K, D	Derivative (δ).
Ctrl+K, <	Less than or equal to ($\leq$).
Ctrl+K, >	Greater than or equal to ($\geq$).
Ctrl+K, T	Times ($\times$).
Ctrl+K, E	Element of ($\in$).
Ctrl+K, Shift+E	Not an element of ($\notin$).
Ctrl+K, C	Contained in ($\subset$).
Ctrl+K, Shift+C	Not contained in ($\subseteq$).

(continued)

Table 22-4 (continued)

Keyboard Shortcut	What It Does
Inserting embellishments	
Ctrl+Shift+-(hyphen)	Overbar.
Ctrl+~	Tilde.
Ctrl+Alt+-(hyphen)	Arrow.
Ctrl+Alt+'	Single prime.
Ctrl+Alt+"	Double prime.
Ctrl+Alt+. (period)	Single dot.
Inserting templates	
Ctrl+9 or Ctrl+0	Parentheses.
Ctrl+[or Ctrl+]	Brackets.
Ctrl+{ or Ctrl+}	Braces.
Ctrl+F	Fraction.
Ctrl+/	Slash fraction.
Ctrl+H	Superscript (high).
Ctrl+L	Subscript (low).
Ctrl+J	Joint superscript/subscript.
Ctrl+I	Integral.
Ctrl+T, |	Absolute value.
Ctrl+R	Root.
Ctrl+T,N	Nth root.
Ctrl+T, S	Summation.
Ctrl+T, P	Product.
Ctrl+T, M	Matrix.
Ctrl+T, U	Underscript (limit).

Editing an equation in a window

Secret

For complex equations, it is often easier to edit the equation in a separate window, which isn't tied to Word's zoom factor. To do that, right-click an existing equation and choose the Open Equation command. A window such as the one shown in Figure 22-8 appears. When you are finished editing the equation, choose the File⇨Exit and Return command.

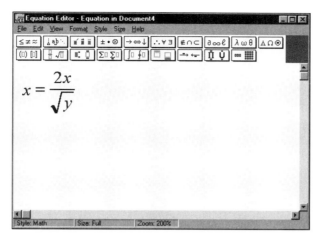

Figure 22-8: Editing an equation in a window.

Microsoft Graph

If you've never worked with a charting program, Microsoft Graph can be a little confusing. It takes a series of numbers and renders them as a graph. You can supply the numbers yourself, or you can copy them from an Excel or Lotus 1-2-3 worksheet. Microsoft Graph can create all kinds of different charts that range from simple bar charts and pie charts to exotic doughnut charts and radar charts. Very cool, but a little confusing for the uninitiated.

Microsoft Graph terms

This list shows some of the jargon you have to contend with when you're working with charts:

- **Chart or graph:** Same thing. These terms are used interchangeably. A chart or graph is nothing more than a bunch of numbers turned into a picture. After all, a picture is worth a thousand numbers.

- **Chart type:** Microsoft Graph supports several chart types: bar charts, column charts, pie charts, line charts, scatter charts, area charts, radar charts, Dunkin' Donut charts, and others. Different types of charts are better suited to displaying different types of data.

- **3-D chart:** Some chart types have a 3-D effect that gives them a jazzier look. Nothing special here; it's mostly a cosmetic effect.

- **Datasheet:** Supplies the underlying data for a chart. After all, a chart is nothing more than a bunch of numbers made into a picture. The numbers come from the datasheet. It works just like a spreadsheet program, so if you know how to use Excel or Lotus 1-2-3, learning how to use the datasheet takes you about 30 seconds. The datasheet is part of the chart object, but it doesn't appear in the document. Instead, the datasheet appears only when you edit the chart object.

■ **Series:** A collection of related numbers. For example, a graph of quarterly sales by region may have a series for each region. Each series has four sales totals, one for each quarter. Each series is usually represented by a row on the datasheet, but you can change the datasheet so that each column represents a series. Most chart types can plot more than one series. Pie charts can chart only one series at a time, however.

■ **Axes:** The lines on the edges of a chart. The X-axis is the line along the bottom of the chart; the Y-axis is the line along the left edge of the chart. The X-axis is usually used to indicate categories. Actual data values are plotted along the Y-axis. Microsoft Graph automatically provides labels for the X and Y axes, but you can change them.

■ **Legend:** A box used to identify the various series plotted on the graph. Microsoft Graph can create a legend automatically if you want one.

Microsoft Graph has its own help system. To see help information for Microsoft Graph, first call up Microsoft Graph by inserting a graph object or double-clicking an existing graph object. Then, press F1 or use the Help menu.

Inserting a chart

Use this procedure to add a chart to a document:

1. Position the insertion point at the location where you want to insert the graph.

2. Choose the Insert⇨Object, select Microsoft Graph 5.0 as the object type, and click OK.

   Either way, Microsoft Graph will come to life, creating a sample chart as shown in Figure 22-9.

3. Type your data in the datasheet. The sample data supplied by Microsoft Graph is interesting, but probably not the same numbers you need to plot.

4. Fiddle with the chart until it's just right by using the editing and formatting techniques described in the remainder of this section.

5. When the chart is just right, click outside it to return control to Word.

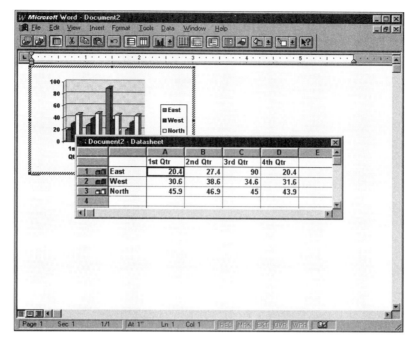

Figure 22-9: Microsoft Graph springs to life.

Finding the Insert Chart button

In Word 6.0, there was an Insert Chart button on the Standard toolbar. In order to make room for the new Insert Address button, the Insert Chart button was bumped from its traditional place on the Standard toolbar. You can, however, reinstate it by following these steps:

1. Choose the Tools⇨Customize command.

2. Click the Toolbars tab.

3. Select Insert from the Categories list.

4. Drag the Insert Chart button from the Customize dialog box onto the Standard toolbar and release it where you want it to appear.

5. Click Close to dismiss the Customize dialog box.

Working with the datasheet

The datasheet contains the numbers plotted in your Microsoft Graph chart and works like a simple spreadsheet program, with values stored in cells that are arranged in rows and columns. Like a spreadsheet, each column is assigned a letter, and each row is assigned a number. You can identify each cell in the datasheet, therefore, by combining the column letter and row number, as in A1 or B17. (Bingo!)

Ordinarily, each series of numbers is represented by a row in the spreadsheet. You can change this orientation so that each series is represented by a column by clicking the By Column button on the toolbar (shown in the margin) or by using the Data⇨Series in Columns command.

To flip back to row orientation, click the By Row button.

The first row and column in the datasheet are used for headings and are not assigned a letter or number.

If you have a large number of data values that you want to chart, you may want to increase the size of the datasheet window. Unfortunately, Microsoft forgot to put the Maximize button on the datasheet window, but you can still increase the size of the datasheet window by dragging any of its corners.

Tip

You can choose an entire column by clicking its column letter or you can choose an entire row by clicking its row number. You also can choose the entire datasheet by clicking the blank box in the top-left corner of the datasheet.

You can change the font used in the datasheet by using the Format⇨Font command. You also can change the numeric format with the Format⇨Number command. Changing the font and number format for the datasheet affects not only the way the datasheet is displayed but also the format of data value labels included in the chart.

Although the datasheet resembles a spreadsheet, you cannot use formulas or functions in a datasheet. If you want to use formulas or functions to calculate the values to be plotted, use a spreadsheet program, such as Excel, to create the spreadsheet and then import it into Microsoft Graph. (Or, create the chart in Excel rather than in Word and then import the Excel chart into the Word document by using the Insert⇨Object command or copy it into Word by way of the Clipboard, as described in Chapter 27.)

If the datasheet disappears, you can summon it again by clicking the Datasheet button on the toolbar (shown in the margin).

Changing the chart type

Microsoft Graph enables you to create 14 basic types of charts. Each type of chart conveys information with a different emphasis. Sales data plotted in a column chart may emphasize the relative performance of different regions, for example, and the same data plotted as a line chart may emphasize the increase or decrease in sales over time. The type of chart that's best for your data depends on the nature of the data and which aspects of it you want to emphasize.

Fortunately, Microsoft Graph doesn't force you to decide the final chart type up front. You can easily change the chart type at any time without changing the chart data. To change the chart type, double-click the chart to activate Microsoft Graph and summon the Format⇨Chart Type command. This will display the Chart Type dialog box, shown in Figures 22-10 and 22-11. From this dialog box, you can choose the chart type you want to use. The chart types are arranged in two groups: two-dimensional and three-dimensional. Figure 22-10 shows the 2-D types; Figure 22-11 shows the 3-D types. To switch from the 2-D group to the 3-D group, click the 3-D radio button.

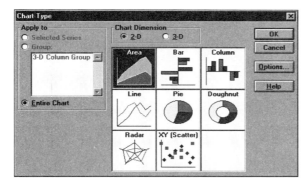

Figure 22-10: The Chart Type dialog box shows the 2-D chart types.

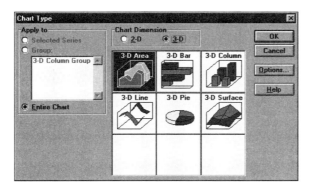

Figure 22-11: The Chart Type dialog box shows the 3-D chart types.

Select the chart type you want and click the Options button to choose the variation of the chart type. For example, Figure 22-12 shows the variants of the 3-D Bar chart type. Pick the variation you'd like to use and click OK.

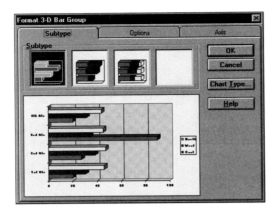

Figure 22-12: Picking the chart variant.

You can change the chart type another way by using the Chart Type button on Microsoft Graph's toolbar. When you click the down arrow next to the button, a palette of chart types appears, as shown in Figure 22-13. All 14 basic chart types are available from this menu, but if you want to choose a subtype, you must use the Format⇨Chart Type command.

Figure 22-13: The Chart Type button is a shortcut for assigning chart types.

One more way to change the chart type is to use an AutoFormat. See the section "Applying an AutoFormat" later in this chapter for more information.

Tip

If you choose one of the 3-D chart types, you can adjust the angle from which you view the chart by using the Format⇨3-D View command. Experiment with this one; it's kind of fun.

Adding chart titles

Microsoft Graph enables you to add two types of titles to your chart: a chart title, which describes the chart's contents, and axis titles, which explain the meaning of each chart axis. Most charts use two axes: the *value axis* and the *category axis*. Some 3-D chart types use a third axis called the *series axis*.

You can add titles via the Insert⬦Titles command, which summons the Titles dialog box shown in Figure 22-14.

Figure 22-14: The Titles dialog box.

This dialog box lets you create a chart title plus all three types of axis titles; just click the type of title you want to create and click OK. You can then click the title and type your own text, and you can move the title by dragging it with the mouse. You can also change the font by using the Format⬦Font command.

Naturally, the chart title should usually provide a title for the entire chart. The value axis title is sometimes handy for pointing out that sales are in thousands or millions or that the number of hamburgers served is in the billions. The category axis title is a good place to add a note, such as Sales by Quarter.

Tip

To remove a title, click it and press the Del key, or call up the Insert⬦Titles command again and uncheck the title you want to remove.

Adding a label

A *label* is the text that's attached to each data point plotted on the chart. You can tell Microsoft Graph to use the actual data value for the label or you can use the category heading for the label.

Use the Insert⬦Data Labels command to add labels. It displays the Data Labels dialog box, shown in Figure 22-15, which allows you to choose whether you want to create a label (from the headings in the data table) or use the actual data value for each point plotted on the chart. Depending on the chart type, you may also be able to show percentages.

Figure 22-15: The Data Labels dialog box.

To change the format used for the labels, choose a label and summon the Format⇨Selected Data Labels command. Then, set the pattern, font, number format, and alignment that you want. If a data label isn't positioned where you want it, move it by clicking it and then drag it to a new location. To remove labels, follow the steps in this section, but check None when the Data Labels dialog box appears. Or, click the label you want to remove and press the Del key.

Adding a legend

A *legend* explains the color scheme used in the chart. If you want a legend to appear in your chart, choose the Insert⇨Legend command. You can then move the legend around by dragging it with the mouse, and you can resize it by clicking on it and dragging one of its control handles if you think that Microsoft Graph made it too big or small or put it in the wrong spot.

To remove the legend, click it and press Del. To change the legend's format, click the legend and then use the Format⇨Selected Legend command.

Applying an AutoFormat

Microsoft Graph's AutoFormats are a combination of a chart type and other chart elements, such as legends, labels, fonts, and colors. Think of AutoFormats as templates for charts.

Tip

Each type of chart format is appropriate for a particular type of data. For example, if your data shows how expenses break down into various categories, use a pie chart. To show how sales have increased or decreased over time, use a column chart or a line chart. Use common sense to pick the chart type that's right for your data.

To apply an AutoFormat, just summon the Format⇨AutoFormat command. This will display the AutoFormat dialog box, shown in Figure 22-16. You can then choose the AutoFormat you want to use. The various formats are arranged in Galleries by chart type. First, choose the basic chart type from the Galleries list and then choose the format you want to use and click OK.

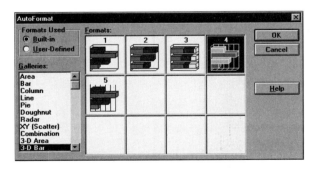

Figure 22-16: Applying an AutoFormat.

You can apply a different AutoFormat to a chart at any time. When you do, the chart type, color scheme, and other characteristics of the chart change, but the data remains the same.

Creating custom AutoFormats

In addition to the predefined AutoFormats that come with Microsoft Graph, you can create your own AutoFormats as well. These are called *user-defined* AutoFormats. To create a user-defined AutoFormat, you must first create a chart that contains all of the formatting you want applied when you select the AutoFormat. Then, use the Format⇨AutoFormat command to create a new user-defined AutoFormat by using the current chart as a model.

Follow these steps to create a user-defined AutoFormat based on the current chart:

1. Choose the Format⇨AutoFormat command.

2. Click the User-Defined option button.

3. Choose the Customize button. This will bring up the User-Defined AutoFormats dialog box, shown in Figure 22-17.

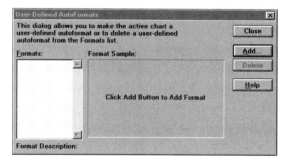

Figure 22-17: The User Defined AutoFormats dialog box.

4. Click the Add button. This will bring up the Add Custom AutoFormat dialog box, shown in Figure 22-18.

5. Type a short name and a description for the custom AutoFormat.

6. Click OK to return to the User Defined AutoFormats dialog box and click Close.

After you've created a custom AutoFormat, you can apply it by calling up the Format⇨AutoFormat command and choosing the User-Defined option. Any custom AutoFormats you have created will appear in the dialog box, as shown in Figure 22-19.

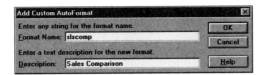

Figure 22-18: The Add Custom AutoFormat dialog box.

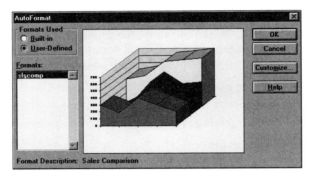

Figure 22-19: A User-defined AutoFormat.

Using the Chart Wizard

Secret

Microsoft Graph includes a Chart Wizard that steps you through the process of creating a simple chart. The only trouble with the Chart Wizard is that it's hard to find. It isn't really documented anywhere, and merely clicking on the Insert Chart button or choosing the Insert⇨Object command and selecting Microsoft Graph 5.0 as the object type won't call it up. There are, that I know of, only two ways to fire up the Chart Wizard:

- Copy the data for the datasheet from another source, such as an Excel spreadsheet or a Word table, by pressing Ctrl+C. Then, insert a Microsoft Graph 5.0 object by using the Insert⇨Object command or by clicking the Chart button. Then, use the Edit⇨Paste Special command to paste the copied data into the datasheet. Surprise! Here comes the Chart Wizard.

- The other method is to create the data to be charted in Word, either by using Word's table feature or simply by delimiting the numbers with tab characters. Then, select the data and click the Insert Chart button. Low and behold, the Chart Wizard once again makes an appearance!

Figure 22-20 shows the Chart Wizard in action. In this first exchange, the Chart Wizard asks you to select the chart type. Next, it asks for the specific format for the chart type you select. It then allows you to set the data series used to plot the chart and allows you to create titles.

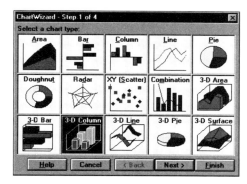

Figure 22-20: The Chart Wizard in action.

Part VII
Secrets of Working with Long Documents

23 Working with Outlines

24 Using Master Documents

25 Creating an Index, Table of Contents, or Other Table

26 Using Footnotes, Endnotes, and Cross-References

Chapter 23

Working with Outlines

In This Chapter

▶ Using Word's Outline feature to view an outline of your document, based on the document's headings

▶ Rearranging your document in Outline view by promoting or demoting headings, deleting whole sections of text, or copying and pasting portions of the outline

▶ Sorting an entire document into alphabetical order by headings

▶ Numbering the headings in a document

Some writers have a knack for creating outlines. They spend days polishing extensive outlines before they write a word. Their outlines are so good that they could write with their eyes closed once the outline is finished. Others jump right into to their writing with nary an outline to guide them. I fall somewhere in between. I spin a fairly decent outline up front, but I try not to be too compulsive about it. I rarely write with my eyes closed and usually revise the outline substantially as I go, sometimes beyond the point of recognition.

Word for Windows has a built-in Outline tool that's useful whether you're an outline fanatic or not. If you use Word to create reports, proposals, or other types of documents that have headings, subheadings, and a semblance of order, you owe it to yourself to learn the basics of working with outlines. I frequently pop back and forth between Normal view and Outline view to keep track of how my documents are evolving.

Understanding Outlines

The key to understanding Word's Outline feature is realizing that an outline is just another way of looking at a document. The Outline is not a separate entity from the document. Instead, when you switch to Outline view, Word takes the headings from your document and presents them in the form of an outline. Any changes you make to your document while in Outline view are automatically reflected in the document when you return to Normal view, and any changes you make in Normal view automatically appear when you switch to outline view. The reason is because Normal view and Outline view are merely two ways of displaying the contents of your document.

There are three ways to switch to outline view so you can see a document's outline:

■ Using the View⇨Outline command.

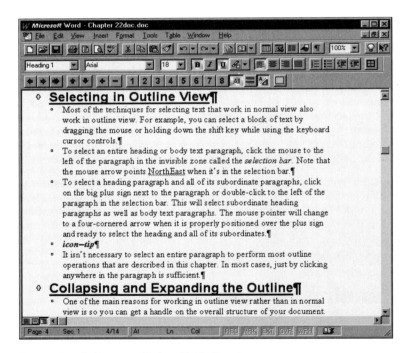

■ Clicking the Outline view button next to the horizontal scrollbar (shown in the margin), near the bottom- left corner of the document window. If you can't find this button, you may have disabled the horizontal scrollbar at the bottom of the window. To redisplay it, use the Tools⇨Options command, click the View tab, and check the Horizontal Scroll Bar box. Then, click OK.

■ Typing the keyboard shortcut Ctrl+Alt+O.

Figure 23-1 shows a document displayed in Outline view. As you can see, the outline consists of the headings and body text of the document. Any paragraph formatted with one of the built-in heading styles (Heading 1, Heading 2, Heading 3, and so on) is considered to be a heading; any other paragraph is considered body text.

Figure 23-1: A document displayed in Outline view.

Outline view isn't just for looking. You can continue to work on your document while in Outline view, typing new text or editing existing text just as you do in Normal view. You can also apply character formatting, such as bold or italic, and you can apply styles to paragraphs. However, you can't apply direct paragraph formats like indentation, tab stops, alignment, and so on. To do that, you must first return to Normal view.

Selecting in Outline View

Most of the techniques for selecting text that work in Normal view also work in Outline view. For example, you can select a block of text by dragging the mouse or holding down the Shift key while using the keyboard cursor controls.

To select an entire heading or body text paragraph, click the mouse to the left of the paragraph in the invisible zone called the *selection bar*. The mouse arrow points northeast when it's in the selection bar.

To select a heading paragraph and all of its subordinate paragraphs, click on the big plus sign next to the paragraph or double-click to the left of the paragraph in the selection bar. This will select subordinate heading paragraphs as well as body text paragraphs. The mouse pointer will change to a four-cornered arrow when it is properly positioned over the plus sign and ready to select the heading and all of its subordinates.

Tip Selecting an entire paragraph isn't necessary for performing most outline operations described in this chapter. In most cases, just clicking anywhere in the paragraph is sufficient.

Collapsing and Expanding the Outline

One of the main reasons for working in Outline view rather than in Normal view is so you can grasp the overall structure of your document. Looking back to Figure 23-1, you might be wondering how Outline view helps you do that. The secret lies in collapsing the outline so that the portions of your document you're not interested in are hidden from view. The following sections show you how to do that.

Collapsing and expanding body text

The first thing you'll want to do after switching to Outline view is to collapse all of the body text paragraphs. There are two ways to do that:

- Click on the All button in the Outlining toolbar.
- Type the keyboard shortcut Alt+Shift+A.

Either way, all of the body text paragraphs are temporally hidden from view so that you can focus on the structure of your document as represented by the document's heading paragraphs. Figure 23-2 shows a sample document after the body text paragraphs have been collapsed.

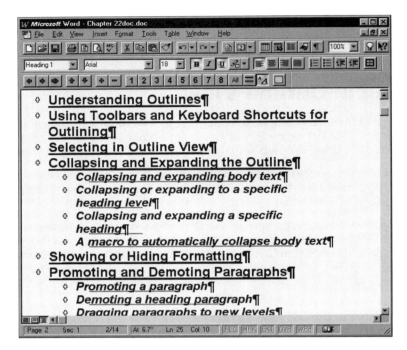

Figure 23-2: A document with body text collapsed.

Notice that some of the headings have fuzzy lines under them. These represent body text that has been collapsed. Also, each heading has either a large plus sign or minus sign next to it. Headings with plus sign, have other headings or body text subordinate to them; headings with minus signs do not. Body text paragraphs have a hollow square bullet next to them.

Collapsing or expanding to a specific heading level

1. The eight numbered buttons on the Outlining toolbar let you collapse or expand an outline to a specific heading level. For example, if you want to see just the top-level headings (paragraphs formatted with the Heading 1 style), click the Show Heading 1 button. Figure 23-3 shows what the document looks like collapsed to Heading 1.

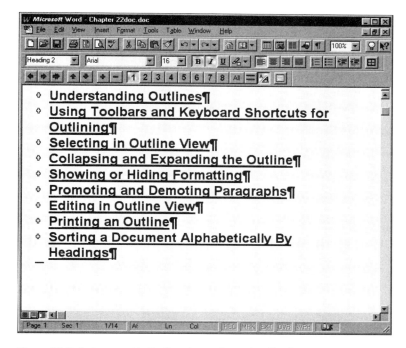

Figure 23-3: A document in Outline view collapsed to Heading 1.

Collapsing and expanding a specific heading

You can also selectively collapse or expand specific headings in Outline view so you can focus on specific portions of your document. For example, you might collapse the entire document down to Heading 1 and then expand just the specific heading where you want to work.

To collapse and expand a specific heading, select the heading you want to collapse and click the Collapse button. All of the subordinate heading and body text paragraphs text for the heading will be hidden temporarily.

To expand the heading again, click on the Expand button. The hidden paragraphs will reappear.

Another way to collapse a heading is to double-click on the big plus sign next to it. Double-click again to expand the heading.

Or, you can use the keyboard shortcuts:

Alt+Shift+Grey-minus	Collapse
Alt+Shift+Grey-plus	Expand

Both of these keyboard shortcuts use keys on the numeric keypad.

A macro to collapse body text automatically

Macro

I work with outlines all the time, and I almost always want to work with body text collapsed. Unfortunately, Word doesn't automatically collapse body text when you switch to Outline view. If you grow tired of always clicking the All button immediately after switching to Outline view, you can create a simple macro that will make the switch for you automatically.

Call up the Tools⇨Macro command, type **ViewOutline** in the Macro Name field, and click Create. Then, type the macro in as follows:

```
Sub MAIN
ViewOutline
ShowHeading9
End Sub
```

Once this macro is in place, it overrides the built-in ViewOutline command, which is invoked when you use the View⇨Outline command or press the Ctrl+Alt+O keyboard shortcut to switch to Outline view. Unfortunately, it does *not* work when you press the Outline View button located down at the bottom of the screen, next to the horizontal scrollbar.

However, there is another way to ensure that Outline view starts out with body text collapsed: by creating an AutoOpen macro. Whenever Word opens a document, it looks in the template attached to the document to see whether there is a macro named AutoOpen. If so, the AutoOpen macro runs. Create an AutoOpen macro that has these commands:

```
Sub MAIN
ViewOutline
ShowHeading9
ViewNormal
End Sub
```

Then, whenever you open a document, Word will momentarily switch to Outline view, collapse the body text, and return to Normal view. You should, however, keep a few caveats in mind:

■ Ordinarily, Word opens a document in the same view that it was in when you last saved it. With this AutoOpen macro in force, Word will always open the document in Normal view, even if it was in Outline or Page Layout view when you last saved it. (If you work more in Page Layout view rather than in Normal view, change the ViewNormal command to ViewPage.)

■ The AutoOpen macro will run only for documents that are attached to a template that contains the macro. If you place the AutoOpen macro in Normal.dot, it will always be available. However, if you open a document that is attached to some other template and that template already contains an AutoOpen macro, the other template's AutoOpen macro will run, not the one in AutoOpen. The bottom line is that if you place the AutoOpen macro in Normal.dot, it will usually run whenever you open a document, but you cannot guarantee that it will always run.

■ If your Normal.dot template already contains an AutoOpen macro, don't mess with it unless you created the AutoOpen macro yourself or you are an experienced WordBasic programmer.

Showing or Hiding Formatting

Collapsing body text from an outline gives you a bird's-eye view of a document's structure, but you can focus even more closely on structure if you remove the formatting associated with each heading style. This will usually allow Word to display more of the outline on the screen so that you can see more of your document's structure. The formatting isn't needed to distinguish among heading levels because indentation does that for you.

To hide formatting from an outline, click the Show Formatting button or press the gray slash key on the numeric keypad. Figure 23-4 shows what an outline looks like with formatting hidden.

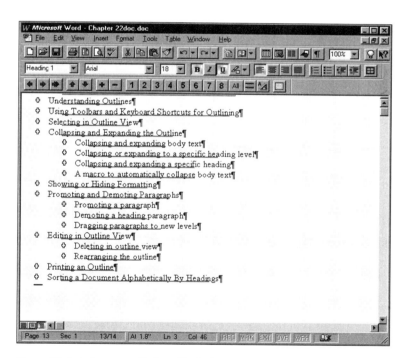

Figure 23-4: A document displayed in Outline view with formatting hidden.

To restore formatting, click the Show Formatting button or press the gray slash key again.

When you hide formatting, you're doing just that: hiding it. You're not actually removing it. After you click the Show Formatting button again or return to Normal view, the hidden formatting will be restored.

Promoting and Demoting Paragraphs

To *promote* a paragraph means to move it up one level in the outline. If you promote a Heading 2 paragraph, it becomes a Heading 1 paragraph. If you promote a body text paragraph, it becomes a heading paragraph at the same level as the heading where it is subordinate. Thus, if you promote a body text paragraph that follows a Heading 2 paragraph, the body text paragraph becomes a Heading 2 paragraph.

To *demote* a paragraph is just the opposite: the paragraph moves down one level in the outline. If you demote a Heading 1 paragraph, it becomes a Heading 2 paragraph. Demote it again and it becomes a Heading 3 paragraph. You cannot demote a body text paragraph, but you can demote any heading paragraph to a body text paragraph.

When you promote or demote heading paragraphs, the body text paragraphs that belong to the heading always go along for the ride. There's no need to worry about losing a heading's body text. Whether subordinate heading paragraphs are swept up in the move depends on how you handle the promotion or demotion.

Promoting a paragraph

To promote a paragraph, place the cursor anywhere in the paragraph and then do one of the following:

- Click the Promote button in the Outlining toolbar.
- Press Shift+Tab.
- Use the keyboard shortcut Alt+Shift+left arrow.

The paragraph moves up one level in the outline pecking order.

You cannot promote a Heading 1 paragraph because it is already at the highest level in the outline hierarchy. If you promote a body text paragraph, it assumes the heading level of the heading paragraph where it used to belong.

If you want to promote a heading paragraph and all of its subordinate heading paragraphs, click the big plus sign next to the paragraph or double-click in the invisible selection bar to the left of the paragraph. Then, promote it.

You can also promote paragraphs by dragging them with the mouse. See the section "Dragging paragraphs to new levels" later in this chapter.

Demoting a heading paragraph

To demote a heading paragraph, place the cursor anywhere in the paragraph and do one of the following:

- Click the Demote button in the Outlining toolbar.
- Press Tab.
- Use the keyboard shortcut Alt+Shift+right arrow.

The paragraph moves down one level in the outline pecking order. You cannot, however, demote a body text paragraph. It's already at the bottom of the rung.

To demote a heading paragraph and any heading paragraphs subordinate to it, click the paragraph's big plus sign or double-click in the hidden selection bar just left of the paragraph. Then, demote it.

You can also demote paragraphs by dragging them with the mouse. See the next section "Dragging paragraphs to new levels."

You can quickly demote a heading paragraph to body text by clicking on the Demote to Body Text button in the Outlining toolbar or by typing the keyboard shortcut Ctrl+Shift+N. (Recognize this shortcut? Demoting a paragraph to body text is accomplished by assigning the Normal style to it.)

Dragging paragraphs to new levels

When you move the mouse pointer over the big plus or minus sign next to a heading or body text paragraph, the pointer changes from a single arrow to a four-cornered arrow. This arrow is your signal that you can click the mouse to select the entire paragraph (and any subordinate paragraphs) and then use the mouse to promote or demote a paragraph along with all its subordinates.

To promote or demote with the mouse, follow these steps:

1. Point to the big plus or minus sign for the paragraph you want to promote or demote. When the mouse is in just the right spot, it will change to a four-cornered arrow.

2. Click and hold the down mouse button .

3. Drag the mouse to the right or left. The mouse pointer changes to a double-pointed arrow, and a vertical line appears that shows the indentation level of the selection. Release the button when the selection is indented the way you want. The text is automatically assigned the correct heading style.

The only limitation is that you cannot demote a heading to body text by using this technique. To demote a heading to body text, you must use the Demote to Body Text button or Ctrl+Shift+N.

Editing in Outline View

Outline view is a great place to do large-scale editing on your document, like rearranging or deleting whole sections of text. If you edit a document while body text is hidden, any edits you perform on a heading are automatically extended to the body text that belongs to them. Thus, if you delete a heading, you delete all of its body text, too. If you move a heading to a new location in the document, the body text is moved as well.

Deleting in Outline view

To delete large portions of your document quickly, switch to Outline view. Select the text you want to delete and press the Delete key. Here are three basic variations of this mass-deletion technique:

- Click the mouse in the hidden selection bar just to the left of a heading paragraph to select the entire paragraph. Then, press Delete. Any body text that belonged to the heading will be subsumed under the previous heading.

- Click on the big plus sign next to a heading paragraph to select it and all of its subordinate headings and body text. Press the Delete key to delete everything, headings and body text alike.

- Drag the mouse over a block of heading paragraphs to select them and press Delete to eliminate everything you selected.

Warning

Using the Delete key in Outline view is risky business, becuase it's easy to delete whole sections of text without realizing it. Don't use the Delete key in Outline view unless you're certain you know whether body text and subordinate paragraphs will be preserved. When in doubt, switch to Normal view and delete text the old-fashioned way. And, if you make a mistake, press Ctrl+Z to undo the errant delete.

Rearranging the outline

To rearrange your document on a large scale, switch to Outline view and move entire headings up or down in the outline. Remember, body text always travels with it's headings. Whether subordinate headings travel as well depends on whether you select them before moving things around.

You can move a single paragraph by clicking anywhere in the paragraph. To move a paragraph along with its subordinates, click the big plus sign next to it. Then, use one of the following techniques.

To move the selected paragraphs up, use one of the following techniques:

- Click the Up button on the Outlining toolbar.
- Press Alt+Shift+up arrow.
- Drag the text with the mouse.

To move the selected text down, use one of the following techniques:

- Click the Down button on the Outlining toolbar.
- Press Alt+Shift+down arrow.
- Drag the text with the mouse.

Printing an Outline

You can print an outline of your document by following this procedure:

1. Switch to Outline view.
2. Click the All button to hide body text.
3. Collapse or expand any other headings you want to include or exclude in the printout.
4. Click the Show Formatting button if you do not want the outline to include heading formats.
5. Click on the Print button in the Standard toolbar.

If you frequently print document outlines, consider creating a PrintOutline macro. Call up the Tools⇨Macro command, type **PrintOutline** in the Macro Name field, and type the macro in exactly as follows:

```
Sub MAIN
If Not ViewOutline() Then ViewOutline
ShowHeading9
FilePrintDefault
ViewNormal
End Sub
```

You can then assign this macro to a toolbar button, menu command, or keyboard shortcut. (One side effect of this macro is that it leaves you in Normal view regardless of what view you were in when you invoked the macro.)

Numbering the Headings in a Document

Word can automatically number the headings in a document to add a formal touch to your outline. To apply heading numbers, choose the Format⇨Heading Numbering command. This will bring up the Heading Numbering dialog box, as shown in Figure 23-5.

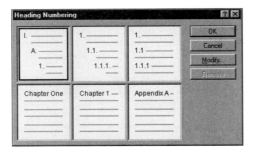

Figure 23-5: The Heading Numbering dialog box.

Pick the numbering scheme you'd like applied to the headings and click OK.

If you'd like to customize the numbering scheme, click the Modify button. This brings up the Modify Heading Numbering dialog box, shown in Figure 23-6. Here, you can change the numbering format that will be used for each heading level. First, set the Level control to the heading level whose number format you want to change. Then, use the other controls on the dialog box to set the format and position of the numbers. When you're done, click OK to return to the Heading Numbering dialog box. Click OK again to apply the heading numbers.

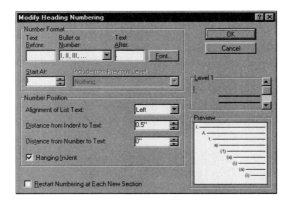

Figure 23-6: Customizing heading numbers.

Sorting a Document Alphabetically by Headings

If you are working on a document with headings that should appear in alphabetical order, Outline view can be a real time-saver. The following procedure will sort an entire document into alphabetical order based on the Heading 1 paragraphs. All body text and Heading 2 and lower headings will travel along with their Heading 1 paragraph when sorted.

1. Use the View⇨Outline command or click the Outline View button to switch to Outline view.

2. Click the Show Heading 1 button to collapse the entire outline so that only Heading 1 paragraphs are shown.

3. Press Ctrl+A to select the entire document.

4. Choose the Table⇨Sort Text command. When the Sort Text dialog box appears, click OK.

5. Click the Normal View button to return to Normal view.

Using Toolbars and Keyboard Shortcuts for Outlining

When you switch to Outline view, an extra toolbar appears on-screen, replacing the ruler (which isn't needed in Outline view). This toolbar contains buttons for performing routine outlining tasks. In addition, several new keyboard shortcuts become available for working with outlines. Table 23-1 summarizes the toolbar buttons, and Table 23-2 summarizes the keyboard shortcuts.

Table 23-1	Tools for Outline View
Toolbar button	*What It Does*
	Promotes the selection to the next higher level.
	Demotes the selection to the next lower level.
	Makes the selection body text.
	Moves the selection up.
	Moves the selection down.
	Expands the selection.
	Collapses the selection.
	Expands or collapses to heading level 1.

(continued)

Table 23-1 *(continued)*

Toolbar button	What It Does
2	Expands or collapses to heading level 2.
3	Expands or collapses to heading level 3.
4	Expands or collapses to heading level 4.
5	Expands or collapses to heading level 5.
6	Expands or collapses to heading level 6.
7	Expands or collapses to heading level 7.
8	Expands or collapses to heading level 8.
All	Shows all headings and body text.
≡	Shows only the first line of body text.
ªA	Shows or hides formatting.
▢	Switches to master document view.

Table 23-2   **Keyboard Shortcuts for Outline View.**

Keyboard Shortcut	What It Does
Ctrl+Alt+O	Switches to Outline View.
Ctrl+Alt+N	Switches back to Normal view.
Alt+Shift+A	Collapses or expands all text.
Alt+Shift+Grey-minus	Collapses the selection.
Alt+Shift+Grey-plus	Expands the selection.
Alt+Shift+1	Collapses/expands to heading level 1.
Alt+Shift+(number)	Collapses/expands to specified heading level.
/ (on numeric keypad)	Hides/shows formatting
Shift-Tab	Promotes the selection.
Alt+Shift+right arrow	Promotes the selection.
Tab	Demotes the selection.
Alt+Shift+right arrow	Demotes the selection.
Ctrl+Shift+N	Demotes to body text by applying Normal style.
Alt+Shift+up arrow	Moves the selection up.
Alt+Shift+down arrow	Moves the selection down.

Chapter 24

Using Master Documents

In This Chapter

▶ Understanding how master documents let you piece together a large publication from many separate Word document files

▶ Creating the master document and the subdocuments

▶ Editing a subdocument

▶ Working with headers and footers in subdocuments

▶ Some tips for avoiding the most common pitfalls of working with master documents

Suppose that you've accepted the dubious honor of moderating the annual Village Idiot Convention and one of your responsibilities is to assemble a little 1,200-page book titled *Proceedings of the 1996 Village Idiot Convention.* Notable idiots from villages throughout the country will be presenting papers on all aspects of village idiocy, and your job is to assemble them all into one huge book. Fortunately, the Village Idiot Association (VIA) has recently settled on Word for Windows 95 as its official word processor, so each idiot of note will be sending you a document on disk. All you have to do is combine all the papers into a single document and print it out.

You have finally found an ideal job for Word's Master Document feature. It lets you create long documents by piecing them together from small documents. It's all very confusing and is worth figuring out only if you have to do this sort of thing often. And, as you will discover, it always has been (and probably always will be) one of Word's more poorly implemented features, with more than a few bugs. Pesky enough, in fact, to give you pause: perhaps a better way to produce the *1996 Village Idiot* proceedings would be with a real desktop publishing program, such as PageMaker or Corel Ventura.

Note Don't mess with Word's Master Document feature until you have mastered working in Outline view. As you will see, the Master Document feature is handled as an advanced form of outlining. If outlining isn't your cup of tea, go back to Chapter 23 before continuing.

Understanding Master Documents

A *master document* is a document that contains special links to other documents, which are called *subdocuments*. For example, if you were putting together a book that consisted of 30 chapters, you probably wouldn't want to put the whole book into one document. Instead, you'd create a separate document for each chapter. That's all well and good, but what happens when you want to print the whole thing out with page numbers that start at page 1 and run through the end of the book, rather than restarting at 1 at the start of each chapter? Or, what if you want to print a table of contents for the entire book or create an index?

Master documents are designed for just such situations. With a master document, you create each chapter as a separate document. Then, you create a master document for the entire book. In this master document, you create links to each of the chapter subdocuments. Then, you can print out the entire book and Word will take care of numbering the pages for you. You can also create a table of contents or index in the master document, and the page numbers will all be correct.

An entirely separate view is devoted to working with master documents. Master Document view is a variation of Outline view, except that the portions of the master document that are actually subdocuments are indicated by little icons. You can double-click on one of these icons to open a subdocument in a separate window to edit it.

Use Master Document view mostly when you want to create a new master document, when you want to change the order in which individual subdocuments appear in the master document, or when you want to add or remove subdocuments. If all you want to do is edit one of the individual chapters in your book, you just open the chapter document as you normally would, without even worrying about its being a subdocument in a master document.

If you open a master document and switch to Normal view or Page Layout view, Word treats the master document and all the subdocuments as if they were actually a part of one large document. For example, you could scroll through the master document all the way to Chapter 12 and start typing, you could use the File⇨Print command to print the entire book, or you could use the Edit⇨Replace command to replace all occurrences of "WordPerfect" with "Word for Windows" throughout the entire document.

There are three ways to assemble a master document:

- If you know that you need a master document beforehand, you can create the master document and all the subdocuments from scratch. This will result in a master document and a collection of empty subdocuments, which you can then call up and edit as you see fit. See the section "Creating a Master Document from Scratch," later in this chapter.

- If you work partway into a project and realize the document is too long, you can break the document into several subdocuments. See the section "How Word Decides Where to Break the Subdocuments," later in this chapter.

- If you already have a bunch of Word documents that you want to assemble into a master document, you can create a master document by using these existing documents as the subdocuments. See the section "Inserting Existing Files into a Master Document," later in this chapter.

Within the master document, each subdocument is contained within its own section. Thus, each subdocument can have its own page layout, headings, column arrangement, and all of the other page formats that apply at the section level.

The Master Document Toolbar

You can switch between Outline view and Master Document view by clicking on the Master Document view button in the Outline toolbar. When you switch to Master Document view, a small toolbar of specialized master document buttons appears next to the Outline toolbar. The function of each of these buttons is summarized in Table 24-1.

Table 24-1	Buttons on the Master Document Toolbar
Button	*What It Does*
	Breaks the selected text into subdocuments by using heading styles to determine where to start each subdocument.
	Copies the contents of a subdocument into the master document and breaks the link to the subdocument file.
	Inserts an existing file as a subdocument.
	Combines two subdocument files into one subdocument file.
	Splits a subdocument into two subdocuments.
	Locks or unlocks a subdocument.

The function of each of these buttons is more fully described in the sections that follow.

Creating a Master Document from Scratch

If none of the documents that you want to combine by using a master document have been created yet, the best way to start is to create the master document and all of its subdocuments all at once. Then, you can call up each subdocument individually to fill in the missing chapters of your book.

Here's the procedure for creating a master document and its subdocuments from scratch:

1. Choose the File⇨New command and start a new document.

2. Choose the View⇨Master Document command to switch to Master Document view.

3. Type the title of the master document and format it as a Heading 1 paragraph. For example, if you're creating a book, type the book's title as a Heading 1 paragraph.

4. Create a Heading 2 paragraph for each subdocument that you want to create. For example, if each subdocument represents a chapter, type the chapter titles as Heading 2 paragraphs.

   Figure 24-1 shows an example of a master document with a Heading 1 paragraph for the master document title and a Heading 2 paragraph for each subdocument title.

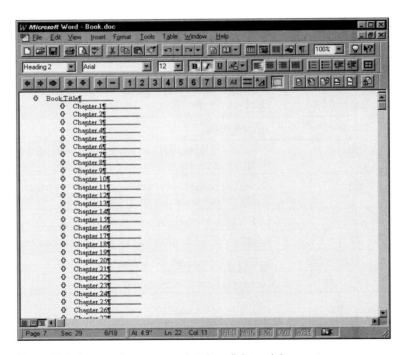

Figure 24-1: A master document, ready to be split into subdocuments.

5. Select the Heading 2 paragraphs. Drag the mouse or hold down the Shift key while moving the cursor with the arrow keys.

6. Click the Create Subdocument button in the Master Document toolbar. Clicking this button tells Word to bust up the selected heading paragraphs into smaller subdocuments, kind of like the Justice Department keeps threatening to do to Microsoft.

Figure 24-2 shows a document that's been busted up. Notice how Word draws a box around each subdocument and adds a little subdocument icon in the top-left corner of the box.

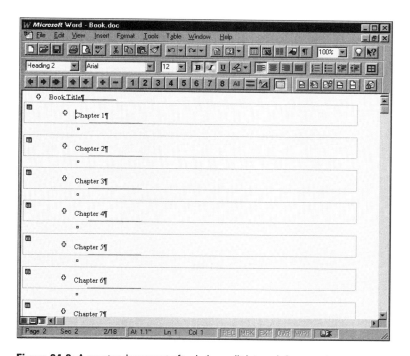

Figure 24-2: A master document after being split into subdocuments.

7. Use the File⊃Save command to save the files. You'll have to provide the name and location of the master document. Word will make up names for all the subdocuments, based on the heading paragraphs.

Once you've created subdocuments, you can edit a subdocument by double-clicking on the little subdocument icon next to the subdocument heading. This opens the subdocument in a separate document window and leaves the master document open in its own window, too. When you're done editing the subdocument, save it and close the window to return to the master document window.

How Word Decides Where to Break the Subdocuments

You don't *have* to use the Heading 1 style for the master document title and Heading 2 for the subdocument titles, but it makes sense to do so. Word examines the text you selected before clicking the Create Subdocument button to find the first heading paragraph. Then, it creates a separate subdocument for each paragraph in the selected text that's formatted with the same heading style as the first heading.

Confused? You're in good company. It took me awhile to figure this out. If the first heading paragraph is formatted with the Heading 3 style, Word creates a separate subdocument for each Heading 3 paragraph. All of the body text and heading paragraphs between one Heading 3 paragraph and the next Heading 3 paragraph will be placed in a subdocument — even it this includes a Heading 2 or Heading 1 paragraph.

Most of the time, using Heading 1 for the master document title and Heading 2 for each subdocument title makes perfect sense.

The subdocuments aren't actually saved as separate document files until you use the File⇨Save command to save the master document. Then, all of the subdocuments are automatically saved in the same folder as the master document.

Inserting Existing Files into a Master Document

If you have already collected a bunch of files that you want to combine together into a larger publication, you can plug each file into a master document as a subdocument. Then, you can create a table of contents or an index for the whole publication, or print the publication with uninterrupted page numbers.

Here is the procedure for creating a master document from a collection of separate subdocuments:

1. In Windows, gather up all of the documents in a folder created just for the master document. This isn't strictly necessary, but life will be simpler all the way around if the master document and all it subdocuments have a folder they can call their own.

2. In Word, choose the File⇨New command or click the New button.

3. Choose the View⇨Master Document command to switch to Master Document view.

 4. Click on the Insert Subdocument button in the Master Document toolbar to bring up the Insert Subdocument dialog box, shown in Figure 24-3.

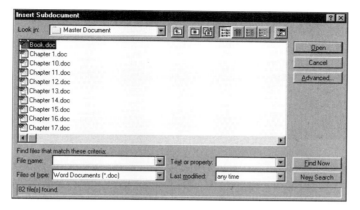

Figure 24-3: The Insert Subdocument dialog box.

5. Locate the file you want to insert as a subdocument, select it, and click Open. The file will be inserted into the master document as a subdocument. Section breaks will be created before and after it.

6. Repeat Steps 4 and 5 for any other subdocuments you want to insert.

7. Use the Save command to save the master document.

Remember that the contents of the subdocument file are not actually copied into the master document. Instead, a link to the subdocument file is created so that whenever you open the master document, the subdocument file is accessed as well. You can still open the subdocument file separately, apart from the master document.

Tip

When you click the Insert Subdocument button, the subdocument will be inserted at the position of the insertion point. Make sure that the insertion point is either at the start or end of the master document or between two previously inserted subdocuments. If the insertion point is within a subdocument when you click the Insert Subdocument button, the subdocument you select will be inserted within the subdocument, not within the master document. If you're not careful, you can end up with subdocuments within subdocuments within subdocuments.

Opening a Subdocument

There are two ways to open a subdocument:

■ You can first open the master document and double-click on the subdocument icon. Word opens the subdocument in a separate window. When you close the document, you will return to the master document.

■ Alternatively, you can ignore the master document and open the subdocument file the way you would open any other Word document by using the File⇨ Open command or by clicking on the Open button in the Standard toolbar.

Removing a Subdocument

You can remove a subdocument but keep its text in the master document by clicking on the subdocument icon and clicking the Remove Subdocument button.

If you want to remove a subdocument and delete its text, click the subdocument icon and press Delete.

Merging and Splitting a Subdocument

Suppose that you create a master document and several subdocuments and decide that you don't like the way the subdocuments are packaged. You discover that two adjacent small subdocuments should be combined into a single larger subdocument, and one large subdocument should be split into two smaller subdocuments.

No problem, that's what the Merge and Split Subdocument buttons do.

To combine two adjacent subdocuments into one, follow these steps:

1. Select both subdocuments by clicking on the first subdocument's subdocument icon and holding down the Shift key while clicking the second's subdocument icon.

2. Click the Merge Subdocument button.

3. Choose the File⇨Save command to save the master document and the newly combined subdocuments.

To split a subdocument into two parts, follow these steps:

1. Place the insertion point at the location where you want the subdocument split.

2. Click the Split Subdocument button.

3. Choose the File⇨Save command to save the new subdocuments.

Headers and Footers in Master Documents

One of the more confusing aspects of how master documents and subdocuments work is the way headers and footers are handled. Because each subdocument is housed within its own section within the master document, each subdocument can have its own headers and footers. However, here's the catch: Word must encounter a section break *within the subdocument* in order for a subdocument's headers to "catch." If the subdocument doesn't contain a section break, any headers or footers set up for the subdocument will be ignored. Instead, the headers and footers that were in effect in the master document just before the section break that marks the subdocument are used.

This makes it easy to assemble a group of documents and provide for continuous page numbering through the documents. If none of the subdocuments contain section breaks, you can create a header or footer in the master document. Then, any page numbers that appear in the master document header or footer will be numbered continuously from the start of the master document to the end.

If you want to have a special header or footer for each subdocument, all you have to do is begin the subdocument with a section break. To start the subdocument at the top of a page, specify Next Page for the section break. Otherwise, insert a continuous section break. Then, create a custom header or footer in the subdocument.

If you want the master document to resume with its original headers or footers after a subdocument with a custom header or footer, copy the master document's header from before the subdocument and paste it into the header in the section following the subdocument.

Tip

Another way to make each subdocument start on a new page is to add the Page Break Before option to the Heading 2 style's Paragraph format or whatever style you use for the title of each subdocument. (The Page Break Before option is found on the Text Flow tab of the Format⇨Paragraph command.) Or, you can press Ctrl+Enter or use the Insert⇨Break command to create a page break at the beginning of each subdocument.

Using Master Documents on a Network

Microsoft recognizes that one of the main reasons for using master documents is so different users can work on individual components of a project. As a result, the master document feature includes some rudimentary provisions for sharing master documents and subdocuments across a network.

Word keeps track of who owns the master document and each of its subdocuments based on the Author Name field of the documents' properties. When you open a master document, you are automatically allowed to open and edit any of the subdocuments that you created. However, you are granted only read-only access to subdocuments that someone else created. Before you can edit a subdocument that someone else created, you must unlock it by clicking the Lock/Unlock button in the Master Document toolbar.

Warning

The Lock/Unlock button is *not* designed as a robust security mechanism. No passwords or other validation is required to unlock a subdocument. Any user who can open the master document can click the Unlock button and open any of the subdocuments. The locking mechanism is provided only as a convenience to prevent users from inadvertently opening and editing documents that other users created.

Tip

For true security control, use the password protection that was described in Chapter 8.

Secrets of Avoiding Trouble with Master Documents

Word's Master Document feature sounds like a good idea, but it is complicated enough that you can easily spend more time fiddling with it than it is worth. While I can't make the master document's feature any easier to use or less error prone, I can offer some general advice that should go a long way toward avoiding the most common pitfalls of master documents.

- Store the master document and all subdocuments in a common folder set aside for the project. Word will let you scatter subdocuments around different folders and network drives, but master documents will be much easier to control if everything is kept in one place.

- If possible, use the same template for the master documents and all of the subdocuments. This will eliminate the problems that occur when a subdocument's template contains styles, macros, and autotext entries that conflict with styles, macros, and autotext entries in the master document's template.

- Do not move any of the subdocuments to another folder or drive. The master document keeps track of the location of each subdocument. If you move a subdocument, the master document won't be able to find it. If you must move a subdocument, do so by opening the master document, opening the subdocument, and using the Save As command to save the subdocument to its new location.

Word 6 had a nasty bug that effectively limited the number of subdocuments you could use to about 20. With Word for Windows 95, this limitation has been removed. However, you should still be cautious when creating master documents with more than 20 subdocuments, especially if a Word 6 user might use the document.

- Word will not AutoSave master documents. As a result, get in the habit of pressing Ctrl+S frequently when working with master documents. (It's a good habit anyway.)

Chapter 25

Creating an Index, Table of Contents, or Other Table

In This Chapter

▶ How to create a table of contents by using styles, a process that is nearly automatic.

▶ How to use field codes, which are more difficult to use than styles but which provide greater flexibility. (A macro is provided to ease the pain of using field codes to generate a table of contents.)

▶ How to create other types of tables, such as tables of figures, tables, equations, and a table of authorities for legal documents.

▶ How to create an index.

O nce upon a time, the preferred method of creating a table of contents for a book, manual, or other long document was a two-step affair. First, you created the table of contents, leaving blanks or X's where the page numbers would eventually go. Then, once the pages of the document were in their final form, you would browse through the entire document, make a list of the page numbers for each chapter, and add the page numbers to the table of contents.

Now, assuming that you format your document properly, creating a table of contents is a matter of clicking the mouse a few times. Word takes care of the drudgery of counting pages and even adjusts the table of contents for you if you make changes to the document that affect page numbers in the table.

This chapter shows you all the ins and outs of making a table of contents. It also shows you how to create a table of figures and a table of authorities, which is often used in legal documents.

Note

The term *table of contents* is a bit cumbersome to use over and over again throughout this chapter. Being a bit of a computer nerd myself, I kind of like using TLAs (Three Letter Acronyms). So I'll frequently use the TLA *TOC* to stand for *table of contents* in this chapter, if for no other reason than to save paper.

Formatting Your Document to Make a Table of Contents Easy to Create

Like many other Word features, the Table of Contents feature depends on the proper use of styles for care-free operation. The Table of Contents feature assumes that you will be using the built-in heading styles (Heading 1, Heading 2, etc.) to identify your heading paragraphs. To compile a TOC, Word simply searches through the documents looking for heading paragraphs identified by the heading styles.

Make sure that you use Heading styles to format your document's headings if you plan on creating a TOC, especially for the headings you want to appear in the TOC. Of course, you should do this anyway: it helps you format all your headings consistently, and it lets you take advantage of Word's Outline view.

Word provides three shortcut keys for applying heading styles:

- Ctrl+Alt+1   Heading 1
- Ctrl+Alt+2   Heading 2
- Ctrl+Alt+3   Heading 3

If you routinely use additional heading styles for more heading levels, you can assign those styles to keyboard shortcuts such as Ctrl+Alt+4, Ctrl+Alt+5, and so on by using the Tools⇨Customize command or the Format⇨Style command.

Tip

If you want, you can tell Word to use different styles to create a TOC. For example, you might format chapter titles with a style named "Chapter Title." Then, you can tell Word to include paragraphs formatted with the Chapter Title style in the TOC. This is a very important technique because it allows you to use the built-in heading styles more freely. For more information, see the section "Using Other Styles to Create a Table of Contents," later in this chapter.

Creating a Table of Contents

Assuming that you flagged all your headings by using built-in heading styles, creating a TOC is a snap. Start by placing the insertion point at the place in the document where you want the table of contents to appear. Usually, the TOC appears on its own page near the beginning of a document. Press Ctrl+Enter to create a new page if necessary and click the mouse to position the insertion point in the empty page.

You may want to add a heading such as "Contents" or "Table of Contents" at the top of the page. Format this however you want, but don't use one of the heading styles unless you want the TOC to include the page number of the table of contents.

Next, choose the Insert⇨Index and Tables command and click the Table of Contents tab. The dialog box shown in Figure 25-1 will appear.

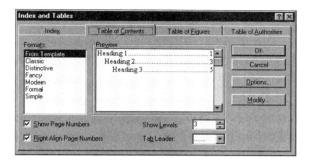

Figure 25-1: The Index and Tables dialog box (Table of Contents tab).

The Index and Tables dialog box lets you select one of several styles for the Table of Contents in the Formats field: Classic, Distinctive, Fancy, Modern, Formal, and Simple. If you'd rather design your own style, select the From Template option in the Formats field. This formats the TOC by using the built-in TOC styles, which you can modify any way you want. See the section "Creating Custom TOC Styles" later in this chapter for more information.

Four options are available to help you fine-tune the appearance of the TOC:

- **Show Page Numbers:** Uncheck this box if you want the TOC to show the document's outline but not page numbers.

- **Right Align Page Numbers:** If this box is checked, page numbers will be aligned by using a right-aligned tab. Uncheck this box if you want the page numbers to be placed next to the corresponding text rather than at the right margin.

- **Show Levels:** Use this field to include more or less detail in the table. It indicates how many heading levels should be included.

- **Tab Leader:** This field allows you to change or remove the dotted line that connects each TOC entry to its page number.

After you have set the options for the TOC, click OK and Word will insert the table of contents into your document.

Note

Word uses field codes to create tables of contents. If your TOC looks like {TOC \o "1-3" \p " "}, call up the Tools⇨Options command, click the View button, and uncheck the Field Codes check box. Click OK and the table should appear as it should. (You can also right-click the table of contents or its field code, whichever appears, and choose the Toggle Field Codes command from the shortcut menu that appears.)

To delete a TOC, select the entire table or its field code — whichever is visible — and press the Delete key. Or, press Ctrl+Z immediately after creating the table.

Using Other Styles to Create a TOC

Using the standard heading styles to create a table of contents is convenient but not always exactly what you want to do. For example, what if you've created a document that consists of several chapters, and you've marked the title of each chapter with a style named "Chapter Title"? Fortunately, Word lets you create a TOC based on paragraphs formatted with any style you want, not just the standard heading styles.

To create a TOC by using styles other than the standard heading styles, follow this procedure: call up the Insert⇨Index and Tables command and click the Table of Contents tab. Then, click the Options button to call up the Table of Contents Options dialog box, shown in Figure 25-2. This dialog box lists all of the styles available in the document and lets you assign a TOC Level to each style.

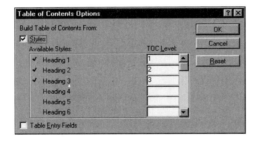

Figure 25-2: The Table of Contents Options dialog box.

Adjust the TOC Level fields to specify the styles you want to use for creating the table of contents. Initially, the TOC Level fields are set to include standard heading styles based on the number of levels you indicated for the TOC in the Show Levels field. To exclude a style from the TOC, select the style's TOC Level field and delete the number in the field. To add a style to the TOC, select the style's TOC Level field and type a number.

Tip

If you plan on excluding the standard heading levels from your TOC, set the Show Levels field to 1 before calling up the Table of Contents Options dialog box. Then, you'll only have to clear the TOC Level field for the Heading 1 style.

You can set up the TOC so that several styles appear at the same level. For example, suppose that you want paragraphs formatted with the Chapter Title, Preface Title, Foreword Title, and Appendix Title styles all included in the TOC at the top level. No problem. Just type **1** in the TOC Level field for each of these styles.

Creating Custom TOC Styles

The entries in a TOC are formatted with a set of standard styles named TOC 1, TOC 2, TOC 3, and so on. If you don't like any of the predefined formats listed in the Formats list, select "Custom Style" and click the Modify button. This will take you to a special version of the Style dialog box, which lists only the standard TOC styles, shown in Figure 25-3.

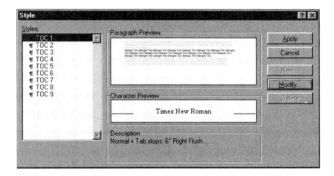

Figure 25-3: Modifying the standard TOC styles.

You can use this dialog box to change the appearance of the Custom Style Table of Contents format by modifying the various TOC styles. For more information about modifying styles, refer to Chapter 18.

Creating a TOC by Using Field Codes

Because of styles, compiling a table of contents in Word is as easy as pie — well, as easy as popping a frozen pie into the oven, anyway. The TOC equivalent of baking a pie from scratch is using fields rather than styles to create the TOC. The only real reason to do this is if you want the text that appears in the TOC to vary slightly from the document text on which the TOC is based. For example, you might want to add "Chapter 1" in front of the title for chapter 1. (Quite frankly, creating a TOC by using field codes is so much harder than using styles that I wouldn't bother, even if I wanted to modify the text in the TOC. Instead, I'd just create the TOC by using styles and type whatever changes I wanted to make directly in the TOC.)

To create a TOC from fields, you must first insert special fields which use the TC field code throughout your document, wherever you want a TOC entry created. Start by placing the insertion point where you want to insert the TC field and call up the Insert⇨Field command. The Insert Field dialog box will appear, as shown in Figure 25-4.

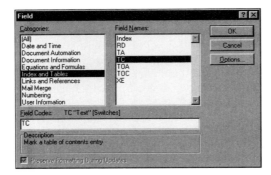

Figure 25-4: The Insert Field dialog box.

Select "Index and Tables" in the Categories list and select "TC" from the field Names list. Type the text you want included in the TOC in quotes immediately after the TC field code, in the Field Codes field. For example:

```
TC "Chapter 1 I Am Born"
```

Then, click OK. The field will be inserted into the document at the cursor location. It should look something like this:

```
{ TC "Chapter 1 I Am Born" }
```

It will be formatted as hidden text, so you may not be able to see it. If you can't, call up the Tools⇨Options command, click on the View tab, check the Hidden Text check box, and click OK.

After you insert all the TC fields, you create the TOC by using the Insert⇨Index and Tables command, same as when you base the TOC on styles. Click the Options button and check the Table Entry Fields check box in the Table of Contents Options dialog box. Click OK to return to the Table of Contents dialog box and click OK again to compile the table.

Secret

You can create a table of contents that is based on both styles *and* field codes. Just check both the Styles and Table Entry Field codes check boxes.

A Macro for Inserting TOC Field Codes

If you're going to create a Table of Contents by using field codes, please don't torture yourself with the Insert⇨Field command. Instead, use the Tools⇨Macro command to create a macro named MarkTOC, as follows:

```
Sub MAIN

On Error Goto UserBail

Begin Dialog UserDialog 352,
148, "Mark TOC Entry"

    CancelButton 242, 105, 88,
21

    OKButton 242, 69, 88, 21

    Text 18, 18, 79, 13, "TOC
Text:", .Text1

    TextBox 18, 34, 307, 18,
.TocText

    Text 18, 73, 73, 13, "Iden-
tifier:", .Text2

    TextBox 115, 72, 65, 18,
.Ident

    Text 18, 107, 53, 13,
"Level: ", .Text3

    TextBox 115, 107, 65, 18,
.Level

End Dialog

Dim dlg As UserDialog

If SelType() = 2 Then
dlg.TocText = Selection$()

dlg.Level = "1"

Dialog dlg

SelType 1
```

```
MarkTableOfContentsEntry .En-
try = dlg.TocText, .Level =
dlg.Level, .TableId = dlg.Ident

UserBail:

End Sub
```

Then, when you run the macro, the following dialog box will be displayed:

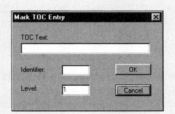

You can type in the text you want to appear in the TOC entry, or you can select the text before you run the macro, and the selected text will appear in the TOC Text field. When you click OK, a TC field code will automatically be inserted at the location of the insertion point.

If you want to use field codes to create more than one table of contents in the same document, you can use the Identifier field to identify each table. Just type a single letter to identify each table. And, if you want to change the level at which the entry appears, type a different level number in the Level field.

To make the MarkTOC macro easier to use, you may want to assign it a keyboard shortcut or toolbar button.

The MarkTOC macro is a bit primitive in its error-checking. In particular, make sure that only the exact text you want to appear in the TC field is selected when you run it. If you have paragraph marks or other special characters selected when you run MarkTOC, you should edit those characters out of the TOC Text field before clicking OK.

Creating a Table of Figures or Other Similar Tables

Tables of contents aren't the only kind of tables you can create with the Insert⇨Index and Tables command. You can also use this command to compile tables of figures, tables, equations, or other similar collectibles. For convenience, I'll refer to all of these tables as "tables of figures," even though they are each somewhat different.

To create a table of figures, you must first mark each figure with a caption. First, select the figure you want to apply the caption to and use the Insert⇨Caption command. This brings up the Caption dialog box, as shown in Figure 25-5. Select the type of caption you want to create (Figure, Table, or Equation) in the Label field. Then, type the caption itself in the Caption field. When you're done, click OK.

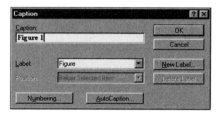

Figure 25-5: The Caption dialog box.

(For more information about creating captions, refer to Chapter 21.) After you have created captions for all the figures, tables, or equations; you can call up the Insert⇨Index and Tables command and click the Table of Figures tab to view the dialog box shown in Figure 25-6.

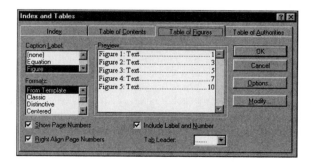

Figure 25-6: The Index and Tables dialog box (Table of Figures tab).

Pick the type of table you want to create from the Caption Label list. The settings in this field correspond to the Label setting in the Caption dialog box. For example, to create a table of all figure captions, select Figure for the Caption Label field.

Next, pick the table style you want to create from the Formats list. As with tables of contents, you can select From Template to format the table according to the styles in the document's template. (Only one style, Table of Figures, is required to format a table of figures.) To modify the Table of Figures style, click the Modify button.

Other controls allow you to fine-tune the table's appearance:

- **Show Page Numbers:** Uncheck this box if you want the table to list the captions but not page numbers.

- **Right Align Page Numbers:** Uncheck this box if you want the page numbers placed right next to the corresponding text rather than at the right margin.

- **Include Label and Number:** Uncheck this check box if you want the table to include the caption text (for example, "A Heffalump and a Woozle" or "Ratio of Red M&Ms") but not the number (for example, "Figure 1" or "Table 3").

- **Tab Leader:** Change this field to add or remove the dotted line that connects each table entry with its page number.

Remember that if the table looks like { **TOC \c "Figure"** }, call up the Tools⇨Options command, click the View button, and uncheck the Field Codes check box. Click OK and the table should appear correctly.

Tip

Word is set up to create captions and tables for equations, figures, and tables. If you want to create other types of captions and tables (for example, for limericks or cartoons), you can add items to the list of labels that appears in the Caption and Table of Figures dialog boxes. Call up the Insert⇨Caption command and click the New Label button. Then, type a new label (such as "Limerick" or "Cartoon") and click OK. Type the caption text and click OK to insert the first caption of the new type. Later, when you call up the Insert⇨Index and Tables command and click the Table of Figures tab, the label you created will appear in the Caption Label list.

Using Styles to Create a Table of Figures

The funny thing about tables of figures is that they are usually created by using field codes that are inserted by the Insert⇨Caption command. Everywhere else in Word for Windows, Microsoft seems to be preaching the virtues of using styles. If you are a style convert and feel that the Insert⇨Caption command is against your new religion, fear not. You can create tables of figures, tables, and equations by using styles just as you can create tables of contents by using styles. Here's how:

1. Type your captions as separate paragraphs and create a style for them. Pick a creative name for your caption style, such as "Caption."

2. When all of the captions have been formatted with the appropriate style, move the insertion point to the location where you want the table inserted, choose the Insert⇨Index and Tables command, and click the Table of Figures tab.

3. Click the Options button. The Table of Figures Options dialog box will appear, as shown in Figure 25-7.

Figure 25-7: The Table of Figures Options dialog box.

4. Make sure that the Style check box is checked and select the style you used to format the captions. In this case, Caption.

5. Click OK to return to the Index and Tables dialog box and click OK to create the table.

Tables of Authorities

The following sections show you how to use Word's Table of Authorities feature. If you're a lawyer or legal secretary, you already know what a Table of Authorities is. If you aren't, you should skip ahead to the section on indexes.

Creating a table of authorities is much like creating a table of figures. First, you mark the citations where they appear within the document. Then, you use the Insert⇨Index and Tables command to compile the table of authorities based on the citations you marked. If necessary, you can then edit the table or adjust its formatting. You can also update the table to make sure that all the entries are up to date.

Marking citations in the document

The first step to creating a table of authorities is reviewing the entire document and marking any citations you want included in the table. To mark a citation, highlight it and press Alt+Shift+I. The Mark Citation dialog box will appear, as shown in Figure 25-8.

Tip

If the screen suddenly changes to Print Preview mode when you try to mark a citation, it's because you pressed Ctrl+Alt+I instead of Alt+Shift+I. Ctrl+Alt+I is the keyboard shortcut for toggling Print Preview on and off. These two keyboard shortcuts are perilously close to one another, but don't panic if you press the wrong one. Just press Ctrl+Alt+I again to return to Normal view and start over.

Note

Another way to summon the Mark Citation dialog box is to call up the Insert⇨Index and Tables command, click on the Table of Authorities tab, and click on the Mark Citation button.

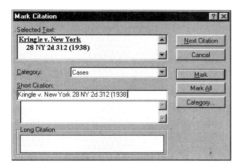

Figure 25-8: The Mark Citation dialog box.

Edit the Selected Text field so that it is exactly the way you want the citation to appear in the table of authorities. This field will initially contain the text that was selected when you pressed Alt+Shift+I. If the citation in the document is not as it should appear in the table of authorities, click in the Selected Text field and type away. If you want to split the citation into two lines, just position the cursor where you want the line to be split and press the Enter key.

The first time you cite an authority, you must provide a complete citation (such as "Kringle v. New York, 28 NY 2d 312 (1938)"), but thereafter you can use the short form ("Kringle v. New York"). Edit the Short Citation field to match the short form of the citation that you will use. That way, Word can automatically locate subsequent citations and mark them.

Next, select the type of authority being cited from the Category list box. Word comes equipped with several common categories: Cases, Statutes, Other Authorities, Rules, Treatises, Regulations, and Constitutional Provisions. You can also create your own categories.

When you are ready to mark the citation, click the Mark button. Word will insert a hidden field code to mark the citation.

Note

If you stumble upon a citation that you know occurs later in your document, click the Mark All button. This creates a citation not only for the selected text but also for any subsequent occurrences of the citation.

The Mark Citation dialog box will remain on the screen so you can continue to mark additional citations. Click the Next Citation button to send Word searching for the next citation. Word will look for text that looks like a citation. Repeat the process of marking citations for each legitimate citation Word finds.

Word marks citations with field codes formatted as hidden text so that they are normally invisible. They jump to life, however, when you compile a table of authorities. See the next section, "Creating a table of authorities," for the procedure.

The field codes for citations look something like this:

```
{ TA \l "Kringle v. New York
28 NY 2d 312 (1938)" \s "Kringle v. New York" \c 1 }
```

These codes are formatted as hidden text, so you don't normally see them. You can edit the long citation text (the part between quotes following \l) or the short citation text (the quoted text that follows \s) if you need to change a citation after you create it.

 The first time you mark a citation, Word activates the All check box of the Tools⇨Options command's View tab. This reveals not only the hidden text used to mark citations but also perverts the screen with dots for spaces, paragraph and tab marks, and other obnoxious codes. To return your display to normal, click the Show/Hide button on the Standard toolbar.

Creating a table of authorities

After you have marked all of the citations in your document, you can create the table of authorities by first positioning the insertion point where you want the table to be located (usually at the front or back of the document), choosing the Insert⇨Index and Tables command, and clicking the Table of Authorities tab. The dialog box shown in Figure 25-9 will be displayed.

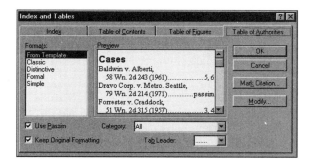

Figure 25-9: Creating a table of authorities.

Pick the style you want from the Formats list. As you click on the various formats, the Preview window shows how the resulting table of authorities will appear.

Here is a description of the other controls on this dialog box:

- **Use Passim:** Check this box if you want Word to use the word *Passim* when a citation occurs on five or more pages. (*Passim* is a Latin word that means "scattered throughout," not an ugly overgrown rat-like creature that hangs upside down by its tail.)

- **Keep Original Formatting:** Check this box if you want character formatting (like underline, italic, and so on) applied to the citation as it appears in the document to be carried over into the table of authorities.

- **Category:** Use this list box to select the citation category you want compiled. Usually, you'll leave this field set to the default, All. If you want to compile a table of one category (cases, rules, regulations, and so on), select the category from the drop-down list.

- **Tab Leader:** Use this field to change or remove the dotted line that connects each citation to its page number.

Once again, if your table shows up as a bunch of codes (like { TOA \h \c "1" \p }), call up the Tools⇨Options command, click the View button, and uncheck the Field Codes check box. Click OK and the table should appear as it should.

Tip

The entries in a table of authorities are formatted with a standard style name "Table of Authorities," and the headings for categories are formatted using a style named "TOA Heading." If none of the predefined formats listed in the Formats list tickles your fancy, select "Custom Style" and click the Modify button. This takes you to a special version of the Style dialog box in which only the standard table of authorities styles are shown. You can customize the Custom Style format by modifying the Table of Authorities and TOA Heading styles.

Adding your own categories

Word comes with seven predefined table of authorities categories: Cases, Statutes, Other Authorities, Rules, Treatises, Regulations, and Constitutional Provisions. If these categories aren't sufficient enough for you, you can add your own. Word has room for up to 16 categories, so you can either add new categories or replace existing categories with new categories of your choosing.

To create your own categories, call up the Mark Citation dialog box by pressing Alt+Shift+I to summon the Mark Citation dialog box and click the Category button. The Edit Category dialog box will appear, as shown in Figure 25-10.

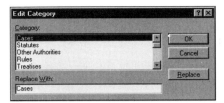

Figure 25-10: Creating a custom category.

Select the category you want to replace in the Category list. (If you don't want to replace one of the seven predefined categories, scroll past them and select one of the dummy categories numbered 8 through 16.) Then, type the name you want to use for the new category in the Replace With field and click the Replace button.

When you add your own categories, those categories will appear in the Category drop-down list box on the Mark Citation dialog box. Then, you can assign citations to the new category as you mark them.

Indexes

Creating an index is a three-stage affair. First, you must mark (one at a time) all the words and phrases within your document that you want to appear in the index. Second, you call on the Insert⇨Index and Tables command to create the index. This command takes all the words and phrases you marked, sorts them in alphabetical order, and combines identical entries. Third, you carefully review the index, lament that Word didn't do a better job, and fix what you can.

Note

I've indexed quite a few books in my day, and I have yet to find a word processor with an indexing feature that really does the trick. Word is no exception. It does a better job than any other word processors I've had the pleasure of working with, but you should still be prepared to do a ton of work yourself.

The most efficient way to create an index is after you've written and edited your document. Set aside some time to work through the document, marking up index entries. Don't bother to create index entries as you write your document. It just slows you down and distracts you from your primary task: writing.

There are two ways to mark the words you want included in an index: manually, marking each word one by one, or automatically, giving Word a list of words that you want in the index and letting it mark the words in the document.

Marking index entries manually

The first (and most important) task in creating an index is to mark the words or phrases that you want included in the index. The most common way to do that is to insert an index marker in the document at each occurrence of each item you want to appear in the index.

To mark index entries, work your way through the document from start to finish. When you find a word or phrase that you want to put into the index, highlight it by using the mouse or keyboard and press the keyboard shortcut Alt+Shift+X (one of Word's more memorable shortcuts). The Mark Index Entry dialog box will appear, shown in Figure 25-11.

Note

Another way to summon the Mark Index Entry dialog box is to call up the Insert⇨Index and Tables command, click the Index tab, and then click the Mark Entry button.

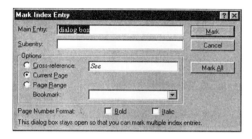

Figure 25-11: The Mark Index Entry dialog box.

If you want, you can edit the text in the Main Entry field any way you want. The text does not have to appear in the index exactly as it appears in the document. You might highlight an abbreviation to include in the index, for example, but then edit the Main Entry field so that the full spelling of the word rather than the abbreviation appears in the appendix. Click the Mark button to mark the entry.

If you want to index the entry under a different word, type the alternative entry in the Main Entry field and click the Mark button again. For example, you might want to create an entry for "cow, sacred" in addition to "sacred cow."

To make it easier to mark up an entire document, the Mark Index Entry dialog box remains on-screen after you click the Mark button. You can mark additional index entries by highlighting them in the document and clicking the Mark button. When you've marked all the index entries you want to mark, click the Close button to dismiss the Mark Index Entry dialog box.

If you come across a word or phrase that you know occurs elsewhere in your document while marking index entries, click the Mark All button. This action creates an index entry not only for the selected text, but also for any other occurrence of the selected text within the document.

Index entries look something like this: { XE "sacred cow " }, formatted as hidden text. You can edit the index entry text (the part between quotation marks) if you want to change an index entry after you create it. (If you can't see the index entries, call up the Tools⇨Options command, click the View tab, and enable the display of hidden text.)

Creating an index

After you have marked the index entries, the process of generating the index is relatively easy. Start by moving the insertion point to the place where you want the index to appear. The index generally begins on a new page near the end of the document. Press Ctrl+Enter to create a new page, if necessary, and click the mouse to position the insertion point on the empty page. You may want to add a heading, such as Index, at the top of the page.

To insert the index, choose the Insert⇨Index and Tables command and click the Index tab. The Index and Tables dialog box appears, as shown in Figure 25-12.

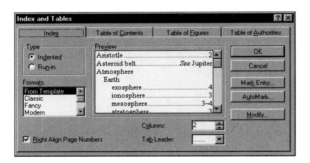

Figure 25-12: Inserting an index.

The Index and Tables dialog box gives you several alternative index styles from which to choose. As you click the various formats listed in the Formats list box, the Preview window shows how the resulting index will appear.

The following controls are also available for fine-tuning the appearance of the index:

- **Type:** These options let you place index subentries on separate indented lines (Indented) or run together (Run-in).

- **Right Align Page Numbers:** Check this option if you want the page numbers placed at the right edge of the index.

- **Columns:** Set this field to the number of columns to include in the index. Two is the norm.

- **Tab Leader:** Use this field to change or remove the dotted line that connects each index entry to its page number. This option is allowed only when the Right Align Page Numbers option is checked.

The entries in an index are formatted with a set of standard styles named Index 1, Index 2, Index 3, and so on. If you don't like any of the predefined formats listed in the Formats list in the Index and Styles dialog box, choose Custom Style and click the Modify button. This step takes you to a special version of the Style dialog box in which only the standard index styles are shown. You can then change the appearance of the Custom Style Index format by modifying the various index styles.

Marking bold and italic page numbers

Some index entries are more important than others. For example, you might include a lengthy discussion of a particular topic on one page and include several passing references to the subject on subsequent pages. Obviously, the reader is more likely to be interested in the lengthy discussion than in the passing references. For this reason, Word lets you highlight page numbers for significant index entries in boldface or italics.

To create a boldface or italic page reference, all you must do is check the Bold or Italic option in the Mark Index Entry dialog box when you create the entry. Then, Word formats the page number for that entry in bold or italic when it generates the index.

Marking a range of pages

If a particular topic is discussed for several pages in your document, you might want to create an index entry that marks a range of pages (for example, *26-29*) rather than each page individually (*26, 27, 28, 29*).

Unfortunately, the procedure for marking page ranges isn't as straightforward as it could be. You have to mess around with bookmarks to make it work. A *bookmark* is a name you can assign to a selection of text. Bookmarks are usually used to mark locations in your document so that you can skip to them later, but they have all sorts of more interesting uses. This is just one.

To mark a range of pages, highlight the entire range of text that refers to the index topic. For a long discussion, this range could extend for many pages. Call up the Edit⇨Bookmark command and assign a name for the bookmark. The name you choose doesn't matter. Click OK to create the bookmark.

Now, move the insertion point back to the beginning of the bookmark you just created and press Alt+Shift+X to summon the Mark Index Entry dialog box. Type the text you want to appear in the index in the Main Entry text box, click the Page Range option button, and choose the bookmark that you just created from the list of bookmark names that appears in the Bookmark drop-down list.

Finally, click Mark to mark the entry. When the index is compiled, the entire range of pages spanned by the bookmark will be listed for the index entry.

Marking index entries automatically from a concordance file

Another way to create index entries is to use a *concordance file*: a list of words you want indexed. You just type a list of words that you want Word to include in the index. Word then creates an index entry for each occurrence of each word in the list. Sometimes (but not always), this can be a great time-saver.

To create the concordance file, start a new document and type the words you want to be indexed, one per line. For example

    Kirk
    Spock
    McCoy
    Scotty

If you want the text in the index to be different from the text in the document, press the Tab key and then type the text exactly as you want it to appear in the index:

    Kirk   Kirk, James T.
    Spock   Spock, Mr.
    McCoy   McCoy, Leonard H.
    Scotty   Scott, Montgomery

Don't worry about keeping the list in alphabetical order; Word will automatically sort it when the time comes. When the word list is finished, save it to a file and close the document.

Tip

If you want, you can use Word's Table feature to create the concordance. Create a two-column table and use the first column for the text to find in the document and the second column for the text to include in the index.

Now, open the document you want indexed, choose the Insert⇨Index and Tables command, and click the Index tab. Click the AutoMark button; the dialog box shown in Figure 25-13 will appear.

Select the concordance file and click OK. Word will proceed to create index marks for each occurrence of each word in the AutoMark file. This might take a while, so patience is in order.

After the automatic index entries have been created, you probably will want to work your way through the document by creating additional index entries. And, if you haven't already done so, you'll need to create an index.

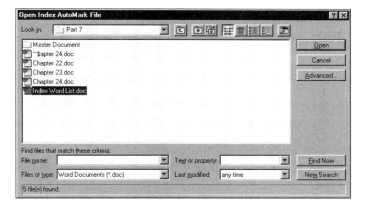

Figure 25-13: The Open Index AutoMark File dialog box.

Tip

Unfortunately, the AutoMark option doesn't account for running discussions of a single topic that span several pages. It results in index entries such as "Vogons, 14, 15, 16, 17, 18" that should read "Vogons, 14-18." The only way around this is to search for such entries manually, go back and create bookmarks for them, and remove the extraneous index marks. Or, don't worry about it until after the index is created; you can always edit the index itself to make such corrections.

Creating subentries

A *subentry* is what happens when a word is used for two different meanings or when a word serves as a category organizer for several related words. For example, you might want to create an index entry that looks like this:

crew
    Kirk, James T., 15
    McCoy, Leonard H., 16
    Scott, Montgomery, 16
    Spock, Mr., 17

Here, the index entries for Kirk, McCoy, Scott, and Spock are all *subentries* of the main entry, crew.

To create index subentries, you follow the normal procedure for marking index entries. Type text for both the main entry and the subentry, however, in the Mark Index Entry dialog box. Each of the index entries shown previously, for example, would have "crew" for the Main Entry field and the individual crew member's name as the Subentry.

Creating cross-references

A cross-reference is one of those annoying messages that means you're about to embark on a wild goose chase:

> crew, *see* cast.

To create a cross-reference, begin marking an index entry as you normally would. On the Mark Index Entry dialog box, click the C̲ross-reference button and type some text in the accompanying text box. Word automatically merges the cross-reference with other index entries for the same text.

Note

If you create a cross-reference such as "crew, *see* cast", be sure you do not also create a cross-reference for "cast, *see* crew". You're sure to receive hate mail if you do.

Formatting an index

Although you can control some of the formatting of an index from the Index and Tables dialog box, you are limited to the predefined formats supplied by Word. The best way to create your own unique index format is to play with the styles that are automatically applied to various parts of the index. The index entries themselves are formatted by using the standard styles Index 1, Index 2, Index 3, and so on. You can modify these styles to control the appearance of your index entries.

Word also inserts text at the beginning of each letter break in the index. To control the formatting that is applied to these letter entries, use the Index Heading style.

For more precise control of the index format, you can play with the actual Index field code that is inserted when you create the index. Various options on the Index field code allow you to control which text is inserted in each letter group heading (\h), change the page range separator (\g), change the page number separator (\l), and change the character that separates the entry from the first page number (\e). You'll find more information about working with field codes in Chapter 28.

Updating Tables of Contents, Tables of Figures, Tables of Authorities, or an Index

As you edit your document, it's likely that a TOC, table of figures, table of authorities, or index you've created will become out of date. The page numbers might change; you might delete headings, captions, or citations; or you might insert new headings, captions, or citations.

You can make sure that your tables and indexes are up to date when you print your document in several ways:

■ Call up the Tools⇨Options command, click the Print tab, check the Update Fields check box, and click OK. Then, tables and indexes (and other fields in the document) will automatically be updated each time you print your document.

■ To update a table or index without printing the document, select the table and press F9. A dialog box will appear asking whether you want to refresh just the page numbers or whether you want to completely rebuild the table or index. Just refreshing the page numbers is faster, but it doesn't account for items you've added or deleted since you created the table or index.

■ If you point to a table or index and click the right mouse button, the short-cut menu that appears will include an Update Field command. Using this command works the same as pressing F9.

■ To update all tables and indexes in your document, press Ctrl+A to select the entire document and press F9.

■ Another way to update a table or index is to select the table or index and use the Insert⇨Index and Tables command to replace the table or index.

Chapter 26

Using Footnotes, Endnotes, and Cross-References

In This Chapter

▶ Creating great-looking footnotes that are properly lined up at the bottom of each page, or endnotes that appear at the end of the document

▶ Changing the appearance of footnotes, including the reference marks and footnote separators

▶ Finding a footnote reference

▶ Creating cross-references

▶ Creating dictionary-style headers that use special cross-reference fields to pick up text from the current page

▶ Using the secret Footnote Wizard to create perfect bibliographic references

Footnotes are one of the best features in modern word processors. In the old, pre-word processor days (when I went to college), you had to count out all the lines on the page and make sure that you allowed enough room at the bottom for any footnotes. With Word, you don't have to worry about footnote positioning at all. Word makes sure that each footnote is properly positioned at the bottom of the page on which the footnote reference appears. All you have to do is mark the footnote references and type in the footnote text.

Word even numbers the footnotes for you, keeping the numbers in sync when you add or remove footnote references. It's enough to make you want to go back to college. (Well, maybe not *quite* enough.)

Adding a Footnote

Footnotes are pretty easy to create unless you want to get fancy with them. To create a basic footnote, follow these easy steps:

1. Move the cursor to the point where you want the footnote referenced.

2. Choose the Insert⇨Footnote command. This summons the Footnote and Endnote dialog box, shown in Figure 26-1. You can choose between footnotes and endnotes. (Footnotes appear at the bottom of the page on which the footnote reference appears; endnotes are printed together at the end of the document.) You can also fiddle with numbering options, but usually you just give this dialog box a bothered glance before clicking OK.

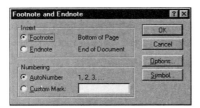

Figure 26-1: The Footnote and Endnote dialog box.

3. Click OK. A separate footnote window, called the *footnote pane,* opens up at the bottom of the screen, as shown in Figure 26-2. (This proves my contention that footnotes are a pain.) Type your footnote in the space provided.

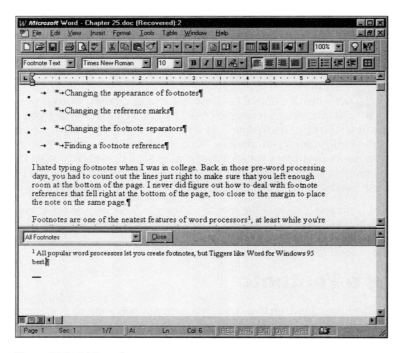

Figure 26-2: Adding a footnote.

4. Click Close when you're finished.

The preceding procedure assumes that you are working in Normal view. If you are working in Page Layout view, the footnote pane is bypassed. Instead, footnotes are placed at the bottom of the page, where they belong. You can edit the footnotes in place at the bottom of the page.

Footnotes are automatically numbered for you as you create them. When you use the Insert⇨Footnote command, Word inserts the superscript footnote reference number in the text and pairs it with a number in the footnote itself. If you go back later and insert a new footnote in front of an existing one, Word automatically juggles the footnote numbers to keep everything in sync.

Tip

For an extra-quick way to create a footnote, use the keyboard shortcut Ctrl+Alt+F. This bypasses the Footnote and Endnote dialog box, and goes directly to the footnote pane.

To delete a footnote, select its footnote reference in the text and press the Del key.

Tip

To bring up the footnote pane so that you can see a document's footnotes, double-click on one of the footnote references, or choose the View⇨Footnotes command to open the footnote pane.

Adding an Endnote

The procedure for adding an endnote is the same as for adding a footnote. In fact, the only difference is that when you call up the Insert⇨Footnote command, you check the Endnote option button rather than the Footnote button.

Word allows you to mix footnotes and endnotes in the same document. Word numbers footnotes and endnotes separately. By default, Word uses Arabic numerals (1, 2, 3...) for footnotes and lowercase Roman numerals for endnotes (i, ii, iii, ...). You can change either numbering format, but be sure that you don't change them to the same format. If you do, you won't be able to tell your footnotes from your endnotes.

When you activate the footnote pane by using the View⇨Footnotes command, you can switch between footnotes and endnotes by using the drop-down list that appears at the top of the footnote pane in Normal view. In Page Layout view, the footnotes are edited directly at the bottom of the page, but endnotes appear at the end of the document.

Displaying and Finding Footnotes

To display a specific footnote quickly, double-click on the footnote reference. If the footnote pane is not yet open, this action will open it.

You can also use the Edit⇨Go To command to find footnotes. Press Ctrl+G to pop up the Go To dialog box as shown in Figure 26-3, and select Footnote in the Go To What box. At this point, you can click Next or Previous to go to the next or previous footnote, or you can type a specific footnote number and click Go To to go to a specific footnote.

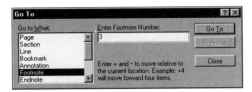

Figure 26-3: Using the Go To command to locate footnotes.

You can also search for footnote marks with the Edit⇨Find command. Press Ctrl+F to call up the Find dialog box, click the Special button, and select Footnote mark from the menu that pops up. Then, click Find Next to find the first footnote.

Changing the Footnote Format

Footnote formatting is controlled by a pair of styles named *Footnote Text* and *Footnote Reference*. Footnote Text style controls the appearance of the footnote at the bottom of the page, while Footnote Reference controls the format of the superscript footnote number that appears in the body of the document. The Footnote Reference style is a character style, so it doesn't affect formatting for the entire paragraph.

The initial setting for Footnote Text is Normal+10 point. As a result, footnotes are formatted with the same font as in your Normal paragraphs, except that they are 10 point regardless of the Normal text size. If you want your footnotes to appear in a different font or in a different size from the rest of the document, change the font for the Footnote Text style.

The initial setting for Footnote Reference is Default Character Format + Superscript. As a result, footnote references are printed with the same font as the rest of the text in the paragraph, except that the superscript attribute applies. If you would rather see footnote references in a different font, just change the Footnote Reference style.

Both Footnote Text and Footnote Reference are applied automatically when you create footnotes, so you shouldn't have any cause to apply these formats directly.

Endnotes are formatted with a similar pair of styles: Endnote Text and Endnote Reference.

Using Different Reference Marks

In most cases, you want footnotes to be numbered 1, 2, 3, and so on. However, Word lets you change this standard numbering format to use letters, Roman numerals, or the special reference symbols *, †, ‡, and §.

To change the reference marks, call up the Insert⇨Footnote command to summon the Footnote and Endnote dialog box and click the Options button. This will bring forth the Note Options dialog box, shown in Figure 26-4.

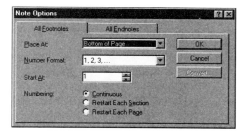

Figure 26-4: The Note Options dialog box.

This dialog box allows you to select from several numbering choices:

> 1, 2, 3 . . .
>
> a, b, c . . .
>
> A, B, C . . .
>
> i, ii, iii . . .
>
> I, II, III . . .
>
> *, †, ‡, § . . .

All the footnotes in a section must use the same numbering scheme. You can't mix and match.

If you want footnotes to be renumbered for each page, choose the Restart Each Page option. To renumber footnotes beginning with each section, choose the Restart Each Section option.

Note

If you choose the special symbols *, †, ‡, and § for your reference marks, Word doubles them if necessary to create unique reference marks. The first four footnotes, therefore, use the symbols singly. The mark for the fifth through eighth notes are **, ††, ‡‡, and §§. After that, the symbols are tripled.

To avoid excessive doubling and tripling of these symbols, choose the Restart Each Page button in the Note Options dialog box. That way, the mark for the first note on each page is always an asterisk (*).

Using a Custom Reference Mark

You can bypass Word's automatic footnote-numbering scheme at any time by checking the Custom Mark button in the Footnote and Endnote dialog box and entering any text you want to use for the mark in the Custom Mark text box. If you want to enter a symbol that's not readily available from the keyboard, click the <u>S</u>ymbol button to bring up the Symbol dialog box, shown in Figure 26-5.

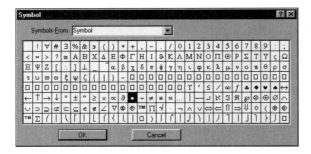

Figure 26-5: The Symbol dialog box.

You can select any of the symbols that appear in the Symbol dialog box to use as a reference mark, or you can pick a different font to display a different set of symbols. The most useful symbols can be found in the Wingdings font that comes with Windows 95 or in the Wingdings 2 or Wingdings 3 fonts that come with Word for Windows 95 or Office 95.

Changing the Footnote Separators

To separate footnotes from the text on a page, Word for Windows automatically adds a short horizontal line called the *footnote separator* above the first foot- note on each page. If the footnote is too long to fit at the bottom of the page, Word automatically continues the footnote to the next page and adds a *footnote continuation separator*, a longer horizontal line that appears on the second page, and a *footnote continuation notice* that appears at the end of the first part of the footnote to indicate that the footnote is being continued to another page.

You can customize the appearance of these separators by opening the footnote pane (choose the <u>V</u>iew➪<u>F</u>ootnotes command or double-click a footnote reference) and choosing the footnote element that you want to modify from the list box that appears at the top of the footnote pane. You can then apply whatever edits and formats you want. For example, you might want to add the word *Footnotes* above or below the line that appears in the footnote separator, or you might want to increase the space above or below the separator. In the continuation notice, you might want to add a bit of text, such as *continues....*

Converting Footnotes to Endnotes

You can convert footnotes to endnotes, and vice versa, by choosing the <u>I</u>nsert➪<u>F</u>ootnotes command, clicking the <u>O</u>ptions button, and clicking the <u>C</u>onvert button. This brings up the Convert Notes dialog box, shown in Figure 26-6.

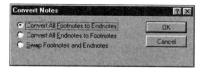

Figure 26-6: The Convert Notes dialog box.

This dialog box allows you to convert all existing footnotes to endnotes, all endnotes to footnotes, or both. Footnote and endnote reference numbers are properly merged and renumbered when you convert one to the other, so the resulting footnotes and endnotes will be numbered consecutively.

Secret

To convert a footnote to an endnote quickly, activate the footnote pane and right-click the footnote you want to convert and select Convert to Endnote in the shortcut menu that appears. Likewise, you can convert an endnote to a footnote by right-clicking the endnote and selecting the Convert to Footnote command.

Two Footnote Styles That Are Beyond Word's Capabilities

I've come across two styles of footnotes that I haven't been able to duplicate in Word for Windows. The first is from an edition of the complete works of Chaucer. The text of this book is set in two columns, but the footnotes (and there are many of them, at least a dozen per page) are set in a single column at the bottom of the page. In Word, once you set the text in two columns, the footnotes are placed in two columns as well. There is no way that I can find to set the footnotes in a single column when the text is in two columns.

The second case is an edition of the Bible that has elaborate footnotes that include at least two features that Word cannot duplicate. The text itself is set in two columns, but there is a narrow column running between the two text columns. The footnotes are contained within this narrow center column. There is no way to accomplish this in Word. To make matters worse, the center column is often not large enough to accommodate all of the footnotes for a given page. When that happens, the excess footnotes are placed at the bottom of the second text column.

The second stumper in this Bible is that the footnotes consist of two separate "threads," one identified by numerals and consisting mostly of cross-references to other passages, the other identified by letters and listing alternative translations. Although Word allows you to create separate sequences of footnotes and endnotes, there is no way to keep two separate sequences, both footnotes.

(continued)

(continued)

For example, consider this excerpt (Isaiah 33:13):

> You who are far away, [a]hear what I have done; and you who are near, [1]acknowledge my Might.

The footnotes read as follows:

[a]Ps. 48:10; Is. 49:1

[1]Lit. *know*

The first provides cross-references to related passages; the second provides an alternative translation for the word *acknowledge*.

To further complicate matters, the footnote numbers are reset for each verse. Word lets you reset footnote numbers for each page or each section, but not for each paragraph. As a result, you would have to place each verse in its own section to duplicate these footnotes properly. (You could abandon the footnote feature altogether, but verses with five or more footnotes are not uncommon.)

The moral of the story is: Word is probably not suitable for publishing referenced texts of Chaucer or the Bible.

Using the Secret Footnote Wizard

One of the sample macros that comes with Word for Windows is called InsertFootnote. In actuality, it is a sophisticated Footnote Wizard that builds bibliographic references in strict accordance with either the Modern Language Association (MLA) standards or the *Chicago Manual of Style*.

Note

The InsertFootnote macro is contained in the Macro7.dot template that comes with Word. To make this template available as a global template so that its macros can be used, follow these steps:

1. Save any open files and exit Word.

2. Double-click on the My Computer icon on your desktop.

3. In the My Computer window, double-click on the C: drive and double-click on MSOffice, then Winword, and then Macros. You will now be looking at the contents of the C:\MSOffice\Winword\Macros folder.

4. Click on the icon for the Macro7.dot file and press Ctrl+C.

5. Press the Backspace key to move back up to the C:\MSOffice\Winword folder and double-click on the Startup icon to move to the C:\MSOffice\Winword\Startup folder.

6. Press Ctrl+V to paste a copy of the Macro7.dot file in the Startup folder.

7. Click the close box to dismiss the My Computer window.

8. Restart Word.

Tip

Alternatively, you can use the Organizer to copy the InsertFootnote macro from the Macro7.dot template to Normal.dot. See Chapter 4 for more information about how to access these macros.

Once the InsertFootnote macro has been made available, you use it by calling up the Insert⇨Footnote command. The normal footnote dialog box is displayed, but when you click OK, the footnote isn't immediately inserted. Instead, the dialog box shown in Figure 26-7 is displayed.

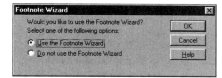

Figure 26-7: The InsertFootnote macro asks whether you want to run the Footnote Wizard.

If you want to use the Footnote Wizard, click OK. Otherwise, select the Do not use the Footnote Wizard option button and click OK.

Assuming that you elect to use the Footnote Wizard, you will next see the dialog box shown in Figure 26-8.

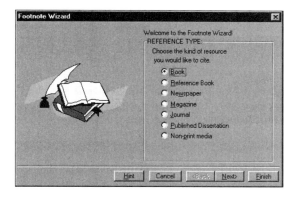

Figure 26-8: The Footnote Wizard asks which kind of publication you want to reference.

In this dialog box, select the type of publication you want to cite: Book, Reference Book, Newspaper, Magazine, Journal, Published Dissertation, or Non-print media. Then, click Next.

The information that appears next depends on which type of publication you select. For a book, the dialog box shown in Figure 26-9 is displayed next. For other publication types, the Footnote Wizard may request different information.

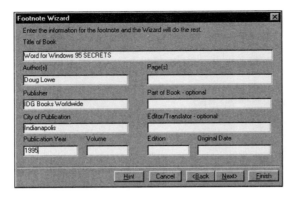

Figure 26-9: The Footnote Wizard asks for the information needed to create a book citation.

Fill in as much information as is available or necessary. If you are unsure about any of the fields, move the insertion point to the field and click the Hint button. The Footnote Wizard will display a message explaining what type of information should be entered in the field.

When you have entered all of the information, click the Next button. The dialog box shown in Figure 26-10 will be displayed.

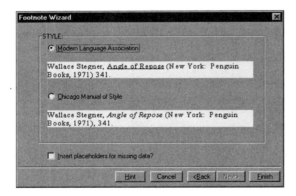

Figure 26-10: The Footnote Wizard asks which kind of footnote format to use.

Here, the Footnote Wizard asks whether it should format the footnote according to the standards of the Modern Language Association (MLA) or the *Chicago Manual of Style*. There is also a check box that enables you to insert blank placeholders in the place of missing information. Set these options however you want and click Finish to create the foonote.

Working with Cross-References

A *cross-reference* is a bit of text that refers to some other text or graphic in your document. For example, if I wanted to refer you back to the instructions on how to create a footnote, I'd say something like this:

> Way back in the section "Adding a Footnote."

Now, what would happen if I decided to rename that section, "Creating a Footnote"? I'd have to remember to change any references to that section, too. Unless, of course, I decided to use a cross-reference to refer to the section rather than just retyping the heading manually.

To complicate matters, suppose that I wanted to let you know what page the section appeared on, too. Then, I'd say something like this:

> Way back in the section "Adding a Footnote" on page ###.

Word lets you create several types of cross-references:

- **Headings,** which let you include the actual heading text, the page number on which the heading appears, or the heading number (if you use the Heading Numbering feature). Headings must be formatted with the standard heading styles for this feature to work.

- **Bookmarks,** which let you include the text identified by the bookmark, the page number the bookmark appears on, or the paragraph number for the bookmark, assuming that you have used Word's Paragraph Numbering feature.

- **Footnotes or Endnotes,** which let you include the footnote or endnote number or its page number.

- **Equations, Figures, or Tables,** which are tied to captions and let you include the complete caption text, the label and number, just the caption text, or just the page number where the caption appears.

To insert a cross-reference, follow these steps:

1. Type the text that leads up to the cross-reference. For example, type **for more information, see the section**.

2. Choose the Insert⇨Cross-reference command. The Cross-reference dialog box will appear, as shown in Figure 26-11.

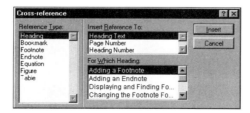

Figure 26-11: The Cross-reference dialog box.

3. Pick the type of cross-reference that you want to create from the Reference Type list.

4. Pick the Insert Reference To option that you want.

5. Select the specific item that you want to reference from the For Which list.

6. Click the Insert button.

Creating a Style Reference

The Insert⇨Cross-reference command lets you create several types of cross-references, but unfortunately Microsoft forgot to add one of the most useful cross-reference types: the capability to insert text formatted by an arbitrary style. Fortunately, you can create this type of cross-reference by using a special field code called *StyleRef*. I won't go into the ins and outs of working with field codes here, but I do want to show you how to work with the StyleRef field code. For more information about working with field codes, see Chapter 28.

A common use for the StyleRef field code is creating headers or footers that include text that appears on the page. For example, dictionaries, phone books, and many reference books have headers of this sort. Suppose that you are working on a reference document that includes detailed information about all of Word's field codes, and you want the first field code listed on each page to appear in the header for that page. The field codes themselves are formatted by using the Heading 1 style.

To create a header such as this, you insert a StyleRef field code in the header. The StyleRef code should refer to the Heading 1 style: **{StyleRef "Heading 1"}**. To create a header with this code, follow these steps:

1. Use the View⇨Header and Footer command to open up the header pane.

2. Choose the Insert⇨Field command. The Field dialog box will appear, as shown in Figure 26-12.

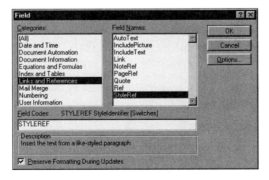

Figure 26-12: The Field dialog box.

3. Select "Links and References" in the Categories list and select StyleRef in the Field Names list.

4. Click the Options button and click the Styles tab. The Field Options dialog box will appear, as shown in Figure 26-13. (The styles listed on your machine will be different from those that are shown in the figure.)

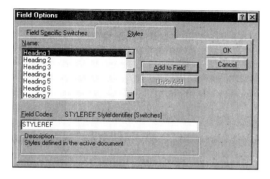

Figure 26-13: The Field Options dialog box.

5. Click the style used to format the text you want to reference and click Add to Field.

6. Click OK to return to the Field dialog box and click OK again to insert the field into the document.

The StyleRef field code will pick up text from the first paragraph on the page formatted with the style you select. If there is no paragraph on the page formatted with the style you select, the StyleRef code will use the most recent occurrence of the style.

For a subtle variation, you can add the \l switch to the StyleRef field code. This causes Word to pick up text from the *last* occurrence of the style on the page. This is useful to create dictionary-style headers or footers that list both the first and last reference found on the page. For example, assuming that the text you want to reference is formatted with the Heading 1 style, you could create a header or footer with two StyleRef codes, like this:

{StyleRef "Heading 1"} - {StyleRef \l "Heading 1"}

This header would show the text from the first Heading 1 paragraph on the page, a hyphen, then the text from the last Heading 1 paragraph on the page. For example, if the first Heading 1 paragraph contained the text **Aardvark** and the second contained the text **Africa**, the header would include the text **Aardvark - Africa**.

If the StyleRef field cannot find any paragraphs formatted with the style you specify, the field code will show the following error message:

```
Error! No text of specified style in document.
```

You'll routinely see this message if you set up the StyleRef field before you enter any text formatted with the style.

Secret

If you don't want the entire paragraph text to be picked up by the StyleRef field, use a character style instead. Create a character style with a name such as Reference Text and then list the character style in the StyleRef field. Then, highlight the text on each page that you want to appear in the heading and apply the character style to it.

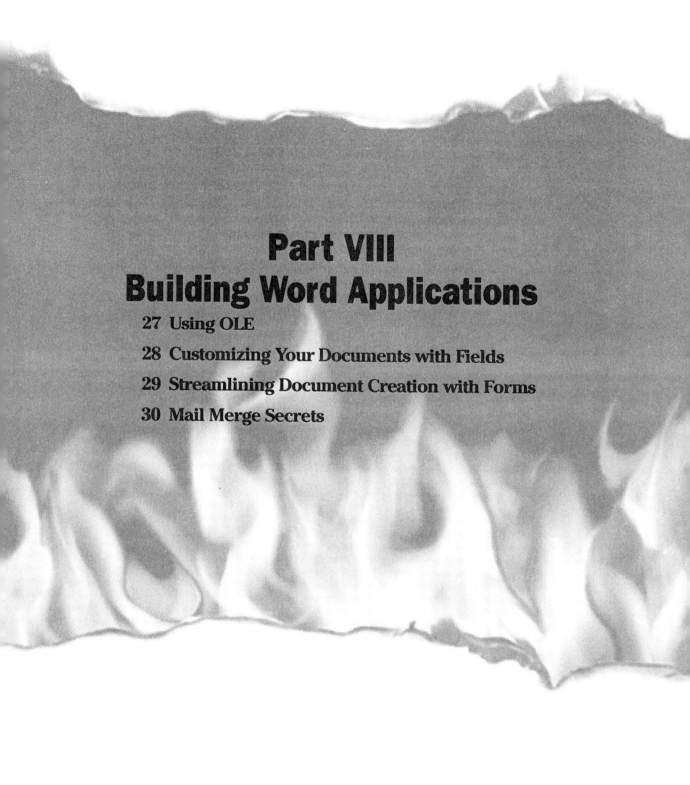

Part VIII
Building Word Applications

27 Using OLE

28 Customizing Your Documents with Fields

29 Streamlining Document Creation with Forms

30 Mail Merge Secrets

Chapter 27

Using OLE

In This Chapter

▶ Understanding what OLE is and how it works

▶ Creating linked and embedded objects

▶ Working with multimedia objects so that your Word documents can play sounds and movies. No one really knows why you would want to do this, but it's really cool anyway.

This chapter covers the ins and outs of OLE, Microsoft's gee-whiz technology that lets programs exchange information by embedding data created by one application in a document created by another.

Understanding OLE

OLE stands for *object linking and embedding*. The basis of OLE is the notion of *compound documents*: documents that consist of bits and pieces that are taken from different applications. For example, a compound word processing document may include portions of a worksheet taken from Excel and a graph created by Microsoft Graph, all embedded within a Microsoft Word document.

How does Word know how to deal with Excel worksheets and Microsoft Graph graphs? It doesn't. But, it does know how to activate Excel and Microsoft Graph to deal with their respective portions of the compound documents, and Excel and Microsoft Graph know how to work with other applications that contain their data in embedded form.

The original version of OLE was first introduced with Windows 3.1. In "classic" OLE, an object embedded within a document appeared either as an icon or as actual data within a frame. If you double-clicked on the object, the program that owned the data was launched so that you could edit the data in a separate window.

OLE 2.0

The newest breed of OLE, called OLE 2.0, allows the various programs responsible for working with objects to work together seemlessly. This means that unless the user is paying attention, he or she won't even realize that another program has been activated. When you double-click on an OLE 2.0 object, the application that owns that object takes over the main program's window, replacing the original program's menus and toolbars with its own. When you finish editing the embedded object, the original menus and toolbars are restored.

Let's put this in terms of a practical example. Suppose that you are working on a monthly report and realize that you'd like to include a spreadsheet to illustrate a crucial point. You could create a Word table and type in the numbers, but Word's table feature is a pretty crude spreadsheet program. You can create simple SUM formulas, but more advanced calculations are out of the question. What you'd really like to do is insert an Excel worksheet right in the middle of the document.

You could do that by launching Excel, creating the worksheet, and then copying and pasting it back into the Word document. But, OLE 2.0 offers a better way: just insert an Excel worksheet object in the document. When you do, an Excel worksheet will appear right in the document. If you double-click the worksheet object, Excel's menus and toolbars will suddenly replace Word's menus and toolbars, and you can edit the worksheet as if you were working in Excel. When you are finished, just click outside of the worksheet object to restore Word's menus and toolbars.

OLE 2.0 makes it seem as if Word and Excel are merged together to create a huge mega-application. In fact, that is precisely the point. Word is already a huge program, with as many or more features than any other word processing program, but Word can't do it all. No matter how much Microsoft improves Word's table feature, Excel will always be better at creating spreadsheets. Also, Microsoft Graph will always be better at creating charts than Word's primitive drawing tools. OLE is a way of allowing individual programs to focus on specific tasks without burdening the user with the details of coaxing the programs to work together.

As an added benefit, OLE 2.0 frees you from tying yourself down to a single software vendor for all your programs. Microsoft could have set up Word so that it would work with Excel and only Excel, but it didn't. Instead, OLE 2.0 allows you to choose any spreadsheet program to embed spreadsheet data in a Word document. Lotus 1-2-3 and Borland's Quattro Pro are every bit as capable as Excel in this regard.

Note

Word 95, as well as all of the other Microsoft Office 95 applications, support OLE 2.0. As a result, this chapter focuses on OLE 2.0, conveniently disregarding the now obsolete OLE 1.

Linking vs. embedding

OLE lets you link or embed objects. The difference between linking and embedding is subtle, but important. When an object is linked, OLE keeps track of the file that contains the object's data. Then, whenever the data in the file changes, OLE automatically updates the linked object. In other words, the linked object is kept synchronized with the source file. When an object is embedded, the object's data is stored right in the Word document rather than in a separate file.

When linking is used, the Word document is smaller than when embedding is used. That's because the object's data doesn't have to be stored along with the Word document. Instead, the object's data is stored in a separate file.

On the other hand, linking is cumbersome because you have to keep track of the linked files. For example, suppose that you create a document that is linked to an Excel file, and then you copy the document to a diskette so a friend or coworker can use it. If you forget to copy the Excel file as well, your colleague won't be able to edit the linked object.

Aside from these differences, linking and embedding work the same. Whether an object is linked or embedded, you still double-click on it to edit its contents.

The Great Componentware Debate

The term *componentware* refers to standards for software that allows objects to be embedded within documents and to software that adheres to these standards. A great debate is currently waging concerning the future of componentware, specifically regarding which of two competing object standards will ultimately prevail: Microsoft's OLE or Apple's OpenDoc.

OLE is Microsoft's Object Linking and Embedding technology, first introduced with Windows 3.1 and now in its second major incarnation (OLE 2). OpenDoc is the alternative to OLE, developed by Apple and embraced by an alliance of just about every major computer company except Microsoft, most notably IBM. In other words, OpenDoc is the rest of the computer industry's answer to Microsoft's OLE.

OLE has the advantage of being in place on millions of Windows-based computers throughout the world, and software developers have been working with OLE for years. OLE has evolved from a simple document-linking standard to a sophisticated object-based architecture that will eventually allow you to distribute objects transparently across a network.

OpenDoc, on the other hand, is brand new. In fact, much of OpenDoc doesn't even really exist yet except on paper. OpenDoc doesn't have the track record that OLE has, but it also doesn't have the evolutionary burdens of OLE. Many experts consider OpenDoc to be technically superior to OLE, but in the real world, technical merit isn't always enough (look where that left OS/2). The smart money is on OLE because of the broad-based acceptance of Windows, the clout of Microsoft, and the substantial head start that OLE has.

Using the <u>I</u>nsert⇨<u>O</u>bject Command

You use the <u>I</u>nsert⇨<u>O</u>bject command to embed an object in a Word document. There are two ways to use this command: by creating a new OLE object that will actually be stored within the Word document file and by embedding an existing file as an object in a Word document. The following sections describe both techniques.

Creating a new OLE object

To create a new OLE object by using the Insert⇨Object command, follow these steps:

1. Position the insertion point where you want to insert the object.

2. Choose the <u>I</u>nsert⇨<u>O</u>bject command and click the <u>C</u>reate New tab. The Object dialog box will appear, as shown in Figure 27-1.

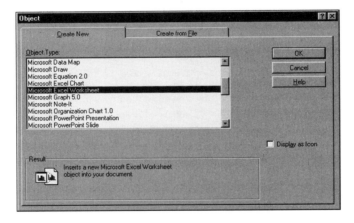

Figure 27-1: The Object dialog box for creating a new OLE object.

3. Choose the type of object you want to insert from the <u>O</u>bject type list. This list shows all of the applications that are installed on your computer and support OLE.

Note

If an application doesn't appear on the list and you know it supports OLE, the application isn't properly registered with Windows 95. The easiest way to remedy this problem is to reinstall the application.

4. If you want the object to appear as an icon rather than as the actual data contained in the object, select the Displ<u>a</u>y as Icon option. This option is usually used for multimedia objects, such as sound or video files.

5. Click OK. Word will insert the object. If the owning application supports OLE 2.0, it will take over Word's menus and toolbars. For example, Figure 27-2 shows how the Word window appears after inserting an Excel object. Notice that the menus and toolbars are those of Excel, not Word.

6. Edit the embedded object by using its application's editing features.

7. When you're done, click anywhere outside the embedded object to restore Word's menus and toolbars.

Inserting an existing file as an object

If you want to embed an existing file as an object, follow these steps:

1. Position the insertion point where you want to insert the file.

2. Choose the Insert⇨Object command and click the Create from File tab. The dialog box shown in Figure 27-3 will be shown.

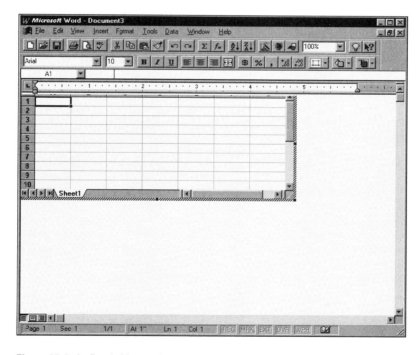

Figure 27-2: An Excel object embedded in a Word document.

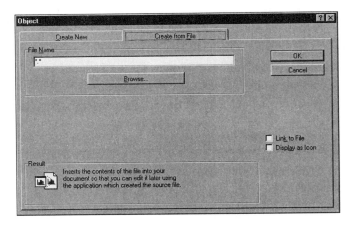

Figure 27-3: Inserting an existing file as an object.

3. Type the name of the file you want to insert as an object. Or, click the Browse button and rummage about until you locate the file.

4. If you want to create a link to the file so that the object will be updated if the file is modified, choose the Link to File option.

5. If you want to display an icon instead of the file's actual data, pick the Display as Icon option.

6. Click OK to insert the file as an object.

Dragging Objects into Word Documents

Another, sometimes simpler, way to insert an existing file as an object is to use the drag-and-drop technique. To use this technique, you simply drag a Windows 95 file icon into the Word document, releasing it at the point where you want to insert it. Drag and drop is easiest if you first arrange your desktop so that the both the icon you want to insert and the Word document are visible. However, arranging the windows to make this possible is not always feasible. In such cases, there is an easier, although little-known, way:

1. Locate the icon for the file you want to insert into a Word document.

2. Point to the icon and then press and hold down the left mouse button. Drag the icon until the mouser pointer changes to indicate that you have begun to drag the object. For example

3. While still holding down the left mouse button, press Alt+Tab to bring up the display of open windows. Release the Tab key, but continue to hold down the Alt key (and the mouse button).

4. While still holding down the Alt key, press the Tab key as many times as necessary until the Word icon is highlighted. When the Word icon is selected, release the Alt key.

5. Move the mouse pointer to the location where you want the object inserted and release the mouse button.

Using the Copy and Paste Special Commands

If you want to insert just a portion of another application's file into a Word document, you must use the Copy and Paste Special commands. Here is the procedure:

1. In the other application, open the file that contains the information you want to embed.

2. Select the information you want to embed and choose the Edit⇨Copy command (or press Ctrl+C or right-click the information and choose the Copy command).

3. Switch to Word and move the insertion point to the location where you want the information embedded.

4. Choose the Edit⇨Paste Special command. The Paste Special dialog box will appear, as shown in Figure 27-4.

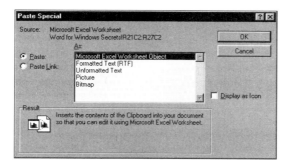

Figure 27-4: The Paste Special dialog box.

5. Select the type of object that you want to insert in the As list. If the information on the Clipboard was copied from an application that supports OLE, an object type will appear first in the As list. The other options in the list represent alternative formats in which you can paste the data.

6. If you want to establish a link to the original file, select the Paste⇨Link option.

7. If you want the object displayed as an icon rather than the file's actual contents, select the Display as Icon option. When you select this option, a Change Icon button will appear. You can click this button to change the icon displayed for the object.

8. Click OK.

Editing an Object

There are several ways to edit an OLE object:

- Double-click the object. If the object supports OLE 2.0, this edits the object in-place. If the object does not support OLE 2.0, a separate window is opened to edit the object.

- Select the object and choose the Edit⇨Object command. For an OLE 2.0 object, this will display a menu that allows you to Edit the object in-place or Open the object for editing in a separate window.

- Right-click the object to bring up its quick menu. Then, select the Edit command to edit the object in place or the Open command to edit the object in a separate window.

Working with Links

When you link an object, Windows 95 maintains a connection between the object and the source file that contains its information. By default, the object is automatically updated with new information from the source file whenever you open the document that contains the linked object or when the information in the source file changes. However, you can change the way the link is maintained by selecting the object and calling up the Edit⇨Links command. This displays the dialog box shown in Figure 27-5.

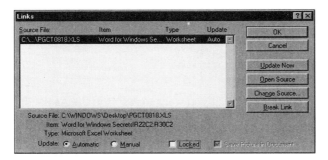

Figure 27-5: The Links dialog box.

Once this dialog box appears, you have the following options:

- **Source File:** If the document contains more than one linked object, you can select the object that you want to work with from the list of objects in the Source File area.

- **Update Now:** Click this button to update the selected links immediately.

- **Open Source:** Click this button to open the selected object in a separate window so that you can edit it.

- **Change Source:** Click this button to change the source file associated with a link.

- **Break Link:** Click this button to break the line with the source file.

- **Automatic:** Select this option to specify that Word should update the selected link when the document is opened or when the source file changes.

- **Manual:** Select this option if you do not want Word to update the selected link automatically. See the next section for information on how to update links manually.

- **Locked:** Select this option to lock the selected link temporarily . The object will not be updated until you unlock the link.

- **Save Picture in Document:** For links to graphics files, select this option to save a bitmapped image of the file in the document.

Manually Updating Links

To update links to objects manually, use one of these techniques:

- Choose the Edit⇨Links command, select the link or links you want to update, and click the Update Now button.

- Click the object you want to update and press F9.

- Right-click the object you want to update and select Update Links from the shortcut menu that appears.

- To update all links quickly, press Ctrl+A to select the entire document and press F9. (This will also update all fields in the document.)

Converting an Object

The Edit⇨Object⇨Convert command performs three functions:

- Converting an object of one type to another type.

- Specifying that an object should be opened as if it were an object of a different type.

- Specifying whether the object should be displayed as data or as an icon.

To use the Edit⇨Object⇨Convert command, select the object you want to convert and choose the Edit⇨Object⇨Convert command. The dialog box shown in Figure 27-6 will be displayed.

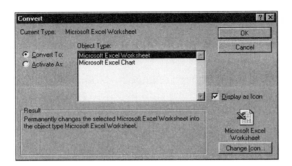

Figure 27-6: The Convert dialog box.

Select whether you want to convert the object to another type (Convert To) or merely activate the object as a different type (Activate As) and click OK. To switch from displaying data to displaying an icon, or vice versa, click the Display as Icon check box. If you want, you can also click the Change Icon button to specify a different icon to be displayed for the object.

Inserting and Playing Multimedia Objects

The following sections explain the procedures for inserting and playing sound and video objects in a Word document.

Inserting a sound object

You can embed a sound file into a Word document just like any other object. To insert an existing sound file, follow these steps:

1. Position the insertion point where you want to insert the sound.

2. Call up the Insert⇨Object command and click the Create From File tab.

3. Click the Browse button and locate the sound file you want to insert.

To display just sound files, type *.**wav** in the File name field.

Note

4. Select the file you want to insert and click OK.

5. The sound file will be inserted into the document and displayed as an icon, as shown in Figure 27-7.

Figure 27-7: Icon displayed for a sound file.

Note

If you click the Display as Icon option, the name of the sound file will be displayed beneath its icon. Either way, you can play the sound by double-clicking it.

Recording a sound in Word

To record a new sound object while working in Word, follow these steps:

1. Position the insertion point where you want to insert the sound.

2. Call up the Insert⇨Object command and click the Create New tab.

3. Choose Wave Sound as the Object Type and click OK. The Sound Object dialog box will appear, as shown in Figure 27-8.

Figure 27-8: The Sound Object dialog box.

4. Click the red Record button.

5. Talk into the microphone.

6. When you're done, click the Stop button.

The sound object will be inserted in the document as an icon. To play the sound, double-click the icon.

Inserting a video file in a Word document

If you have a stunning video clip you'd like to insert into a Word document, use the Insert⇨Object command, click the Create from File tab, and browse for the file. The file will be inserted into the document along with a graphical representation (unless you choose Display as Icon) that you can double-click to play. It's a bit strange to watch a video play in the middle of a Word document, but you can do it. See Figure 27-9.

Figure 27-9: An Eddie Brickell video playing in the middle of a Word document.

Tip

If you want to experiment with this but aren't sure where to obtain video files, you're in luck if you purchased the CD-ROM edition of the Windows 95 upgrade. It includes several videos that you can use for this purpose. Look in the \Funstuff\Videos folder. The video shown in Figure 27-9 is called Goodtimes.avi (Avi is the standard extension for video files). It's a music video produced by Edie Brickell.

Chapter 28

Customizing Your
Documents With Fields

In This Chapter

▶ How to work with fields, which let you customize your documents with values such as the current date, the number of pages in the document, and many other values

▶ A complete reference to all of Word's fields

A *field* is a special placeholder code that tells Word to insert something (usually text of some sort) into the document. A date field, for example, tells Word to insert the current date into the document. No matter when you edit or print the document, the date field causes the document to contain the current date.

Fields are everywhere in Word. Many of the commands you have come to know and love rely on fields to do their business. Fields let you put the page number in a header or footer, create a table of contents or an index, and print mail-merged letters. These fields are often inserted into your document without your knowledge, as a result of your using some other command, such as Insert⇨Page Numbers or Tools⇨Mail Merge.

This chapter shows you what you need to know to insert fields directly, by using the Insert⇨Field command. Word provides many different types of types of fields (more than 60). At the end of this chapter, you'll find a complete reference to all of them.

Understanding Fields

A *field* is a code that Word translates into some result, usually text, which is then inserted into the document. When you insert a date field, for example, you're really saying to Word, "Insert the current date right here, and make sure that you get the date right. When I print this document, I want to see today's date. If I print it tomorrow, I want to see tomorrow's date. Next week, I want to see next week's date. A year from now... ." You get the idea. A date field is like a placeholder for an actual date, which Word inserts automatically.

Other fields work in the same way. The text Word inserts in place of the field code is called the *result.* For a date field, the result is the current date. For a page-number field, the result is the current page number. Other field types produce more complicated results, such as a table of contents or an index. For some fields, the result isn't text at all, but a picture or a chart.

When you print a document, there's no way to distinguish between text you typed directly into the document and text that is a field result. Consider, for example, the following text you might use in a letter:

> As of today, Saturday, August 26, 1995, you have been banished from Remulak and sentenced to live out the remainder of your existence among the Blunt Skulls of Earth.

You can't tell that *Saturday, August 26, 1995,* is a field result.

When you edit a document in Word, you must have some way to distinguish between regular text and field results. Word normally displays field results so that the document appears on-screen just as it does when you print it. If the result isn't quite what you expected, however, or if you want to make sure that you used the correct field to produce a result, you can switch the display to show field codes.

Secret

Word also has an option that displays field results but shades them so that you can distinguish field results from ordinary text. Call up the Tools⇨Options command and click from the View tab. Then, select one of the following three values for the Field Shading drop-down list box:

- **Never:** Field results are displayed as normal, with no shading.
- **Always:** Field results are shaded with a gray background.
- **When Selected:** Field results are shown with a gray background when selected.

Then, click OK to put the option you selected into effect.

The preceding letter fragment with field codes displayed looks like this:

> As of today, { TIME \@ "dddd, MMMM dd, yyyy" }, you have been banished from Remulak and sentenced to live out the remainder of your existence among the Blunt Skulls of Earth.

The field is the stuff marked by the curly braces ({ }), which are called *field characters.* Their whole purpose in life is to tell Word that a field lives there. They look just like the curly braces you can type from the keyboard, but they're not. The only way you can create these field characters is by using the Insert⇨Field command or some other Word command that inserts a field.

Sandwiched between the field characters is the field itself. Each field begins with a *field type* that tells you what type of field you have there. In the preceding example, you're looking at a TIME field, which provides the current date or time in many different formats.

Following the field type are *instructions,* which tell the field what to do. The TIME field in the preceding example contains an instruction that tells Word how to format the time: *ddd, MMMM dd, yyyy.* The hard part about using fields is figuring out what to do with the instructions. Each field type has its own array of instruction codes. The reference section at the end of this chapter provides the instruction codes for every Word field.

Inserting a Field

Many Word commands, such as Insert⇨Date and Time and Insert⇨Index and Tables, quietly insert fields into your document without boasting. But, Word provides many other fields you can insert only by using the Insert⇨Field command.

Follow this procedure to insert a field in your document:

1. Move the cursor to the point where you want to insert the field.

2. Call up the Insert⇨Field command. The Field dialog box appears, as shown in Figure 28-1.

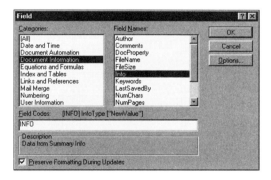

Figure 28-1: The Field dialog box.

3. Choose the field type you want by scrolling through the Categories and Field Names lists. Because so many field types exist, Word breaks them down into categories so that you can find them easier. First, pick the category that contains the field you want to use. Then, pick the field from the Field Names list. If the field you want doesn't appear, try a different category. If you're not sure which category contains the field you want to insert, choose (All) as the category. This action lists all of Word's field types in the Field Names list.

4. In the Field Codes box, add any additional instructions required by the field. Word automatically adds the field type to the Field Codes text box. Then, it gives you a hint about how to complete the field code by listing, just above the Field Codes box, which instructions the selected field type accepts. Look back at Figure 28-1. You can see that Word added the field type INFO to the Field Codes box and shows that you can include an InfoType (whatever that is) and a NewValue (huh?). This is very helpful, if you happen to know what an InfoType and NewValue are.

5. If you aren't sure what additional instructions to use for the field, click the Options button. A Field Options dialog box appears, which looks something like Figure 28-2. The options presented in the dialog box will vary depending on the field.

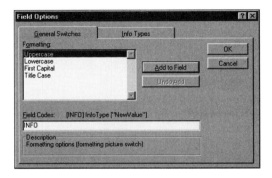

Figure 28-2: The Field Options dialog box.

6. Add options to the field codes by choosing an option you want to add in the Name list and then clicking Add to Field. Every time you click the Add to Field button, the selected option is added to the Field Codes box. Also, a terse description of each field option appears at the bottom of the Field Options dialog box.

7. When you have added all the options you need, click OK to return to the Field dialog box.

8. Click OK to insert the field into the document.

Note

When you insert a field, either the field code or the result is displayed, depending on whether the Field Codes view option is set. You can switch between field codes and field results by pressing Alt+F9, or you can right-click the field to select the Toggle Field Codes command.

If you see something like **Error! Unknown switch argument** rather than the field result you expected, you made a mistake when you composed the field instructions. You have to edit the field directly by pressing Alt+F9 to reveal the field codes and then clicking in the field and typing your correction. (Or, once again, right-click the field and choose the Toggle Field Codes command.)

Keyboard Shortcuts for Working with Fields

A whole bevy of specialized keyboard shortcuts are available for working with fields. Table 28-1 summarizes them for your convenience.

Table 28-1	Keyboard Shortcuts for Fields
Keyboard Shortcut	*What It Does*
F9	Updates the selected field or fields.
Shift+F9	Switches the display between field codes and field results for the selected field or fields. You must place the insertion point in a field to use this command.
Alt+F9	Switches the display between field codes and field results for all fields in the document. You do not have to select a field before using this command.
Ctrl+F9	Inserts a blank field into a document.
Ctrl+Shift+F9	Converts a field to text (unlinks the field).
F11	Finds the next field in the document.
Shift+F11	Finds the previous field in the document.
Ctrl+F11	Locks a field so that it cannot be updated.
Ctrl+Shift+F11	Unlocks a field.

Another Way to Insert Fields

If you are good at typing commands, you can insert a field by typing it directly in your document. Just follow these steps:

1. Position the cursor where you want to insert the field.

2. Type the field name and instructions for the field you want to insert. Don't worry about the curly braces for now.

3. Select the text you typed in Step 2.

4. Press Ctrl+F9.

Ctrl+F9 converts the selected text to a field by enclosing it in field codes: those curly little braces that look just like the curly braces you can type on the keyboard but aren't the same thing at all. If you prefer, you can reverse these steps: position the cursor where you want to place the field and press Ctrl+F9 and an empty field appears, which you can select. Then, you can type the field name and instructions within the braces.

Formatting Field Results with Switches

Word provides several switches that you can use on almost any field to control the formatting applied to the field result. You don't have to use any of these fields if you don't want to. If you omit them, Word makes an educated guess about the format of the field result.

You can use three switches to format a field's result:

- The Format switch (\·) tells Word whether to capitalize the field results and, for fields that produce numeric results, which type of numbers to create (Arabic or Roman numerals, for example).
- The Numeric Picture switch (\#) controls the format of numbers.
- The Date-Time Picture switch (\@) sets the format of dates and times.

Each of these switches has numerous options that you can mix and match to format the field in just about any way you want. The various uses of these three switches are explained in the following sections.

Preserving formatting when you update fields: the * mergeformat switch

When you update a field, Word usually removes any formatting, such as bold or italics, that you have applied to a field result. If you want Word to keep this type of formatting, include the * mergeformat switch in the field. It's usually a good idea to preserve formatting, so I recommend you use this switch most of the time.

You can tell Word to add a * mergeformat switch automatically to a field by checking the Preserve Formatting During Updates check box in the Field dialog box.

Capitalizing field results

Use the Format switch (*) options listed in Table 28-2 to control capitalization in a field result. The following field, for example, inserts the name of the current file in lowercase letters:

{ filename \n lower \n mergeformat }

Table 28-2	Capitalizing Field Results
Switch	*What It Means*
* caps	The First Letter Of Each Word Is Capitalized.
* firstcap	The first letter of the first word is capitalized.
* lower	all the letters are lowercase.
* upper	ALL THE LETTERS ARE UPPERCASE.

Setting the number format

Numbers are usually displayed with Arabic numerals. You can change the format of numbers in field results, however, by using the switches listed in Table 28-3. Consider this text, for example:

This is the { page \n ordtext \n mergeformat } page.

This line produces a result like this:

This is the thirty-third page.

In this case, the * ordtext switch caused the page number to be spelled out as a number.

Table 28-3	Setting The Number Format
Switch	*What It Means*
\n alphabetic	Converts numbers to their corresponding letters of the alphabet (*1* becomes *A, 2* becomes *B,* and so on).
\n arabic	The usual number format (nothing special here).
\n cardtext	Spells out the number (for example, *1994* becomes *one thousand nine-hundred ninety-four*).
\n dollartext	Spells out a dollar amount the way you would write it on a check (*289.95* becomes *two hundred eighty-nine and 95/100*).
\n hex	A favorite of computer nerds, converts numbers from the normal earth dweller base 10 numbering system to base 16 (for example, *492* becomes *1EC*).

(continued)

Table 28-3 *(continued)*

Switch	What It Means
\n ordinal	Adds *st, nd, rd,* or whatever is appropriate to the end of the number (for example, *307* becomes *307th*).
\n ordtext	Spells out the number and adds *st, nd, rd,* or whatever is appropriate to the end (for example, *307* becomes *three hundred seventh*).
\n roman	Converts the number to Roman numerals. This is used by film directors to mark copyright dates (for example, *1953* becomes *mcmliii*). To get the true motion picture copyright effect, use this in combination with the \n upper switch.

Creating custom number formats

If you don't like the way Word displays numbers, you can create your own custom number formats by using the Numeric Picture switch (\#). Numeric pictures are created by stringing together a bunch of pound signs, zeros, commas, decimal points, plus or minus signs, dollar signs, and other characters to show how you want numbers to appear. Table 28-4 lists the numeric picture switches you're most likely to use.

Tip

You can automatically add the numeric pictures listed in Table 28-4 to formulas if you use the Table⇨Formula command rather than the Insert⇨Field command to create the formula. The Table⇨Formula command provides a drop-down list box that lists these pictures. You just choose the number format you want, and Word inserts the appropriate switch into the field.

Table 28-4	Sample Numeric Picture Switches
Picture Switch	Description
\# #,##0	Prints whole numbers with commas to separate groups of thousands (for example, 1,024 and 1,244,212).
\# #,##0.00	Prints numbers with commas to separate groups of thousands and two decimal positions. Both decimal positions are printed, even if one or both of them is zero (for example, 1,024.00 and 8.47).
\# $#,##0.00; ($#,##0.00)	Prints numbers as money: commas to separate groups of thousands, two decimal positions, and a leading dollar sign. Negative numbers are enclosed in parentheses: for example, $1,024.00 and ($97.38).

Picture Switch	Description
\# 0	Prints whole numbers without commas (for example, 38 and 124873345).
\# 0%	Prints whole numbers without commas, followed by a percent sign (for example, 98%).
\# 0.00	Prints numbers without commas but with two decimal positions (for example, 1024.00 or 3.14).
\# 0.00%	Prints numbers without commas, with two decimal positions, and followed by a percent sign (for example, 97.99%).

Creating custom date and time formats

When you use the Insert⇨Field command to insert a date field, you can click the Options button and choose from one of 14 different formats. If you don't like any of the 14 formats, you can compose your own custom date format by using the Date-Time Picture switch (\@). You just string together the various components of the date or time by using combinations of characters, such as MMM to stand for the three-letter month abbreviation, and dddd to stand for the day of the week, spelled out.

You'd think that with 14 date formats to choose from, you'd always be able to find the one you need. That's not always the case, though. For example, if you want the current year (as in 1995), you have to create a custom date format using the switch \@ **"yyyy"**. This seemingly basic date format isn't among the 14 formats provided by Word.

Updating a Field

When you first insert a field, Word calculates the field's result. Thereafter, the field result may become out of date. To recalculate a field result to make sure that it is up to date, follow one of these procedures:

- Call up the Tools⇨Options command and choose the Print tab. Check the Update Fields check box and click OK. This action tells Word to automatically update all fields every time it prints the document.

- To update a specific field, select the field and press F9. If you select several fields, pressing F9 updates all of them. You can quickly update all the fields in a document by pressing Ctrl+A to select the entire document and then pressing F9 to update the fields.

- If you point to a field and click the right mouse button, a shortcut menu appears. Choose the Update Field command from this menu to update the field.

Preventing a Field from Being Updated

If you do *not* want a field to be updated, you can either lock the field or unlink the field. If you lock the field, Word prevents it from being updated until you *unlock* the field. If you *unlink* the field, Word deletes the field code and replaces it with the result text. Locking a field temporarily prevents it from being updated; unlinking the field is permanent.

To lock, unlock, or unlink a field, first select it. Then, use the following keyboard shortcuts shown in Table 28-5:

Table 28-5 Keyboard Shortcuts for Locking, Unlocking, or Unlinking a Field

Keyboard Shortcut	*What It Does*
Ctrl+F11	Locks the field.
Ctrl+Shift+F11	Unlocks the field.
Ctrl+Shift+F9	Converts the field to results text (unlink the field).

Field Code Reference

The following sections describe the various field codes you can use with Word. As you use this reference, keep in mind that all of the fields can use the * Format switch, the date-related fields can use the \@ Date-Time Picture switch, and any of the numeric fields can use the \# Numeric Picture switch.

In the following sections, text enclosed in brackets is optional. For example, in the following field code,

{ INCLUDETEXT "*filename*" [*bookmark*] [\c *classname*] [\!] }

bookmark, \c *classname*, and \! are all optional. In addition, text that must appear exactly as typed is shown in regular type; text that must be replaced with your own values appears in italics.

Advance

Moves the text that follows the ADVANCE field to the right or left, up or down, or to a specific position. In most cases, it's better to adjust positioning with the Format⇨Font, Format⇨Paragraph, or Format⇨Tabs command or by framing the text. The Advance field takes the following form:

{ ADVANCE [\d *points*] [\u *points*] [\l *points*] [\r *points*]
[\x *points*] [\y *points*] }

Option	What It Does
\d *points*	Moves the text down the specified number of points.
\u *points*	Moves the text up the specified number of points.
\l *points*	Moves the text left the specified number of points.
\r *points*	Moves the text right the specified number of points.
\x *points*	Moves the text to a specific position (in points) from the left margin. You can think of this as a special type of tab character that is capable of moving text both forward and backward.
\y *points*	This switch does not seem to work the way that the on-line help says it does. According to the on-line help, this switch moves the text "to the specified vertical position relative to the current line position," whatever that means. What it actually does is move the text down to the specified vertical position measured in points from the top of the page, unless the field code appears *below* the specified point. In that case, it appears to have no effect. In other words, the \y switch moves text down to the specified position, but does not move text up. Note, too, that there is the inconsistency between \x and \y: \x positions text relative to the left margin. \y positions text relative to the top of the page.

Ask

Prompts for information from the user and stores the result in a bookmark. A separate dialog box is displayed to ask the question. The Ask field takes the following form:

```
{ ASK Bookmark "prompt" [\d "default"] [\o] }
```

Option	What It Does
Bookmark	Specifies the name of the bookmark that will be used to hold the response entered by the user. The existing contents of the bookmark will be erased. To include the user's response somewhere in the document, reference the bookmark name.
"prompt"	Specifies the text that will appear to prompt the user for input.
\d *"default"*	Specifies the default value that will be assigned to the bookmark if the user does not enter a response.
\o	Allows you to include an Ask field in a mail merge main document and avoid having the user prompted for each merged record. Instead, the prompt is displayed just once, when the first record is merged. The same response is used for each subsequent record.

Author

Obtains the Author name from the document properties or sets the Author property to a new value. The Author field takes the following form:

```
{ AUTHOR ["newname"] }
```

Option	What It Does
"newname"	Supplies a new author name for the document.

AutoNum

Automatically numbers the paragraph. This field has been made obsolete by the Format⇨Bullets and Numbering command. AutoNum has no options, and takes the following form:

```
{ AUTONUM }
```

AutoNumLgl

Automatically numbers heading paragraphs using legal or technical format (for example, 1.1, 1.2, and so on). Place an AutoNumLgl field at the beginning of each paragraph that you want to be numbered. This field has been rendered obsolete by the Format⇨Bullets and Numbering command. AutoNumLgl has no options, and takes the following form:

```
{ AUTONUMLGL }
```

AutoNumOut

Automatically numbers heading paragraphs using outline form. Place an AutoNumOut field at the beginning of each paragraph that you want to be numbered. This field has been rendered obsolete by the Format⇨Bullets and Numbering command. AutoNumOut has no options, and takes the following form:

```
{ AUTONUMOUT }
```

AutoText

Inserts an AutoText entry. AutoText takes the following form:

```
{ AUTOTEXT autotextentry }
```

Option	What It Does
autotextentry	The name of the AutoText entry to insert. If the AutoText entry does not exist, the message **"Error! AutoText entry not defined"** will be inserted in your document.

BarCode

Inserts a postal bar code based on an address. You can do this more easily by using the Tools⇨Envelopes and Labels command. BarCode takes the following form:

```
{ BARCODE "address" [\b] [\f "char"] [\u] }
```

Option	What It Does
"address"	Specifies the address that is used to create the barcode.
\b	Indicates that address is actually a bookmark. The value of the bookmark is used to create the bar code.
\f"char"	Inserts a Facing Identification Mark (FIM). Char should be "A" to insert a courtesy reply mark (FIM-A) or "C" to insert a business reply mark (FIM-C).
\u	Identifies the bar code as a United States postal address. This switch should always be specified if you are mailing in the United States.

(Bookmark)

See the Ref field.

Comments

Shows the contents of the Comments field from the document's properties, and allows you to change the comments. Comments takes the following form:

```
{ COMMENTS ["new comments"] }
```

Option	What It Does
"new comments"	Sets the Comments property for the current document. If omitted, the document's comments are displayed.

Compare

Compares two expressions and returns a value of 1 if the comparison is true and 0 if false. It is similar to the If field. Compare takes the following form:

```
{ COMPARE Expression1 Operator Expression2 }
```

Option	What It Does
expression1	Specifies the first expression to compare.
operator	Specifies one of the following comparison operators.
	= Equal to
	<> Not equal to
	> Greater than
	< Less than
	>= Greater than or equal to
	<= Less than or equal to
expression2	Specifies the other expression to compare.

Tip

Placing 1 or 0 in your document probably won't be very meaningful to your reader. As a result, you are more likely to use this field if it is nested within another field that performs additional calculations that are based on the result of the comparison.

CreateDate

Inserts the document's creation date. CreateDate takes the following form:

```
{ CREATEDATE [ \@ "Date Picture " ] }
```

Option	What It Does
\@ "Date Picture "	The format in which the creation date will be displayed. See the section "Creating custom date and time formats" earlier in this chapter for more information.

Database

Inserts the result of a database query into the document as a table. Database takes the following form:

```
{ DATABASE [\l "autoformat"] [\b "sum"] [\h] [\c "connect "]
[\d "location "] [\f "start "] [\t "end "] [\s "SQL-text "]}
```

Option	What It Does
\l *"autoformat"*	Applies an AutoFormat to the resulting table. Refer to the T<u>a</u>ble⇨Table Auto<u>F</u>ormat command to determine the number associated with each AutoFormat: Simple 1 is 1, Simple 2 is 2, Classic 1 is 4, and so on.
\b *"sum"*	Further qualifies the setting of the \l switch by indicating which attributes of the AutoFormat set by the \l switch apply to the table. Adds any combination of the following values to determine the value for the switch.
0	None
1	Borders
2	Shading
4	Font
8	Color
16	AutoFit
32	Heading Rows
64	Last Row
128	First Column
256	Last Column
	For example, the switches "\l "3" \b "11" apply only the borders, shading, and color attributes of the table format set by the \l switch.
\h	Uses the field names from the database to create column headings in the resulting table.
\c *"connect "*	Specifies the connection to the database. This should be a valid ODBC connection string. (ODBC only.)
\d *"location "*	Specifies the path and filename of the database. This is not used for ODBC.
\f *"start "*	Specifies the record number of the first data record to insert.
\t *"end "*	Specifies the record number of the last data record to insert.
\s *"SQL-text "*	SQL instructions. Oh boy. If I started to explain SQL here, the book would run another 200 pages at least. (To include a quotation mark in the SQL text, type a backslash before the quotation mark.)

Date

Inserts the current date into the document. Date takes the following form:

```
{ DA⁻E [\@Date-picture] [\l] }
```

Option	What It Does
[\@*Date-picture*	Specifies the format for the date. If omitted, the date format specified in the Windows Control Panel Regional Settings is used.
|	Uses the date format from the last time the date was inserted.

DDE

Establishes a Dynamic Data Exchange (DDE) link with another application. DDE is an older form of linking that has been superseded by OLE. Therefore, the DDE field is considered obsolete. DDE takes the following form:

`{ DDE appname filename [placeref] }`

Option	What It Does
appname	Specifies the name of the application with which to establish the link.
filename	Specifies the name of the file.
placeref	Specifies a portion of the file to be linked to, such as a range of cells or text. This setting is application-specific.

DDEAuto

Establishes a Dynamic Data Exchange (DDE) automatic link with another application. DDE is an older form of linking that has been superseded by OLE. Therefore, the DDE field is considered obsolete. Automatic links are updated automatically whenever the source document changes. DDEAuto takes the following form:

`{ DDEAuto appname filename [placeref] }`

Option	What It Does
appname	Specifies the name of the application with which to establish the link.
filename	Specifies the name of the file.
placeref	Specifies a portion of the file to be linked to, such as a range of cells or text. This setting is application-specific.

DocProperty

Retrieves a specified document property. Many of these document properties are also available via their own field codes, such as Author, TotalEditingTime, and so on. Some are also available via the Info field. DocPropertytakes the following form:

```
{ DOCPROPERTY "name" }
```

Option	What It Does	
name	The name of the property to insert. The standard document Properties include:	
	Author	Bytes
	Category	Characters
	Comments	Company
	CreateTime	Keywords
	LastPrinted	LastSavedBy
	LastSavedTime	Lines
	Manager	NameOfApplication
	Pages	Paragraphs
	RevisionNumber	Security
	Subject	Template
	Title	TotalEditingTime
	Words	

EditTime

Inserts the total editing time in minutes since the document was created. Don't be fooled into thinking that this number somehow reflects a meaningful measure of how long you spent working on the document because the clock continues to run while a document is open whether you're working on it or not. If you are paid based on this field, I recommend you leave your documents open overnight. EditTime takes the following form:

```
{ EDITTIME }
```

Embed

Sets up an embedded OLE object. You cannot enter this field manually. You can only create this field via the Insert⇨Object command, the Edit⇨Paste Special command or by any of the many other means of creating embedded objects. Embed takes the following form:

```
{ EMBED classname [\s] }
```

Option	What It Does
classname	Specifies the classname for the application associated with the embedded object.
\s	Indicates that whenever the field is updated, the object should be returned to its original size.

Eq

Before Microsoft added the Equation Editor to Word, the Eq field was the only way to create equations. The Equation Editor is much easier to use and has many more options, so you won't want to bother with this field. If you need to create equations, install the Equation Editor and be done with it. Eq takes the following form:

```
{ EQ equation }
```

Option	What It Does
equation	Consists of a sequence of special equation switches that you can use to build equations. For more information, see the on-line help.

Secret

One good use for the EQ field code is to place a border around an individual word or phrase. For example:

Sometimes it is nice to place a ⌐border⌐ around a single word.

If you placed the insertion point in the bordered word and pressed Alt+F9, the line would appear as follows:

Sometimes it is nice to place a { EQ \x(border) }around a single word.

As you can see, the text that is to be given a border is placed within parentheses following an \x switch.

FileName

Inserts the filename of the current document, with or without the complete path. FileName takes the following form:

```
{ FILENAME [\p] }
```

Option	What It Does
\p	Includes the complete path with the filename.

FileSize

Inserts the size of the document file in bytes, kilobytes, or megabytes. FileSize takes the following form:

```
{ FILESIZE [\k] [\m] }
```

Option	What It Does
\k	Shows the size in kilobytes.
\m	Shows the size in megabytes.

Fillin

The Fillin field prompts the user for text and inserts the text into the document as the field result. It is similar to Ask, except that Ask places the user's input in a bookmark rather than in the document. Fillin takes the following form:

```
{ FILLIN "prompt" [\d "default"] [\o] }
```

Option	What It Does
"prompt"	Specifies the text that will appear to prompt the user for input.
\d "default"	Specifies the default value that will be assigned to the bookmark if the user does not enter a response.
\o	Allows you to include an Ask field in a mail merge main document and avoid having the user prompted for each merged record. Instead, the prompt is displayed just once, when the first record is merged. The same response is used for each subsequent record.

FormCheckBox

Creates a check box field for a form. You can insert this field only by the Insert⇨Form Field command or by the Check Box Form Field button on the Forms toolbar.

FormDropDown

Creates a drop-down list field for a form. You can insert this field only by the Insert⇨Form Field command or by the Drop-Down Form Field button on the Forms toolbar.

FormText

Creates a text box field for a form. You can insert this field only by the Insert⇨Form Field command or by the Text Box Form Field button on the Forms toolbar.

GoToButton

Creates a button that moves the insertion point to a specified location when clicked. GoToButton takes the following form:

```
{ GOTOBUTTON destination text }
```

Option	What It Does
destination	Specifies the location that the insertion point is moved to when the button is clicked. It may be a bookmark name, a page number, or one of the following items:
	s*n* A section, for example, s3 to go to the third section.
	l*n* A line, for example, l20 to go to line 20.
	f*n* A footnote, for example, f10 to go to the tenth footnote.
	a*n* An annotation, for example, a1 to go to the first annotation.
text	Specifies the text used to represent the button. You can format the text in any way you wish to make it resemble a button or a hypertext link. For example, apply a border to the text to create a button-like appearance or display the text in an alternate color to create a hypertext link. You can also include a graphic button image.

Secret

Where do you obtain graphic button images for GOTOBUTTON fields? You can draw them yourself using Paint, but you can also steal any of the toolbar button images that come with Word. Call up the Tools⇨Customize command, click the Toolbars tab, right-click any button on the screen with an image that you want to use, and choose the Copy Button Image command. This places the button image on the Clipboard. Close the Customize dialog box and press Ctrl+V to paste the button image into the GOTOBUTTON field.

If

This is one of Word's trickiest fields. It compares the results of two expressions and supplies one of two result values depending on the outcome of the comparison. The If field takes the following form:

```
{ IF expression1 operator expression2 truetext falsetext }
```

Option	What It Does
expression1	Specifies the first expression to compare.
operator	Specifies one of the following comparison operators:
	= Equal to
	<> Not equal to
	> Greater than
	< Less than
	>= Greater than or equal to
	<= Less than or equal to
expression2	Specifies the other expression to compare.
truetext	Specifies the text value to be used if the result of the comparison is true.
falsetext	Specifies the text value to be used if the result of the comparison is false.

IncludePicture

Inserts a picture into the document. IncludePicture takes the following form:

```
{ INCLUDEPICTURE filename [\c converter] [\d] }
```

Option	What It Does
filename	Specifies the name of the picture file to be inserted. Use double-slashes to indicate slashes in a path: for example, "c:\\Windows\\arcade.bmp".
\c *converter*	Indicates the name of the graphics converter. Word can usually determine which converter to use, so this field shouldn't be necessary.
\d	Does not store the graphics file in the document. This reduces the size of the document but requires Word to access the graphics file before the file can be displayed.

IncludeText

Inserts another document into the current document. IncludeText takes the following form:

`{ INCLUDETEXT "filename" [bookmark] [\c classname] [\!] }`

Option	What It Does
"filename"	Specifies the filename of the document to be inserted. Use double-slashes to indicate slashes in a path: for example, "c:\\winword\\readme.doc".
bookmark	Specifies the name of a bookmark in the source document to be included. If omitted, the entire document is included.
\c converter	Specifies the name of the converter used to import the text. The following converters are supplied with Word:

Document Format	Converter Name
Microsoft Excel	MSBiff
Lotus 1-2-3	Lotus123
WordPerfect version 6.x	WordPerfect6x
WordPerfect version 5.x	WrdPrfctDos
WordStar versions 3.3–7.0	WordStar
WordStar versions 1.0–2.0 for Windows	WordStarWin
RFT-DCA	RFTDCA
Word version 4–5.x for the Macintosh	MSWordMac
Word version 3.x–5.x for MS-DOS	MSWordDOS
Word version 6 for MS-DOS	MSWordDOS6
Word version 2.x for Windows	MSWordWin2
Works version 3.0 for Windows	MSWorksWin3
Works version 4.0 for Windows	MSWorksWin4
MS-DOS Text with Layout	MS-DOS Text With Layout
Text with Layout	Text with Layout
Windows Write version 3.x	MSWinWrite

Index

Inserts an index. The easiest way to do this is with the Insert⇨Index and Tables command. You must first mark entries to be included in the index with XE fields. Index takes the following form:

```
{ INDEX [\b bookmark] [\c cols] [\d "sep"] [\e "sep"] [\f "id"] [\g
"sep"] [\h "heading"] [\l "sep"] [\p "range"] [\r] [\s seqname] }
```

Option	What It Does
\b *bookmark*	Creates an index just for the text marked by the specified bookmark.
\c *cols*	Creates an index with the specified number of columns. The default is 1.
\d *"sep"*	Used in conjunction with the /s switch, specifies a separator that appears between page numbers and sequence numbers. Can be up to five characters long. The default is a hyphen.
\e *"sep"*	Specifies up to five characters used to separate an index entry from the page number. The default is ", ".
\f *"id"*	Creates an index only for XE fields that contain the corresponding \f field. *Id* can is a single character.
\g *"sep"*	Specifies up to five characters used to separate page ranges. The default is an en dash.
\h *"heading"*	Inserts the specified text between letter groups in the index. Any single letter in the *heading* string will be replaced by the actual letter for the group.
\l *"sep"*	Specifies up to five characters used to separate multiple pages. The default is ", ".
\p *"range"*	Creates an index just for the specified range of letters. For example, \p"a-m" creates an index for the letters *a* through *m*. Use an exclamation mark (!) to include special characters.
\r	Places index subentries on the same line as the main entry. If omitted, subentries are placed on separate lines.
\s *seqname*	Includes the sequence numbers indicated by *seqname* in the page references. See the SEQ section for more information about sequence numbers.

Info

Retrieves the specified document information. Many of these document properties are also available via their own field codes, such as Author, TotalEditingTime, and so on. Most are also available via the DocProperty field. The Info field also lets you set a new value for several of the properties. Info takes the following form:

```
{ INFO name ["newvalue"] }
```

Option	What It Does
name	Specifies the name of the property to insert. The standard document Properties include:

Author	Comments	CreateTime
EditTime	FileName	FileSize
Keywords	LastSavedBy	NumChars
NumPages	NumWords	PrintDate
RevNumber	SaveDate	Subject
Template	Title	

Option	What It Does
"newvalue"	Specifies a new value for the property. Valid only with Author, Comments, Keywords, Subject, and Title.

Keywords

Displays the keywords from the document properties. Keywords takes the following form:

```
{ KEYWORDS ["newkeywords"] }
```

Option	What It Does
"newkeywords"	Specifies text that should replace the existing value of the keywords property.

LastSavedBy

Displays the name of the user who last saved the document. LastSavedBy has no options, so it has a simple form:

```
{ LASTSAVEDBY }
```

Link

Establishes an OLE link with another application. The Link field itself is inserted by the Insert⇨Object command or the DDE takes the following form:

```
{ LINK classname "filename" [placeref] [\a] [\b] [\d] [\p] [\r] [\t] }
```

Option	What It Does
appname	Specifies the name of the application with which to establish the link.
filename	Specifies the name of the file.
placeref	Specifies a portion of the file to be linked to, such as a range of cells or text. This setting is application-specific.
\a	Updates the link field automatically whenever the source file changes.
\b	Inserts the object as a bitmap.
\d	Does not store the data in the document. This reduces the size of the document, but slows access to the data.
\r	Inserts the object in RTF format.
\t	Inserts the object in text format.

MacroButton

Inserts a button that, when clicked, runs a macro. MacroButton takes the following form:

`{ MACROBUTTON `*`macroname displaytext`*` }`

Option	What It Does
macroname	Specifies the name of the macro to be run.
displaytext	Specifies the text to be displayed as the macro button. You can format the text in any way you wish to make it resemble a button. For example, you can apply a border to the text to create a button-like appearance, or you can also include a graphic button image.

MergeField

Sets up a merge field that will be replaced by data from the data source when the mail merge is processed. MergeField takes the following form:

`{ MERGEFIELD `*`fieldname`*` }`

Option	What It Does
fieldname	Specifies the name of the merge field to be inserted.

MergeRec

Sets up a merge field that displays the number of the data record being processed during a mail merge. MergeRec has no options, so it has this simple format:

```
{ MERGEREC }
```

MergeSeq

Displays a count of the number of records that have been merged so far. MergeSeq has no options, so it has this simple format:

```
{ MERGESEQ }
```

Next

Instructs Word to skip to the next record in the data source without starting a new merge document. Use this field if you want each merge document to include data from two or more records. Next has no options, so it has this simple format:

```
{ NEXT }
```

NextIf

The NextIf field skips to the next merge record if the specified condition is true. Conditional merging can be better handled by the Mail Merge Helper (Tools⇨Mail Merge). NextIf takes the following form:

```
{ NEXTIF expression1 operator expression2 }
```

Option	What It Does
expression1	Specifies the first expression to compare.
operator	Specifies one of the following comparison operators:
	= Equal to
	< > Not equal to
	> Greater than
	< Less than
	> = Greater than or equal to
	< = Less than or equal to
expression2	*Specifies* the other expression to compare.

NoteRef

Allows you to refer to a footnote or endnote that has already been marked so that if the footnote or endnote changes, the reference changes along with it. NoteRef takes the following form:

`{ NOTEREF bookmark [\f] }`

Option	What It Does
bookmark	Specifies the name of the bookmark that marks the footnote you want to reference.
\f	Uses the Footnote Reference or Endnote Reference character style to format the reference. That way, the reference will be formatted the same as the original footnote or endnote.

NumChars

Inserts the number of characters in the document. NumChars has no options, so it has this simple form:

`{ NUMREF }`

NumPages

Inserts the number of pages in the document. NumPages has no options, so it has this simple form:

`{ NUMPAGES }`

Tip

Use this field along with the Page field in a header or footer to indicate the page number in the "*x* of *y*" form like this:

`{ PAGE } of { NUMPAGES }`

NumWords

Inserts the number of words in the document. NumWords has no options, so it has this simple form:

`{ NUMWORDS }`

Page

Inserts the current page number. This field is inserted into the header or footer when you click on the Page Number button. Page has no options, so it takes this simple form:

```
{ PAGE }
```

PageRef

Inserts the number of the page on which a specified bookmark appears. PageRef takes the following form:

```
{ PAGEREF bookmark }
```

Option	What It Does
bookmark	Specifies the name of the bookmark with the page number that you want to reference.

Tip

This is the field to use to the page number of a heading or some other portion of text. First, mark the heading or other text with a bookmark. Then, use a PAGEREF field as in this example:

```
For more information, refer to page { PAGEREF InfoRef }.
```

Print

Sends printer codes directly to the printer when the document is printed. To use this field properly, you need to be an expert in the printer codes used by your printer. It works best with HP LaserJet printers or PostScript printers. Unfortunately, the printer codes used by these printers are beyond the scope of this book. The Print command has this format:

```
{ PRINT "printercodes" }
```

PrintDate

Displays the date the document was last printed. PrintDate has the following format:

```
{ PRINTDATE \@"Date-picture" }
```

Option	What It Does
\@ *"Date Picture "*	Specifies the format in which the print date is to be displayed. See the section "Creating custom date and time formats" earlier in this chapter for more information.

Private

Holds information stored when a document is converted from one format to another. This field is intended for use only by the document converters.

```
{ PRIVATE }
```

Quote

Inserts text into a document. Quote takes the following format:

```
{ QUCTE "text" }
```

Option	What It Does
"text"	*Specifies* the text to be quoted. It can include other fields as well.

Tip

Word's on-line Help says that the Quote field "inserts the specified text in the document." Why not just type the text into the document instead of bothering with the Quote field? Because the Quote field actually does more than that. It allows you to fool another field into thinking that the text that is being quoted is actually the result of a field (which, I guess, it is), and therefore should be subject to being formatted according to other switches.

For example, the following field could be used by the RainMan to tell you what day of the week any date in history (or in the future) occurs on:

```
That would be a { quote { fillin "What date are you interested in?" {
date }} \@"dddd" }
```

When you update this field, a dialog box will appear asking you for a date (the default is the current date). When you click on OK, the text changes to "That would be a Saturday" (or whatever day is correct for the date you type).

RD

Allows you to create a table of contents or index for a multifile project without dealing with Word's master document feature. Unfortunately, this method does not automatically number pages consecutively from one document to the next. Instead, you must manually set the page numbers and update any TOC, TOA, or Index fields in the separate documents. The RD field has the following format:

```
{ RD filename }
```

Option	What It Does
filename	Specifies the filename of the document to be inserted. Use double-slashes to indicate slashes in a path (for example, "c:\\winword\\readme.doc").

Ref

Inserts the contents of the specified bookmark. This is the only field for which the field code itself is optional. As a result, you can just cite the name of the bookmark if you wish. The Ref field takes the following form:

```
{ [REF] bookmark [\f] [\n]}
```

Option	What It Does
bookmark	Specifies the name of the bookmark to be inserted.
\f	If the bookmark is a footnote, endnote, or annotation, inserts the corresponding note text and assigns the next footnote, endnote, or annotation number.
\n	If the paragraphs referred to by the bookmark are numbered, includes the paragraph numbers.

RevNum

Inserts the number of times the document has been saved. Unfortunately, this is probably not what you or I think of as a true revision number, as most users frequently save their work. Thus, if you save a document 10 times in the course of an hour (not an unreasonable rate), you will have produced 10 revisions. RevNum has no options, so it has this simple form:

```
{ REVNUM }
```

SaveDate

Inserts the date the document was last saved. SaveDate takes the following form:

```
{ SAVEDATE \@"Date-picture" }
```

Option	What It Does
\@ "Date Picture "	Specifies the format in which the save date is to be displayed. See the section "Creating custom date and time formats" earlier in this chapter for more information.

Section

Inserts the current section number. Section has the following format:

```
{ SECTION }
```

SectionPages

Inserts the total number of pages in the current section. SectionPages has the following format:

```
{ SECTIONPAGES }
```

Seq

Creates sequence numbers, such as a numbered list, chapter or heading numbers, and so on. For simple lists, it's best to use the Format⇨Bullets and Numbering command or the Format⇨Heading Numbering command. However, the Seq field can be useful as a more general numbering tool. It takes the following format:

```
{ SEQ ident [bookmark] [\c] [\h] [\n] [\r n] }
```

Option	What It Does
ident	Specifies a name, up to 40 characters in length, that uniquely identifies each sequence numbering series. This allows you to keep track of more than one series of sequence numbers.
bookmark	Allows you to cross-reference a particular sequence number. An example of how to do this is given as follows. If you include a bookmark name in the Seq field, you should not use any of the remaining switches.
\c	Repeats the closest preceding sequence number.
\h	Does not display the field result. This allows you to increment the sequence number invisibly. When used in conjunction with the \r switch, you can reset the sequence number without inserting the new sequence number in the document.
\r n	Resets the sequence number to *n*. If you have a single document with more than one chapter, you may want to reset the figure numbers at the start of each chapter. The best way to do that is to use the \r 0 and \h switches together, as in **{ SEQ figs \r0 \h }**. This invisibly resets the figs numbering sequence to 0. Then, the next **{ SEQ figs }** field will insert the number 1.

Note

Unlike sequence numbers created by the Format⇨Bullets and Numbering command, sequence numbers created by Seq fields are not updated automatically when fields are added, deleted, or rearranged. To update sequence numbers, select the entire document and press Ctrl+F9.

Tip

Seq is one of my favorite fields because it lets me create a type of numbered list that I use all the time and that can't be done by using the Format⇨Bullet and Numbering command. When I plan the table of contents for a book, I have to create a list that looks something like this:

Part One   Welcome to Word 95

Chapter 1   What's New with Word 95

Chapter 2   Welcome to Windows 95

Chapter 3   Fundamental Word Secrets

Part Two   Secrets of Customizing Word

Chapter 4   Using Templates

Chapter 5   Customizing Word's Startup and Appearance

Chapter 6   Customizing Keyboard Shortcuts, Toolbars, and Menus

Chapter 7   Automating Your Work with Macros

Do you see in this example how the chapters are numbered sequentially (1 through 7) and the parts also are numbered sequentially (One, Two, and so on)? You cannot create this type of list by using the Format➪Bullet and Numbering command. If you use the multilevel list option, the chapter numbers reset to 1 following each part. So you end up with this:

Part One   Welcome to Word 95

Chapter 1   What's New with Word 95

Chapter 2   Welcome to Windows 95

Chapter 3   Fundamental Word Secrets

Part Two   Secrets of Customizing Word

Chapter 1   Using Templates

Chapter 2   Customizing Word's Startup and Appearance

Chapter 3   Customizing Keyboard Shortcuts, Toolbars, and Menus

Chapter 4   Automating Your Work with Macros

But you can do it if you use a Seq field. For the part numbers, use the Seq field like this:

```
{ seq part \n cardtext \n mergeformat }
```

For the chapter numbers, use the Seq field like this:

```
{ seq chapter \n mergeformat }
```

The *part* and *chapter* in the fields let Word keep track of two separate lists at the same time. With field codes revealed, the list looks like this:

Part { seq part \n cardtext \n mergeformat }   **Welcome to Word 95**

Chapter { seq chapter \n mergeformat }   What's New with Word 95

Chapter { seq chapter \n mergeformat }   Getting the Most from
                                                Windows 95

Chapter { seq chapter \n mergeformat }   The Tao of Word

Part { seq part \n cardtext \n mergeformat } Secrets of Customizing Word

Chapter { seq chapter \n mergeformat }   Using Document Templates

Chapter { seq chapter \n mergeformat }   Customizing Word's Startup
                                                and Appearance

Chapter { seq chapter \n mergeformat }   Creating Custom Keyboard
                                                Shortcuts, Toolbars, and Menus

Chapter { seq chapter \n mergeformat }   Automating Your Work with
                                                Macros

I don't want to have to type these field codes every time I need them, of course, so I've created macros to insert the Seq fields for parts and chapters.

Another common use for the Seq field is to insert cross-references to figure numbers or other sequence numbers. For example, "See Figure 12." To do that, you must first mark the Seq field for the figure you want to reference with a bookmark. Let's say the figure is numbered with the field { SEQ figs }, and you've marked that field with a bookmark named Fig_K. Then, you would create the cross-reference as follows:

See figure { SEQ figs Fig_K }

Here, the Seq field inserts the fig sequence number that is indicated by the Fig_K bookmark name. If the figure number changes because you add, remove, or rearrange figures, the cross-reference will change, too.

Set

Allows you to create a bookmark for text that isn't visible in the document. Set takes the following form:

`{ SET bookmark "text" }`

Option	What It Does
bookmark	Specifies the name of the bookmark to be assigned.
"text"	The text assigned to the bookmark. This text may actually be another field code.

Tip

One excellent use for this field is to set a "variable" that you can use in other fields in the document. For example, suppose you want to calculate a cash discount using a percentage that can change periodically. You could use the field { SET discount 10 } to set the discount to 10 and use the discount bookmark in other fields to calculate the discount. If the discount changes, you merely change the Set field and the other fields will automatically reflect the new cash discount.

SkipIf

Conditionally skips the next merge record during a mail merge, based on the results of a comparison. Conditional merging can be better handled by the Mail Merge Helper (Tools⇨Mail Merge), so you should avoid using this field. SkipIf has the following format:

`{ SKIPIF expression1 operator expression2 }`

Option	What It Does	
expression1	Specifies the first expression to compare.	
operator	Specifies one of the following comparison operators:	
	=	Equal to
	< >	Not equal to
	>	Greater than
	<	Less than
	> =	Greater than or equal to
	< =	Less than or equal to
expression2	Specifies the other expression to compare.	

StyleRef

Inserts text that is formatted with a particular style. This is most useful for creating dictionary-style headers or footers that cite the first or last heading on the page. See Chapter 26 for more information. StyleRef takes the following form:

{ STYLEREF *style* [\l] [\n] }

Option	What It Does
style	Specifies the style to be referenced.
\l	Inserts text from the last paragraph on the page highlighted by *style* rather than the first.
\n	Inserts any paragraph numbering associated with the paragraph.

Subject

Inserts the document subject taken from the document's properties. Subject uses the following format:

{ SUBJECT "*newsubject*" }

Option	What It Does
"*newsubject*"	Sets a new subject for the document.

Symbol

Inserts a symbol into the document. This is far easier to accomplish by using the Insert⇨Symbol command. Symbol takes the following form:

{ SYMBOL *charnum* [\f "*fontname*"] [\h] [\s *size*] }

Option	What It Does
charnum	Specifies the number of the character to be inserted. You can use a decimal number or a hexadecimal number preceded by 0x, such as 0x4F.
\f "*fontname*"	Specifies the font to be used. If omitted, the font used to format the Symbol field code is used.
\h	Instructs Word to not adjust the line spacing to accommodate the symbol.
\s *size*	Specifies the size in points for the symbol to be inserted.

TA

Marks a citation to be included in a table of authorities. This field is inserted when you use the Alt+Shift+I keyboard shortcut to mark a citation. The TA field uses the following format:

```
{ TA [\c category [\i] [\b] [\l "long"] [\s "short"] [\r bookmark] }
```

Option	What It Does
\c cat	Indicates the category for the table. *cat* must be a number that corresponds to the categories from the Mark Citation dialog box. The standard categories are the following:
	1 Cases
	2 Statutes
	3 Other Authorities
	4 Rules
	5 Treatises
	6 Regulations
	7 Constitutional provisions
	8-16 User defined
\i	Marks the page reference in italics when the table of authorities is compiled.
\b	Marks the page reference in boldface when the table of authorities is compiled.
\l "*long*"	Supplies the long citation, which is the one used in the table of authorities. For example:
	Kringle v. New York 28 NY 2d 312 (1938)" \s "Kringle v. New York
\s "*short*"	The short form of the citation, such as "Kringle v. New York."
\r bookmark	The name of a bookmark that is used to determine a range of pages for the table. If the citation is discussed for a range of pages, mark the entire discussion with the bookmark, and include the bookmark in TA field.

Note

TA codes are formatted as hidden text. To see them, you must use the Tools⇨Options command to show hidden text.

TC

Marks an entry to be included in a table of contents. You can more easily compile tables of contents based on heading styles, but if you must do it the hard way, use the TC field instead. The TC field uses the following format:

```
{ TC "text" [\f type] [\l level] [\n] }
```

Option	What It Does
text	Specifies the text to be included in the table.
\f type	Specifies a letter (A-Z) used to identify items to be included in a table of contents. This allows you to create two or more separate tables in a single document. The default is "c" for "contents."
\l level	Indicates the level at which the entry will appear in the table. If omitted, level 1 is assumed.
\n	Omits the page number for the entry. This allows you to build a table in which some entries have page numbers, while others do not. (This is not possible when compiling a table from styles.)

TC codes are formatted as hidden text. To see them, you must use the Tools⇨Options command to show hidden text.

Template

Inserts the filename of the template attached to the document. Template takes the following form:

```
{ TEMPLATE [\p] }
```

Option	What It Does
\p	Includes the complete path with the template filename.

Time

Inserts the current time. Time takes the following form:

```
{ TIME [\@Date-picture]}
```

Option	What It Does
[\@Date-picture	Specifies the format for the date. If omitted, the time format specified in the Windows Control Panel Regional Settings is used.

Title

Inserts the document title taken from the document's properties. Title uses the following format:

```
{ TITLE "newtitle" }
```

Option	What It Does
newtitle	Sets a new title for the document.

TOA

Compiles a table of authorities based on TA fields inserted into the document. This field is inserted when you use the Insert⟹Index and Tables command. TOA takes the following form:

```
{ TOA \c "cat" [\b bookmark] [\e "sep"] [\g "sep"] [\l "sep"] [\s
ident] [\e "sep"] [\h] [\p] [\f] }
```

Option	What It Does
\c *"cat"*	Compiles a table of authorities for the specified category. See the TA field for a list of standard categories.
\b *bookmark*	Searches for TA fields only in the range indicated by the bookmark.
\e *"sep"*	Specifies up to five characters that separate the entry from its page number. The default is a tab with leader dots.
\g *"sep"*	Specifies up to five characters used to separate page ranges. The default is an en dash.
\l *"sep"*	Specifies up to five characters used to separate multiple pages. The default is ", ".
\s *ident*	Specifies an identifier used in a Seq field to provide case numbers.
\e *"sep"*	Used with the \s switch, provides up to five characters used to separate the case number from the citation number. The default is a hyphen.
\h	Includes the category heading in the table.
\p	Replaces five or more occurrences of the citation with "passim."
\f	Removes formatting from the citation.

TOC

Compiles a table of contents. This field is inserted when you use the Insert⟹Index and Tables command. TOC takes the following form:

```
{ TOC [\a ident] [\b bookmark] [\c SEQident] [\f type] [\l levels]
[\n levels][\o "headings"] [\p "sep"] [\s ident] [\d "sep"]
[\t "style,level,style,level..." }
```

Option	What It Does
\a *ident*	Compiles a table from entries that are numbered with Seq fields. The table does not include the sequence numbers themselves. *Ident* refers to the identifier in the Seq fields.
\b *bookmark*	Compiles a table only from entries within the bookmark.
\c *SEQident*	Compiles a table from entries that are numbered with Seq fields. Unlike \a, \c includes the entire paragraph, sequence number and all.
\f *type*	Compiles a table based on TC fields. Only those TC fields that have a matching \f switch are included in the table.
\l *levels*	Specifies the range of levels as specified in the TC fields to include in the table. For example, \l 1-4 builds a table that includes levels 1 through 4.
\n *levels*	Specifies the range of levels for which page numbers should be omitted. If you specify \n without including a range of levels, all page numbers are omitted.
\o *"headings"*	Compiles a table of contents using built-in heading styles. *Headings* is a range of levels to include in the table. For example, \o "1-2" builds a table using the built-in heading styles Heading 1 and Heading 2.
\p *"sep"*	Specifies up to five characters that separate the entry from the page number. The default is a tab with leaders.
\s *ident*	Includes a sequence number marked by Seq fields before the page reference. Use this if page numbers take the form "2-12," where 2 is the chapter number and 12 is the page number. *Ident* must match the *ident* specified in the Seq field.
\d *"sep"*	*Specifies* up to five characters used to separate the sequence number from the page number. Used in conjunction with the \s switch. The default is a hyphen.
\t *"style,level, style,level..."*	Allows you to compile a table of contents using styles other than the built-in heading styles. For example, "Part,1,Chapter,2" compiles a table of contents using paragraphs formatted with the Part style for level 1 and paragraphs formatted with the Chapter style as level 2.

UserAddress

Inserts the user's address taken from the Tools➪Options command, User Info tab. UserAddress takes the following form:

```
{ USERADDRESS ["address"] }
```

Option	What It Does
address	Specifies an address to use instead of the UserAddress. This is a weird option, in that you may as well just type in the address. Word's on-line help calls this field *NewAddress*, which implies that the address will update the UserAddress field in Tools⇨Options, but it doesn't.

UserInitials

Inserts the user's initials taken from the Tools⇨Options command, User Info tab. UserName takes the following form:

```
{ USERINITIALS ["initials"] }
```

Option	What It Does
"initials"	Specifies a set of initials to use instead of the UserInitials. This is really useful. For example, rather than type the three-letter JFK, why not use the field **{ USERINITIALS "JFK" }**. The result is the same. Once again, the on-line help refers to this field as *NewInitials*, which sort of implies that this might update the UserInitials field, but it doesn't.

UserName

Inserts the user's name taken from the Tools⇨Options command, User Info tab. UserName takes the following form:

```
{ USERNAME ["name"] }
```

Option	What It Does
"name"	Specifies a name to use instead of the UserName. The on-line help calls this field *NewName*, but once again, it doesn't update the UserName. I am now convinced that this field, along with UserAddress and UserInitials, was at one time going to allow you to update the user information, but then the Word developers changed their minds.

XE

Marks an entry for inclusion in an index. XE fields are inserted when you use the Alt+Shift+X keyboard shortcut. XE has the following format:

```
{ XE "text" [\f type] [\b] [\i] [\r bookmark] [\t "text" }
```

Option	What it Does
"text"	Specifies the text to be included in the index.
\f type	Specifies a letter (A-Z) used to identify items to be included in the index. This allows you to create two or more separate indexes in a single document. The default is "i".
\b	Marks the page reference in boldface when the index is compiled.
\i	Marks the page reference in italics when the index is compiled.
\r bookmark	Specifies the name of a bookmark that is used to determine a range of pages for the index entry. If the entry is discussed for a range of pages, mark the entire discussion with the bookmark and include the bookmark in XE field.
\t "text"	Specifies the text to include for the entry instead of a page number. Use this to create a cross-reference, such as "See magnesium."

Note

XE fields are formatted as hidden text. To see them, you must use the Tools⇨Options command to show hidden text.

= (Formula)

Lets you insert formulas into your documents. It takes the following format:

```
{= formula [\# numeric-picture] }
```

Formulas can use the following operators:

Operator	Operation
+	Addition
−	Subtraction
n	Multiplication
/	Division
%	Percentage
^	Powers and roots
=	Equal to
<	Less than
< =	Less than or equal to
>	Greater than
> =	Greater than or equal to
< >	Not equal to

Formulas may also use the following functions:

ABS(x)	Absolute value.
AND(x,y)	True (1) if both expressions are true; otherwise false (0).
AVERAGE( )	Average of a list of values.
COUNT( )	The number of items in the list.
DEFINED(x)	True (1) if the expression x is valid. False (0) if the expression cannot be computed.
FALSE	0.
IF(x,y,z)	y if the result of evaluating the conditional expression x is true; otherwise, z.
INT(x)	The numbers to the left of the decimal place in the value or formula x.
MIN( )	The smallest of a list of values.
MAX( )	The largest of a list of values.
MOD(x,y)	The remainder that results when the value x is divided by the value y.
NOT(x)	False (0) if expression x is true, or true (1) if the expression x is false.
OR(x,y)	True (1) if either expressions are true, or false (0) if both expressions are false.
PRODUCT( )	The product of the list: that is, the result of multiplying the values in the list.
ROUND(x,y)	The value of x rounded to the specified number of decimal places y.
SIGN(x)	1 if x is a positive number, 0 if it is zero, and -1 if it is a negative number.
SUM( )	The sum of a list of values.
TRUE	1.

When the field is used in a table, you can also include references to other table cells. These references can take the following forms:

Cell Reference	Explanation
A1	A single cell identified by its row and column.
A1-B5	A range of cells.
A2,B5,D9	A list of individual cells.
ABOVE	All the cells in the column above the current cell.
BELOW	All the cells in the column below the current cell.
LEFT	All the cells in the row to the left of the current cell.
RIGHT	All the cells in the row to the right of the current cell.

As you can imagine, formulas can get pretty complex. Here are some examples of simple ones:

{ = 3/4 }	The result is 0.75.
{ = 1024 n 1024 }	The result is 1,048,576.
{ = SUM(1, 2, 3) }	The result is 6.
{ = { PAGE} + 1 }	If the current page is 13, the result is 14.

Chapter 29

Streamlining Document Creation with Forms

In This Chapter

▶ Understanding and creating forms, including the various types of fields they can include

▶ Filling in a form

▶ Creating a custom menu for your form templates

▶ Using macros in a form, including a sample form that uses macros to perform calculations on form fields

Microsoft Word includes a Forms feature that lets you create sophisticated fill-in-the-blanks forms. This chapter explains how to create forms, and shows you how you can use forms in conjunction with WordBasic to create complete applications.

Understanding Forms

A *form* is a special type of document in which parts of the document are protected from being modified by the user. The user can enter information only in predefined fill-in-the-blank portions of the document, which are called *form fields*.

Figure 29-1 shows an example of a form that I created with Word. Most of the text you see in the document is protected. The only parts of the document that the user can modify are the shaded parts: the name and address fields, the answers to the two questions, and the check boxes.

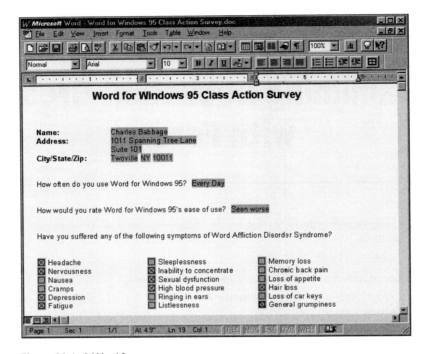

Figure 29-1: A Word form.

I provide the exact steps for creating and filling out a blank form later in this chapter, but the general idea goes something like this. First, you must create a new template. Then, you add any text that you want to appear in the form to the template and you add the form fields by using the Insert⇨Form Field command. When the blank form is finished, you use the Tools⇨Protect Document command to prevent the user from modifying any part of the document other than the form fields, and finally, you save the template.

To fill in a blank form, you have to create a new document based on the form template and fill in the blanks. If the form has been set up properly, Word won't allow you to move the insertion point anywhere outside the form fields, so you don't have to worry about accidentally messing up the form. After you have filled out the form, you can print it and/or save it as a normal document.

Although you can't really tell from Figure 29-1, the form fields for the first two questions are actually drop-down list boxes. Instead of typing in a response to the question, the user selects one of several permissible responses. If, for example, the user clicks the mouse in the form field for the second question ("How would you rate Word's ease of use?"), the drop-down list shown in Figure 29-2 appears.

Figure 29-2: A drop-down form field.

Word comes with three prefabricated form templates: an invoice (Invoice.dot), a purchase order (Purchase Order.dot), and a weekly time sheet (Weekly Time Sheet.dot). To see what you can do with forms, try creating a new document based on one of these templates and start exploring.

Creating a Form Template

Before you can fill out a form, you must create a template. The template contains any text and graphics that appear on the blank form, as well as the form fields, in which the user enters information.

To create a form template, follow these steps:

1. Call up the File⇨New command to access the New dialog box. Clicking the New button in the Standard toolbar is insufficient because this action bypasses the New dialog box.

2. Check the Template button. This action tells Word that you are creating a new template rather than a new document.

3. Select the template on which you want to base the new template. Usually, Normal works fine. If the new form is similar to a form you've previously created or one of the forms that comes with Word, select the appropriate template.

4. Click OK. A document window for the new template opens.

5. Create the outline and structure of your form by typing whatever text you want to appear on the form. Insert graphics where you want graphics to appear. If you're converting a paper form to Word, create the Word form so that it looks as much like the current paper form as possible. Work in Page Layout view so that you can see how things line up.

   If you want the form to be laid out on a grid with ruled lines and boxes, use tables, frames, borders, shading, and whatever other Word features you can muster. See Chapter 17 for more information about working with tables and Chapter 20 for information about working with frames.

Save your work often!

6. Insert fields where you want the user to enter information. There are three basic types of fields that you can insert into a form: text fields, list box fields, and check box fields. To create any of these, call up the

Insert⇨Form Field command, check whichever field type you want to create, and click OK. If you're creating a check box field, set the default value (Checked or Not Checked); if you're creating a list box field, add as many items to the drop-down list as you want. For more specific information on creating these fields, see the following three sections.

7. Call up the Tools⇨Protect document command. The Protect Document dialog box appears, as shown in Figure 29-3.

Figure 29-3: The Protect Document dialog box.

8. Check the Forms option and click OK. This action protects the document so that the user can enter data into the form fields only.

9. Use the File⇨Save command to save the template. Assign a meaningful name to the template file. Store it in the same folder with the Normal.dot template, or store it in the Other Documents template folder.

Note

If this is your first time creating a template, you may want to refer back to Chapter 4 to make sure that you know the ins and outs of working with templates.

If you protect the template by using the Tools⇨Protect Document command, you'll have to unprotect the template if you need to change the layout of the form later. Call up the Tools⇨Unprotect Document command. Don't forget to protect the form again when you're finished.

Using the Forms Toolbar

Word provides a Forms toolbar, shown in Figure 29-4. To activate this toolbar, call up the View⇨Toolbars command, check the Forms check box, and click OK.

Figure 29-4: The Forms toolbar.

Table 29-1 lists the toolbar buttons that appear on the Forms toolbar.

Table 29-1	Buttons on the Forms Toolbar
Button	**What It Does**
abl	Inserts a text field
☒	Inserts a check box field
🔲	Inserts a drop-down field
🔲	Calls up the Form Field Options dialog box for a field
🔲	Inserts a table
🔲	Inserts a frame
ⓐ	Turns field shading on or off
🔒	Protects or unprotects a form

Creating a Text Field

A *text field* is a form field where the user can type information. You use text fields to provide a space on the form where the user can enter information, such as a name or address. The form shown in Figure 29-1 uses four text fields: one for the name and three for the address lines.

To create a text field in a form, position the insertion point on the template where you want the text field to appear and choose the Insert⇨Form Field command. The Form Field dialog box will appear, as shown in Figure 29-5.

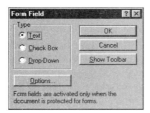

Figure 29-5: The Form Field dialog box.

Select the Text option and click the Options button to call up the Text Form Field Options dialog box.

If you want to provide a *default value* for the text field (that is, a value that the field assumes if the user doesn't type anything into the field), select the Text option and then click the Options button. The Text Form Field Options dialog box appears, as shown in Figure 29-6. Type a default value for the field in the Default Text box and click OK.

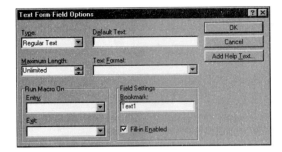

Figure 29-6: The Text Form Field Options dialog box.

The Text Form Field Options dialog box also lets you set the following options:

■ **Type:** Lets you set one of six different text field types, as summarized in Table 29-2.

■ **Maximum Length:** Lets you set the maximum number of characters that can be entered into the field. The default setting is "Unlimited."

■ **Default Text:** Lets you set a default value for the field.

■ **Text Format:** Lets you set the capitalization for the field: Upper Case, Lower Case, First Cap, or Title Case. The default is to leave the text formatted as typed by the user.

■ **Run Macro On Entry:** Supplies the name of a macro that is run whenever the insertion point enters this field.

■ **Run Macro On Exit:** Supplies the name of a macro that is run whenever the insertion point leaves this field.

■ **Bookmark:** Assigns a bookmark to the form field. This allows you to refer to the field in a macro.

■ **Fill-in Enabled:** If this option is unchecked, the user cannot modify the field. This is useful when you want to create a macro to calculate the field value, and you don't want the user to modify the result.

Table 29-2	The Six Types of Text Fields
Text Field Type	*What It Does*
Regular Text	This field consists of ordinary text, such as a name or address. The user can type anything into the field.
Number	The user must type a number into the field.

Text Field Type	What It Does
Date	The user must type a date into the field. The date must be in the usual date format (for example, *05/31/94* or *6-24-94*) or may include the month spelled out (as in *March 28, 1994*).
Current Date	Word automatically inserts the current date into the field. The user can't type anything in the field.
Current Time	Word automatically inserts the current time into the field. The user can't type anything in the field.
Calculation	The field contains a formula field ($=$) to calculate a result value, usually based on the value of one or more number fields. The user also can't type anything into this field.

Tip

After you've created a text field, you can call up the Text Form Field Options dialog box by double-clicking the field or right-clicking the field (that is, pointing to the field and clicking the right mouse button) and selecting the Form Field Options command from the shortcut menu that appears.

Creating a Check Box Field

A *check box field* is a field that the user can check or uncheck to provide a yes or no answer. Check box fields work just like regular check boxes in dialog boxes: you click them with the mouse to check or uncheck them.

You use the Insert⇔Form Field command to insert a check box field. Click the Check Box option and click the Options button to bring up the Check Box Form Field Options dialog box, as shown in Figure 29-7.

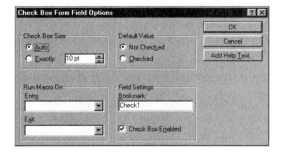

Figure 29-7: The Check Box Form Field Options dialog box.

The Check Box Form Field Options dialog box gives you the following options:

- **Check Box Size:** Set to <u>A</u>uto, which sets the size of the check box automatically to match the point size of the surrounding text, or <u>E</u>xactly, which lets you set a specific point size for the check box so that you can increase or decrease the size of the check box relative to the surrounding text.

- **Default Value:** Choose Not Chec<u>k</u>ed or <u>C</u>hecked.

- **Run Macro On:** Lets you specify macros to run when the insertion point enters (Entr<u>y</u>) or leaves (E<u>x</u>it) the field.

- **<u>B</u>ookmark:** Assigns a bookmark to the form field so that you can determine the field's setting in a macro.

- **Check Box E<u>n</u>abled:** You can uncheck this option to prevent the user from modifying the field's setting.

Unless you're into writing macros, the only thing you can do with a check box is check it or uncheck it. If you want to roll up your sleeves and do some heavy-duty macro programming, you can come up with all sorts of exotic uses for check box fields.

Note

You can call up the Check Box Form Field Options dialog box after you've inserted a check box field by double-clicking the field or right-clicking the field (that is, pointing to it and clicking the right mouse button) and selecting the Form Field Options command from the shortcut menu that appears.

Creating a Drop-Down Field

A *drop-down field* is like a text field, except that the user isn't allowed to type text directly into the field. Instead, the user must select from a list of preset choices that are given in a list box. List boxes are great for fields like marital status, shipping instructions, or gender. In other words, fields that have only a limited set of correct answers.

Once again, the <u>I</u>nsert⇨ For<u>m</u> Field command is the tool of choice here. To create a drop-down list field, follow these steps:

1. Position the insertion point where you want the text field to appear.

2. Choose the <u>I</u>nsert⇨For<u>m</u> Field command to summon the Form Field dialog box.

3. Check the <u>D</u>rop-Down option button and click the Options button to call up the Drop-Down Form Field Options dialog box, as shown in Figure 29-8.

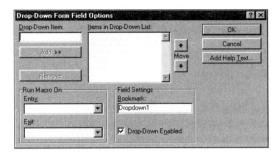

Figure 29-8: The Drop-Down Form Field Options dialog box.

4. To add an item to the drop-down list, type text in the Drop-Down Item box and then click the Add button. The text will appear in the Items in Drop-Down List field. Repeat this step for each item you want to include in the drop-down list.

5. To rearrange items in the drop-down list, select the item that you want to move to another position in the list and click the up or down Move buttons.

6. To delete an item from the list, select the item and click the Remove button.

Secret

To correct a mistake in a list item, delete the incorrect item. Word copies the deleted item to the Drop-Down Item field, where you can correct the mistake and click the Add button to reinsert the item.

7. When you've added all the items you want in the list, click OK. The drop-down field will be added to the document.

Note

The first item in the drop-down list is the default selection (that is, the item that is initially selected for the field).

Adding Help to a Form Field

Word lets you add your own help text to form fields. Then, if you forget what a field is for when you're filling out a form, the help text reminds you.

You can create two types of help text for each field. The status bar help is a single line of text that appears in the status bar whenever the insertion point moves into the field. Word limits this help text to 138 characters so that it can fit in the space provided on the status bar. If the status bar help isn't enough, you can supply help text, which the user can summon by pressing F1. You can provide up to 256 characters for help text. Figure 29-9 shows an example of help text.

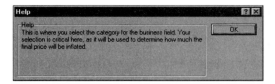

Figure 29-9: Help text for a form field.

You create help text from the field's Options dialog box for the field in question (double-click the field if the Options dialog box isn't already visible). Click the Add Help Text button to summon the Form Field Help Text dialog box, shown in Figure 29-10.

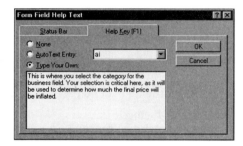

Figure 29-10: Adding help text to a form field.

This dialog box allows you to create help text to appear in the status bar or when the user presses F1.

Filling Out a Form

Once you've created a form template and protected it, you should put it to good use by collecting the vital information it was so carefully designed to record. In other words, it's time to fill out the form.

To fill out a form by using a form template that you or someone else created, follow these steps:

1. Call up the File➪New command. The New dialog box appears, listing all of the available templates.

2. Select the correct form template from the Template list.

3. Click OK.

4. Fill in the form fields. When you fill in the form fields, you can use any of the keyboard actions listed in Table 25-3.

5. Print the document. Use the <u>F</u>ile⇨<u>P</u>rint command or click the Print button in the Standard toolbar.

6. Save the file, if you want, by using the <u>F</u>ile⇨<u>S</u>ave command or by clicking the Save button in the Standard toolbar.

Table 25-3	**Keys You Can Use When Filling Out a Form**
Key	*What It Does*
Enter, Tab, or down arrow	Moves the insertion point to the next field
Shift+Tab, or up arrow	Moves the insertion point to the previous field
Alt+down arrow, or F4	Displays a drop-down list
Up arrow or down arrow	Moves up or down in a drop-down list
Space or X	Checks or unchecks a check box field
F1	Displays the help text for a field
Ctrl+Tab	Inserts a tab character into a text field

Using Preprinted Forms

If you are creating an on-line form for a document for which you have pre-printed forms that you can use with your printer, format the form template so that its fields align exactly with the form fields on the preprinted form. Then, when you want to print to the preprinted form, call up the Print options by choosing <u>T</u>ools⇨<u>O</u>ptions, clicking the Print tab (or choosing <u>F</u>ile⇨<u>P</u>rint), and clicking the <u>O</u>ptions button. Then, select the <u>P</u>rint Data Only For Forms option. This will cause Word to print just the data you enter into the form fields, not the form template itself. If your preprinted forms and your form template are lined up properly, the data will fit snugly in the fields on the preprinted form.

Creating a Custom Form Menu

If you have developed a slate of forms that you use routinely, you might want to consider adding a special Form menu to Word's standard menu bar, with commands to create new documents based on each of your form templates. Figure 29-11 shows just such a custom Form menu in action.

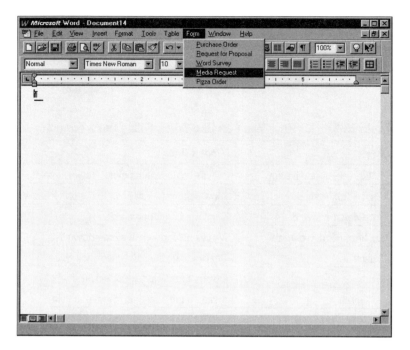

Figure 29-11: A custom Form menu in action.

Macro

To create a Form menu such as this, you must first create a macro for each form you want to add to the menu. Each macro should look something like this:

```
Sub MAIN
FileNew .Template = "C:\MSOffice\Templates\Forms\Pizza Order.dot"
End Sub
```

You can use any names you want for the macro. I suggest naming each macro Form, followed by the name of the template with spaces removed, for example, FormPizzaOrder.

Secret

The File⇨New command is a little picky about how you specify the name of the template. If the form template is in the default template directory (normally C:\MSOffice\Templates), you can just specify the template name. However, if the template is in one of the subfolders under the Templates folder, you must specify the complete path for the template.

Next, use the Tools⇨Customize command to create a new menu named Form (specify Fo&rm for the menu name so that the r becomes the hot key for the menu) and add each macro to the menu.

Using Macros in a Form

I've mentioned several times in this chapter that you can use macros to create forms with an extra punch. You'll find detailed information about using WordBasic later in this book, so I won't go into a complete course in writing WordBasic macros here. I do, however, want to show you a simple example of a form that uses two macros to calculate form field results automatically based on values entered into certain fields.

Word lets you attach two macros to each form field: an entry macro and an exit macro. The entry macro runs whenever the insertion point moves into the form field. Likewise, the exit macro runs whenever the insertion point leaves the form field. Exit macros are more commonly used than entry macros because they let you take action based on what's typed into the field. For example, if you attach an exit macro to a check box field, the macro can determine whether the check box field was checked or unchecked.

Here are the steps to follow to attach either an entry or an exit macro:

1. Create the macro you want to attach by using the Tools⇨Macro command. You will almost certainly need to create the macro manually. There is little you can do of value in a Form field macro that can be recorded.

Warning

Make sure that you create your macros in the form template, not in the global Normal.dot template. You don't want to clutter up Normal.dot with these macros. Also, you want the macros to travel with the template, just in case you decide to share the form with your friends. (If you accidentally create the macros in Normal.dot, call up the Organizer and move them to the appropriate template.)

2. Double-click the form field where you want to attach the macro. The appropriate Form Field Options dialog box appears, depending on whether the field is a text field, a check box field, or a drop-down field.

3. Select the macro in the Entry or Exit fields. Both fields offer drop-down lists that list every available macro. The macro you created in Step 1 should appear on the list.

4. Click OK to attach the macro to the field.

A Sample Form That Uses Macros

Figure 29-12 shows a simple form that one might use when bidding for government contracts. To fill out this form, simply select which customer category you're working with — for example, Local Government, State Government, Federal Government, or Military. Then, you type the actual value of the services provided in the contract. The form automatically determines the markup factor based on the category and then multiplies the actual value by the markup to determine the amount to bid for the contract. For example, if you select Military for the category, the form assumes 10 for the markup and bids $50,000 for a $5,000 job.

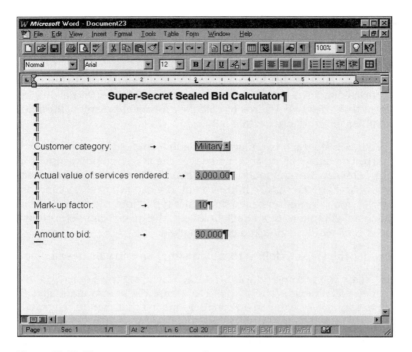

Figure 29-12: The government contract form.

Please do *not* call Mike Wallace or anyone else at CBS News concerning this form. They already know about inflated government contracts.

How does this form work? Simple. The form itself has four fields:

- **Category:** A drop-down list field that has five items defined: Regular, Local Government, State Government, Federal Government, and Military. I changed the bookmark name of this field to "Category" and specified the macro named CategoryExit as an exit macro.

- **Value:** A text field formatted to accept numbers. I changed the bookmark name of this field to "Value" and specified the macro named ValueExit as an exit macro.

- **Markup:** A text field that I disabled by unchecking the Fill-in Enabled box. The bookmark name for the field is "Markup." The value of the field is set by the CategoryExit macro whenever the insertion point leaves the Category field.

- **Total:** Another text field that I disabled by unchecking the Fill-in Enabled box. In the Text Form Field Options dialog box, I specified Formula for the text field Type and provided the following formula for the field:

```
= Value * Markup
```

The bookmark name for the field is "Total." The value of the field is set by the CategoryExit macro whenever the insertion point leaves the Category field and by the ValueExit macro whenever the insertion point leaves the Cost field.

The form in Figure 29-12 uses two macros. The first, named CategoryExit, runs whenever the insertion point leaves the Category drop-down field. This macro determines which category was selected, sets the Markup field accordingly, and updates the Total field. To accomplish these feats, the CategoryExit macro contains these instructions:

```
Sub MAIN
Category = GetFormResult("Category")
Select Case Category
    Case 0
        Markup = 1
    Case 1
        Markup = 2
    Case 2
        Markup = 2.5
    Case 3
        Markup = 3
    Case 4
        Markup = 7
End Select
SetFormResult "Markup", Str$(Markup)
SetFormResult "Total"
End Sub
```

The first instruction, `GetFormResult`, sets the Category variable to a number that represents the item selected from the Category drop-down field. Then, a Select Case statement sets the `Markup` variable based on the category selected: for category 0 (Regular), Markup is set to 1; for category 1 (Local Government), Markup is set to 2; and so on, all the way up to category 4 (Military), for which Markup is set to 7.

After the Markup variable is set, a `SetFormResult` statement sets the result of the Markup field to the value of the Markup variable. Then, another `SetFormResult` statement sets the result of the Total field. Because the Total field uses a formula (`= Cost * Total`), this statement simply updates the formula result.

The other macro, named ValueExit, is much simpler:

```
Sub MAIN
SetFormResult "Total"
End Sub
```

This macro simply updates the Total field's calculation. This macro runs whenever the insertion point leaves the Value field. That way, any change to the cost is reflected in the total.

Exporting Form Data to a Text File

Word lets you save the data you enter into a form in a comma-delimited text file that can then be used as input to another program, such as a database program. To use this feature, choose the Tools⇨Options command, click the Save tab, and select the Save Data Only for Forms option. Then, when you save the file, it will be saved to a text file rather than to a document file.

All of the fields in the form will be written to the text file, whether the user enters data into the field or not. The fields are separated from one another with commas, and text values are enclosed in quotation marks. List fields are given the text value for the item selected for the field, and check boxes are written as 1 if they are selected, 0 if they are not.

Chapter 30

Mail Merge Secrets

In This Chapter

▶ Using the Mail Merge feature to prepare form letters

▶ Using fields to customize mail merge

▶ Printing labels and envelopes for your form letters

▶ Working with the data source

This chapter covers Word's Mail Merge feature, including not just the basics of printing mass quantities of irritating personalized form letters but also some of the more interesting things you can do with Word's Mail Merge feature, such as print mailing labels, choosing just certain names to print letters for, and using data from sources other than Word for Windows.

Understanding Mail Merge

When most people say *mail merge*, they mean merging a file that contains a list of names and addresses with another file that contains a model letter to produce a bunch of personalized form letters. For example, suppose that you want to mail a letter to all of your customers telling them about a new special offer that is so good they cannot refuse. Mail merge allows you to create *form letters*: personalized copies of the letter for each customer, with the customer's name and address printed right on the letter.

The beauty of the whole thing is that you can keep the names and addresses in a separate file and use them over and over again.

Mail merge involves three basic steps:

1. Create the *main document*. The main document contains the form letter. It includes the text that will be printed for each letter, plus special *merge fields* that indicate exactly where in each letter information from your mailing list will be placed.

2. Identify the *data source*, the list of names and addresses that will be used to create the form letters. The data source is represented in Word as a table, with one row for each name and address. Individual fields, such as name, address, city, state, zip code, and so on, are stored in separate columns. Word lets you create the table yourself, or you can import it from a database program or your Microsoft Exchange address book.

3. *Merge* the main document with the data source. This creates a form letter for each row in the data source table. You can create the form letters as a separate document, with one letter on each page, or you can send the form letter directly to the printer.

You can use mail merge to produce more than form letters. You can also use it to print envelopes or mailing labels or even documents that don't have anything to do with mailing, such as directories or catalogs. In short, mail merge is useful for any application in which a list of repeating data must be converted into a document in which each record in the data source is formatted in a similar way.

Using the Mail Merge Helper

Mail merge is a pretty complicated process, but fortunately Word provides some help in the form of the Mail Merge Helper dialog box, which appears when you summon the Tools⇨Mail Merge command. The Mail Merge Helper isn't quite as thorough as a wizard, but it does guide you through the basic mail merge steps.

The following sections guide you through the mail merge process step-by-step.

Preparing the main document

The first step in doing a mail merge is creating the main document. Follow this procedure:

1. Choose the Tools⇨Mail Merge command to summon the Mail Merge Helper, shown in Figure 30-1.

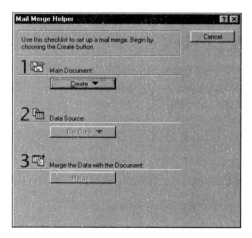

Figure 30-1: The Mail Merge Helper.

2. Click the Create button, the only button that isn't grayed out when the Mail Merge Helper starts. This will reveal a drop-down menu offering the following choices:

Form Letters

Mailing Labels

Envelopes

Catalog

Choose Form Letters to create a form letter main document. Word responds by displaying the dialog box shown in Figure 30-2.

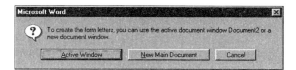

Figure 30-2: Deciding whether to use an existing document or a new document for your data source.

3. Click New Main Document to open a new, empty main document window. The Mail Merge Helper lights up with a few additional choices, as shown in Figure 30-3.

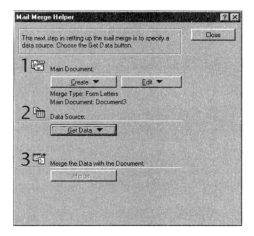

Figure 30-3: More choices appear on the Mail Merge Helper dialog box.

4. Click the Edit button. A drop-down menu will appear with only one choice on it, Form Letter: Document 1 (or whatever number it assigned to your new document). Choose this menu option. Word will switch to the main document window, as shown in Figure 30-4. Notice that a new toolbar has appeared.

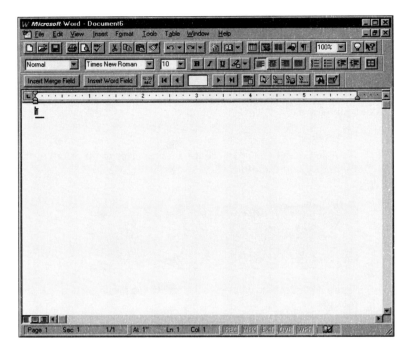

Figure 30-4: A new main document.

5. Type the form letter, leaving blank spaces where you eventually want information from the data source to appear, such as the inside address, salutation ("Dear John..."), and so on. You'll add special codes called *merge fields* to insert that information later.

6. Use the File⇨Save command to save the document to disk and use the Ctrl+S keyboard shortcut frequently as you work to save your changes.

Preparing the data source

After the main document is all set up (except for the merge fields, which will be added later), the next step is to prepare the data source. The following procedure assumes that the data source does not already exist in a separate file. The procedures for using an existing mail list are covered later in this chapter.

 1. Choose the Tools⇨Mail Merge command again to bring up the Mail Merge Helper, or click the Mail Merge Helper button in the Mail Merge toolbar.

2. Click the Get Data button. A drop-down menu listing the following choices will appear:

Create Data Source

Open Data Source

<u>U</u>se Address Book

<u>H</u>eader Options

3. Choose <u>C</u>reate Data Source from the menu that appears. The Create Data Source dialog box will appear, as shown in Figure 30-5.

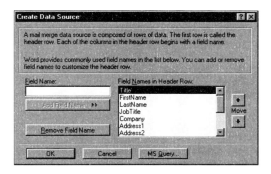

Figure 30-5: The Create Data Source dialog box.

4. The data source will initially be set up with the following fields:

Title

FirstName

LastName

JobTitle

Company

Address1

Address2

City

State

PostalCode

HomePhone

WorkPhone

If you want, you can add or remove fields included in the data source. To remove a field, click on the field to select it and click the <u>R</u>emove Field Name button. To add a field, type a name in the <u>F</u>ield Name box and click the <u>A</u>dd Field Name button. To change the order in which the fields appear, click on the field you want to move to select it and click the up- or down-arrow move buttons to move the field.

Note

Merge field names can be up to 40 characters long. They must start with a letter, and can consist only of letters, numerals, and the underscore character (_). Spaces and other punctuation are not allowed.

5. Click OK when you're satisfied with the fields to be included in the data source.

6. When Word displays the Save As dialog box, type an appropriate name to save your mailing list document and click OK. The dialog box shown in Figure 30-6 will appear.

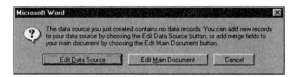

Figure 30-6: Word kindly points out that it ain't over yet.

7. Click the Edit Data Source button to begin adding names and addresses to the data source. A Data Form dialog box similar to the one shown in Figure 30-7 will appear.

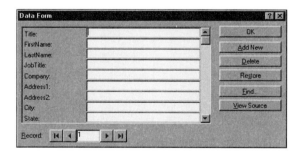

Figure 30-7: The Data Form dialog box.

8. Type the information for one person that you want to add to the data source. Use the Tab key to move from field to field or to skip over those fields that you don't want to enter. (You don't have to enter a value for every field.)

9. When you've typed all the data for the person, click Add New to add that person's data to the table in the data source.

10. Repeat Steps 8 and 9 for each person you want to add to the data source.

11. When you've added all the names you want to add, click OK.

You can use the arrow buttons at the bottom of the Data Form dialog box to move forward or backward through the data source. Thus, you can recall a previously entered record to correct a mistake if necessary.

To delete a record, use the arrow buttons at the bottom of the Data Form dialog box to move to the record you want to delete and click the <u>D</u>elete button.

Inserting field names in the main document

When you finish adding names and addresses to the data source, you return to the main document. Now is the time to add field names to the main document so that Word will know where to insert data from the data source into the form letter. If the main document isn't already displayed, select it from the <u>W</u>indow menu and follow this procedure:

1. Move the insertion point where you want to insert a field from the data source.

2. Click the Insert Merge Field button in the Mail Merge toolbar. A menu of field names from the data source will appear, as shown in Figure 30-8.

Figure 30-8: The Insert Merge Field button lists all the fields in the data source.

3. Click the field you want inserted into the document.

4. Repeat Steps 1 through 3 for each field you want inserted. Remember that the fields themselves do not contain any punctuation or spacing, so be sure to type any necessary punctuation or spacing in the document before inserting the fields. Figure 30-9 shows how the document appears with fields inserted.

5. When you're finished, use the <u>F</u>ile⇨<u>S</u>ave command to save the file.

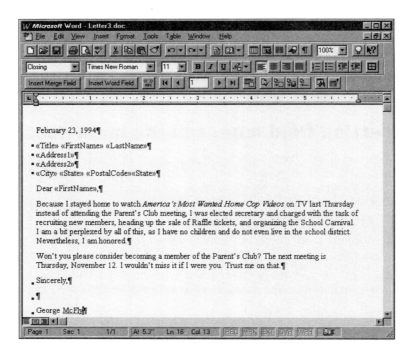

Figure 30-9: A document with fields inserted.

Notice that merge fields are displayed within special chevron characters, for example, «FirstName». You can insert these chevron characters by using the keyboard shortcuts Ctrl+`, < and Ctrl+`, > (note that ` is the backwards apostrophe, found to the left of the numeral 1), but that will not create a field code. That's because Merge fields are actually special Word fields, where the field code is MERGEFIELD. For example, the «FirstName» merge field is actually a { MERGEFIELD FirstName } field. The field result for a MERGEFIELD field is the merge field name enclosed in chevrons.

In fact, if the Show Field Codes option is on, you won't see the field names in chevrons. Instead, you'll see the MERGECODE fields in their place.

Secret

The Word documentation suggests that the only way to enter Merge fields into the document is by using the Insert Merge Field button. This isn't the case. Another way to insert a merge field is to compose the MERGEFIELD fields that reference the merge fields manually. Press Ctrl+F9 to insert a pair of field codes and type MERGEFIELD *fieldname*, where *fieldname* is the name of the merge field you want to insert. If the fieldname is FirstName, the result will look like this:

```
{ MERGEFIELD FirstName }
```

Now, press F9, and the result «FirstName» will be displayed.

Why would you bother doing this? Ordinarily, you wouldn't because just using the Insert Merge Field button is much easier. But, if you are composing a main document *before* you have a data source available, the Insert Merge Field button will not list any merge fields. In that case, you can create the MERGEFIELD fields manually.

Verifying your merge codes

 You can verify that you have set up the merge codes in your main document correctly by clicking the View Merged Data button in the Mail Merge toolbar. This replaces the merge field with data obtained from the first record in the data source. You can then inspect the main document to make sure that the data appears in the document the way you expected it to.

If the first record checks out, you can use the Mail Merge toolbar buttons summarized in Table 30-1 to view data from other data source records. If the data source is manageable in size, you can review each record to make sure that the mail merge will work as you expect. If the data source has too many records to feasibly check every one, spot check it by displaying randomly selected records.

Tip

If you discover a record that doesn't merge properly with the main document, the trouble could be in the main document or in the way the data is entered into the data source itself. For example, you may have entered the customer's last name in the FirstName field and vice versa. If so, you'll have to edit the data source to correct the error. On the other hand, the problem may be with the way the merge fields are set up in the main document. In that case, click the View Data button again to display the field codes, and make whatever adjustments are necessary.

Table 30-1	Mail Merge Toolbar Buttons Used to Retrieve Records from the Data Source
Button	*What It Does*
▶	Displays the next record in the data source.
◀	Displays the previous record.
◀◀	Displays the first record
▶▶	Displays the last record.
▭	Lets you select any record to display by entering its record number.

Merging the Documents

Now that you've set up the main document and the data source, you're ready for the show. Use the Tools⇨Mail Merge command to summon back the Mail

Merge Helper or click the Mail Merge Helper button on the Mail Merge toolbar. Then, click the Merge button to bring up the Merge dialog box, as shown in

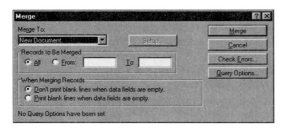

Figure 30-10: The Merge dialog box.

From this dialog box, you have several ways to proceed, as outlined in the following sections.

Merging directly to the printer

If you are confident that that the data source and the main document are set up properly and will merge as you expect, select Printer in the Marge To field and click the Merge button. The data source will be merged with the main document, and the results sent directly to the printer.

If you are in the Main Document window and are ready to merge directly to the printer, you don't have to call up the Mail Merge Helper. Instead, you can just click the Merge to Printer button in the Mail Merge toolbar.

Merging to a new document

If you want to review the complete mail merge before printing it, select New Document for the Merge To field and click Merge. This will send the merged letters to a new document. You'll end up with a new document that contains one page for each merged letter (or two pages if the main document consists of two pages). You can then browse through the document to verify that the pages have been merged properly before printing the document.

If you are in the Main Document window, you can merge to a new document by clicking the Merge New button in the Mail Merge toolbar.

Merging to e-mail or fax

If you want the merged letters to be delivered via e-mail or a fax, select Electronic Mail for the Merge To field. Then, click the Setup button to bring forth the Merge To Setup dialog box, shown in Figure 30-11.

Figure 30-11: The Merge To Setup dialog box.

In the Data Field with Mail/Fax Address drop-down list box, you must select the name of the merge field that contains the address which will be used to deliver each message via e-mail or fax; the drop-down lists provides a list of the available merge fields. You can use the Mail Message Subject Line field to provide a subject line that will be used for every message, and you can check Send Document as an Attachment if you want the formatting in the main document to be preserved.

When you have filled in these fields, click OK. Then, back in the Merge dialog box, click Merge. The data source and main document will be merged, and the resulting letters will be delivered to e-mail or fax via Microsoft Exchange.

Tip

The contents of the merge field you specify in the Data Field with Mail/Fax Address drop-down list box should contain an address that Microsoft Exchange can locate in your Address Book. However, you can bypass the Address Book and provide a fax number directly in the field, provided that you enter the fax numbers in the following format:

```
[FAX:number]
```

For example, if the fax number is 555-1234, enter [FAX: 555-1234]. For a long distance number, enclose the area code in parentheses and preface the number with +1. For example: [FAX: +1(209) 555-1234].

Merging a range of records

If the data source contains many records — say, more than 100 — you may want to consider merging them in batches. Click the From option button and type a range of record numbers in the two text fields. For example, to merge letters 100 at a time, set the fields to merge records 1 to 100, then 101 to 200, then 201 to 300, and so on until the entire data source has been merged.

Secret

This technique is also useful if your dot-matrix printer goes haywire on you in the middle of a print merge and some of the letters get crunched up in the printer. Stop the printer, clear the paper jam, realign the forms in the printer, and finish the job. Then, count from the beginning of the merge output to determine which letters were unusable and remerge just those records. For example, if the printer jammed at record 70 and ruined 10 letters before you were able to stop it and fix the jam, remerge records 70 to 80.

Using Merge Fields in the Body of a Letter

Suppose that you are sending a letter to all of the parents at your kid's school, and that in addition to all the names and addresses of parents, you have the names of their children. To make the letter seem more personalized, why not drop the kids' names into the body of the letter?

Figure 30-12 shows how this type of letter looks. As you can see, I included the merge field *Children* in the body of the paragraph. When you merge the letters, the contents of each record's *Children* field is inserted into the middle of the sentence, as in these examples:

```
I hope that Susie won't be too embarrassed by your involvement.
I hope that Jack and Jill won't be too embarrassed by your
involvement.
I hope that Huey, Dewey, and Louie won't be too embarrassed by your
involvement.
```

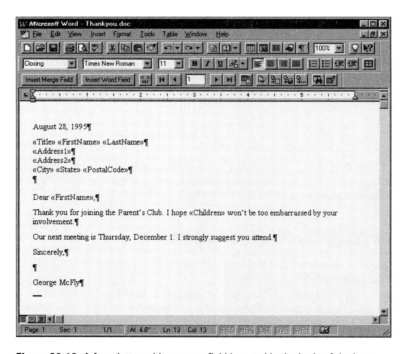

Figure 30-12: A form letter with a merge field inserted in the body of the letter.

The secret to inserting fields in the middle of sentences is carefully planning all of the grammatical possibilities to avoid an embarrassing faux pas. Suppose that you write the sentence as "I hope that your children «Children» are not too embarrassed by your involvement." You will end up with sentences like these:

```
I hope that your children Susie are not too embarrassed by your in-
volvement.
I hope that your children Jack and Jill are not too embarrassed by
your involvement.
I hope that your children Huey, Dewey, and Louie are not too embar-
rassed by your involvement.
```

The second two sentences come out fine, but the first one looks like it was written by one of the children in question.

On the other hand, if you change the sentence to "I hope that your child «Children» is not too embarrassed by your involvement," the opposite grammatical error will occur:

```
I hope that your child Susie is not too embarrassed by your involve-
ment.
I hope that your child Jack and Jill is not too embarrassed by your
involvement.
I hope that your child Huey, Dewey, and Louie is not too embarrassed
by your involvement.
```

Here are some suggestions for avoiding such traps:

- Write the sentence in such a way that it is not dependent on the whether the merge field is singular or plural. For example, "I hope that «Children» won't be too embarrassed by your involvement."

- Be consistent about how you enter information into the data source.

- If the merge field is a number, include an IF field that yields a singular or plural result based on whether the field is greater than one. For example: { IF { MERGEFIELD Quantity } > 1 "copies" "copy" }. This example inserts the word "copies" if the merge field Quantity is greater than one; otherwise, it inserts the word "copy." See the section "Using an If Field" later in this chapter for more information.

 People have been desensitized to personalized mail by Publishers Clearing House. Don't overdo the personalization; most people see right through it.

Tip

Using Word Fields

The Insert Word Field button on the Mail Merge toolbar allows you to insert several specific types of fields that are especially useful in mail merges:

- **Ask:** Displays a dialog box prompting the user for input and stores the user's input in a bookmark.

- **Fill-in:** Displays a dialog box prompting the user for input and adds the user's input to the document.

- **If-Then-Else:** Tests the value of a merge field and inserts one of two text values into the document based on the result of the condition test.

- **Merge Record #:** Inserts the record number of the current merge record into the document.

- **Merge Sequence #:** Inserts the number of records that have been merged so far.

- **Next Record:** Skips to the next merge record, allowing you to insert data from two or more records on the same page. This function is usually handled by creating a catalog-style main document instead.

- **Next Record If:** Conditionally skips to the next merge record.

- **Set Bookmark:** Sets a bookmark to any value you want.

- **Skip Record If:** Skips the current record if a condition is true. This function is easier to accomplish by using a merge query.

The most useful of these fields are Fill-In and If-Then-Else; they are described in the following sections.

Using a Fill-In field

Suppose that you want to add a little personal note to each letter. You can merge the letters to a document, edit the resulting document, and add a personal note to each merged letter. That's the easy way and probably the best way if you want to do it only once. But, if you want to add a personal note to each letter of a mail merge you run every Friday, consider adding a FILLIN field to your main document.

A FILLIN field causes Word to prompt you for text to be inserted into each document as the mail merge proceeds. A dialog box like the one in Figure 30-13 appears for each letter as it is merged. When you type a personalized message here, it is inserted into the letter.

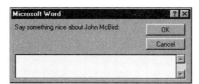

Figure 30-13: A prompt resulting from a FILL-IN field.

 The FILLIN field was covered in Chapter 29, but when you use the mail merge feature, Word provides an easier way to create the FILLIN field. To include a FILLIN field in a main document, just click the Insert Word Field button. This reveals a drop-down menu that lists several Word field codes. When you choose Fill-in, the Insert Word Field: Fill-in dialog box appears, as shown in Figure 30-14.

Type the prompt you want displayed and a default value, if you want to supply one.

Figure 30-14: The Insert Word Field: Fill-in dialog box.

If you want the prompt displayed only once for each merge job, check the **Ask Once** option. This causes Word to prompt you for the Fill-in field only when the first data source record is processed. Then, the same value will be used for all subsequent records. This procedure is useful if you want to insert a different message every time you run a mail merge, but the message is the same for each letter in the merge run.

You will want to include a merge field in the Fill-in prompt so that the user will know which record is being processed when the prompt is displayed. There is no way to do that from the Insert Word Field dialog box, so you must manually edit the FILLIN field code yourself. Go to the Tools⇨Options command and set the View Field Codes option on (it's in the View tab) and look for the Fill-in field. It should look something like this:

```
{ FILLIN "Say something nice about:" }
```

Move the cursor to the point in the field's prompt text where you want the name inserted (in this case, just before the colon), press Ctrl+F9 to insert field code brackets, and type **MERGEFIELD** followed by the name of the field you want to include. To include two fields (such as FirstName and LastName), repeat the procedure for both fields and remember to insert a space before each field. When you're finished, the FILLIN field should look like this:

```
{ FILLIN "Say something nice about { MERGFIELD FirstName } {
MERGEFIELD LastName }:" }
```

This field will display the first and last name for each record in the data source as a part of the Fill-in field prompt.

Using an If-Then-Else field

Word allows you to insert different text into a merge letter based on the contents of some field in the data source. If you have a field named *Party,* for example, you may include one message for records in which the Party field is Republican and a completely different message for records in which the field is Democrat. (I would offer appropriate messages for both cases, but I would probably offend half my loyal readers, so I'll pass.) To do that, you use an IF field code.

When you set up your data source, make sure that it provides a field which you can use as the basis for a condition test. For example, if you want to include one message for people who owe you money and another for people who are all paid up, make sure that the data source has a field that provides the balance due.

Insert Word Field   To insert conditional text, position the cursor where you want the text to appear, click the Insert Word Field button, and choose If...Then...Else from the drop-down menu that appears. The Insert Word Field: IF dialog box will appear, as shown in Figure 30-15.

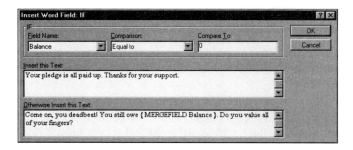

Figure 30-15: The Insert Word Field: IF dialog box.

This dialog box allows you to construct the condition test by selecting any of the merge fields available in the data source. Start by choosing in the Field Name field the field you want to test. Then, set the conditional equation in the Comparison field and the value to be compared in the Compare To field. In Figure 30-15, I compare the contents of the Balance field to the value zero.

Type the text that you want inserted if the condition is true in the Insert This Text field. For example, in Figure 30-15, I typed, *Your pledge is all paid up. Thanks for your support.* In the Otherwise Insert This Text field, type the text you want inserted if the condition is *not* true.

Notice in Figure 30-15 that I included a { MERGEFIELD } field in Otherwise text. To insert a merge field in either of the text areas of the IF dialog box, just press Ctrl+F9 to insert the field code brackets. Then, type **MERGEFIELD** followed by the name of the field you want inserted.

Printing Mailing Labels

To use the mail merge feature to print mailing labels rather than form letters, call up the Tools⇨Mail Merge command to display the Mail Merge Helper. When you click the Create button, select Mailing Labels rather than Form Letters and click the Get Data Source button to open the data source as usual. When the data source has been opened, Word will complain that the main document has to be set up. Click the Set Up Main Document button to display the Label Options dialog box, shown in Figure 30-16.

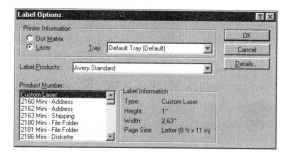

Figure 30-16: The Label Options dialog box.

This dialog box allows you to select the labels you want to use. If the labels you want to use aren't in the list, choose Custom Dot Matrix or Custom Laser as the label type and then click the Details button. A dialog box will appear that allows you to type detailed measurements for the labels. Measure your labels carefully, type the measurements, and click OK.

Word will then display the Create Labels dialog box, as shown in Figure 30-17. This dialog box allows you to specify which merge fields you want to appear on the labels. To add a merge field, click the Insert Merge Field button. As you insert each merge field, it is copied into the Sample Label box. If you include more than one field on a line, be sure to press the Spacebar to leave a space between the fields. To begin a new line, press Enter.

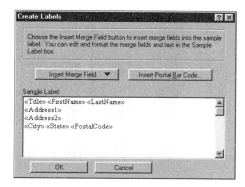

Figure 30-17: Adding merge fields to labels.

If you want to include a postal bar code on your labels, click the Insert Postal Bar Code on the Create Labels dialog box. This code is not a secret password that gets you into pubs where mail carriers hang out: it's a bar code that speeds mail delivery. If you do bulk mailing and have the proper permits, using this bar code can earn postage discounts.

When you are finished, click OK. Figure 30-18 shows how the main document will appear once it has been set up for labels. From this point, you complete the merge as usual: call up the Mail Merge Helper if it isn't displayed, click the <u>M</u>erge button, and merge to a new document or directly to the printer.

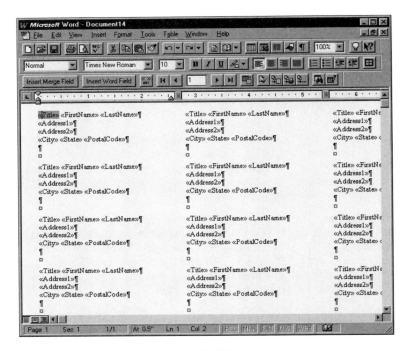

Figure 30-18: A main document set up for labels.

Printing Envelopes

Mail merge can also be used to print envelopes, although I wouldn't mess with it unless I had a printer that is capable of reliably feeding mass quantities of envelopes without jamming, curling, or sealing them. Printing envelopes is similar to printing labels. In the Mail Merge Helper, select Envelopes as the main document type when you click the <u>C</u>reate Main Document button.

As when you merge labels, Word will complain that the main document has to be set up after you open the data source. Click the <u>S</u>et Up Main Document button to display the Envelope Options dialog box, shown in Figure 30-19.

From this dialog box, you can select the envelope size you want to use. You can also click the Printing Options tab to select the method you want your printer to use when printing the envelopes, as shown in Figure 30-20.

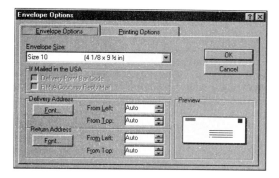

Figure 30-19: The Envelope Options dialog box (Envelope Options tab).

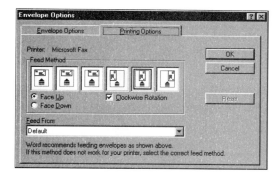

Figure 30-20: The Envelope Options dialog box (Printing Options tab).

Word then displays the Envelope Address dialog box, as shown in Figure 30-21. As you can see, this dialog box is similar to the Create Labels dialog box, which was shown in Figure 30-17. It allows you to add fields to the envelope one at a time by clicking the Insert Merge Field button and by selecting the field that you want to insert. You can include more than one field on each line, but be sure to separate the fields with spaces. You can press the Enter key to begin a new line, and you can click the Insert Postal Bar button to add a bar code.

Figure 30-22 shows how the main document looks that has been set up to print envelopes. To print the envelopes, return to the Mail Merge Helper and click the Merge button.

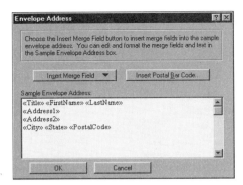

Figure 30-21: Adding merge fields to envelopes.

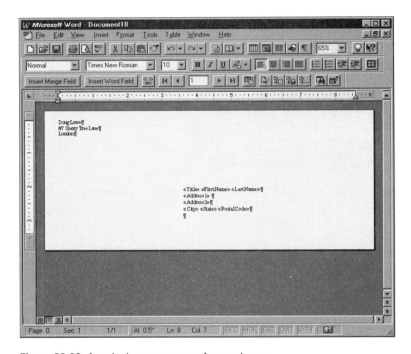

Figure 30-22: A main document set up for envelopes.

Fun Things to Do with the Data Source

Mail merge would be useful enough if all you could do with the data source was use it to store your names and addresses. But Word's data sources have more tricks up their sleeves. With a little chutzpah and a bit of wrestling with the dialog boxes, you can do several cute and moderately useful tricks with the data source. The following sections explain these amazing feats.

Sorting data

Suppose that you enter all the names in whatever sequence they were sitting in the pile, but you want to print the letters in alphabetical order. No problem. Just sort the data source. Set up the merge as you normally would, but before you click the Mail Merge Helper's Merge button, click the Query Options button to summon the Query Options dialog box. Click the Sort Records tab to display the Sort options, shown in Figure 30-23.

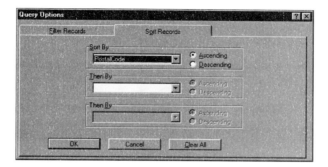

Figure 30-23: Sorting the data source.

You can sort the data source on any field by choosing the field in the Sort By list box.

If you want a second or third sort field, set them in the Then By and Then By fields. For example, if you use LastName for the Sort By field and FirstName for the Then By field, the FirstName field will be used as a tie-breaker when two or more records have the same LastName fields, such as this:

```
King    Larry
King    Martin Luther
King    Stephen
```

If you have a third field you can use as a tie-breaker, set it in the Then By field.

If you want to sort records in reverse order, click the appropriate Descending button. Records are then sorted on that field in reverse order, beginning with the *Z*s and working back up to the *A*s.

Using a merge query

Merge query lets you send letters only to a certain select group of names from your data source. You may want to send letters only to bald-headed starship captains of French descent, for example. Sending letters to this group is possible if you have fields in your data source for degree of hair coverage, rank, and ethnic background.

Note

Word uses the term *filter* to mean the process of choosing the records you want to include in a mail merge. Unlike the filters in your car, mail merge filters don't fill up with gunk, so you don't have to change them every 3,000 miles. You do have to be careful about how you set them up, though, to be sure that they choose just the records you want included in your mail merge.

To apply a filter to your mail merge, click the Mail Merge Helper's Query Options button before performing the merge. Click the Filter Records tab to display the filter options, as shown in Figure 30-24.

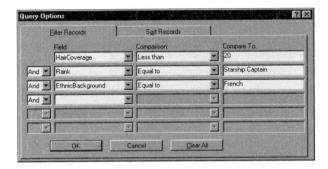

Figure 30-24: Filtering records.

Set the criteria for including records in the mail merge by specifying a Field, Comparison, and Compare To value for each criteria. For example, Figure 30-24 says to select only those records where the HairCoverage field is less than "20", Rank field is equal to "Starship Captain," and EthnicBackground is equal to "French."

Table 30-2 lists the relational tests you can perform when filtering records.

You can set up complicated queries that check the contents of several fields. For example, you may want to mail letters only to people who live in a particular city and state. You set up the query like this:

```
        City Equal to Bakersfield
And     State Equal to CA
```

In this query, only records whose City field is equal to "Bakersfield" and whose State field is equal to "CA" are included in the merge.

You can also set up queries that test the same field twice. To mail to addresses with ZIP codes 93711 or 93722, for example, set up the query like this:

```
        PostalCode Equal to 93711
Or      PostalCode Equal to 93722
```

Table 30-2	Relational Tests
Comparison Setting	*What It Means*
Equal To	Selects only those records in which the value of the specified Field exactly matches the Compare To value.
Not Equal To	Selects only those records in which the value of the specified Field does not exactly match the Compare To value.
Less Than	Selects only those records in which the value of the specified Field is less than the Compare To value.
Greater Than	Selects only those records in which the value of the specified Field is greater than the Compare To value.
Greater Than or Equal To	Selects only those records in which the value of the specified Field is greater than or equal to the Compare To value.
Is Blank	Selects only those records in which the value of the specified Field is blank.
Is Not Blank	Selects only those records in which the value of the specified Field is not blank.

Notice that I change the And/Or field from And to Or. That way, a record is selected if its PostalCode field is 93711 or 93722. If you test the same field for two or more specific values, do not leave the And/Or field set to And. If I had left the And/Or field set to And in the preceding example, a record would be selected only if its PostalCode was equal to 93711 and if it was also equal to 93722. Obviously, this can't be: each record in the data source can have only one value for the PostalCode field. It's natural to want to leave the And/Or field set to And because you want to "mail letters to everyone in the 93711 *and* 93722 ZIP codes." But, when you fill in the Query dialog box, you have to use Or, not And.

On the other hand, suppose that you want to mail to anyone whose ZIP Code is 93711, 93722, or any value in between. In that case, you use two condition tests linked by And, as shown in this example:

```
     PostalCode Greater Than or Equal to 93711
And  PostalCode Less Than or Equal to 93722
```

Understanding precedence

Be careful when you set up a query that uses three or more field tests and mixes And and Or. You're going to be confronted with the issue of precedence, which means, in layman's terms, "what to do first." You may suppose that Word would test the conditions you list in the Query Options dialog box in the order in which you list them. Not necessarily. Word groups any condition tests linked by And and checks them out before combining the results with tests linked by Or.

Confused? So am I. Let's walk through an example to see how it works. Suppose that you open the menu at a restaurant and see that the fried chicken dinner comes with a "leg or wing and thigh." Which of the following statements represents the two possible chicken-dinner configurations the restaurant will sell you:

- You can order a meal with a leg and a thigh, or you can order a meal with a wing and a thigh.

- You can order a meal with a leg, or you can order a meal with a wing and a thigh.

According to the way Word processes queries, the answer is the second one. Word lumps together as a group the two options linked by And. If you were a computer science grad student, you would put parentheses around "wing and thigh," like this: "leg or (wing and thigh)."

If you want the first example to be the right answer, you have to state the menu choice as "leg and thigh or wing and thigh."

For a more realistic Word for Windows example, suppose that you want to mail to everyone who lives in Olympia, WA, and just across the way in Aberdeen, WA. You might be tempted to set the query up like this:

```
        State Equal to WA
And     City Equal to Olympia
Or      City Equal to Aberdeen
```

Unfortunately, that won't work. You'll end up with everyone who lives in Olympia, WA, plus anyone who lives in any town named Aberdeen, regardless of the state (Aberdeens can also be found in Maryland and South Dakota.) To do this filter up properly, you have to mention the state twice:

```
        State Equal to WA
And     City Equal to Olympia
Or      State Equal to WA
And     City Equal to Aberdeen
```

Editing the data source directly

When you edit the data source by clicking the E_dit button in the Data Source portion of the Mail Merge Helper dialog box, you are presented with the Data Form dialog box, which provides a convenient way to add names and addresses to your mailing list. If you want, you can fiddle directly with the data in the data source by clicking the _View Source button in the Data Form dialog box. When you do, the data source document is displayed in a document window so that you can edit it just like any other document.

Data is stored in the data source as a Word table, as shown in Figure 30-25. Each field is represented by a table column, and each record is represented by a row. The first row of the table contains the field names. You can edit data directly in the table if you want, but I find it easier to edit the table data by using the Data Form dialog box.

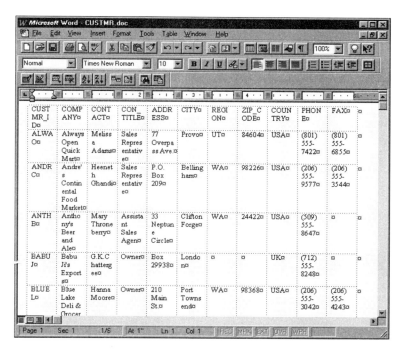

Figure 30-25: Editing the data source directly.

Tip

Word formats the table so that most of the columns are not wide enough to display their contents on one line. However, the line breaks in the fields don't affect the way the merged letters are printed. If you want, you can adjust the width of each field by dragging the boxes between columns in the ruler.

When you view the data source, Word activates the Database toolbar, just beneath the Formatting toolbar. The function of each button on the Database toolbar is summarized in Table 30-3.

Table 30-3	**Buttons on the Database Toolbar**
Button	**What It Does**
▦	Calls up the Data Form dialog box so that you can quickly enter new records.
▦	Calls up the Manage Fields dialog box so that you can add new fields to the table or delete fields from the table.
▦	Adds a new record to the table.
▦	Deletes the chosen record.
▦	Sorts the table into ascending sequence.
▦	Sorts the table into descending sequence.
▦	Imports data from a database program.
▦	Updates the contents of any Word fields included in the data source.
▦	Finds data in a specific field.
▦	Switches to the Mail Merge main document.

To add or delete fields (columns) from the table, click the Manage Fields button. This brings up the Manage Fields dialog box, as shown in Figure 30-26. To add a field to the table, type the field name in the Field Name box and click the Add button. To remove a field, choose the field in the Field Names in Header Row list and click the Remove button.

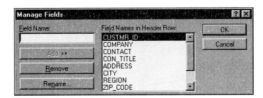

Figure 30-26: The Manage Fields dialog box.

Importing data from another source

Word for Windows enables you to use name and address records that you created with another program for your mail merges. If you use Paradox for Windows to keep a customer list, for example, you can open the Paradox database file as the data source. Word supports the following database formats:

- Microsoft Excel
- Microsoft Access
- Microsoft FoxPro
- Lotus 1-2-3
- WordPerfect
- dBASE
- Paradox
- earlier versions of Microsoft Word

To use a file created by one of the programs just listed as a mail merge data source, just change the Files of Type field in the Open Data Source dialog box, which appears when you choose the Mail Merge Helper's Get Data button to open an existing data source.

When you open a Microsoft Access file as a data source, Word for Windows asks whether you want to include the entire file or access specific records based on an Access query. If the data table is large and you don't need all the records, consider setting up an Access query to select just the records you want to include in the mail merge. This procedure is more efficient than importing the entire file into Word for Windows and then using a Mail Merge query.

If the file you open is a Microsoft Excel worksheet, Word for Windows asks whether you want to include the entire worksheet file or whether you want to include only those cells that fall within a certain range.

Tip

You can also open text files in which the data for each field is separated by commas, tabs, or other characters. This is your bridge to foreign database programs that aren't included in the List Files of Type field. Almost all database programs let you *export* data to a text file. You can use the export feature to create a file that Word for Windows can open as a text file data source.

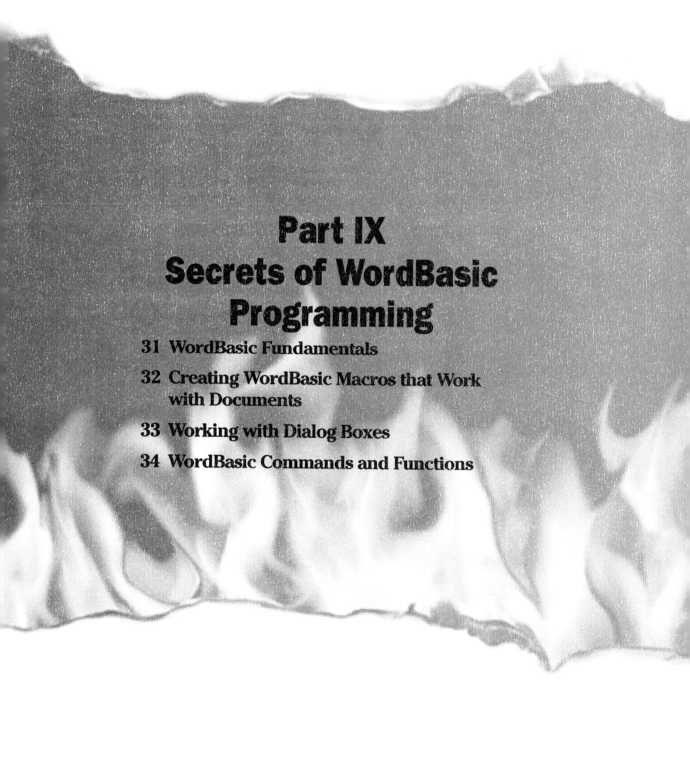

Part IX
Secrets of WordBasic Programming

31 WordBasic Fundamentals

32 Creating WordBasic Macros that Work with Documents

33 Working with Dialog Boxes

34 WordBasic Commands and Functions

Chapter 31

WordBasic Fundamentals

In This Chapter

▶ The basics of coding WordBasic commands, including how to use variables, strings, functions, and other WordBasic elements

▶ Controlling the execution of a WordBasic macro with commands such as If, While, and Select Case

▶ Displaying information and obtaining input from the user

▶ Working with user-defined subroutines and macros

T he basics of recording and playing back macros was covered way back in Chapter 7. Chapter 7 began to touch on the subject of WordBasic programming, just enough to whet your appetite and give you the skills needed to create and use the various macros that appear throughout this book. But the real meat of WordBasic programming has been reserved for this chapter. It is here that we will look at WordBasic in-depth so that, with a little practice and a lot of trial and error, you'll be able to create WordBasic macros of your own.

WordBasic is a peculiar dialect of the BASIC programming language, with capabilities that fall somewhere between the original BASIC language, which many of us cut our teeth on decades ago, and Visual Basic, the object-oriented programming language that may work its way into Word 8.

Warning

This chapter is admittedly a bit of a whirlwind introduction to WordBasic programming. If you have absolutely no programming experience, this chapter may seem a bit overwhelming. Don't let the details of WordBasic bog you down. Study the sample macros that appear in this chapter and throughout this book, experiment a lot, and keep your chin up. You'll catch on soon enough. If you're not sure about how to use the Tools⇔Macro command to create and edit macros, better review Chapter 7 before proceeding.

The Basic Structure of WordBasic Macros

When you first create a macro by calling up the Tools⇔Macro command, typing a macro name, and clicking on the Create button, the macro will consist of only two lines:

```
Sub MAIN
End Sub
```

These two lines, `Sub MAIN` and `End Sub`, mark the beginning and end of the macro's main routine. As you'll see later, a macro can consist of other subroutines and user-defined functions. However, the simplest macros consist of these two lines (`Sub MAIN` and `End Sub`) with WordBasic instructions in between. For example, the following macro contains two WordBasic instructions, one to make the selected text bold and the other to make it italic:

```
Sub MAIN
Bold
Italic
End Sub
```

The net effect of this command makes the selected text both bold and italic.

Note

Well, not quite. Actually, the effect of this macro changes both the bold and italic attributes of the selected text. If the text isn't already bold or italic, the macro will make it bold and italic. But, if the text is already formatted as bold but not italic, the macro will turn off the bold attribute but turn on the italic. And, if no text is selected at all, the macro sets the bold and italic attributes for text that you subsequently type.

So here, just a page into this chapter, we already have an example of the Undeniable Truth of WordBasic Programming: Even simple macros sometimes don't work the way you expect them to. The outcome of a macro usually very much dependends on whether text is selected, how the selected text (if any) is formatted, the view (Normal, Page Layout, or Outline), and many other factors. The moral of the story: *Test everything.*

There are two broad categories of WordBasic instructions you will encounter:

- **Word commands**, which correspond to the commands that are built in to Word. For the most part, anything that you can do with a menu command, keyboard shortcut, or toolbar button has a corresponding WordBasic statement. This includes such obvious statements as FileOpen, which corresponds to the File⇨Open command, and CharLeft, which corresponds to pressing the left arrow key.

- **WordBasic commands**, which are commands of the WordBasic programming language, such as `If`, `For`, `Goto`, `Dim`, and so on. These commands control the execution of the macro.

You must also contend with functions, which have a variety of uses ranging from returning information about the document to manipulating string variables to obtaining input from the user.

Many of the Word and WordBasic commands have corresponding functions, which perform the same operation as the command but return a value that the macro can act on. For example, the `MsgBox` command displays a message in a dialog box. The `MsgBox()` function also displays a message in a dialog box, but returns a number that indicates which button the user pressed to dismiss the dialog box. The macro can then act on this number to take different actions depending on which button the user presses.

In WordBasic, functions are followed by parentheses, which may or may not contain *arguments* — values that are used as input by the function. For example, Len(FirstName$) returns a number that indicates how many characters are in the string contained in the variable named FirstName$ (more on variables in a moment). The parentheses are always required when calling a function, even if no arguments are passed. For example, the function AtEndOfDocument() returns a number that indicates whether the insertion point is at the end of the document. No arguments are required for this function, but the parentheses are required nevertheless.

Rules for Writing WordBasic Instructions

The normal way to write WordBasic instructions is one per line. You can gang up several instructions on a single line by separating the instructions with colons, as in this example:

```
Sub MAIN
Bold : Italic
End Sub
```

You can indent lines to show the relationships among instructions by using tabs or spaces.

Spacing *within* a WordBasic instruction generally isn't important. You can omit spaces when different elements of an instruction are separated by a comma, colon, or other punctuation. However, the first time you run the macro, WordBasic will insert spaces around such elements.

If a line is longer than what will fit in the window at one time, Word will automatically wrap the macro to the next line, as in this example:

```
FormatParagraph .LeftIndent = "0" + Chr$(34), .RightIndent = "0" +
Chr$(34), .Before = "12 pt", .After = "0 pt", .LineSpacingRule = 0,
.LineSpacing = "", .Alignment = 0, .WidowControl = 0, .KeepWithNext =
0,
.KeepTogether = 0, .PageBreak = 0, .NoLineNum = 0, .DontHyphen = 0,
.Tab =
"0", .FirstIndent = "0" + Chr$(34)
```

If you want to change the line endings of a macro to make the macro instruction easier to read, you can insert a backslash character at the end of a line and pressing the Enter key, as in this example:

```
FormatParagraph .LeftIndent = "0" + Chr$(34), \
.RightIndent = "0" + Chr$(34), .Before = "12 pt", \
.After = "0 pt", .LineSpacingRule = 0, .LineSpacing = "", \
.Alignment = 0, .WidowControl = 0, .KeepWithNext = 0, \
.KeepTogether = 0, .PageBreak = 0, .NoLineNum = 0, .DontHyphen = 0, \
.Tab = "0", .FirstIndent = "0" + Chr$(34)
```

The backslash characters indicate to Word that the instruction is continued on the next line, so the successive lines should be treated as a single instruction. While this might seem to be a good idea at first, it can lead to problems if you decide to edit the instruction later. As a result, I suggest you just let Word break the lines where they fall.

Secret

There is no way to change the formatting used for macro instructions (such as the indentation, font, point size, or paragraph margins) while editing a macro. However, you can modify these settings by changing the built-in style named Macro Text. To change the Macro Text style, open any document window, call up the Format⇨Style command, and adjust the Macro Text style however you see fit. When you return to the macro window, the macro text will reflect any changes you made to the style. (If Macro Text doesn't appear in the style list, make sure the List drop-down list box is set to All Macros.)

Comments

Comments are used in macros to remind you and others of what the macro, or portions of it, does. Comments are especially useful when the WordBasic instructions required to carry out a task are obscure enough that you can't tell immediately what the instructions do just by looking at them. In such cases, a succinct comment can often save you hours of troubleshooting time later.

You can insert comments into a WordBasic macro in two ways. The first is to use a REM statement, such as this:

```
Sub MAIN
Rem This macro applies both bold and italic.
Bold
Italic
End Sub
```

The second is to use apostrophes. When you use an apostrophe anywhere on a line, WordBasic completely ignores everything on the line after the apostrophe. This allows you to place comments directly on the lines where they relate:

```
Sub MAIN
' This macro applies both bold and italic.
Bold        ' Apply the bold attribute.
Italic      ' Apply the italic attribute.
End Sub
```

Tip

It's a good idea to preface each of your nontrivial macros with a block of comments that gives basic information about the macro. For example:

```
' ****************************************************************
' ConvertForPub
' Date written:   August 3, 1995
' Last Modified:  August 10, 1995 DAL
' Author:         Doug Lowe
' Converts document into a format that can be more easily imported
' into desktop publishing programs.
' ****************************************************************
```

Variables

A *variable* is a name that is assigned to a bit of computer memory and which can be used to hold a value. Variables are one of the key features of any programming language, and WordBasic is no exception. Variables play an important role in all but the most trivial WordBasic macros.

WordBasic provides two kinds of variables: numeric and string. You can tell whether a variable is a numeric variable or a string variable because string variable names end with a dollar sign ($). Thus, `Counter` is a numeric variable, and `DisplayText$` is a string variable.

For the hardened programmers in the audience who won't sleep well unless they know, numeric variables are stored as double-precision, 64-bit floating point numbers. Values for numeric variables can be as large as 1.79 followed by 308 zeros, which is probably larger than any number you're likely to deal with in WordBasic programming unless you're working on the Federal budget.

String variables can hold at most 65,280 characters, though some string functions limit the string size to half that, and some have a 255-character limit.

Variable names can be up to 40 characters, must start with a letter, and can contain only letters, numerals, and the underscore (_). Also, you cannot use any of WordBasic's reserved words, such as function names, the names of WordBasic instructions, and so on.

You use an assignment statement to assign values to variables. For example

```
Pi = 3.14159
x=0
MessageText$="Hello from Planet Earth"
```

In a concession to the 30-year-old legacy of BASIC programming, WordBasic allows you to preface assignment statements with the word `Let`:

```
Let Pi = 3.14159
Let x=0
Let MessageText$="Hello from Planet Earth"
```

Unlike many other programming languages such as C and Pascal, you do not have to "define" variables before you can use them. The first time you use a variable in a WordBasic macro, the variable is automatically defined and assigned a default value: 0 if the variable is a numeric variable, an empty string ("") if the variable is a string variable. Also, WordBasic can tell whether the variable is numeric or string by the presence or absence of the dollar sign at the end of the variable name: the dollar sign signifies that the variable is a string variable.

Warning

Most experienced programmers consider the fact that variables do not have to be defined to be *the* major weakness in BASIC and all of its dialects, including WordBasic and VisualBasic. The trouble is that you never know when you've misspelled a variable name, because if you misspell a variable name, WordBasic assumes that you want to create a new variable. For example, suppose at the start of a macro you ask the user to enter a string value, and you store the value entered by the user in a variable named `InputString$`. Then, later in the macro, you use the variable in an instruction but misspell it `InputStrign$`. Does WordBasic point out your error? No. It just assumes that you wanted to create a new variable named `InputStrign$`. Like any new string variable, this `InputStrign$` variable will be given a value of "" rather than the value entered by the user.

Such problems are very common in WordBasic programming. Anytime you are faced with a macro that looks like it should work, but doesn't, carefully double-check all your variable names to see if any are misspelled.

Arrays

An array is a collection of variable values that are stored under the same name. To access a specific variable value, called an *element,* you must specify not only the variable name, but a number called a *subscript.* For example, the following line adds the first two elements of an array named `SomeArray` and stores the result in a variable named `TheSum`:

```
TheSum = SomeArray(0) + SomeArray(1)
```

Notice that the subscript for the first element is 0; for the second element, 1. Next to misspelling variable names, this peculiarity is probably the second leading cause of bugs in WordBasic macros.

Using the Dim instruction to define arrays

Before you can use an array, you must define it using a `Dim` statement. The `Dim` statement specifies one or more *dimensions* for the array. Most arrays have just one dimension, as follows:

```
Dim Recipient$(50)
```

Here, an array of string variables is created. The dimension specifies that the largest subscript that can be used by the array is 50. Because array subscripts begin with 0, this means that the array can hold up to 51 string values.

To create an array of numeric variables, leave the dollar sign off the array variable name, as in this example:

```
Dim GridCoordinates(4)
```

Here, an array of numeric variables that can hold up to five values is created.

When accessing specific array elements, you can use another variable to provide the subscript, as in `Recipient$(Counter)`. In this case, the current value of the `Counter` variable indicates to which element the `Recipient$` array refers.

WordBasic allows you to create more than one array on a single Dim statement. Just separate the arrays with commas, like this:

```
Dim Recipient$(50), GridCoordinates(4)
```

Note

Remember that WordBasic arrays always have one more element that is indicated in the Dim statement because array subscripts always begin with 0 to refer to the first element of the array. An array dimensioned with 50 elements would have subscripts that range from 0 to 50, for a total of 51 elements. Because of this peculiarity, it is common practice to simply ignore the first element and program your WordBasic macros so that subscripts are indexed from 1 to the number of elements defined.

This practice of skipping subscript 0 works in most cases, but in one specific case — when the array is used to supply values to a list field that appears in a dialog box — it can lead to unexpected bugs. I'll have more to say about that in Chapter 33, when I describe the WordBasic techniques for creating and displaying your own dialog boxes.

Arrays with more than one dimension

You can create arrays with more than one dimension. For example:

```
Dim Grid(10, 10)
```

Here, an array of numeric variables is created, with 11 rows and 11 columns.

You can think of a two-dimensional array as a table with rows and columns. A three-dimensional array, such as the following,

```
Dim Cube(10, 10, 10)
```

can be thought of as a cube. While arrays of more than three dimensions are possible, they are difficult to visualize, so most programmers avoid them. In any event, it's difficult to conceive of applications for arrays of more than three dimensions in WordBasic macros.

Secret

An array can have 8,142 elements at most. To figure out how many elements an array has, add one to each dimension and multiply all the dimensions together. For example, the following array has 6,561 elements:

```
Dim Threes(2, 2, 2, 2, 2, 2, 2, 2)
```

Remember that array subscripts start at 0, so each dimension in this array actually has 3 elements. The larger each dimension, the fewer the number of dimensions allowed. For example, the following Dim statement erupts with an "Invalid Array Dimension" error:

```
Dim Threes(2, 2, 2, 2, 2, 2, 2, 3)
```

The only difference is that the last dimension is 3 instead of 2. That raises the number of elements to 8,748, just a tad above the 8,142 element limit.

Sorting array values

WordBasic includes a `SortArray` function that sorts array elements into alphabetical order. In its simplest form, it looks like this:

```
SortArray List()
```

See the on-line help for information about how to use `SortArray` to sort in descending sequence, to sort two-dimensional arrays, and to sort only a portion of the array.

Strings

I've already mentioned that WordBasic distinguishes between string variables and numeric variables by virtue of the dollar sign that must be affixed to the end of string variable names. In addition to knowing how to create variable names for string variables, you also need to know how to manipulate string values if you hope to accomplish anything in WordBasic.

For starters, you can create string *literals:* that is, strings that are simply quoted in your macro. To use a string literal, enclose a string value in quotation marks: full-fledged double quotes, not apostrophes. For example:

```
Message$ = "Hi there!"
```

Here, the value `"Hi there!"` is assigned to the string variable named `Message$`.

You can use an apostrophe within a string literal with no ill effects, as in the following example:

```
Message$ = "Hi y'all"
```

But, you cannot include quotes within quotes. For example, the following will produce an error:

```
Message$ = "Say, "Cheeseburger!""
```

To see how to create a string value that includes quotation marks, read the following sections on concatenation and string functions.

Concatenation

A technique called *concatenation* allows you to join two or more strings together end to end to make a single, larger string. For example:

```
Entre$ = "Cheese" + "burger"
```

results in the string `"Cheeseburger"` being assigned to `Entre$`. The plus sign (+) is used for this purpose. (The spaces around the plus sign are optional; if you leave them out, Word will add them in when you run the macro.)

Concatenation becomes very useful when combined with string variables and, as you'll see in a moment, string functions. For example, consider this instruction:

```
Message$ = "Could not deliver message to " + Recipient$
```

Here, a literal string value is concatenated with a variable string value. If the value of the `Recipient$` variable were `"Jimmy Hoffa"`, the `Message$` variable would have been set to `"Could not deliver message to Jimmy Hoffa"`.

There is no limit to the number of concatenations you can string together in a single instruction.

String functions

WordBasic provides several built-in functions that work on strings. Table 31-1 summarizes these functions. Most of these functions will come in handy from time to time.

One of the most commonly used string functions is `Chr$`. It lets you generate any character by specifying its ANSI code number, which ranges from 0 to 255. You can use concatenation along with the `Chr$()` function to create strings that contain quotation marks. For example:

```
Message$ = "Say, " + Chr$(34) + "Cheeseburger!" + Chr$(34)
```

Here, `Chr$(34)` is used to insert the quotation marks.

Another commonly used string function is `Len`: it returns the number of characters in a string. For example:

```
Message$="Hello world!"
LengthOfMessage = Len(Message$)
```

In this example, the `LengthOfMessage` variable is assigned the value 12, the number of characters in the string `Message$`. The `Len` function returns a number, not a string. That's why the `Len` function doesn't have a dollar sign appended to its name.

A final group of string functions that you need are those used to clean up string values that may contain unnecessary leading or trailing spaces or unprintable characters. These functions include `LTrim$()`, `RTrim$()`, and `CleanString$()`. For example, to remove unprintable characters from the string `InputText$` and assign the cleaned-up string to the string variable `Clear$`, you would use this instruction:

```
Clear$ = CleanString$(InputText$)
```

Because the result of the `CleanString$()` function is a string value, you can use the `CleanString$` function as the argument to another string function such as `LTrim$()`:

```
Clear$ = LTrim$(CleanString$(InputText$))
```

Note that two sets of parentheses are used, and that the parentheses must be properly balanced: the innermost set of parentheses contains the argument for the `CleanString$()` function: `InputText$`. The outer set of parentheses contains the argument for the `LTrim$()` function: `CleanString$(InputText$)`.

The following cluster of functions is often used to remove both leading and trailing spaces, plus unprintable characters:

```
Clear$ = LTrim$(RTrim$(CleanString$(InputText$)))
```

Here, the string variable `InputText$` is passed as an argument to the `CleanString$()` function, which removes any unprintable characters. Then, the string with unprintable characters removed is passed as an argument to the `RTrim$()` function, which removes trailing spaces. Finally, the string with unprintable characters and trailing spaces removed is passed as an argument to the `LTrim$()` function, which removes leading spaces.

Table 31-1   WordBasic Functions for Manipulating Strings

Function	What It Does	
Chr$(*value*)	Generates the character that corresponds to the ANSI code *value*. Common uses are:	
	Chr$(9)	Tab
	Chr$(11)	New line
	Chr$(13)	Carriage return
	Chr$(30)	Non-breaking hyphen
	Chr$(32)	Space
	Chr$(34)	Quotation mark (")
	Chr$(160)	Non-breaking space
CleanString$(*string$*)	Removes unprintable characters from *string$*.	
InStr([*n*,]*string1$*,*string2$*)	Returns the character position within *string1$* at which *string2$* begins, or 0 if *string2$* is not found in *string1$*. If *n* is used, the first *n-1* characters of *string1$* are ignored.	
Lcase$(*string$*)	Converts *string$* to lowercase.	
Left$(*string$*,*n*)	Returns the leftmost *n* characters of *string$*.	
Len(*string$*)	Returns the length of *string$*.	
Ltrim$(*string$*)	Removes leading spaces from *string$*.	

Function	What It Does
Mid$(*string$,x,y*)	Returns *y* characters from *string$* starting at character *x*.
Right$(*string$,n*)	Returns the rightmost *n* characters of *string$*.
Rtrim$(*string$*)	Removes trailing spaces from *string*.
Str$(*n*)	Converts the number *n* to a string variable. For example, Str$(3.15) becomes the string " 3.15".
Ucase$(*string$*)	Converts *string$* to uppercase.
Val(*string*)	Returns the numeric value of *string*. For example, Val("3.15") becomes the numeric value 3.15.

Control Structures

The simplest macros start at the beginning and execute their instructions one at a time, in the sequence in which the instructions are listed in the macro, until the `End Sub` instruction is reached.

More sophisticated macros need more control over the sequence in which instructions are executed. For example, you may need to skip over some instructions based on the result of a condition test. Or, you may need to create a loop of instructions that repeats itself a given number of times, or until a certain condition — such as reaching the end of the document — is met.

The following sections describe the WordBasic statements that let you control the flow of execution in your macro.

The Goto Instruction and Labels

The Goto instruction jumps to the instruction indicated by a label. Labels follow the same naming rules as variables, are coded at the beginning of a line, and are followed by a colon. For example:

```
Goto Gitaround
x=0
Gitaround: Print x
```

There's only one problem with the previous bit of code: the second line (x=0) will never be executed under any circumstances. This is one of the reasons that programmers have argued vehemently for the outright banning of `Goto` statements for nearly 25 years now.

As a general rule, anytime you use a `Goto` statement, the next statement in sequence should be a label. For example:

```
Goto Gitaround
Comearound: x=0
Gitaround: Print x
```

Then, some other instruction would hopefully branch to the Comearound label, so that the x=0 instruction can be executed.

Goto statements are rarely used by themselves in WordBasic macros. Instead, you'll use them in combination with the other flow-control instructions that are described in the following sections.

The If Statement

Do you remember that Robert Frost poem that begins, "Two roads diverged in a yellow wood..."? That poem is an apt description of how the If statement works. The macro is rolling along, executing one instruction after another, until it comes to an If statement. The If statement represents a fork in the road, and a choice must be made about which path to take.

Many macros need to make such decisions as they execute. For example, a macro that creates an index entry for text selected by the user would have to first determine whether the user has indeed selected any text. If so, the macro would proceed to create the index entry. If not, the macro would do nothing, or perhaps display an error message saying something along the lines of, "You didn't select any text!" To handle this decision processing, the macro would use an If statement.

WordBasic's If statement is remarkably flexible, with several formats to choose from. All of these forms involve three basic parts:

- A *condition test,* which is evaluated to yield a value of "true" or "false."

- A *then part*, which supplies one or more instructions that are executed only if the result of the condition test is "true."

- An *else part*, which supplies one or more instructions that are executed only if the result of the condition test is "false."

For example, consider these lines that might be used in an index-marking macro:

```
If SelType() = 2 Then
    InsertField "XE " + Chr$(34) + Selection$() + Chr$(34)
Else
    MsgBox "You didn't select any text!"
End If
```

Here, the If statement begins with a condition test: SelType() = 2. The SelType() function returns a number that indicates whether the user has selected text; 2 indicates that text is selected, 1 that text is not selected. If the condition test is true — that is, if the SelType() function returns 2 — the InsertField command is executed, which inserts an XE field code used to mark an index entry based on the user's selection. Otherwise, the MsgBox command is executed, which displays the message, "You didn't select any text!"

The basic If statement

The general form of this type of If statement looks like this:

```
If expression Then
    instructions executed if true
[ Else
    instructions executed if false ]
End If
```

Each component of the If instruction must fall on a separate line, as shown in the above structure. In other words, you cannot place the instructions on the same line as the Then or Else keywords.

The brackets around the Else lines indicate that the Else clause is optional. Note, however, that End If is not optional: every If instruction must have a corresponding End If. (The only exception to this is the single-line If format which I'll explain in a moment.)

Tip

While it is not strictly required that you indent the instructions, using such indentation makes the structure of the If statement much more apparent. Consider the preceding example without any indentation:

```
If SelType() = 2 Then
InsertField "XE " + Chr$(34) + Selection$() + Chr$(34)
Else
MsgBox "You didn't select any text!"
End If
```

Now, imagine that instead of a single instruction between the Then and Else lines, there were a dozen, with a dozen more lines between the Else and End If lines. Indentation is the only way to keep track of the overall structure of the If instruction.

Nested If statements

If statements can be nested: that is, you can include one If statement within the Then or Else part of another. For example:

```
If expression Then
    If expression Then
        instructions
    Else
        instructions
    End If
Else
    If expression Then
        instructions
    Else
        instructions
    End IF
End If
```

Nesting can be as complex as you wish. Just remember that you need an End If for every If, and be certain to use indentation so that each set of matching If, Else, and End If lines are properly aligned.

The ElseIf structure

WordBasic supports a special type of If structure, using the ElseIf keyword. The ElseIf form is a shorthand notation that allows you to simplify If structures that follow this form:

```
If expression Then
    instructions
Else
    If expression Then
        instructions
    Else
        If expression Then
            instructions
        End If
    End IF
End If
```

Using the ElseIf keyword, you could express the same structure like this:

```
If expression Then
    instructions
ElseIf expression Then
    instructions
ElseIf expression Then
    instructions
End If
```

If that's a little too abstract, let's consider a macro that displays one of three messages, depending on the day of the week. For Sunday, the macro displays "Time for Football!" For Saturday, it displays "Time to mow the lawn!!" And, for any other day, it displays "Time to go to work!!!"

Here's how this macro might be coded using ordinary If statements:

```
DayOfWeek=Weekday(Now())
If DayOfWeek = 1 Then
    MsgBox "Time for football!"
Else
    If DayOfWeek = 7 Then
        MsgBox "Time to mow the lawn!!"
    Else
        MsgBox "Time to go to work!!!"
    End IF
End If
```

Notice that the first Else clause contains a nested If statement. By using the ElseIf keyword, the second If statement can be subsumed into the first, so the whole thing can be handled by a single If statement:

```
DayOfWeek=Weekday(Now())
If DayOfWeek = 1 Then
    MsgBox "Time for football!"
ElseIf DayOfWeek = 7 Then
    MsgBox "Time to mow the lawn!!"
Else
    MsgBox "Time to go to work!!!"
End If
```

In this example, only one End If line is required because there is only one If statement. In other words, the ElseIf keyword does not require its own matching End If.

Secret

In most cases, If structures that require ElseIf clauses can often be implemented more easily using a Select Case statement, which will be described later in this chapter.

The single-line If

WordBasic also allows you to use a single-line form of the If statement, which looks like this:

```
If condition Then instruction [Else instruction]
```

To use this form of the If statement, the condition, Then clause, and Else clause (if any) must all be coded on the same line. For example:

```
If x > 0 Then MsgBox Message$(x)
```

The above example displays a message using an element of the Message$ array, but only if the variable used for the subscript (x, in this case) is greater than 0.

You can include more than one instruction in the Then or Else part by separating the instructions with colons, as follows:

```
If x > 0 Then Beep : MsgBox Message$(x)
```

In this example, the Beep command will cause the computer to beep as the message is displayed.

For/Next Loops

For/Next loops allow you to set up a basic looping structure, in which a series of instructions is executed over and over again, with the value of a counter variable increased by one each time, until the counter variable reaches a certain value.

As a simple, if not very practical, example, the following snippet inserts the numbers 1 through 100 in the current document, one number on each line:

```
For x = 1 to 100
    Insert Str$(x) + Chr$(13)
Next x
```

This For/Next loop will cause the Insert instruction it contains to execute 100 times. The first time through, the variable x will be set to the value 1. The second time, x will be 2; the third time, 3; and so on, all the way up to 100.

Note

Within the For/Next loop, an Insert instruction inserts the counter variable x followed by a paragraph mark into the document. The Str$() function is required because the Insert command requires a string value, not a numeric value. All the Str$() function does is convert numeric value to a string value; for example, 1 becomes "1". The Chr$(13) function is used to insert the paragraph mark. The purpose of this example is to explain how the For/Next loop works, so don't get bogged down if the Insert instruction is confusing. There's a whole section devoted to how the Insert instruction works in Chapter 32.

The general form of a For/Next loop is:

```
For counter-variable = start To end [Step increment]
    instructions...
Next [counter-variable]
```

As you can see, you can specify any starting and ending value you wish for the counter variable. In addition, you can specify an increment value using the Step clause. You can use Step to create For/Next loops that count by twos, threes, or any other value you wish. If you omit Step, the default is 1.

Note

The term *iteration* is often used to refer to each execution of a For/Next loop. For example, a For/Next loop that starts with the line For x = 1 To 10 would iterate 10 times.

Using For/Next loops with arrays

For/Next loops are often used with arrays, because they provide a convenient way to set up a loop that will enable you to access every element in the array. For example, suppose you have managed to fill an array named MonthlySales with the total sales for your company for each of the past 12 months. You could calculate the average sales per month by using these instructions:

```
TotalSales = 0
For x = 1 to 12
    TotalSales = TotalSales + MonthlySales(x)
Next x
AverageSales = TotalSales / 12
```

In this example, the 12 elements of the MonthlySales array are added up in the TotalSales variable and then the sum is divided by 12 to yield the average.

When you use a `For/Next` loop with an array, it is always critical that you know whether the first element — subscript 0 — has been used. In the previous example, I ignored `MonthlySales(0)`, presumably because that element was also ignored when the array was loaded with the monthly sales data. If the 12 monthly sales values were stored in elements 0 through 11, you would code the routine like this instead:

```
TotalSales = 0
For x = 0 to 11
    TotalSales = TotalSales + MonthlySales(x)
Next x
AverageSales = TotalSales / 12
```

Here, elements 0 through 11 are added up rather than elements 1 through 12.

Secret

A common programming technique with arrays that might contain a variable number of meaningful entries is to store the number of entries in the first element of the array. For example, suppose the `MonthlySales` array has been `Dim`'d with enough entries to hold up to 100 months of sales information, and the first element, `MonthlySales(0)`, indicates how many months of information are actually available in the array. Then, you could calculate the average like this:

```
TotalSales = 0
For x = 1 to MonthlySales(0)
    TotalSales = TotalSales + MonthlySales(x)
Next x
AverageSales = TotalSales / MonthlySales(0)
```

Here, the end value for the `For/Next` loop and the value used in the division to calculate the average is obtained from `MonthlySales(0)`.

Nested For/Next loops

A `For/Next` loop can contain another `For/Next` loop. When you nest `For/Next` loops in this way, the inner `For/Next` loop is processed in its entirety for each iteration of the outer `For/Next` loop.

Nesting is often used to handle two-dimensional arrays. For example, suppose two arrays have been dimensioned as follows:

```
Dim MonthlySales(12,6), AverageSales(6)
```

The `MonthlySales` array will be used to keep track of the 12 months of sales for each of six company divisions. The `AverageSales` array will be used to hold the calculated average monthly sales for each of the six divisions.

Once the sales data has been loaded into the `MonthlySales` array, you could calculate the averages using this code:

```
For Division = 1 To 6
    TotalSales = 0
    For x = 1 To 12
        TotalSales = TotalSales + MonthlySales(x, Division)
    Next x
    AverageSales(Division) = TotalSales / 12
Next Division
```

Here, each iteration of the first `For/Next` loop calculates the average sales for one of the six divisions.

While/Wend loops

`While/Wend` loops provide a more sophisticated form of looping, in which the loop continues as long as a specified condition remains true. The general form is

```
While condition
    instructions
Wend
```

The `While` loop starts by evaluating the condition. If it is true, the instructions in the loop are executed. When the `Wend` statement is encountered, the condition is evaluated again. If it is still true, the instructions in the loop are executed again. This continues until the condition evaluates as False.

Secret

At this point, you really need to know just what it means to say a condition is "true." In WordBasic, "false" is defined as the numeric value 0, and any nonzero value is considered to be "true." For example, consider this `While` loop:

```
x = 5
While x
    MsgBox Str$(x)
    x = x - 1
Wend
```

This loop continues to execute as long as x is not 0. The moment x becomes 0, WordBasic considers the condition expression to be false and the loop terminates. As a result, this `While` loop displays five message boxes, showing the values 5, 4, 3, 2, 1, and then it terminates.

Many WordBasic functions return the value -1 to represent "true" and 0 to represent "false." Thus, you can use such functions directly in a `While` condition. Here is an example:

```
While EditFindFound()
    Count = Count + 1
    RepeatFind
Wend
```

To continue a loop as long as an expression evaluates to "false," test for a 0 value, as in this example, which scrolls through the entire document, one paragraph at a time:

```
StartOfDocument
While AtEndOfDocument() = 0
    instructions go here
    ParaDown
Wend
```

In the previous example, you can insert whatever instructions you want to manipulate each paragraph in the document.

The Select Case statement

Life would be easy if it consisted entirely of either/or choices. But, in the real world, we are often faced with many alternatives from which to choose. And so it is in WordBasic. More than a few WordBasic functions return more complicated results than a simple yes/no, true/false, 0/1. For example, the StyleName$() function returns the name of the style applied to the current paragraph. You could use this information to cause your macro to take different actions depending on which style is applied to the current paragraph.

The Select Case statement is designed just for such situations. It lets you test an expression for various values, executing different instructions depending on the result. Its general form is

```
Select Case expression
    Case case-condition
        instructions
  [ Case case-condition
        instructions ]
  [ Case Else
        instructions ]
End Select
```

The Select Case statement starts by evaluating the expression. Then, it compares the result with the case conditions listed in the Case clauses, one at a time. When it finds a match, it executes the instructions listed for the Case clause that matches, and skips the rest of the Select Case statement. If none of the case conditions match, the instructions in the Case Else clause execute. The key point is that only one of the Case clauses is selected for execution.

For each Case clause, *values* can be any of the following:

- A single value, such as Case 4. The Case clause is selected if the expression is equal to the value.

- A list of expressions, such as Case 4, 8, 12, 16. The Case clause is selected if the expression equals any of the listed values.

- A range of values, separated with the keyword To, such as Case 4 to 8.

The Case clause is selected if the expression falls between the two values, inclusively.

■ The word Is followed by a relational comparison, such as Is > 4. The relation is tested against the expression, and the Case clause is selected if the result of the comparison is true.

Here is an example of a While loop that includes a Select Case statement to count the number of Heading 1, Heading 2, and Heading 3 styles in a document:

```
Heading1Count = 0
Heading2Count = 0
Heading3Count = 0
StartOfDocument
While AtEndOfDocument() = 0
    Select Case StyleName$()
        Case "Heading 1"
            Heading1Count = Heading1Count + 1
        Case "Heading 2"
            Heading2Count = Heading2Count + 1
        Case "Heading 3"
            Heading3Count = Heading3Count + 1
        Case Else
    End Select
    ParaDown
Wend
```

In this example, the variables Heading1Count, Heading2Count, and Heading3Count are used to count the number of headings for each level. The Select Case statement invokes the StyleName$() function, which returns the name of the style for the current paragraph. Then, the Case clauses check for the values "Heading 1", "Heading 2", and "Heading 3". If the StyleName$() function returns one of these three values, 1 is added to the appropriate counter variable.

Note

The preceding routine could have been implemented using an If/ElseIf structure, as follows:

```
Heading1Count = 0
Heading2Count = 0
Heading3Count = 0
StartOfDocument
While AtEndOfDocument() = 0
    If StyleName$() = "Heading 1" Then
        Heading1Count = Heading1Count + 1
    ElseIf StyleName$() = "Heading 2" Then
        Heading2Count = Heading2Count + 1
    ElseIf StyleName$() = "Heading 3" Then
        Heading3Count = Heading3Count + 1
    EndIf
    ParaDown
Wend
```

Either method will get the job done, but the `Select Case` method is more flexible.

Tip You should always provide `Case Else` to handle any values that aren't specifically mentioned in `Case` clauses. If you do not include `Case Else`, and none of the `Case` clauses result in a match, an error will result.

Error Handling

If an error occurs while a Word instruction is being processed, Word's default behavior displays a terse error message and terminates the macro. For example, Figure 31-1 shows a typical WordBasic error message. As you can imagine, most users aren't too thrilled to see such a message.

Figure 31-1: A WordBasic error message.

To avoid such error messages, you can use the `On Error` command so that your program can handle any errors that might occur.

Unfortunately, the `On Error` command is pretty limited. It provides you with just three options for error handling:

- `On Error Resume Next`: This command deactivates error checking so that any errors that occur are completely ignored.

- `On Error Goto label`: This command tells Word to jump to a specified label if an error occurs. The instructions at the label can then figure out what to do based on the type of error that occurred.

- `On Error Goto 0`: This command reactivates Word's built-in error handling so that dialog boxes such as the one in Figure 31-1 will once again be displayed.

Unless you are developing professional-quality macros, you will probably leave Word's default error handling in place most of the time. Whenever you use a WordBasic command that is likely to raise an error condition, however, you should precede the command with an `On Error Goto` command that jumps to an error handler if the anticipated error occurs.

If you use an `On Error Goto` command to set up an error routine, make sure you use an `On Error Goto 0` command when you no longer want the error routine to be in effect. Otherwise, your error routine will end up being invoked from unexpected places.

User Input and Output

The following sections describe various methods of displaying information and obtaining input from the user.

Print and Input

If you have programmed in BASIC, you know all about the `Print` and `Input` commands. In WordBasic, you can forget about these commands. They are available, but they are designed to display output and obtain input via the Status bar, down at the bottom of the Word Windows. As a result, they aren't particularly useful. You might use the `Print` command now and then to display a status message, but you should avoid the `Input` command at all costs: the user will never notice the ? prompt down at the bottom of the screen.

MsgBox and MsgBox()

The `MsgBox` command and the `MsgBox()` function allow you to display a dialog box containing an informative message. `MsgBox` temporarily halts the macro until the user closes the message dialog box. The only difference between the command and function versions of `MsgBox` is that the `MsgBox()` function tells you which button the user clicked to close the dialog box. If you don't care which button the user clicks, use the `MsgBox` command instead of the function.

The `MsgBox` command has the following form:

MsgBox *message$* [,*title$*] [,*type*]

message$* is the text to be displayed in the message, *title$ is the title displayed in the dialog box title bar, and *type* is a number that determines what type of icon is displayed in the message box, what buttons are present, and which button is the default button.

To display a simple message, use a command such as this:

```
MsgBox "It's Saturday Night!", "Live From New York"
```

This displays the dialog box shown in Figure 31-2.

Here's a more complex `MsgBox` command:

```
MsgBox "Heading counts..." + Chr$(13) + Chr$(13) + "   Heading 1: " +
Str$(Heading1Count) + Chr$(13) + "   Heading 2: " +
Str$(Heading2Count) + Chr$(13) + "   Heading 3: " +
Str$(Heading3Count), " Count Headings ", 64
```

Figure 31-2: A MsgBox dialog box.

Here, the message consists of several lines of text, each line terminated by a carriage return: Chr$(13). It's output is shown in Figure 31-3.

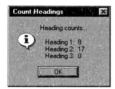

Figure 31-3: A more complicated MsgBox dialog box.

The *type* argument is a number that controls three things at once: what buttons appear in the dialog box, what icon appears in the dialog box, and which button is the default. Table 31-2 lists the values for these settings. The *type* value is the sum of three values, one from each group in the table. For example, to display an OK and Cancel button (1), a Stop symbol (16), and make the Cancel button the default (256), specify 1 + 16 + 256. (You could add them all up and specify 273, but then you'd have to scratch your head every time you looked at the code from then on, trying to figure out what 273 means.)

Table 31-2		MsgBox Type Values
Group	*Value*	*Meaning*
Buttons	0	OK only
	1	OK and Cancel
	2	Abort, Retry, and Ignore
	3	Yes, No, and Cancel
	4	Yes and No
	5	Retry and Cancel
Symbol	0	None
	16	Stop
	32	Question

(continued)

Table 31-2 (continued)

Group	Value	Meaning
	48	Attention
	64	Information
Default button	0	First button (OK, Yes, or Abort)
	256	Second button (Cancel, No, or Retry)
	512	Third button (Cancel or Ignore)

If you use the `MsgBox()` function rather than the `MsgBox` display, your macro can determine which button was used to dismiss the dialog box. For example:

```
While MsgBox("Do you want to try again?","The Loopmaster", 4 + 32)
```

This `MsgBox` function causes the `While` loop to continue as long as the user keeps clicking Yes.

The return values for the `MsgBox()` function are summarized in Table 31-3.

Table 31-3	MsgBox() Return Values
Return Value	**Which Button Was Pressed**
-1 First button	(OK, Yes, or Abort)
0 Second button	(Cancel, No, or Retry)
1 Third button	(Cancel or Ignore)

InputBox$( )

The `InputBox$()` displays a dialog box that includes a single text field into which the user can type a response. The user's input is then returned to the macro as the function's return value.

The `InputBox$()` function has the following form:

```
InputBox$(prompt$ [,title$] [,default$])
```

For example, the following `InputBox$()` function asks the user to enter a name, conveniently displaying the user's own name as the default choice (assuming that the `UserName$` variable has been previously set to the user's name):

```
Name$=InputBox$("Type a name:","The Name Game",UserName$)
```

The user's response is returned in the `Name$` variable. Figure 31-4 shows the dialog box that is displayed.

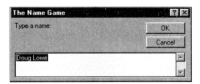

Figure 31-4: An InputBox$( ) dialog box

`InputBox$` has two annoying problems that you must program around. The first is that if the user enters a two-line response by pressing Shift+Enter, the `InputBox$( )` function will add the sequence `Chr$(11) + Chr$(13)` to the response. You can strip away the extraneous characters by nesting your `InputBox$( )` functions within a `CleanString$( )` function, like this:

```
Name$=CleanString$(InputBox$("Type a name:","The Name
Game",UserName$))
```

The second annoying problem is that `InputBox$( )` throws up a Cancel button. Unfortunately, if the users presses it, you'll see the error message shown in Figure 31-5.

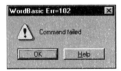

Figure 31-5: But all I did was press Cancel!

The only way to avoid this message is to use an `On Error` command before the `InputBox$( )` function. If you want to bail out of the macro if the user selects Cancel, place a label immediately before the `End Sub` line, and specify it in the `On Error Goto` command. For example:

```
On Error Goto UserExit
Name$=CleanString$(InputBox$("Type a name:","The Name
Game",UserName$))
the rest of the macro goes here
UserExit:
End Sub
```

Getting a Word Command's Dialog Settings

Many Word commands have corresponding dialog boxes. For example, the `FormatParagraph` command sets the format of a paragraph, but it also has a corresponding dialog box that is displayed when the command is invoked from a menu, toolbar button, or keyboard shortcut. The Format Paragraph dialog box is not displayed when you use the `FormatParagraph` command from within a macro.

However, WordBasic does provide a mechanism for obtaining the current settings of each command's dialog box. This can be an extremely useful technique in Word macros, as it lets your macro obtain almost any information that would ordinarily be visible in a Word dialog box. For example, you can find out what indentation is applied to the current paragraph by examining the settings of the `FormatParagraph` dialog box.

To obtain the values from a dialog box, you use a special form of the `Dim` command along with the `GetCurValues` command. For example, the following macro snippet determines whether the current paragraph has a forced page break:

```
Dim fp As FormatParagraph
GetCurValues fp
PageBreakBefore = fp.PageBreak
```

The `Dim` command defines fp as a *dialog record,* which is a special type of variable that can store the values returned by each field in the `FormatParagraph` command. The general form of this command is

```
Dim DialogRecord As DialogName
```

DialogRecord is a WordBasic variable name that will be assigned to the dialog record. *DialogName* is the name of a WordBasic command that has a dialog box, such as `FormatParagraph`. The name you use for *DialogRecord* doesn't matter. I usually use a short, two-or three-character abbreviation of *DialogName*.

`GetCurValues` fills the dialog record with the current values from the dialog box. Once the values have been retrieved, you can access them individually using the syntax *DialogRecord.DialogBoxOption*. For example, to obtain the value of the `PageBreak` option, I specified `fp.PageBreak`.

Working with Word Commands

All of the commands that are available from Word's menus, toolbars, and keyboard shortcuts are also available as macro commands, plus many more commands that are built in to Word but aren't immediately accessible to the user except through the Tools⇨Customize command or via macros. You'll find a complete list of Word commands in Chapter 34.

Finding the right command

One of the most common questions that comes up is, which command is used to perform a given Word function? If you can perform a Word function from a menu command, you can usually quickly figure out the name of the corresponding WordBasic command: it is usually the name of the menu followed immediately by the name of the command, with no intervening spaces. Table 31-4 lists the WordBasic commands that are assigned to menu commands. As you can see, only a few of the commands vary from this naming rule.

For commands that are available only through keyboard actions or toolbar buttons, use the Tools⇨Customize command to find the command name.

Table 31-4	WordBasic Commands That Appear in Word Menus
Menu	*Command*
File Menu	
File⇨New...	FileNew
File⇨Open...	FileOpen
File⇨Close	FileCloseOrCloseAll
File⇨Save	FileSave
File⇨Save As	FileSaveAs
File⇨Save All	FileSaveAll
File⇨Properties	FileProperties
File⇨Templates...	FileTemplates
File⇨Page Setup...	FilePageSetup
File⇨Print Preview	FilePrintPreview
File⇨Print...	FilePrint
File⇨Send	FileSendMail
File⇨Add Routing Slip	FileRoutingSlip
File⇨Exit	FileExit
Edit Menu	
Edit⇨Undo	EditUndo
Edit⇨Redo	EditRedoOrRepeat
Edit⇨Cut	EditCut
Edit⇨Copy	EditCopy
Edit⇨Paste	EditPaste

(continued)

Table 31-4 (continued)

Menu	Command
Edit⇨Paste Special...	EditPasteSpecial
Edit⇨Clear	EditClear
Edit⇨Select All	EditSelectAll
Edit⇨Find...	EditFind
Edit⇨Replace...	EditReplace
Edit⇨Go To...	EditGoTo
Edit⇨AutoText...	EditAutoText
Edit⇨Bookmark...	EditBookmark
Edit⇨Links...	EditLinks
Edit⇨Object	EditObject
View Menu	
View⇨Normal	ViewNormal
View⇨Outline	ViewOutline
View⇨Page Layout	ViewPage
View⇨Master Document	ViewMasterDocument
View⇨Full Screen	ToggleFull
View⇨Toolbars...	ViewToolbars
View⇨Ruler	ViewRuler
View⇨Header and Footer	ViewHeader
View⇨Footnotes	ViewFootnotes
View⇨Annotations	ViewAnnotations
View⇨Zoom...	ViewZoom
Insert Menu	
Insert⇨Break...	InsertBreak
Insert⇨Page Numbers...	InsertPageNumbers
Insert⇨Annotation	InsertAnnotation
Insert⇨Date and Time...	InsertDateTime
Insert⇨Field...	InsertField
Insert⇨Symbol...	InsertSymbol
Insert⇨Form Field...	InsertFormField

Menu	Command
Insert⇨Footnote...	InsertFootnote
Insert⇨Caption...	InsertCaption
Insert⇨Cross-reference...	InsertCrossReference
Insert⇨Index and Tables...	InsertIndexAndTables
Insert⇨File...	InsertFile
Insert⇨Frame	InsertFrame
Insert⇨Picture...	InsertPicture
Insert⇨Object...	InsertObject
Insert⇨Database...	InsertDatabase
Format Menu	
Format⇨Font...	FormatFont
Format⇨Paragraph...	FormatParagraph
Format⇨Tabs...	FormatTabs
Format⇨Borders and Shading...	FormatBordersAndShading
Format⇨Columns...	FormatColumns
Format⇨Change Case...	FormatChangeCase
Format⇨Drop Cap...	FormatDropCap
Format⇨Bullets and Numbering...	FormatBulletsAndNumbering
Format⇨Heading Numbering...	FormatHeadingNumbering
Format⇨AutoFormat...	FormatAutoFormatBegin
Format⇨Style Gallery...	FormatStyleGallery
Format⇨Style...	FormatStyle
Format⇨Frame...	FormatFrame
Format⇨Picture...	FormatPicture
Format⇨Drawing Object...	FormatDrawingObject
Tools Menu	
Tools⇨Spelling	ToolsSpelling
Tools⇨Grammar	ToolsGrammar
Tools⇨Thesaurus	ToolsThesaurus
Tools⇨Hyphenation	ToolsHyphenation
Tools⇨Language...	ToolsLanguage
Tools⇨Word Count...	ToolsWordCount
Tools⇨AutoCorrect...	ToolsAutoCorrect

(continued)

Table 31-4 *(continued)*

Menu	Command
Tools⇨Mail Merge...	MailMergeHelper
Tools⇨Envelopes and Labels...	ToolsEnvelopesAndLabels
Tools⇨Protect / ToolsÍUnprotect	ToolsProtectUnprotectDocument
Tools⇨Revisions...	ToolsRevisions
Tools⇨Macro...	ToolsMacro
Tools⇨Customize...	ToolsCustomize
Tools⇨Options...	ToolsOptions
Table Menu	
Table⇨Insert	TableInsertGeneral
Table⇨Delete	TableDeleteGeneral
Table⇨Merge Cells	TableMergeCells
Table⇨Split Cells...	TableSplitCells
Table⇨Select Row	TableSelectRow
Table⇨Select Column	TableSelectColumn
Table⇨Select Table	TableSelectTable
Table⇨Table AutoFormat...	TableAutoFormat
Table⇨Cell Height and Width...	TableFormatCell
Table⇨Headings	TableHeadings
Table⇨TableToOrFromText	TableToOrFromText
Table⇨TableSort	TableSort
Table⇨Formula...	TableFormula
Table⇨Split Table	TableSplit
Table⇨Gridlines	TableGridlines
Window Menu	
Window⇨New Window	WindowNewWindow
Window⇨Arrange All	WindowArrangeAll
Window⇨Split	DocSplit
Help Menu	
Help⇨Microsoft Word Help Topics	HelpSearch
Help⇨Answer Wizard	Help

Menu	Command
Help⟹The Microsoft Network...	HelpMSN
Help⟹WordPerfect Help...	HelpWordPerfectHelp
Help⟹About Microsoft Word	HelpAbout

Using WordBasic Help

Once you have determined which WordBasic command you want to use, you need to figure out the exact syntax for the command. Fortunately, Word comes with complete on-line help that thoroughly (well, almost, anyway) documents WordBasic commands.

To call up the help for a WordBasic command, type the command name while working in a macro window and press F1. This brings up a Help window that offers a complete description of the command, complete with an explanation of each of its parameters, examples, and links to other related commands. See Figure 31-6.

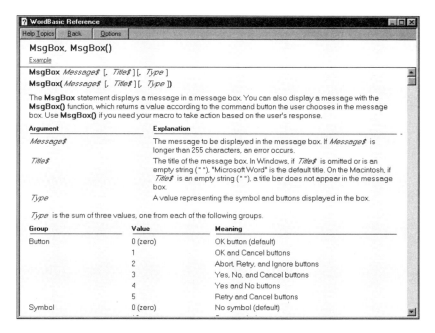

Figure 31-6: WordBasic help.

You can copy examples from the help by highlighting them with the mouse and pressing Ctrl+C. Then, you can paste the examples directly into your macro and adjust them as necessary.

Secret

Recording the next command

One of the most useful tricks for creating macros is to use the Record Next Command button to record a single WordBasic command and insert it into your macro. Start by positioning the insertion point where you want to insert the command. Then, switch to an active document or create a new document (most Word commands are unavailable while you are working in a macro window).

Next, click the Record Next button and invoke the command you want recorded using a menu, toolbar, or keyboard shortcut. For example, to record a FileOpen command, use the File⇨Open command to open a file. Then, you can return to the macro window to see the command inserted into your macro. For example:

```
FileOpen .Name = Chr$(34) + "Jr Magic Mountain Trip.doc" + Chr$(34),
.ConfirmConversions = 0, .ReadOnly = 0, .AddToMru = 0, .PasswordDoc =
"", .PasswordDot = "", .Revert = 0, .WritePasswordDoc = "",
.WritePasswordDot = ""
```

When Word records a macro command, it includes all of the parameters accepted by the command, even if you did not explicitly set a value for each option. This serves as a form of help, at least giving you the names of each parameter accepted by the command. If you need additional information about a command parameter, position the insertion point in the command name (for example, "FileOpen") and press F1 to summon the help.

In most cases, you'll want to clean up the macro command that was inserted by removing unnecessary parameters, possibly by replacing recorded parameter values with values that are more appropriate for your macro. For example, to open a file with a name supplied in a variable named FileToOpen$, you'd edit the command down to its bare essentials:

```
FileOpen .Name = FileToOpen$
```

User-Defined Subroutines and Functions

Most WordBasic macros consist of a single routine, named Main and marked with the Sub Main and End commands. However, WordBasic lets you create additional subroutines and functions that you can call from within the Main routine. Subroutines and functions are useful when you have a series of WordBasic commands or a complex calculation that you need to call upon several times in a macro. By placing these commands in a subroutine or function, you can code them once and call upon them as many times as needed.

Using subroutines

To create a subroutine, use a `Sub`/`End Sub` command pair *outside* of the `Sub Main`/`End Sub` command pair. The instructions that make up the subroutine go between the `Sub` and `End Sub` commands, and the `Sub` command supplies the name of the subroutine and any arguments that can be passed to the subroutine. For example:

```
Sub MAIN
    BeepMsg "Hello World!"
End Sub

Sub BeepMsg(Message$)
    Beep
    MsgBox Message$, 48
End Sub
```

In this example, the `BeepMsg` subroutine displays a message and sounds a tone to get the user's attention. In the `Main` routine, you can use `BeepMsg` as if it were a built-in WordBasic command.

If you wish, you can type the keyword `Call` before the subroutine name when calling the subroutine. For example:

```
Call BeepMsg "Hello World!"
```

The `Call` keyword is optional, but some WordBasic programmers like to use it to help distinguish user-written subroutines from built-in WordBasic commands.

Using functions

A function is similar to a subroutine, with one crucial difference: a function returns a value. Here's an example:

```
Sub Main
    If GetYesNo("Yes, or no?") Then
        BeepMsg "You said yes."
    Else
        BeepMsg "You said no."
    End If
End Sub

Sub BeepMsg(Message$)
    Beep
    MsgBox Message$, 48
End Sub

Function GetYesNo(Message$)
    GetYesNo = MsgBox(Message$, 36)
End Function
```

Here, the GetYesNo function uses a MsgBox function to display a message box with Yes and No buttons. The return value from the MsgBox function is used directly as the return value for the GetYesNo function. Back in the Main routine, the GetYesNo function is used in an If statement to display "You said yes." if the user clicks Yes or "You said no." if the user clicks No.

Using shared variables

Ordinarily, variables used within subroutines and functions are known only to those subroutines and functions. Thus, if you use the same variable name in two subroutines, you are actually referring to two separate variables. For example, consider this macro:

```
Sub Main
    StringVar$ = "Original Value"
    BeepMsg "Hello"
    MsgBox StringVar$
End Sub

Sub BeepMsg(Message$)
    Beep
    MsgBox Message$, 48
    StringVar$ = "New Value"
End Sub
```

Here, both Main and BeepMsg refer to a variable named StringVar$. However, these are two distinct variables. As a result, when the MsgBox command is executed in the Main routine, "Hello" is displayed. The statement StringVar$="New Value" in the BeepMsg subroutine has no impact on the value of the StringVar$ variable in Main.

If you want to refer to a variable in more than one subroutine or function, you must list each variable you want to share in a Dim Shared command, which is placed *outside* of any of the macro's subroutines or functions, including Main. For example:

```
Dim Shared StringVar$

Sub Main
    StringVar$ = "Original Value"
    BeepMsg "Hello"
    MsgBox StringVar$
End Sub

Sub BeepMsg(Message$)
    Beep
    MsgBox Message$, 48
    StringVar$ = "New Value"
End Sub
```

This time, the `MsgBox` command in `Main` will display the `"New Value"` rather than `"Original Value"` because `StringVar$` now refers to the same variable in both `Main` and `BeepMsg`.

Call-by-reference vs. call-by-value

You can pass subroutines and functions to arguments in two ways: by reference and by value. When arguments are passed by reference, the calling routine passes the address of the variable in memory to the subroutine or function. That way, if the subroutine or function changes the contents of the variable, the change is reflected when the subroutine or function ends and control returns to the calling program.

For example, consider this snippet:

```
Sub Main
    StringVar$ = "Original Value"
    BeepMsg StringVar$
    MsgBox StringVar$
End Sub

Sub BeepMsg(Message$)
    Beep
    MsgBox Message$, 48
    Message$ = "New Value"
End Sub
```

Notice that after displaying the string variable passed to it as an argument, the `BeepMsg` subroutine assigns a new value to the variable. When the `MsgBox` command in the `Main` routine is processed, the value displayed will be `"New Value"`. This is how call-by-reference works.

Call-by-value means that instead of passing the address of argument variables to subroutines and functions, WordBasic makes a copy of the arguments and passes the copies. As a result, any change made to an argument in a subroutine or function will *not* be reflected in the calling routine.

To use call-by-value instead of call-by-reference, simply enclose the arguments you want to pass by value in parentheses. For example:

```
Sub Main
    StringVar$ = "Original Value"
    BeepMsg (StringVar$)
    MsgBox StringVar$
End Sub

Sub BeepMsg(Message$)
    Beep
    MsgBox Message$, 48
    Message$ = "New Value"
End Sub
```

Here, StringVar$ is passed by value rather than by reference to BeepMsg. As a result, the MsgBox command in Main will display "Original Value" rather than "New Value".

Call-by-value looks peculiar when used with a function call, because the parentheses must be doubled. For example:

```
Sub Main
    Prompt$ = "Yes, or no?"
    Reply = GetYesNo((Prompt$))
    MsgBox Prompt$
End Sub

Function GetYesNo(Message$)
    GetYesNo = MsgBox(Message$, 36)
    Message$ = "New Value"
End Function
```

Here, Prompt$ is passed by value to the GetYesNo function, so its value is unchanged.

Chapter 32

Creating WordBasic Macros That Work With Documents

In This Chapter

▶ Working with the text that the user has selected and moving the insertion point around to select different text.

▶ Inserting text into the document, including special characters such as tabs and paragraph marks

▶ Deleting text

▶ Using WordBasic's formatting commands to apply formatting to document text

▶ Working with bookmarks, including Word's predefined bookmarks that are hidden from the user but are very useful when working with macros

▶ Secrets of working with the EditFind command in macros

▶ Using even more useful macro techniques!

This chapter describes the techniques that you will use most frequently when creating macros that interact with documents.

Making Sure You're In a Document Window

Before your macros start inserting text and otherwise fiddling around with documents, you'd better make sure that the macro was invoked from a document window that you can edit. Otherwise, you'll leave the user faced with unpleasant error messages about commands that failed because you weren't in a document editing window.

There are no hard-and-fast rules for how much checking should be done; it varies from macro to macro. The following is a list of some of the things your macro may need to check for before proceeding:

What view is the document in? To find out, test the ViewNormal( ), ViewOutline( ), and ViewPage( ) functions. One — and only one — of these functions will return -1 to indicate which view you are currently in. Whether your macro is sensitive to the current view depends on what functions the macro performs.

Is the document protected? If the user has used the Tools⇨Protect Document command to protect a form or allow annotations only, the macro should not proceed. Use the DocumentProtection( ) function, checking for return values of 1 (forms) or 2 (annotations only).

Is the document dirty? That is, has the user changed the document since it was last saved? If your macro makes extensive changes to the document, you may want to suggest that the user save it before running the macro. IsDocumentDirty( ) will return -1 if the document is dirty.

Is the insertion point in a header, footer, footnote, endnote, or annotation pane? If your macro would not be safe to run in one of these panes, use the SelInfo( ) function. The following SelInfo( ) functions return -1 if the insertion point is in the specified pane:

SelInfo(28)   Header or Footer pane

SelInfo(25)   Footnote or Endnote pane

SelInfo(26)   Annotation pane

Is the insertion point at a table end-of-row marker? When the insertion point is placed just before the end-of-row marker in a table, most editing functions are disabled. Macros that insert text into the document should not run when the insertion point is at that location. To find out if it is, check SelInfo(31) for a -1 value.

Are you in a macro window? Most document-related WordBasic functions won't work if the macro is invoked from a macro-editing window. IsMacro( ) will return -1 if you are in a macro window.

As an example of how a macro might apply these tests, consider the following code taken from the InsertFootnote macro supplied with Word 95 on the Macro7.dot template (the code has been modified a bit to make it more readable):

```
If IsMacro() Or SelInfo(25) = - 1 Or SelInfo(26) = - 1 \
 Or SelInfo(31) = - 1 Then
    Beep
    Print "This command is not available"
    Goto bye
End If
```

In other words, the Footnote Wizard will not run if it is invoked from a macro window, if it is invoked from a footnote or endnote pane, or annotation pane, or if it is at the end of row mark in a table.

Getting the Selection

One of the most basic WordBasic actions is transforming the currently selected text into a variable. WordBasic includes the Selection$( ) function expressly for this purpose:

```
SelectedText$ = Selection$()
```

This will return the plain text for whatever is selected in the document at the time.

Secret

If no text is selected, `Selection$()` returns the character immediately following the insertion point. As a result, you cannot use a test such as `If Selection$() = ""` or `If Len(Selection$()) = 0` to determine whether anything is selected.

You can, however, use the `SelTyp()` function to determine whether text is selected. The `SelType` requires no parameters and returns 1 if no text is selected, 2 if text is selected.

The following function returns the contents of the selection or, if no text is selected, an empty string:

```
Function CleanSel$
  If SelType() = 2 Then
    CleanSel$ = CleanString$(Selection$())
  Else
    CleanSel$ = ""
  End If
End Function
```

The `CleanSel$` function also uses the `CleanString$()` function to remove extraneous characters from the selection.

Using SelInfo( )

You can use the `SelInfo()` function to determine various types of information about the selection and other interesting information. The `SelInfo()` function accepts as an argument a number that indicates which type of information you want returned. The argument values and the information each returned is listed in Table 32-1. For example, `SelInfo(1)` returns the page number of the end of the selection.

Table 32-1	SelInfo( ) Argument Values
Value	**Information Returned**
1	Page number of the end of the selection.
2	Section number of the end of the selection.
3	Page number of the end of the selection, counting from the beginning of the document and disregarding any manual page number changes.
4	Number of pages in the document.
5	Horizontal position of the selection, measured from the left edge of the page, in twips (20 twips = 1 point). Valid only in Page Layout view.

(continued)

Table 32-1 *(continued)*

Value	Information Returned
6	Vertical position of the selection, measured from the top edge of the page, in twips (20 twips = 1 point). Valid only in Page Layout view or when background repagination is on.
7	Horizontal position of the selection, measured from the text boundary that encloses it, in twips (20 twips = 1 point).
8	Vertical position of the selection, measured from the text boundary that encloses it, in twips (20 twips = 1 point).
9	Character column position of the first character of text. Same as the Col value shown in the Status bar.
10	Line number of the first line in the selection.
11	Returns -1 if an entire frame is selected.
12	Returns -1 if the selection is in a table.
13	The row number of the start of the selection. Valid only in a table.
14	The row number of the end of the selection. Valid only in a table.
15	The number of rows in the table. Valid only in a table.
16	The column number of the start of the selection. Valid only in a table.
17	The column number of the end of the selection. Valid only in a table.
18	The number of columns in the table. Valid only in a table.
19	The current zoom setting.
20	The selection mode: 0 if normal, 1 if extended, 2 if column.
21	Returns -1 if Caps Lock is on.
22	Returns -1 if Num Lock is on.
23	Returns -1 if Overtype mode is on.
24	Returns -1 if revision marking is on.
25	Returns -1 if the selection is in a footnote.
26	Returns -1 if the selection is in an annotation pane.
27	Returns -1 if the selection is in a macro window.
28	Returns -1 if the selection is in a header or footer.
29	The number of the bookmark enclosing the selection; 0 if the selection is not enclosed within a bookmark.
30	The number of the last bookmark at or before the selection.
31	Returns -1 if the insertion point is at the end-of-row mark in a table.

Value	Information Returned
32	Indicates whether the selection is in a reference: 0 if none, 1 if a footnote reference, 2 if an endnote reference, 3 if an annotation reference. If the selection spans the start or end of a reference so that only a part of the selection is within a reference, -1 is returned.
33	Indicates the kind of header or footer that contains the selection: -1 if the selection is not in a header or footer, 0 if an even-page header, 1 if an odd-page header or the only header if there are not odd and even headers, 2 if an even-page footer, 3 if an odd-page footer or the only footer if there are not odd and even footers, 4 if the first-page header, and 5 if the first-page footer.
34	Returns -1 if the current document is a master document.
35	Returns -1 if the selection is in the footnote pane or in a footnote in Page Layout view.
36	Returns -1 if the selection is in the endnote pane or in an endnote in Page Layout view.
37	Returns a value that indicates whether the selection is in a WordMail message: 0 if the selection is not in a WordMail message, 1 if the selection is in a WordMail send note, and 2 if the selection is in a WordMail read note.

Moving and Selecting

WordBasic provides a whole suite of commands and functions for moving the insertion point around and selecting text. Many macros depend heavily on these commands to position the insertion point to the proper location so that text can be inserted, deleted, formatted, or otherwise manipulated.

Table 32-2 summarizes the basic movement commands.

Table 32-2	Commands for Moving and Selecting
Command/Function	**What It Does**
CharLeft [*count*][,*select*]	Moves the insertion point to the left *count* characters.
CharRight [*count*][,*select*]	Moves the insertion point to the right *count* characters.
WordLeft [*count*][,*select*]	Moves the insertion point to the left *count* words.
WordRight [*count*][,*select*]	Moves the insertion point to the right *count* characters.
SentLeft [*count*][,*select*]	Moves the insertion point to the left *count* sentences.
SentRight [*count*][,*select*]	Moves the insertion point to the right *count* sentences.

(continued)

Table 32-2 (continued)

Command/Function	What It Does
LineDown [count][, select]	Moves the insertion point down count lines.
LineUp [count][, select]	Moves the insertion point up count lines.
ParaDown [count][, select]	Moves the insertion point down count paragraphs.
LineUp [count][, select]	Moves the insertion point up count paragraphs.
PageDown [count][, select]	Moves the insertion point down count screens.
PageUp [count][, select]	Moves the insertion point up count screens.
StartOfLine [select]	Moves the insertion point to the beginning of the current line.
EndOfLine [select]	Moves the insertion point to the end of the current line.
StartOfWindow [select]	Moves the insertion point to the start of the first visible line on the screen.
EndOfWindow [select]	Moves the insertion point to the end of the last visible line on the screen.
StartOfDocument [select]	Moves the insertion point to the beginning of the first line of the document.
EndOfDocument [select]	Moves the insertion point to the end of the last line of the document.

In each command listed in Table 32-2, you can use the *select* parameter to extend the selection to the specified location rather than just moving the insertion point. This is the equivalent of holding down the Shift key while using the cursor movement keys.

WordBasic also offers a function version of each of the commands in Table 32-2. The function versions of the cursor movement commands have the added capability to let you know if the insertion point was actually moved. Each of the functions returns one of two values:

  0   The insertion point was not moved.

  -1   The insertion point was moved.

To use the function version, specify the same arguments as the command version, but enclose them in parentheses. For example, LineDown(2) moves the insertion point down two lines, returning -1 if the insertion point was moved and 0 if it was not.

Note

The cursor movement functions return -1 if the insertion point was moved at all, even if it was not moved as far as requested by the *count* parameter. For example, if you use the function ParaDown(20), but there are only 18 paragraphs left in the document, the insertion point will be moved to the last paragraph and -1 will be returned.

WordBasic offers two functions that tell you whether you are at the start or end of the document but don't actually move the insertion point:

AtStartOfDocument( )	Returns -1 if the insertion point is at the start of the document. Otherwise returns 0.
AtEnd( )	Returns -1 if the insertion point is at the end of the document. Otherwise returns 0.

You can go directly to a bookmark, including one of Word's built-in bookmarks, by using the EditGoto command:

EditGoto *bookmark*	Moves the insertion to the specified bookmark, and selects the entire bookmark.

I'll have more to say about bookmarks and the EditGoto command in the section "Working with Bookmarks" later in this chapter, but I wanted to mention it here because it provides an often essential function WordBasic does not provide a command for: moving to the start of the current paragraph. To go to the start of the current paragraph, use this sequence of commands:

```
EditGoto "\Para"
StartOfLine
```

The EditGoto command selects the entire paragraph. Then, the StartOfLine moves the insertion point to the beginning of the first line of the selection, deselecting the paragraph in the process. (\Para is a predefined bookmark name that represents the current paragraph. It and other predefined bookmarks are explained later in this chapter, in the section "Working with Bookmarks.")

You can extend the selection to the next occurrence of a specific character by using the ExtendSelection command:

ExtendSelection *char$*	Extends the selection to the next occurrence of *char$*.

For example, the following sequence of commands selects text from the beginning of the current paragraph up to and including the first tab character:

```
EditGoto "\Para"
StartOfLine
ExtendSelection Chr$(9)
```

If you use the ExtendSelection command without specifying a character, WordBasic throws Word into Extend mode. Then, any subsequent cursor movement commands will have the effect of extending the selection rather than just moving the insertion point. Extend mode remains in effect until the macro issues a Cancel command (the Cancel command is equivalent to the user pressing the Esc key to end Extend mode). For example, the following sequence of commands selects the next three words:

```
ExtendSelection
WordRight(3)
Cancel
```

You could have achieved the same effect with a single command:

```
WordRight(3,1)
```

Inserting Text

You can easily insert text into the document at the current position of the insertion point by using the `Insert` command:

> `Insert` *text$*   Inserts *text$* at the current location.

The text to be inserted can be a string variable or a literal text value and can be concatenated from several variables or literals strung together by plus signs (+). The following are all valid examples of Insert commands:

```
Insert "Hello World"
Insert TextToBeInserted$
Insert "Document filename: " + FileName$()
```

In the last example, the WordBasic `FileName$()` function is used to insert the name of the document file.

You can use the `Chr$(13)` function to insert a paragraph mark, as follows:

```
Insert "Document filename: " + FileName$() + Chr$(13)
```

Alternatively, you can insert the paragraph mark using an `InsertPara` command:

```
Insert "Document filename: " + FileName$()
InsertPara
```

These two commands have the same effect as the single `Insert` command listed previously.

To insert a tab character, you must use the `Chr$(9)` function:

```
Insert "Document filename: " + Chr$(9) + FileName$() + Chr$(13)
```

There is no `InsertTab` command to insert tab characters for you.

Deleting Text

To delete text, select the text you want deleted and use the `EditClear` command:

> `EditClear [count]`   Deletes the selected text. If *count* is specified, deletes the specified number of characters.

`EditClear` is equivalent to pressing the Del key.

To delete the current paragraph, use this sequence of commands:

```
EditGoto "\Para"
EditClear
```

The first command selects the entire paragraph that contains the insertion point, or, if text is already selected, the beginning of the selection.

The `EditClear` command has an interesting behavior that may throw you or your users off if you aren't careful. If you specify a *count* parameter and text is selected, Word deletes the entire selection and counts it as one character. Then, the remaining characters specified by *count* are deleted. For example, suppose you select an entire word and issue the command `EditClear 5`. This deletes the selected word and deletes the next four characters.

You can use two additional commands to delete entire words:

> `DeleteWord`   Deletes from the insertion point to the end of the current word.

> `DeleteBackWord`   Deletes from the insertion point to the beginning of the current word.

These are the macro command equivalents of Ctrl+Del and Ctrl+Backspace.

Formatting Text

Any formatting that you can apply through the F̲ormat menu can also be applied with corresponding WordBasic commands. For example, you can use the `FormatParagraph` command to set paragraph indentation and spacing, the `FormatTabs` command to set tab stops, and the `FormatBulletsAndNumbering` command to control bullets and numbering.

Each of these commands has arguments that correspond to the fields on the dialog box that is displayed when you activate the command from the menus. For example, to set the font of the selected text to Times New Roman, use this command:

```
FormatFont .Font="Times New Roman"
```

The period before Font indicates that Font is a parameter for the FormatFont command and can also be accessed as a dialog record variable, as described in Chapter 31.

Tables 32-3 through 32-6 show the arguments used by the `FormatFont`, `FormatParagraph`, `FormatTabs`, and `FormatBordersAndShading` commands. Consult the on-line help or use the `Record Next Command` feature as described in Chapter 31 for details on using the other formatting commands.

Table 32-3	Arguments for the FormatFont Command		
Argument	*Explanation*		
.AllCaps=*number*	If 1, the text is formatted as all caps.		
.Bold=*number*	If 1, the text is formatted as bold.		
.Color=*color*	The text color:		
	0	Auto	9	Dark Blue
	1	Black	10	Dark Cyan
	2	Blue	11	Dark Green
	3	Cyan	12	Dark Magenta
	4	Green	13	Dark Red
	5	Magenta	14	Dark Yellow
	6	Red	15	Dark Gray
	7	Yellow	16	Light Gray
	8	White		
.Default	Updates the Normal style to reflect new character formats.		
.Font=*font$*	The name of the font.		
.Hidden=*number*	If 1, the text is formatted as hidden.		
.Italic=*number*	If 1, the text is formatted as italic.		
.Kerning=*number*	If 1, automatic kerning is enabled.		
.KerningMin=*size*	Specifies the minimum font size for kerning to be applied.		
.Points=*size*	Specifies the font size in points.		
.Position=*position*	The character's position relative to the baseline, specified in units of 0.5 point or as a text measurement. Positive values raise the text, negative values lower it.		
.SmallCaps=*number*	If 1, the text is formatted as small caps.		

Argument	Explanation
.Spacing=*spacing*	The spacing between characters, in twips (20 twips = 1 point; 72 points = 1 inch) or as a text measurement. Positive values expand text, negative values condense text.
.Strikethrough=*number*	If 1, the text is formatted as strikethrough.
.Subscript=*number*	If 1, the text is formatted as subscript.
.Superscript=*number*	If 1, the text is formatted as superscript.
.Tab	Used only when displaying the dialog box with a Dialog instruction to specify which tab is displayed: 0 Font 1 Character spacing
.Underline=*type*	Specifies the underlining to be applied: 0 None 1 Single 2 Words Only 3 Double 4 Dotted

Table 32-4	Arguments for the FormatParagraph Command
Argument	**Explanation**
.After=*size*	The space after the paragraph, specified in points or as a text measurement.
.Alignment=*type*	Sets the paragraph alignment: 0 Left 1 Centered 2 Right 3 Justified
.Before=*size*	The space before the paragraph, specified in points or as a text measurement.
.DontHyphen=*number*	If 1, the paragraph is not included in automatic hyphenation.
.FirstIndent=*size*	The first-line indent specified in points or as a text measurement.
.KeepTogether=*number*	If 1, all lines in the paragraph are kept on the same page.

(continued)

Table 32-4 *(continued)*

Argument	Explanation
.KeepWithNext=*number*	If 1, all lines in the paragraph are kept on the same page as the following paragraph that follows.
.LeftIndent=*size*	The left indent, specified in points or as a text measurement.
.LineSpacing=*size*	The line spacing, specified in points or as a text measurement, used when .LineSpacingRule is At Least, Exactly, or Multiple.
.LineSpacingRule=*spacing*	Line spacing: 0 or omitted — Single 1 — 1.5 Lines 2 — Double 3 — At Least 4 — Exactly 5 — Multiple
.NoLineNum=*number*	If 1, line numbering is not used for the paragraph.
.PageBreak=*number*	If 1, the paragraph always appears at the top of a new page.
.RightIndent=*size*	The right indent, specified in points or as a text measurement.
.Tab=*tab*	Used only when displaying the dialog box with a Dialog instruction to specify which tab is displayed: 0 — Indents And Spacing 1 — Text Flow
.WidowControl=*number*	If 1, single lines will not be orphaned at the bottom or top of the page.

Table 32-5   Arguments for the FormatTabs Command

Argument	Explanation
.Align=*type*	Specifies the tab stop alignment: 0 — Left 1 — Center 2 — Right 3 — Decimal 4 — Bar

Argument	Explanation
.Clear	Clears the specified custom tab stop.
.ClearAll	Clears all custom tab stops.
.DefTabs=*size*	The spacing of default tab stops in the document, specified in points or as a text measurement.
.Leader=*type*	Specifies the leader character to use for the tab stop:
	0 None
	1 Period
	2 Hyphen
	3 Underscore
.Position=*size*	Specifies the position of the tab stop using a text measurement.
.Set	Sets the specified custom tab stop.

Table 32-6   Arguments for the FormatBordersAndShading Command

Argument	Explanation
.ApplyTo=*type*	Specifies which item or items the border is applied to, when the selection includes more than one type of item:
	0 Paragraphs
	1 Graphic
	2 Cells
	3 Whole table
.Background=*color*	The color to be applied to the background. For allowable values, see the .Color field in the FormatFont command (Table 32-3).
.FineShading=*amount*	The shading pattern in the range 0 to 40, corresponding to actual shading percentages in increments of 2.5. If .FineShading is nonzero, the .Shading argument is ignored.
.Foreground=*color*	The color to be applied to the foreground. For allowable values, see the .Color field in the FormatFont command (Table 32-3).
.FromText=*size*	The distance of the border from adjacent paragraph text, specified in points or as a text measurement. Valid only for paragraphs.
.HorizBorder=*type*	The line style for the horizontal border that appears between paragraphs or table rows. Specify a value in the range 0 through 11.

(continued)

Table 32-6 *(continued)*

Argument	Explanation
.Shading=*type*	The shading pattern to be applied to the selection, specified in the range from 0 (Clear) through 25.
.Shadow=*type*	Controls the border shadow style: 0 No shadow 1 Shadow
.Tab=*tab*	Used only when displaying the dialog box with a Dialog instruction to specify which tab is displayed: 0 Borders 1 Shading
.TopBorder=*type*, .LeftBorder=*type*, .BottomBorder=*type*, .RightBorder=*type*	The line style for the border on the top, left, bottom, and right. Specify a value in the range 0 (no border) through 11.
.TopColor=*color*, .LeftColor=*color*, .BottomColor=*color*, .RightColor=*color*, .HorizColor=*color*, .VertColor=*color*	The color to be applied to the specified borders. For allowable values, see the .Color field in the FormatFont command (Table 32-3).
.VertBorder=*type*	The line style for the vertical border between table cells, specified in the range 0 (no border) through 11.

Word also provides a variety of shortcut commands that apply common formats to the selected text without the bother of going through the full Format commands. These commands are listed in Table 32-7.

Table 32-7	Shortcut Formatting Commands
Command	**Explanation**
AllCaps [*on*]	Makes the selection all capitals (toggle).
Bold [*on*]	Makes the selection bold (toggle).
CenterPara	Centers the paragraph between the indents.
CharColor *color*	Sets the color of the selected characters to the specified color.
DottedUnderline [*on*]	Underlines the selection with dots (toggle).

Command	*Explanation*
DoubleUnderline [*on*]	Double underlines the selection (toggle).
Font *font$* [*,size*]	Changes the font and optionally the size of the selection.
FontSize	Changes the size of the selection.
Hidden [*on*]	Makes the selection hidden text (toggle).
Italic [*on*]	Makes the selection italic (toggle).
JustifyPara	Aligns the paragraph at both the left and the right indent.
Language *language$*	Sets the language for a text selection.
LeftPara	Aligns the paragraph at the left indent.
ParaKeepLinesTogether [*on*]	Prevents a paragraph from splitting across page boundaries.
ParaKeepWithNext [*on*]	Keeps a paragraph and the following paragraph on the same page.
ParaPageBreakBefore [*on*]	Makes the current paragraph start on a new page.
ParaWidowOrphanControl [*on*]	Prevents a page break from leaving a single line of a paragraph on one page.
RightPara	Aligns the paragraph at the right indent.
SmallCaps [*on*]	Makes the selection small capitals (toggle).
SpacePara1	Sets the line spacing to single space.
SpacePara15	Sets the line spacing to one-and-one-half space.
SpacePara2	Sets the line spacing to double space.
Subscript [*on*]	Makes the selection subscript (toggle).
Superscript [*on*]	Makes the selection superscript (toggle).
Underline [*on*]	Formats the selection with a continuous underline (toggle).
WordUnderline [*on*]	Underlines the words but not the spaces in the selection (toggle).

For the functions that include the *on* argument, you can specify one of two values:

0   Removes the specified format

1   Applies the specified format

If you omit the *on* argument, the format is toggled.

With just a few exceptions, you can use all of the commands in Table 32-6 as functions to determine whether or not the selection is formatted with the indicated attribute. The return values for these functions are all the same:

0	The selection does not contain the format.
1	All of the selection contains the format.
-1	Only part of the selection contains the format.

Here are the exceptions:

- `CharColor( )`: Returns the color used to format the selection. If the selection is formatted with more than one color, -1 is returned.

- `Font$( )`: Returns the name of the font used to format the selected text. If the selection is formatted with a mixture of fonts, `font$( )` returns an empty string.

- `FontSize( )`: Returns the point size of the selection.

Working with Bookmarks

Word provides several predefined bookmarks that you can use to access key parts of a document. These bookmarks are listed in Table 32-8.

Table 32-8	Predefined Bookmarks
Bookmark	**What It Is**
\Sel	The current selection.
\PrevSel1	The most recent selection that was edited.
\PrevSel2	The second most recent selection.
\StartOfSel	The start of the current selection.
\EndOfSel	The end of the current selection.
\Line	The current line. If the selection spans more than one line, the first line of the selection.
\Char	The current character. If there is no selection, the character following the insertion point.
\Para	The current paragraph. If the selection spans more than one paragraph, the first paragraph in the selection.
\Section	The current section. If the selection spans more than one section, the first section in the selection.
\Doc	The entire document.
\Page	The current page.

Bookmark	What It Is
\StartOfDoc	Start of the document.
\EndOfDoc	End of the document.
\Cell	The current cell. If the selection spans more than one cell, the first cell in the selection.
\Table	The entire table.
\HeadingLevel	If the insertion point or selection is in a heading paragraph, the entire heading paragraph plus all subordinate headings and body text.

You can move directly to any of these bookmarks or to a user-defined bookmark by using the `EditGoTo` command. For example, the command `EditGoto "\Para"` selects highlights all of the current paragraph.

To copy the contents of a bookmark into a variable, use a command sequence such as this:

```
EditGoto "\Para"
ParagraphText$=CleanString$(Selection$())
```

To apply formatting to the text indicated by a bookmark, use a sequence such as this:

```
EditGoto "\Para"
Bold
```

In both examples, the first command selects the text indicated by the bookmark.

Creating your own bookmarks to serve as markers is useful so that your macro can return to specific locations. You can do this using the `EditBookmark` command, with arguments summarized in Table 32-9.

Table 32-9	Arguments for the EditBookmark Command
Argument	**Explanation**
.Name=*text$*	Specifies the name of the bookmark.
.SortBy=*number*	Specifies how the list of bookmarks should be sorted when you display the Bookmark dialog box with a Dialog or Dialog( ) instruction: 0 Sort by name 1 Sort by location
.Add	Adds a bookmark at the insertion point or selection.
.Delete	Deletes the bookmark.
.Goto	Moves the insertion point or selection to the bookmark. This is the same as using the EditGoto command.

You can specify only one of the arguments .Add, .Delete, and .Goto.

To create a bookmark, move the insertion point to the location where you want the bookmark created, and use a EditBookmark similar to the following:

```
EditBookmark .Name="TempBookmark", .Add
```

To delete the same bookmark, use this command:

```
EditBookmark .Name="TempBookmark", .Delete
```

Deleting any bookmarks you create is a good idea so that your macro doesn't leave unnecessary bookmarks strewn about the document. (Unless, of course, the purpose of the macro is to create a bookmark that the user can access.)

Secret

The .Add argument adds the bookmark you specify, whether a bookmark with the same name already exists in the document or not. If there is an existing bookmark with the same name, EditBookmark deletes it without fanfare. As a result, you should be careful to avoid using bookmark names that the user has already chosen. One way to do this is to use the Now() function, which returns a number representing the date and time, to append a time stamp to your bookmark names. You can use the following function for this purpose:

```
Function MakeBookmarkName$
    TimeStamp$ = LTrim$(Str$(Now()))
    Dot = InStr(TimeStamp$, ".")
    bm$ = "Temp" + Left$(TimeStamp$, Dot - 1)
    MakeBookmarkName$ = bm$ + Right$(TimeStamp$, Len(TimeStamp$) -
Dot)
End Function
```

This function returns a string consisting of the word "Temp" followed by a unique timestamp. For example, Temp34945373043981. You can be pretty confident that the user hasn't created a macro with the same name. Plus, the MakeBookmarkName$() function will return a different name each time your macro runs. (You can't, however, rely on MakeBookmarkName$() to create a different value if you run it several times within the same macro. Date serial number has a precision of only one second, and there is no guarantee that a full second has elapsed between executions of the MakeBookmarkName$() function.)

You might be tempted to use the MakeBookmarkName$() function directly in an EditBookmark command, like this:

```
EditBookmark .Name=MakeBookmarkName$(), .Add
```

This is ill-advised, however, because it provides no way of retaining the generated bookmark name so you can delete the bookmark later. It's better to use a variable:

```
NewBookmark$ = MakeBookmarkName$()
EditBookmark .Name=NewBookmark$ .Add
```

Then, you can use NewBookmark$ later to delete the bookmark.

Tip

`BookmarkName$()` is the name of a built-in WordBasic function. As a result, you cannot use `BookmarkName$` as a variable. The following command will result in a syntax error:

```
BookmarkName$ = MakeBookmarkName$()
```

You must think of a more creative variable name to hold your bookmark names.

Using the EditFind Command

Programming around the `EditFind` command can be a bit tricky. The command itself works pretty much the way it works when invoked from the menus. However, when you use it in a macro, you'll often want to include it in a loop that processes every occurrence of text that meets the search criteria. Keep the following points in consideration when creating such a loop:

- If you want the search to start from the beginning of the document, use a `StartOfDocument` command. If you want to return to the original position, drop a bookmark before using the `StartOfDocument` command. Then, when the find loop is completed, you can return to the bookmark using `EditGoto` and drop the bookmark. (Use the `MakeBookmarkName$()` function described earlier in this chapter to create a unique bookmark name. Be sure to delete the bookmark when you're finished. No reason to leave bookmarks lying around.)

- You have no way of knowing what the user has done with the `Find` command before running your macro. As a result, you should always use an `EditFindClearFormatting` command to wipe out any special format options that have been set up, such as searching for a particular font or style.

- Before running `EditFind`, you can use `EditFindFont`, `EditFindLang`, `EditFindPara`, and `EditFindStyle` to set up searches for specific formats.

- To find the first occurrence of the search criteria, use an `EditFind` command. If anything was found, the `EditFindFound()` function will return True (-1). You can use `EditFindFound()` to determine whether another `EditFind` command should be issued.

- The text found by the `EditFind` command will be automatically selected. You can access the text only (no formatting) using `Selection$()`. To work with the found text formatting and all, use the `\Sel` bookmark.

- After using EditFind, you should clean up by issuing `EditFindClearFormatting` again.

The arguments for the EditFind command are shown in Table 32-10. For the `EditFindFont`, `EditFindLang`, `EditFindPara`, and `EditFindStyle` commands, you can use the same arguments as with the corresponding `EditFont`, `EditLang`, `EditPara`, and `EditStyle` commands. `EditFindClearFormatting` has no arguments.

Table 32-10	Arguments for EditFind
Argument	**Explanation**
.Find=*text*	The text for which to search. To search for formatting only, specify an empty string ("").
.Direction=*direction*	The search direction:
	0 Forward
	1 Backward
.WholeWord=*number*	If 1, only whole words will be found.
.MatchCase=*number*	If 1, the capitalization must match for text to be found.
.PatternMatch=*number*	If 1, wildcard characters can be used.
.SoundsLike=*number*	If 1, Word searches for words that sound like the .Find text.
.FindAllWordForms=*number*	If 1, Word searches for alternate forms of the .Find word.
.Format=*number*	Specifies whether formatting should be taken into consideration:
	0 Ignores formatting
	1 Searches for formatting set up by the other EditFind commands
.Wrap=*number*	Specifies what to do when the search reaches the end or beginning of the document or selection:
	0 Ends the search
	1 Continues the search with the rest of the document
	2 Prompts the user

The following is a skeleton of the coding that you would typically use to use the EditFind command for finding all occurrences that match the find criteria:

```
EditBookmark to create a bookmark
StartOfDocument
EditFindClearFormatting
EditFindFont, EditFindLang, EditFindPara, or EditFindStyle if needed
EditFind to find first occurrence
While EditFindFound()
    process the found text using Selection$() or \Sel bookmark
    EditFind to find the next occurrence
Wend
EditFindClearFormatting
EditGoto to return to bookmark created earlier
EditBookmark to delete the bookmark
```

Typically, both EditFind commands would be identical.

To demonstrate these techniques, here's a macro that counts all occurrences of a word entered by the user:

```
Sub MAIN
SearchWord$ = InputBox$("Enter the word to count:", "WinWord Secrets")
EditBookmark .Name = "CountWord", .Add
StartOfDocument
EditFindClearFormatting
EditFind .Find = SearchWord$, .Direction = 0, .Format = 0
While EditFindFound()
    Count = Count + 1
    EditFind .Find = SearchWord$, .Direction = 0, .Format = 0
Wend
EditFindClearFormatting
EditGoTo "CountWord"
EditBookmark .Name = "CountWord", .Delete
MsgBox "Occurrences of " + SearchWord$ + ": " + Str$(Count)
End Sub
```

In the previous macro, I hard-coded the bookmark name as "CountWord". Before I unleashed this macro on unsuspecting users, I'd probably change that to a name generated by the MakeBookmarkName$() function that was described earlier in this chapter.

Using the EditReplace command is similar to using EditFind, the biggest difference being that with EditReplace allows you to use a .Replace argument that specifies text that is used to replace the .Find text. Another important difference is that you can use the EditReplaceFont, EditReplaceLang, EditReplacePara, and EditReplaceStyle commands to change the formatting of found text.

Creating a Temporary Document

Many macros need a place where they can compile bits of text culled from various locations throughout a document. For example, consider a macro that compiles a list of all the words that are formatted in italics throughout an entire document, placing the list (sorted into alphabetical order) at the end of the document. One way to perform this search would be to work through the document one word at a time (using WordRight), checking for italicized words, and moving them to the end of the document. A faster way would be to use the EditFind command to search for italicized words and copying the found words to the end of the document.

Either way, the macro involves a lot of back-and-forth movement, moving from the found text to the end of the document and back again. You could accomplish this back-and-forth movement by using bookmarks, but another (and sometimes easier) way is to create a new document in which to compile the text. Then, when the text has been gathered up, you can insert it into the original document, and you can close the temporary document.

To work with a temporary document, the following WordBasic commands and functions are likely to be beneficial:

- **FileNew .Name=*doc-name***: Creates a new document.

- **FileClose *save-option***: Closes the current document. Save-option can be 0 to ask the user about saving the file, 1 to always save the file, and 2 to discard the file without saving it.

- **Activate *window-name***: Switches to the window identified by *window-name*.

- **WindowName$( )**: Returns the name in the title bar of the current window, often for use with Activate.

Macro

Here is a macro that uses these commands to create a list of all italicized words:

```
Sub MAIN
ScreenUpdating 0                                          '1
DocWindow$ = WindowName$()                                '2
FileNewDefault
NewDocWindow$ = WindowName$()
Activate DocWindow$                                       '3
StartOfDocument
EditFindClearFormatting                                   '4
EditFindFont .Italic = 1
EditFind .Find = "", .Direction = 0, .Format = 1          '5
While EditFindFound()                                     '6
    ItalText$ = Selection$()                              '7
    Activate NewDocWindow$                                '8
    Insert ItalText$ + Chr$(13)
    Activate DocWindow$                                   '9
    EditFind .Find = "", .Direction = 0, .Format = 1
Wend
EditFindClearFormatting                                   '10
Activate NewDocWindow$                                    '11
EditSelectAll
TableSort
EditCopy                                                  '12
FileClose 2
Activate DocWindow$
ScreenUpdating 1                                          '13
EndOfDocument                                             '14
InsertPageBreak
EditPaste
End Sub
```

This macro might seem a bit daunting at first, but if you pick it apart one piece at a time, it turns out to be pretty straightforward. The following numbered comments correspond to the reference numbers in the macro:

1. The macro starts by turning off screen updating. Otherwise, all the flashing that results from finding text and switching between windows can give the user a severe headache.

2. The macro next collects the window title of the current document in `DocWindow$`, creates a new document, and stores the window title of the new document in `NewDocWindow$`. This enables the macro to subsequently switch between the two documents using an `Activate` command.

3. The macro switches back to the original document window.

4. The macro next begins the process of setting up a `Find` command. First, it clears any existing `Find` settings. Then, it uses the `EditFindFont` command to set up a search for *italicized* text.

5. The macro invokes the EditFind command, which locates the first occurrence of italicized text.

6. The macro enters a `While` loop, which repeats as long as the `EditFound()` function indicates that the most recent `EditFind` command successfully found italicized text.

7. The macro stores the selection — in this case, the text found by the `EditFind` command — in the variable `ItalText$`.

8. The macro switches to the other document window and inserts the contents of `ItalText$` as a new paragraph.

9. The macro switches back to the original document window and issues an `EditFind` command to find the next italicized word. Assuming that another word is found, the loop repeats with step 6. Otherwise, the macro continues with step 10.

10. The macro issues an `EditFindClearFormatting` command to reset the `Find` command's settings.

11. The macro switches back to the new document, selects the entire contents of the document, and copies it to the Clipboard.

12. The macro closes the new document without saving it and returns to the original document.

13. The macro resumes screen updating so the user will be able to see the changes made by the remaining macro commands.

14. The macro moves to the end of the document, inserts a page break and pastes the italicized word list from the Clipboard.

Lists of Useful Stuff

The last category of WordBasic commands I want to cover in this chapter are those commands that let you access various lists of information. These lists include

■ Global templates and add-ins

■ AutoText entries

■ Bookmarks

- Document variables
- Subdirectories of a given directory
- Files in a given directory
- Files found by a `FileFind` command
- Custom keyboard assignments
- Available language formats
- Available fonts
- Macros
- Menus on the menu bar
- Menu items in a given menu
- Merge fields in a data source
- Styles
- Toolbars
- Buttons on a given toolbar
- Open document and macro windows

Each of these lists has a macro that returns the number of items available in the list and one or more macros that returns items from the list. You can use the first macro to set up a For...Next loop that iterates through the entire list, retrieving each item using the other macros. Table 32-11 lists these macros.

Table 32-11	Macros That Let You Retrieve Lists
Count Macro	*Retrieval Macros*
CountAddIns()	AddInState(*count*) GetAddInName$(*count*)
CountAutoTextEntries([*context*])	AutoTextName$(*count* [,*context*])
CountBookmarks()	BookmarkName$(*count*)
CountDocumentVars()	GetDocumentVarName$(*count*)
CountFonts()	Font$(*count*)
CountFoundFiles()	FoundFileName$(*count*)
CountKeys([*context*])	KeyCode(*count* [,*context*] [*firstorsecond*]) KeyMacro$(*count* [,*context*])
CountLanguages()	Language$(*count*)
CountMacros([,*context*] [,*all*] [,*global*])	MacroName$(*count* [,*context*] [,*all*] [,*global*])

Count Macro	*Retrieval Macros*
CountMenuItems(*menu$, type,* [*,context*])	MenuItemMacro$(*menu$, type, count,* [*,context*]) MenuItemText$(*menu$, type, count,* [*,context*])
CountMenus(*type* [*,context*])	MenuText$(*type, count* [*,context*])
CountMergeFields()	MergeFieldName$(*count*)
CountStyles([*,context*] [*,all*])	StyleName$(*count* [*,context*] [*,all*])
CountToolbarButtons(*toolbar$* [*,context*])	ToolbarButtonMacro$(*toolbar$, count* [*,context*])
CountToolbars([*context*])	ToolbarName$(*count* [*,context*])
CountWindow()	WindowName$(*count*)

The following `For...Next` loop inserts the names of all available fonts into the current document:

```
For count = 1 To CountFonts()
    Insert Font$(count) + Chr$(13)
Next count
```

Some of the functions have additional arguments that control which items are included in the list. For example, `CountStyles()` has two arguments: *Context* and *All*. *Context* can be set to 0 to retrieve styles from the active document or 1 to retrieve styles in the document's template. *All* can be set to 0 to omit built-in styles or 1 to include built-in styles.

Using these arguments, the following `For...Next` loop inserts the name and description of every style in the current document, including built-in styles:

```
For count = 1 To CountStyles(0, 1)
    Bold 1
    Insert StyleName$(count, 0, 1) + Chr$(13)
    Bold 0
    Insert StyleDesc$(StyleName$(count, 0, 1)) + Chr$(13) + Chr$(13)
Next count
```

Notice in this example that the `StyleDesc$()` function accepts the `StyleName$()` function as an argument. This type of indirection is common when processing these lists.

For specific details on using the remaining functions listed in Table 32-11, consult the on-line help.

Using Document Variables

You can use the `Dim Shared` command to create variables that can be shared among the subroutines and functions within a macro. You can't, however, share ordinary WordBasic variables among two or more macros. That's because when a macro ends, the memory occupied by its variables is freed and the contents of the macro's variables is lost.

To share variables among two or more macros or to create variables with values that persist from one execution of a macro to the next, you must use document variables. Document variables are similar to document properties. They are stored along with the document, but unlike document properties, the user cannot view them. They are accessible only to WordBasic macros.

Document variables are created with the `SetDocumentVar` command or function. The command version has this format:

```
SetDocumentVar VariableName$, VariableText$
```

For example, to create a document variable named `"Version Number"` and assign it a value of 1.0, you'd use this command:

```
SetDocumentVar "Version Number", "1.0"
```

Notice that the document variable name does not have to conform to WordBasic's variable naming conventions. You can use any string value you wish for the document variable name.

Note

Unlike normal WordBasic variables, all document variables are strings. To store a numeric value in a document variable, you must convert the value to a string using the `Str$()` function. You can later convert the value back to a number using the `Val()` function.

The `SetDocumentVar()` function accepts the same arguments as the command:

```
SetDocumentVar(VariableName$, VariableText$)
```

However, `SetDocumentVar()` returns -1 if the document variable was success-fully created. Don't be misled into thinking that this will tell you if you are using a document variable name that is already in use — it won't. Both `SetDocumentVar` and `SetDocumentVar()` blindly overwrite the value of an existing variable if one happens to have the same name. As a result, the `SetDocumentVar()` function is of little value.

To retrieve a document variable's value, you must use the `GetDocumentVar$()` function. It accepts the name of the document variable you want to retrieve as an argument and returns the value of the corresponding variable. For example:

```
VersionNum$ = GetDocumentVar$("Version Number")
```

The variable name must be enclosed in quotes. If the document variable doesn't exist, `GetDocumentVar$()` returns an empty string.

Secret

WordBasic does not provide a `DeleteDocumentVar` command or function. However, you can easily delete a document variable by simply assigning it an empty string. For example:

```
SetDocumentVar "Version Number", ""
```

This command deletes the Version Number document variable.

WordBasic provides two other commands for handling document variables: `CountDocumentVars()` and `GetDocumentVarName$()`. These commands are used to access the entire list of document variables for the current document. For example, the following command inserts the name and value of every document variable into the current document:

```
Sub MAIN
For count = 1 To CountDocumentVars()
    Insert GetDocumentVarName$(count) + " = "
    Insert GetDocumentVar$(GetDocumentVarName$(count)) + Chr$(13)
Next count
End Sub
```

Notice how the GetDocumentVar$() macro uses the result of the `GetDocumentVarName$()` function as an argument.

The following macro deletes all document variables:

```
Sub MAIN
For x = 1 To CountDocumentVars()
    SetDocumentVar GetDocumentVarName$(x), ""
Next x
End Sub
```

Macros such as these can be very useful when you are developing a macro that uses document variables, as you periodically need to view the document variables to ensure that they have been created properly, and you may need to delete all of a document's variables so you can rerun the macro on a document without variables.

Using a Private Settings File (INI File)

Document variables are useful for storing variables that you want associated with a particular document, but what about variables you want to be truly global and not dependent on any single document? That's where private settings files come in. Private settings files are the same as INI files, and are a familiar part of the Windows landscape.

A Revision Tracking Macro

Microsoft's *Word Developer's Kit* for Word 6.0 contains an interesting macro that uses document variables to track the revision history of a document. Unfortunately, the macro has a minor bug: it makes the outrageous assumption that it and only it is allowed to create document variables. The following is a macro that is based on the one that is printed in the Developer's Kit, but with this annoying oversight corrected:

```
Sub MAIN
Version$ =
GetDocumentVar$("SECRETS Version")
If Version$ = "" Then
    Version = 0
    Dim docVarArray$(0)
Else
    Version =
Val(LTrim$(Version$))
    Dim
docVarArray$(CountDocumentVars())
    For count = 1 To
CountDocumentVars()
        DocVarName$ =
GetDocumentVarName$(count)
        If Left$(DocVarName$, 11)
= "SECRETS Rev" Then
            docVarArray$(ArrayIndex)
= GetDocumentVar$(DocVarName$)
            ArrayIndex =
ArrayIndex + 1
        End If
    Next
End If
Begin Dialog UserDialog 508, 214,
"Revision History - Version " +
Version$
    Text 12, 133, 105, 13, "New
Revision", .Text2
    TextBox 12, 149, 453, 18,
.NewRevision
    OKButton 380, 186, 88, 21
    CancelButton 282, 186, 88, 21
    Text 12, 6, 80, 13, "Revi-
sions:", .Text1
    ListBox 12, 21, 473, 106,
docVarArray$(), .ListBox1
End Dialog
```

```
Dim dlg As UserDialog
x = Dialog(dlg)
If dlg.NewRevision <> "" Then
    revVarName$ = "SECRETS Rev" +
LTrim$(Str$(Version + 1))
    revText$ = Date$() + " - " +
dlg.NewRevision
    SetDocumentVar revVarName$,
revText$
    SetDocumentVar "SECRETS
Version", LTrim$(Str$(Version +
1))
End If
End Sub
```

Each time the macro runs and the user types in a comment to identify a new version, a new variable named `"SECRETS  Revn"` is added, where *n* represents the version number, and the variable `"SECRETS   Version"` is incremented. The macro uses these variables to fill a list box in a user-defined dialog box with the complete revision history. In addition, the version number is displayed in the dialog box title bar.

Here is how this dialog box will appear after several revisions have been recorded:

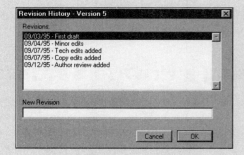

A *private settings file* is a plain text file in which keyword-value combinations are organized into sections. The sections themselves are enclosed in brackets. For example, here is a settings file with just one section:

```
[MsgBox Defaults]
Title=Hello!
Buttons=2
Symbols=1
Default Button=2
```

The section is named `MsgBox Defaults`, and it contains four keywords: `Title`, `Buttons`, `Symbols`, and `Default Button`.

To write an entry to a private settings file, you use the `SetPrivateProfileString` command, as follows:

```
SetPrivateProfileString "MsgBox Defaults","Buttons","2","WORDSEC.INI"
```

This command will create the `Buttons` keyword in the `MsgBox Defaults` section of Wordsec.ini, assigning it a value of 2. If the keyword already exists, it will be overwritten. The filename refers to an .ini file in the \Windows folder. You can use any name you wish for this file, but it must have the .ini extension.

To retrieve an entry from a private settings file, use the `GetPrivateProfileString$()` function. For example:

```
Title$=GetPrivateProfileString$("MsgBox Defaults", "Title",
    "WORDSEC.INI")
Buttons=Val(GetPrivateProfileString$("MsgBox Defaults", "Buttons",
    "WORDSEC.INI"))
Symbols=Val(GetPrivateProfileString$("MsgBox Defaults", "Symbols",
    "WORDSEC.INI"))
DefaultButton=Val(GetPrivateProfileString$("MsgBox Defaults", "Default
    Button", "WORDSEC.INI"))
```

Here, the `Title`, `Buttons`, `Symbols`, and `Default Button` strings are read into variables.

Secret

Microsoft has officially denounced private INI files in favor of the more generalized, system wide registry. You still use the `SetPrivateProfileString` command and `GetPrivateProfileString$()` function to access the Registry, but you leave the `filename$` argument (the last one) empty. The first parameter must specify the complete path to the key you want to access. For example:

```
Key$ = "HKEY_CURRENT_USER\software\WordSecrets\Preferences\MsgBox"
SetPrivateProfileString Key$, "Title", "Hello!", ""
SetPrivateProfileString Key$, "Buttons", "2", ""
SetPrivateProfileString Key$, "Symbols", "1", ""
SetPrivateProfileString Key$, "Default Button", "2", ""
```

Notice that unlike sections in a settings file, keys in the registry have a tree structure. It's best to place your private settings in keys under HKEY_CURRENT_USER\software\.

You must use a similar technique to retrieve the settings:

```
Title$ = GetPrivateProfileString$(Key$, "Title", "")
Buttons = Val(GetPrivateProfileString$(Key$, "Buttons", ""))
Symbols = Val(GetPrivateProfileString$(Key$, "Symbols", ""))
DefaultButton = Val(GetPrivateProfileString$(Key$, "Default Button",
""))
```

Again, the filename$ argument (the last one in the
GetPrivateProfileString$() function call) is left empty to access the
registry.

You can access the registry directly by running the regedit program from the
Windows 95 Start\Run command. Regedit allows you to navigate the registry
tree and display and set registry entries. Figure 32-1 shows how the keys added
in the previous examples appear in when displayed by regedit.

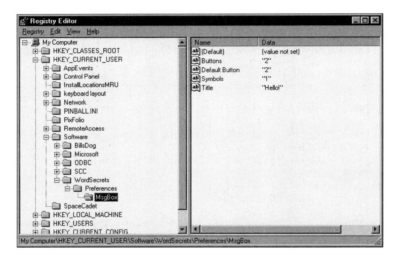

Figure 32-1: Regedit displays private profile strings created in the registry.

Chapter 33

Working with Dialog Boxes

In This Chapter

▶ Displaying Word's built-in dialog boxes

▶ Creating your own dialog boxes with the Dialog Editor, a free program that comes with Word for Windows 95

▶ Using dynamic dialog boxes to create dialog boxes that change on-the-fly, enabling and disabling their controls at will, changing their appearance, and even behaving like the tabbed dialog boxes that are found throughout Word

T his chapter shows you how to create macros that display and use dialog boxes. It starts by quickly showing you how to access Word's built-in dialog boxes and launches into the more interesting topic of creating your own dialog boxes.

Using Built-in Dialog Boxes

As you know, many Word commands display dialog boxes when run from the menus, toolbars, or keyboard shortcuts. However, the corresponding WordBasic commands do not display dialog boxes. For example, if you choose the File⇨Open menu command, the Open dialog box is displayed. But, if you use the FileOpen command in a macro, a dialog box is not displayed.

That only makes sense. After all, the reason for putting the command in a macro is most likely so that you can automate its function by opening a file without interacting with the user. Displaying the dialog box would defeat the purpose.

But, what if you want the user to see the dialog box for a WordBasic command? Not to worry. WordBasic provides a `Dialog` command and a `Dialog()` function just for this purpose. They allow you to display the dialog box for a given WordBasic command so that the user can change the command's settings before proceeding.

Here is an example of how you might display the FileOpen dialog box:

```
Dim dlg As FileOpen
GetCurValues dlg
Dialog dlg
FileOpen dlg
```

The first two commands are familiar; I explained how to use them in Chapter 31. The Dim...As command declares the variable dlg as a dialog record, corresponding to the built-in dialog box for the FileOpen command. The GetCurValues command then fills the dialog record with the current settings for the FileOpen dialog box.

The next command, Dialog dlg, actually displays the FileOpen dialog box. Users will be able to interact with the dialog box as if they had invoked the File⇨Open command directly. When the user closes the dialog box by clicking Open or Cancel, control returns to the macro. Any new values the user entered into the dialog box will be reflected in the dialog record. For example, the name of the file selected by the user will be available in dlg.Name.

The last command, FileOpen dlg, uses a special command form in which all of the command's arguments are obtained from a dialog record rather than set individually. In other words, in this line the FileOpen command is using the settings specified by the user when the FileOpen dialog box was displayed.

The only problem with the previous example is that it provides no error checking. Unfortunately, WordBasic raises an error condition when the user closes a dialog box by clicking the Cancel button or pressing the Esc key. Thus, the error message "WordBasic Error=102 Command Failed" will be displayed and the macro terminated if the user cancels out of the dialog box.

One way to remedy this problem is to include an On Error Goto command immediately before the Dialog command. For example:

```
Dim dlg As FileOpen
GetCurValues dlg
On Error Goto UserCancel
Dialog dlg
On Error Goto 0
FileOpen dlg
UserCancel:
```

If an error occurs when the Dialog command is processed, the macro skips the FileOpen command by branching to the UserCancel label. Notice that the command On Error Goto 0 is used following the Dialog command to reinstate normal error handling.

Another way to avoid the Cancel button error is to use the Dialog() function rather than the Dialog command to display the dialog box. You can use the Dialog () function like this:

```
ReturnVal = Dialog(dlg)
```

Then, you can determine which button the user pressed to close the dialog box by examining the ReturnVal variable. The Dialog() function returns -1 if the user presses the OK button or 0 if the user presses the Cancel button. If the dialog box provides other buttons that close the dialog box, Dialog() returns a positive number to indicate which button was pressed: 1 for the first button, 2 for the second, and so on.

Sometimes, you can get away with using the `Dialog()` function call directly in an `If` command condition test. For example:

```
If Dialog(dlg) Then FileOpen dlg
```

Here, the dialog box is opened when the `Dialog()` function is processed by the `If` command. The result of the `Dialog()` function is used as the condition test so that the `FileOpen` command is executed if `Dialog()` returns any nonzero value.

Understanding Custom Dialog Boxes

Custom dialog boxes let you obtain any kind of information you need from the user in a single interaction. For example, suppose that you need to know a person's name, company, and fax number. You could obtain this information with a series of `InputBox$` commands:

```
Name$ = InputBox$("Name:")
Company$ = InputBox$("Company:")
FaxNumber$ = InputBox$("Fax Number:")
```

Wouldn't it be more convenient to the user if you could simply display a dialog box like the one shown in Figure 33-1? With custom dialog boxes, you can.

Figure 33-1: A custom dialog box.

Word's custom dialog boxes are not as powerful as dialog boxes created with a full-fledged programming language such as Visual Basic. However, you can create the dialog box controls listed in Table 33-1.

Table 33-1	WordBasic Dialog Box Controls	
What It Looks Like	*What It's Called*	*Description*
OK	OK button	Accepts the dialog box settings and processes them.
Cancel	Cancel button	Cancels the dialog box and does not process its settings.
Button	Push button	Invokes an alternative dialog box function *(continued)*

Table 33-1 *(continued)*

What It Looks Like	What It's Called	Description
⦿ Option Button	Option button	Selects one of several alternative settings.
☑ Check Box	Check box	Supplies a yes/no or on/off setting.
Text Field	Text box	Supplies a text label for the dialog box.
Type text here	Text field	Allows the user to enter text input.
Abadi MT Condensed / Algerian / Arial / Arial Black / Arial Narrow / Arial Rounded MT Bc / Augsburger Initials	List box	Allows the user to choose from a list of items.
Arial / Abadi MT Condense / Algerian / Arial / Arial Black / Arial Narrow / Arial Rounded MT E / Augsburger Initials	Combo box	Allows the user to choose from a list of items or enter a value not on the list.
Arial ▼	Drop-down list box	Allows the user to choose from a list that appears when the arrow is clicked.
(picture of a cat)	Picture	Includes a picture from a file, a bookmark, an AutoText entry, or the Clipboard.

There are two basic ways to use custom dialog boxes in a macro. The first, and simplest, is to create and use a *static dialog box* that has a fixed set of controls. When the dialog box is displayed, the user can type information into text fields, choose option buttons and check boxes, and make selections from list boxes. Then, the user clicks one of the command buttons (OK, Cancel, or a push button) to return control to the macro. The macro then determines which values the user entered into the dialog box and acts accordingly.

The second way to use a dialog box is to set up a *dynamic dialog box*. A dynamic dialog box is a custom dialog box that has a special function that enables the macro to respond as the user works with the dialog box controls. For example, you can disable certain controls if the user unchecks a check box control. With a bit of effort, you can even create "tabbed" dialog boxes that resemble the ones used extensively in Word 95, such as the Font or Customize dialog boxes.

Dialog Box Commands

Before you can display a custom dialog box, you must define it by using WordBasic's dialog box commands. For example, here are the commands used to define the dialog box that was shown in Figure 33-1:

```
Begin Dialog UserDialog 505, 72, "Microsoft Word"
    Text 11, 9, 49, 13, "Name:", .Text5
    Text 11, 30, 75, 13, "Company:", .Text6
    Text 10, 50, 96, 13, "Fax Number:", .Text7
    TextBox 114, 6, 263, 18, .Name
    TextBox 114, 27, 263, 18, .Company
    OKButton 405, 6, 88, 21
    CancelButton 405, 33, 88, 21
    TextBox 114, 48, 263, 18, .FaxNumber
End Dialog
```

As you can see, the dialog box definition begins with a `Begin Dialog` command and ends with an `End Dialog` command. Each of the commands in between creates a dialog box control. The numbers supply position and size information for each control: the first pair of numbers is an x, y coordinate relative to the top left corner of the dialog box, and the second pair specifies the width and height of the control.

Fortunately, WordBasic doesn't require you to type in these commands manually. The commands themselves are difficult, but determining the position and size information is tedious. That's why Microsoft includes a program called Dialog Editor, which lets you set up dialog boxes visually. Dialog Editor converts the dialog box you create visually to WordBasic commands, which can be included in your macro.

Using the Dialog Editor

To activate Dialog Editor, click on the Dialog Editor button on the Macros toolbar. The Dialog Editor window will appear, as shown in Figure 33-2.

Dialog Editor starts up with a blank dialog box, ready for you to populate with dialog box controls. The first thing to do is to give the dialog box a more meaningful name than "Microsoft Word." Double-click the dialog box title bar to summon the Dialog Information dialog box, shown in Figure 33-3. Then, type a more meaningful name for the dialog box in the Text$ field and click OK. You should now see the title you typed appear in the dialog box title.

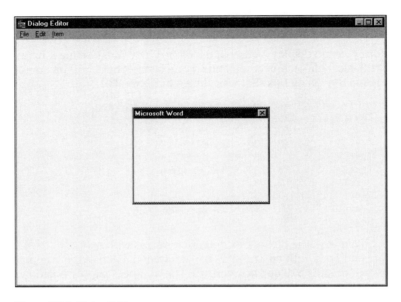

Figure 33-2: Dialog Editor.

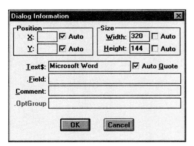

Figure 33-3: The Dialog Information dialog box.

Secret

Dialog Editor is unfortunately an old-style Windows application; Microsoft did not see fit to upgrade it for Windows 95. As a matter of fact, Dialog Editor isn't even up to Windows 3.1 and Word 6.0 standards. Much to your dismay, you will quickly discover that Dialog Editor has no Help command, no toolbars, no keyboard shortcuts, and no alignment grid or snap-to feature. The sad truth is that building custom dialog boxes is harder than it should be because of the limitations in Dialog Editor.

Adding button controls

Now you're ready to start adding dialog box controls. Most dialog boxes will require both an OK button and a Cancel button, so you may as well start with them. Choose the Item⇨Button command to summon the New Button dialog box, shown in Figure 34-4. Then, select the type of button you want to create (OK) and click OK. The button will be added to the dialog box. You can then drag the button to the location at which you want it to appear.

Figure 33-4: The New Button dialog box puts buttons on your dialog box.

After you create the OK button, you can create a Cancel button simply by pressing Enter. The Cancel button will appear immediately beneath the OK button.

Figure 33-5 shows a dialog box with OK and Cancel buttons in place.

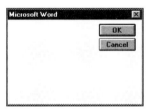

Figure 33-5: A dialog box with the buttons correctly placed.

To create a custom push button control, press Enter again. The push button will be inserted immediately beneath the Cancel button, and you can type whatever text you want to appear on the button. You can continue creating buttons in this manner by pressing the Enter key. Each new button will be lined up beneath the previous button.

To create a hot key for the button (a letter the user can press while holding down the Alt key to activate the button) select the button and type an ampersand immediately before the letter you want to use. For example, to create a Start button, where the hot key is Alt+S, type &Start for the button text.

Tip

As a general rule, the Enter key creates a duplicate of the last control you created. However, if the last control was an OK button, Dialog Editor creates a Cancel button instead because a dialog box can have only one OK button. Similarly, if the last control you created was a Cancel button or if a Cancel button already exists, pressing Enter creates a push button because a dialog box can have only one Cancel button. If you want to add an OK, Cancel, or push button after you have added other controls, call up the Item⇨Button command and select the type of button you want to create.

Using the Information dialog boxes

You can move and resize dialog box items by using the mouse, and you can change the text that is displayed for a dialog box control by selecting the control and typing. But, for more precise control, you can double-click the item to bring up an Information dialog box similar to the one shown in Figure 33-6. The figure shows the Information dialog box for an OK button control, but the same information is shown for other types of controls as well.

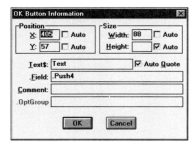

Figure 33-6: Adjusting dialog box item information.

Using this dialog box, you can change the following information:

■ **Position:** The X and Y position of the item, measured from the top-left corner of the dialog box. The measurements are relative to the size of the system font used to display the dialog box, which seems strange until you realize that this enables the dialog box to scale properly for different screen resolutions and system font sizes. Each X unit is 1/8 of the system font, and each Y unit is 1/12 of the system font.

If you check Auto for either X or Y position, you won't be able to use the mouse to drag the item to a new location. Instead, Dialog Editor will choose the positioning of the item for you. You probably won't use Auto for the Position settings.

- **Size:** The width and height of the item, using the same units of measure as used by the X and Y position settings.

  If you check Auto for either <u>W</u>idth or <u>H</u>eight, Dialog Editor will pick the size of the item for you. Unlike the X and Y Auto settings, Auto is a good idea for certain types of dialog controls. For example, using Auto Height for a text box ensures that the text box will always be one line in height. And using Auto Width for a text item automatically sizes the control to fit the text you type.

Note

Because Dialog Editor uses such strange units of measure, the best approach to positioning and sizing dialog box items is to use the mouse to move and size each item as accurately as possible. Then, you can use the Information dialog box to make minor changes to the position and size settings. For example, if you want to make sure that a row of controls are aligned horizontally, line them up as closely as you can with the mouse. Double-click on the first one and note its Y position. Then, double-click on the remaining items in the row, setting each one's Y position to the Y position of the first item in the row.

- `Text$:` The text that is displayed in the dialog box. With the Auto Quote option enabled, the `Text$` value is treated as a literal string. If you uncheck Auto Quote, `Text$` must be a variable name.

- `.Field:` The name that will be assigned to the dialog item, so you can access its value in your macro. Dialog Editor will pick a generic name, such as TextBox4 or OptionButton8. If you prefer to use more meaningful names, type them here.

- `Comment:` A comment that will be associated with the dialog item but not displayed to the user.

- `OptGroup:` Used to indicate to which group an option button belongs.

Adding option buttons and check boxes

To add an option button or a check box control, choose the <u>I</u>tem⇨<u>B</u>utton, select Option or Check Box for the button type, and click OK. Then, type the text for the button. To create additional option buttons or check boxes, press Enter.

Once again, use an ampersand to mark the hot key for each option button or check box. For example, to create a F<u>o</u>rmat check box, type F&ormat for the check box text.

Secret

A quick way to add a group of option buttons is to add a Group Box first by choosing the <u>I</u>tem⇨<u>G</u>roup Box command. With the group box selected, simply press the Enter key to add an option button within the group box. To add more than one option button, keep pressing the Enter key: each time you press the Enter key, a new option button is added beneath the previous one.

Adding text and text boxes

To add text to a dialog box, choose the Item⇨Text command. Dialog Editor will place a simple text object on the dialog box, consisting of the word "text." You can immediately begin typing to replace "text" with the text you want to appear on the dialog box for instructions. To add another line of text, press the Enter key. This will create another text object immediately beneath the first one.

To create a text box in which the user can enter information, use the Item⇨Text Box command. This creates a relatively short text box control, which you can resize by positioning the mouse pointer over the right or left edge and dragging right or left. Don't worry about changing the text that appears within the text box ("Edit text"). It is there only to provide a representative sample of how text will appear.

Text items and text box items are usually paired, the text item providing a caption for the text box so that the user knows what information to enter. To create a hot key for a text box, use an ampersand in the text item that immediately precedes the text box. Create the text item first and then create the text box item. That way, Dialog Editor will know that the text item and the text box item should be paired.

Figure 33-7 shows an example of a dialog box with several text and text box items.

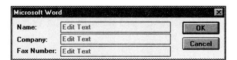

Figure 33-7: A dialog box with several text and text box items.

Secret

For text fields, Dialog Editor sets Auto Width and Auto Height by default so that the text item will automatically be sized to fit a single line of text, and the width of the item will grow as you type text. To create a text item that spans several lines, double-click the text item, uncheck Auto Height, and click OK. You can then resize the text item's height by dragging it by the top or bottom edge.

Similarly, Dialog Editor uses Auto Height (but not Width) for text box items. This allows you to change the text box width without accidentally changing its height. To create a text box that allows for more than one line of input, double-click the text box item, uncheck the Auto Height setting, click OK, and drag the top or bottom edge of the text box to change its height.

Adding a group box

A group box is used to group related items in a dialog box. It displays as a rectangle with text in the top-left corner. Group boxes are often used to house a group of option buttons, but you can place any types of controls you want in a group box. For excellent examples of how group boxes can be used to clarify the relationships of controls in a dialog box, browse through the various panels of Word's Tools⇨Options command.

Secret

You should create a group box before you create any controls that go in it. If you place a group box over the top of existing controls, the existing controls will be hidden. When you display the dialog box in your macro, the hidden controls will magically reappear. In other words, group boxes are transparent in Word, but opaque in Dialog Editor. To avoid confusion, always create the group box before you create the controls that go in it.

Tip

You don't have to provide text for a group box. If you remove the Text$ setting, the group box will display as a simple rectangle. You can also use this to create an unlabeled border around other fields.

Adding a picture field

The only complication involved with placing a picture field on a dialog box is specifying where the picture will originate. WordBasic will allow you to display pictures obtained from one of four sources:

- **A file:** Can be any of the file types supported by the Insert⇨Picture command. A good source of pictures to start with is c:\msoffice\clipart.

- **An AutoText entry:** Anything that can be stored as AutoText can be included in a picture field. For example, Figure 33-8 shows a WordArt object displayed as an AutoText picture field.

Figure 33-8: WordArt as a picture field in a dialog box.

- **A bookmark.:** Mark a graphic within your document with a bookmark before displaying the document.

- **The Clipboard:** When the dialog box is displayed, the contents of the Clipboard will be shown in the picture field.

When you use the Item⇨Picture command, you will be asked which type of picture item to create. To specify the name of the picture source, double-click the picture item and type the filename, AutoText name, or bookmark name in the Text$ field.

Deleting dialog box controls

To delete a dialog box control, all you have to do is select the control and press the Delete key.

Copying the dialog box into the macro

After you have created the dialog box, you can copy it into your WordBasic macro by following these steps:

1. Choose the Edit⇨Select Dialog command.

2. Choose the Edit⇨Copy command or press Ctrl+C.

3. Press Alt+Tab as many times as necessary to return to Word.

4. In the macro editing window, position the insertion point where you want the dialog box commands to insert. If you want to replace an existing version of the same dialog box, select the entire range of commands that define the dialog box, from `Begin Dialog` to `End Dialog.`

5. Press Ctrl+V to paste the WordBasic definition of the dialog into your macro.

Copying a dialog box from a macro to Dialog Editor

After you have copied the dialog box into your macro, you may realize that it has some mistakes, such as items that aren't aligned properly or missing items. Fortunately, you can copy the dialog box back to Dialog Editor, where you can correct the problems. Then, you can copy the dialog box definition back into your macro, overwriting the previous version of the dialog box definition.

To copy a dialog box back to Dialog Editor, follow these steps:

1. Select the entire dialog box definition, including the `Begin Dialog` and `End Dialog` commands.

2. Press Ctrl+C to copy the dialog definition to the Clipboard.

3. Click the Dialog Editor button in the Macro toolbar, or press Alt+Tab to switch to Dialog Editor if it is already running.

4. Press Ctrl+V to paste the dialog definition from the Clipboard. You can then edit the dialog box any way you want.

Editing the dialog box definition commands

You don't have to go to all the trouble of copying the dialog definition back to Dialog Editor if you only need to make minor dialog box changes. Instead, just edit the dialog box controls directly. The following are some of the edits you might consider making directly to the dialog box commands:

- Changing the names used for fields in the dialog box record. These names begin with a period and are listed as the last argument on each dialog box control except `OKButton` and `CancelButton`.

- Changing the text displayed for a dialog box control.

- Making minor position adjustments to align fields.

- Changing the tab order. The Tab key cycles through dialog box controls in the order in which they are listed. You can easily use cut-and-paste to rearrange the order of the fields to correct problems with the tab order.

The good news is that if you edit the dialog definition directly and then copy the definition back to Dialog Editor to make more substantial changes, your edits will be preserved.

Using a Custom Dialog Box in a Macro

Once the dialog box has been defined, you can write the macro instructions that will display the dialog box and respond to the user's input. The following sections explain how.

Displaying the dialog box

Displaying a custom dialog box is similar to displaying one of Word's built-in dialog boxes. You must first define a dialog box record that specifies `UserDialog` and use a `Dialog` command or `Dialog()` function to display the dialog box. For example:

```
Dim dlg As UserDialog
ResponseVal = Dialog(dlg)
```

You can determine which button the user clicked to dismiss the dialog box by examining the value returned by the Dialog function:

-1   The user pressed OK.

0   The user pressed Cancel.

>0   The user pressed a push button. The number indicates which button was pressed: 1 for the first button, 2 for the second button, and so on.

If you use the Dialog command rather than the Dialog() function, an error will result if the user selects Cancel. You can trap this error by using an On Error Goto command before the Dialog command. You cannot tell, however, which button the user pressed if the dialog includes push buttons. As a result, I recommend that you use the Dialog() function rather than the Dialog command.

Accessing the user's input

After the Dialog command or Dialog() function has been executed, you can retrieve the values entered by the user from the dialog record fields. The field names are supplied by the Dialog Editor .Field setting for each dialog box item and are listed as the last argument on each of the dialog control commands within the Begin Dialog and End Dialog commands.

For example, consider again the Dialog definition commands for the dialog box that was shown in Figure 33-1:

```
Begin Dialog UserDialog 505, 72, "Microsoft Word"
    Text 11, 9, 49, 13, "Name:", .Text5
    Text 11, 30, 75, 13, "Company:", .Text6
    Text 10, 50, 96, 13, "Fax Number:", .Text7
    TextBox 114, 6, 263, 18, .Name
    TextBox 114, 27, 263, 18, .Company
    OKButton 405, 6, 88, 21
    CancelButton 405, 33, 88, 21
    TextBox 114, 48, 263, 18, .FaxNumber
End Dialog
```

Here, the field names for the TextBox controls are .Name, .Company, and .FaxNumber. (For the Text controls, the field names are .Text5, .Text6, and .Text7. Dialog Editor generated these names automatically, and I didn't change them because I didn't plan on referencing them in the macro.)

To move the data entered into the three text box controls into variables, you'd use commands such as these:

```
CustomerName$ = dlg.Name
CustomerCompany$ = dlg.Company
CustomerFax$ = dlg.FaxNumber
```

Check boxes return a value of 1 or 0, indicating whether the box is checked. You can test the setting of a check box named CheckBox1 as follows:

```
If dlg.CheckBox1 Then
    MsgBox "CheckBox1 is checked"
Else
    MsgBox "CheckBox1 is not checked"
End If
```

This example will display a message box with the message "CheckBox1 is checked" if the check box is checked. Otherwise, "CheckBox1 is not checked" will be displayed.

Option buttons work a little differently. Instead of each option button having a separate value, the option group returns a value that indicates which of the buttons in the group was selected: 0 for the first button in the group, 1 for the second, 2 for the third, and so on. These options are easily tested with a `Select Case` command. For example, to test an option group named `OptionGroup6` that has four buttons, you'd set up a `Select Case` structure like this:

```
Select Case dlg.OptionGroup6
    Case 0
            'commands for processing first option button
    Case 1
            'commands for processing second option button
    Case 2
            'commands for processing third option button
    Case 3
            'commands for processing fourth option button
End Select
```

Setting default values

You can also supply default values to dialog box controls by assigning values to their dialog record fields before using the `Dialog` command or `Dialog()` function. For example:

```
dlg.TextBox1 = "Any text string"
dlg.CheckBox1 = 1          'Sets CheckBox1 to checked
dlg.CheckBox2 = 0          'Sets CheckBox2 to unchecked
dlg.OptionGroup3 = 2       'Sets the third option button in OptionGroup3
```

Once again, remember that the values used for option button groups begin with 0.

Secret

If you want default values to persist from one execution of the macro to the next, use the `SetPrivateProfileString` command and `GetPrivateProfileString$()` function to store the settings in a private settings file or the Windows 95 registry, as explained in Chapter 32.

Putting it all together

Now that you've seen how to create a dialog box, display it, and retrieve information from it, it's time to examine a macro that combines all of these actions to perform a useful function. The following paragraphs explain the operation of a dialog box named CreateMsgBox, which you can use to add MsgBox() function calls to your macros. The CreateMsgBox macro displays a dialog box that presents the various MsgBox() options in the form of text fields and option buttons. Then, the macro uses Insert commands to build an appropriate MsgBox() function call based on the values entered by the user.

Figure 33-9 shows a dialog box displayed by the CreateMsgBox macro. When the dialog box is displayed, the user types the MsgBox title in the Title field and the message itself in the message text field. Then, the user selects which button configuration to use, which symbol to display, and which button to make the default. When the user clicks the OK button, an appropriate MsgBox() function call will be created.

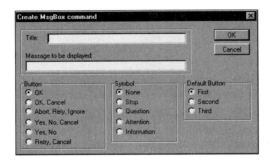

Figure 33-9: The dialog box displayed by the CreateMsgBox macro.

Here is the actual WordBasic code for the macro:

```
Sub MAIN
Begin Dialog UserDialog 569, 222, "Create MsgBox command"
    GroupBox 10, 6, 407, 83, ""
    Text 22, 20, 40, 13, "Title:"
    TextBox 73, 18, 330, 18, .Title
    Text 22, 49, 193, 13, "Message to be displayed:"
    TextBox 22, 65, 381, 18, .MessageText
    GroupBox 10, 97, 204, 119, "Button"
    OptionGroup  .ButtonGroup
        OptionButton 20, 109, 52, 16, "OK", .BG1
        OptionButton 20, 126, 115, 16, "OK, Cancel", .BG2
        OptionButton 20, 143, 173, 16, "Abort, Rety, Ignore", .BG3
        OptionButton 20, 160, 152, 16, "Yes, No, Cancel", .BG4
        OptionButton 20, 177, 89, 16, "Yes, No", .BG5
        OptionButton 20, 194, 132, 16, "Retry, Cancel", .BG6
    GroupBox 226, 97, 158, 108, "Symbol"
    OptionGroup  .SymbolGroup
        OptionButton 236, 109, 69, 16, "None", .SG1
        OptionButton 236, 126, 64, 16, "Stop", .SG2
        OptionButton 236, 143, 96, 16, "Question", .SG3
        OptionButton 236, 160, 97, 16, "Attention", .SG4
        OptionButton 236, 177, 113, 16, "Information", .SG5
    GroupBox 397, 97, 161, 71, "Default Button"
    OptionGroup  .DefaultGroup
        OptionButton 407, 109, 61, 16, "First", .DG1
        OptionButton 407, 126, 87, 16, "Second", .DG2
        OptionButton 407, 143, 68, 16, "Third", .DG3
```

```
        OKButton 469, 12, 88, 21
        CancelButton 469, 36, 88, 21
    End Dialog
    Dim dlg As UserDialog
    If Dialog(dlg) Then
        Insert "MsgBox("
        Insert Chr$(34) + CleanString$(dlg.MessageText) + Chr$(34) + ","
        Insert Chr$(34) + CleanString$(dlg.Title) + Chr$(34) + ", "
        Select Case dlg.ButtonGroup
            Case 0              'OK
                Insert " 0 "
            Case 1              'OK, Cancel
                Insert " 1 "
            Case 2              'Abort, Retry, Ignore
                Insert " 2 "
            Case 3              'Yes, No, Cancel
                Insert " 3 "
            Case 4              'Yes, No
                Insert " 4 "
            Case 5              'Retry, Cancel
                Insert " 5 "
        End Select
        Insert "+"
        Select Case dlg.SymbolGroup
            Case 0              'None
                Insert " 0 "
            Case 1              'Stop
                Insert " 16 "
            Case 2              'Question
                Insert " 32 "
            Case 3              'Attention
                Insert " 48 "
            Case 4              'Information
                Insert " 64 "
        End Select
        Insert "+"
        Select Case dlg.DefaultGroup
            Case 0              'First
                Insert " 0 "
            Case 1              'Second
                Insert " 256 "
            Case 2              'Third
                Insert " 512 "
        End Select
        Insert ")" + Chr$(13)
    End If
    UserCancel:
    End Sub
```

The heart of the macro is found within the If command structure that follows the Dim...As command midway through the macro. This If command includes a Dialog() function call which displays the dialog box and then builds the MsgBox() function call if the user doesn't cancel.

The MsgBox() function call is inserted into the active document or macro editing window by a series of Insert commands.The first three build the MsgBox() call up to and including the title text. For example, if the user enters "This Is A Test" in the Title field and "Of the Emergency Broadcasting System" in the second, the first three Insert commands will insert the following text:

```
MsgBox("Of the Emergency Broadcasting System","This Is A Test",
```

To finish the MsgBox() function call, three Select Case commands build a numeric expression that adds up the values used by the MsgBox function to indicate the message box type. For example, if the user selects OK, Cancel from the Buttons group, Attention from the Symbol group, and First from the Default Button group, " 1 + 48 + 0" will be added to the MsgBox function call. Then, the final Insert command will complete the call by adding the closing parenthesis and the paragraph mark. The complete function call inserted into the document or macro will look like this:

```
MsgBox("Of the Emergency Broadcasting System","This Is A Test",
1 + 48 + 0 )
```

If the user includes this MsgBox() call in the macros, the message box shown in Figure 33-10 will be displayed.

Figure 33-10: A MsgBox generated by the CreateMsgBox macro.

Working with List Fields

List fields are a little more difficult to work with than other dialog box controls. WordBasic supports three kinds of list fields: list boxes, drop-down list boxes, and combo boxes. A *list box* is a simple list of items, displayed with a scrollbar if necessary, from which the user can select one item. A *drop-down list box* is similar, except that the list itself is shown only if the user clicks the arrow next to the field. A *combo box* is a combination of a list box and a text box. It allows the user to pick an item from the list or to type any arbitrary string into the text box.

Figure 33-11 shows a small custom dialog box that displays a list of all the available fonts, allowing the user to pick one from the list.

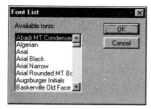

Figure 33-11: A custom dialog box that lists available fonts.

List fields such as the one in Figure 33-11 wouldn't be much use if they didn't allow you to fill them with values prior to displaying the dialog box. You do that by associating an array with the list field and filling the array with values *before defining the dialog box*. For example, the following snippet of code displays the dialog box shown in Figure 33-11 by filling an array named FontArray$() with the names of all available fonts, sorted into alphabetical order:

```
Dim FontArray$(CountFonts() - 1)
For Count = 0 To CountFonts() - 1
    FontArray$(Count) = Font$(Count + 1)
Next Count
SortArray FontArray$()
Begin Dialog UserDialog 320, 144, "Font List"
    OKButton 222, 7, 88, 21
    CancelButton 222, 31, 88, 21
    ListBox 12, 25, 160, 106, FontArray$(), .Fonts
    Text 12, 8, 119, 13, "Available fonts:", .Text1
End Dialog
Dim dlg As UserDialog
Dialog dlg
UserFont$=FontArray$(dlg.Fonts)
```

Here, the FontArray$() array is defined to contain as many elements as there are fonts. When working with arrays in WordBasic, you can often ignore the first element, accessed by the subscript 0 (zero). However, you cannot ignore the 0 entry when working with dialog box list controls. That's because the end of the list is indicated by a null entry in the array. If you ignore the 0 entry, WordBasic will consider the list to be empty.

As a result, the For...Next loop in this example counts from 0 to one less than the number of fonts, and the array is dimensioned accordingly. If you plan on sorting the array, you must be careful to dimension the array with exactly the number of entries you need. Otherwise, empty entries will be sorted to the beginning of the array, and once again, WordBasic will consider the array to be empty.

When you access the dialog record field associated with a list box or a drop-down list box, the value returned is the number of the item chosen. If the user chooses the first item, 0 is returned, 1 is returned for the second item, and so on. As a result, the following command:

```
UserFont$=FontArray$(dlg.Fonts)
```

sets the variable `UserFont$` to the name of the font selected by the user.

Combo boxes behave a little differently because they allow the user to enter a value directly rather than select a value from the list. The dialog record field for a combo box returns the actual text selected or entered by the user.

Using Dynamic Dialog Boxes

A *dynamic dialog box* is a dialog box that can react on-the-fly to the user's actions. Common uses of dynamic dialog boxes include the following:

- Enabling or disabling some dialog controls based on the settings of other dialog controls.

- Showing or hiding dialog controls based on the settings of other controls.

- Changing the contents of a picture field based on the setting of a control.

- Calling up a built-in Word dialog box without dismissing the user-defined dialog box.

- Switching from one "panel" of controls to another to simulate Word's tabbed dialog box style.

- Adjusting the array entries for a list box, drop-down list box, or combo box control.

This section shows you the basics of creating dynamic dialog boxes and illustrates several of the techniques using a more advanced version of the CreateMsgBox macro, which was presented earlier in this chapter.

Setting up a dialog function

To create a dynamic dialog box, you must first set up a *dialog function*, a user-defined function which WordBasic calls whenever a dialog box event occurs. Word calls your dialog function whenever any of the following events occurs:

- The dialog box is initialized.

- The user chooses a command button, an option, or check box, or makes a selection from a list box or drop-down list box.

- The user changes the value of a text box or combo box.

- The input focus moves to another dialog box control, as when the user presses the Tab key.

- Nothing has happened in a while and Word wonders if your dialog box would like to take advantage of the idle time.
- The user moves the dialog box.

When Word calls the dialog function, it passes three arguments which the dialog function can use to ascertain the situation and respond accordingly. The three arguments are as follows:

- `ControlID$`: A string that corresponds to the identifier of the control for which an event has occurred. These strings are identical to the dialog record field names for each control, except that the period is omitted. Thus, if an event occurs for an option button named .Option1, "Option1" will be passed to the dialog function via this argument.

- `Action`: A number indicating what event has occurred. The action numbers are listed in Table 33-2.

- `SuppValue`: An additional number that contains additional information about the event when action 2 or 3 occurs. The information passed via this argument varies depending on the type of control passed in the `ControlID$` argument, as described in Table 33-3.

Table 33-2	Action Values for Dialog Functions
Value	*Meaning*
1	Dialog box initialization.
2	The user has selected a button or list field item.
3	The user has typed information into a text box or combo box.
4	A control has received the input focus.
5	Idle loop.
6	The dialog box has moved.

Table 33-3	SuppValues
Type of Control	*Meaning of SuppValue Argument*
List box, drop-down list box, or combo box	The number of the item selected, starting with 0.
Check box	1 if checked, 0 if cleared.
Option button	The number of the option button in the group, starting with 0.
Text box	The number of characters entered.
Combo box	For action 3, the number of characters in the combo box.
Command button	The button chosen.

The same dialog function is called for all controls and actions, so the dialog function must determine what action to take based on the arguments passed to it. Usually, a Select Case command is used for this purpose. For example, the following is a typical form for dialog box functions:

```
Function DlgFunction(ID$, action, suppval)
Select Case action
    Case 1          'Initialization
        place your initialization code here
    Case 2          'User select
        Select Case ID$
            place one or more Case clauses here
            to process specific user events
        End Select
    Case 3          'User changed data
        Select Case ID$
            place one or more Case clauses here
            to process specific user events
        End Select
    Case Else
End Select
End Function
```

Here, a Select Case action command controls the dialog function's processing based on the event that triggered the call. Within the Case clauses for actions 2 and 3, another Select Case command determines with which control each event is associated. The actual commands that deal with specific user events, such as when the user clicks a specific button or types data into a specific text box, are coded within the Case clauses of these Select Case commands.

After your dialog function has been set up, you have to let Word know that your dialog box will need to use it. To do that, you must add the dialog box function name to the Begin Dialog command that starts the definition of your user dialog, like this:

```
Begin Dialog UserDialog 591, 222, "Create MsgBox command",
.DlgFunction
```

Here, the dialog function named DlgFunction will be called when the dialog box is displayed. Notice that a period is required before the dialog box function name on the Begin Dialog command, but not on the Function command that defines the dialog function.

Secret

If your dialog box suddenly stops responding to user events, make sure that the dialog function name hasn't been yanked from the Begin Dialog command. This happens sometimes when copying and pasting the dialog box definition between a Word macro editing window and the Dialog Editor.

Note

One other detail about dialog functions you should know is that the return value from the function determines whether Word keeps the dialog box open when the user presses a command button (OK, Cancel, or a push button). Ordinarily, pressing a command button will close the dialog box, and that's the way the dialog function works by default. If you want to leave the dialog box open after a user presses a command button, just set the dialog function name to -1, like this:

```
DlgFunction = -1
```

Commands used in dialog functions

So, just what can you *do* in the dialog function? Just about anything, with the possible exception of displaying another custom dialog box: WordBasic only allows one custom dialog record to exist at a time, so there's no way to display one custom dialog box from within another. Short of that, the possibilities are limitless.

WordBasic provides a small suite of commands that are designed specifically for use within a dialog function. These commands, summarized in Table 33-4 , are designed to let you modify the appearance of the dialog box. For example, you can show or hide and enable or disable controls, change the setting of a text field, or display a different picture in a picture field. To disable a control named BG2, you would use the following command:

```
DlgEnable "BG2",0
```

The control identifier must be typed exactly as it is listed in the dialog box definition. Dialog control identifiers are case-sensitive, so BG2 and bg2 might represent different controls.

Table 33-4	Dynamic Dialog Commands	
Command	*What It Does*	
DlgEnable *id$* [, *on*]	Enables (*on*=1) or disables (*on*=2) the control identified by *id$*. If *on* is omitted, toggles the control between enabled and disabled.	
DlgFilePreview [*id$l*] [*filename$*]	Displays a preview of the *filename$* in the file preview box, if one is provided. *Id$* is optional because a dialog box can have only one file preview control.	
DlgFocus *id$*	Sets the input focus to the control identified by *id$*.	
DlgListBoxArray *id$,array$()*	Fills the list box *id$* with the contents of the array *array$()*.	
DlgSetPicture *id$,picture$,type*	Sets the picture control identified by *id$* to the picture indicated by *picture$*. *Type* indicates the picture type:	
	0	File
	1	AutoText

(continued)

Table 33-4 *(continued)*

Command	What It Does	
	2	Bookmark
	3	Clipboard (*picture$* is ignored)
DlgText *id$,text$*	Sets the text of the control identified by *id$* to *text$*.	
DlgUpdateFilePreview [*id$l*]	Updates the file preview. *Id$* is optional because a dialog box can have only one file preview control.	
DlgValue *id$, value*	Sets the dialog control identified by *id$* to *value*.	
DlgVisible *id$*, [*on*]	Shows (*on*=1) or hides (*on*=2) the control identified by *id$*. If *on* is omitted, toggles the control between visible and invisible.	

Most of these commands also have a corresponding function, which is listed in Table 33-5. Notice also the addition of the DlgControlId() function, which is sometimes used to improve performance in macros that process dialog boxes with many controls.

Table 33-5	Dynamic Dialog Functions
Command	*What It Does*
DlgControlId$(*id$*)	Returns the numeric control identifier for the control identified by the string *id$*. This number can be used in any dialog box commands or functions in place of the string *id$* to improve performance.
DlgEnable(*id$*)	Returns -1 if the control is enabled, 0 if not.
DlgFilePreview$()	Returns the name of the file being previewed.
DlgFocus$()	Returns the control *id$* of the control that has the focus.
DlgListBoxArray(*id$* [,*array$()*])	Fills the specified array variable with the contents of the list control, and returns the number of items in the list.
DlgText$(*id$*)	Returns the text of the control identified by *id$*.
DlgValue(*id$*)	Returns the value of the dialog control identified by *id$*.
DlgVisible(*id$*)	Returns -1 if the control is visible, 0 if not.

A dynamic version of the CreateMsgBox macro

The CreateMsgBox macro, which was presented earlier in this chapter, has two weaknesses that can be improved by using a dynamic dialog box. First, several combinations of option buttons are inappropriate. For example, if only an OK button is selected, it doesn't make sense to set the second button as the default button. Specifically, the Second and Third options in the Default Button group should be disabled if the user selects a single OK button, and the Third button option should be disabled if the user picks a two-button configuration. The second weakness is that you can't tell by looking what the symbols look like.

This section presents an enhanced version of the CreateMsgBox macro that uses a dialog function to remedy these problems. The new macro (named CreateMsgBoxDynam) displays the dialog box shown in Figure 33-12. You can see here that the symbol corresponding to the select symbol option is displayed in a picture field in the top-left corner of the dialog box. In addition, the Second and Third default button options are disabled because the user has chosen a single button for the MsgBox dialog box.

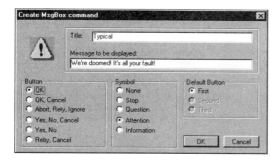

Figure 33-12: The dynamic version of the CreateMsgBox macro displays this dialog box.

Here is the complete code for the CreateMsgBoxDynam macro:

```
Sub MAIN
Begin Dialog UserDialog 591, 222, "Create MsgBox command",
.DlgFunction
    GroupBox 114, 6, 462, 83, ""
    Text 126, 20, 40, 13, "Title:"
    TextBox 177, 18, 382, 18, .Title
    Text 126, 49, 193, 13, "Message to be displayed:"
    TextBox 126, 65, 433, 18, .MessageText
    GroupBox 10, 97, 204, 119, "Button"
```

```
        OptionGroup  .ButtonGroup
            OptionButton 20, 109, 52, 16, "OK", .BG1
            OptionButton 20, 126, 115, 16, "OK, Cancel", .BG2
            OptionButton 20, 143, 173, 16, "Abort, Rety, Ignore", .BG3
            OptionButton 20, 160, 152, 16, "Yes, No, Cancel", .BG4
            OptionButton 20, 177, 89, 16, "Yes, No", .BG5
            OptionButton 20, 194, 132, 16, "Retry, Cancel", .BG6
        GroupBox 226, 97, 158, 118, "Symbol"
        OptionGroup  .SymbolGroup
            OptionButton 236, 109, 69, 16, "None", .SG1
            OptionButton 236, 126, 64, 16, "Stop", .SG2
            OptionButton 236, 143, 96, 16, "Question", .SG3
            OptionButton 236, 160, 97, 16, "Attention", .SG4
            OptionButton 236, 177, 113, 16, "Information", .SG5
        GroupBox 396, 98, 182, 67, "Default Button"
        OptionGroup  .DefaultGroup
            OptionButton 407, 109, 61, 16, "First", .DG1
            OptionButton 407, 126, 87, 16, "Second", .DG2
            OptionButton 407, 143, 68, 16, "Third", .DG3
        Picture 29, 28, 58, 41, "picture_0", 1, .SymbolPic
        OKButton 396, 193, 88, 21
        CancelButton 492, 193, 88, 21
    End Dialog
    Dim dlg As UserDialog
    If Dialog(dlg) Then
        Insert "MsgBox("
        Insert Chr$(34) + CleanString$(dlg.MessageText) + Chr$(34) + ","
        Insert Chr$(34) + CleanString$(dlg.Title) + Chr$(34) + ", "
        Select Case dlg.ButtonGroup
            Case 0                    'OK
                Insert " 0 "
            Case 1                    'OK, Cancel
                Insert " 1 "
            Case 2                    'Abort, Retry, Ignore
                Insert " 2 "
            Case 3                    'Yes, No, Cancel
                Insert " 3 "
            Case 4                    'Yes, No
                Insert " 4 "
            Case 5                    'Retry, Cancel
                Insert " 5 "
        End Select
        Insert "+"
        Select Case dlg.SymbolGroup
            Case 0                    'None
                Insert " 0 "
            Case 1                    'Stop
                Insert " 16 "
            Case 2                    'Question
                Insert " 32 "
            Case 3                    'Attention
                Insert " 48 "
            Case 4                    'Information
                Insert " 64 "
        End Select
```

```
        Insert "+"
        Select Case dlg.DefaultGroup
            Case 0                    'First
                Insert " 0 "
            Case 1                    'Second
                Insert " 256 "
            Case 2                    'Third
                Insert " 512 "
        End Select
        Insert ")" + Chr$(13)
    End If
    UserCancel:
    End Sub

    Function DlgFunction(ID$, action, suppval)
    Select Case action
        Case 1            'Initialization
            DlgEnable "DG2", 0
            DlgEnable "DG3", 0
        Case 2            'User select
            Select Case ID$
                Case "BG1"
                    DlgEnable "DG2", 0
                    DlgEnable "DG3", 0
                Case "BG2", "BG5", "BG6"
                    DlgEnable "DG2", 1
                    DlgEnable "DG3", 0
                Case "BG3", "BG4"
                    DlgEnable "DG2", 1
                    DlgEnable "DG3", 1
                Case "SG1"
                    DlgSetPicture "SymbolPic", "picture_0", 1
                Case "SG2"
                    DlgSetPicture "SymbolPic", "picture_1", 1
                Case "SG3"
                    DlgSetPicture "SymbolPic", "picture_2", 1
                Case "SG4"
                    DlgSetPicture "SymbolPic", "picture_3", 1
                Case "SG5"
                    DlgSetPicture "SymbolPic", "picture_4", 1
                Case Else
            End Select
    Case Else
    End Select
    End Function
```

Most of this macro is identical to the original version. In the dialog box definition, the only difference is that I have moved the fields around a bit, added a Picture field to display the symbol, and specified DlgFunction as the dialog box function. Other than these changes, the Sub MAIN routine here is identical to the Sub MAIN routine in the original version. So, you can focus your attention on the dialog box function itself, DlgFunction.

The dialog box function consists of a large `Select Case` construct that provides specific handling for action codes 1 (initialization) and 2 (user select). For action 1, the dialog function disables the two extraneous Default Button option buttons by using these commands:

```
DlgEnable "DG2", 0
DlgEnable "DG3", 0
```

That way, these option buttons will initially be disabled when the dialog box is first displayed.

For action 2, another `Select Case` construct is used to provide processing for specific controls as they are selected by the user. The first group of controls to be dealt with are the option buttons in the Buttons group. They are handled by these lines:

```
Case "BG1"
    DlgEnable "DG2", 0
    DlgEnable "DG3", 0
Case "BG2", "BG5", "BG6"
    DlgEnable "DG2", 1
    DlgEnable "DG3", 0
Case "BG3", "BG4"
    DlgEnable "DG2", 1
    DlgEnable "DG3", 1
```

If the user chooses option button BG1 ("OK"), the second two default button choices are disabled. If the user chooses options BG2, BG5, or BG6 ("OK, Cancel," "Yes, No," or "Retry, Cancel"), the second default option button is enabled and the third is disabled. If the user chooses option buttons BG3 ("Abort, Retry, Ignore") or BG4 ("Yes, No, Cancel"), the second and third default buttons are both enabled.

The rest of the action 2 statements are responsible for changing the picture displayed in the SymbolPic control:

```
Case "SG1"
    DlgSetPicture "SymbolPic", "picture_0", 1
Case "SG2"
    DlgSetPicture "SymbolPic", "picture_1", 1
Case "SG3"
    DlgSetPicture "SymbolPic", "picture_2", 1
Case "SG4"
    DlgSetPicture "SymbolPic", "picture_3", 1
Case "SG5"
    DlgSetPicture "SymbolPic", "picture_4", 1
```

Whenever the user chooses one of the symbol option buttons, the appropriate `Case` clause is selected and the correct picture is displayed.

The pictures themselves are stored in the template as AutoText entries, named "picture_0," "picture_1," and so on. I constructed these AutoText entries by displaying a MsgBox with the appropriate symbol, pressing Shift+PrintScreen to copy the screen to the Clipboard, pasting the Clipboard image into Paintbrush, and then copying and pasting just the icon back into a Word document. I then highlighted the icon and used the Edit⊅AutoText command to create the AutoText entry. (Until you set up these AutoText entries, the picture fields will display "Missing picture.")

Solving a problem with drop-down list fields

Secret

Many of Word's built-in dialog boxes contain drop-down list boxes that, when opened, extend below the bottom of the dialog box. For example, call up the File⊅Open command and activate the Files of Type drop-down list box. The list of file types hangs well below the bottom of the dialog box. Remarkably, Windows is even smart enough to make sure that there is enough room underneath to open the drop-down list box. If you move the dialog box too close to the bottom of the screen, the drop-down list flies *up* instead of down.

The on-line help text for the DropListBox command says that you can create WordBasic dialog boxes with drop-down list boxes that behave this way: "When a drop-down list box is dropped down, the portion that is dropped down can cover other controls in the dialog box or fall outside the dialog box." But, it doesn't work. Try creating a dialog box that has a drop-down list box positioned near the bottom of the window, and you'll get the message "WordBasic Error 512: Value Out Of Range."

Reposition the drop-down list box so that it falls within the dialog box and the error will go away. With a little experimentation, you'll discover that you can make a small amount of the drop-down list to extend over the line, but not by much. Clearly, the on-line help is wrong: you cannot create a drop-down list box that hangs outside of the dialog box.

At least not without help from a dialog function. As it turns out, you can create a drop-down list box that hangs below the dialog box. It just takes a little hacking. (The technique was suggested by Romke Soldaat, developer of MegaWord 95.)

Start by creating an oversized dialog box, tall enough to accommodate the drop-down list box without generating the Value Out Of Range error. Figure 33-13 shows how such a dialog box would appear in Dialog Editor.

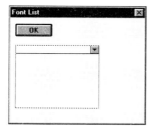

Figure 33-13: Creating an oversized dialog box to accommodate a low-flying drop-down list box.

Before leaving Dialog Editor, resize the dialog box to the size you would like it to be displayed, allowing the drop-down list box to spill outside of the dialog box. Then, double-click the dialog box to show the dialog box information, and make a note of the height of the dialog box.

Now, in your macro, create the dialog box as dynamic by providing a dialog function. In the dialog function, use the WordBasic AppWindowHeight command to change the size of the dialog box to the adjusted size. You may also want to use the AppWindowPosTop command to relocate the dialog box back to the center of the screen because reducing its size will skew it toward the top.

It all sounds easy enough, except that the AppWindowHeight and AppWindowPosTop commands use a different unit of measure than the WordBasic commands you use to create dialog boxes: the AppWindow functions use points, but the dialog definition commands use a relative measurement that's based on the size of the system font. So, you have to do a little calculation to make it work out. The easiest way to accomplish this is to divide the desired size of the dialog box by the size you actually defined it as to yield a percentage. Then, use the AppWindowHeight() function to obtain the window height in points and multiply it by the percentage you calculated.

Here is a simple example of a macro that displays a dialog box which includes a drop-down list box that extends below the dialog box boundaries:

```
Sub MAIN
Dim FontArray$(CountFonts() - 1)
For Count = 1 To CountFonts()
    FontArray$(Count - 1) = Font$(Count)
Next Count
SortArray FontArray$()
Begin Dialog UserDialog 320, 180, "Font List", .DlgFunction
    DropListBox 12, 46, 200, 108, FontArray$(), .FontList
    OKButton 12, 10, 88, 21
End Dialog
Dim dlg As UserDialog
If Dialog(dlg) Then
    MsgBox FontArray$(dlg.FontList)
End If
End Sub

Function DlgFunction(ID$, action, suppvalue)
Select Case action
    Case 1                'Initialization
        WindowHeight = AppWindowHeight("Font List")
        WindowPos = AppWindowPosTop("Font List")
        AppWindowHeight "Font List", WindowHeight * 0.5
        AppWindowPosTop "Font List", WindowPos + WindowHeight * 0.25
    Case Else
End Select
End Function
```

In this example, the dialog box is defined exactly twice as large as I really want it to be when displayed. The dialog function handles initialization by first determining the height and vertical position of the dialog box and setting a new height and vertical position for the dialog box. Notice that the `AppWindow` functions provide the name that appears in the dialog box title bar to identify the dialog box. Figure 33-14 shows how this dialog box appears when the drop-down list box has been activated.

Figure 33-14: Yes, you CAN create a drop-down list that drops below the dialog box.

A dynamic dialog box that simulates tabbed dialog boxes

The final example in this chapter demonstrates the technique for creating tabbed dialog boxes that resemble those used throughout Microsoft Word itself. Unfortunately, there is no quick-and-easy way to create tabbed dialog boxes. WordBasic does not provide a control that is similar to the tab buttons used to switch from one panel of dialog box controls to another. Nor does Dialog Editor provide an easy way to edit dialog boxes that are loaded with controls on top of controls as tabbed dialog boxes are. Still, with some patience and an occasional spurt of clever thinking, you can create dialog boxes that bear a striking resemblance to Word's tabbed dialog boxes.

The basic technique is to provide a row of buttons across the top of the dialog box that the user clicks to move from panel to panel. You can use option buttons for this purpose, but I prefer to use normal push buttons. A bit of extra work is involved, but the effect more closely resembles the real thing.

In the dialog function, you respond to the "tab" buttons by using the `DlgVisible` command to show the dialog controls that are parts of the panel selected and hide those that are not. In addition, you may need to make other adjustments, such as changing the value displayed in text controls.

To let the user know which of the dialog tabs is selected, create a text field that overlaps the bottom edge of each tab's button. Fill this text field with spaces and adjust its positioning until it just covers the bottom edge of the button but not the sides. Only one of these fields will be visible at a time, the one corresponding to the tab that is selected by the user.

Figure 33-15 shows two panels of dialog controls for yet another enhanced version of the CreateMsgBox macro, called CreateMsgBoxTabs. This version of the macro can create not only a MsgBox function call, but also an InputBox function call. The controls used to set up each type of call are provided on separate panels of dialog box controls, activated by clicking the push buttons at the top of the dialog box.

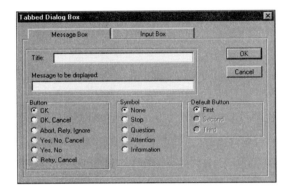

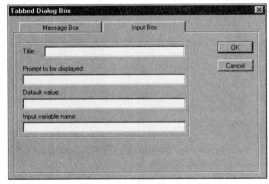

Figure 33-15: Dialog boxes that display two panels of dialog controls, mimicking Word's tabbed dialog boxes.

Here is the complete WordBasic code for the CreateMsgBoxTabs macro:

```
Dim Shared TabSelected
Sub MAIN
Begin Dialog UserDialog 607, 273, "Tabbed Dialog Box", .DlgFunction
    PushButton 22, 9, 200, 21, "Message Box", .Tab1
    PushButton 221, 9, 200, 21, "Input Box", .Tab2
    GroupBox 10, 23, 586, 244, ""
    Text 24, 27, 196, 7, "                              ", .Blank1
    Text 223, 27, 196, 7, "                              ", .Blank2

    GroupBox 18, 39, 410, 85, "", .Box1
    GroupBox 18, 39, 412, 166, "", .Box2

    Text 32, 53, 40, 13, "Title:"
    TextBox 83, 51, 334, 18, .Title

    Text 32, 82, 193, 13, "Message to be displayed:", .MsgPrompt
    TextBox 32, 98, 387, 18, .MessageText

    Text 32, 122, 108, 13, "Default value:", .Label1
    TextBox 32, 138, 387, 18, .Default

    Text 32, 162, 156, 13, "Input variable name:", .Label2
    TextBox 32, 178, 387, 18, .VariableName


    GroupBox 18, 129, 199, 124, "Button", .Box3
    OptionGroup  .ButtonGroup
        OptionButton 28, 141, 52, 16, "OK", .BG1
        OptionButton 28, 158, 115, 16, "OK, Cancel", .BG2
        OptionButton 28, 175, 173, 16, "Abort, Rety, Ignore", .BG3
        OptionButton 28, 192, 152, 16, "Yes, No, Cancel", .BG4
        OptionButton 28, 209, 89, 16, "Yes, No", .BG5
        OptionButton 28, 226, 132, 16, "Retry, Cancel", .BG6

    GroupBox 234, 129, 158, 118, "Symbol", .Box4
    OptionGroup  .SymbolGroup
        OptionButton 244, 141, 69, 16, "None", .SG1
        OptionButton 244, 158, 64, 16, "Stop", .SG2
        OptionButton 244, 175, 96, 16, "Question", .SG3
        OptionButton 244, 192, 97, 16, "Attention", .SG4
        OptionButton 244, 209, 113, 16, "Information", .SG5

    GroupBox 404, 130, 182, 67, "Default Button", .Box5
    OptionGroup  .DefaultGroup
        OptionButton 415, 141, 61, 16, "First", .DG1
        OptionButton 415, 158, 87, 16, "Second", .DG2
        OptionButton 415, 175, 68, 16, "Third", .DG3

    OKButton 495, 44, 88, 21
    CancelButton 495, 74, 88, 21

End Dialog
```

```
Dim dlg As UserDialog
If Dialog(dlg) Then
  Select Case TabSelected
    Case 1   'Create MsgBox()
        Insert "MsgBox("
        Insert Chr$(34) + CleanString$(dlg.MessageText) + Chr$(34) + ","
        Insert Chr$(34) + CleanString$(dlg.Title) + Chr$(34) + ", "
    Select Case dlg.ButtonGroup
        Case 0               'OK
            Insert " 0 "
            Case 1                 'OK, Cancel
            Insert " 1 "
            Case 2                 'Abort, Retry, Ignore
            Insert " 2 "
        Case 3               'Yes, No, Cancel
            Insert " 3 "
        Case 4               'Yes, No
            Insert " 4 "
        Case 5               'Retry, Cancel
            Insert " 5 "
    End Select
    Insert "+"
    Select Case dlg.SymbolGroup
        Case 0               'None
            Insert " 0 "
        Case 1               'Stop
            Insert " 16 "
        Case 2               'Question
            Insert " 32 "
        Case 3               'Attention
            Insert " 48 "
        Case 4               'Information
            Insert " 64 "
    End Select
    Insert "+"
    Select Case dlg.DefaultGroup
        Case 0               'First
            Insert " 0 "
        Case 1               'Second
            Insert " 256 "
        Case 2               'Third
            Insert " 512 "
    End Select
        Insert ")" + Chr$(13)
  Case Else   'Create InputBox$()
    Insert CleanString$(dlg.VariableName) + " = InputBox$("
    Insert Chr$(34) + CleanString$(dlg.MessageText) + Chr$(34) + ","
    Insert Chr$(34) + CleanString$(dlg.Title) + Chr$(34) + ", "
    Insert Chr$(34) + CleanString$(dlg.Default) + Chr$(34) + ")"
End Select
End If
UserCancel:
End Sub
```

```
Function DlgFunction(ID$, action, suppval)
Select Case action
    Case 1          'Initialization
        TabSelected = 1
        DlgVisible "Blank2", 0
        DlgVisible "Label1", 0
        DlgVisible "Label2", 0
        DlgVisible "Default", 0
        DlgVisible "VariableName", 0
        DlgVisible "Box2", 0
        DlgEnable "DG2", 0
        DlgEnable "DG3", 0
        DlgFocus "Title"
    Case 2          'User select
        Select Case ID$
            Case "Tab1"
                TabSelected = 1
                DlgVisible "Blank1", 1
                DlgVisible "Blank2", 0
                DlgText "MsgPrompt", "Message to be displayed:"
                DlgVisible "ButtonGroup", 1
                DlgVisible "BG1", 1
                DlgVisible "BG2", 1
                DlgVisible "BG3", 1
                DlgVisible "BG4", 1
                DlgVisible "BG5", 1
                DlgVisible "BG6", 1
                DlgVisible "SymbolGroup", 1
                DlgVisible "SG1", 1
                DlgVisible "SG2", 1
                DlgVisible "SG3", 1
                DlgVisible "SG4", 1
                DlgVisible "SG5", 1
                DlgVisible "DefaultGroup", 1
                DlgVisible "DG1", 1
                DlgVisible "DG2", 1
                DlgVisible "DG3", 1
                DlgVisible "Box1", 1
                DlgVisible "Box2", 0
                DlgVisible "Box3", 1
                DlgVisible "Box4", 1
                DlgVisible "Box5", 1
                DlgVisible "Label1", 0
                DlgVisible "Label2", 0
                DlgVisible "Default", 0
                DlgVisible "VariableName", 0
                DlgFunction = - 1
                DlgFocus "Title"
            Case "Tab2"
                TabSelected = 2
                DlgVisible "Blank1", 0
                DlgVisible "Blank2", 1
                DlgText "MsgPrompt", "Prompt to be displayed:"
                DlgVisible "ButtonGroup", 1
```

```
                              DlgVisible "BG1", 0
                              DlgVisible "BG2", 0
                              DlgVisible "BG3", 0
                              DlgVisible "BG4", 0
                              DlgVisible "BG5", 0
                              DlgVisible "BG6", 0
                              DlgVisible "SymbolGroup", 0
                              DlgVisible "SG1", 0
                              DlgVisible "SG2", 0
                              DlgVisible "SG3", 0
                              DlgVisible "SG4", 0
                              DlgVisible "SG5", 0
                              DlgVisible "DefaultGroup", 0
                              DlgVisible "DG1", 0
                              DlgVisible "DG2", 0
                              DlgVisible "DG3", 0
                              DlgVisible "Box1", 0
                              DlgVisible "Box2", 1
                              DlgVisible "Box3", 0
                              DlgVisible "Box4", 0
                              DlgVisible "Box5", 0
                              DlgVisible "Label1", 1
                              DlgVisible "Label2", 1
                              DlgVisible "Default", 1
                              DlgVisible "VariableName", 1
                              DlgFunction = - 1
                              DlgFocus "Title"
                         Case "BG1"
                              DlgEnable "DG2", 0
                              DlgEnable "DG3", 0
                         Case "BG2", "BG5", "BG6"
                              DlgEnable "DG2", 1
                              DlgEnable "DG3", 0
                         Case "BG3", "BG4"
                              DlgEnable "DG2", 1
                              DlgEnable "DG3", 1
                         Case Else
                    End Select
               Case Else
          End Select
    End Select
    End Function
```

Although it's long, this macro isn't really that complicated. I'll just mention some of the highlights here:

■ The hardest part of creating a macro of this sort is drawing the dialog box itself. The easiest way is to draw each panel separately and selectively copy and paste elements from each panel together to create a single `Begin Dialog...End Dialog` group that includes all of the controls.

■ In the CreateMsgBoxTabs macro, I added blank lines here and there to separate groups of related commands in the dialog box definition. This makes the dialog definition easier to pick apart.

- The `Main` subroutine needs to know which dialog tab was selected when the user pressed OK so that it can figure out whether to generate a `MsgBox()` function call or an `InputBox$()` function call. It does this by defining a shared variable named TabSelect, which can be accessed from the `Main` subroutine and from the `DlgFunction` function. The `DlgFunction` function sets this variable whenever the user clicks on of the push buttons. Then, after the dialog box is completed, the `Main` subroutine uses the variable to determine which button was pressed last.

- In the dialog function, the initialization routine sets the `TabSelected` variable to 1, hides the controls that aren't supposed to be visible on the MsgBox tab, and hides the blank text field `.Text2`.

- When the user clicks one of the push buttons, the `TabSelected` variable is set, the controls that are supposed to be visible on the tab are shown, the controls that are supposed to be hidden are hidden, and the `.Blank1` and `.Blank2` fields are alternately shown and hidden so that the user can tell which "tab" is active.

- `DlgFunction` is set to -1 when the user presses a push button so that this action does not dismiss the dialog box.

Chapter 34

WordBasic Commands and Functions

In This Chapter

▶ A complete listing of all WordBasic commands and functions

▶ Commands and functions by category

This chapter is simply a list of WordBasic commands and functions, along with a one-line description of what each command does. There isn't room enough in this book for a complete reference to each command, but once you've identified the command you want to use, you can quickly call up Word's on-line help for the command or function by typing the command's name in a macro window and pressing F1.

After the table of WordBasic commands, you'll find several lists that group commands by category.

Note

If the command has an associated dialog record, it is shown here in boldface type. Also, if the command or function is new with Word for Windows 95, or if it has been given new options, a Word for Windows 95 icon appears next to the command.

Table 34-1	**WordBasic Commands and Functions**
Command	*What It Does*
Abs()	Returns the absolute value of a number.
Activate	Activates a window.
ActivateObject	Activates an object.
AddAddIn AddAddIn()	Adds a template or add-in library as a global template or add-in.
AddAddress	Adds an entry to an Address Book.
AddButton	Adds a button to a toolbar.
AddDropDownItem	Adds an item to a drop-down form field.

(continued)

Table 34-1 *(continued)*

Command	What It Does
AddInState AddInState()	Loads a global template or add-in library.
AllCaps AllCaps()	Makes the selection all capitals (toggle).
AnnotationRefFromSel$()	Returns the annotation mark for the selection.
AppActivate	Activates an application.
AppClose	Closes an application.
AppCount()	Returns the number of open applications.
AppGetNames AppGetNames()	Obtains the names of open applications.
AppHide	Hides an application.
AppInfo$()	Returns information about an application.
AppIsRunning()	Determines whether an application is running.
AppMaximize AppMaximize()	Enlarges the application window to full size.
AppMinimize AppMinimize()	Minimizes the application window to an icon.
AppMove	Changes the position of the application window.
AppRestore AppRestore()	Restores the application window to normal size.
AppSendMessage	Sends a Windows message to an application.
AppShow	Shows a hidden application.
AppSize	Changes the size of the application window.
AppWindowHeight AppWindowHeight()	Adjusts the height of an application window.
AppWindowPosLeft AppWindowPosLeft()	Adjusts the left position of a window.
AppWindowPosTop AppWindowPosTop()	Adjusts the top position of a window.
AppWindowWidth AppWindowWidth()	Adjusts the width of a window.
Asc()	Returns the character code for a single character.
AtEndOfDocument()	Returns true if positioned at the end of the document.
AtStartOfDocument()	Returns true if positioned at the start of the document.

Command	*What It Does*
AutoMarkIndexEntries	Inserts index entries by using an automark file.
AutomaticChange	Automatically makes changes suggested by the Tip Wizard.
AutoText	Creates or inserts an AutoText entry depending on the selection.
AutoTextName$()	Returns the name of an AutoText entry.
Beep	Sounds a tone on the computer's speaker.
Begin Dialog...End Dialog	Marks a user-defined dialog box.
Bold Bold()	Makes the selection bold (toggle).
BookmarkName$()	Returns the name of a bookmark.
BorderBottom BorderBottom()	Changes the bottom border of the selected paragraphs, table cells, and pictures.
BorderInside BorderInside()	Changes the inside borders of the selected paragraphs, table cells, and pictures.
BorderLeft BorderLeft()	Changes the left border of the selected paragraphs, table cells, and pictures.
BorderLineStyle BorderLineStyle()	Changes border line styles of the selected paragraphs, table cells, and pictures.
BorderNone BorderNone()	Removes borders from the selected paragraphs, table cells, and pictures.
BorderOutside BorderOutside()	Changes the outside borders of the selected paragraphs, table cells, and pictures.
BorderRight BorderRight()	Changes the right border of the selected paragraphs, table cells, and pictures.
BorderTop BorderTop()	Changes the top borders of the selected paragraphs, table cells, and pictures.
Call	Calls a user-written subroutine.
Cancel	Terminates an action.
CancelButton	Defines a Cancel button in a dialog box.
CenterPara CenterPara()	Centers the paragraph between the indents.
ChangeCase ChangeCase()	Changes the case of the letters in the selection.
CharColor CharColor()	Sets the color of the selected characters.
CharLeft CharLeft()	Moves the insertion point to the left one character.

(continued)

Table 34-1 *(continued)*

Command	What It Does
CharRight CharRight()	Moves the insertion point to the right one character.
ChDefaultDir	Changes one of Word's default directories.
ChDir	Changes the current directory.
CheckBox	Creates a check box control in a dialog box.
CheckBoxFormField	Inserts a check box form field.
ChooseButtonImage	**Selects a button image for a custom toolbar.**
Chr$()	Returns the character for a given ANSI code.
CleanString$()	Removes unprintable characters from a string.
ClearAddIns	Unloads all global templates and add-ins.
ClearFormField	Clears a form field.
Close	Closes a sequential file.
ClosePane	Closes the active window pane.
ClosePreview	Exits Print Preview.
CloseUpPara	Removes extra spacing above the selected paragraph.
CloseViewHeaderFooter	Returns to document text.
CmpBookmarks()	Compares two bookmarks.
ColumnSelect	Selects a columnar block of text.
ComboBox	Creates a combo box in a dialog box.
CommandValid()	Determines if a command is valid in the current context.
Connect	**Connects to a network drive.**
ControlRun	**Displays the Control Panel or the Clipboard.**
Converter$()	Returns the class name of a specified converter.
ConverterLookup()	Returns the file format for a given converter.
ConvertObject	**Converts or activates an object as another type.**
CopyBookmark	Copies a bookmark.
CopyButtonImage	Copies the image of the selected button to the Clipboard.
CopyFile	**Copies a file.**
CopyFormat	Copies the formatting of the selection to a specified location.
CopyText	Makes a copy of the selection at a specified location.

Command	What It Does
CountAddIns()	Returns the number of global templates and add-ins.
CountAutoCorrectExceptions()	Returns the number of exceptions listed in the AutoCorrect Exceptions dialog box.
CountAutoTextEntries()	Returns the number of AutoText entries.
CountBookmarks()	Returns the number of bookmarks.
CountDirectories()	Returns the number of subdirectories in a directory.
CountDocumentProperties()	Returns the number of document properties that are available.
CountDocumentVars()	Returns the number of document variables in a document.
CountFiles()	Returns the number of files in the most-recently-used list on the File menu.
CountFonts()	Returns the number of available fonts.
CountFoundFiles()	Returns the number of files found by FileFind.
CountKeys()	Returns the number of custom keyboard assignments.
CountLanguages()	Returns the number of available languages.
CountMacros()	Returns the number of macros.
CountMenuItems()	Returns the number of items on a menu.
CountMenus()	Returns the number of menus on the menu bar.
CountMergeFields()	Returns the number of merge fields in the data source.
CountStyles()	Returns the number of available styles.
CountToolbarButtons()	Returns the number of buttons on a toolbar.
CountToolbars()	Returns the number of toolbars.
CountToolsGrammarStatistics()	Returns the number of grammar statistics recorded by the `ToolsGrammar` command.
CountWindows()	Counts the number of open document and macro windows.
CreateSubdocument	Transforms the selected outline items into subdocuments.
Date$()	Converts a date serial number to a date string.
DateSerial()	Converts a date string to a date serial number.
DateValue()	Returns the serial number for a date string.
Day()	Returns the day of the month for a given date serial number.
Day360()	Calculates dates based on a 360-day year.

(continued)

Table 34-1 (continued)

Command	What It Does
DDEExecute	Sends a command to an application via DDE.
DDEInitiate	Initiates a DDE exchange.
DDEPoke	Sends data to an application via DDE.
DDERequest	Requests information from an application via DDE.
DDETerminate	Closes a DDE channel.
DDETerminateAll	Closes all DDE channels.
Declare	Declares a Windows API routine.
DefaultDir$()	Returns the path for any of 16 different default locations.
DeleteAddIn	Deletes a global template or an add-in.
DeleteBackWord	Deletes the previous word without putting it on the Clipboard.
DeleteButton	Deletes a button in a dynamic dialog box.
DeleteDocumentProperty	Deletes a custom document property.
DeleteWord	Deletes the next word without putting it on the Clipboard.
DemoteList	Demotes the selection one level.
DemoteToBodyText	Applies the Normal style and converts the selected headings to body text.
Dialog Dialog()	Creates a user-defined dialog box.
DialogEditor	Opens the macro Dialog Editor.
Dim	Defines an array, dialog record, or shared variable.
DisableAutoMacros	Disables AutoOpen, AutoClose, AutoNew, AutoExit.
DisableInput	Ignores the Esc key during macro execution.
DlgControlId()	Returns the ID of a dialog control.
DlgEnable DlgEnable()	Enables a dialog box control.
DlgFilePreview DlgFilePreview()	Previews a file in a dialog box.
DlgFocus DlgFocus()	Sets the focus to a dialog box control.
DlgListBoxArray DlgListBoxArray()	Fills a list box with values from an array.

Command	*What It Does*
DlgSetPicture	Sets the graphic for a dialog box picture control.
DlgText DlgText()	Sets the text for a dialog box control.
DlgUpdateFilePreview	Updates a file preview control.
DlgValue DlgValue()	Sets the value for a dialog box control.
DlgVisible DlgVisible()	Shows or hides a dialog box control.
DocClose	Prompts to save the document and then closes the active window.
DocMaximize DocMaximize()	Enlarges the active window to full size.
DocMinimize DocMinimize()	Minimizes the active window to an icon.
DocMove	Changes the position of the active window.
DocRestore	Restores the window to normal size.
DocSize	Changes the size of the active window.
DocSplit DocSplit()	Splits the active window horizontally and then adjusts the split.
DocumentHasMisspellings()	Determines whether any uncorrected spelling errors are present in the document.
DocumentPropertyExists()	Determines if a specified document property exists.
DocumentPropertyName$()	Returns the name of a document property.
DocumentPropertyType()	Returns the type of a document property.
DocumentProtection()	Returns the level of protection in place for the current document.
DocumentStatistics	**Displays the statistics of the active document.**
DocWindowHeight DocWindowHeight()	Adjusts the height of a document window.
DocWindowPosLeft DocWindowPosLeft()	Adjusts the left position of a document window.
DocWindowPosTop DocWindowPosTop()	Adjusts the top position of a document window.
DocWindowWidth DocWindowWidth()	Adjusts the width of a document window.
DoFieldClick	Executes the action associated with the button fields.

(continued)

Table 34-1 (continued)

Command	What It Does
DOSToWin$()	Translates a string from DOS character set to Windows character set.
DottedUnderline DottedUnderline()	Underlines the selection with dots (toggle).
DoubleUnderline DoubleUnderline()	Double underlines the selection (toggle).
DrawAlign	**Aligns the selected drawing objects with one another or the page.**
DrawArc	Inserts an arc drawing object.
DrawBringForward	Brings the selected drawing objects forward.
DrawBringInFrontOfText	Brings the selected drawing objects forward one layer.
DrawBringToFront	Brings the selected drawing objects to the front.
DrawCallout	Inserts a callout drawing object.
DrawClearRange	Clears the drawing range.
DrawCount()	Returns the number of drawing objects anchored in a drawing range.
DrawCountPolyPoints()	Returns the number of points in a drawing object.
DrawDisassemblePicture	Disassembles the selected metafile picture into drawing objects.
DrawEllipse	Inserts an ellipse drawing object.
DrawExtendSelect	Selects a drawing object.
DrawFlipHorizontal	Flips the selected drawing objects from left to right.
DrawFlipVertical	Flips the selected drawing objects from top to bottom.
DrawFreeformPolygon	Inserts a freeform drawing object.
DrawGetCalloutTextbox	Determines the boundary coordinates for a callout textbox.
DrawGetPolyPoints	Obtains the coordinates for the endpoints of a drawing object.
DrawGetType()	Returns the drawing type for an object.
DrawGroup	Groups the selected drawing objects.
DrawInsertWordPicture	Opens a separate window for creating a picture object or inserts the selected drawing objects into a picture.
DrawLine	Inserts a line drawing object.

Command	*What It Does*
DrawNudgeDown	Moves the selected drawing objects down.
DrawNudgeDownPixel	Moves the selected drawing objects down one pixel.
DrawNudgeLeft	Moves the selected drawing objects to the left.
DrawNudgeLeftPixel	Moves the selected drawing objects to the left one pixel.
DrawNudgeRight	Moves the selected drawing objects to the right.
DrawNudgeRightPixel	Moves the selected drawing objects to the right one pixel.
DrawNudgeUp	Moves the selected drawing objects up.
DrawNudgeUpPixel	Moves the selected drawing objects up one pixel.
DrawRectangle	Inserts a rectangle drawing object.
DrawResetWordPicture	Sets document margins to enclose all drawing objects on the page.
DrawReshape	Displays resizing handles on selected freeform drawing objects. Drags a handle to reshape the object.
DrawRotateLeft	Rotates the selected drawing objects 90 degrees to the left.
DrawRotateRight	Rotates the selected drawing objects 90 degrees to the right.
DrawRoundRectangle	Inserts a rounded rectangle drawing object.
DrawSelect DrawSelect()	Selects a drawing object.
DrawSelectNext	Selects the next drawn object.
DrawSelectPrevious	Selects the previous drawn object.
DrawSendBackward	Sends the selected drawing objects backward.
DrawSendBehindText	Sends the selected drawing objects back one layer.
DrawSendToBack	Sends the selected drawing objects to the back.
DrawSetCalloutBox	Sets the coordinates of a callout box.
DrawSetInsertToAnchor	Moves the insertion point to the paragraph where an object is anchored.
DrawSetInsertToTextbox	Moves the insertion point to the text area of a text box or callout box.
DrawSetPolyPoints	Sets the coordinates of the endpoints of an object.
DrawSetRange DrawSetRange()	Sets the drawing range.
DrawSnapToGrid	**Sets up a grid for aligning drawing objects.**

(continued)

Table 34-1 *(continued)*

Command	What It Does
DrawTextbox	Inserts a text box drawing object.
DrawUngroup	Ungroups the selected group of drawing objects.
DrawUnselect	Unselects a drawn object.
DropDownFormField	Inserts a drop-down form field.
DropListBox	Creates a drop-down list box in a dialog box.
EditAutoText	**Inserts or defines AutoText entries.**
EditBookmark	**Assigns a name to the selection.**
EditButtonImage	Edits the image on the selected button.
EditClear	Performs a forward delete or removes the selection without putting it on the Clipboard.
EditConvertAllEndnotes	Converts all endnotes into footnotes.
EditConvertAllFootnotes	Converts all footnotes into endnotes.
EditConvertNotes	Converts selected footnotes into endnotes, or converts selected endnotes into footnotes.
EditCopy	Copies the selection and puts it on the Clipboard.
EditCopyAsPicture	Copies the selection and puts it on the Clipboard as a picture.
EditCut	Cuts the selection and puts it on the Clipboard.
EditFind	**Finds the specified text or the specified formatting.**
EditFindClearFormatting	Clears the formats in the Find dialog box.
EditFindFont	**Sets up EditFind or EditReplace to search for a specific font.**
EditFindFound()	Indicates whether the most recent EditFind was successful.
EditFindHighlight	Finds text that is highlighted.
EditFindLang	**Sets the language for EditFind or EditReplace.**
EditFindNotHighlight	Finds text that is not highlighted.
EditFindPara	**Sets the paragraph formatting for EditFind or EditReplace.**
EditFindStyle	**Sets the style formatting for EditFind or EditReplace.**
EditGoTo	**Jumps to a specified place in the active document.**

Command	*What It Does*
EditLinks	**Allows links to be viewed, updated, opened, or removed.**
EditObject	**Opens the selected object for editing.**
EditPaste	Inserts the Clipboard contents at the insertion point.
EditPasteSpecial	**Inserts the Clipboard contents as a linked object, embedded object, or other format.**
EditPicture	Uses the specified drawing application to edit the selected picture.
EditRedo	Redoes the last action that was undone.
EditRepeat	Repeats the last action.
EditReplace	**Finds the specified text or the specified formatting and replaces it.**
EditReplaceClearFormatting	Clears the formats for replacement text.
EditReplaceFont	**Sets the replacement font.**
EditReplaceHighlight	Replaces text that is highlighted.
EditReplaceLang	Sets the replacement language.
EditReplaceNotHighlight	Replaces text that is not highlighted.
EditReplacePara	Sets the replacement paragraph formatting.
EditReplaceStyle	Sets the replacement style.
EditSelectAll	Selects the entire document.
EditSwapAllNotes	Changes all footnotes to endnotes and all endnotes to footnotes.
EditTOACategory	Modifies the category names for the table of authorities.
EditUndo	Reverses the last action.
EmptyBookmark()	Determines whether a bookmark is empty.
EnableFormField	Enables a form field.
EndOfColumn EndOfColumn()	Moves the insertion point to the last cell in the current column.
EndOfDocument EndOfDocument()	Moves the insertion point to the end of the last line of the document.
EndOfLine EndOfLine()	Moves the insertion point to the end of the current line.
EndOfRow EndOfRow()	Moves the insertion point to the last cell in the current row.
EndOfWindow EndOfWindow()	Moves the insertion point to the end of the last visible line on the screen.

(continued)

Table 34-1 *(continued)*

Command	What It Does
EndOfWindowExtend	Extends the selection to the end of the last visible line on the screen.
Environ$()	Returns the MS-DOS environment string.
Eof$()	Determines when the end of a sequential file has been reached.
Err	Sets the error code.
Error	Raises an error condition.
ExistingBookmark()	Determines whether a bookmark exists.
ExitWindows	Quits Windows.
ExtendMode()	Determines if Extend Selection mode is on.
ExtendSelection	Turns on Extend Selection mode and then expands the selection with the direction keys.
FieldSeparator$ FieldSeparator$()	Sets the field separator used by the TextToTable command.
FileClose	Closes all of the windows of the active document.
FileCloseAll	Closes all of the windows of all documents.
FileClosePicture	Closes the picture editing window.
FileConfirmConversions FileConfirmConversions()	Toggles asking the user to confirm the conversion when opening a file.
FileExit	Quits Microsoft Word and prompts to save the documents.
FileFind	Locates the documents in any directory, drive, or folder.
FileList	Opens one of the files in the recently used file list on the File menu.
FileName$()	Returns the filename of the active document.
FileNameFromWindow$()	Obtains the filename for a specified window.
FileNameInfo$()	Returns information extracted from a filename.
FileNew	Creates a new document or template.
FileNewDefault	Creates a new document based on the NORMAL template.
File*number*	Opens the selected file from the recently used list.
FileOpen	Opens an existing document or template.
FilePageSetup	Changes the page setup of the selected sections.

Command	What It Does
FilePost	Puts the active document into an Exchange folder.
FileProperties	Displays the Properties dialog box.
FilePreview	Previews a file.
FilePrint	Prints the active document.
FilePrintDefault	Prints the active document using the current defaults.
FilePrintPreview FilePrintPreview()	Displays full pages as they will be printed.
FilePrintPreviewFullScreen	Toggles the full screen.
FilePrintPreviewPages FilePrintPreviewPages()	Displays one or two pages in Print Preview mode.
FilePrintSetup	Changes the printer and the printing options.
FileProperties	Shows the properties of the active document.
FileRoutingSlip	Adds or changes the electronic mail routing slip of the active document.
Files$()	Returns a filename that matches a wildcard spec.
FileSave	Saves the active document or template.
FileSaveAll	Saves all open files, macros, and AutoText entries, prompting for each one separately.
FileSaveAs	Saves a copy of the document in a separate file.
FileSendMail	Sends the active document through electronic mail.
FileSummaryInfo	Shows the summary information about the active document.
FileTemplates	Changes the active template and the template options.
Font Font()	Changes the font of the selection.
FontSize FontSize()	Sets the font size of the selection.
FontSizeSelect	Changes the font size of the selection.
FontSubstitution	Changes the document's font mapping.
For...Next	Loops through a set of instructions, incrementing a variable on each iteration.
FormatAddrFonts	Formats the delivery address font for envelopes.
FormatAutoFormat	Automatically formats a document.
FormatBordersAndShading	Changes the borders and shading of the selected paragraphs, table cells, and pictures.
FormatBullet	Adds bullets to selected paragraphs.

(continued)

Table 34-1 (continued)

Command	What It Does
FormatBulletDefault	Creates a bulleted list based on the current defaults.
FormatBulletsAndNumbering	Creates a numbered or bulleted list.
FormatCallout	Formats the selected callouts or sets callout defaults.
FormatChangeCase	Changes the case of the letters in the selection.
FormatColumns	Changes the column format of the selected sections.
FormatDefineStyleBorders	Sets the border and shading format for styles.
FormatDefineStyleFont	Sets the font for styles.
FormatDefineStyleFrame	Sets the frame for styles.
FormatDefineStyleLang	Sets the language for styles.
FormatDefineStyleNumbers	Sets the number format for styles.
FormatDefineStylePara	Sets the paragraph format for styles.
FormatDefineStyleTabs	Sets the tabs for styles.
FormatDrawingObject	Changes the fill, line, size, and position attributes of the selected drawing objects.
FormatDropCap	Formats the first character of current paragraph as a dropped capital.
FormatFont	Changes the appearance of the selected characters.
FormatFrame	Changes the options for frame formatting.
FormatHeaderFooterLink	Links this header/footer to the previous section.
FormatHeadingNumber	Applies heading numbers.
FormatHeadingNumbering	Changes numbering options for heading level styles.
FormatMultilevel	Sets options for multilevel headings.
FormatNumber	Creates a numbered list.
FormatNumberDefault FormatNumberDefault()	Creates a numbered list using default settings.
FormatPageNumber	Changes the appearance of page numbers.
FormatParagraph	Changes the appearance and line numbering of the selected paragraphs.
FormatPicture	Changes the picture scaling, size, and cropping information.
FormatRetAddrFonts	Formats the return address font for envelopes.
FormatSectionLayout	Changes the page format of the selected sections.
FormatStyle	Applies, creates, or modifies styles.

Command	*What It Does*
FormatStyleGallery	Applies styles from templates.
FormatTabs	Sets and clears the tab stops for the selected paragraphs.
FormFieldOptions	Changes the options for a form field.
FormShading	Changes shading options for the current form.
FoundFileName$()	Returns the name of a file found by the `FileFind` command.
Function...End Function	Marks the beginning and end of a user-defined function.
GetAddInID()	Obtains the ID of a global template or add-in.
GetAddInName$()	Obtains the name of a global template or add-in.
GetAddress$()	Retrieves an address from an Address Book.
GetAttr()	Obtains file attributes.
GetAutoCorrect$()	Obtains AutoCorrect replacement text.
GetAutoCorrectException$()	Obtains an AutoCorrect exception.
GetAutoText$()	Obtains AutoText replacement text.
GetBookmark$()	Obtains the text for a bookmark.
GetCurValues	Obtains the current values from a dialog record.
GetDirectory$()	Returns the name of a subdirectory.
GetDocumentVar$()	Returns the value of a document variable.
GetDocumentName$()	Returns the name of a document variable.
GetDocumentProperty() GetDocumentProperty$()	Obtains a document property setting.
GetFieldData$()	Obtains data from an ADDIN field.
GetFormResult() GetFormResult$()	Obtains result values from a form field.
GetMergeFields$()	Obtains data for a merge field.
GetPrivateProfileString$()	Obtains a value from the registry.
GetProfileString$()	Obtains a value from the registry.
GetSelEndPos()	Returns the character position of the last character in the selection.
GetSelStartPos()	Returns the character position of the first character in the selection.
GetSystemInfo() GetSystemInfo$()	Obtains information about the system.
GetText$()	Obtains text from the document.

(continued)

Table 34-1 *(continued)*

Command	What It Does
GoBack	Returns to the previous insertion point.
Goto	Jumps to a label.
GotoAnnotationScope	Highlights the text associated with an annotation reference mark.
GoToHeaderFooter	Jumps between a header and footer.
GoToNextAnnotation	Jumps to the next annotation in the active document.
GoToNextEndnote	Jumps to the next endnote in the active document.
GoToNextFootnote	Jumps to the next footnote in the active document.
GoToNextPage	Jumps to the next page in the active document.
GoToNextSection	Jumps to the next section in the active document.
GoToPreviousAnnotation	Jumps to the previous annotation in the active document.
GoToPreviousEndnote	Jumps to the previous endnote in the active document.
GoToPreviousFootnote	Jumps to the previous footnote in the active document.
GoToPreviousPage	Jumps to the previous page in the active document.
GoToPreviousSection	Jumps to the previous section in the active document.
GrowFont	Increases the font size of the selection.
GrowFontOnePoint	Increases the font size of the selection by one point.
Help	Locates Help topics based on an entered question or request.
HelpAbout	Displays the program information, Word version number, and the copyright.
HelpMSN	Connects to a desired forum on The Microsoft Network.
HelpPSSHelp	Displays information about the support available for Microsoft Word.
HelpTipOfTheDay	Displays a Word Tip of the Day.
HelpTool	Lets you obtain help on a command or screen region or examine text properties.
HelpUsingHelp	Displays the instructions for how to use Help.
HelpWordPerfectHelp	Shows the equivalent for a WordPerfect command.
HelpWordPerfectHelpOptions	Customizes WordPerfect Help.

Command	What It Does
Hidden Hidden()	Makes the selection hidden text (toggle).
Highlight	Applies color highlighting to the selection.
HighlightColor HighlightColor()	Sets the highlight color.
HLine	Scrolls horizontally.
Hour()	Returns the hour for a date serial number.
HPage	Scrolls horizontally one page at a time.
HScroll HScroll()	Scrolls horizontally.
If...Then...Else	Sets up conditional processing.
Indent	Moves the left indent to the next tab stop.
Input	Reads data from the status bar or a file.
Input$()	Reads a specific number of characters from a sequential file.
InputBox$()	Obtains input from a standard dialog box.
Insert	Inserts text into the document.
InsertAddCaption	Adds a new caption type.
InsertAddress	Inserts an address from your Personal Address Book.
InsertAnnotation	Inserts a comment and opens the annotation pane.
InsertAutoCaption	Defines which objects are inserted with a caption.
InsertAutoText	Replaces the name of the AutoText entry with its contents.
InsertBreak	Ends a page, column, or section at the insertion point.
InsertCaption	Inserts a caption above or below a selected object.
InsertCaptionNumbering	Sets the number for a caption type.
InsertChart	Inserts a Microsoft Graph object.
InsertColumnBreak	Inserts a column break at the insertion point.
InsertCrossReference	Inserts a cross-reference.
InsertDatabase	Inserts information from an external data source into the active document.
InsertDateField	Inserts a date field.
InsertDateTime	Inserts the current date and/or time into the active document.
InsertDrawing	Inserts a Microsoft Draw object.

(continued)

Table 34-1 *(continued)*

Command	What It Does
InsertEquation	Inserts a Microsoft Equation object.
InsertExcelTable	Inserts a Microsoft Excel worksheet object.
InsertField	Inserts a field in the active document.
InsertFieldChars	Inserts a field with the enclosing field characters.
InsertFile	Inserts the text of another file into the active document.
InsertFootnote	Inserts a footnote or endnote reference at the insertion point.
InsertFormField	Inserts a new form field.
InsertFrame	Inserts an empty frame or encloses the selected item in a frame.
InsertIndex	Collects the index entries into an index.
InsertMergeField	Inserts a mail merge field at the insertion point.
InsertObject	Inserts an equation, chart, drawing, or some other object.
InsertPageBreak	Inserts a page break at the insertion point.
InsertPageField	Inserts a page number field.
InsertPageNumbers	Adds page numbers to the top or the bottom of the pages.
InsertPara	Inserts a paragraph mark.
InsertPicture	Inserts a picture from a graphics file.
InsertSectionBreak	Ends a section at the insertion point.
InsertSound	Inserts a sound object into the document.
InsertSpike	Empties the spike AutoText entry and inserts all of its contents into the document.
InsertSubdocument	Opens a file and inserts it as a subdocument in a master document.
InsertSymbol	Inserts a special character.
InsertTableOfAuthorities	Collects the table of authorities entries into a table of authorities.
InsertTableOfContents	Collects the headings or the table of contents entries into a table of contents.
InsertTableOfFigures	Collects captions into a table of figures.
InsertTimeField	Inserts a time field.

Command	What It Does
InsertWordArt	Inserts a Microsoft WordArt object.
InStr()	Locates one string within another.
Int()	Rounds to an integer value.
IsAutoCorrectException()	Determines whether a string appears in the list of AutoCorrect exceptions.
IsCustomDocumentProperty()	Determines whether a document property is a custom property.
IsDocumentDirty()	Determines whether the document has been changed since it was last saved.
IsDocumentPropertyReadOnly()	Determines whether a document property is read-only.
IsExecuteOnly()	Determines if a macro has been encrypted.
IsMacro()	Determines if a specified window is a macro window.
IsTemplateDirty	Determines whether the template has changed since it was last saved.
Italic Italic()	Makes the selection italic (toggle).
JustifyPara JustifyPara()	Aligns the paragraph at both the left and the right indent.
KeyCode()	Returns the number representing a custom key assignment.
KeyMacro$()	Returns the name of the macro assigned to a key.
Kill	Deletes a file.
Language Language()	Sets the language for a text selection.
Lcase$()	Converts to lowercase.
Left$()	Returns the leftmost characters of a string.
LeftPara LeftPara()	Aligns the paragraph at the left indent.
Len()	Returns the length of a string.
Let	Returns optional keyword on assignment statements.
Line Input	Reads an entire line from a text file.
LineDown LineDown()	Moves the insertion point down one line.
LineUp LineUp()	Moves the insertion point up one line.
ListBox	Creates a list box in a user-defined dialog box.

(continued)

Table 34-1 *(continued)*

Command	What It Does
LockDocument LockDocument()	Toggles the file lock state of a document.
LockFields	Locks the selected fields to prevent updating.
Lof()	Returns the length of an open file.
Ltrim$()	Removes space from the left of a string.
MacroCopy	Copies a macro from one template to another.
MacroDesc$()	Returns the description text of a macro.
MacroFileName$()	Returns the name of the template that contains the specified macro.
MacroName$()	Returns the name of a macro.
MacroNameFromWindow$()	Returns the name of the macro in the specified window.
Magnifier Magnifier()	Toggles zoom-in, zoom-out mode.
MailCheckNames	Validates names against an Address Book.
MailHideMessageHeader	Shows or hides the message header.
MailMerge	Combines files to produce form letters, mailing labels, envelopes, and catalogs.
MailMergeAskToConvertChevrons MailMergeAskToConvertChevrons()	Toggles asking the user about converting Word for the Macintosh mail merge chevrons.
MailMergeCheck	Checks for errors in a mail merge.
MailMergeConvertChevrons MailMergeConvertChevrons()	Toggles converting Word for the Macintosh mail merge chevrons.
MailMergeCreateDataSource	Creates a new mail merge data source.
MailMergeCreateHeaderSource	Creates a new mail merge header source.
MailMergeDataForm	Edits a list or table in a form.
MailMergeDataSource$()	Returns information about the data source.
MailMergeEditDataSource	Opens a mail merge data source.
MailMergeEditHeaderSource	Opens a mail merge header source.
MailMergeEditMainDocument	Switches to a mail merge main document.
MailMergeFindRecord	Finds a specified record in a mail merge data source.
MailMergeFirstRecord	Displays the first record in the active mail merge data source.
MailMergeFoundRecord()	Indicates whether the record was found.

Command	What It Does
MailMergeGoToRecord MailMergeGoToRecord()	Displays the specified record in the active mail merge data source.
MailMergeHelper	Prepares a main document for a mail merge.
MailMergeInsertAsk	Inserts a Word Ask field at the insertion point.
MailMergeInsertFillIn	Inserts a Word Fillin field at the insertion point.
MailMergeInsertIf	Inserts a Word Field at the insertion point.
MailMergeInsertMergeRec	Inserts a Word Record field at the insertion point.
MailMergeInsertMergeSeq	Inserts a Word Sequence field at the insertion point.
MailMergeInsertNext	Inserts a Word Next field at the insertion point.
MailMergeInsertNextIf	Inserts a Word Next if field at the insertion point.
MailMergeInsertSet	Inserts a Word Set field at the insertion point.
MailMergeInsertSkipIf	Inserts a Word Skip if field at the insertion point.
MailMergeLastRecord	Displays the last record in the active mail merge data source.
MailMergeMainDocumentType MailMergeMainDocumentType()	Makes the active window a main document.
MailMergeNextRecord	Displays the next record in the active mail merge data source.
MailMergeOpenDataSource	Opens a data source for mail merge or database.
MailMergeOpenHeaderSource	Opens a header source for mail merge.
MailMergePrevRecord	Displays the previous record in the active mail merge data source.
MailMergeQueryOptions	Sets the query options for a mail merge.
MailMergeReset	Resets a mail merge main document to a normal document.
MailMergeState()	Returns the current state of a mail merge setup.
MailMergeToDoc	Collects the results of the mail merge in a document.
MailMergeToPrinter	Sends the results of the mail merge to the printer.
MailMergeUseAddressBook	Opens an address book as a data source for mail merge.
MailMergeViewData() MailMergeViewData	Toggles between viewing merge fields and actual data.
MailMessageDelete	Deletes a mail message.
MailMessageForward	Forwards a mail message.
MailMessageMove	Moves a mail message.
MailMessageNext	Goes to the next mail message.

(continued)

Table 34-1 *(continued)*

Command	What It Does
MailMessagePrevious	Goes to the previous mail message.
MailMessageProperties	Sets the properties of the mail message.
MailMessageReply	Replies to a mail message.
MailMessageReplyAll	Replies All to a mail message.
MailSelectNames	Selects the recipients of a mail message.
MarkCitation	Marks the text you want to include in the table of authorities.
MarkIndexEntry	Marks the text you want to include in the index.
MarkTableOfContentsEntry	Marks the text you want to include in the table of contents.
MenuItemMacro$()	Returns the macro assigned to a menu item.
MenuItemText$()	Returns the text assigned to a menu item.
MenuMode	Makes the menu bar active.
MenuText$()	Returns the text assigned to a menu.
MergeFieldName$()	Returns the name of a merge field.
MergeSubdocument	Merges two adjacent subdocuments into one subdocument.
MicrosoftAccess	Starts or switches to Microsoft Access.
MicrosoftExcel	Starts or switches to Microsoft Excel.
MicrosoftFoxPro	Starts or switches to Microsoft FoxPro.
MicrosoftMail	Starts or switches to Microsoft Mail.
MicrosoftPowerPoint	Starts or switches to Microsoft PowerPoint.
MicrosoftProject	Starts or switches to Microsoft Project.
MicrosoftPublisher	Starts or switches to Microsoft Publisher.
MicrosoftSchedule	Starts or switches to Microsoft Schedule+.
MicrosoftSystemInfo	Executes the Microsoft System Info application.
Mid$()	Extracts data from the middle of a string.
Minute()	Returns the minute for a date serial number.
MkDir	Makes a new folder.
Month()	Returns the month for a date serial number.
MoveButton	Moves a toolbar button.

Command	What It Does
MoveText	Moves the selection to a specified location.
MsgBox MsgBox()	Displays a message in a dialog box.
Name	Renames a file.
NewToolbar	Creates a new toolbar.
NextCell NextCell()	Moves the insertion point to the next table cell.
NextField NextField()	Moves the insertion point to the next field.
NextMisspelling	Finds the next spelling error.
NextObject	Moves the insertion point to the next object on the page.
NextPage NextPage()	Moves the insertion point to the next page.
NextTab()	Returns the position of the next tab stop.
NextWindow	Switches to the next document window.
NormalFontPosition	Removes the raised or lowered font attribute.
NormalFontSpacing	Removes the expanded or condensed font attribute.
NormalStyle	Applies the Normal style.
NormalViewHeaderArea	Shows a list of headers and footers for editing.
NoteOptions	Changes the options for footnotes or endnotes.
Now()	Returns the serial number of the current date and time.
OK	Confirms a location for copying or moving the selection.
OKButton	Creates an OK button in a user dialog box.
On Error	Sets up an error handler.
On Time	Sets up a timer event.
Open	Opens a text file.
OpenSubdocument	Opens a subdocument in a new window.
OpenUpPara	Sets extra spacing above the selected paragraph.
OptionButton	Creates an option button in a dialog box.
OptionGroup	Creates an option group in a dialog box.
Organizer	Manages AutoText entries, styles, macros, and toolbars.
OtherPane	Switches to the other window pane.

(continued)

Table 34-1 *(continued)*

Command	What It Does
OutlineCollapse	Hides the lowest subtext of the selection.
OutlineDemote	Demotes the selected paragraphs one heading level.
OutlineExpand	Displays the next level of subtext of the selection.
OutlineLevel()	Returns the outline level of the selection.
OutlineMoveDown	Moves the selection below the next item in the outline.
OutlineMoveUp	Moves the selection above the previous item in the outline.
OutlinePromote	Promotes the selected paragraphs one heading level.
OutlineShowFirstLine OutlineShowFirstLine()	Toggles between showing the first line of each paragraph only or showing all of the body text in the outline.
OutlineShowFormat	Toggles the display of character formatting in Outline view.
Overtype Overtype()	Toggles the typing mode between replacing and inserting.
PageDown PageDown()	Moves the insertion point and document display to the next screen of text.
PageUp PageUp()	Moves the insertion point and document display to the previous screen of text.
ParaDown ParaDown()	Moves the insertion point to the beginning of the next paragraph.
ParaKeepLinesTogether ParaKeepLinesTogether()	Prevents a paragraph from splitting across page boundaries.
ParaKeepWithNext ParaKeepWithNext()	Keeps a paragraph and the following paragraph on the same page.
ParaPageBreakBefore ParaPageBreakBefore()	Makes the current paragraph start on a new page.
ParaUp ParaUp()	Moves the insertion point to the beginning of the previous paragraph.
ParaWidowOrphanControl ParaWidowOrphanControl()	Prevents a page break from leaving a single line of a paragraph on one page.
PasteButtonImage	Pastes the image on the Clipboard onto the selected button.
PasteFormat	Applies the previously copied formatting to selection.
PasteFromMacPath$()	Converts a Macintosh pathname.

Command	What It Does
PauseRecorder	Pauses the macro recorder (toggle).
Picture	Creates a picture control in a dialog box.
PrevCell PrevCell()	Moves the insertion point to the previous table cell.
PrevField PrevField()	Moves the insertion point to the previous field.
PrevObject	Moves the insertion point to the previous object on the page.
PrevPage PrevPage()	Moves the insertion point to the previous page.
PrevTab()	Returns the position of the previous tab stop.
PrevWindow	Switches back to the previous document window.
Print	Displays information in the status bar.
PromoteList	Promotes the selection one level.
PushButton	Creates a button in a dialog box.
PutFieldData	Stores data in an Addin field.
Read	Reads data from a text file.
Redim	Changes the dimensions of an array.
REM	Treats the entire line as a remark.
RemoveAllDropDownItems	Empties a drop-down list control.
RemoveBulletsNumbers	Removes numbers and bullets from the selection.
RemoveDropDownItem	Removes a drop-down item.
RemoveFrames	Removes frame formatting from the selection.
RemoveSubdocument	Merges the contents of the selected subdocuments into the master document that contains them.
RenameMenu	Changes the name of a menu.
RepeatFind	Repeats Goto or Find to locate the next occurrence.
ResetButtonImage	Resets the image on the selected button to the built-in image.
ResetChar ResetChar()	Makes the selection the default character format of the applied style.
ResetNoteSepOrNotice	Resets a separator, continuation separator, or continuation notice to the Word default.
ResetPara ResetPara()	Makes the selection the default paragraph format of the applied style.
Right$()	Returns the rightmost characters from a string.

(continued)

Table 34-1 *(continued)*

Command	What It Does
RightPara RightPara()	Aligns the paragraph at the right indent.
RmDir	Removes a directory.
Rnd()	Returns a random number.
Rtrim$()	Removes white space from the right of a string.
SaveTemplate	Saves the document template of the active document.
ScreenRefresh	Refreshes the display.
ScreenUpdating ScreenUpdating()	Controls how the screen is updated during macro execution.
Second()	Returns the seconds for a date serial.
Seek Seek()	Finds a record in a text file.
Select Case	Sets up conditional processing.
SelectCurAlignment	Selects all paragraphs with the same alignment.
SelectCurColor	Selects all characters with the same color.
SelectCurFont	Selects all characters with the same font name and point size.
SelectCurIndent	Selects all paragraphs with the same indentation.
SelectCurSpacing	Selects all paragraphs with the same line spacing.
SelectCurTabs	Selects all paragraphs with the same tabs.
SelectCurWord	Selects the current word.
SelectDrawingObjects	Selects drawing objects: drag to create a rectangle enclosing the objects.
Selection$()	Returns the current selection.
SelectionFileName$()	Returns the name of the file.
SelInfo()	Returns various items of information about a selection.
SelType SelType()	Indicates whether text is selected.
SendKeys	Sends keystrokes to another application.
SentLeft SentLeft()	Moves the insertion point to the beginning of the previous sentence.
SentRight SentRight()	Moves the insertion point to the beginning of the next sentence.

Command	What It Does
SetAttr	Sets file attributes.
SetAutoText	Sets an AutoText entry.
SetDocumentDirty	Sets the document as dirty (changed since last saved) so that a Close will prompt to save.
SetDocumentProperty	Sets a document property.
SetDocumentPropertyLink	Sets a document property that is linked to a bookmark.
SetDocumentVar SetDocumentVar()	Sets a document variable.
SetEndOfBookmark	Assigns a new bookmark to the end of an existing bookmark.
SetFormResult	Sets the result of a form field.
SetPrivateProfileString SetPrivateProfileString()	Assigns a value to a setting in the registry. (In previous versions of Word, this command is assigned a value to a line in a private INI file.)
SetProfileString SetProfileString()	Assigns a value to a setting in the registry. (In previous versions of Word, this command is assigned a value to a line in Win.ini.)
SetSelRange	Selects a range of characters based on their character position relative to the start of the document.
SetStartOfBookmark	Assigns a new bookmark to the beginning of an existing bookmark.
SetTemplateDirty	Specifies whether Word should consider the current document dirty: that is, changed since the last time it was saved.
Sgn()	Determines whether a number is negative, positive, or zero.
ShadingPattern ShadingPattern()	Changes shading pattern of the selected paragraphs, table cells, and pictures.
Shell	Starts another Windows application.
ShowAll ShowAll()	Shows/hides all nonprinting characters.
ShowAllHeadings	Displays all of the heading levels and the body text.
ShowAnnotationBy	Shows annotations created by a specific user.
ShowHeading1	Displays the level 1 headings only.
ShowHeading2	Displays the level 1 and 2 headings.
ShowHeading3	Displays the level 1 through 3 headings.

(continued)

Table 34-1 *(continued)*

Command	What It Does
ShowHeading4	Displays the level 1 through 4 headings.
ShowHeading5	Displays the level 1 through 5 headings.
ShowHeading6	Displays the level 1 through 6 headings.
ShowHeading7	Displays the level 1 through 7 headings.
ShowHeading8	Displays the level 1 through 8 headings.
ShowHeading9	Displays the level 1 through 9 headings.
ShowMe	Gives an in-depth explanation of the suggested tip.
ShowNextHeaderFooter	Shows the next section's header/footer in Page Layout view.
ShowPrevHeaderFooter	Shows the previous section's header/footer in Page Layout view.
ShowVars	Lists the active macro's variables.
ShrinkFont	Decreases the font size of the selection.
ShrinkFontOnePoint	Decreases the font size of the selection by one point.
ShrinkSelection	Shrinks the selection to the next smaller unit in the following order: document, section, paragraph, sentence, word, single point (no selection).
SizeToolbar	Changes the size of a toolbar.
SkipNumbering SkipNumbering()	Makes the selected paragraphs skip numbering.
SmallCaps SmallCaps()	Makes the selection small capitals (toggle).
SortArray	Sorts an array.
SpacePara1 SpacePara1()	Sets the line spacing to single space.
SpacePara15 SpacePara15()	Sets the line spacing to one and one-half space.
SpacePara2 SpacePara2()	Sets the line spacing to double space.
SpellChecked SpellChecked()	Identifies the selected text as either spell checked or not spell checked.
Spike	Deletes the selection and adds it to the special AutoText entry.

Command	*What It Does*
SplitSubdocument	Splits the selected part of a subdocument into another subdocument at the same level.
StartOfColumn StartOfColumn()	Moves the insertion point to the first cell in the current column.
StartOfDocument StartOfDocument()	Moves the insertion point to the beginning of the first line of the document.
StartOfLine StartOfLine()	Moves the insertion point to the beginning of the current line.
StartOfRow StartOfRow()	Moves the insertion point to the first cell in the current row.
StartOfWindow StartOfWindow()	Moves the insertion point to the beginning of the first visible line on the screen.
Stop	Stops the macro.
Str$()	Returns a string representing the numeric value of a variable. For example, Str$(3.1415) = " 3.1415" (note the leading space).
Strikethrough Strikethrough()	Makes the selection strikethrough (toggle).
String$()	Creates a string consisting of a specified number of a single character.
Style	Applies an existing style or records a style by example.
StyleDesc$()	Returns the description of a specified style.
StyleName$()	Returns the name of a specified style.
Sub...End Sub	Marks the beginning and end of a subroutine.
Subscript Subscript()	Makes the selection subscript (toggle).
Superscript Superscript()	Makes the selection superscript (toggle).
SymbolFont	Applies the Symbol font to the selection.
TabLeader$()	Returns the leader tab for a tab stop.
TableAutoFormat	**Applies a set of formatting to a table.**
TableAutoSum	**Inserts an expression field that automatically sums a table row or column.**
TableColumnWidth	**Changes the width of the columns in a table.**
TableDeleteCells	**Deletes selected cells.**
TableDeleteColumn	Deletes the selected columns from the table.

(continued)

Table 34-1 *(continued)*

Command	What It Does
TableDeleteRow	Deletes the selected rows from the table.
TableFormula	**Inserts a formula in a cell.**
TableFormula()	Inserts a formula field into a table cell.
TableGridlines TableGridlines()	Toggles table gridlines on and off.
TableHeadings TableHeadings()	Toggles the table headings attribute on and off.
TableInsertCells	**Inserts cells.**
TableInsertColumn	Inserts one or more columns into the table.
TableInsertRow	**Inserts one or more rows into the table.**
TableInsertTable	**Inserts a table.**
TableMergeCells	Merges the selected table cells into a single cell.
TableRowHeight	**Changes the height of the rows in a table.**
TableSelectColumn	Selects the current column in a table.
TableSelectRow	Selects the current row in a table.
TableSelectTable	Selects an entire table.
TableSort	**Rearranges the selection into a specified order.**
TableSort AToZ	Sorts records in ascending order (A to Z).
TableSort ZToA	Sorts records in descending order (Z to A).
TableSplit	Inserts a paragraph mark above the current row in the table.
TableSplitCells	**Splits the selected table cells.**
TableToText	**Converts the text to table form.**
TableUpdateAutoFormat	Updates the table formatting to match the applied formatting set.
TabType()	Returns the alignment for a tab stop.
Text	Creates a text label in a custom dialog box.
TextBox	Creates a text box in a custom dialog box.
TextFormField	Inserts a text form field.
TextToTable	**Converts selected text to a table.**
Time$()	Returns the time corresponding to a date serial number.
TimeSerial()	Returns a serial number for a specified time.

Command	What It Does
TimeValue()	Returns the serial number for a string that contains a time.
TipWizard	Shows or hides the TipWizard toolbar.
Today()	Returns the serial number of the current date.
ToggleFieldDisplay	Shows the field codes or the results for the selection (toggle).
ToggleFull	Toggles full screen mode on/off.
ToggleHeaderFooterLink	Links or unlinks this header/footer to or from the previous section.
ToggleMainTextLayer	Toggles showing the main text layer in Page Layout view.
TogglePortrait	**Toggles between portrait and landscape mode.**
ToggleScribbleMode	Inserts a pen annotation at the location of the insertion point.
ToolbarButtonMacro$()	Returns the name of the macro associated with a toolbar button.
ToolbarName$()	Returns the name of a specified toolbar.
ToolbarState()	Indicates whether a toolbar is displayed.
ToolsAddRecordDefault	Adds a record to a database.
ToolsAdvancedSettings	**Changes Word settings.**
ToolsAutoCorrect	**Adds or deletes AutoCorrect entries.**
ToolsAutoCorrectCapsLockOff ToolsAutoCorrectCapsLockOff()	Selects or clears the AutoCorrect Caps Lock Off check box.
ToolsAutoCorrectDays ToolsAutoCorrectDays()	Selects or clears the AutoCorrect Days check box.
ToolsAutoCorrectExceptions	Adds or deletes AutoCorrect Capitalization exceptions.
ToolsAutoCorrectInitialCaps ToolsAutoCorrectInitialCaps()	Selects or clears the AutoCorrect InitialCaps check box.
ToolsAutoCorrectReplaceText ToolsAutoCorrectReplaceText()	Selects or clears the AutoCorrect ReplaceText check box.
ToolsAutoCorrectSentenceCaps ToolsAutoCorrectSentenceCaps()	Selects or clears the AutoCorrect SentenceCaps check box.
ToolsAutoCorrectSmartQuotes ToolsAutoCorrectSmartQuotes()	Selects or clears the AutoCorrect SmartQuotes check box.
ToolsBulletListDefault	Creates a bulleted list based on the current defaults.
ToolsBulletsNumbers	**Changes the numbered and bulleted paragraphs.**

(continued)

Table 34-1 *(continued)*

Command	What It Does
ToolsCalculate ToolsCalculate()	Calculates expressions in the selection.
ToolsCompareVersions	**Compares the active document with an earlier version.**
ToolsCreateEnvelope	**Creates or prints an envelope.**
ToolsCreateLabels	**Creates or prints a label or a sheet of labels.**
ToolsCustomize	**Customizes the Word user interface (menus, keyboard, and toolbars).**
ToolsCustomizeKeyboard	**Customizes the Word key assignments.**
ToolsCustomizeMenuBar	**Customizes the Word menu bar.**
ToolsCustomizeMenus	**Customizes a menu.**
ToolsEnvelopesAndLabels	**Creates or prints an envelope, a label, or a sheet of labels.**
ToolsGetSpelling ToolsGetSpelling()	Returns an array of suggested spellings for a misspelled word.
ToolsGetSynonyms ToolsGetSynonyms()	Returns an array of synonyms for a word.
ToolsGrammar	Checks the grammar in the active document.
ToolsGrammarStatisticsArray	Returns an array of statistics generated by the grammar checker.
ToolsHyphenation	**Changes the hyphenation settings for the active document.**
ToolsHyphenationManual	Hyphenates the selection of the entire document.
ToolsLanguage	**Changes the language formatting of the selected characters.**
ToolsMacro	**Runs, creates, deletes, or revises a macro.**
ToolsManageFields	**Adds or deletes a field from a database.**
ToolsMergeRevisions	**Merges revisions from the active document to an earlier version.**
ToolsNumberListDefault	Creates a numbered list based on the current defaults.
ToolsOptions	**Displays the Options dialog box.**
ToolsOptionsAutoFormat	**Changes the AutoFormat options.**
ToolsOptionsCompatibility	**Changes the document compatibility options.**

Command	What It Does
ToolsOptionsEdit	**Changes the editing options.**
ToolsOptionsFileLocations	**Changes the default locations Word uses to find files.**
ToolsOptionsGeneral	**Changes the general options.**
ToolsOptionsGrammar	**Changes the grammar options.**
ToolsOptionsPrint	**Changes the printing options.**
ToolsOptionsRevisions	**Changes revision marking options.**
ToolsOptionsSave	**Changes the save settings.**
ToolsOptionsSpelling	**Changes the spelling options.**
ToolsOptionsUserInfo	**Changes the user information options.**
ToolsOptionsView	**Sets the specific view mode options.**
ToolsProtectDocument	**Sets the protection for the active document.**
ToolsProtectSection	**Sets the protection for a section or sections.**
ToolsRemoveRecordDefault	Removes a record from a database.
ToolsRepaginate	Recalculates the page breaks.
ToolsReviewRevisions	**Reviews revisions to the active document.**
ToolsRevisionAuthor$()	Returns the name of a specific revision.
ToolsRevisionDate()	Returns the serial number for the date a specific revision was made.
ToolsRevisionDate$()	Returns the date a specific revision was made as a string.
ToolsRevisions	**Sets revision marking for the active document.**
ToolsRevisionType()	Indicates whether the revision is an insertion or deletion.
ToolsShrinkToFit	Attempts to make the document fit on one less page.
ToolsSpelling	Checks the spelling in the active document.
ToolsSpellingRecheckDocument	Rechecks the document for spelling errors.
ToolsSpellSelection	Checks the spelling of the selected text.
ToolsThesaurus	Finds a synonym for the selected word.
ToolsUnprotectDocument	**Unprotects a document.**
ToolsWordCount	**Displays the word count statistics of the active document.**
UCase$	Converts a string to uppercase.

(continued)

Table 34-1 *(continued)*

Command	What It Does
Underline Underline()	Formats the selection with a continuous underline (toggle).
UnHang	Decreases the hanging indent.
UnIndent	Moves the left indent to the previous tab stop.
UnlinkFields	Permanently replaces the field codes with the results.
UnlockFields	Unlocks the selected fields for updating.
UpdateFields	Updates and displays the results of the selected fields.
UpdateSource	Copies the modified text of a linked file back to its source.
Val()	Returns the numeric value (ANSI code) for a character.
ViewAnnotations ViewAnnotations()	Opens the annotation pane for reading annotations (toggle).
ViewBorderToolbar	Shows or hides the Borders toolbar.
ViewDraft ViewDraft()	Displays the document without formatting and pictures for faster editing (toggle).
ViewDrawingToolbar	Shows or hides the Drawing toolbar.
ViewEndnoteArea ViewEndnoteArea()	Opens a pane for viewing and editing the endnotes (toggle).
ViewEndnoteContNotice	Opens a pane for viewing and editing the endnote continuation notice.
ViewEndnoteContSeparator	Opens a pane for viewing and editing the endnote continuation separator.
ViewEndnoteSeparator	Opens a pane for viewing and editing the endnote separator.
ViewFieldCodes ViewFieldCodes()	Shows the field codes or results for all fields (toggle).
ViewFooter ViewFooter()	Displays the footer in Page Layout view.
ViewFootnoteArea ViewFootnoteArea()	Opens a pane for viewing and editing the footnotes (toggle).
ViewFootnoteContNotice	Opens a pane for viewing and editing the footnote continuation notice.
ViewFootnoteContSeparator	Opens a pane for viewing and editing the footnote continuation separator.
ViewFootnotes ViewFootnotes()	Opens a pane for viewing and editing the footnotes (toggle).

Command	*What It Does*
ViewFootnoteSeparator	Opens a pane for viewing and editing the footnote separator.
ViewHeader ViewHeader()	Displays the header in Page Layout view.
ViewMasterDocument ViewMasterDocument()	Switches to Master Document view.
ViewMenus()	Indicates whether the full menu bar or the abbreviated no-document menu bar is displayed.
ViewNormal ViewNormal()	Changes the editing view to Normal view.
ViewOutline ViewOutline()	Displays a document's outline.
ViewPage ViewPage()	Displays the page as it will be printed and allows editing.
ViewRibbon ViewRibbon()	Displays or hides the Formatting toolbar. This is for compatibility with earlier versions.
ViewRuler ViewRuler()	Shows or hides the ruler.
ViewStatusBar ViewStatusBar()	Shows or hides the status bar.
ViewToggleMasterDocument	Switches between Outline and Master Document views.
ViewToolbars	**Shows or hides the Word toolbars.**
ViewZoom	**Scales the editing view.**
ViewZoom100	Scales the editing view to 100% in Normal view.
ViewZoom200	Scales the editing view to 200% in Normal view.
ViewZoom75	Scales the editing view to 75% in Normal view.
ViewZoomPageWidth	Scales the editing view to see the width of the page.
ViewZoomWholePage	Scales the editing view to see the whole Page in page Layout view.
VLine	Vertically scrolls a specified number of lines.
VPage	Vertically scrolls a specified number of pages.
VScroll VScroll()	Vertically scrolls by a percentage of the entire document.
WaitCursor	Switches to or from the dreaded hourglass cursor.
Weekday()	Returns a number representing the day of the week for a given date serial number.
While...Wend	Sends up a conditional loop.

(continued)

Table 34-1 *(continued)*

Command	What It Does
Window()	Returns the number of the current window.
WindowArrangeAll	Arranges windows as non overlapping tiles.
WindowList	Switches to the window containing the specified document.
Window*n*	Switches to the specified window.
WindowName$()	Returns the title of the specified window.
WindowNewWindow	Opens another window for the active document.
WindowPane()	Determines whether a window is split.
WinToDOS$()	Translates a string from DOS character set to Windows character set.
WordLeft WordLeft()	Moves the insertion point to the left one word.
WordRight WordRight()	Moves the insertion point to the right one word.
WordUnderline WordUnderline()	Underlines the words but not the spaces in the selection (toggle).
Write	Writes information to a text file.
Year()	Returns the year for a given date serial number.

WordBasic Commands and Functions by Category

The following lists show many of the WordBasic commands and functions arranged by category. The following is not intended to be a comprehensive list, but rather serves as a guide to helping you find the right command for common programming tasks.

String functions

```
Asc()              Right$()
Chr$()             RTrim$()
CleanString$()     Selection$()
InStr()            SortArray
Lcase$()           Str$()
Left$()            String$()
Len()              UCase$()
Ltrim$()           Val()
Mid$()
```

Numeric functions

```
Abs()       Sgn()
Int()       Val()
Rnd()
```

Cursor movement

```
AtEndOfDocument()              PageDown, PageDown()
AtStartOfDocument()            PageUp, PageUp()
CharLeft, CharLeft()
CharRight, CharRight()         ParaDown, ParaDown()
EndOfColumn, EndOfColumn()     ParaUp, ParaUp()
EndOfDocument, EndOfDocument() PrevField, PrevField()
EndOfLine, EndOfLine()         PrevObject
EndOfRow, EndOfRow()           PrevPage, PrevPage()
EndOfWindow, EndOfWindow()     PrevWindow
GetText$()                     SentLeft, SentLeft()
GoBack                         SentRight, SentRight()
GoToAnnotationScope            StartOfColumn,StartOfColumn()
GoToHeaderFooter               StartOfDocument,StartOfDocument()
GoToNextItem                   StartOfLine, StartOfLine()
GoToPreviousItem               StartOfRow, StartOfRow()
LineDown, LineDown()           WordLeft, WordLeft()
LineUp, LineUp()               WordRight, WordRight()
NextField, NextField()
```

Scrolling

```
VLine       HLine
VPage       HPage
VScroll, VScroll()   HScroll, HScroll()
```

Selecting

```
ColumnSelect        SelectCurSentence
EditSelectAll       SelectCurSpacing
ExtendMode          SelectCurTabs
ExtendSelection     SelectCurWords
GetSelEndPos()      SelType, SelType()
GetSelStartPos()    SetSelRange
SelectCurAlignment  ShrinkSelection
SelectCurColor
```

Table handling

```
Fieldseparator$, Fieldseparator$()     TableInsertRow
NextCell, NextCel()                     TableInsertTable
PrevCell, PrevCell()                    TableMergeCells
TableAutoFormat                         TableRowHeight
TableAutoSum                            TableSelectColumn
TableColumnWidth                        TableSelectRow
TableDeleteCells                        TableSelectTable
TableDeleteColumn                       TableSort
TableDeleteRow                          TableSortAToZ
TableFormula                            TableSortZToA
TableFormula()                          TableSplit
TableGridlines, TableGridlines()        TableSplitCells
TableHeadings, TableHeadings()          TableToText
TableInsertCells                        TableUpdateAutoFormat
TableInsertColumn                       TextToTable
```

Styles

```
CountStyles()                           FormatStyle
FormatDefineStyleBorders                FormatStyleGallery
FormatDefineStyleFont                   NormalStyle
FormatDefineStyleFrame                  Organizer
FormatDefineStyleLang                   Style
FormatDefineStyleNumbers                StyleDesc$()
FormatDefineStylePara                   StyleName$()
FormatDefineStyleTabs
```

Paragraph formatting

```
CenterPara, CenterPara()                JustifyPara
CloseUpPara                             JustifyPara()
CopyFormat                              LeftPara, LeftPara()
FormatBullet                            NextTab()
FormatBulletDefault                     OpenUpPara
FormatBulletDefault()                   ParaKeepLinesTogether
FormatDefineStyleNumbers                ParaKeepLinesTogether()
FormatDropCap                           ParaKeepWithNext
FormatNumberDefault                     ParaKeepWithNext()
FormatNumberDefault()                   ParaPageBreakBefore
FormatParagraph                         ParaPageBreakBefore()
FormatTabs                              ParaWidowOrphanControl
HangingIndent                           ParaWidowOrphanControl()
Indent                                  PasteFormat
InsertPara                              PrevTab()
```

(continued)

RemoveBulletsNumbers
ResetPara, ResetPara()
RightPara, RightPara()
SpacePara1, SpacePara1()
SpacePara15
SpacePara15()

SpacePara2
SpacePara2()
TabLeader$()
TabType()
UnHang
UnIndent

Character formatting

AllCaps, AllCaps()
Bold, Bold()
CharColor, CharColor()
CopyFormat
CountFonts()
CountLanguages()
DottedUnderline
DottedUnderline()
DoubleUnderline
DoubleUnderline()
Font, Font$()
FontSize, FontSize()
FontSizeSelect
FontSubstitution
FormatAddrFonts
FormatChangeCase
FormatDefineStyleFont
FormatDefineStyleLang
FormatFont
FormatRetAddrFonts
GrowFont

GrowFontOnePoint
Hidden, Hidden()
Italic, Italic()
Language, Language$()
NormalFontPosition
NormalFontSpacing
PasteFormat
ResetChar, ResetChar()
ShrinkFont
ShrinkFontOnePoint
SmallCaps, SmallCaps()
Strikethrough
Strikethrough()
Subscript, Subscript()
Superscript
Superscript()
SymbolFont, SymbolFont()
ToolsLanguage
Underline, Underline()
WordUnderline
WordUnderline()

View

ClosePreview
CloseViewHeaderFooter
FilePrintPreview
FilePrintPreview()
FilePrintPreviewPages
FilePrintPreviewPages()
Magnifier
Magnifier()
ShowAll, ShowAll()
ToggleFull
TogglePortrait
ToolsOptionsView
ViewAnnotations
ViewAnnotations()

ViewDraft
ViewDraft()
ViewEndnoteArea
ViewEndnoteArea()
ViewFieldCodes
ViewFieldCodes()
ViewFooter
ViewFooter()
ViewFootnoteArea
ViewFootnoteArea()
ViewFootnotes
ViewFootnotes()

(continued)

ViewHeader, ViewHeader( )
ViewMasterDocument
ViewMasterDocument( )
ViewMenus, ViewMenus( )
ViewNormal, ViewNormal( )
ViewOutline, ViewOutline( )
ViewPage, ViewPage( )
ViewRuler, ViewRuler( )

ViewStatusBar
ViewStatusBar( )
ViewZoom
ViewZoom100
ViewZoom200
ViewZoom75
ViewZoomPageWidth
ViewZoomWholePage

Appendix A

The *Word for Windows 95 SECRETS* CD-ROM

Word for Windows 95 SECRETS contains a CD-ROM that contains hundreds of valuable shareware and public domain files featuring shareware programs and both shareware and public domain fonts, clip art, and templates. In addition, the CD-ROM includes *the Word for Windows 95 SECRETS* template, which contains all of the sample macros presented throughout this book.

What Is Shareware?

Shareware is software that is distributed on a "try before you buy" basis. The software is distributed freely via on-line services such as CompuServe, America Online, and The Microsoft Network, as well as privately run bulletin boards. In addition, shareware is often made available on CD-ROMs such as the one that comes with this book.

Shareware is *not* free software. Each shareware package comes with a specific licensing agreement that authorizes you to use the software for a trial period, typically 30 days, before deciding whether you would like to purchase the software. If you decide to purchase the software, you must follow the registration procedures included with each offering to properly register the software with its author. If you decide *not* to purchase the software, you must discontinue using it and remove it from your hard disk.

Shareware programs are copyrighted by the authors of the programs and cannot be freely distributed. I have obtained permission from each of the shareware program authors to include evaluation copies of their programs on the CD-ROM.

Note

The purchase price of this book does *not* include the registration or license fees for any of the shareware programs that are included on the accompanying CD-ROM. Your purchase of this book entitles you to evaluate the shareware programs on the CD-ROM under the terms that are specific to each shareware program or font. If you want to continue using a shareware program beyond the trial period, you must properly register with the program's author.

What Is Freeware?

Freeware is software that does not require a registration fee for use. If the author of the software has completely released his or her interest in the software, the software is referred to as *public domain* and may be freely used and distributed. However, not all freeware software has been released to the public domain. In many cases, the author of the freeware software has retained the copyright to the software and has placed restrictions on its use. So, please read the licensing agreement for all freeware files to see what use is permitted.

In some cases, freeware is offered to provide samples of a software publisher's offerings. For example, the CD-ROM contains 15 beautiful clip art images from the Harter Image Archive. You can use these images any way you want. If you like them, you'll find that Harter Image Archive sells CD-ROMs with hundreds of similar images at very reasonable prices.

The CD-ROM Itself Is Copyrighted

Please notice that the CD-ROM itself, including its installation routines, are copyrighted by IDG Books Worldwide. You may install the software from the CD-ROM on your personal computer, and you may redistribute the software contained within the CD-ROM, in accordance with the licensing terms listed for each program (most shareware authors *want* their programs to be distributed to as many people as possible), but you may not duplicate or distribute the CD-ROM itself or its installation routines without written permission from IDG Books.

Installing the CD-ROM

Installing the software from the CD-ROM is easy. If you have not disabled the Windows 95 AutoPlay feature, simply insert the CD-ROM disk into your CD-ROM drive, and the setup program will start automatically. If the setup program doesn't start automatically when you insert the CD-ROM, follow these steps:

1. Insert the CD-ROM into your CD-ROM drive.
2. Click the Windows 95 Start button and click Run.
3. Type the drive letter of your CD-ROM drive, followed by a colon and the word **START**. For example, if your CD-ROM drive is drive D:, type the following:

   ```
   d:start
   ```

When the Word for Windows 95 CD-ROM Setup Program starts, the screen shown in Figure A-1 will be displayed.

Figure A-1: The *Word for Windows 95 SECRETS* CD-ROM Setup Program.

You can click on any of the following buttons on the Setup Program to view information about the CD-ROM or to install software:

- **Start Here:** Displays late-breaking information about the programs on the CD-ROM.

- **SECRETS:** Installs the *Word for Windows 95 SECRETS* template, which includes all of the sample macros that appear throughout this book.

- **MegaWord 95:** Installs MegaWord 95, a brilliant shareware program that adds significant functionality to Word for Windows.

- **ThumbsUp:** Installs ThumbsUp, a shareware program that allows you to view thumbnail images of your clip art.

- **TopDraw:** Installs TopDraw, a shareware drawing program that lets you create complicated drawings that you can incorporate into Word documents.

- **Grab-It Pro:** Installs Grab-It Pro, a shareware program that captures images from your computer's screen and saves them in bitmap files that you can insert into your documents.

- **Paint Shop Pro:** Installs Paint Shop Pro, a shareware image drawing program that includes sophisticated rendering features normally found only in high-end imaging software that sells for hundreds of dollars.

- **Fonts:** Installs several collections of shareware and public domain fonts that are supplied on the CD.

- **Clip Art:** Installs several collections of shareware, freeware samples, and public domain clip art.

- **Prank Macro!:** Displays information about the notorious Word Concept macro virus and installs a program that can remove the macro from your system.

- **Browse:** Opens a Windows 95 window that allows you to browse the contents of the CD-ROM directly.

- **Exit:** Quits the Setup Program.

None of the buttons install software onto your computer without first displaying information about the software, its usage terms, the disk space it requires, and so on. For example, the dialog box shown in Figure A-2 is displayed if you click the Paint Shop Pro button.

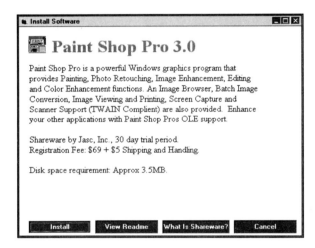

Figure A-2: Installing a program from the CD-ROM.

From this dialog box, you can display the Readme file that is distributed with the program to learn more about the program before installing it. Then, you can click Install to install the program, or Cancel to return to the main Setup Program window.

Appendix B

The Word Document Virus Threat

About a month before the final deadline for this book, I began to notice something strange about the way Word for Windows was behaving. I couldn't change the template attached to my documents, and I couldn't save my documents under a different format. I soon realized that many of my somehow my documents had somehow been switched from normal Word document format to template format. In other words, even though my documents all had filenames that ended with ".doc," they were actually templates rather than documents.

An old Word for Windows trick is to create a template, then rename it to a filename that has a DOC extension. The templates will then appear to be documents, with just a few restrictions: you won't be able to attach a template to the document, because the document already *is* a template; and you won't be able to use the Save As command to change the file format.

Why go to all this trouble? Because template files have several capabilities that normal document files do not, most notably the ability to carry macros. In particular, the template-documents can carry an AutoOpen macro that will be run automatically when the template-document is opened.

Computer virus experts have known for years that application programs (such as Microsoft Word) that support AutoOpen macros are wide-open targets for virus infections. All one has to do is create a template-document with an AutoOpen macro that contains the instructions necessary to "infect" other documents — that is, to copy the AutoOpen macro itself into other documents. In fact, the programming required to create such a virus is pretty trivial. Any competent programmer should be able to create such a virus in a matter of hours.

A support engineer from Microsoft suggested that I might have such a virus. He advised me to look for the following macros in my Normal.dot template:

AAAZAO

AAAZFS

AutoOpen

FileSaveAs

Payload

Sure enough, all five of these macros were present in my Normal.dot. I had been infected by a new virus, now known as "Winword.Concept Virus" or the "Prank Macro," as Microsoft prefers to call it.

Once your Normal.dot template has been infected by Winword.Concept, any document you subsequently save is stored in template format and carries the macros necessary to infect other systems. As a result, this virus can be spread merely by sharing Word documents. If you save a Word document, then pass the document to a friend, whether over a network or via diskettes, your friend's system will be infected when he or she opens the document. The old adage that viruses can only be transmitted via executable programs no longer applies.

Fortunately, the Winword.Concept virus is pretty benign. It does manage convert your document files to template format, which is definitely a major inconvenience. But other than that, it doesn't do any real damage to your computer. The Winword.Concept virus was apparently created just to prove the point that a virus could be spread in this way.

However, the macro does provide the mechanism of delivering a "payload," perhaps to demonstrate that the virus writer could just as easily have done some major damage. Take a look at the Payload macro which is copied to Normal.dot by the Winword.Concept virus:

```
Sub MAIN
    REM That's enough to prove my point
End Sub
```

The Payload macro is merely an ominous comment statement that doesn't do anything. It could just as easily consisted of statements that delete files from your hard disk. So even though the Winword.Concept virus isn't malicious, other such viruses could be.

Is it a Virus or a Prank?

Microsoft insists that Word.Concept is not a virus. They refer to it instead as a "prank macro." Their rationale for this is that Word.Concept isn't a true virus, in that it doesn't spread by attaching itself to executable program files.

I disagree. The technical definition of a virus is any program that is (1) self-replicating and (2) spreads by means of attaching itself to an executable program which serves as a "host". Word.Concept easily meets these two criteria: it is self-replicating; that is, it can create copies of itself, and it is spread by attaching itself to a document file which serves as a host. For all intents and purposes, Word templates (and templates masquerading as documents) *are* a type executable program files, because they can contain executable programs in the form of macros.

Calling this virus a "prank macro" is kind of like congress referring to a tax increase as "revenue enhancement." As they say, if it walks like a duck and quacks like a duck, it's a duck.

How to Tell If You Have the Winword.Concept Virus

When the Winword.Concept virus first strikes, it displays the dialog box shown in Figure B-1.

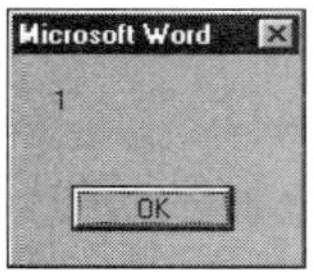

Figure B-1: The dialog box displayed when the Winword.Concept virus infects your computer.

If you ever see this dialog box immediately after opening a document, drop everything, reread this chapter, and remove the virus before the infection spreads.

If for some reason this dialog box slips by unnoticed (amazingly, it does — even I didn't notice it), you can find out if you have been infected by the virus by choosing the Tools⇨Macro command and looking for macros with the following names:

AAAZAO

AAAZFS

AutoOpen

FileSaveAs

Payload

If your Normal.dot template contains these macros, you have been infected.

How to Remove the Infection

You can easily remove the virus from your Normal.dot template by deleting the five macros listed in the previous section. To remove the virus from an infected document, delete the macros, then use the Save As command to save the document in document format rather than in template format.

Microsoft has created a document, named Scan828.doc, that contains macros which will do this clean-up for you automatically. You'll find this document on the *Word for Windows 95 SECRETS* CD-ROM. After copying the document to your hard disk, open it in Word for Windows.

Scan828.doc is actually a template, not a document. It contains an AutoOpen macro that will automatically perform the following safeguards:

1. Scan828.doc will check your Normal.dot template for the virus and remove it if discovered.

2. Next, Scan828.doc offers to scan your entire C: drive, removing the virus from any infected DOC and DOT files. If you want, you can change the drive or path used for this scan.

3. Finally, Scan828.doc installs two macros, Payload and AutoClose, which are designed to prevent further Word.Concept infections.

Be sure to read the entire contents of the Wvfix.doc file; it contains additional information on the Word.Concept virus and tips on removing it and preventing subsequent infections.

Preventing Document Virus Infections

The Scan828.doc document installs a dummy macro named Payload into your Normal.dot template to prevent your Normal.dot from being infected. This works pretty well against the Word.Concept virus, because Word.Concept checks to see if a Payload macro exists before it infects your computer. If a Payload macro already exists, Word.Concept assumes that your computer is already infected, so it stops.

However, it won't be long before more robust variants of Word.Concept start to appear. A simple change to the Word.Concept macro — which any experienced WordBasic programmer could make — would circumvent Scan828.doc's method of preventing infection.

The root cause of the problem is the very existence of AutoOpen macros. Any time you open a document, you need to realize that that document may actually be a template that contains an AutoOpen macro. The solution is to disable AutoOpen macros. You can do that by creating a macro named AutoExec in your Normal.dot template. Follow these steps:

1. Choose the Tools⇨Macro command.

2. Choose "Normal.dot (Global Template)" in the Macros Available In list box.

3. Type AutoExec in the Macro Name field.

4. Click Create.

5. Type the macro in exactly as follows:

```
Sub MAIN
    DisableAutoMacros
    MsgBox "Auto Macros are disabled to prevent virus infections!"
End Sub
```

6. Choose the File⇨Close command. When asked if you want to keep the changes to the macro, click Yes.

7. Exit Word, then restart Word.

The *Word for Windows 95 SECRETS* CD-ROM contains a test document that contains AutoOpen, AutoNew, and AutoClose macros. These macros display dialog boxes indicating that the macro has run. You can use this document to verify that you have successfully disabled Auto macros. Just open the document; if a dialog box appears indicating that AutoOpen has run, you have not disabled the Auto macros. If the dialog box does not appear, the Auto macros have been disabled.

If you routinely use documents that contain legitimate AutoOpen, AutoNew, or AutoClose macros, avoiding this type of virus requires a different approach. Rather than disable all Auto macros, you can bypass the AutoOpen and AutoClose on a document-by-document basis, when you open and close the documents:

- ■ To bypass the AutoOpen macro, hold down the Shift key while opening the document.

- ■ To bypass the AutoClose macro, hold down the Shift key while closing the document.

As a precaution, I recommend you get into the habit of holding down the Shift key whenever you open or close a document.

What About RTF Files? Are They Safe?

It has been suggested that files stored in the Rich Text Format (RTF) are safe from infection of this type because RTF files cannot carry macros. That is only half true. Although RTF files cannot store macros, it is not true that any file with an .rtf extension is an RTF file, any more than it is true that all files with a .doc extension are document files. To prove my point, open the RTF file named AutoTest.rtf on the CD-ROM. If you haven't disabled Auto macros, a dialog box displayed by an AutoOpen macro will appear, proving that a Word template can masquerade as an RTF file just as easily as a DOC file.

Index

Numbers and Symbols

32-bit processing, 19
= field (Formula), 655–657

A

accents, allowing over capital
letters, 275
AccessExporter macro, 184, 415
Accessories menu, customizing as
toolbar, 125
acronyms, ignoring for spell
checks, 315
Add Printer Wizard, 230–233
Address Book dialog box, 258
Add to Favorites button (File Open
dialog box), 195–196
Adobe Type Manager (ATM), 442
Advanced Find dialog box, 204–211
Advance field, 624–625
Agenda Wizard, 113
Algerian typeface, 456
aligning
  caution on use of spaces for, 54
  drawings, 511–512
  frames, 474–475
  searching for, 289
  specifying, 336
  typographical considerations,
    452–453
  vertically, 365
  See also indenting
all caps
  specifying, 333
  toolbar button for, 154
Alt key combinations
  advantages, 139
  Alt+arrow keys, 280, 281
  Alt+Enter for file properties
    display, 35
  Alt+F4 to close active window, 35
  Alt+F9 for switching between field
    code and result, 619
  Alt+M to minimize all windows,
    36
  Alt+NumPad5 to select entire
    table, 276
  Alt+Shift+arrow to promote
  outline paragraphs, 548
  Alt+Shift+A to collapse all outline
    body text, 543
  Alt+Shift+Grey-minus, to collapse
    outline headings, 545
  Alt+Shift+Grey-plus, to expand
    outline headings, 545
  Alt+Shift+I for Mark Citation
    dialog box, 574–575
  Alt+Shift+right arrow to demote
    outline paragraphs, 549
  Alt+Shift+X for Mark Index Entry
    dialog box, 579
  Alt+Tab for switching among
    open applications and
    windows, 35
  caution on using established, 141
  for selecting options from
    menus, 3
ampersand (&) in custom
  menus, 162
anchors of objects
  for drawings, 508
  for frames, 475
  showing, 134, 475
And condition in "Advanced Find"
  searches, 209
animation, 15
annotation panes, 262
Annotation Reference paragraph
  style, 423
annotations
  advantages, 255, 259, 262
  copying into documents, 264
  inserting, 262–263
  printing, 223, 235, 264
  removing, 264–265
  viewing, 263–264
  voice, 263
Annotations toolbar, accessing, 149
Annotation Text paragraph style,
  420
.ANS extensions, 203
Any Word command, 140, 155, 161
applets
  Equation Editor, 154, 520–527
  Microsoft Graph, 527–527
  WordArt, 515–519
  See also programs

applications. See applets;
  WordBasic
Apply to: This Point Forward
  option (Columns dialog
  box), 467
appointment book, 25
arcs, 500
Arial typefaces, 446, 457
ArrangeWindows macro, 186
arrow keys, 280, 281
ascenders, 445
.ASC extensions, 203
.ASD extensions, 215
Ask field, 625, 687
associations of programs with
  filenames/extensions, 31
asterisk (*)
  on numeric keypad for expanding
    folder tree, 39
  as wildcard character, 52, 202
ATM (Adobe Type Manager), 442
@functions, fields as, 64
attributes for formatting
  of characters, 56
  importance of, 55
  of paragraphs, 57–58
Author field, 371, 626
authorities tables. See Tables of
  Authorities
author of documents
  inserting as author field, 371
  master documents on networks,
    563
  as property of document, 193
AutoBackup macros, 178, 216–217
AutoCAD file imports, 485–488
AutoCaption dialog box, 493
AutoClose macro, 174, 857
AutoCorrect
  adding words as entries, 313
  capitalization,
    correcting misuse of Caps
      Lock key, 297
    correcting two initial caps,
      294–295
    of first word of sentences,
      295–296
    of names of days, 296

(continued)

AutoCorrect *(continued)*
compared to AutoText, 304
   creating entries, 298–299
   described, 65, 293–294
   macro for toggling, 299–300
   as user types, 297
   See also spell checking
AutoExec macro, 129, 174, 856–857
AutoExit macro, 174
AutoFormat
   for documents, 300–303, 354–358
   for Microsoft Graph, 534–536
Automatic Save Every *n* minutes
   option, 215
Automatic Spell Checking, 18
AutoNew macro, 174, 857
AutoNum field, 626
AutoNumLgl field, 626
AutoNumOut field, 626
AutoOpen macro, 174, 546, 857
   caution on possible virus, 213,
   853, 856, 857
AutoTest.rtf file, 857
AutoText
   assigning to toolbar button, menu
    or keyboard shortcut, 305
   compared to AutoCorrect, 304
   copying elements to/from
    templates, 80–81
   creating entries, 303–305
   custom toolbar buttons for, 155
   described, 65, 303
   editing entries, 305
   inserting, 626
   keyboard shortcuts for, 140
   on custom menus, 161
   printing entries, 223
   in templates, 78
AutoText field, 626
AVERAGE table formula, 410
Award Wizard, 113
axes of graphs, 528

B

background pagination, 137
background printing, 220, 234
Backspace key
   for opening parent folder, 35, 36
   for Up One Level, 192
backups
   with AutoBackup macros, 178
   option to create automatically,
   214
backward compatibility with Word
   6, 19

.BAK extensions, 214, 216
BarCode field, 627
bar codes on envelopes, 244
BaseShiftDown/Up macros, 187
BASIC programming language, 705
   See also WordBasic
BatchConversion macro, 188
bibliographic references. *See*
   footnotes; Tables of
   Authorities
billing form from Invoice.dot
   template, 103, 110, 661
binders in Microsoft Office suite,
   23–24
bitmaps
   described, 486
   importing, 485–488
   importing for toolbar button
    images, 157–158
blocks of text
   macro for saving as text file, 182
   printing, 222
.BMP extensions, 485
body text, 420, 443, 455
Body Text Indent paragraph style,
   420
Body Text paragraph style, 420
boilerplate text, 62
   in templates, 70, 77, 79
   See also AutoText; mail merge
    operations
boldface
   specifying, 332
   as used in this book, 3
Book Antiqua typeface, 458
Bookman Old Style typeface, 458
bookmarks
   advantages, 284
   improving on, with macros,
    285–286
   inserting, 284–285
   inserting as Ref field, 371
   inserting contents of, 644
   inserting page number of, 642
   for invisible text, 648
   as option of view modes, 134
borders, 58
   applying to words or phrases,
    350
   formatting from borders toolbar,
    349–350
   formatting from Format menu,
    346–348
   formatting with AutoFormat, 301
   for headers and footers, 370
   for pictures, 489

   in tables, 406
Borders toolbar, 148, 349–350
Bormuth Grade Level readability
   statistics, 324
Braggadacio typeface, 458
Briefcase. *See* My Briefcase
Britanic Bold typeface, 459
Brush Script MT typeface, 459
Bullet button, 378–379
bullets
   caution on bugs, 384–386
   described, 58, 377–378
   formatting with AutoFormat,
    301, 357
   specifying with Bullet button,
    378–379
business form templates, 103
   invoice, 110
   press release, 103, 104–106
   purchase order, 111
   weekly time sheet, 112
business organization charts,
   182, 183
buttons
   for browsing folders, 33–34
   creating for WordArt, 518–519
   customizing in dialog boxes,
    777–778, 779
   for equation symbols and
    templates, 523
   inserting for running macros, 639
   for moving to specified location,
    634
   for open windows, 40
   Start, 40, 43
   Up One Level, 36
   See also icons; toolbars
Buttons Galore toolbar, 158–159

C

Calendar Wizard, 113
callouts, 500, 504–506
Cancel button in dialog boxes, 773
capitalization
   as all caps, 154, 333, 335
   allowing accents over, 275
   correcting erroneous doubled,
    294–295
   correcting misuse of Caps Lock
    key, 297
   correcting two initial caps,
    294–295
   drop caps, 154
   for field results, 620–621
   for first word of sentences,
    295–296

for names of days, 296
as small caps, 154, 333, 335
toolbar button for, 154
See also case
Caption dialog box, 492–493
Caption paragraph style, 420
captions for graphics, 491–493
Cascade macro, 186
case
changing, 351–353
in filenames, 47
keyboard shortcuts for
changing, 335
macro for changing, 352–353
in searches, 208, 287, 292
See also capitalization
category as document
property, 631
category axes for graphs, 532
CD accompanying this book, 849,
851–852
AutoClose macro, 857
AutoNew macro, 857
AutoOpen macro, 857
AutoTest.rtf, 857
Buttons Galore toolbar, 158–159
ChangeCase macro, 352–353
clip art from Harter Image
Archive, 850
copyright protections, 850
CopyStyles macro, 82–83
DecreaseBothIndents macro, 340
EditGoTo macro, 283–284
FileOpen macro, 197
IncreaseBothIndents macro,
339–340
InsertStats macro, 326
installing, 850
macros, 2
opening screen, 851
RemoveAnnotations macro, 265
Reports Wizard, 87
ShiftPrint macro, 228
ToggleAutoCorrect macro,
299–300
ToggleFormat macro for toggling
Formatting toolbar, 150–151
WordBorder macro, 350
Wvfix.doc for virus fixes, 855–856
.CDR extensions, 485
CD-ROM drive icons, 30
CD-ROM version of Windows 95,
videos included, 614
cells in tables, 389–390
end-of-cell markers, 390
inserting or deleting, 401–402

merging to create headings,
406–407
navigating to and selecting,
398–399
See also tables
centered alignment, 336
See also aligning
center tabs, 343
centimeters as unit of
measurement, 138, 337
Century Gothic typeface, 459
Century Schoolbook typeface,
450, 460
.CGM extensions, 485
Change Case dialog box, 351
ChangeCase macro, 352–353
chapter numbers in page
numbers, 368
characters
deleting formatting, 331, 335
described, 56–57, 329–330
formatting, 331–335
inserting total count into
documents, 641
kerning, 56, 334, 453–454
proportional versus
monospaced, 54, 443
spacing, 56, 332, 333–334, 454–455
See also special characters
character styles, 59, 60, 330, 419,
433–434
CharacterTrackIn/Out macros, 187
charts. *See* graphs
Chart Wizard, 536–537
check boxes in dialog boxes, 774
check box fields in forms, 665–666
circles, 500, 502
citations. *See* Tables of Authorities
clashing typefaces, 443, 455–456
clip art, 485–486, 493–495
from Harter Image Archive, 850
on CD accompanying this book,
851
ClipArt Gallery, 493–495
Clipboard
cutting or copying documents to,
198
Spike as SuperClipboard, 305–307
clock on taskbar, 41
Close button, 237
Closing paragraph style, 420
codes. *See* fields and field codes
Coleman-Liau Grade Level
readability statistics, 324
collating multiple printed
copies, 220

Colona MT typeface, 460
color
as character attribute, 56
for characters/fonts, 332
as fill for drawings, 507
for Highlighted text, 261
for lines in drawings, 507
for toolbar buttons, 151
Columns button, 466
Columns dialog box, 467
columns in documents
breaks, 361, 468
creating, 58, 360, 465–467
hyphenation, 469–471
length balancing, 469
markers, 468
tab stops for bars between, 345
viewing, 134, 466
width adjustments, 467, 468
columns in tables, 389
adding, 400–401
selecting, 399
width adjustments, 402–404
See also tables
combo boxes in dialog boxes,
774, 788
command-line switches for starting
Word from MS-DOS, 127–128
commands
customizing with macros, 64
options for selecting, 62–63
toolbar button for repeating
last, 153
See also buttons; dialog boxes;
keyboard shortcuts; macros;
menus; toolbars; WordBasic
Commands and Settings button,
199–200, 213
commas in numbers, 622, 623
comments
with Comments field, 627
See also annotations
Compare field, 627–628
componentware, 605
Compose New Fax Wizard, 198
CompuServe file imports, 485–488
concordances, 582
contact lists, 25
Contemporary Fax.dot template,
87, 88
Contemporary Letter.dot template,
83, 84
Contemporary Memo.dot template,
87, 91
Contemporary Press Release.dot
template, 103, 104

Contemporary Report.dot template, 87, 94–96
Contemporary Resume.dot template, 103, 107
Control Panel icon, 30
Convert dialog box, 612
Convert.dot template macros, 188
converting files
  backward compatibility with Word 6, 19
  macros for, 188
Convert Notes dialog box, 592–593
Convert Text to Table dialog box, 414–415
cooperative multitasking, 19
copying
  files or folders, 34
  formats with Format Painter, 358
  template elements to/from styles, 80–81
  See also cut/copy/paste operations
copyright protections
  for CD accompanying this book, 850
  for software, 849
CopyStyles macro, 82–83
CorelDraw file imports, 485–488
counts, of words, pages or characters, 193, 641
COUNT table formula, 410
cover pages for faxes, 252–253
crashes, recovering files from ASD versions, 215–216
Create Data Source dialog box, 679
CreateDate field, 628
CreateMsgBox macro, 785–788, 795–799, 803–807
Create New Folder button, 213
Create Picture button, 512–513
cropping graphics, 489–481
cross-referencing
  footnotes, 597–598
  in indexes, 584
Ctrl key combinations
  advantages, 139
  Ctrl+= for subscripts, 335
  Ctrl+Alt+1 for Heading 1 Style, 430, 566
  Ctrl+Alt+2 for Heading 2 Style, 430, 566
  Ctrl+Alt+3 for Heading 3 Style, 430, 566
  Ctrl+Alt+= for customizing menus, 163–164
  Ctrl+Alt+A for Annotation command, 262

Ctrl+Alt+- for customizing menus, 165
Ctrl+Alt+N for Normal view mode, 130
Ctrl+Alt+NumPlus for keyboard shortcuts creation, 142
Ctrl+Alt+O for Outline view, 542
Ctrl+Alt+O for Outline view mode, 130
Ctrl+Alt+P for Page Layout view mode, 130
Ctrl+A to select all, 35
Ctrl+A to select entire document, 276
Ctrl+B for bold, 334
Ctrl+click for selecting multiple files or folders, 35
Ctrl+C to copy to Clipboard, 35, 277
Ctrl+Esc to activate taskbar, 43
Ctrl+F3 as "Cut-to-Spike" key, 306
Ctrl+F9 to insert blank field, 619–620
Ctrl+F11 to lock fields, 619
Ctrl+F12 for Open command, 191
Ctrl+F for Find command, 286
Ctrl+- for optional hyphen, 452–453, 471
Ctrl+[for point size decrease, 335
Ctrl+] for point size increase, 335
Ctrl+H for Replace command, 291
Ctrl+I for italics, 334
Ctrl+I to copy annotation into text, 264
Ctrl+N for New command, 71, 72
Ctrl+N for Normal Style, 430
Ctrl+NumPad5 to select entire document, 276
Ctrl+O for Open command, 191
Ctrl+P for Print command, 220
Ctrl+S for Save command, 212, 216
Ctrl+Shift+< for point size decrease, 335
Ctrl+Shift+= for superscripts, 335
Ctrl+Shift+> for point size increase, 335
Ctrl+Shift+A for all caps, 335
Ctrl+Shift+D for double underlining, 334
Ctrl+Shift+Enter for column break, 468
Ctrl+Shift+F3 as "Put-Spike-here" key, 306
Ctrl+Shift+F8 to extend column selection, 276

Ctrl+Shift+F9 to convert field to text, 619
Ctrl+Shift+F11 to unlock fields, 619
Ctrl+Shift+F for font change, 335
Ctrl+Shift+I for Print Preview, 575
Ctrl+Shift+K for small caps, 335
Ctrl+Shift+N for Normal style, 549
Ctrl+Shift+N to demote outline heading level, 549
Ctrl+Shift+P for point size change, 335
Ctrl+Shift+Q for Symbol font, 335
Ctrl+Shift+S for style change/add, 335, 423
Ctrl+Shift+W for word underlining, 334
Ctrl+Shift+Z for removing character formatting, 335
Ctrl+Spacebar for removing character formatting, 335
Ctrl+U for underlining, 334
Ctrl+V to paste from Clipboard, 35, 274, 277
Ctrl+X to cut to Clipboard, 35, 277
Ctrl+Y for Repeat command, 279
Ctrl+Z for Undo command, 279
currency formats, 622
Custom Button dialog box, 155–156
custom dictionary, 315
Customize dialog box, 141–142, 152, 162
customizing
  dialog boxes. *See* dialog boxes; Dialog Editor
  envelopes, 245–246
  Grammar Checker, 324–326
  interface for Word, 129–138
  keyboard shortcuts, 63, 139–146
  labels, 248–249
  menus, 63, 161–167
  menus for forms, 669–670
  New button and Ctrl+N keyboard shortcut, 72–73
  Office Shortcut Bar (OSB or SuperMOM), 124–126
  Spell Checker dictionary, 314, 315–316
  Start menu, 44–45
  styles for tables of contents, 569
  taskbar, 40–42
  toolbar buttons for hanging indents, 339
  toolbar for tables, 412–414
  toolbars, 63, 147–161
  via templates, 70, 78
Word for Windows 95, 2, 4

cut/copy/paste operations
  keyboard shortcuts for, 277
  on folders, 32
  with Spike, 305–307

D

dashed lines as tab leaders, 344
dashed underlining, 332
data
  option for printing apart from
    form, 235
  option for saving apart from
    form, 215
  toolbar button for summing
    values, 155
Database field, 628–629
databases
  inserting queries as tables,
    628–629
  See also mail merge operations;
    tables
Database toolbar, accessing, 148
Data Form dialog box, 680
Data menu, Series in Columns
  command, 530
datasheets for graphs, 527–528, 530
data values, toolbar button for
  summing, 155
Date field, 629–630
dates
  inserting by means of Date Field,
    64, 371, 629–630
  inserting from toolbar
    button, 154
  inserting last saved for
    document, 644
days, automatic capitalization of
  names, 296
DDEAuto field, 630
DDE field, 630
decimals
  formats in tables, 411
  in number fields, 623
decimal tabs, 343
DecreaseBothIndents macro, 340
DecreaseCrop macro, 497
DecreaseFont macro, 187
DecreaseLeftAndRightIndent
    macro, 186
Default Paragraph Font paragraph
    style, 423
defaults
  for document location, 196
  for margin settings, 362

Normal.dot template, 62, 70–71
Normal style, 59
  for printer paper tray, 235
  restoring for Wizards, 119
  for tab stops, 342
  for typefaces and margins, 450
Default Tray option, 235
Delete key, 35
deleting, files or folders, 34, 198
descenders, 445
Desdemona typeface, 460
desktop
  creating documents from, 124
  placing document scrap on, 278
  replacing Program Manager, 28
  returning to, 36–37
  See also folders
Desktop folder, in Windows
    directory, 36–37
desktop publishing effects
  design considerations, 476–479
  with frames, 471–476
  icons, 482–483
  pull quotes, 479–480
  side headings, 481–482
  See also columns
Detail button, 193, 213
Details view, 30, 193
dialog box customization, 773–774
  copying from macros to Dialog
    Editor, 782
  defining, 775, 783
  dynamic (reactive),
    advantages, 790
    dialog function commands,
      793–794
    dialog function setup,
      790–793
    drop-down list field problem,
      799–801
    sample (CreateMsgBox),
      795–799, 803–807
    tabbed, 801–802
    versus static, 774
  list fields, 788–790
  static versus dynamic, 774
  using in macro,
    accessing user input, 784–785
    displaying, 783–784
    sample (CreateMsgBox),
      785–788
    setting default values, 785
  See also Dialog Editor
dialog boxes, built-in to Word,
    771–773

Dialog Editor
  activating, 775
  button controls, 777–778
  check boxes, 779
  copying dialog box into
    macro, 782
  deleting controls, 782
  group boxes, 781
  limitations of, 776
  moving, resizing or rewording
    dialog boxes, 778–779
  naming, 775
  option buttons, 779
  picture fields, 781–782
  text and text boxes, 780
Dial-Up Networking icon, 30
dictionaries. *See under* spell
    checking
dictionary-type word ranges in
    headers and footers, 371
dingbats, 449
direct formatting, 59, 61, 427
  in templates, 78
directories
  longer names, 47
  referencing parents in MS-DOS,
    51–52
  See also folders
DisableAutoBackup macro, 178
disk drives
  icons for, 30
  mapping to networks, 200
  viewing contents, 30
display options. *See* View menu
display type, 443, 456
.DOC extensions, 203, 853
docking toolbars, 150
DocProperty field, 631
documents
  adding to menus, 201
  building blocks of, 56–62
  collaborating over networks to
    produce, 255
  comments in, 627
  comparing versions, 268
  converting to templates, 77
  creating from desktop, My
    Computer or Explorer, 124
  creation date insertion, 628
  cutting or copying to Clipboard,
    198
  deleting, 198
  editing, 273–280
  finding and replacing text,
    formats or special
    characters, 286–291

(continued)

documents *(continued)*
  keyboard shortcuts in, 46
  last print date display, 642
  macro for converting formats in
    batches, 188
  macro for displaying statistics
    on, 183–184
  mail-merging directly to, 684
  navigating, 280–286
  navigating as in WordPerfect, 137
  opening multiple, 192
  opening outside of Word, 202
  opening recently used, 137, 200
  options for opening, 192–194,
    195–202
  printing, 198, 199
  properties. *See* properties of
    documents
  Thesaurus lookups, 319–320
  toolbar button for closing, 153
  viewing with Quick view, 198
  See also annotations;
    AutoCorrect; fields and field
    codes; files; formatting;
    forms; master documents;
    OLE (Object Linking and
    Embedding); outlines;
    paragraphs; Revision Marks;
    spell checking; tables;
    templates; text
Documents command (Start
  menu), 44
document scrap, 278
Documents menu, Start button, 122
dollar amounts, spelling out, 621
DOS. *See* MS-DOS
.DOT extensions, 13, 70
dotted lines as tab leaders, 344
dotted underlining, 333
double spacing, 57
  toolbar button for, 154
double-underlining
  specifying, 333
  toolbar button for, 154
Draft Font, 133
draft mode for printer, 234
dragging mouse
  for copying files or folders, 34
  and dropping items, 277–278
DrawDisassemblePicture
  macro, 513
Drawing button, 498
Drawing object dialog box, 507–509
drawings
  aligning, 511–512
  callouts, 504–506

converting to pictures, 512–513
creating, 500
with Drawing toolbar, 498
fill color, 507
flipping, 509
grouping, 512
importance of frequent saves, 500
keyboard shortcuts, 501
in layers, 510
lines, 501–502
line style and color, 507
polygons or freeform shapes,
  502–504
printing, 235
rectangles, squares and
  circles, 502
rotating, 509
selecting, 506–507
showing, 134
text boxes, 504
toolbar buttons, 500–501, 510
undoing keystrokes, 500
zooming in on, 498–499
See also graphics; pictures
Drawings option of Page Layout
  view mode, 134
Drawing toolbar, 148, 498
drives. *See* disk drives
drop caps, toolbar button for, 154
drop-down fields on forms, 666–667
drop-down list boxes in dialog
  boxes, 774, 788
.DRW extensions, 486
.DXF extensions, 485
Dynamic Data Exchange (DDE)
  links, 630
dynamite icon, 7

E

EditConversionOptions macro, 188
EditGoTo macro, 283–284
Edit menu
  AutoText command, 303
  Find command, 286–291
    Special⟳Footnote mark
     option, 590
    Style option, 434–435
  Go To command, 282–283
    macro replacing, 283–284
  Links command, 610–611
  Object command, 610
    Convert option, 611–612
  Paste command, 274
  Paste Link command, 610
  Paste Special command, 609–610

Picture command, 491
Redo command, 279
Replace command, 291–292
Select Dialog command, 782
Undo command, 279–280
EditTime field, 631
Elegant Fax.dot template, 87, 89
Elegant Letter.dot template, 83, 85
Elegant Memo.dot template, 87, 92
Elegant Press Release.dot template,
  103, 105
Elegant Report.dot template, 87,
  97–99
Elegant Resume.dot template,
  103, 108
e-mail
  enabling attachment of files
    to, 137
  in Inbox, 29
  keyboard shortcuts in, 46
  mail-merging directly to, 684
  sending, 198, 255–260
  toolbar button for sending, 153
embedding. *See* OLE (Object
  Linking and Embedding)
Embed field, 631–632
EnableAutoBackup macro, 178
End key, 281
Endnote Reference paragraph
  style, 423
endnotes
  converting from footnotes,
    592–593
  creating, 589
  specifying, 58
  updating references, 641
Endnote Text paragraph style, 420
end-of-cell markers, 390
end-of-section marks, 360
Enter key
  for ending paragraphs, 330
  for opening/running files/
    programs, 35
  as Return key, 54
Envelope Address paragraph
  style, 420
Envelope Options dialog box,
  245, 693
Envelope Return paragraph
  style, 420
envelopes
  printing, 242–246, 692–694
  printing barcodes, 627
  toolbar button for printing, 154
Envelopes and Labels dialog box,
  243, 244

.EPS extensions, 485
Eq field, 632
Equation Editor, 154, 520–527
equations
    adding text, 524
    editing, 526–527
    inserting with fields, 64
    macro for overscores, 186
"Error! Unknown switch argument"
        message, 619
even-numbered pages. *See*
        odd-even pages
Exchange. *See* Microsoft Exchange
ExitAll macro, 178–179
Explore command, 198
Explorer
    creating documents from, 124
    described, 37–38
    how to use, 39
    starting, 38–39
    starting Word from, 122–123
    view of template folders, 76
exporting
    data from forms, 215, 674
    tables to Microsoft Access, 184
expressions
    comparing, 627–628
    comparing conditionally, 635
extension handling
    icon display determination, 29, 31
    selecting for display in File Open
        dialog box, 203

F

favorite folders, 195–196
Fax Cover Page Editor, 252
faxes
    mail merging directly to, 684–685
    sending, 198, 249–253
fax templates, 87, 88, 89, 90
Fax Wizard, 113
Field dialog box, 617–619
Field Option dialog box, 618
fields and field codes
    for border on word or
        phrase, 350
    complete reference list, 624–657
    described, 64–65, 615–617
    field characters, 616
    formatting with switches,
        620–623
    in headers and footers, 370–371
    inserting, 617–620
    keyboard shortcuts, 619
    Names, inserting, 681

printing, 235
results, 616
shading, 134
showing or hiding, 153
for tables of contents, 569–570
types, 616
update prevention, 624
updating, 155, 234, 623
viewing with Field Codes option
        of view modes, 134
Field Shading option of view
        modes, 134
figures tables. *See* Tables of Figures
File Manager, 37, 39
    See also Explorer
File menu
    Add Routing Slip command,
        257–259
    Delete command, 34
    Empty Recycle Bin command, 29
    Explorer command, 38
    New command,
        File or Folder options, 35
        Microsoft Word Document
        option, 124
        running Wizards, 113
        Template option, 13, 71–72,
        77, 661
    Open command. *See* Open
        command (File menu)
    Page Setup command, 58, 360
        layout, 365–366
        line length adjustments, 451
        margins, 362–363
        paper size, 363–364
        paper source, 364
    Print command, 220
        Key Assignments option, 143
        Macrosoft Fax option,
        249–253
        Name option, 229
    Print Preview command, 235–242
    Properties command, 14–15
    Rename command, 34
    Save All command, 214
    Save As command, 12–13,
        211–213
        Document Template option,
        77
    Save Template command, 175
    Send command, 255–260
    Templates command, 74, 79
        Automatically Update
        Document Styles option, 435
filename extensions. *See* extensions
FileName field, 632

filenames
    inserting as filename field, 371
    longer length with Windows 95,
        12, 20, 47–52
    referencing in MS-DOS, 51–52
File Open dialog box, 191–192
FileOpen macro, 197
files
    associating with programs, 31
    caution on deleting with wildcard
        characters, 52
    converting from foreign formats,
        137
    copying, 34
    creating, 35
    creating at print time, 224–227
    deleting, 34
    displaying most recently opened,
        137, 200
    displaying properties of, 14–15,
        193, 198, 199
    finding "lost," 202–204
    password protecting, 217–218
    renaming, 34, 194
    saving with different name/
        format/location, 13, 211–213
    selecting multiple, 35
    sorting, 199
    viewing as preview, 194
    viewing details, 30, 193
    viewing icons, 193
    viewing properties, 193
    See also documents; folders
files finding with advanced search
        techniques, 204–211
FileSize field, 633
fill color for drawings, 507
Fillin field, 633, 687, 688–689
Find command (Start menu), 44
    toolbar button for, 153
Find dialog box, 286–287
finding
    files or folders, 44, 202–204
    files or folders with advanced
        techniques, 204–211
    formats, 289
    and saving search patterns, 200,
        211
    special characters, 289–281
    text, 286–289
finding and replacing
    enhancements with Word 6,
        16–17
    symbols with macro, 179–180
    text, 291–292
Find Style dialog box, 434–435
FindSymbol macro, 179–180

first line indents, with paragraph attribute, 57
Flesch Reading Ease statistics, 323
flipping, drawings, 509
folders
    browsing favorites, 195–196
    browsing for files, 192
    copying, 34
    creating, 13, 35
    cut/copy/paste operations, 32
    deleting, 34, 198
    described, 29
    for document scraps on desktop, 278
    grouping files by, 200
    renaming, 34, 194
    returning to parent, 35, 36
    searching subfolders for files, 199–200, 208
    selecting multiple, 35
    sharing on networks, 260
    for templates, 75
    viewing contents, 30–31
    viewing details, 30, 193
    viewing icons, 193
    See also directories
fonts
    affecting document length, 241
    applying or deleting, 331–335
    as character attribute, 56
    custom toolbar buttons for, 155
    defined, 442
    finding, 289
    keyboard shortcuts for, 140, 142
    macro for generating samples, 180, 181
    macro for listing all printable characters, 186
    on CD accompanying this book, 851
    on custom menus, 161
    PostScript and TrueType, 442
    proportional versus monospaced, 54, 443
    size, 56
    style, 56
    versus typefaces, 332, 442, 443
    See also typography
FontSampleGenerator macro, 180, 181
Footer paragraph style, 420
footers. *See* footnotes; headers and footers
Footlight MT typeface, 461
Footnote and Endnote dialog box, 588

footnote pane, 588
Footnote Reference paragraph style, 423
footnotes
    changing formats, 590
    choosing numbers or symbols, 590–591
    continuation notices, 592
    converting to endnotes, 592–593
    creating, 587–589
    creating with InsertFootnote macro (Footnote Wizard), 594–596
    cross-referencing, 597–598
    customizing numbers or symbols, 591–592
    displaying, 589
    finding, 589–590
    inserting from toolbar button, 154
    macro for inserting, 180
    separators, 592
    specifying, 58
    with StyleRef field code, 598–600
    updating references, 641
    See also sub/superscripts
Footnotes toolbar, accessing, 149
Footnote Text paragraph style, 420
Footnote Wizard, 1, 594–596
Format Callout dialog box, 506
Format Frame dialog box, 474–475
Format menu
    3-D View command, 532
    AutoFormat command, 300–303, 354–358
    Borders and Shading command, 345–348, 418
    Bullets and Numbering command, 379–380, 381–382, 418
    Change Case command, 351
    Chart Type command, 531–532
    Columns command, 58, 360, 466–468
    Drawing Object command, 501–502
    Font command, 61, 331–334, 418
        Character Spacing tab, 453–455
    Frame command, 418, 473–475
    Heading Numbering command, 368
    Paragraph command, 57–58, 330, 335–339, 418
        with picture imports, 488, 489
    Picture command, 490–491

Style command, 60, 424–426, 429–423
    Modify⇨Shortcut Key option, 142, 431
Style Gallery command, 436–438
Tabs command, 58, 343–344, 418
Format Painter, 358
Format Picture dialog box, 490–491
formatting
    applying, 60–61
    with AutoFormat, 300–303, 354–358
    by means of attributes, 55
    datasheets for graphs, 530
    direct, 59, 61, 427
    field results, 620–623
    finding, 289
    footnotes, 590
    with Format Painter, 358
    importance of end-of-section marks, 360
    importance of paragraph marks (¶), 58, 330
    indexes, 584
    layers of, 56–59
    margins, 58, 134, 359, 362–363
    overriding with direct formatting, 59, 61, 427–428
    with styles, 59–60
    See also paragraph styles; styles; templates
Formatting toolbar, 60
    accessing, 148
    macro for toggling, 150–151
FormCheckBox field, 633
FormDropDown field, 634
Form Field dialog box, 663
Form Field Help Text dialog box, 668
form fields, 659
form letters. *See* mail merge operations
forms
    check box fields, 665–666
    creating template for, 661–662
    customizing form menus, 669–670
    data only,
        printing, 235, 669
        saving or exporting, 215, 674
    described, 659–660
    drop-down fields, 666–667
    filling out, 668–669
    filling out, on networks, 260
    help text, 667–668
    macros in, 671
    preprinted, 669

printing, 669
   data only, 235, 669
provided with Word, 661
sample with macros, 671–673
saving, 669
   data only, 215, 674
text fields, 663–665
toolbar, 662–663
Forms toolbar, 148, 662–663
FormText field, 634
formulas
   examples, 657
   functions for use with, 656
   inserting with = field, 655–657
   macro for creating, 185
   operators for use with, 655
   references to other cells, 656
   using in tables, 409–411
fractions, formatting with
      AutoFormat, 302, 358
frames
   adding to pictures, 488–489
   aligning, 473–475
   anchoring, 475
   deleting, 475–476
   inserting, 471–473
   searching for formats, 289
freeform shape drawing, 500,
      502–504
freeware, 850
Full Screen toolbar, accessing, 149
Full Screen view, 130–132
   toolbar button for toggling, 153
function keys
   F2 for renaming file, 35
   F3 for Find command, 35
   F5 for Go To command, 282
   F8 to extend selection, 276
   F9 for field display, 619
   F11 for next field, 619
   F12 for Save As command, 211
functions
   in tables, 410
   in WordBasic, 809–844

G

Galleries
   of ClipArt, 493–495
   of styles, 436–438
games
   MindBender macro, 181–182
   Scrabble solver, 318–319
   word-jumble solutions, 318–319
   WordPuzzler macro, 184
Garamond MT typeface, 461

gears icon, 7
.GIF extensions, 486
global templates, 70, 78–80, 140
Glossary, 65
   See also AutoText
GoToButton field, 634
Go To dialog box, 282
   footnotes, 589–590
Grab-It Pro, 851
Grammar Checker
   advantages and disadvantages,
      320–321
   customizing, 324–325
   how to use, 321–323
   readability statistics, 323–324,
      326
graphics
   adding to envelopes, 245–246
   captions, 491–493
   clip art, 485–486, 493–495
   cropping, 489–481
   editing, 491
   importing, 485–488
   option to save only Windows
      version of, 215
   resizing, 489–481
   in templates, 70, 72
   See also drawings; pictures
graphs
   AutoFormatting, 534–536
   changing type, 530–532
   ChartWizard, 536–537
   from datasheets, 527–528, 530
   inserting, 528–529
   labels, 533–534
   legends, 528, 534
   terminology, 527–528
   titles, 532–533
   types of charts, 527
gridlines in tables, 390
group boxes in custom dialog
      boxes, 781
grouping of drawings, 512
gutters, 362

H

Haettenschweller typeface, 461
hanging indents
   with bullets, 378
   with paragraph attribute, 57
   and side headings, 481–482
   specifying, 336, 337, 338
Harter Image Archive clip art, 850
Header and Footer toolbar,
      accessing, 149

Header paragraph style, 420
headers and footers
   creating, 369–371
   creating toolbar button for,
      371–372
   dictionary-type word ranges, 371
   lifting page text using character
      styles, 434
   macro for editing, 182
   margin settings, 363
   in master documents, 562–563
   specifying, 58, 360
heading paragraphs
   in master documents, 558, 560
   numbering, 58, 386–387
headings
   formatting with AutoFormat,
      301, 357
   Heading 1, 2, 3, etc. styles, 59, 420
   in tables, 406–407
   use for TOC, 566
   See also outlines
head serifs, 445
help
   for converts from WordPerfect,
      137, 138
   with forms, 667–668
   from Help command of Start
      menu, 44
   from Tip of the Day feature,
      128–129
   from Tip Wizard, 17, 138
   from ToolTips, 151
Help buttons, 18, 61, 237
Help command (Start menu), 44
Helvetica typeface, 446
hexadecimal conversions from
      decimal numbers, 621
.HGL extensions, 485
hidden text, 136
   printing, 235
hiding
   screen "Clutter" in Full Screen
      view, 130–132
   taskbar, 41
Highlighter
   advantages, 15–16, 260
   how to use, 260–261
   searching for highlighted
      text, 289
   turning on/off with Highlight
      option of view modes, 134
Highlighter button, 260
Home key, 281
hot keys, 162
HP Graphics file imports, 485–488

hyphenation
   automatic, 469–470
   disabling, 57
   displaying optional hyphens, 136
   manual, 470
   non-breaking, 471
   optional, 136, 452–453, 471
   problems in columns, 465
Hyphenation dialog box, 469–470

I

icons
   for CD-ROM drives, 30
   for disk drives, 30
   for documents, 28
   for document scrap on desktop,
      278
   for files, 29
   Inbox, 29
   Microsoft Network, 28
   My Computer, 28, 29–34
   Network Neighborhood, 28
   for OLE object files, 608
   on Windows 95 desktop, 28
   printing in documents, 482–483
   Recycle Bin, 29
   reducing size, 41
   resizing, 30
   for subdirectories, 29
   for subdocuments of master
      documents, 556
   See also buttons; keyboard
      shortcuts; toolbars
If field, 635
If-Then-Else fields in mail merge
   operations, 687, 689–690
images. *See* graphics
Impact typeface, 462
importing
   data for mail merge operations,
      701
   documents by opening outside of
      Word, 202
Inbox, icon, 29
inches as unit of measurement,
   138, 337
IncludePicture field, 635
IncludeText field, 636
IncreaseBothIndents macro,
   339–340
IncreaseCrop macro, 497
IncreaseFont macro, 187
IncreaseLeftAndRightIndent macro,
   186

indenting
   automatic with Tab key at
      beginning of paragraph,
      57, 341
   caution on use of spaces for, 54
   with hanging indents, 336, 337,
      338
   macros for altering, 186
   macros for double indenting,
      339–340
   with ruler, 337–338
   searching for, 289
   specifying, 336
   unavailability of intra-paragraph,
      330
   See also aligning
Index 1, 2, 3, etc. styles, 584
Index and Tables dialog box, 567
indexes
   creating, 578, 580–581
   creating for multifile prjects, 643
   creating from concordance,
      582–583
   cross-references, 584
   formatting, 584
   formatting with paragraph styles,
      420–421
   highlighting page numbers, 581
   inserting into documents with
      field code, 636–637
   marking entries, 579, 654–655
   specifying ranges of pages, 581
   subentries, 583
   updating, 584–585
   use of fields, 65
Index field, 636–637
Index paragraph styles, 420–421
Info field, 637–638
Insert Cell button, 402
Insert Chart button, 529
Insert Field dialog box, 570
InsertFootnote macro, 180, 594–596
Insert key, specifying for Paste
   operations, 274
Insert menu
   Annotation command, 262
   Break command, 360, 361, 468
   Caption command, 491–493
      for tables of figures, 572–573
   Cross-reference command, 598
   Data Labels command, 533
   Field command, 570, 617–619
   Footnote command, 57, 58,
      360, 588
   Form Field command, 660, 662,
      665–667

   Frame command, 471–473
   Index and Tables command,
      Index tab, 580–581
      Tables of Authorities tab,
         575, 576–577
      Tables of Contents tab, 567,
         568
      Tables of Figures tab, 572,
         574
   Legend command, 534
   Object command,
      for embedding OLE objects,
         606–608
      for importing clip art, 494
      Microsoft Equation option,
         521–522
      Microsoft Graph option, 528
      WordArt option, 515–517
   Page Numbers command, 58, 360,
      367–368
   Picture command, 482, 486–488
   Selected Data Labels command,
      533
   Selected Legend command, 534
   Symbol command, 329–330
   Titles command, 533
Insert Picture command, 486–487
InsertStats macro, 326
Insert Subdocument button, 560
Insert Subdocument dialog box, 561
Insert Table button, 391–392
Insert Word Field:IF dialog box, 690
interface customization for Word,
   129–138
Invoice.dot template, 103, 110, 661
italics, 332

J

JPEG file imports, 485–488
.JPG extensions, 486
justified alignment, 336

K

kerning of characters, 56, 334,
   453–454
keyboard shortcuts
   for character formatting, 334–335
   creating for Highlighter, 260
   customizing, 63, 139–146
   for cut/copy/paste operations,
      277
   determining function of, 143
   displaying with ToolTips, 151

for document navigation, 280–281
for drawing, 501
for Equation Editor, 524–526
for fields and field codes, 619
for form fillouts, 669
for going to next annotation, 264
as links between files/programs,
44, 46–47
for outlines, 554
for paragraph styles, 60
printing, 143, 223
resetting, 143
for selecting text, 276
for starting Word, 123
for styles, 430–432
for tables, 398–399
See also toolbars
key combinations
assigning for keyboard shortcuts,
140–141
how to press, 3
Keywords field, 638
Kino MT typeface, 462
Kodak file imports, 485–488

L

Label Options dialog box, 247, 691
labels, printing, 246–249
landscape orientation of page,
359, 364
language
as character attribute, 57
searching for, 289
laptops, My Briefcase folder for,
192, 198
LastSavedBy field, 638
layers in drawings, 510
Layout7.dot template, 373–374
Layout.dot template macros,
184–187, 373–374
leaders from tabs, 344
leading, 452
left alignment, 336
left indents, with paragraph
attribute, 57
left tabs, 343
legal documents with Pleading
Wizard, 113
legends on graphs, 528, 534
letterhead, storing in templates, 72
letter templates, 83–86
Letter Wizard, 83, 113

license and registration fees for
CD-ROM software, 849
lightbulb icon, 6
line length considerations, 450–451
Line Number paragraph style, 423
lines
between columns, 345
dotted or dashed, as tab
leaders, 344
drawing, 500, 501–502
as gridlines in tables, 390
for overscoring, 186
lines of text
first line indents for paragraphs,
57
numbering, 57, 58, 366
spacing between, 57, 336
typographical
considerations, 451–452
Widow/Orphan control, 57
LineSpaceIn/Out macros, 187
Link field, 638–639
linking
compared to embedding, 605
with Dynamic Data Exchange
(DDE) links, 630
files/programs with shortcuts, 44,
46–47
updating fields before printing,
234, 623–624
updating links automatically, 137
See also OLE (Object Linking and
Embedding)
list boxes in dialog boxes, 774, 788
List button, 213
ListKeys macro, 144–146
List paragraph styles, 421–422
lists
formatting with AutoFormat, 357
formatting with styles, 421–422
providing in dialog boxes,
774, 788
List view, 193
.LNK extensions, 47
logo, creating with WordArt,
515–518
logos
in templates, 70
with WordArt, 1
"Look in" drop-down list box, 192,
196
Look in Favorites button (File Open
dialog box), 195, 213

M

Macintosh file imports, 485–488
MacroButton field, 639
Macro icon, 7
Macro Recorder, 63
Macro Record toolbar, accessing,
149
Macros7.dot template, 178–184
macros
AccessExporter, 415
AutoBackup, 216–217
AutoClose, 174, 857
AutoExec, 129, 856–857
Auto macros, 174
AutoNew, 174, 857
AutoOpen, 174, 213, 546, 857
caution on possible virus,
213, 853, 856, 857
ChangeCase, 352–353
CreateMsgBox, 785–788, 795–799,
803–807
DecreaseBothIndents, 340
DecreaseCrop, 497
DrawDisassemblePicture, 513
GoToWhereWasI, 285–286
IncreaseBothIndents, 339–340
IncreaseCrop, 497
InsertFootnote, 180, 594–596
InsertStats, 326
ListKeys, 144–146
MarkTOC, 571
Payload, 853, 854
PresentIt, 188
RemoveAnnotations, 265
ResetPicture, 496
revision tracking, 768
SectionManager, 373–375
ShiftPrint, 228
TableAutoFit, 413–414
TableMath, 415
TableNum, 415
Tables7.dot template, 415
ToggleAutoCorrect, 299–300
ToggleFormat, 150–151
UnJumbler, 318–319
ViewOutline, 546
virus fixes on Scan828.doc,
855–856
WhereWasI, 285–286
WordBorder, 350
Macro Text paragraph style, 422
Macro toolbar, accessing, 148

macro use
  assigning to toolbar, menu or
    keyboard shortcut, 171
  copying elements to/from
    templates, 80–81
  custom toolbar buttons for, 155
  described, 63–64, 169–170
  editing, 174–175
  in forms, 664, 666, 671–673
  included with Word, 177–188
  keyboard shortcuts for, 140, 141
  naming, 171
  on custom menus, 161
  recording, 170–173
  running, 173–174
  from templates, 70, 78, 79, 170
  testing, 172
  virus fixes, 855–856
  with WordBasic, 2
  for word-jumble solutions,
    318–319
  See also WordBasic
Magnifier button, 236
Mail Merge Helper, 676–673
  Create Main Document
    button, 692
  Data Source option, 699
  Get Data button, 678
  Mailing Labels option, 690
  Merge button, 684, 693
  Query option, 695, 696
mail merge operations
  conditional record skipping,
    640, 648
  conditional word insertions,
    687–688, 689–690
  data source, 675
    editing, 699–700
    filtering with merge queries,
      695–698
    preparing, 678–681
    skipping records, 640
    sorting, 695
  described, 675–676
  importing data, 701
  main document, 675
  main document preparation,
    676–678, 681–683
  merge fields, 65, 675
  merge field setup, 639, 640
  merge fields in body of letter,
    686–687
  merging documents, 683–685
  printing envelopes, 692–694
  printing mailing labels, 690–692
  record counts, 640

verifying codes, 683
word fields, 687–688
Mail Merge toolbar, accessing, 149
main dictionary, 315
Manage Fields dialog box, 700
Manual Hyphenation dialog box,
  470
margins
  showing, 134
  specifying, 58, 359, 362–363
Mark Index Entry dialog box, 579
MarkTOC macro, 571
master documents
  advantages and disadvantages,
    555
  assembling, 556–557
  creating from scratch, 557–559
  headers and footers, 562–563
  inserting existing files, 560–561
  on networks, 563
  storing in separate folders, 564
  subdocuments, 556
    breaks by Heading styles, 560
    merging or splitting, 562
    opening, 561
    removing, 562
  templates for, 564
  tips for avoiding trouble, 564
  toolbar, 557
  value of frequent saves, 564
Master Document toolbar,
  accessing, 149
Master Document view, 556
Master Document view mode
  (View menu), 130
mathematical operations. *See*
  formulas
mathematical operators, in
  tables, 410
MathType, 520
  See also Equation Editor
Matura MT Script Capitals
  typeface, 463
MAX table formula, 410
measurement units, 138, 337
MegaWord 95, 851
memo templates, 87, 91, 92, 93
Memo Wizard, 113
Menu Bar dialog box, 166
menus
  adding, 165–166
  adding documents to, 201
  customizing, 63, 161–167
  customizing for forms, 669–670
  hiding for Full Screen view,
    130–132

removing commands from,
  164–165
restoring default settings, 167
selecting options from, 3
shortcut menus, 35, 166–167
WordBasic version for all
  commands, 731–735
See also Edit menu; File menu;
  Format menu; Insert menu;
  Tools menu; View menu
Merge dialog box, 684
Merge Field button, 681
MergeField field, 639, 682–683, 689
MergeRec field, 640
MergeSeq field, 640
Merge Subdocument button, 562
Merge To Setup dialog box, 685
Message Header paragraph style,
  422
metafile imports, 485–488
metric system for units of
  measurement, 138, 337
Micrographx file imports, 485–488
Microsoft ClipArt Gallery, 493–495
Microsoft Excel files as OLE
  objects, 603
Microsoft Exchange
  activating with Send To option,
    198
  described, 255–256
Microsoft Fax, 249–253
Microsoft Fax Cover Page Editor,
  252
Microsoft Graph
  graphs as OLE objects, 603
  See also graphs
Microsoft Network
  icon, 28
  keyboard shortcuts to, 46
Microsoft Office Binder, 23–24
Microsoft Office Manager (MOM),
  20–23, 125
Microsoft Office suite, 1
  binders, 23–24
  Schedule+, 25
  shortcut bar (MOM and OSB
    SuperMOM), 20–23
Microsoft toolbar, accessing, 148
MindBender macro, 181–182
Minimize All Windows command,
  36
MIN table formula, 410
minus key (–) for collapsing folder
  trees, 39
modification date property,
  displaying files by, 204

Modify Bulleted List dialog box, 380
Modify Style dialog box, 430
monitors, size considerations and
    taskbar behavior, 40
monospaced fonts, 54, 443
Monotype Sorts dingbats, 449
mouse
    actions unrecordable in macros,
        173
    drag-and-drop technique,
        277–278
    dragging for copying files or
        folders, 34
mouse pointer as arrowhead, 506
moving
    files/documents, 13, 196, 211–213
    items to Clipboard, 198, 305–307
    text. See cut/copy/paste
        operations
    toolbars, 150
MRK indicator on status bar, 267
MS-DOS
    future of, 50
    long-to-short filename
        conversions, 48–49
    printing from, 225–227
    starting Word for Windows 95
        from, 126–128
MS Linedraw typeface, 462
multimedia (video and sound
    objects), 612–614
Multiple pages button, 236
multitasking
    cooperative, 19
    preemptive, 19
My Briefcase, 192
    sending documents to, 198
My Computer
    creating documents from, 124
    icon, 28, 29–34
    starting Word from, 122–123

N

names of days, automatic
    capitalization, 296
navigating
    documents, 280–286
    drives with Explorer, 39
    Equation Editor, 525
    tables, 398–399
negative number formats in tables,
    411
networking
    for collaborations on documents,
        255

See also Microsoft Office suite
Network Neighborhood, icon, 28
networks
    advantages, 255
    mapping disk drives to, 200
    master documents on, 563
    storing Workgroup Templates, 76
New button, customizing, 72–73
New dialog box, 13, 35, 71–72
New in 95 icon, 6
newsletters. See desktop
    publishing effects
Newsletter Wizard, 113, 476
newspaper-style columns. See
    columns
Next field, 640
NextIf field, 640
non-breaking hyphens, 471
nonprinting characters display,
    135–136
Normal.dot template, 62, 70–71
    default font, 449
    option to confirm when saving to,
        215
    possible viruses and fixes in,
        853–854, 855, 856
Normal Indent paragraph style, 422
Normal style, 59, 331, 422
NormalViewHeaderFooter macro,
    182
Normal view mode (View menu),
    130
Note icon, 6
notepad icon, 6
NoteRef field, 641
novelty typefaces, 448
numbering
    footnotes, 590–591
    heading paragraphs, 58, 386–387
    lines, 57, 58, 366
    of lines, 57, 58, 366
    outline headings, 551–552
    pages. See page numbering
    paragraphs or lists, 58
        with AutoFormat, 301
        caution on bugs, 384–386
        with multiple levels, 382–384
        with Numbering button,
            380–381
    paragraphs with AutoNum field,
        626
    with Seq field, 645–648
Numbering button, 380
numbers
    formatting in fields, 621–622
    formatting in tables, 411

ignoring in words for spell
    checks, 315
ordinals, 302, 358, 622
Roman numerals, 368, 589, 622
spelling out, 621
NumChars field, 641

O

Object Anchors option of Page
    Layout view mode, 134
odd-even pages printing, 223
    specifying sections for, 361, 365
Office Shortcut Bar (OSB or
    SuperMOM), 20–23
    customizing, 124–126
    for starting Word, 124
OK button in dialog boxes, 773
OLE-enabled applications.
    See applets
OLE (Object Linking and
    Embedding) advantages,
    603–605
    establishing links, 638–639
    linking versus embedding, 605
    version 2.0, 604
OLE objects
    converting, 611–612
    copying and pasting, 609–610
    creating, 606–607
    dragging and dropping existing
        files as, 608–609
    editing, 610
    inserting existing files as, 607–608
    linking, 610–611
    multimedia (video and sound
        objects), 612–614
    setting up, 631–632
    WordArt objects as, 517
One Page button, 236
Open a Document button (OSB),
    124
Open command (File menu)
    accessing, 191
    browsing favorite folders,
        195–196
    changing views of files, 193–194
    Commands and Settings button,
        199–200, 213
    default settings for document
        locations, 196
    deleting files or folders, 194
    renaming files or folders, 194
    selecting files, 192
    shortcut menu, 197–199

OpenDoc, 605
Open Index AutoMark Field dialog
box, 582–583
open shapes, drawing, 504
optional hyphens, 136, 452–453, 471
option buttons in dialog boxes, 774
Options command (Tools menu)
"Always use this profile" setting,
256
Edit tab, 273–275
First Line Indentation
option, 57
File Locations tab, 75, 76, 196, 197
General tab, 136–138
Grammar tab, 324–326
Print tab, 234–235
Update Fields option,
584–585, 623
Save tab, 214–218
Spelling tab, 310, 312
View tab,
Field Codes option, 64
Horizontal Scroll Bar box, 542
Nonprinting Characters
options, 135–136
Normal View Options dialog
box, 132
Page Layout View Options
dialog box, 133
Paragraph Marks option,
58, 330
Show options, 133–134
Style Area Width option,
432–433
Tab Characters option, 58
Window options, 135
Or condition in "Advanced Find"
searches, 209
ordinals
formatting with AutoFormat, 302,
358
providing with field codes, 622
OrganizationalChartMaker macro,
182, 183
Organize ClipArt dialog box, 495
orientation of page, 58, 359, 364
OSB. See Office Shortcut Bar (OSB
or SuperMOM)
outlines
advantages, 541
collapsing and expanding,
543–547
editing, 550–551
keyboard shortcuts, 554
macro to collapse body text
automatically, 546–547

numbering headings, 551–552
printing, 551
promoting or demoting
paragraphs, 548–549
showing or hiding formatting,
547–548
sorting headings alphabetically,
553
switching betwen Normal and
Outline view, 541–542
toolbar, 553–554
Outline view button, 542
Outline view mode (View menu),
130
selecting text in, 543
Outlining toolbar, accessing, 148
ovals, 500
Overscore macro, 186
Overtype Mode, 274
OVR indicator in status bar, 274

P

.PAB extensions, 203
padlock icon, 6
page breaks. See pagination
page count for documents, 641
Page field, 642
page layout
orientation, 359, 364
specifying, 58
See also formatting; pagination
Page Layout view mode (View
menu), 130
Page Layout View Options dialog
box, 132, 133
Page Number Format dialog box,
368
page numbering
displaying with total number of
pages, 371
for indexes, 580, 581
inserting with fields, 64, 642
specifying, 58
specifying in headers and footers,
367
for tables of contents, 567
for tables of figures, 573
varying from section to section,
372–373
Page Number paragraph style, 423
Page Numbers dialog box, 367–368
PageRef field, 642
Page Up/Page Down keys, caution
on use in macros, 173

pagination
with Background Repagination
feature, 137
with Page Break Before, 57, 341
with paragraph attributes, 57
Paintbrush file imports, 485–488
Paint Shop Pro, 851
paper size, 58, 359, 363–364
paper source, 364
paper tray, 364
Paragraph Borders and Shading
dialog box, 346–347
Paragraph dialog box, 336
paragraph marks (¶), 58, 136, 330
paragraphs
described, 56, 57–58, 330
ending with Return, 54
numbering, 58
numbering as headings, 58,
386–387
numbering with AutoNum field,
626
spacing, 57, 336
Widow/Orphan control, 57
paragraph styles
described, 331, 419
See also styles
parent folders, 35, 36
Passim in tables of authorities, 577
password protecting files, 217–218
pasting, 274, 609–610
See also cut/copy/paste
operations
Pattern Matching option, 287, 292
Payload macro virus, 853, 854
.PCD extensions, 486
PC Paintbrush file imports, 485–488
.PCT extensions, 485
.PCX extensions, 485
performance considerations
of Background Repagination, 137
Page Layout view mode, 130
Picture Placeholders, 134
periods in filenames, 48
personalized form letters. See mail
merge operations
picas as unit of measurement, 138,
337
Picture Placeholders option of view
modes, 134
pictures
clip art, 485–486, 493–495
converting drawings to, 512–513
inserting with field code, 635
macros for handling, 495–497
See also drawings; graphics

Picture shortcut menu, customizing, 495–497
pictures in dialog boxes, 774
pixels, 486
Playbill typeface, 463
Pleading Wizard, 113
.PLT extensions, 485
Plug and Play, printers, 219
plus key (+) for expanding folder trees, 39
points as unit of measurement, 138, 337
point size for type, 449–450
polygons, 502–504
portrait orientation of page, 359, 364
position as character attribute, 56
postal barcodes, 627
PostScript file imports, 485–488
PostScript fonts, 442
PowerPoint presentations, macro for converting documents to, 188
Prank Macro!, 852, 853–854
preemptive multitasking, 19
presentations, macro for converting documents to, 188
Present.dot template macros, 188
PresentIt macro, 188
press release templates, 103, 104–106
Preview mode, 194
PrintableCharacters macro, 186
Print button, 236
Print Data Only for Forms option, 235
PrintDate field, 642
Print dialog box, 221
printer drivers, macro for overriding, 182
printers
    adding, 230–233
    changing default, 229–230
    icon for, 30
    mail-merging directly to, 684
    paper tray default, 235
    selecting, 229
    sending print codes to, 642
    setup, 233–234
Print field, 642
print files, 224–227
printing
    annotations, 223, 235, 264
    in background, 220, 234
    canceling, 254

current page, 221
document information, 223
documents, 198, 199
drawing objects, 235
drawings, 235
envelopes, 242–246, 692–694
envelopes from toolbar button, 154
fields and field codes, 235
to files, 224–225
forms, 669
hidden text, 235
keyboard shortcuts list, 143
labels, 246–249
macro for, 228
mailing labels, 690–692
managing jobs in print spooler, 253–254
from MS-DOS prompt, 225–227
multiple copies, 220–221
odd- or even-numbered pages, 223
to other printers, 224–225
outlines, 551
pausing, 254
ranges of pages, 221
in reverse page order, 234
selected text, 222
setting options, 234–235
Summary Info, 223, 235
viewing status, 254
Print Manager, 219, 253
Print Preview, 235–237
    editing, 242
    shrinking to fit, 240–242
    toolbar, 236–237
    zoom feature, 237–240
Print Preview toolbar, accessing, 149
print spooler, 219, 253–254
Print to File dialog box, 224
Private field, 643
PRODUCT table formula, 410
Professional Fax.dot template, 87, 90
Professional Letter.dot template, 83, 86
Professional Memo.dot template, 87, 93
Professional Press Release.dot template, 103, 106
Professional Report.dot template, 87, 100–102
Professional Resume.dot template, 103, 109
profiles for Microsoft Exchange, 256

Program Manager, replaced by desktop, 28
programs
    adding/deleting to/from Start menu, 44–45
    starting from Start menu, 43–44
    starting with Ctrl+Escape, 43
    starting with documents open, 44
    starting with Run command of Start menu, 44
    starting with Start button, 40
    See also applets; WordBasic
Programs command (Start menu), 43
Programs menu
    customizing as toolbar, 125
    Start button, 122
prompting users. *See* user prompts
proofing tools, 309
Properties button, 213
properties of documents
    for advanced searches, 205–208
    Author field, 371, 626
    Comments field, 627
    CreateDate field, 628
    displaying, 14–15, 193, 198, 199
    displaying keywords, 638
    EditTime field, 631
    Info field, 637–638
    Keywords field, 638
    LastSavedBy field, 638
    option to prompt for, 215
    PrintDate field, 642
    retrieving with fields, 631, 637–638
    RevNum field, 644
    SaveDate field, 644
    Subject field, 649
    Title field, 651–652
Properties view, 193
proportional spacing of characters, 54, 443
public domain software, 850
publishing. *See* desktop publishing effects
pull quotes, 479–480
Purchase Order.dot template, 103, 111, 661
push buttons in dialog boxes, 773

Q

Quick view, 198
quotation marks
    formatting with AutoFormat, 358
    as SmartQuotes, 294, 302
Quote field, 643

R

RD field, 643
read-only mode for opening documents, 198, 199
Reapply Style dialog box, 428
Recently Used File List, 137, 200
REC indicator on status bar, 170, 172
recording
  sounds, 613
  voice annotations to documents, 263
rectangles, squares and circles, 500, 502
Recycle Bin icon, 29
Redo command, 279
Ref field, 644
Registry
  macro for changing options, 182
  macro for overriding printer drivers, 182
RegOptions macro, 182
relative pages, 282
RemoveAnnotations macro, 265
renaming files or folders, 34, 194
replacing text. *See* finding and replacing
Reports Wizard, on CD accompanying this book, 87
report templates, 87, 94–102
requisitions, with Purchase Order.dot template, 103, 111, 661
ResetPicture macro, 496
resizing
  icons, 30
  taskbar, 43
  toolbar buttons, 151
resolution, considerations for video and multiple pages zoom feature, 239–240
resume templates, 103, 107–109
Resume Wizard, 103, 113–118
return address on envelopes, 244
Return key
  as Enter key, 54
  pressing for ends of paragraphs (*not* lines), 54
Reveal Codes command of WordPerfect, 55
reverse text (white-on-black), 347
Revision Marks
  accepting or rejecting revisions, 267–268
  advantages, 255, 259, 265
  as character attribute, 57

comparing document versions, 268
merging revisions, 268–269
  and Revision Numbers, 371
tracking revisions, 266–267, 644
  See also strikethrough
RevNum field, 644
right alignment, 336
right indents, with paragraph attribute, 57
right tabs, 343
Roman numerals
  converting numbers to, 622
  for footnotes or endnotes, 589
  for page numbers, 368
rotating drawings, 509
Routing Slip dialog box, 258
rows in tables, 389
  adding, 399–400
  as headings, 407
  selecting, 399
  See also tables
.RTF extensions, 203, 857
RTF files, macro for converting to and opening as PowerPoint presentation, 188
rulers
  hiding for Full Screen view, 130–132
  indenting with, 337–338
  making visible, 342
  for tab stops, 342
  toolbar button for, 153
Rulers button, 236
Run command (Start menu), 44

S

sans serif type, 446–447
Save As dialog box, 212
SaveDate field, 644
Saved Searches command, 200
Save Options dialog box, 214–218
SaveSelectionToTextFile macro, 182
saving
  automatically, 215
  with automatic backups (.BAK files), 214
  with AutoSave, 215–216
  "fast" option, 214–215
  files with different name/format/ location, 13, 211–213
  importance before changing templates, 74
  importance of frequent, 216

Scan828.doc, 856
.SCD extensions, 203
Schedule+, Microsoft Office suite, 25
scrollbars
  hiding, 135
  hiding for Full Screen view, 130–132
searches, saving, 200, 211
search operators, 287–288
Search Subfolders command, 199, 208
"Secret" icon, 6
"Secrets" of Word for Windows, 1, 95
SECRETS template, 851
Section field, 644
SectionManager macro, 187, 373–375
SectionPages field, 645
sections
  inserting number of current, 644
  inserting number of pages in current, 645
sections of binders, 23
sections of documents
  creating, 361–362
  described, 56, 58–59, 359
  end-of-section marks, 360
  formatting, 330
  printing ranges of, 222
  specifying, 360
security considerations
  master documents on networks, 563
  password protecting files, 217–218
  See also viruses
selecting
  multiple files, 192
  text, 275–276
selection bar, 276, 543
sending e-mail, 198, 255–260
sentences, automatic capitalization of first word, 295–296
separators
  in custom menus, 165
  for footnotes, 592
Seq field, 645–648
sequence numbers, 645–648
series of data for graphs, 528
  axes for, 532
serifs, 445
serif type, 444–446, 455
Set field, 648
SetPrintFlags macro, 182

Settings command (Start menu), 44
shading, 58
    of field results, 616
    in tables, 406
shared folders, 260
shareware, 849
Shift key combinations
    Shift+click for multiple selections,
        192
    Shift+click for opening folders,
        38–39
    Shift+Delete for file deletion, 35
    Shift+Enter to open Explorer, 35
    Shift+F3 to change case, 335,
        351–352
    Shift+F5 for Go Back command,
        285–286
    Shift+F7 for Thesaurus, 319
    Shift+F9 for switching between
        field code and result, 619
    Shift+F11 for previous field, 619
ShiftPrint macro, 228
shortcut menus, 35, 166–167
    customizing Picture, 495–497
    for tables, 398
shortcuts
    creating, 198
    to favorite folders, 195
    See also keyboard shortcuts
Show options
    of Normal or Outline view mode,
        Draft Font, 133
        Wrap to Window, 133
    of Page Layout view mode, 134
shrinking documents to fit page,
        237, 240–242
Shut Down command (Start menu),
        44
sidebars. See frames
Signature paragraph style, 422
Single MS-DOS mode, 50
single spacing, 57
    toolbar button for, 154
single underlining, 333
SkipIf field, 648
small caps
    specifying, 333
    toolbar button for, 154
SmartQuotes, 294, 302
Snap to Grid option for
        drawings, 511
soft page breaks, 137
software
    copyright protections, 849
    freeware, 850
    public domain, 850
    shareware, 849

sorting
    files, 199
    mail merge data, 695
    outline headings alphabetically,
        553
    toolbar button for, 155
sound effects, Beep on Error
        Actions, 137
sound object insertion into
        documents, 612–613
sounds, recording, 613
Sounds Like option, 288, 292
spaces
    caution on use for aligning or
        indenting, 54
    displaying as dots, 136
    in filenames, 12, 47
spacing
    characters, 56, 332, 333–334
    lines, 57, 336
    paragraphs, 57, 336
special characters
    for bullets, 380
    entering with AutoCorrect, 297
    in filenames, 48
    finding, 289–281
    See also characters
Special indentation, 336
spell checking
    automatic, 18
    completed documents, 312–313
    dictionary modification, 314,
        315–316
    excluding text from, 317
    on-the-fly, 310–312
    options, 314–315
    solving word jumbles, 318–319
    Spelling icon, 313–314
    with wildcard characters,
        317–318
    See also AutoCorrect
Spelling dialog box, 312
Spelling icon, 313–314
Spike, 305–307
Split Subdocument button, 562
spreadsheets for graphs, 530
squares and circles, 502
Standard toolbar, accessing, 148
Start a New Document button
        (OSB), 124
Start button, 40, 43, 122
starting
    Explorer, 38–39
    Word for Windows 95, 28,
        123–127
    Word from Explorer, 122–123

Start menu, 43–44
    customizing, 44–45
    customizing as toolbar, 125
    Settings command, Printers
        option, 229–230, 253–254
status bars, 40
    hiding, 135
    hiding for Full Screen view,
        130–132
    MRK indicator, 267
    OVR indicator, 274
    REC indicator, 170, 172
    Spelling icon, 313–314
strikethrough
    applying, 332
    toolbar button for, 154
    See also Revision Marks
style area, 135
Style Area Width option, 135
Style Gallery, 436–438
StyleRef field, 598–600, 649
styles
    advantages, 59–60, 417
    applying, 60, 427
    assigning keyboard shortcuts,
        430–432
    automatic updates to documents,
        435
    built-in with Word, 419–423
    character, 59, 60, 330, 419,
        433–434
    copying, 425
    copying elements to/from
        templates, 80–81
    creating, 423–426
    custom toolbar buttons for, 155
    deleting, 430
    finding, 289
    finding and replacing, 434–435
    gallery of, 436–438
    how to use for formatting, 59–60,
        330–331, 418–419
    for index entries, 584
    inserting pre-formatted text, 649
    keyboard shortcuts for, 140, 141,
        142, 430–432
    modifying, 428–430
    on custom menus, 162
    overriding, 427–428
    preventing AutoFormat from
        altering paragraphs, 358
    printing, 223
    specifying for following
        paragraph, 60, 426
    for tables of contents, 566,
        568–570

                        (continued)

styles *(continued)*
   in templates, 78, 426
   viewing, 427, 432–433
   See also paragraph styles
subdocuments, 556
   · *See also* master documents
subentries in indexes, 583
subfolders, searching for files,
   199, 208
Subject field, 649
sub/superscripts
   keyboard shortcuts for, 335
   specifying, 333
   toolbar button for, 154
   See also footnotes
Subtitle paragraph style, 422
Summary Info, printing, 223, 235
SUM table formula, 410
SuperDocStatistics macro, 183–184
Symbol dialog box, 180
Symbol field, 649
symbols
   dingbats, 449
   entering with AutoCorrect, 297
   in equations, 521–522, 525
   finding and replacing, 179–180
   for footnotes or endnotes,
      590–592
   formatting with AutoFormat,
      303, 358
   inserting with field, 649
   keyboard shortcuts for, 140
   Wingdings, 449

T

tab leaders, 344
   in indexes, 580
   in tables of authorities, 577
   in tables of contents, 567
   in tables of figures, 573
TableAutoFit macro, 413–414
Table AutoFormat dialog box, 405
TableFillDown macro, 185
TableFillRight macro, 185
Tablemath macro, 185, 415
Table menu
   Cell Height and Width command,
      403–404
   Convert Text to Table command,
      414–415
   Delete commands, 402
   Formula command, 409–411
   Gridlines command, 390
   Insert command, 399–401

Insert Table command, 392–393
   Merge Cells command, 406
   Sort command, 408–409
   Split Cells command, 407
   Split Table command, 407–408
   Table AutoFormat command, 405
TableNumber macro, 185
TableNum macro, 415
Table of Figures Options dialog
   box, 574
Tables7.dot macro template, 415
tables
   accessing shortcut menu with
      right-clicks, 398
   adding rows or columns, 399–401
   AutoFormatting, 405
   borders and shading, 406
   column width adjustments,
      402–404
   compared to tabs, 390
   creating from text, 414–415
   creating with Insert Table button,
      391–392
   creating with Insert Table
      command, 392–393
   creating with Table Wizard,
      393–398
   customizing toolbar for, 412–414
   database queries as, 628–629
   as databases. *See* mail merge
      operations
   deleting cells, 402
   described, 389–391
   formatting numbers, 411
   formulas in, 409–411
   headings, 406–407
   inserting cells, 401–402
   macro for exporting to Microsoft
      Access, 184
   macro for numbering rows or
      columns, 185
   navigating, 398
   selecting cells or ranges, 399
   sorting rows, 408–409
   splitting, 407–408
   tabs, 404
Tables.dot template macros,
   184–185
Tables of Authorities
   adding categories, 577–578
   creating, 576–577
   creating with field, 652
   marking citations, 574–576, 650
   paragraph style, 422
   updating, 584–585

Tables of Contents (TOC)
   creating, 565, 566–568
   creating for multifile projects, 643
   creating with field, 652–653
   creating with field codes, 569–570
   creating with non-heading styles,
      568–569
   custom TOC styles, 569
   formatting documents for, 566
   macro for field code insertion,
      571
   marking entries, 650–651
   paragraph style, 422
   updating, 584–585
   use of fields, 65
Tables of Figures
   creating, 572–573
   creating with styles, 573–574
   paragraph style, 422
   updating, 584–585
tablet icon, 6
Table Wizard, 113, 393–398
Tabs dialog box, 342
tab stops, 58, 341
   for bars between columns, 345
   deleting, 342, 344
   displaying as arrows, 136
   searching for, 289
   specifying with ruler, 342
   styles, 343
   variability of, 54
   See also tables
TA field, 650
Targa file imports, 485–488
taskbar
   activating (Ctrl+Escape), 43
   customizing, 40–42
   moving, 42–43
   resizing, 43
   setting for automatic startup of
      Word, 126
Taskbar Properties dialog box, 52
Task Manager, 28
TC field, 650–651
Template field, 651
templates
   backward compatibility with
      Word 6, 19–20
   boilerplate text in, 70
   caution on changing attached, 74
   caution on possible virus
      infection, 853–857
   changing for documents, 73–74
   converting documents to, 77
   copying elements to/from styles,
      80–81

creating new, 77
creating new documents from, 71–73
described, 62, 69–70
for equations, 522
for forms, 661–662
gallery of, 83–112
global, 70, 78–80, 140
inserting name of, 651
modifying, 78
modifying with macro, 82–83
Organizer, 80–82
as storage for custom menus, 161
as storage for keyboard shortcuts, 140, 142
as storage for macros, 170
storing, 13, 75–76
styles in, 78, 426
as Wizards, 72
Templates and Add-ins dialog box, 74, 79
text
    boilerplate, 62, 70, 77, 79
    converting to tables, 414–415
    in equations, 524
    excluding from spell checking, 317
    finding, 286–289
    flow and page breaks, 340–341
    hidden, 136
    inserting as quotation into documents, 643
    inserting with field code, 636
    moving with Advance field, 624–625
    selecting, 275–276
    Thesaurus word lookups, 319–320
    typing automatically with AutoText, 65, 626
    white-on-black, 347
    See also finding and replacing
Text Boundaries option of Page Layout view mode, 134
text boxes
    in dialog boxes, 774
    in drawings, 500, 504
text fields
    in dialog boxes, 774
    in forms, 663–665
Text Form Field Options dialog box, 664
.TGA extensions, 485
Thesaurus, 319–320
3D charts or graphs, 527, 531–532

ThumbsUp, 851
.TIF extensions, 485
tildes, in filenames, 48, 49
TileHorizontally macro, 187
TileVertically macro, 187
time
    displaying clock on taskbar, 41
    inserting by means of Time Field, 64, 371, 651
    inserting from toolbar button, 154
Time field, 651
timesheets, with Weekly Time Sheet.dot template, 103, 112, 661
Times New Roman typeface, 445, 449, 451, 455, 463
Times Roman typeface, 445
Tip icon, 6
TipWizard, 17
    disabling, 138
    Tip of the Day feature, 128–129
TipWizard toolbar, accessing, 148
title bar, hiding for Full Screen view, 130–132
Title field, 651–652
Title paragraph style, 422
titles
    on graphs, 532
    spanning multiple columns, 467
titles of documents
    choosing typeface for, 443, 456
    inserting, 651–652
    inserting as Title field, 371
    as property of document, 193
TOA field, 652
TOC 1,, 2, 3, etc. styles, 569
TOC. See Tables of Contents (TOC)
TOC field, 652–653
ToggleAutoCorrect macro, 299–300
ToggleFormat macro for toggling Formatting toolbar, 150–151
toolbars
    adding to OSB, 125
    for borders and shading, 349–350
    buttons,
        adding, 152–155
        adding custom, 155–156
        adding for Find command, 286
        for browsing folders, 33–34
        customizing New, 72–73
        for hanging indents, 339
        for headers and footers, 370–372

list of favorite obscure, 153–155
    removing, 152
    spacing, 159
copying elements to/from templates, 80–81
creating new, 160
customizing, 63, 147–161
customizing for tables, 412–414
Database, 700
deleting, 160
display options, 151
for drawing, 500–501, 510
Forms, 662–663
hiding for Full Screen view, 130–132
list of, 148–149
Mail Merge, 683
Master Document, 557
moving, 150
Outline view, 553–554
renaming, 160
resetting to defaults, 161
showing and hiding, 32, 149–150
using button actions in WordBasic macros, 731
WordArt, 518–519
See also buttons; keyboard shortcuts
Toolbars dialog box, 149–150
Tools menu
    AutoCorrect command, 293–294
    Customize command, 63
        for assigning AutoText, 305
        Insert Chart button, 529
        Keyboard tab, 141–142
        Menus tab, 162–167, 201
        Toolbars tab, 152–153, 155, 157, 159
        WordArt button, 518–519
    Envelopes and Labels command, 242–249
    Grammar command, 321–323
    Hyphenation command, 469–470
    Language command, 317, 418
    Macros command, 170–172, 173, 175
    Mail Merge command, 676, 678, 683
    Protect Document command, 660, 662
    Revision command, 266–269
    Spelling command, 312–313
    Unprotect Document command, 662

ToolTips, 151
TopDraw, 851
tracking (character spacing), 454
TrueType fonts, 442
    option to embed, 215
.TXT extensions, 203
typeface families, 442
typefaces, 332, 442
    choosing, 455–456
    clashing, 443, 455–456
    novelty, 448
    provided with Windows and
        Word, 456–464
    scripts, 447–448
typeover mode, 273
typewriters, compared to Word for
        Windows 95, 53–54
typography
    alignment, 452–453
    character spacing, 454–455
    dingbats, 449
    kerning, 56, 334, 453–454
    leading, 452
    line length, 450–451
    line spacing, 451–452
    novelty typefaces, 448
    point size, 449–450
    sans serif type, 446–447
    scripts, 447–448
    serif type, 444–446, 455
    typeface clash, 443, 455–456
    See also fonts

U

underlining
    as character attribute, 56
    dashed, 332
    specifying, 333
    toolbar button for, 154
underlining of misspelled words,
        310
Undo command, 279–280
Undo Minimize All command, 36
units of measurement, 138, 337
UnJumbler macro, 318–319
Up One Level button, 192, 212
uppercase
    ignoring acromymns in spell
        checks, 315
    See also capitalization; case
UserAddress field, 653–654
UserInitials field, 654
UserName field, 654

user prompts
    with Ask field, 625
    with Fillin field, 633
utilities. *See* applets

V

value axes for graphs, 532
VBA (Visual Basic for
        Applications), 20
vector images, 486
video files in Word documents,
        613–614
View menu
    Annotations command, 263–264
    Details command, 30
    Footnotes command, 589
    Full Screen command, 131–132
    Header and Footer command,
        58, 360, 369
    Master Document command,
        130, 558
    Normal command, 130
    Options command,
        Browse folders option, 32
        dialog box, 33
        View options, 37
    Outline command, 130, 542
    Page Layout command, 130
    Ruler command, 342
    Toolbars command, 32, 148,
        149–150, 160
View Merged Data button, 683
ViewOutline macro, 546
View tab. *See under* Options
        command (Tools menu)
viruses
    in AutoOpen macro, 213, 853,
        856, 857
    detecting and removing, 853–857
    protection from Prank Macro!,
        852
    protection from Scan828.doc, 856
Visual Basic, 705
Visual Basic for Applications
        (VBA), 20
voice annotations, 263

W

Warning icon, 7
Weekly Time Sheet.dot template,
        103, 112, 661
Whole Screen button, 237

Wide Latin typeface, 464
Widow/Orphan control, 57, 340
wildcard characters, 52
    in searches for files, 202
    in spell checking, 317–318
Win16, 19
Win32, 19
Window menu, Arrange All
        command, 278
Windows 95
    shutting down, 44
    See also desktop
windows
    macros for arranging, 186, 187
    minimizing all, 36
    multiple for viewing multiple
        documents, 278
    scrolling, 135
Windows Explorer. *See* Explorer
Windows metafile imports, 485–488
Winword.Concept virus, 854, 855
Wizard handling
    resetting defaults, 119
    running, 113–118
    as templates, 72
Wizards
    Add Printer, 230–233
    Agenda, 113
    Award, 113
    Calendar, 113
    Chart, 536–537
    Compose New Fax, 198
    Fax, 113
    Footnote, 1, 594–596
    Letter, 83, 113
    Memo, 113
    Newsletter, 113, 476
    Pleading, 113
    Resume, 103, 113–118
    Table, 113, 393–398
    Tip, 17
.WIZ extensions, 72, 113
.WK*n* extensions, 203
.WMF extensions, 485
Word 6, 3
    compatibility with Word for
        Windows 95, 19–20
WordArt, 515–519
    described, 1
    inserting objects from toolbar
        button, 154
WordBasic
    arrays, 710–712
    bookmarks, 756–759

call-by-reference versus
    call-by-value, 739–740
character formatting functions,
    847
commands,
    for accessing useful lists,
        763–765
    availability, 730–731
    choosing, 731–735
    complete list, 809–844
    EditClear, 748
    EditFind, 759–761
    Format*xxxxx*, 748–754
    help with syntax, 735–736
    Insert, 748
    for moving and selecting,
        745–748
    recording with Record Next
        Command button, 736
    shortcut formatting, 754–756
comments (REM statements), 708
concatenation of strings, 712–713
control structures, 715
cursor movement functions, 845
described, 2, 63–64, 169, 705
dialog box settings retrieval, 730
ElseIf statements, 718–719
error handling, 725
For/Next loops, 719–722
functions, 736, 737–738, 739–740
functions operation, 706–707
Goto instruction and labels,
    715–716
If statements, 716–719
InputBox$ function, 728–729
Input command, 726
macros,
    being sure of document
        window, 741–742
    converting text into variable,
        742–743
    editing, 175–177
    structure, 705–708
MsgBox functions, 726–728
numeric functions, 845
On Error command, 725
paragraph formatting functions,
    846–847
Print command, 726
private settings (INI) files, 767,
    769–770
scrolling functions, 845
Select Case statements, 723–725
Selection$( ) function, 742–743
selection functions, 845
SelInfo function, 743–745

string functions, 713–715, 844
strings, 712–713
style functions, 846
subroutines, 736, 737, 739–740
syntax of commands/macros,
    705–708
table handling functions, 846
temporary documents, 761–763
testing, importance of, 706
user input and output, 726–729
variables, 709–710
    document, 766–767
    shared, 738–739
view functions, 847–848
While/Wend loops, 722–723
See also dialog box customization
WordBorder macro, 350
word count
    inserting into documents, 641
    as property of document, 193
Word for Windows 2.0 toolbar,
    accessing, 148
Word for Windows 95
    bugs in, 2
    command selection, 62–63
    compared to typewriters, 53–54
    compared to WordPerfect, 55
    compatibility with Word 6, 19–20
    exiting with macro to close all
        open documents, 178–179
    history, 1
    interface customization, 129–138
    starting automatically, 126
    starting by clicking document
        icon, 28
    starting from desktop shortcut,
        123
    starting from MS-DOS prompt,
        126–127
    starting from My Computer or
        Explorer window, 122–123
    starting from Office Shortcut Bar
        (OSB), 124–126
    starting from Start buttons, 122
    Tip of the Day feature, 128–129
    See also commands; documents;
        WordBasic
Word for Windows 95's new
    features
    32-bit processing, 19
    animation, 15
    File menu enhancements, 12–13
    file properties, 14–15
    file search capability
        enhancement, 13

Find and Replace enhancements,
    16–17
folder creation enhancement, 13
Help buttons, 18
Highlighter, 15–16
longer filename capability, 12, 13
overview, 11
spell checking on-the-fly, 18
template assignment
    enhancement, 13–14
Tip Wizard, 17
word jumble solutions, 318–319
WordPerfect
    compared to Word for Windows
        95, 55, 330
    file imports, 485–488
    help options for converts from,
        137, 138
WordPuzzler macro, 184
words
    Thesaurus lookups, 319–320
    See also text
Wordwiz.ini file, 119
Workgroup Templates, 76
.WPD extensions, 203
.WPG extensions, 485
.WPS extensions, 203
Wrap to Window, 133
.WRI extensions, 203
.WSD extensions, 203
.WS extensions, 203

X

XE field, 654–655
X-height, 445
.XLS extensions, 203
.XLW extensions, 203

Z

zero suppression in tables, 411
Zoom Control button, 236
zoom feature, 237–240
    drawings, 498–499

IDG BOOKS WORLDWIDE LICENSE AGREEMENT

Important — read carefully before opening the software packet. This is a legal agreement between you (either an individual or an entity) and IDG Books Worldwide, Inc. (IDG). By opening the accompanying sealed packet containing the software disc, you acknowledge that you have read and accept the following IDG License Agreement. If you do not agree and do not want to be bound by the terms of this Agreement, promptly return the book and the unopened software packet(s) to the place you obtained them for a full refund.

1. **License.** This License Agreement (Agreement) permits you to use one copy of the enclosed Software program(s) on a single computer. The Software is in "use" on a computer when it is loaded into temporary memory (i.e., RAM) or installed into permanent memory (e.g., hard disk, CD-ROM, or other storage device) of that computer.

2. **Copyright.** The entire contents of this disc and the compilation of the Software are copyrighted and protected by both United States copyright laws and international treaty provisions. You may only (a) make one copy of the Software for backup or archival purposes or (b) transfer the Software to a single hard disk, provided that you keep the original for backup or archival purposes. The individual programs on the disc are copyrighted by the authors of each program respectively. Each program has its own use permissions and limitations. To use each program, you must follow the individual requirements and restrictions detailed for each in either Appendix A of this Book or the program's online documentation. Do not use a program if you do not want to follow its Licensing Agreement. None of the material on this compact disc or listed in this Book may ever be distributed, in original or modified form, for commercial purposes.

3. **Other Restrictions.** You may not rent or lease the Software. You may transfer the Software and user documentation on a permanent basis provided you retain no copies and the recipient agrees to the terms of this Agreement. You may not reverse engineer, decompile, or disassemble the Software except to the extent that the foregoing restriction is expressly prohibited by applicable law. If the Software is an update or has been updated, any transfer must include the most recent update and all prior versions. Each shareware program has its own use permissions and limitations. These limitations are contained in the individual license agreements that are on the CD-ROM. The restrictions include a requirement that after using the program for a period of time specified in its text, the user must pay a registration fee or discontinue use. By opening the package which contains the CD-ROM, you will be agreeing to abide by the licenses and restrictions for these programs. Do not open the Software package unless you agree to be bound by the license agreements.

4. Limited Warranty. IDG Warrants that the Software and disc are free from defects in materials and workmanship for a period of sixty (60) days from the date of purchase of this Book. If IDG receives notification within the warranty period of defects in material or workmanship, IDG will replace the defective disc. IDG's entire liability and your exclusive remedy shall be limited to replacement of the Software, which is returned to IDG with a copy of your receipt. This Limited Warranty is void if failure of the Software has resulted from accident, abuse, or misapplication. Any replacement Software will be warranted for the remainder of the original warranty period or thirty (30) days, whichever is longer.

5. No Other Warranties. To the maximum extent permitted by applicable law, IDG and the author disclaim all other warranties, express or implied, including but not limited to implied warranties of merchantability and fitness for a particular purpose, with respect to the Software, the programs, the source code contained therein and/or the techniques described in this Book. This limited warranty gives you specific legal rights. You may have others that vary from state/jurisdiction to state/jurisdiction.

6. No Liability For Consequential Damages. To the extent permitted by applicable law, in no event shall IDG or the author be liable for any damages whatsoever (including without limitation, damages for loss of business profits, business interruption, loss of business information, or any other pecuniary loss) arising out of the use of or inability to use the Book or the Software, even if IDG has been advised of the possibility of such damages. Because some states/jurisdictions do not allow the exclusion or limitation of liability for consequential or incidental damages, the above limitation may not apply to you.

7. U.S.Government Restricted Rights. Use, duplication, or disclosure of the Software by the U.S. Government is subject to restrictions stated in paragraph (c) (1) (ii) of the Rights in Technical Data and Computer Software clause of DFARS 252.227-7013, and in subparagraphs (a) through (d) of the Commercial Computer—Restricted Rights clause at FAR 52.227-19, and in similar clauses in the NASA FAR supplement, when applicable.

Installation Instructions

The installation instructions for the CD-ROM are included in Appendix A of this book and on the CD itself.

IDG BOOKS WORLDWIDE REGISTRATION CARD

RETURN THIS REGISTRATION CARD FOR FREE CATALOG

Title of this book: Word for Windows 95 SECRETS

My overall rating of this book: ❏ Very good [1] ❏ Good [2] ❏ Satisfactory [3] ❏ Fair [4] ❏ Poor [5]

How I first heard about this book:

❏ Found in bookstore; name: [6] _____

❏ Advertisement: [8] _____

❏ Word of mouth; heard about book from friend, co-worker, etc.: [10] _____

❏ Book review: [7] _____

❏ Catalog: [9] _____

❏ Other: [11] _____

What I liked most about this book:

_____
_____
_____

What I would change, add, delete, etc., in future editions of this book:

_____
_____
_____

Other comments:

_____
_____

Number of computer books I purchase in a year: ❏ 1 [12] ❏ 2-5 [13] ❏ 6-10 [14] ❏ More than 10 [15]

I would characterize my computer skills as: ❏ Beginner [16] ❏ Intermediate [17] ❏ Advanced [18] ❏ Professional [19]

I use ❏ DOS [20] ❏ Windows [21] ❏ OS/2 [22] ❏ Unix [23] ❏ Macintosh [24] ❏ Other: [25] _____

(please specify)

I would be interested in new books on the following subjects:

(please check all that apply, and use the spaces provided to identify specific software)

❏ Word processing: [26] _____

❏ Data bases: [28] _____

❏ File Utilities: [30] _____

❏ Networking: [32] _____

❏ Other: [34] _____

❏ Spreadsheets: [27] _____

❏ Desktop publishing: [29] _____

❏ Money management: [31] _____

❏ Programming languages: [33] _____

I use a PC at (please check all that apply): ❏ home [35] ❏ work [36] ❏ school [37] ❏ other: [38] _____

The disks I prefer to use are ❏ 5.25 [39] ❏ 3.5 [40] ❏ other: [41] _____

I have a CD ROM: ❏ yes [42] ❏ no [43]

I plan to buy or upgrade computer hardware this year: ❏ yes [44] ❏ no [45]

I plan to buy or upgrade computer software this year: ❏ yes [46] ❏ no [47]

Name: _____   Business title: [48] _____   Type of Business: [49] _____

Address (❏ home [50] ❏ work [51] /Company name: _____)

Street/Suite# _____

City [52] /State [53] /Zipcode [54]: _____   Country [55] _____

❏ **I liked this book!** You may quote me by name in future IDG Books Worldwide promotional materials.

My daytime phone number is _____

IDG BOOKS

®

THE WORLD OF COMPUTER KNOWLEDGE

☐ YES!

Please keep me informed about IDG's World of Computer Knowledge.
Send me the latest IDG Books catalog.